DICTIONARY OF MANITOBA BIOGRAPHY

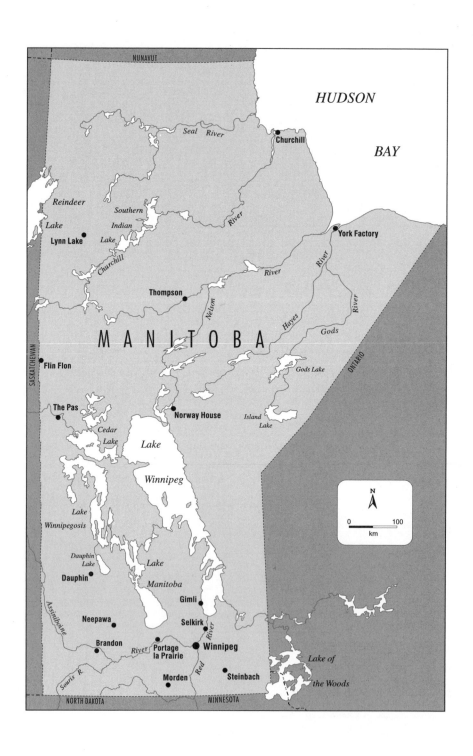

DICTIONARY OF MANITOBA BIOGRAPHY

J.M. BUMSTED

THE UNIVERSITY OF MANITOBA PRESS

The University of Manitoba Press
Winnipeg, Manitoba Canada R3T 2N2
www.umanitoba.ca/uofmpress

Printed in Canada

Printed on recycled, acid-free paper

Cover and text design: Doowah Design
Map: Weldon Hiebert
For credits to cover illustrations, see page 275.

Canadian Cataloguing in Publication Data

Bumsted, J.M., 1938—

      Dictionary of Manitoba Biography
      Includes bibliographical references.
      ISBN 0-88755-169-6 (bound)—ISBN 0-88755-662-0 (pbk.)

1.   Manitoba—Biography—Dictionaries.   I. Title.
FC3355.B85 1999   920.07127   C99-920213-8
F1061.8.B85 1999

The University of Manitoba Press gratefully acknowledges the financial support provided for its publishi
program by the Government of Canada through the Book Publishing Industry Development Progra
(BPIDP); the Canada Council for the Arts; the Manitoba Department of Culture, Heritage and Citizenshi
and the Manitoba Arts Council.

For Jeremy and Thomas,
two new Manitobans

INTRODUCTION

This volume has its origins in a long-time fascination I have had with biography. I began researching and writing biographical sketches for various reference works while in graduate school. One of my earliest books was an extended biographical sketch of the Nova Scotia evangelist Henry Alline. For some years I prepared a good many longer sketches for various volumes of the *Dictionary of Canadian Biography*, nearly 100 in total. That great work always seemed to me to have several very serious weaknesses. For one thing, it was difficult to use as a reference work, partly because of its multiple volumes, partly because of the size of the biographies, partly because of its organization by death date, partly because of its national focus. In more recent volumes, it is possible to find at the end a list of biographies broken down by region and province, but that was not true of earlier ones. In any case, one needs an entire library shelf to store a complete set of the *DCB*, hardly recommending it to the occasional user. Moreover, the slow pace at which the twentieth-century volumes of the *DCB* are being produced has meant that there is an enormous hiatus of up-to-date biographical reference material for much of recent Canadian history. For me, an equally serious weakness of the *DCB* was its concentration on major figures of national and regional importance, to the relative neglect of the second- and third-rank people who often operated on only the local, regional, or provincial level. The *DCB* was simply not designed for anyone wanting a quick reference work to identify an individual or to find some birth dates and death dates, especially within a provincial or regional context.

Conscious of the weaknesses of the existing reference system for Canadian biography, when I prepared for publication my study of the Winnipeg General Strike in 1994 I decided to include an appendix that would offer some biographical material on the major players in the strike. I did not want to burden the text with a plethora of material on the lives of the participants, although few were household names. Most of those involved had died fairly recently, or were still alive; their biographical details simply were not readily available. For many, the General Strike represented their major moment of historical prominence. The appendix was such a success with readers that I repeated a similar effort in my history of the Red River Rebellion. As with the Strike book, it was the relative obscurity of many of the major actors that made such an appendix necessary. My research for these two appendices further highlighted to me the need for a biographical reference work for Manitoba. This *Dictionary of Manitoba Biography* is the result.

A few words must be said about principles of inclusion. I started with three basic principles. Those whose lives would be sketched had to be deceased, they had to have set foot — at least briefly — upon Manitoba soil, and they had either to have made some impact upon Manitoba or to have had their lives seriously formed or influenced by Manitoba residence. The restriction on residence was essential to keep from overloading the text with individuals whose actions and decisions somehow impinged upon the history of the province but who had no direct connection with it. I ended up breaking this rule several times, once in the case of George-Étienne Cartier, whose involvement in the creation of Manitoba was central, and who actually was elected to represent a Manitoba constituency in the House of Commons in 1872, although he never visited the province. The other exceptions were individuals whose relationship with the Hudson's Bay Company or the Selkirk Settlement made their inclusion seem essential. The insistence on some influence of residence on the life seemed necessary to avoid including individuals (Deanna Durbin, the Hollywood actress, is a good example) who were born in Manitoba but who left the province at a very early age.

There are doubtless very important individuals whose names have been omitted through oversight; no reference work is ever perfect, and most readers will turn to it in the first instance to play the game "Who Has Been Omitted?" The real challenge in this work, however, was in deciding who among the slightly less important should be included. To produce a biographical sketch for every Member of Parliament from Manitoba, for every MLA who sat in the provincial legislature, for every judge who sat on the bench, for every local reeve and school board chair, for every businessman, for every university professor, or for every cleric — much less every writer, artist, or architect — would have made this work considerably longer than it is already. Instead, I have tried to include elected officials and judges, as well as such people as businessmen, doctors, professors, and clerics, only when they did something special in their careers. Mere progression towards the top of one's field is thus for this volume not enough. The space saved I have devoted to individuals who once made an impression on their society in the often-neglected social and cultural arenas. I have worked very hard at finding out about artists, architects, educators, musicians, writers, poets, journalists, performers, reformers, and agitators. I have also worked hard at finding out about members of the neglected communities: of immigrants, of women, of Aboriginals, of Métis. For every individual possible I have tried to list some important writings or other creative productions, if there were any, and also to suggest sources for further biographical or critical information if available. I would hardly claim that every Manitoban who deserves a biographical sketch is included here. But this is a start.

There are some real problems inherent in preparing a biographical dictionary of one province. The lives and careers of many individuals are not constrained by geography. For a province like Manitoba, which experienced a continual influx of new immigrants, the early lives of many of its prominent people are shrouded in obscurity. On the other hand, many people passed through Manitoba on their way someplace else, usually further west in Canada, where they really became prominent. If they did not retain some connection with the province after their departure, they sometimes became lost to it, their later careers and deaths unrecorded. While there are thus some people who virtually disappear, the more common problem with those who move is deciding how much of their non-Manitoba lives and careers ought to be included in a Manitoba volume. My instincts were to be generous in this regard.

Further and sometimes related problems result from the nature of the sources, particularly for those who were not prominent Manitobans. To a large extent, a researcher of a volume of this nature is dependent on the biographical information generated by others, the accuracy and coverage of which is fairly variable. One might think that the presence of a lengthy obituary in a local newspaper, for example, would virtually guarantee certain minimal biographical details and accuracy. But such is simply not the case. Many obituaries say little about the early life, others little about the later life. Some obituary writers seem unable to produce dates for the important events in their subject's life, perhaps because they don't really know them. Some obituary writers are really not concerned about the details of the background or career of the subject, but only about offering an effusive assessment of how beloved he or she was. I am indebted to the biographical scrapbooks and vertical files at the Legislative Library of Manitoba. These 20 volumes of newspaper clippings and supplementary files contain thousands of obituaries and other biographical clippings on the well-known and the obscure alike. Without their existence this book could not have been prepared.

While I have employed obituaries extensively, they are hardly my only sources of information. The Provincial Archives of Manitoba provided a good deal of material in its manuscript collections, and I have listed collections of personal papers held by the archives in the sketches themselves. I have also relied heavily on other biographical directories, reference books, and historical works. The most useful of these sources are listed in a brief bibliography at the end of this introduction. Whenever possible, I have in addition employed specialist material, including journal articles, unpublished theses, and books; these references are commonly listed in the biographical sketch itself. The sketches contained herein are doubtless riddled with factual errors, which I would hope to be able to correct in subsequent editions. But all sketches are based on the best information presently available to me. If people have better information, I hope they will let me or the University of Manitoba Press know about it.

Unlike the *Dictionary of Canadian Biography*, this work is not particularly designed for the casual browser, although I hope browsing will prove possible — and illuminating. The sketches are for the most part too short to be works of literary art. On the other hand, I have extended beyond bare bones the sketches of some Manitobans whose lives I have found unusually fascinating and revealing of the development of the province, or who have been forgotten and deserve to be remembered. The residents of Red River and early Manitoba often led more fascinating lives than most of us realize, and this is reflected in the coverage. Size of sketch is therefore not always a guide to importance. In any case, I hope that the user finds some value in perusing this book's pages beyond the search for the facts of a single life. Manitoba has produced an incredible number of interesting people, many of whom are worthy of more attention than is given them here. I hope this work calls attention to the province's rich collection of achievers — and failures.

J.M. Bumsted
Winnipeg, September 1999

Select Bibliography

Baker, Marilyn. *The Winnipeg School of Art: The Early Years.* Winnipeg: University of Manitoba Press, 1984.

Benson, Eugene, and William Toye, eds. *The Oxford Companion of Canadian Literature.* 2nd ed. Toronto: Oxford University Press, 1997.

Carbone, Stanislao. *Italians in Winnipeg: An Illustrated History.* Winnipeg: University of Manitoba Press, 1998.

Dictionary of Canadian Biography. 14 vols. to date. Toronto: University of Toronto Press, 1969- .

Kalman, Harold. *A History of Canadian Architecture.* Don Mills: Oxford University Press, 1994.

Kallman, Helmut, Gilles Potvin, Kenneth Winters, eds. *Encyclopedia of Music in Canada.* 2nd ed. Toronto: University of Toronto Press, 1992.

Manitoba Agricultural Hall of Fame. Brandon: Manitoba Agricultural Hall of Fame, n.d.

Manitoba Library Association. *Pioneers and Early Citizens of Manitoba: A Dictionary of Manitoba Biography from the Earliest Times to 1920.* Winnipeg: Peguis Publishing, 1971.

Marsh, James, ed. *The Canadian Encyclopedia.* Edmonton: Hurtig Publishers, 1985.

McFee, Janice, and Bruce Sealey, eds. *Famous Manitoba Métis.* Winnipeg: Manitoba Métis Federation Press, 1974.

McRaye, Walter, ed. *Pioneers and Prominent People of Manitoba.* Winnipeg: Canada Publicity, 1925.

Morgan, Henry James, ed. *The Canadian Men and Women of the Time: A Handbook of Canadian Biography of Living Characters.* 2nd ed. Toronto: William Briggs, 1912.

Peel, Bruce Braden. *A Bibliography of the Prairie Provinces to 1953, with bibliographical index.* 2nd ed. Toronto: University of Toronto Press, 1973.

Ribling, John E., ed. *Encyclopedia Canadiana.* 10 vols. Ottawa: Canadiana Company Ltd., 1957-58.

Ripley, Gordon, and Anne Mercer. *Who's Who in Canadian Literature.* Toronto: Reference Press, 1985.

Schofield, Frank Howard. *The Story of Manitoba.* Winnipeg: S.J. Clarke, 1913.

The 1997 Canadian Encyclopedia Plus [cd rom]. Toronto: M&S Multimedia, 1997.

Wallace, W. Stewart, ed. *The Macmillan Dictionary of Canadian Biography.* 4th ed. rev. by W.A. McKay. Toronto: Macmillan of Canada, 1978.

Editorial Notes

Personal Names. Entries in *The Dictionary of Manitoba Biography* are arranged by family name. The title "Sir" is used only when the subject is best known by this form of address (e.g., Smith, Sir Donald). All other professional or religious titles are excluded. Maiden names are in parentheses. When it has not been possible to determine with certainty that a woman's middle name was her maiden name, no maiden name is indicated. Names beginning with "Mac" or "Mc" are in a section of their own.

Dates. When it has not been possible to determine with accuracy either a birth or death date for a subject, the abbreviation "fl." (flourished) is used to indicate the period of a person's greatest activity.

Cross-references. Persons who have their own entries in the *DMB* are indicated by an asterisk when their names are first mentioned in another entry. There is one important exception to this. There are so many references to Louis Riel throughout this work, and it is so obvious that his entry would be included here, that his name has not been cross-referenced with an asterisk.

Place and Institutional Names. The names "Upper Canada" and "Lower Canada" are used here to refer to those two regions up to 1840. The terms that identified those regions from 1840 to Confederation are not as well known nor as commonly used, and to avoid confusion, the name "Canada," rather than "Canada West" or "Canada East," is used here when referring to the period from 1840 to 1867. Some institutions are commonly known by both the French and English versions of their names. One example is the institution known as both St. Boniface College and Collège de Saint-Boniface. In such cases, the French name of the institution is used when the subject of the entry is a Francophone, and the English name is used when the subject is an Anglophone.

References and Other Sources. Whenever possible, other sources for more detailed information are listed at the end of the entries. These include published materials as well as unpublished theses and dissertations and collections of papers at either the Public Archives of Manitoba (PAM), the National Archives of Canada (NAC), or the University of Manitoba Library Archives (UML Archives). Entries in the *Dictionary of Canadian Biography* are indicated by the abbreviation *DCB*, followed by the appropriate volume and page number.

A Request to Readers

Future editions of the *Dictionary of Manitoba Biography* will attempt to correct any omissions or errors in these biographical sketches. Suggestions from readers for future editions are welcome. These should include information such as birth and death dates and major accomplishments, as well as references to other sources of information, both published and unpublished, and should be sent to:

The Dictionary of Manitoba Biography
c/o The University of Manitoba Press
University of Manitoba, Winnipeg, Manitoba
Canada R3T 2N2

ABBREVIATIONS

a.k.a. also known as
b. born
BA Bachelor of Arts
BBC British Broadcasting Corporation
BLitt Bachelor of Literature
BMI Broadcast Music Incorporated
BMus Bachelor of Music
BNA Britsh North America
BSc Bachelor of Science
c. *circa*
CBC Canadian Broadcasting Corporation
CCF Co-operative Commonwealth Federation
CFL Canadian Football League
CNE Canadian National Exhibition
CNIB Canadian National Institute for the Blind
CNR Canadian National Railway
CPR Canadian Pacific Railway
d. died
DCB Dictionary of Canadian Biography
DD Doctor of Divinity
diss. dissertation
DSc Doctor of Science
fl. (*floriat*) flourished
HBC Hudson's Bay Company
HBCA Hudson's Bay Company Archives
HSSM Historical and Scientific Society of Manitoba
IODE Imperial Order of Daughters of the Empire

IOOF International Order of Odd Fellows
KC King's Counsel
LLB Bachelor of Laws
LLD Doctor of Laws
LLM Master of Laws
MA Master of Arts
MLA Member of the Legislative Assembly
MP Member of Parliament
MPP Member of Provincial Parliament
MSc Master of Science
NAC National Archives of Canada
NDP New Democratic Party
NHL National Hockey League
NWC North West Company
NWMP North-West Mounted Police
PAM Provincial Archives of Manitoba
PhD Doctor of Philosophy
QC Queen's Counsel
RCAF Royal Canadian Air Force
RCMP Royal Canadian Mounted Police
RCN Royal Canadian Navy
RNWMP Royal North-West Mounted Police
UML University of Manitoba Library
UN United Nations
WWI World War I
WWII World War II

DICTIONARY OF MANITOBA BIOGRAPHY

Abishabis (d. 1843) Native prophet. Born near York Factory to Cree parents, he was converted to Methodism by James Evans. Later, in 1842, he assumed a role as a spiritual prophet around Moose Factory and Fort Albany. Accused of being a *windigo*, he was arrested by the HBC at Severn House. He was subsequently killed by three of his people on 30 August 1843. See Norman J.W. Williamson, "Abishabis the Cree," *Studies in Religion* 9, no. 2 (1980): 216-45. *DCB* VII, 3-4.

Abraham, John (fl. 1672-89) Mariner. Little is known of his life except for his service with the HBC, mainly in maritime capacities until 1684, when he was briefly appointed governor of Port Nelson. He explored the Churchill River in 1686 and later became a buccaneer preying on English shipping in the St. Lawrence River. *DCB* I, 39.

Accetti, Angelo (d. 1955) Cameraman and photographer. Little is known of his background. He began with a studio in St. Boniface, and between 1920 and 1954 he supplied Fox Movie-Tone News with Winnipeg film footage. Accetti was an early pioneer in aerial filming. He later moved to the Film Exchange Building at 361 Hargrave Street. He weighed over 300 pounds.

Ackland, Clifford Maxwell (1886-1957) Businessman and soldier. Born in Almonte, Ontario, Ackland came west with his parents in 1891, went east for schooling, and returned to Manitoba in 1901. He became manager of D. Ackland and Son Limited and president of Ackland Hardware Company. He enlisted in the Canadian Expeditionary Force in December 1915 and served as major and second-in-command in the 222nd battalion. He was awarded the Military Cross. During WWII he commanded the 100th Canadian Army Basic Training Centre at Portage la Prairie.

Adams, David Elder (d. 1919) Businessman. He immigrated to Winnipeg in 1882 and entered the coal business. He helped organize the Souris Valley Coal Company, selling out his interest in 1900 and moving into the development of Alberta coal. He was a charter member of the Winnipeg Rowing Club Building Committee. He later became involved with the Canada West Coal and Coke Company, which ultimately became a stock company known as the D.E. Adams Coal Company Limited. He died in Pasadena, California.

Adamson, John Evans (1884-1961) Judge. Born in Nelson, Manitoba, he was educated at St. John's College at the University of Manitoba (where he won the Governor General's Gold Medal for philosophy) and Osgoode Hall. He ran for the Liberals in the 1921 federal election and was appointed to the Court of King's Bench in 1922. He became chief justice of Manitoba in 1954, serving until 1961, when a new amendment to the BNA Act forced him to retire against his will.

Agnew, John Hume (1863-1908) Lawyer, politician. Born at Whitby, Canada, and educated at Upper Canada College, he accompanied his family to Winnipeg in 1879. He studied law, articling with J.A.M. Aikins.* He later practised with the firm of Agnew, Craig, and Ross, and from 1886 to 1904 practised law at Virden, where he was active in local politics. He was elected to the Manitoba legislature in 1904 as a Conservative from Virden and became provincial treasurer. Agnew was Manitoba vice-president of the Upper Canada College Old Boys' Association.

Agur, Robert Henry (1856-1913) Businessman. Born in Oxford County, Canada, he was educated at Ingersoll High School, Upper Canada College, and the Toronto Business College. He moved to Winnipeg in 1882 and became involved with a series of farm implement manufacturers, becoming a partner in the firm of Massey and Company. In 1898 he became manager of the North West Department of what was by then Massey-Harris Limited.

Aikins, James Albert Manning ("Jam," 1851-1929) Lawyer, politician. A son of James C. Aikins,* he was born in Peel County, Ontario, and educated at Upper Canada College and the University of Toronto. He began practising law in Winnipeg in 1879, serving as Manitoba counsel for the Department of Justice from 1879 to 1896. He also was counsel for the western division of the CPR from 1880 to 1911. Elected MP from Brandon in 1911, he served until 1915, when he resigned to reorganize the Conservative Party in Manitoba. In 1914 he took the lead in reviving the Canadian Bar Association, serving as president to 1923. He was knighted in 1914. He and his party were badly defeated in the 1916 election. He was president of the Canadian Bar Association from 1914 to 1923 and lieutenant-governor of Manitoba from 1916 to 1926. His lieutenant-governor's papers are in the PAM.

Aikins, James Cox (1823-1904) Politician. Born in Toronto to Irish immigrant parents, he was educated at Victoria College, Cobourg. A successful farmer, he was elected to the Legislative Assembly in 1854 as a Clear Grit. Despite his lukewarm support for Confederation — he objected to it as a coalition measure — he was called to the Senate in 1867. He served as secretary of state from 1869 to 1873, helped organize the Dominion Lands Bureau, and wrote the Public Lands Act of 1872. He was reappointed as secretary of state as a concession to reform voters when the Conservatives returned to power in 1878. Aikins was a fervent supporter of temperance throughout his life, and this made him a political liability after 1880. He was appointed lieutenant-governor of Manitoba in 1882, at which time he resigned from the Senate, and he served until 1888. He was recalled to the Senate in 1896. He died in Toronto. His correspondence (1882-93) and other papers are in the PAM. *DCB* XIII, 6-9.

Aikins, John Somerset (1850-1911) Businessman, politician. The eldest son of James C. Aikins,* he was educated at Upper Canada College and the University of Toronto. He migrated to the Prairies in 1875, settling in Winnipeg in 1879. In 1880 he sat for Rockwood in the Manitoba legislature. He was an early director of the Winnipeg General Hospital and a member of the real estate firm of Aikins and Montgomery.

Aird, Alexander A. (1855?-1916) Civil servant. Born in Cranston, Canada, he taught school in Ontario before coming to Winnipeg, where he became secretary of the Police Commission and clerk of the Police Court. He held these posts for 35 years.

Aird, John (1855-1938) Banker. Born in Longueil, Canada, he was educated at the Model School, Toronto. He joined the Canadian Bank of Commerce as a stenographer in 1878, and rose to become president in 1924. He was manager of the Commerce bank in Winnipeg from 1899 to 1908, and superintendent of Western Canadian operations from 1908 to 1911 before returning to Toronto. Knighted in 1917, he chaired the Aird Commission on Radio Broadcasting 1928-29. The Aird Commission recommended the nationalization of broadcasting in Canada, leading to the establishment of the Canadian Radio Broadcasting Commission, which in 1936 became the Canadian Broadcasting Corporation.

Aldous, Montague (1850-1946) Surveyor. Born in Charlottetown and educated at Prince of Wales College and Bowdoin College in Maine, he owned a coasting schooner on the Island before he came to Winnipeg in 1874 to work as a government surveyor on one of the boundary commissions. He joined the HBC as surveyor and then was in charge of its land department until his resignation in 1907. After his retirement from the HBC, he lived during the winter at the Manitoba Club, summered at Lake of the Woods, and between seasons spent time in Montreal and Barbados, where he was regarded as a "character." Fond of fast cars, golf, and sailboats, he was a huge bear of a man, 6 feet 4 inches tall and weighing 300 pounds.

Aldrick, Albert Alexander (1894-1972) Music critic. Born in Coventry, England, he was music critic for the *Winnipeg Tribune* from 1921 to 1928 and the *Winnipeg Free Press* from 1938 to 1955. His byline was "A.A.A."

Alexander, Louise (d. 1946) Painter. She studied at the Winnipeg School of Art from 1913 to 1917 and was secretary of the Winnipeg Art Students Sketch Club from 1914 to 1916, later serving as vice-president in 1927 and president in 1928. Alexander came to specialize in portraiture, winning first prize in a Sketch Club exhibition in 1920 and exhibiting at the Royal Canadian Academy of Arts exhibition in 1924, both with portraits. She solicited and received a number of commissions for portraits of Winnipeg mayors, including one of Mayor Parnell and another of Mayor McLean, both in 1928. She died in Vancouver.

Alexander, William (1880-1917) Soldier. Born in London, England, he came to Winnipeg after service with the British army and worked for the Auto Tire and Vulcanizing Company. He joined the 103rd Regiment in 1914 and served under fire for several years before he was found wandering behind the lines after an assault. He was court-martialled for desertion and shot by a firing squad on 18 October 1917. *DCB* XIV, 13-14.

Allan, George William (1860-1940) Lawyer, businessman, politician. Born at Moss Park, Toronto, he was educated at Upper Canada College, Galt Collegiate Institute, Trinity College School, and Trinity College University. He came to Winnipeg in 1879 and was called to the Manitoba bar in 1882, establishing the law firm of Munson and Allan. He became president of Great-West Life Assurance Company and chair of the Canadian Committee of the HBC. Elected to the House of Commons in 1917 as a conscriptionist, he served until 1921. In 1917 Allan was Food and Fuel Control administrator for Manitoba.

Allemand, Pierre (c. 1662-1691) Pilot, cartographer. Born in France, he first achieved prominence as pilot in an expedition of Radisson and Groseilliers to Hudson Bay in 1682-83. He served in subsequent expeditions and was responsible for several maps of Hudson Bay. In 1687 he also proposed hydrographic surveys of the St. Lawrence River. *DCB* I, 56.

Allen, Frank (1874-1965) Professor. Born in Meductic, New Brunswick, he graduated from the University of New Brunswick in 1895, receiving the Alumni Gold Medal. He received an MA in 1902 and a PhD in 1905 from Cornell University. In 1904 he was appointed first professor of physics and mineralogy at the University of Manitoba, where he headed the Physics Department until 1944. He was a member of the Polish Army in France Relief Commission in 1918. He published 300 scientific research papers and was made a fellow of the Royal Society of Canada in 1944. The new physics building at the University of Manitoba was named for him in 1961. His papers are at the UML Archives.

Allen, John Jacob (1867-1959) Musician. Born in Manchester, England, he was educated in English choir schools and was a solo chorister at Gloucester Cathedral. In 1906 he came to Winnipeg. A double bassist, he played in many Winnipeg theatre and hotel orchestras over the years and was secretary of the Musicians Union.

Allen, Lillian B. (1889-1985) Painter, teacher. Graduating in arts from the University of Manitoba in 1926, she then enrolled at the Winnipeg School of Art until 1928, teaching there in the Saturday morning classes in 1927-28. Much influenced by Lemoine Fitzgerald, she went to Toronto to attend the Ontario College of Education. Allen eventually returned to the University of Manitoba, teaching housing and design, and retiring in 1971. She helped found the Volunteer Committee of the Winnipeg Art Gallery and was awarded "Woman of the Year" by the YWCA in 1980. Her papers are at the UML Archives.

Allen, Ralph (1913-1966) Journalist, writer. Born in Winnipeg, he began his journalistic career with the *Winnipeg Tribune.* He moved to Toronto and the *Toronto Globe* in 1938, then to *Maclean's* and finally to the *Toronto Star.* He wrote five novels, three of which dealt with men at war. He also wrote several works of history, including *Ordeal by Fire: Canada 1910-1945* (1961). None of his writing was set in Manitoba. See Christina McCall Newman, ed., *The Man from Oxbow: The Best of Ralph Allen* (1967).

Allison, Frederick Gerard (1904-1989) Physician. Born in Stayner, Ontario, he came to Winnipeg in 1910, graduating in arts (1924) and medicine (1929) from the University of Manitoba. Son of William Allison,* he did postgraduate work in Vienna and London before returning to Winnipeg to specialize in internal medicine. He became president of the Manitoba Medical Association in 1960 and chair of Manitoba Medical Services in 1961. He served on the Canadian Medical Association committee that proposed a pension plan for doctors.

Allison, William Talbot (1874-1941) Cleric, professor. Born in Ontario, he was educated at the University of Toronto and Yale University. He served as pastor of the Presbyterian Church in Stayner, Ontario, until his appointment to Wesley College, Winnipeg, in 1910. Ten years later he became assistant professor at the University of Manitoba. Allison was active in journalism, syndicating a weekly book review feature in leading Canadian newspapers. He was a founder of the Canadian Authors' Association and one of the first educators to take advantage of the medium of radio, lecturing over CKY as early as 1924. He was the author of *Bolshevism in English Literature* (1921). A scrapbook of newspaper clippings is in the PAM.

Alloway, Charles Valentine (1850-1929) Banker. Born in Ireland, he moved to Hamilton with his parents in 1855, residing there until 1871, when he came to Manitoba with the second contingent of the Canadian expeditionary force. He hunted buffalo on the Prairies in the 1870s. Active in scrip speculation, he carried the first mail from Calgary to Edmonton. He went into partnership with his brother William* in the banking business.

Alloway, William Forbes (1852-1930) Businessman, financier, philanthropist. Born in Ireland, he came to Canada with his parents at age three. He came west with the Wolseley Expedition as a private and worked briefly as a veterinarian. Then, beginning with a tobacco store, he soon moved into freighting and was an active dealer in Métis scrip. After 1879 he was a partner in the banking business of Alloway and Champion, which was transferred to the

Canadian Bank of Commerce in 1923. In 1921 he established the Winnipeg Foundation with a gift of $100,000, and he gave it most of his fortune. Alloway was a silent partner in many business ventures, especially in the milling industry. He boasted that he had paid cash for everything throughout his life.

Allum, William James Douglas (1917-1992) Hockey player. Born in the Winnipeg neighbourhood of Elmwood, he attended Lord Selkirk School. He played professional hockey for many years, including a stint with the New York Rangers in their 1940 Stanley Cup season. Allum also played lacrosse for several Mann Cup teams. He coached several sports after retirement.

Allward, John Raphael (1856-1929) Craftsman, artist. He studied stained glass with John La Farge and worked in Manitoba from 1902 to 1916, creating many windows. He helped found the Manitoba Society of Artists. After service in the Canadian army in WWI, he moved to Seattle.

Almazoff, Solomon (b. 1890) Editor, radical. He came to Winnipeg from Russia in 1913. While a student at the University of Manitoba, he became the editor of the radical paper *Die Volke Stimme*. During the crackdown on radicals during the Winnipeg General Strike, he was arrested 17 June 1919, four days after writing his exams. After his release, he left for the United States, where he worked as a labour organizer in the Minneapolis region for many years.

Almey, J. Robert (1895-1988) Horticulturalist. Born in Leicester, England, he came to Canada at age 16 and graduated from the Ontario Agricultural College. He was appointed Manitoba's first provincial horticulturalist in 1921, then joined the CPR as chief horticulturalist of the western lines in 1928. He was promoted to general agriculture agent in 1946, and he retired in 1960. He was responsible for most of the landscaping at CPR railway depots. A rosybloom ornamental crabapple developed at the Morden station in 1945, named for him, was chosen Canada's centennial tree in 1967.

Alsip, William (1833-1912) Businessman. Born in Pittsburgh, Pennsylvania, he was in the brick-making business in several states before founding the Alsip Brick, Tile and Lumber Company in Winnipeg around 1900.

Anderson, Charles Daniel ("Flatboat," 1829-1914) Boat captain. Born in Sweden, he arrived in Chicago in 1851. He came to Fort Garry in 1872 to captain boats running on the Red River between Minnesota and Fort Garry. He was the first grand master of the IOOF in Manitoba.

Anderson, Cyril Leonard (1904-1977) Businessman. Born in Winnipeg, he moved to Chicago and returned to Manitoba in 1927, where he joined Canada Packers' Feed Division. He made many improvements to animal feed by introducing modern nutritional concepts, and in 1939 formed his own company, Feed-Rite Mills. Anderson pioneered in the use of canola and soybean meal, always advocating the economic value of proper feeding practices, particularly for hogs and poultry. He was honoured by the Canadian Feed Industry Association in 1977, and received the Buffalo Rooster award from the Manitoba Hatchery Association. He is a member of the Manitoba Agricultural Hall of Fame.

Anderson, David (1814-1885) Clergyman. Born in London, England, he was educated at the Edinburgh Academy and at Exeter College, Oxford. Consecrated as first bishop of the Anglican diocese of Rupert's Land in 1849, his incumbency was a turbulent one, as he battled with the colony's Presbyterians, its government, and his own clergy. He increased the number of clergy in the colony and regularized the educational system, including the St. John's Collegiate School, before his resignation in 1864. See *The Net in the Bay. A Journal by the Bishop of Rupert's Land* (1854) and his published diary of the 1852 flood. Consult also M.P. Wilkinson, "The episcopate of the Right Reverend David Anderson, DD," (MA diss., University of Manitoba, 1950). There are scattered papers in the PAM and extensive papers in the Rupert's Land Archives. *DCB* XI, 18-20.

Anderson, Edward (b. 1867) Lawyer. Born in Dorchester, Quebec, he came to Winnipeg in 1879. He attended the University of Manitoba, then practised law in Portage la Prairie before becoming a junior partner in the law firm of Moran, Anderson, and Guy. He was for many years general counsel for the Winnipeg Electric Company.

Anderson, George (b. 1890) Soccer organizer. Born in Fraserburgh, Scotland, he came to Canada in 1911 and played soccer for clubs across Manitoba. He served with the Winnipeg Rifles in WWI, and after the war he became secretary of the Manitoba Minor Soccer Association, Manitoba Senior Soccer Association, and Canadian Soccer Football Association. He was employed by the Veterans' Press in Winnipeg. After WWII he organized Canadian tours by European soccer teams for the Dominion Football Association. He was inducted into the Canadian Sports Hall of Fame in 1973 and is a member of the Manitoba Sports Hall of Fame.

Anderson, John Ogle (1912-1969) Cleric. Born in Rathwell, Manitoba, he graduated from St. John's College and was ordained in 1937. He served many Manitoba parishes. During WWII he was an armed forces chaplain, and he was wounded in Holland when his jeep hit a land mine. He served as rector of Christ Church Cathedral in Ottawa from 1949 to 1962, then returned to Manitoba as suffragan bishop of Rupert's Land, becoming bishop of British Columbia in 1968. He died in Victoria.

Anderson, Samuel (1839-1881) Surveyor. Born in London, England, he attended the Royal Military Academy at Woolwich in 1857-58, and was appointed to the staff of the North American Boundary Commission which was to survey the 49th parallel from the Gulf of Georgia to the Rockies. He worked on the survey from 1859 to 1865, and in 1872 was appointed chief astronomer to the British commission charged with surveying the boundary from Lake of the Woods to the Rockies. Based at Pembina, he did most of the work of organization for the working engineers of the commission in surveying Manitoba's southern boundary. He died in Scotland. There are Anderson letters in the Yale University Library. See also his "The North-American Boundary from Lake of the Woods to the Rocky Mountains," *Royal Geographical Society Journal*, 46 (1876), 228-62; *DCB* XI, 20-22.

Anderson, William Henry (1882-1955) Musician. Born in London, England, he came to Winnipeg in 1910. He served as choir director, teacher, and composer of carols and anthems. He directed the St. Andrew's River Heights United Church choir from 1934 to 1954.

Andrews, Alfred A. (1865-1912) Businessman. Born in Augusta, Canada, he moved to Winnipeg in 1881, becoming vice-president and general manager of the

Winnipeg Rubber Company. He was one of the city's most active boosters, serving as president of the Winnipeg Industrial Bureau.

Andrews, Alfred Joseph (1865-1950) Lawyer, civic politician. Born in Franklin, Canada, the son of a Methodist minister, he came with his family to Winnipeg in 1881. Articled as a lawyer, he was admitted to the Manitoba bar in 1886. He was a founding member of the Winnipeg Humane Society in 1894. He was elected mayor of Winnipeg in 1898 and re-elected in 1899. One of the leading members of the Citizens' Committee of 1,000 in the 1919 Winnipeg General Strike, he was appointed representative of the federal justice department on 26 May 1919, charged with ascertaining whether the activities of the strike leaders were seditious or treasonable. He became special deputy minister of justice and chief Crown counsel in subsequent court trials of the strike leaders. See Tom Mitchell, ed., "A.J. Andrews to Arthur Meighen: Winnipeg General Strike Correspondence," *Manitoba History,* no. 24 (autumn 1992): 29-35.

Andrews, George William (1869-1943) Businessman, politician. Born in Oxfordshire, England, he immigrated to Manitoba in 1890, settling in Springfield to farm. He later moved to Winnipeg and entered the real estate business. He was elected to the Union Parliament in 1917 from Winnipeg Centre as a conscriptionist.

Andrusyshen, Constantine H. (1907-1983) Scholar, educator. Born in Winnipeg, he founded the Department of Slavic Studies at the University of Saskatchewan. He compiled a *Ukrainian-English Dictionary* (1953). With Watson Kirkconnell he translated the *Complete Poetical Works of Taras Shevchenko,* as well as *Ukrainian Poets* (1963). He also translated Wasyl Stefanyk's *The Stone Cross.* There are papers at the NAC.

Anehereo See Bernard, Gertrude.

Antonovych, Kateryna (1887-1975) Artist. Born in Ukraine, she was an internationally known artist who studied in western Europe, immigrated to Prague in 1923, and joined her daughter in Winnipeg in 1949. She opened an art school in 1954. Antonovych was active in Ukrainian women's and community organizations. Her papers are at the NAC.

Appleton, John (1867-1937) Labour leader, journalist. Born in Yorkshire, England, he came to Canada in 1890. He became president of the Winnipeg Trades and Labor Council in 1896. In 1898 he was appointed financial and municipal editor of the *Manitoba Free Press.* He resigned in 1912 to become editor of the *Financial Post* in Toronto.

Archibald, Adams George (1814-1893) Lawyer, politician. Descended from Ulster Scots who settled Colchester County, Nova Scotia, he was born in Truro and educated at Pictou Academy. Called to the Prince Edward Island bar in 1838 and the Nova Scotia bar in 1839, he was first elected to Nova Scotia's Assembly in 1851 as a Liberal (reformer). He served as solicitor general of Nova Scotia in 1856-57 and as attorney general from 1860 to 1863. Archibald was an ardent pro-confederate who attended all the major conferences. He served as lieutenant-governor of Manitoba from 1870 to 1873 and as lieutenant-governor of Nova Scotia from 1873 to 1883. While lieutenant-governor of Manitoba he negotiated several Indian treaties and attempted to settle the Métis land question. He was criticized by many as too favourably disposed to the Native peoples and their claims. See Neil Edgar Allan Ronaghan, "The Archibald Administration in Manitoba, 1870-72" (PhD diss., University of Manitoba, 1987). There are extensive papers at the PAM. *DCB* XII, 30-36.

Armes, Henry P. (1885-1951) Professor, soldier. Born in England, he graduated from the University of Leeds in 1905 and received a PhD from the University of Strasbourg in 1909 in organic chemistry. He came to Winnipeg and the University of Manitoba in 1911. He served with the Western Universities Battalion in WWI, losing a leg at Passchendaele. Armes was commanding officer of the Canadian Officers' Training Corps in Manitoba from 1932 to 1938. He was appointed dean of the University of Manitoba in 1945 and president two years later. He retired in 1949. The Armes Building at the University of Manitoba is named for him.

Armington, Frank Milton (b. 1876) Artist. Born in Fordwich, Ontario, he studied art in France at L'académie Julian, Paris. While briefly in Winnipeg, he was vice-president of the Manitoba Society of Artists upon its founding in 1903. He later became a distinguished etcher, residing in Paris.

Armstrong, George (1870-1956) Union leader, radical. A native of Scarborough, Ontario, he came to Winnipeg in 1905. A member of the Carpenters' Union, he was a one-time organizer of that union, as well as a founding member of the Socialist Party in Winnipeg. He ran against F.W. Dixon for the provincial legislature in 1914, gaining 953 votes. A prominent exponent of Marxism and regarded as one of Canada's leading soap-box orators, Armstrong was highly critical of the Canadian government for its repressive policies toward dissent. He was married to Helen Armstrong.* One of the leaders of the Winnipeg Strike of 1919, he was arrested on 17 June, tried on seven counts of seditious conspiracy, found guilty, and sentenced to one year in prison. In 1920 he won election to the provincial legislature as a Socialist Party of Canada candidate. Armstrong and his family left Canada for Chicago in 1922, depriving Manitoba of two of its most influential radical leaders. He died in Concord, California. See Harry and Mildred Gutkin, *Profiles in Dissent: The Shaping of Radical Thought in the Canadian West* (1997), 181-192.

Armstrong, Helen (Jury) (1875-1947) Union leader, radical. Leader of the local chapter of the Women's Labor League, she was referred to as "business manager for the Women's Unions" and later dubbed by eastern newspapers "the Wild Woman of the West." In 1917 she intervened on behalf of "aliens" arrested for breach of contract, and mounted public platforms to demonstrate against conscription. In April, 1918 she was elected president of the Hotel and Household Workers' Union in Winnipeg. Armstrong resigned as president of the Women's Labor League in February 1919 when it supported the Minimum Wage Board. She was in charge of arrangements for the kitchen maintained by the Women's League during the Winnipeg General Strike. Arrested several times during the strike for disorderly conduct, "Ma" Armstrong was an ardent feminist as well as a socialist. She ran unsuccessfully for Winnipeg City Council in 1923. She was married to George Armstrong.* She died in California. See Harry and Mildred Gutkin, *Profiles in Dissent: The Shaping of Radical Thought in the Canadian West* (1997), 213-50.

Armstrong, Hugh (1858-1926) Politician. Born in New York state, he came to Carleton County, Upper Canada, at age two. He moved to Manitoba in 1883. He was elected to the provincial Parliament as representative for Woodlands in 1892 and then was elected MLA for Portage la Prairie in 1905, 1907, and 1911, serving as provincial treasurer from 1908 to 1915. He was a pioneer fish exporter.

Armstrong, Ida Manning (1905-1982) Physician, sportswoman. Born in Gladstone, Manitoba, she came to Winnipeg in 1915 when her father James* joined the Norris cabinet. She attended Kelvin High School and graduated with a BSc from the University of Manitoba in 1926. She completed her medical degree at the University of Manitoba in 1936, studied in England in 1937-38, and entered private practice in Winnipeg as an obstetrician and gynecologist. She gave radio lectures for women on medical emergencies during WWII. She was active in golf, curling, and bowling. Her papers are at the PAM.

Armstrong, James William (1860-1928) Physician, politician. Born in Nova Scotia, he graduated from Acadia College. After teaching in Brandon he studied at the Manitoba Medical College and did postgraduate work in Edinburgh. He became health officer for the Municipality of Gladstone and was elected its MPP as a Liberal from 1897 to 1922, serving as provincial secretary, minister of health, and, from 1915 to 1922, municipal commissioner in the Norris government. Extensive papers are at the PAM.

Arnold, Alfred Edwin (b. 1898) Horse breeder. Born in Toronto, he was educated in Shoal Lake, Manitoba, and soon entered the heavy horse business, specializing in Clydesdales. Throughout his life, he not only bred prize-winning horses but helped others raise and show them. He is a member of the Manitoba Agricultural Hall of Fame.

Aronovitch, A. Herman (b. 1882) Businessman. Born in Russia and educated in Grand Forks, North Dakota, he joined the New York Life insurance company in 1905 and came to Winnipeg in 1907 to found the firm of Aronovitch and Leipsic.

Arpin, Maurice J. (1923-1983) Lawyer. Born in Lorette, Manitoba, he was educated at Collège de Saint-Boniface and the University of Manitoba law school. He served as a lieutenant in the RCN during WWII. Called to the bar in 1950, he was a prominent lawyer, serving as chair of the University of Manitoba board of governors from 1969 to 1971. He was the author of *The Law and You* (1966). His papers are at the PAM.

Arsenych, Jaroslaw (1889-1953) Judge. Born in Galicia, he came to Winnipeg in 1904 virtually penniless. He worked in quarries at Stony Mountain to raise money to learn English. He taught school in Dauphin and attended the University of Manitoba, studying arts. He was encouraged to study law when he served as interpreter in a law case in 1913. He attended the University of Manitoba law school from 1914 to 1917 and practised law until 1948, when he was appointed as a county court judge, the first Canadian judge of Ukrainian descent.

Arsin, Jean (fl. 1909-20) Filmmaker. He came to Winnipeg around 1909 and was the chief filmmaker in the city between that date and 1920. He was also a pioneer animator. He moved to Montreal in 1920 and became a well-known documentary filmmaker.

Ashdown, James Henry (1844-1924) Businessman, financier, civic leader. Born in London, England, he came to Canada with his parents at age eight and grew up in small-town Ontario. He was apprenticed to a tinsmith and first went west to Kansas. After coming to Winnipeg by oxcart in 1868 he bought out Winnipeg's tinsmith in 1869, establishing his small hardware store ("James H. Ashdown Hardware Merchant and Tinsmith") and building it into a major wholesale and retail business. He supported J.C. Schultz in the Red River Rebellion of 1870 and was imprisoned by Louis Riel. He constructed his large house in Point Douglas in 1878. Real estate speculation added to his wealth. He built his second warehouse (today an apartment block) in 1896. An original member of the Winnipeg Board of Trade, he served as mayor of Winnipeg in 1907 and 1908. He was a prominent member of many boards of directors in both the business and the non-business world. His estate was valued at $1,634,000. See Lorne A. Shropshire, "A Founding Father of Winnipeg: James Henry Ashdown 1844-1924," *Manitoba History*, no. 19 (spring 1990): 23-26. There are scattered papers at the PAM.

Ashmore, Cyril Frank (b. 1894) Watercolourist. Born in Sheffield, England, he grew up in Liverpool before coming to Manitoba in 1911. He farmed until 1915, took a correspondence course in applied art, was wounded in WWI, and joined Brigden's for 53 years upon demobilization in 1918. He joined the Manitoba Society of Artists in 1925. Ashmore was best known for his delicate watercolours.

Atakawinin (d. 1916) Warrior. A leading Saulteaux warrior in the fighting against the Sioux around Portage la Prairie in the 1850s and 1860s, he moved to Lizard Point in 1863 and later to Valley River.

Atchison, John D. (1870-1959) Architect. Born at Monmouth, Illinois, he was trained at the Chicago Art Institute and the Chicago Manual Training School before moving to Winnipeg in 1905. He served on the Art Committee of the Winnipeg School of Art from 1913 to 1924. Atchison was the most important "Chicago Style" architect in Winnipeg, designing nearly 100 buildings, including the Great West Life Insurance Building, the Winnipeg General Hospital, the Boyd Building, and the Manitoba School for the Deaf, as well as the Winnipeg Industrial Bureau in 1911 and its addition that accommodated the Art Gallery in 1912. He moved to California in 1922.

Atkinson, George (d. 1913) Ornithologist. Born in Toronto, he first came west to Port Arthur, where he became an expert on the turkey buzzard, before moving to Winnipeg and then to Portage la Prairie. A leading Manitoba taxidermist and ornithologist with a store at Portage la Prairie, he was the author of *Manitoba Birds of Prey* and *Rare Bird Records of Manitoba*. He drowned after suffering an epileptic fit while rowing on the Assiniboine River.

Aubert, Pierre (1814-1890) Cleric. Born at Digné, France, he entered the Oblate Order in 1830 and came to Canada in 1844. A year later he was appointed superior and founder of the first Oblate mission at Red River, based in St. Boniface. Upon his arrival at St. Boniface, he also became priest of the cathedral and vicar general. But his French origins made it impossible for him to advance to a bishopric in Red River, and he moved east to Bytown in 1850 and then to Montreal until his return to France in 1865. *DCB* XI, 33-34.

Auld, William (c. 1770-c. 1830) Surgeon, fur trader. Born in Scotland, he possibly studied medicine at the University of Edinburgh. He first joined the HBC in 1790 as a surgeon. In 1795 he became an "inland trader" at Fort Churchill. Auld had enormous difficulty in coming to terms with the new management system introduced by the family of the Earl of Selkirk after 1810. He did not get on well with Miles Macdonell and seemed unable to execute the instructions sent to him by Selkirk. He resigned in 1814 and fought with the Company for another year before retiring to Leith in Scotland. *DCB* VI, 17-18.

Aulneau, Jean Pierre (1705-1736) Cleric. Born in France, he entered the Jesuit order in 1720. He came to Canada in 1734 and travelled west with La Vérendrye in 1735. Aulneau was murdered with a party of 20 French by Sioux Indians in 1736 at Fort St. Charles. He is buried in the St. Boniface Cathedral cemetery. *DCB* II, 30-40.

Austin, Albert William (1857-1934) Businessman. Born in Toronto, the son of the founder of the Dominion Bank, Toronto, he came to Winnipeg in 1880 and organized the Winnipeg Street Railway Company in 1881, opening the line with horse-drawn cars in 1882. The cars were operated on runners in the winter. Austin electrified the system in 1891 to produce the first commercial electric transit system in Canada. He returned to Toronto in 1894.

Bachysky, Nicolas Volodymir (1888-1969) Politician. Born in Celo Serafinily, Western Ukraine, he came to Canada in 1904 and to Manitoba in 1909 to homestead at Fisher Branch. He subsequently attended Brandon Teachers College and became a teacher. He was elected a MLA in 1922, and served until 1958. He was first elected as a member of the United Farmers Movement, became a Progressive in 1932 and from 1949 sat as a Liberal-Progressive. He was Speaker of the House from 1950 to 1958. Bachysky was active in many Ukrainian organizations.

Back, George (1796-1878) Explorer, artist. Born in Stockport, England, he joined the Royal Navy at the age of 12. He was a French prisoner of war from 1809 to 1814. In 1817 Back volunteered for duty aboard one of the first of the arctic expeditions of the post-Napoleonic period. This service brought him the acquaintanceship of Lieutenant John Franklin, who chose Back to accompany his 1819 expedition to Repulse Bay. This expedition spent a winter at Cumberland House. For this and subsequent expeditions, Back's watercolours and drawings became essential to Franklin's published narratives. The originals on which the Franklin illustrations were based still survive, virtually unknown. In 1833 Back himself led another expedition, which began from Lake Winnipeg and explored extensively in the Back River region. Another expedition in HMS Terror in 1836-7 was less successful. Back settled down to become the London doyen of arctic exploration, serving on innumerable committees that advised the admiralty on search expeditions for Sir John Franklin. He had a reputation as a womanizer. Back's principal publication was his *Narrative of the Arctic Land Expedition to the Mouth of the Great Fish River* (1836), which went through several editions and was translated into a number of languages including French and German. *DCB* X, 26-29.

Bain, Donald H. (1874-1962) Athlete and sportsman. Born in Belleville, Ontario, he came west to Winnipeg with his family at the age of six. He won the Three Mile Roller Skating Championship of Manitoba in 1887 and played centre for the Winnipeg Victorias from 1895 to 1902, serving as team captain for three campaigns. He retired from hockey after the Victorias won their second Stanley Cup in 1901. Bain won many figure-skating titles, played lacrosse, and won the Canadian trapshooting title in 1903. He was an early proponent of marshland management for wildfowl. He founded the wholesale firm of Donald H. Bain Limited, with branches in major Canadian cities. Bain took the lead in founding both the old and new Winter Clubs. He was fond of automobiles and at one point owned 13. He is a member of the Manitoba Sports Hall of Fame.

Bain, John Farquhar (1849-1905) Lawyer, judge. Born in Perth, Canada, he graduated from Queen's University in 1867 and was called to the bar in 1871, the year he migrated to Manitoba. In 1873 he went into partnership with Sedley Blanchard in a pioneer law firm. Bain served as treasurer of the Manitoba Law Society and in 1887 was appointed puisne judge of the Court of Queen's Bench. He died unmarried.

Baird, Andrew Browning (1855-1940) Professor. Born in Motherwell, Canada, in October 1855, he attended Upper Canada College, graduating from the University of Toronto in 1873. He then attended Knox College in Toronto, then the University of Edinburgh (graduating in 1881), then Leipzig. He received his DD from Knox College. He was ordained in 1881, and he left for the Canadian West immediately. He was called to Manitoba College as professor of church history in 1887. Baird served as president of the Manitoba Historical Society (1892-95) and Manitoba Horticultural Society (1896-99). He was moderator of the Presbyterian Church of Canada in 1916-17. His extensive papers are at the University of Winnipeg, with additional papers at the PAM. For a biography, see John A.M. Edwards, *Andrew Baird of Manitoba College* (1965).

Baird, Hugh Northcote (1878-1948) Grain merchant. He came to Winnipeg in 1901, becoming a member of the firm of Baird and Botterell, and he was president of the Winnipeg Grain Exchange in 1909-10. In 1919 he was chair of the Finance Committee of the Citizens' Committee of 1,000. In 1924 he became head of the National Steel Car Company of Montreal.

Baird, James Bryson (1859-1939) Businessman, politician. Born in Appleton, Canada, he came to Manitoba in 1879, settling at Pilot Mound. Baird owned a general store, then went into the cattle business. Mayor of Pilot Mound at the time of its incorporation, he was elected to the Manitoba legislature in 1907, 1910, 1914, and 1915, serving as Speaker from 1916 to 1921.

Baker, George William (1854-1917) Lawyer, municipal politician. Born and educated in Ottawa, he came to Winnipeg in 1881 and was called to the Manitoba bar in 1882. A municipal politician, he was frequently elected to the Winnipeg City Council and was a Winnipeg police magistrate from 1901 to 1903. A diary (1881-82) and papers are at the PAM.

Baldwinson, Baldwin Lárus (1856-1936) Newspaper editor, politician. Born in Iceland, he first settled in Toronto and then came to Winnipeg in 1882. In 1883 he became the Dominion government's Icelandic immigration agent, serving until 1896. During those years more than 7,000 people immigrated from Iceland to Canada, many under his direction. From 1898 to 1913 he was proprietor and editor of the newspaper *Heimskringla*. A Conservative, he represented Gimli in the Manitoba legislature from 1899 to 1907 and from 1910 to 1913 and served as deputy provincial secretary of Manitoba from 1913 to 1922.

Balfour, David (1937-1991) Community leader. Born in Winnipeg, he was raised in Flin Flon and graduated from the University of Manitoba in arts in 1961. He received a law degree from the University of Manitoba and joined the firm of Thompson Dorfman Sweatman in 1966. Active in the Manitoba Red Cross for many years, he was Canadian president from 1975 to 1977. He was president of the Canadian Disaster Relief Fund from 1978 to 1983 and president of Winnipeg Meals on Wheels from 1979 to 1981. He died in Winnipeg.

Ball, Jimmy (b. 1903) Track athlete. Born in Dauphin, he attended Dauphin College and the University of Manitoba, where he studied pharmacy. He won Manitoba and western Canadian intercollegiate track titles in 1925 and won a place on the 1928 Canadian Olympic team, finishing second in the 400 metre race at the Olympics. He also won a bronze medal with the Canadian relay team. He won another bronze medal in the relay in the 1932 Olympics, and in 1933 he won the Norton H. Crowe Trophy as "Canada's Outstanding Athlete." He is a member of the Canadian Sports Hall of Fame and the Manitoba Sports Hall of Fame.

Ballantyne, Robert Michael (1825-1894) Fur trader, author. Born in Edinburgh, Scotland, he joined the HBC at age 16 and spent six years as clerk with the Company at Hudson Bay and the Lower St. Lawrence. His first book, *Every-day Life in the Wilds of North America, During Six Years' Residence in the Territories of the Hon. Hudson Bay Company* (1848), was autobiographical, assembled from his letters home and his journals. With it he began a distinguished career as a writer of adventure books for boys, many of them (20 out of 120) set in the Northwest, which serves as an unusual locale for heroic derring-do by his young heroes. For a biography, consult Eric

Quayle, *Ballantyne the Brave: A Victorian Writer and His Family* (1967). *DCB* XII, 53-54.

Ballenden, John (c. 1812-1856) Fur trader. Born in Stromness, Scotland, Ballenden joined the HBC as apprentice clerk in 1829. He rose to accountant at Upper Fort Garry by 1836, the year he married Sarah McLeod.* Ballenden spent several years after 1840 in the Company's service in Upper Canada. In 1848 he was promoted to chief factor and placed in command of Lower Fort Garry, suffering a paralytic stroke on his way to take up his post. Ballenden was unable to staunch the growing free trade movement. He was also unable to keep his wife away from the company of Captain Christopher Foss,* who in the summer of 1850 sued several local residents for defamatory conspiracy for spreading stories of his adultery with Mrs. Ballenden. Ballenden's health went downhill steadily, despite a transfer to Fort Vancouver in 1851. He returned to Red River in 1854 but soon retired to Edinburgh, where he died. *DCB* VIII, 59-60.

Ballenden, Sarah (McLeod) (1818-1853) Fur-trade wife. Born in Rupert's Land, she was the daughter of Chief Trader Alexander McLeod and his "half-breed wife." In the 1930s she was sent for education to Red River, where she met and married John Ballenden.* Pretty and vivacious, she chafed during Ballenden's posting to Upper Canada and rejoiced at his return in 1848. The pleasure was considerably reduced by her husband's stroke, but Sarah enjoyed the status of the wife of a chief factor, including a "dalliance" with an English officer who often ate at the HBC mess table. Those who regarded Sarah Ballenden's ancestry as tainted led the attempts to blacken her character by spreading rumours of adultery, and the tiny settlement chose sides as Captain Christopher Foss* went to court in 1850 "to clear the reputation of a lady." Despite a jury finding in Foss's favour with an assessment of high damages against the defendants, those who had criticized Sarah refused to be chastised. An incriminating note allegedly from Sarah to Foss that was intercepted by George Simpson* hardly helped. Alexander Ross reported, "If there is such a thing as dying of a broken heart, she cannot live long." She died in Edinburgh shortly after being reunited with her husband. See Sylvia Van Kirk, *"Many Tender Ties": Women in Fur Trade Society in Western Canada, 1670-1870* (1980) and her "The Reputation of a Lady," *Manitoba History*, no. 11 (1986): 4-11. *DCB* VIII, 573-75.

Balsillie, Gladys (1919-1987) Burlesque agent. Born in Franklin, Manitoba, she attended St. Mary's Academy. She opened a restaurant on Main Street in Winnipeg and ended up running a restaurant consultancy firm and a bartending school, as well as managing a stable of 100 dancers. For years she was known as Winnipeg's "Queen of Burlesque" because of the agency for exotic dancers she operated in the province.

Balsillie, John (1839-1906) Fur trader. Born in Scotland, he joined the HBC in 1855. He was made chief trader at Fort Garry in 1872, soon becoming an accountant in the HBC land department.

Banfield, Armine Frederick (1850-1908) Merchant. Born in Quebec City to a leading merchant family, he came to Winnipeg in 1882 and soon established a dry-goods firm. In 1893 he founded A.F. Banfield and Company, one of the largest household furnishing firms in the West. Banfield was an active member of the Winnipeg Board of Trade.

Bannatyne, Andrew Graham Ballenden (1829-1889) Fur trader, merchant, politician. Born in South Ronaldsay, Orkney Islands, he joined the HBC service at age 14, later becoming a free trader. According to Walter Traill, he quit the Company to marry Annie McDermott,* since junior clerks were not allowed to wed. In 1857 he was arrested by the HBC for illegal trading but was released by recorder Francis Johnson in a decision agreed with by the HBC's London Committee. By 1868 he was in partnership with Alexander Begg, running what quickly became the largest merchant firm in Red River. Bannatyne sought to act as a conciliator during the troubled times of 1869-70, serving as postmaster in Louis Riel's provisional government on the condition that it seek terms from Canada. Although the English-speaking community was critical of him, he was appointed Winnipeg's first postmaster in 1871. That same year he helped found the St. Andrew's Society and an early lodge of Freemasons in Manitoba. For several years, beginning in 1873, he supported Louis Riel's political pretensions and helped seek the release from prison of Ambroise Lépine.* He was himself elected to Riel's House of Commons seat in 1875, but he devoted most of his attention to business and local philanthropy, helping to organize the Winnipeg General Hospital, for example. He also played in Winnipeg's first curling match in December 1876. Although at first he became wealthy in the Manitoba land boom of the early 1880s, he held on too long and lost virtually everything. He subsequently became involved in dubious dealings in Métis scrip. He died on vacation in St. Paul, Minnesota. His ledger book (1867-69) is at the PAM on microfilm. *DCB* XI, 44-47.

Bannatyne, Annie (McDermott) (c. 1830-1908) Hostess and charity organizer. The mixed-blood daughter of Andrew McDermott* and wife of A.G.B. Bannatyne,* she was a noted hostess and charity organizer in the village of Winnipeg. In February 1869 she horsewhipped Charles Mair* (either in her husband's store or on its front steps, depending on who tells the story) over slurs Mair had published about mixed-blood women in Red River. Her later energy was devoted to the Winnipeg General Hospital, built on land owned by her family.

Bannerman, Donald (1803-1880) Merchant and businessman. Born in Kildonan, Scotland, he came to Red River with his parents as part of the third party of Selkirk settlers in 1815. He ran a general store in Kildonan and owned York boats running on the Red River.

Barber, Charles Arnold (1848-1915) Architect. Born in Upper Canada, he apprenticed as an architect and opened his own practice in 1870. He moved to Winnipeg in 1876 and was one of two brothers who headed an architectural firm there and designed many buildings before, during, and after the city's first boom, which ended in the early 1880s. Many of their buildings were ornate, often with Italianate flourishes. They designed the Winnipeg City Hall (1884-86) in Victorian eclectic style. There were constant rumours of corruption and dishonesty against Barber, a rival architect describing him as "an artist truly whose canvas is that of cunning and whose tools are those of deception." He left Winnipeg in 1887 following a charge of election bribery, and returned in 1892. In Montreal in 1903 he and his wife were arrested for extortion with violence, and the court heard that they had behaved similarly before in many other cities. He was sentenced to seven years' imprisonment. He died in New Westminster, British Columbia. *DCB* XIV, 32-34.

Barber, Earle William (1855-1915) Architect. He was the brother of Charles Barber,* a partner in Barber and Barber.

Barber, Edmund Lorenzo (1834-1909) Businessman. Born in Hamden, Connecticut, Barber received his education via a voyage around Cape Horn to California. He moved to St. Paul in 1854 and began doing business in Red River in 1859. In 1869 he went into partnership with John Schultz* for the development of the Point Douglas area. In 1873 he purchased the *Nor'-Wester* from Schultz, but the paper did not flourish. Barber became involved in many business ventures, although his dealings in later years were dominated by real estate. There are extensive papers at the PAM.

Barbour, Charles Arthur (1906-1975) Recreation director. Born in Mosa Township, Ontario, he graduated from Northwestern University. He was director of physical education at Lower Canada College and several other Montreal educational institutions in the 1930s, and served as trainer for the Montreal Maroons in 1934-35. As summer recreational director for the town of Mount Royal, he employed the motto, "The family that plays together stays together." He came to Winnipeg in 1946 to become the City's director of recreation, serving until his death in 1970. Barbour was associated with many developments during his tenure with the city, including the expansion of the community-club concept, the introduction of the Little League, and the establishment of Rainbow Stage. He was awarded the City of Winnipeg's Citizen's Award in 1974. He died in Winnipeg. See Catherine Macdonald, *A City at Leisure: An Illustrated History of Parks and Recreation Services in Winnipeg 1893-1993* (1995).

Barfoot, Walter Foster (1893-1978) Cleric. Born in Collingwood, Ontario, he was educated at Wycliffe College. During WWI he served in the British army as a second lieutenant in the Royal Sussex Regiment, later claiming "the war taught me basically to know and understand men." His first parish was in Melita, Manitoba, in 1923, and he was appointed to the faculty of Emmanuel College in Saskatoon in 1926. He subsequently served as warden of St. John's College from 1935 to 1941 and canon of St. John's Cathedral from 1934 to 1941 before becoming bishop of Edmonton. He was Anglican Primate of All Canada in 1951 and was elected archbishop of the Diocese of Rupert's Land in 1953. See William E. Harrison, *I Have Chosen You: The Life and Ministry of Walter Foster Barfoot* (1986). There are extensive papers at the Rupert's Land Archives.

Barker, William George (1894-1930) Soldier, aviator, war hero. Born in Dauphin, Manitoba, he joined the First Canadian Mounted Rifles as a private, later becoming a machine-gunner. Barker went to France with his unit in September 1915, and after weeks of trench warfare he transferred to the Flying Corps as an observer with the rank of corporal. In April 1916 he was promoted to lieutenant and soon after was awarded the Military Cross for his deeds as an observer-gunner. He then trained in England as a pilot, returning to action in January 1917. During his career, flying mainly Sopwith Camels, he destroyed 52 enemy planes, winning a number of medals, including the Victoria Cross, the Distinguished Flying Cross, and the French Croix de Guerre, and earning promotion to the rank of lieutenant-colonel at age 24. He joined the RCAF in 1920, resigning in 1924. After the war he suffered from post-traumatic stress disorder (then known as neurasthenia). In 1930 he became president of an aviation corporation in Montreal, and he was killed when a plane he was demonstrating to the Department of National Defence crashed at Rockcliffe Airport in Ottawa. There are a clippings file and papers at the PAM. See Wayne Ralph, *Barker VC: William Barker, Canada's Most Decorated War Hero* (1997).

Barnardo, Thomas John (1845-1905) Philanthropist. The founder of one of many child-saving institutions in Britain devoted to the care of orphans and waifs, he established an industrial farm of 10,000 acres at Russell, Manitoba, which provided work for about 40 boys. When a boy had saved $150 and taken up a homestead, the farm manager outfitted him with a house and supplies, including farm machinery, which could be paid off by easy instalments. There were charges that Barnardo's people often separated children from their parents and generally rode roughshod over what remained of family life in Britain's slum districts. By 1893, however, his operation had sent more than 6,500 children to Canada. For a biography, see J.H. Barr, *Dr. Barnardo: The Foster Father of Nobody's Children* (1904).

Barnston, George (c. 1800-1883) Fur trader, botanist. Born in Edinburgh, Scotland, he joined the NWC in 1820 and stayed on with the HBC after the two companies merged, serving as clerk at York Factory and Red River before being transferred to the Columbia District in 1826. He resigned in 1831 and was rehired in 1832, working in the Albany District until he was put in charge of Norway House in 1851, where he served until 1858. He then served on Lake Superior and retired to Montreal in 1862. He actively pursued scientific research, especially in botany and entomology, and he gave the British Museum, the Smithsonian Institution, and McGill College collections of specimens. He became a fellow of the Royal Society of Canada in 1882. He was the author of *The Oregon Treaty and the Hudson's Bay Company* (c. 1865). See Debra Lindsay, *Science in the Subarctic: Trappers, Traders, and the Smithsonian Institution* (1993). *DCB* XI, 52-53.

Barnston, James (1831-1858) Botanist, physician. Born at Norway House, he was educated at Red River and then at Lachine, Lower Canada, before attending the University of Edinburgh, from which he received his medical diploma in 1852. One of the first medical practitioners born in Western Canada, he began practising medicine in Montreal in 1853, at the same time beginning a herbarium. In 1857 he was appointed first professor of botany at McGill University. He died in Montreal. *DCB* VIII, 61-62.

Barone, George (1916-1992) Sculptor. Born in Italy, he came to Winnipeg in 1949. After several years with CBC-TV as a set designer, he set off on his own as a sculptor. He was responsible for the white horse sculpture near Headingley, the Viking in Gimli, the turtle in Boissevain and the ski bum in McCreary. He used a technique that enabled him to create statues from resins and steel rods that could withstand the Canadian climate. He died in Kelowna, British Columbia.

Barraud, Cyril (1877-1965) Painter, art teacher. Born in Barnes, a suburb of London, he came to Canada in 1913 with his art skills fully developed. He soon began exhibiting with the Royal Canadian Academy and taught at the Winnipeg School of Art, where he influenced a number of subsequently locally-important artists. His métiers were landscape painting and etching. He left for England with the Canadian Expeditionary Force in 1915 as a lieutenant in the 43rd Battalion, teaching grenade weaponry. By 1916 he was in France, where he did much painting of the wartorn landscape and suffering, particularly at Ypres, Mont St. Eloy and Vlamerlinghe. He remained in Britain after demobilization and died in obscurity there.

Barrett, John Kelly (1850-c.1921) Educator, civil servant, editor. A local superintendent and inspector of separate schools in Ontario, Barrett held various federal posts with Inland Revenue. As well, he became managing director and chief editor of the *North West Review*. A Catholic, Barrett was the Winnipeg taxpayer who refused to pay his school taxes because the Manitoba School Act of 1890 denied his constitutional rights. This suit, *Barrett v. the City of Winnipeg*, brought with federal government support, touched off the legal aspects of the Manitoba School Question. After losing in a Manitoba court, Barrett won in the Supreme Court of Canada, which declared that the Manitoba act plainly set up a denominational system. Along with another similar case, the suit was appealed in 1892 to the Judicial Committee of the Privy Council, which overturned the Supreme Court decision. See Paul Crunican, *Priests a n d Politicians: Manitoba Schools a n d the Election of 1896* (1974).

Barron, John (1850-1926) Shorthorn breeder. Born in Elora, Canada, he came to Manitoba in 1878 to homestead near Carberry. In 1882 he established one of the province's first shorthorn herds at what became known as Fairview Stock Farm. He won prizes all over Canada for his cattle, topping the field at the Winnipeg Industrial Exhibition in 1879. He served as president of the Dominion Shorthorn Breeders' Association. Barron was active in local government, serving for years as reeve and councillor of the Municipality of North Cypress. He was a director of the Carberry Agricultural Society. He is a member of the Manitoba Agricultural Hall of Fame.

Barrowclough, Samuel Lees (1869-1944) Musician. Born in Birkenhead, England, he came to Canada in 1884 and became director of the Winnipeg Citizen Band, continuing as director after it merged with the 90th Rifles Regiment Band. He took the band overseas during WWI. Barrowclough operated a music store in Winnipeg. After the war he moved to Detroit to become a music publisher. He died in Detroit.

Barsky, Percy (1921-1989) Pediatrician. Born in Winnipeg, he graduated from the Manitoba Medical College and practised pediatrics in Winnipeg all his life. He was professor of pediatrics at the University of Manitoba and president of the Winnipeg Children's Hospital medical staff. Barsky established Winnipeg's Poison Control Centre and was involved in a number of neighbourhood and social issues. He received the Jubilee Award of the University of Manitoba Alumni Association in 1986 and a humanitarian award from Shaarey Zedek Medical Centre in Israel in 1987. He was chosen by *The Canadian Doctor* magazine in 1987 as one of the nation's 50 top doctors during the previous half century. He died in Winnipeg.

Bartlett, J.W. (d. 1892) Journalist, civil servant. Born in Glencoe, Canada, he came to Manitoba from London, Ontario, as western manager of the *Farmer's Advocate*. In November 1892 he became chief clerk in the Manitoba Department of Agriculture, taking the lead in organizing the first Winnipeg Industrial Exhibition.

Basker, August (1828-1912) Miller, farmer. Born in Breslau, Germany, he immigrated to Canada in 1861 and then to Portage la Prairie in 1873 as a miller. He was a pioneer farmer at Rapid City from 1875, one of the first German-born agriculturalists in the province.

Battaglia, Frankie (1910-1971) Boxer. Born in Winnipeg, he became a professional prizefighter on the advice of Jack Dempsey. In the early 1930s he was regarded as one of the best middleweight fighters in the world, although he never won a world championship, losing in title fights to Ben Jeby at Madison Square Garden in 1933 and to Freddy Steele in 1936. He retired from the ring and moved to California. He returned to Winnipeg in the 1950s to manage a restaurant at the corner of Pembina and Stafford but later went back to California, where he died.

Baudoux, Maurice (1903-1988) Cleric. Born in Belgium, he came to Canada at age nine, entering the Collège de Saint-Boniface in 1919, then studying at Laval, where he received a doctorate in theology. He began as a priest at Prud'homme, Saskatchewan, in 1919. In 1948 he became bishop of St. Paul, Alberta, and then he became archbishop of St. Boniface in 1952, although he didn't take over the functions of the post until 1955 upon the death of Archbishop Arthur Beliveau. An extremely tall man — he was six feet four inches — Baudoux devoted himself to the preservation of local Francophone culture. He died of cancer.

Bawlf, Nicholas (1849-1914) Grain merchant. Born in Smiths Falls, Canada, he moved to Winnipeg in

1877 and established a feed and flour business on Princess Street. He helped found the Winnipeg Grain Exchange in 1887, serving as its president in 1887 and 1890. Active in the grain elevator business, he joined with other Winnipeg merchants (including Rodmond Roblin*) to form the Northern Elevator Company in 1893. He was Northern Elevator's president from 1903 to 1909. Bawlf sold out to the Peavy Company of Minneapolis in 1909, then founded N. Bawlf Grain Company, and in 1912 became president of the Alberta Pacific Grain Company of Calgary. He was one of the first traders to ship grain to Japan via Pacific ports. Bawlf held many directorships of Canadian corporations. A devout Catholic, he opposed the Manitoba School Act of 1890 and lobbied in Ottawa for more Anglo-Catholic senators. He died in Winnipeg. *DCB* XIV, 39-40.

Bawlf, William Richard (1881-1972) Grain merchant. Born in Winnipeg, he was educated at St. Mary's School and the University of Ottawa. He became president of the Winnipeg Grain Exchange in 1917. He was president of the Winnipeg Hockey Club in 1929-30, when the team won the Allan Cup. He was also vice-president of the Canadian Wheat Board. He wrote extensively on grain marketing.

Bayly, Charles (fl. 1630-80) HBC governor. Born in London, England, to French Catholic parents, he was educated in France before journeying to Virginia as an indentured servant and spending 14 years of suffering there. He was converted to the Quaker faith in the late 1650s, and he returned to Europe as a missionary around 1660. He was frequently imprisoned for his faith and was released from the Tower of London in 1669 only on condition that he depart for Hudson Bay, where he headed a successful trading party in 1670 as resident governor. He was in England in 1671-72, but then he returned to the Bay until 1674, when he was recalled but instead served under the command of his successor. In 1675 he resumed the governorship, holding this position until 1679. He died in London while under investigation for mismanagement. His Virginia sojourn is described in his *A True and Faithful Warning unto the People and Inhabitants of Bristol . . . with a Brief Account of Some Tryalls and Sufferings* (1663). *DCB* I, 81-84.

Beachell, Percy (1874-1969) Merchant, politician. Born in Yorkshire, England, one of 15 children, he immigrated with his family to Canada in 1889, first to Portage la Prairie, then to Rosser, Manitoba. Active in local government, Beachell served as a councillor of the Rural Municipality of Rosser from 1914 to 1921, then as reeve from 1922 to 1953. He became involved in all aspects of life in Rosser, serving as its first postmaster, its agricultural implement dealer, its insurance agent, and warden of the Anglican church from 1902 to 1926. He was active in rural electrification and in improving rural medical facilities.

Beale, Anthony (c. 1664-1731) HBC governor. He first joined the HBC in 1678 as an apprentice, and he returned in 1687. He was captured and imprisoned by the French on several occasions over the next few years. He rose gradually through the ranks at Albany Fort, becoming governor in 1705. His contract expired in 1714, and he was subsequently hired for lesser positions after 1718 until his death. *DCB* II, 49-52.

Beard, Gordon W. (1921-1972) Politician. Born in Neepawa, Manitoba, he moved to Thompson in 1960. He had many business interests in Thompson and the North. Elected MLA for Churchill as an Independent, he was a strong spokesman for the North, advocating a separate provincial department of northern affairs.

Beardy, Jackson (1945-1984) Artist, writer. Born at the Garden Hill Reserve, Manitoba, he was a Cree artist, a pioneer in expressing the new iconography of his people by reconceptualizing Native symbolism. Beardy made headlines when he was denied admission to his own exhibit at the National Arts Centre in Ottawa in 1970. He compiled *Cree Indian Legends from Northern Manitoba* (1971). For a biography, see Kenneth James Hughes, *Jackson Beardy: Life and Art* (1979).

Beattie, Thomson (1875-1912) Land manager. Born in Fergus, Ontario, he apprenticed as a banker but came to Winnipeg in 1897 to become a partner in the Haslam Land Company. He died in the *Titanic* disaster.

Beatty, Frank W. Moore (b. 1900) Commercial artist. Born in Winnipeg, he studied at the Winnipeg School of Art from 1917 to 1924, after which he left for Chicago and a career in commercial art. He worked for many years for *Popular Mechanics Magazine* as an illustrator.

Beauchemin, André (1824-1902) Politician. He was a delegate to the November 1869 council from St. Vital. Later he was a French delegate from St. Vital to the Convention of Forty (1870) and a councillor in the provisional government of 1870. Subsequently elected to the provincial legislature, he delivered the famous Riel/Lépine letter to Lieutenant-Governor Morris in 1873.

Beaven, Alan (1903-1988) Conservationist. Born in Ottawa, he began working for the Canadian Forestry Association in 1922. From 1925 to 1945 he planted trees across the Prairies from a "tree-planting car" that traversed the railways. He was manager of the Prairie Forestry Association from 1945 to 1978. In 1957 he assisted in founding Sandilands Forestry Centre near Hadashville. He was awarded an honorary degree from the University of Manitoba.

Beddome, Henry L. (1830-1881) Surgeon. Born in London, England, he studied medicine at Guy's Hospital, London, and entered the employment of the HBC as surgeon in 1851. In 1852 he qualified as a member of the Royal College of Surgeons of England. From 1852 to 1857 he was chief medical officer of the HBC, based at York Factory. Upon completion of his term of service he moved to Upper Fort Garry, then in 1859 returned to York Factory for five years before permanently settling into medical practice at Red River in a home just south of St. Andrew's Church. In 1871 he was one of the founders of the Medical Health Board of Manitoba, which became the College of Physicians and Surgeons in 1877. *DCB* XI, 63-64.

Bedford, Spencer Argyle (1851-1933) Land surveyor, educator. Born in Sussex, England, he came to Ontario with his family in 1862. He trained as a surveyor, worked for the CPR in surveying its holdings, and moved into a CPR house at Moosomin. He also helped Dr. W. Saunders in selecting proper sites for the establishment of experimental farms in the West. In 1888 he became the first superintendent of the Brandon Experimental Farm, subsequently becoming professor of field husbandry at the Manitoba Agricultural College. He was appointed deputy minister of agriculture in 1915. Bedford received an honorary LLD from the University of Manitoba in 1921. He is a member of the Manitoba Agricultural Hall of Fame.

Bedson, Derek (1921-1989) Civil servant. Born in Manitoba, he studied modern history at Balliol, Oxford, after serving in the Royal Canadian Army Service Corps during WWII. He moved to Ottawa and was a minor civil servant from 1949 to 1955. He then became George Drew's private secretary, then John Diefenbaker's. In 1958 he was appointed clerk of the Manitoba Privy Council, a position he held until his retirement. He was president of the Manitoba Record Society.

Bedson, Samuel Lawrence (1842-1891) Soldier, prison warden. Born in England, Bedson came to Manitoba with the Wolseley Expedition as quartermaster sergeant of the Second Quebec Battalion after being posted to Canada as a non-commissioned officer with the 16th Regiment. He remained in charge of prisoners at Lower Fort Garry after the troops departed in 1870 and was named warden of the Manitoba Penitentiary in 1871. In 1885 he was placed in charge of the transport service required by the North-West Rebellion. He was an ardent golfer and curler, and he probably established the province's first golf course at Stony Mountain. In 1891 he became an aide-de-camp to the governor general and served briefly on the Alaska Boundary Commission before his sudden death in Ottawa. *DCB* XII, 74-75.

Beech, Arthur (b. 1876) Artist. Born in England, he studied at the Oldham School of Art before immigrating to Winnipeg in 1904. He taught manual arts at many Winnipeg Schools, including Kelvin High School. From 1916 to 1919 and from 1920 to 1921 he was enrolled in the Winnipeg School of Art. He was president of the Winnipeg Sketch Club in 1923 and one of those who re-formed the Manitoba Society of Artists in 1925. His work was executed in a variety of mediums.

Begg, Alexander (1825-1905) Journalist, civil servant, historian. Born in Caithness, Scotland, he was a journalist in Upper Canada when he was appointed by William McDougall as collector of customs in the Manitoba government to be set up in 1870 under McDougall's governorship. He spent the fall and winter of 1870 in Pembina waiting for Canada to take over Red River so that he could assume office. He returned to Ontario and later became Ontario's immigration commissioner in Scotland, then British Columbia's commissioner (1888-97), before moving to Victoria. In later years he wrote a number of histories of British Columbia.

Begg, Alexander (1839-1897) Merchant, diarist, author. Born in Quebec City, he was educated at St. John's and Aberdeen, Scotland. He came to Red River in 1867 as business agent for Upper Canadian firms, and a year later he went into partnership with A.G.B. Bannatyne.* Like Bannatyne, Begg was active during the Red River Rebellion in support of the Métis effort to secure terms from Canada. His diary (upon which his 1871 book, *The Creation of Manitoba, o r, The History of the Red River Troubles*, was based) is one of the principal sources for the events of 1869-70. Less well known is a series of letters he wrote recounting Red River affairs to the *Globe* of Toronto between November 1869 and March 1870 under the *nom de plume* "Justitia." He was the author of what was arguably the province's first novel, *Dot-It-Down* (1871), a thinly disguised satire of the pre-rebellion period in Red River. In 1879 he also published *Ten Years in Winnipeg* Begg was appointed Queen's Printer in 1877, and from 1884 to 1888 he was immigration agent for the CPR in London. He then moved to British Columbia, where he resumed his writing career, producing his *History of the North-West* (3 vols.) in 1894. *DCB* XII, 81-84. His journal 1869-70 (in microfilm) is at the PAM.

Beioley, Joseph (1785-1864) Fur trader. Born in Essex, England, he joined the HBC in 1800, serving at Albany Factory until 1808. He subsequently was stationed at Brandon House and Moose Lake before becoming accountant of the Southern Department at Moose Factory from 1814 to 1819. Upon the merger of the HBC and NWC in 1821 he was made a chief factor. In 1822 he was appointed a councillor of Rupert's Land. Most of his subsequent service was in the Moose River and Rupert River Districts. He retired in 1843.

Belaney, Archibald Stansfeld See Grey Owl.

Belcourt, Georges-Antoine (1803-1874) Cleric. Born in Lower Canada and educated at the Collège de Nicolet, he came west as a missionary in 1831 and stayed until 1858, returning east in 1859. He was a supporter of the Métis and their land claims, drawing up a petition to London in French in 1846. He thereafter withdrew to Pembina, from where he advised the Métis in the Sayer trial of 1849. After

his enforced departure from the Red River Valley he was sent to Rustico on Prince Edward Island, where he helped found the Farmers' Bank of Rustico in 1864, perhaps the smallest bank ever chartered in Canada. He drove the first steam-driven vehicle on the island. Father Belcourt wrote *Principes d e la langue sauvagés appeles sauteux* (1839). See Manitoba Historic Resources Branch, *Georges-Antoine Belcourt* (1984) and James Michael Belcourt, *George Anthony Belcourt: Pioneer Catholic Missionary of the Northwest, 1803-1874* (1955). *DCB* X, 46-48.

Bell, Charles Napier (1854-1936) Trader, real estate speculator, historian. Born in Lanark, Canada, he enlisted in the Wolseley Expedition in 1870 as a bugler. He began trading and freighting in 1872, becoming heavily involved in real estate speculation. He served as secretary of the Winnipeg Board of Trade from 1887 to 1916 and of the Winnipeg Grain Exchange in 1887. A noted local historian, he was the author of *The Selkirk Settlement a n d Settlers* (1887) and *The Old Forts of Winnipeg, 1738-1927* (1927). An avid skater, he introduced family skating to Winnipeg and trained many in the sport. Bell became a fellow of the Royal Geographical Society in 1885 and was a founder of the Manitoba Historical and Scientific Society. There are extensive papers at the PAM.

Bell, Gordon (1863-1923) Ophthalmologist, bacteriologist. Born in Pembroke, Canada, he was educated at Pembroke Collegiate, the University of Toronto, and the Manitoba Medical College. He lost a leg as a result of a severe bout with diphtheria. He served as superintendent of the Brandon Hospital for the Insane from 1890 to 1893 before becoming Manitoba's first ophthalmologist. In 1896 he was appointed provincial bacteriologist, and in 1897 he set up a laboratory near the first Medical College building, which became the diagnostic and epidemiological centre for the province. He was chair of the provincial Board of Health from 1913 to 1927. He resided at Fox Lake, Manitoba, from 1914 to 1923. He died of streptococcal sore throat, probably contracted from specimens he had examined in Brandon. A Winnipeg high school is named after him.

Bell, James Reynolds (1891-1979) Civil servant. Born in Clearwater, Manitoba, he attended the Manitoba Agricultural College and graduated with a BSA. He then became a Manitoba agricultural representative for the Portage la Prairie district, becoming a livestock field man with the extension service in 1923, and eventually livestock commissioner, in which capacity he worked to upgrade quality and extend diversification. From 1949 to 1962 he was deputy minister of agriculture, latterly assisting in the implementation of the Agricultural Credit Act and the Crop Insurance Act. The University of Manitoba gave him an honorary LLD in 1956. He is a member of the Manitoba Agricultural Hall of Fame.

Bell, John (1799-1868) Fur trader. Born in Mull, Scotland, he joined the NWC in 1818 and remained in the HBC after the 1821 merger, stationed in the Winnipeg District until 1824. Thereafter he was in the Mackenzie River department and active in Arctic exploration until late in his life, when he served at Oxford House, Fort Chipewyan, and Montreal. He was made a chief trader in 1840, and he retired in 1860.

Bell, John Headingly (1840-1897) Farmer, politician. Born in London, Canada, he settled on a farm in Kildonan in 1871, subsequently working for J.H. Ashdown* as a bookkeeper. He was active in Kildonan municipal affairs and was elected MPP for Springfield from 1883 to 1886. He then became assistant to the clerk of the House and served the Winnipeg Exhibition Association in the summer months. He was a prominent Mason, serving as a grand secretary and a grand master.

Bell, Lennox Gordon ("Buzz," 1903-1973) Physician. Born in Winnipeg, he graduated from University of Manitoba Medical School in 1928, then did graduate work at Grey's Hospital, London. Returning to Winnipeg in 1930, he was in charge of outpatients at Winnipeg General Hospital from 1933 to 1949. Appointed a professor of medicine at the University of Manitoba, he became dean of the faculty in 1949, and physician-in-chief at Winnipeg General Hospital in 1950. During WWII he served as a wing commander in the medical branch of the RCAF. In later years he retired to Fox Lake, Manitoba, and wrote *Fox Lake: An Informal History* (n.d.); the copy at UML Archives has original photographs.

Bell, Robert (1841-1917) Scientist. Born in Toronto Township, Canada, he was appointed to the Geological Survey of Canada in 1856, later graduating from McGill University and studying at the University of Edinburgh. In 1869 he became a permanent member of the Geological Survey, rising to acting director in 1901. He surveyed extensively in the northern and the eastern Arctic, naming over 3,000 geological features across Canada. He was a fellow of the Geological Society of London, the Royal Society of Canada (1882) and the Royal Society of London (1897). In 1903 he became a companion of the Imperial Service Order, and he was awarded several distinguished medals. Officially retiring in 1908, he spent his last years mainly at his farm at Rathwell, Manitoba, where he died. *DCB* XIV, 55-56.

Bell, William Robert (1845-1913) Farmer, soldier. Born in Brockville, Canada, he was active in the Ontario militia, retiring in 1875 as major of the 41st Regiment. He supervised transport in the 1885 North-West Rebellion. He had come to Manitoba in 1882 and walked west from Brandon to Indian Head in present-day Saskatchewan to operate a large 50,000-acre model farm. He remained there until 1895 and then moved to Winnipeg, where he held a seat on the Winnipeg Grain Exchange and was associated with the Winnipeg Coal Company. He died in Winnipeg. *DCB* XIV, 56-58.

Benard, Aimé (1873-1938) Rancher, politician. Born in Henryville, Quebec, he owned large farms and ranches in Manitoba. He was elected to the Manitoba legislature for the constituency of Assiniboia, serving from 1907 to 1917, and was appointed to the Senate in 1917.

Benedictson, Margjret (Jonsson) (1866-1956) Journalist. Born in Hrappsstaðir in Viðidalur, Iceland, she immigrated to North Dakota in 1887, where she attended Bathgate College. Four years later she came to Manitoba. Benedictson first lectured on women's rights in 1893 and she later founded an Icelandic women's suffrage society in Winnipeg. She served as editor, with her husband Sigfus, of *Freyja*, "the only women's suffrage paper published in Canada," from 1898 to 1910. She divorced her husband in 1910 and moved in 1912 with her three children to Blaine, Washington. She died in Anacortes, Washington.

Benham, Mary Lile (Love) (1914-1991) Journalist, author. Born in Winnipeg, she was educated at Rupertsland School. She started writing for the

Winnipeg Free Press during WWII. After retirement, she wrote a number of biographies of famous Canadians for schoolchildren, as well as much local history, including a history of St. George's Church in the Winnipeg neighbourhood of Crescentwood. She won the 1984 YWCA Woman of the Year award.

Bennett, Leslie James (1893-1972) Journalist. Born in North Dakota to Canadian parents, he learned about the printing business in Morden, Manitoba. He published the *Roland News* before moving to Oregon, where he worked on a number of newspapers. In 1925 he returned to Carman, Manitoba, and purchased the *Leader* newspaper.

Benoit, Joseph Paul Augustin (1850-1915) Priest, colonizer. Born in Le Nans, France, he was ordained at the French Seminary in Rome in 1874, subsequently receiving a doctorate in philosophy from the Gregorian University and a doctorate in theology from St. Thomas College. He entered the Canons Regular of the Immaculate Conception in 1877. He toured Canada in 1890, and in 1891 he established his first colony of French in the Pembina Hills. His order ministered to a number of parishes and missions in southern Manitoba. He wrote extensively during his years in Manitoba, his works including a two-volume *Vie de Mgr Taché*, published in 1904. He retired in 1910, much disappointed with the results of his colonizing activities. He died in France. *DCB* XIV, 59-60.

Benson, Edward (1843-1904) Physician. Born in Peterborough, Canada, he studied medicine in Kentucky before receiving a Canadian medical diploma at Toronto. In 1874 he moved to Winnipeg, where he served as city jail surgeon, coroner for Winnipeg, and medical officer of the Deaf and Dumb Institute. He was a founder of the Winnipeg General Hospital.

Berens, Jacob (Nah-wee-kee-sick-quah-yash) (c. 1832-1916) Native chief. Probably born in Berens River, he was baptized at Norway House by George McDougall in 1860. He settled with his family at Pigeon Bay and was a leader of his people both in negotiating Treaty Five and in dealing with the arrival of Icelanders in 1875. He became a prominent lay Methodist and served his people as chief for 40 years. He died in Berens River. *DCB* XIV, 63-64.

Bergman, H. Eric (1893-1958) Commercial artist. Born in Dresden, Germany, where he studied at the Art and Trade School, he came to Canada in 1913. A year later he joined Brigden's Limited in Winnipeg, where he spent many years as a wood engraver for the Eaton's catalogue. He and Charles Comfort exhibited together in 1922 and 1924. Fond of tempera and watercolour landscapes, Bergman taught a generation of Winnipeg artists (including Walter J. Phillips) the techniques of wood-block printing. See Nancy E. Dillow, *Transformation of Vision: The Works of H. Eric Bergman* (1983).

Bergmann, Fridrik Jonsson (c. 1858-1918) Professor. Born in Iceland, he went to the United States in 1874 and graduated from Decorah College, Iowa. He was invited to become a professor of Icelandic at Winnipeg's Wesley College in 1902, and was noted as a littérateur. He was hit by an automobile on Sherbrook Street and died almost instantly.

Bernard, Gertrude, a.k.a. Anahareo (1906-1987) Animal rights activist. Born at Mattawa, Ontario, she married Archibald Belaney (Grey Owl*) and helped convert him to environmentalism while the couple were living in Riding Mountain National Park in the early 1930s. She remained involved in animal rights after the couple divorced in 1936. She wrote an autobiography, *Devil in Deerskins: My Life with Grey Owl* (1972).

Bernier, Alexandre (1886-1961) Lawyer, judge. Born in St. Boniface, he graduated in arts from the Collège de Saint-Boniface. He was called to the bar in 1910 and was appointed to the Manitoba County Court in 1950. He was president of the Société Saint-Jean-Baptiste of St. Boniface.

Bernier, Joseph (1852-1934) Lawyer. Born at St. Jean d'Iberville, Canada, he came to Winnipeg in 1880 and was educated at the Collège de Saint-Boniface. He was called to the bar in 1896, and he eventually joined Andrews and Pitblado before founding his own firm of Bernier and Bernier in 1902. Elected to the provincial legislature for St. Boniface as a Conservative in 1901, he was appointed provincial secretary in the Roblin government in 1912. During WWI he was an honorary colonel who was active in recruiting activities.

Bernier, Thomas-Alfred (1844-1908) Lawyer, municipal politician, civil servant. Born at Henryville,

Canada, he was educated at the Séminaire de Saint-Hyacinthe from 1857 to 1865 and was called to the bar in 1869. He moved to Manitoba in 1880 under the influence of Father Albert Lacombe. After farming in Ste. Agathe, he became superintendent of Catholic education in Manitoba in 1881, working hard to maintain high standards. He served on the 1881 commission on "half-breed" lands. He served frequently as mayor of St. Boniface (1883, 1884, 1886, 1891, and 1897) and was registrar of the University of Manitoba from 1882 to 1893. He also was French clerk of the Manitoba legislature and chair of the Eastern Judicial District Board. The Greenway government abolished the dual educational system in 1890, but in 1892 Bernier was appointed to the Senate as a Conservative, and there he spoke often on the Manitoba School Question. He wrote several pamphlets, including *Le Manitoba, champ d'immigration* (1887). He died in St. Boniface. His papers are at the PAM and the St. Boniface Historical Society. *DCB* XIII, 63-64.

Bétournay, Louis (1825-1879) Lawyer, judge. Born in St. Lambert, Lower Canada, he was called to the bar of Canada in 1849, later practising in a firm with George-Étienne Cartier. Through Cartier's influence he was appointed a puisne judge of the Court of Queen's Bench of Manitoba in 1872. He had no knowledge of English law before his appointment, and his only asset was his fluency in French. He ordered Ambroise Lépine* to stand trial in 1873 but refused to rule on the question of whether the court had jurisdiction in the matter. Despite this reticence, the Francophone community was unhappy with his behaviour in the Lépine case. He had a fondness for fine horses and rode well. A Winnipeg street is named for him.

Beynon, Frances Marion (1884-1951) Journalist, writer, feminist. Born in Streetsville, Ontario, she moved with her family to Manitoba at an early age, settling in the Hartney district of the province, where her father farmed. The family was of staunch Methodist background, which she came to reject. Like her siblings, Beynon earned a teaching certificate. She taught near Carman before moving to Winnipeg in 1908 to work in the T. Eaton Company's advertising department. She was an active member of the Quill Club. In 1912 she became the first full-time women's editor of the *Grain Growers' Guide*, holding the post until 1917. She and her sister Lillian* fought

for a variety of women's issues, including suffrage, dower legislation, and homesteading rights for women, but she lost much public credibility when she began to criticize the war. She left Manitoba in 1917 for the United States, where she wrote a semi-autobiographical novel, *Aleta Day*, and continued her journalistic work. See Anne Hicks, "Frances Beynon and The Guide," in *First Days Fighting Days: Women in Manitoba History*, ed. Mary Kinnear (1987), 41-52. Beynon is one of the protagonists (with Nellie McClung) of Wendy Lill's play *The Fighting Days*.

Beynon, Lillian See Thomas, Lillian (Beynon).

Bigelow, Wilfred (1878-1967) Physician. Born in Kingsport, Nova Scotia, he came to Winnipeg in 1897 and worked in a doctor's office for three dollars per week sweeping floors. Lamed for life at the age of 16, he learned Latin on his own and graduated from the University of Manitoba in 1903. He first set up medical practice in Souris, then in Brandon in 1906, where in 1915 he founded Canada's first medical clinic. Bigelow's clinic was modelled on the Mayo Clinic, and consisted of a group of specialists who worked together to provide medical treatment and who presented the patient with a joint bill. Bigelow travelled across southwestern Manitoba by horse and later by automobile for many years

Biggs, Samuel Clarke (1851-1911) Lawyer, journalist, politician. Born in Ancaster, Canada, he graduated from the University of Toronto in 1872. He came to Winnipeg in 1875 to practise law, helping to found the Manitoba Law Society and the University of Manitoba in 1877. He was a proprietor of the *Winnipeg Daily Sun*. He was MPP for St. Paul's in 1878 and was acting minister of public works in 1879. He moved to St. Paul, Minnesota, in 1886, then to Toronto in 1892.

Bird, Curtis James (1838-1876) Physician, politician. Born in Birds Hill, he was baptized in St. John's Parish and was the son of Chief Factor James Curtis Bird and the former Mary Lowman, a teacher at the Red River Academy. After his education at St. John's College he studied medicine at Guy's Hospital, London, before returning to Red River. In 1862 he married Frances Ross, daughter of another senior HBC official. He later married his sister-in-law, Annabella Ross McDermott, widow of Charles Edward McDermott. Bird became coroner of Assiniboia in

1861, receiving formal appointment in 1862. He held this post until the 1870s, advocating publicly supported medical care in the settlement. He was appointed to the Council of Assiniboia in 1868. He served as delegate to the November 1869 council from St. Paul's and as English delegate to the 1870 Convention of Forty, appearing on a subcommittee to propose the officers of government and on the committee to draft a bill of rights. Nominated both federally and provincially in 1870, he took up his seat in the provincial legislature, representing Baie de Saint-Paul. He was elected Speaker in 1873. In 1874 Bird was involved in a controversy over a bill to incorporate the city of Winnipeg, which resulted in an attack upon him with heated oil. He never really recovered from the incident, and he died in London, where he had gone in search of better health care. *DCB* X, 67-68.

Bird, Frederick Valentine (1885-1977) Physician, local politician. Born in St. Andrews to Scottish-Indian parents, he taught school to put himself through the Faculty of Medicine at the University of Manitoba, from which he graduated in 1913. He set up practice in Boissevain, where he became famous as a general practitioner, delivering more than 3,500 babies and often accepting pay in butter and eggs. In 1935 Bird cancelled all debts owed to him by farmers. He was a member of the Boissevain Town Council for many years, mayor from 1929 to 1939, and health officer for 40 years. He is a member of the Manitoba Agricultural Hall of Fame.

Bird, George (c. 1792-1856) Fur trader, interpreter. Born in Rupert's Land, he joined the HBC in 1805, becoming assistant trader in 1812 and company clerk in 1815, in which capacity he served at Carlton House from 1815 to 1818 and at Edmonton House from 1818 to 1821. He served as an interpreter after the merger of the HBC and NWC in 1821, retiring to the Red River Settlement in 1825.

Bird, James Curtis (c. 1773-1856) Fur trader. Born in London, England, he joined the HBC in 1788, serving at York Factory for four years before heading inland to Saskatchewan. He headed Carlton House from 1795 to 1799 and Edmonton House from 1799 to 1816, organizing the Peter Fidler* expedition of 1799. Beginning in 1816, he acted as governor of Rupert's Land until William Williams* arrived in 1818. After the merger of the HBC and

NWC he was made chief factor in charge of Lower Red River. He served there only briefly, then was equally briefly in charge of Upper Red River. He retired in 1824 to Red River and received a large company grant (1,245 acres) on the east side of the Red River. The village of Birds Hill is named after him. He served on several early councils and was appointed a councillor of Assiniboia in 1839. In 1836 he was made registrar for land sales and grants. Known for his harshness, he was never popular in the settlement. *DCB* VIII, 90-91.

Bjarnason, Jón (1844-1914) Educator, journalist, cleric. Born in Iceland, he went to the United States in 1874, becoming a professor of theology at Dekora College in Minnesota. He then served as an editor of several Scandinavian journals before being called to Lake Winnipeg as a pastor in 1877. In New Iceland, Bjarnason led the liberal "Association of Icelandic Lutheran Churches in America" in opposition to the conservatives headed by Paul Thorlaksson. After returning to Iceland for family reasons, he settled in Winnipeg as pastor of the Icelandic Lutheran Church of Winnipeg, helping to found the Icelandic Evangelical Lutheran Synod. He established the journal *Sameiningin* in 1885, serving as editor until his death. He was active in the formation of an Icelandic Academy in Winnipeg, which opened its doors in 1913 and was named the Jón Bjarnason Academy after his death in the city. *DCB* XIV, 73-74.

Black, Alexander (1847-1913) Businessman, municipal politician, curler. Born in Edinburgh, Scotland, he came to Winnipeg in 1882, and in 1893 he formed the Alex. Black Lumber Company. He was a Winnipeg alderman from 1885 to 1895 and a pioneer curler in the city at the Thistle Curling Club.

Black, Elinor F.E. (1905-1982) Physician. Born in Nelson, British Columbia, she moved to Winnipeg with her family at the age of 12. She was educated at Kelvin High School and the University of Manitoba Medical School, graduating in 1930. After a year in Britain she set up practice in Winnipeg in 1931. In 1937 she received a six-month appointment as house surgeon at the South London Hospital for Women, following which she took the examination to become, in 1938, the first Canadian woman member of the British Royal College of Obstetricians and Gynaecologists. During the Manitoba Flood in 1950, she handled the opening of the Women's Pavilion at the Winnipeg General Hospital with considerable aplomb. In 1951 she was appointed professor of obstetrics and gynaecology and chair of the Department of Obstetrics and Gynaecology at the University of Manitoba, resigning from the chair in 1960. In 1961, she was elected the first woman president of the Society of Obstetricians and Gynaecologists of Canada. She retired from the University in 1964, although she continued to teach for many years thereafter. Black died in Winnipeg. Her research papers are at the UML Archives, as is her correspondence with Arthur Stoughton. See Julie Vandervoort, *Tell the Driver: A Biography of Elinor F.E. Black, M.D.* (1992).

Black, Francis Mollison (1871-1941) Civil servant, politician. Born in Kilmarnock, Scotland, he was educated at Perth Academy. He came to Canada in 1891 with the Bank of British Columbia, then worked with the P. Burns Company in Calgary. In 1917 he was appointed treasurer of the United Grain Growers. In 1922 he became provincial treasurer of Manitoba and minister of telephones. He was elected MPP from Rupertsland that same year. In 1924 he resigned his posts to become vice-president of finance with Winnipeg Electric, and in 1927 he became chair of the fruit control board of British Columbia. See Donald M. Black, "Francis Mollison Black 1870-1941," unpublished article at the PAM.

Black, George (d. 1919) Merchant, civil servant, Masonic leader. Born in Montreal, he was educated at McGill University and came west with Wolseley as a member of the Second Battalion of Quebec Rifles. He was stationed at Lower Fort Garry, and he opened a store at Selkirk upon his discharge. He became assistant auditor in the Manitoba government in 1885 and was promoted to auditor in 1888, serving until 1915. He was a pioneer Mason in Selkirk, serving as first master of the Selkirk lodge in 1870-71, then as deputy grand master for Manitoba in 1874 and grand master in 1875. He founded the Civil Service Lawn Bowling Club.

Black, Hugh (1846-1918) Steamboat operator. Born at Fergus, Canada, he came to Red River in 1869, initially farming at Springfield. He crewed on HBC steamboats until he acquired his own vessel in 1876 to ply Lake Winnipeg. He operated a number of steamers before retiring to a farm near Petersfield in 1909.

Black, John (1817-1879) Fur trader, judge. Born in Scotland, he accompanied Adam Thom* to Red River in 1839, entering the service of the HBC and rising to the post of chief trader. In 1845 Black married Margaret, daughter of Alexander Christie,* governor of Assiniboia. From 1850 to 1852 he served as chief accountant of the Upper Red River District, but Governor Eden Colvile* did not much like him. After his wife's death in 1854 he went to Scotland and Australia, returning to Red River in 1862 to become recorder and president of the General Quarterly Court of Assiniboia. He apparently had acquired some legal training in Scotland; his procedures in the court were Scottish rather than English. In 1862 he joined the Council of Assiniboia. He was ready to resign as recorder in 1868 after much criticism of his judicial activities, but agreed to stay on. He was still in office when the Red River Rebellion began. He kept a moderate course. He was elected English delegate from St. Andrew's to the Convention of Forty in 1870 and was chosen as its chair. On 4-5 February he spoke at length against the immediate creation of a province and the continued use of an appointed council. He was subsequently chosen as a delegate of the provisional government to the Canadian government to negotiate terms of entrance into Confederation. In Ottawa he was far less enthusiastic than his colleagues about a large land settlement for the Métis. He left Ottawa for the United Kingdom before the agreement with Canada had been fully implemented. He retired in Scotland with a chief trader's pension, although he died in St. Andrew's Parish, Manitoba. See Roy St. George Stubbs, *Four Recorders of Rupert's Land* (1967); James Cowan to Archer Martin, 1 October 1890, PAM MG 2 C15-1. *DCB* X, 69-70.

Black, John (1819-1882) Cleric. Born in Scotland and privately educated, he emigrated with his family in 1841 to Bovina Township, New York, where he prepared for the ministry. In 1843 he decided to attend the Free Church's college (later Knox College) in Toronto, and he was one of its first students in 1844. Ordained in 1851, he agreed temporarily to serve the Presbyterian community in Red River, and he remained at Kildonan until his death. He opened a church building at Kildonan in 1853 and soon established a school beside it. That same year he married Henrietta Ross, the daughter of Alexander Ross.* In 1868 he built a church in the village of Winnipeg, and he helped found Manitoba College in 1871.

During the Red River Rebellion of 1869-70 he preached for the preservation of law and order but against open resistance to Louis Riel and the provisional government. He resigned from the Board of Education of Manitoba in 1876 in opposition to the efforts of some of his Protestant colleagues to dissolve the province's denominational school system. Black received an honorary DD from Queen's College in 1876. See Olive Knox, *John Black of Old Kildonan* (1958); James D. Marnoch, "John Black," in *Prairie Spirit: Perspectives on the Heritage of the United Church of Canada in the West*, ed. Dennis Butcher et al. (1985), 65-84. There are papers in the United Church Archives, Toronto, and the PAM. *DCB* XI, 79-80.

Black, William John (1872-1941) Journalist, educator, civil servant. Born in Dufferin County, Ontario, he attended the Ontario Agricultural College, receiving his BSA in 1901, and came west to Winnipeg to become editor-in-chief of the *Farmer's Advocate*. In 1905 he became deputy minister of agriculture, first president of the Manitoba Agricultural College, and professor of animal husbandry. During WWI he became federal commissioner of the Agricultural Instruction Act from 1916 to 1918, while also serving as chair of the Soldier Settlement Board of Canada and deputy minister of immigration and colonization. After some time in Europe as manager of the CNR's department of colonization, in 1924 he became director of the CNR's Colonization and Development Department, from which he retired in 1938.

Black, William R. (1855-1919) Lawyer, land registrar. Born in Kildonan, the son of Rev. John* and Henrietta Ross Black, he graduated with honours from the University of Toronto, winning the Governor General's Medal and a medal in classics. He practised law in Portage la Prairie before becoming registrar of the Land Titles Office in Morden, where he served from 1899 to 1919. He died in Winnipeg.

Blain, Joseph (1859-1925) Cleric, professor. A member of the Jesuit Order, he came in 1885 to Collège de Saint-Boniface, where he was professor of science and mathematics. He maintained the province's only seismograph and monitored earthquakes for many years, and he discovered the site of Fort St. Charles in 1908.

Blake, Emily Hilda (1877-1899) Murderer. Born in England, she was sent to Manitoba by an English benevolent society. She became a nursemaid or nanny to the Lane family of Brandon and in 1899 shot Mrs. Lane with a pistol, claiming she was jealous of the mother's relationship with her children. Tried for murder, she was convicted in five minutes and sentenced to be hanged. Amelia Yeomans* began a movement for clemency, which insisted Blake was "morally degenerate" and suffered from "moral insanity." Blake was hanged on 27 December 1899, the last woman executed in Manitoba.

Blake, Matthew Robert (1876-1937) Physician, politician. Born in Ashfield Township, Ontario, he studied medicine in London and Dublin. He was medical officer and captain of the 106th Winnipeg Light Infantry. Blake was elected to the Union Parliament in 1917 as a Conservative MP for Winnipeg North. He vociferously opposed the Winnipeg General Strike in the House of Commons. He lived at 275 Burrows Avenue in Winnipeg.

Blakely, Frank D. (1865-1918) Photographer, editor. Born in Owen Sound, Canada, he came to Winnipeg as a boy. He worked as a photographer in the United States before returning to Canada as the CPR photographer. In 1897 he became managing editor of the *Nor'West Farmer* and in 1904 publisher of *Canadian Farm Implements*. He died in Winnipeg.

Blanchard, Kathleen (Barrett) (1872-1954) Music historian. Born in England, she came to Winnipeg with her husband around 1920. In 1940 she began writing for the *Free Press* about the history of church music; her column was called "Romance of Our Hymns." She ultimately published five books, including *The Gossamer Thread* (1937) and *Stories of Popular Hymns* (c. 1939). She moved to Vancouver in 1953, and died there.

Blanchard, Robert Johnston (1853-1928) Surgeon. Born in Truro, Nova Scotia, he graduated from the University of Edinburgh in 1878 and came to Winnipeg in 1879. He served as medical adviser to the CPR from 1889 to 1905, and then as chief surgeon to 1914. He was president of the Canadian Medical Association in 1908-9 and was a founding member of the Manitoba Medical College. In 1911 he opened a private hospital at the corner of Donald and Broadway. He commanded No. Three Canadian Casualty Clearing Station in France from 1915, returning to Canada with impaired health. He never fully recovered.

Bland, Salem (1859-1950) Cleric, professor, reformer. Born in Lachute, Canada, Bland was educated at Queen's University. He taught at Wesley College in Winnipeg from 1903 until 1917, when he was dismissed for his unorthodox opinions. He was very influential in Winnipeg social gospel and labour reform circles before and during WWI. He served as a columnist for the *Grain Growers' Guide* from 1917 until he moved to Toronto in 1919. An influential popularizer of the linkage between liberal theology and socialism, he urged a constant battle against slums, monopolies, and unearned profits. He was an exponent of Henry George's single tax ideology and was an influential teacher of J.S. Woodsworth,* William Ivens,* and other social gospellers. Despite his radical enthusiasm, Bland was generally wary of general strikes and labour militancy. His major work was *The New Christianity, or the Religion of the New Age* (1920), which associated Protestantism and capitalism and argued for a reformed Christian religion. His papers are in Victoria University, Toronto. See A.R. Allen, *The Social Passion: Religion and Social Reform in Canada 1914-28* (1971). There are papers at the United Church Archives, Toronto.

Blankstein, Cecil (1908-1989) Architect. Born in Winnipeg, he graduated from the University of Manitoba in 1929 and helped found Green Blankstein Russell Associates, which designed many Winnipeg buildings between 1931 and 1978, including the Winnipeg International Airport and Polo Park Shopping Centre. He later moved to Israel and designed high-density housing projects in Jerusalem. He was president of the Manitoba Association of Architects and a fellow of the Royal Architectural Institute. He died in Jerusalem.

Bletcher, Henry Ernest (1869-1949) Pharmacist, professor. Born in Peterborough, Ontario, he attended the Toronto College of Pharmacy and received a BA from the University of Manitoba in 1891. He was appointed instructor to students of the Pharmaceutical Association in 1898, then was made principal of the Manitoba College of Pharmacy in 1899. After the amalgamation of the College of Pharmacy with the University of Manitoba in 1914, he became the first professor of pharmacy in the British Empire.

Blewett, George John (1873-1912) Professor, author. Born in Yarmouth Township, Ontario, he graduated a medal winner from Victoria University, Toronto, in 1897 and was ordained in 1898. He lectured in philosophy at Wesley College from 1901 to 1906 before becoming Ryerson professor of moral philosophy at Victoria College, Toronto. A theological liberal, he wrote several works important to the social gospel, especially *The Study of Nature and the Vision of God* (1907) and *The Christian View of the World* (1912). He died in Go Home Bay, Ontario. *DCB* XIV, 92-3.

Blick, John Oliver (1915-1981) Radio pioneer. Born in Edmonton, he served in the RCAF in WWII. In 1946 he founded radio station CJOB, selling it in 1961. He introduced many broadcasting innovations to CJOB, including news on the hour and simultaneous FM broadcasting (1948). He was very active in community cultural organizations.

Blondal, Patricia (Jenkins) (1926-1959) Writer. Born in Souris, Manitoba, she moved to Winnipeg with her family in the 1930s and attended United College from 1944 to 1947 where she was a classmate of Margaret Laurence.* After her graduation she lived in Winnipeg, and later moved to Chalk River, Ontario, and then to Montreal. She began serious writing in 1955. In the 1950s she wrote that her coat of arms was "a typewriter rampant on a field of rejection slips." She finally had one novel (*From Heaven with a Shout,* published in book form in 1963) serialized by *Chatelaine* and another (*A Candle to Light the Sun*) accepted by McClelland and Stewart. She died of cancer in Montreal before the latter book was published in 1960 to considerable critical acclaim. *A Candle to Light the Sun* was probably autobiographical, describing the constraints of living in the small town of "Mouse Bluffs." Blondal has been described as one of the most promising Canadian writing talents of the half century.

Blondeau, Maurice-Régis (1734-1809) Fur trader. Born in Montreal, he entered the fur trade in the 1750s and headed for the *pays d'en haut* in 1769. By 1770 he was working in the area south of Lake Winnipeg, and he later went into partnership with James McGill and others to mount a major trade to Grand Portage. He received a seigneury on the St. Lawrence River in 1773. In 1785 he was one of the founders of the Beaver Club in Montreal, and he was an active reformer in the 1780s in Quebec. *DCB* V, 89-90.

Blumberg, John ("Jack," 1892-1961) Municipal politician. Born in Hull, England, he came to Winnipeg in 1910. He worked as a streetcar motorman from 1912 until 1919, when he was elected to city council as an anti-communist. During WWI he served overseas in the King's Rifles. He served on the council almost continuously until his death, being defeated only in 1950. As acting mayor in Winnipeg in 1933 he refused to read the riot act to demonstrators against unemployment. He served as chair of the Greater Winnipeg Transit Commission from 1956.

Blumenberg, Sam (fl. 1900-1919) Businessman, Socialist. One of Winnipeg's most popular Socialists, he told a meeting at the Columbia Theatre in Winnipeg in 1918 that "we are going to run this city." His business establishment, the Minneapolis Dye House (a cleaning shop), was wrecked by rampaging veterans in January 1919. He was arrested in June 1919, and he left for the United States rather than be deported to Europe. He subsequently worked as a labour organizer in Duluth and Minneapolis.

Bole, D.W. (1856-1933) Pharmacist, businessman, politician. Born in Lambton County, Canada, he was educated there before graduating from the University of Toronto in pharmacy. He opened a Regina drugstore in 1882 and came to Winnipeg in 1889. He founded the National Drug and Chemical Company in 1905 and was its president until 1922. He moved to Montreal in 1905, although he represented Winnipeg in the Commons until 1911. He returned to Winnipeg in 1922.

Bolus, Malvina (d. 1997) Editor, author. Born in the Falkland Islands, she came to Ottawa to work with the Canadian Geographical Society. She later moved west and became assistant editor of *The Beaver,* and then its editor from 1958 to 1972. She was the author of *Image of Canada* (1953). She retired to Victoria.

Bonami, Alexis (dit Lesperance) (1796-1890) Fur trader. Born in Lower Canada to a fur-trading family, he began his career with the HBC as a voyageur. He became noted for his leadership of the difficult Portage La Loche canoe brigade. He opened this route in 1832, travelling from Red River in York boats across Lake Winnipeg to Norway House, then along the Saskatchewan River, then the Churchill River, then to Lac La Loche, then to Methy Portage, where he met a crew from the Mackenzie River district and furs were exchanged for provisions. The route covered 4,000 miles on a tight schedule using dangerous waterways. Bonami supervised the brigade until his retirement, when he received a pension from the HBC. He was eulogized at the time of his death as "an imposing figure among the host of intrepid voyageurs." *DCB* XI, 88-89.

Bond, Annie (Crisp) (1854-1943) Nurse, philanthropist. Born in Warwickshire, England, she trained at Queen's Hospital before joining the nursing sisters in the British army. She served in a series of imperial campaigns in locations that included South Africa during the Zulu War, Egypt, and the Sudan. She was decorated in each of these campaigns, receiving the Royal Red Cross Medal in 1884. In that same year she moved to Auckland, New Zealand, to establish New Zealand's first school of nursing, and in 1886 she married Dr. J.H.R. Bond.* She went to the United States with her husband, administering the British exhibit at the Chicago World's Fair in 1896. The couple eventually settled in Winnipeg in 1903. She began urging the foundation of a children's hospital in 1906, and in 1909 she began one on Beaconsfield Street which became the Winnipeg Children's Hospital. She died there as one of the few patients over the age of 14 ever admitted. See Harry Medovy, *A Vision Fulfilled: The Story of the Children's Hospital of Winnipeg 1909-1973* (1979).

Bond, John Henry Richard (1859-1945) Physician, radiologist. Born in Portsmouth, England, he attended the United Services College and graduated from Edinburgh University in medicine in 1881. He travelled to New Zealand in 1882 and remained to practise medicine until 1890, receiving the master's chair of the District Grand Lodge of Masons in Auckland. He moved to Chicago and practised medicine there from 1890 to 1903, heading to the Klondike in 1898-99. In 1903 he came to Winnipeg with his wife Annie* and set up a practice and private hospital at 167 Donald Street. He brought a portable X-ray machine with him from Chicago and was a pioneer in the use of X-rays in Canada. His blindness of later years probably resulted from his exposure to the X-rays. He served as secretary of the Manitoba Cricket Association. There are travel journals in private hands. See Andrew Taylor, "The Bond Papers," *Manitoba History,* no. 22 (autumn 1991): 23-29.

Bonnar, Robert Andrew (1860-1932) Lawyer. Born in Canada and educated at Osgoode Hall law school, Bonnar came to Winnipeg in 1882. He was called to the bar in 1889 and was a partner in the legal firm of Bonnar, Trueman, Hollands, and Robinson. In 1919 and 1920 he served as counsel for the defence in the trials of the leaders of the Winnipeg General Strike who were charged with sedition. Bonnar was known as one of the great theatrical criminal lawyers of his generation and was often criticized for his methods. His clients escaped the gallows in all but one of the trials he defended.

Bonnycastle, Arthur Lorne (1873-1941) Judge. Born in Campbellford, Ontario, he came to Manitoba in 1893 to teach school at Shellmouth. He then studied law in Winnipeg and was called to the bar in 1905. Elected as a Conservtive MLA from Russell in 1907, he served as deputy provincial secretary from 1910 to 1913. In 1913 he was appointed provincial police magistrate in Winnipeg, remaining until 1916, when he resigned to raise, take overseas, and lead (as lieutenant-colonel) the 207th Battalion ("Bonny's Buccaneers"). Upon demobilization he served as a county court judge in Dauphin until 1941. He died in Dauphin. There are extensive papers at the PAM.

Bonnycastle, Richard (1903-1968) Business executive, publisher. Born near Binscarth, Manitoba, he was educated at Trinity College in Toronto and Oxford University. At Oxford he played ice hockey with Lester Pearson and Roland Michener. He joined the HBC in 1925 and travelled extensively in the North. In 1945 he became president of Stovel-Advocate Press, and in the 1950s he created Harlequin Books Limited to publish romance novels. He was the first chair of the Metropolitan Corporation of Greater Winnipeg (Metro) in 1960 and the first chancellor of the University of Winnipeg in 1957. See Heather Robertson, ed., *R.H.G. Bonnycastle, A Gentleman Adventurer: The Arctic Diaries of Richard Bonnycastle* (1984); Paul Grescoe, *The Merchants of Venus: Inside Harlequin and the Empire of Romance* (1996).

Boon, Thomas Charles Boucher (1887-1979) Professor, cleric, historian, archivist. Born in Worcester, England, he was educated at the Worcester Royal Grammar School, University College Reading, the University of London, and the University of Manitoba. In 1921 he joined St. John's College, and he served as registrar and as lecturer in chemistry from 1928 to 1940. He was ordained a priest in 1937 and served parishes in Alberta and Winnipeg. From 1947 to 1960 he was provincial archivist of the Ecclesiastical Diocese of Rupert's Land. He wrote many works of church history, notably *The Anglican Church from the Bay to the Rockies* (1962). There are extensive papers at the Rupert's Land Archives.

Borebank, John James (1870-1912) Businessman. Born in West Hallam, Derbyshire, England, he moved to Canada as a child. He came to Winnipeg in 1896 and opened a business before returning to Toronto. He died in the sinking of the *Titanic*. There is a plaque in his memory in Winnipeg City Hall, and a street in the Winnipeg neighbourhood of River Heights is named after him.

Borowski, Joseph (1933-1996) Politician, anti-abortion crusader. Born in Wishart, Saskatchewan, he worked as a cook in mines and owned a Saskatoon restaurant. He became a miner in Thompson, then opened a souvenir shop where in 1965 he refused to collect provincial sales tax. He was elected NDP MLA for Thompson in 1969 and became minister of highways in the Schreyer government. He resigned in 1971 over the abortion issue and became the most prominent pro-lifer in Canada. He went on a hunger strike and carried on a long constitutional battle with the Canadian Supreme Court, which he lost in 1989.

Borthwick, Hugh Jamieson (1824-1916) School inspector, missionary. Born in Midlothian, Scotland, he was educated at Edinburgh University and came to Canada in 1845. He served for years in education, becoming Ottawa school inspector. He attended Queen's University and was ordained a missionary in the Presbyterian Church. In 1876 he was sent as a missionary to Manitoba by the Home Missionary Committee of the Presbyterian Church of Canada, and he served the Pembina Mountain district until 1911. He became a school inspector for southern Manitoba and worked for several years as editor of the *Morden Herald.*

Boswell, Charles Musgrave (1849-1907) Soldier. Born in Cobourg, Canada, he was educated at Upper Canada College before joining the Cobourg Infantry Company in 1864. After active militia service during the Fenian period, he was employed at the Cobourg post office from 1871 until 1881, when he was transferred to Winnipeg. In Manitoba he helped organize the 90th Regiment and served as its first adjutant. He commanded the 90th in the North-West Rebellion and was mentioned in dispatches. He became lieutenant-colonel of the 90th in 1887 and was aide-de-camp for Manitoba to the governor general from 1887 to 1895.

Botterell, John E. (1880-1924) Grain broker. He migrated to Winnipeg in 1913 to become a partner of Baird and Botterell. In 1919 he was president of the Winnipeg Grain Exchange and a leading member of the Citizens' Committee of 1,000.

Boucher de Niverville, Joseph Claude (1715-1804) Soldier. Born in Chambly, Canada, he served as a cadet in the colonial regular troops and worked his way up the officer ranks. In 1750 he was one of a party led by Jacques Légardeur de Saint-Pierre to search for the "western sea." The expedition left Montreal in 1750 and established bases at present-day Portage la Prairie and The Pas. He became ill at the latter base and did not manage to get further west. He left the region in the spring of 1753. *DCB* V, 97-100.

Boulton, Charles Arkoll (1842-1899) Surveyor, soldier, politician. Born at Cobourg, Canada, Boulton was educated at Upper Canada College. He served with the Royal Canadian Regiment in Gibraltar and Wales before his appointment as a member of the Canadian survey party in Red River. Boulton attempted to organize military support for Governor William McDougall* in December 1869 and reluctantly led an armed party from Portage la Prairie in its attempt to free prisoners held by Riel in February 1870. Captured by Riel, he was threatened with execution. His reprieve was a major quid pro quo in the complex negotiations between Riel and Canadian envoy Donald A. Smith.* After the rebellion, Boulton went back to Ontario, failed in business there, and then returned with his family to the Shellmouth region in 1880. In 1885 he raised Boulton's Scouts for service in the North-West Rebellion. After the uprising was suppressed, he

immediately returned home, hired a stenographer, and dictated his best-selling *Reminiscences of the North-West Rebellion*, which led directly to his appointment as senator from Manitoba in 1889. For a biography, see Keith Wilson, *Charles Arkoll Boulton* (1984). *DCB* XII, 119-20. There are family papers at the PAM.

Bourgeaux, Eugene (1813-1877) Botanist. Born in Brizon, France, he was employed by the Botanic Garden at Lyons before becoming botanist in Paris for a French botanical society. The British appointed him botanist to the Palliser Expedition in 1857, and he was the first botanist to carefully examine much of the Prairies and the Rocky Mountains. He collected over 1,200 specimens and was popular with the Métis. He became a friend of Father Lacombe. In 1859 he went to the Royal Botanic Gardens at Kew to sort his specimens, unfortunately not re-transcribing his habitat notes. He subsequently did fieldwork in Asia Minor, Spain, Mexico, and Rhodes. Bourgeaux insisted that much of the Canadian West was more suitable for grain farming "than one would be inclined to believe." *DCB* X, 81-82.

Bourke, Edwin (1835-1915) Farmer, politician, soldier. Born in Red River, he inherited the Hay Field Farm in St. James from his father, John.* Beginning in 1870, he represented St. James in the legislature, serving until 1878. He was also a captain of the volunteers during the Fenian raids of 1871. He was active in the St. James municipal government. He died in Ocean Park, California.

Bourke, John (1823-1887) Buffalo hunter. A mixed-blood buffalo hunter from St. James Parish, he married Elizabeth Fidler. With William Hallett,* he helped James Stewart* break out of jail in 1863. He was also one of a party that met on 7 December 1869 in Winnipeg at the office of Bannatyne and Begg. The gathering decided to tell John Schultz* that he was endangering the whole settlement and that he needed to withdraw his party from the fortified houses it was holding.

Bourke, John Palmer (b. 1791) Settler. Born in Sligo, Ireland, he accompanied the 1812 party of Selkirk settlers, wintered at York Factory, and arrived in the Red River Settlement to become a storekeeper in 1813. He came with cannon to Seven Oaks in 1816 after the skirmish was over, but was wounded in the retreat. He subsequently was captured by the NWC and was tried in Montreal in 1818 for his part in the conflict. He returned to Red River in 1819, served as a clerk for the HBC for several years, and retired to the settlement in 1822. George Simpson* described him as sober but untalented, with "a quarrelsome irritable temper." He was part of the 1833 expedition to the United States to procure sheep, and in 1835 he purchased the HBC experimental farm in present-day St. James. In 1845 he became head of the HBC's newly established post at Pembina.

Boutal, Pauline (LeGoff) (1894-1992) Artist, theatrical designer. Born in Brittany, she immigrated to Manitoba with her family in 1907, settling first on Lake Manitoba and later in Winnipeg. Her family members were active workers in stained glass, and she learned to draw in childhood. In 1918 she joined Brigden's as a fashion artist, and she remained there until 1941, in charge of designs for the Eaton's catalogue. In those days, she later recalled, "all the clothes and other items for sale in the catalogue were drawn by artists." She joined Le Cercle Molière with her husband in 1925, and the Boutals soon became responsible for most of the design work of the group. She replaced her husband as artistic director upon his death in 1941, the same year she resigned from Brigden's. She was later awarded the Order of Canada.

Bowles, Richard (1912-1988) Lawyer, lieutenant-governor. Born in Winnipeg, he graduated from the University of Manitoba in arts and law. A prominent Winnipeg lawyer, he was president of the Manitoba Law Society in 1964-65 and chair of the Winnipeg Board of Parks and Recreation in 1955-56. He served as lieutenant-governor of Manitoba from 1965 to 1970 and subsequently was chancellor of the University of Manitoba from 1974 to 1977.

Bown, Walter (1828-1903) Dentist, publisher. Born in England, Bown was raised in Brantford, Upper Canada. He trained as a dentist, then immigrated to the Midwestern United States, where he became involved in the 1862-63 Sioux uprising. Bown moved to Red River in 1863, and soon became involved with John Schultz,* an association which lasted for nearly three decades. He first became editor of the *Nor'-Wester* when Schultz was jailed in 1868. Bown purchased the newspaper from Schultz on 1 July 1868. It continued to advocate Canadian annexation until it was shut down by Louis Riel. Bown was forced to hide from Riel's wrath, and stories circulated of his escape from Red River in disguise. He accompanied Schultz to the United States in 1872 in an abortive plot to steal Riel's papers. In 1873 he was appointed to the Council of the North-West Territories. He continued to serve as Schultz's factotum, including a term as private secretary while Schultz was lieutenant-governor of Manitoba. At the end of his life, he was involved in a demeaning court case in which his sister tried unsuccessfully to prove him incompetent to manage his own affairs. He died in Battle Creek, Michigan. *DCB* XIII, 103-104.

Boyd, Alfred (1836-1908) Merchant, politician. Born in England, Boyd was in Red River by 1858. He owned a store in St. John's Parish that was managed by Maurice Lowman,* and he engaged in fur trade with the Inkster interests. Boyd was elected as an English delegate to the 1870 Convention of Forty from St. Andrew's. Although he was not a leading member, Louis Riel later described him as "one of the most decided against us." Boyd certainly opposed Riel's election as president and favoured territorial over provincial status. His critics later charged that he had received inflated reimbursement for "rebellion losses" (he claimed $55,500 in general damages and was awarded $2,505.18 for guns seized by the insurgents), but he always insisted that real goods had been involved. In any event, he was appointed provincial secretary in September 1870 and was elected to the Legislative Assembly from St. Andrew's North in December 1870. He resigned the secretaryship to become minister of public works and agriculture. He is sometimes regarded as Manitoba's first premier. Boyd was heavily criticized by incoming settlers for his failure to make public improvements, and he resigned in 1871 to be replaced by John Norquay.* He subsequently became a founding member of the Council of the North-West Territories. He was a clever cartoonist, and according to J.H. O'Donnell* he "drew many laughable sketches of members of the House that were grotesquely funny." He left Manitoba about 1889, dying in England a wealthy man. *DCB* XIII, 104-6.

Boyd, John Mackenzie (1859-1939) Journalist, school administrator, art critic. Born in Scotland, Boyd served in the Marines and rattled around eastern Canada as a journalist before settling down as registrar of the Winnipeg School of Art in 1914. A regular contributor to the *Manitoba Free Press* on art and activities at the school, Boyd was regarded by many students as the person who held the school together.

Boyd, Stella (d. 1945) Contralto, vocal teacher. The daughter of W.J. Boyd,* she was a leading contralto soloist and vocal teacher in Winnipeg, having studied in France, Germany, and England. She was a vocal examiner for many years. She was an executive member of the Women's Musical Club and the Registered Music Teachers' Association.

Boyd, William (1885-1979) Pathologist. Born in Portsoy, Scotland, he studied medicine at the University of Edinburgh and worked in hospitals in the English Midlands. After a brief period as a pathologist in Wolverhampton, he was appointed professor of pathology at the University of Manitoba. Before taking up his post in Manitoba, he served in Flanders as a captain with the Third Field Ambulance Unit, writing of the experience in the book *With a Field Ambulance at Ypres* (1915). Boyd spent 22 years in Winnipeg, achieving an international reputation in pathology before becoming professor and head of pathology at the University of Toronto in 1937. After retirement from Toronto he was the first professor of pathology at the new medical school at the University of British Columbia, 1951-1954. Boyd was a Fellow of the Royal Society of Canada and a Companion of the Order of Canada (1968). He wrote extensively; his medical textbooks, written mainly in Manitoba, were professional best-sellers for many years. See Ian Carr, *William Boyd: Silver Tongue and Golden Pen* (1993).

Boyd, William J. (1861-1943) Businessman. Born in Kemptville, Ontario, he came to Winnipeg in 1885 and soon entered the confectionery business, later opening a bread firm. He went into the wholesale confectionery business in 1912 and built the Boyd Building in 1913. He retired in 1934. He was an active Conservative and a Master Mason.

Bozyk, Pantelemon (1879-1944) Cleric, poet. Born at Omut, Bukovina, he was ordained a priest in the Orthodox Church in 1911. By special papal dispensation in 1922 he was allowed to become a Catholic priest although he was married. He came to Canada in 1924 as the country's only married Catholic priest and proceeded to Winnipeg in 1925, becoming priest at St. Andrew's Church. As a poet, he published extensively in Ukrainian.

Bracken, John (1883-1969) Professor, politician. Born in Ellisville, Ontario, Bracken graduated from the Ontario Agricultural College. He was a government employee until he became a professor of field husbandry at the University of Saskatchewan in 1910. Ten years later he took an appointment as principal of the Manitoba Agricultural College. One of his activities was a major survey of farm conditions in Manitoba. Within two years he had become premier of the province, his seat in the legislature representing The Pas. Although he regarded himself as a Progressive, most of his governments were of the coalition variety, distinguished for their cautious nonpartisanship and reflection of the rural interests of the province. In 1943 Bracken reluctantly became the leader of the federal Conservative Party, insisting that it add the word "Progressive" to its name. He was not a successful leader. He did not actually enter the House of Commons until 1945 (from Neepawa), and he lacked charisma. On the other hand, he did push the party towards acceptance of the welfare state. Bracken stepped down from the leadership in 1948, subsequently serving as chair of a royal commission on the liquor laws of Manitoba. He wrote two books, *Crop Production in Western Canada* (1920) and *Dry Farming in Western Canada* (1921), the latter book appearing just as the worst drought in Prairie history began. He is a member of the Manitoba Agricultural Hall of Fame. For a biography, consult John Kendle, *John Bracken* (1979). There are papers at the PAM.

Braithwaite, Charles (1850-1910) Reformer. Born in Foston, England, he came to Canada in the early 1870s and arrived in Portage la Prairie in 1881, where he eventually settled. He was an early member of the Patrons of Husbandry and was elected grand president in 1891. He was a superb orator who toured Manitoba with the slogan "Manitoba for Manitobans." The most important "Grange" leader in the province, he advocated organization against "the financial, commercial and manufacturing classes, who by a system of combines and monopolies are exacting from us an undue proportion of the fruits of our toil." He offered to resign from the Patrons in 1894 because they were not strongly supporting cooperatives, but was prevailed upon to remain. He began to advocate political organization and the fielding of farmer candidates. In 1894 he again toured the province, criticizing rail rates and high tariffs. By the end of the year 5,000 members belonged to 330 lodges. The organization was probably broken by the Manitoba school question, which divided its Catholic and Protestant members. Braithwaite campaigned for Parliament in Macdonald riding in 1896 on a platform of non-sectarian schools, electoral and civil service reform, free trade, public ownership of utilities, universal suffrage, and prohibition. In 1896, Braithwaite and other Patron candidates helped the Conservatives win four of seven seats despite the national Liberal sweep. He became a provincial weed inspector in, and then moved his family to Chilliwack, British Columbia in 1904. He died in Chilliwack. *DCB* XIII, 108-110.

Bray, Roger E. (fl. 1903-1950) Socialist, veterans' leader. Born in Sheffield, England, Bray immigrated to Winnipeg in 1903, working in the butcher trade. He was a former Methodist lay preacher and an active socialist, who had discovered "that Christianity was not the means of correcting social injustice." Bray joined the Canadian army in 1916 while unemployed, later explaining he had "no job and a large family." He returned to Winnipeg from England on 31 December 1918, serving in 1919 as spokesman for a returned soldiers meeting in Victoria Park, and as chair of an informal group of returned soldier strikers. On 14 June 1919 a secret agent of the RNWMP informed the superintendent of the Winnipeg District that Bray was "at the present time the most dangerous person in the City." He was arrested on 17 June 1919 by the government on charges of seditious conspiracy. He became vice-president of the Winnipeg Labour Council formed by the One Big Union on 5 August 1919. At his sedition trial in 1920, he was acquitted on most charges and convicted only on the charge of conspiracy to commit a common criminal nuisance. He was sentenced to six months in prison. Bray subsequently became an organizer for the One Big Union. He eventually moved to North Vancouver where he raised gladioli and was an organizer for the CCF. See Harry and Mildred Gutkin, *Profiles in Dissent: The Shaping of Radical Thought in the Canadian West* (1997), 193-203.

Breau, Lenny (1941-1984) Musician. Born in Auburn, Maine, to a family of country and western performers, he came to Winnipeg in 1957. He was self-taught on the guitar, developing an amazing technical proficiency that was much admired by fellow musicians. He was discovered by Chet Atkins but spent virtually his entire career battling drug addiction. He died by drowning in a Los Angeles apartment swimming pool.

Bredt, Paul Frederick (1883-1940) Livestock breeder, company executive. Born in Leipzig, Germany, he came to Canada with his family in 1900, entering the Manitoba Agricultural College and graduating in 1914 with highest honours. He served as assistant livestock commissioner and later livestock commissioner in Saskatchewan until 1919, when he established a farm at Kemnay, Manitoba, that specialized in livestock and registered grains. After several years as a director of the Manitoba Wheat Pool and Manitoba Pool Elevators, he became president of the Manitoba Pool Elevators, adding the presidency of the Canadian Cooperative Wheat Producers Limited and Canadian Pool Agencies Limited in 1937 and becoming president of the Pool Insurance Company in 1940. He served as a governor of the University of Manitoba and on several major national grain committees. He is a member of the Manitoba Agricultural Hall of Fame. See F.W. Hamilton, *Service at Cost: A History of Manitoba Pool Elevators 1925-1975* (1975).

Breen, William Wright ("Billy," 1883-1927) Hockey player. Born in Winnipeg, he played hockey for several Winnipeg clubs, including the Winnipeg Assiniboines. A centre, he was noted as a checker as well as a goal scorer. He also was an alley bowler of distinction. Breen refused to turn professional and always retained his amateur standing. He worked in the automotive industry in its early days in Winnipeg.

Bréland, Pascal (1811-1896) Farmer, politician. Born in the Saskatchewan Valley to a French-Canadian fur trader and a Métisse, he moved with his family to Red River around 1828 and took up farming. In 1836 he married a daughter of Cuthbert Grant* and gradually acquired most of Grant's property in the St. François Xavier district. He received an official grant to this land in 1882. Bréland was also active as a free trader and a freighter. In 1851 he was appointed magistrate for White Horse Plains, and in 1857 he became a member of the Council of Assiniboia. During the 1869-70 insurrection he withdrew to the Qu'Appelle Valley, reappearing in St. François Xavier in April 1870 to warn that "men should now refrain from associating themselves with the murderers of a helpless prisoner." Not surprisingly, the new leaders of Manitoba found him useful. He was elected MPP from St. François Xavier in the first elections of 1870, and in 1872 he was appointed to the North-West Council, where he served until 1887. In 1874 he became a member of the executive of the North-West Council, serving actively in treaty negotiations from 1874 to 1876. His later utility was somewhat limited by his difficulty in speaking English, and by the 1880s events had passed him by. He died in St. François Xavier. See Manitoba Historic Resources Branch, *Pascal Bréland* (1984). *DCB* XII, 124-25. There are scattered papers at the PAM.

Brereton, Alexander Picton (1892-1976) War hero. Born in Oak River, Manitoba, he was educated in Hamiota. As a member of the 85th Battalion, Winnipeg Rifles (the "Little Black Devils"), he won a Victoria Cross at Aubrecourt (Battle of Amiens) in 1918 by single-handedly capturing an enemy machine-gun post. He moved to Elnora, Alberta, after the war, where he farmed 640 acres. He later served in WWII as a quartermaster sergeant based in Red Deer. He died in Three Hills, Alberta.

Bridgman, Wellington (1853-1922) Cleric, writer. He came to Manitoba in 1881 as assistant to Rev. Dr. George Young* and served as a Methodist missionary in the West for many years. He was appointed garrison chaplain in 1916 and was later chaplain to the 251st Battalion of the Canadian Expeditionary Force. From 1909 to 1913 he was superintendent of the Manitoba Boys' Reformatory. Both of his sons were killed in WWI. In 1920 he published a memoir, *Breaking Prairie Sod: The Story of a Pioneer Preacher in the Eighties.* The book contained "A Discussion on the Burning Question of To-Day, 'Shall the Alien Go?'" and advocated the deportation of enemy aliens from the West.

Brigden, Arnold Oliver (1886-1972) Commercial artist. Born in England, Brigden came to Canada as an apprentice with the Brigden firm in Toronto. In 1914 he was sent to manage Brigden's in Winnipeg, which he quickly made into a major commercial art producer in the Canadian West. Brigden's employed many young Canadian artists. The firm specialized in catalogues, both of hard goods and of fashion articles. Brigden was for many years a member of the Winnipeg School of Art's Art Committee. He retired from the business in 1956. His wide-ranging art collection is now a basis of the Winnipeg Art Gallery. Consult Winnipeg Art Gallery, *The Brigden Collection: A Winnipeg Centennial Exhibition* (1974). See also Angela Davis, "Business, Art and Labour: Brigden's and the Growth of the Graphic Arts Industry, 1870-1959" (PhD diss., University of Manitoba, 1986).

Brigden, Beatrice Alice (1894-1977) Politician. Born in Manitoba, she spent her early years in eastern Canada and was educated at the Toronto Conservatory School. After returning to Brandon she was active in the Independent Labor Party (later the CCF, then the NDP). She was a frequent candidate in elections. Brigden organized the Manitoba Women's Model Parliament and was a member of the Manitoba Human Rights Commission. A letter of hers, on labour matters in 1919, is reprinted in *Manitoba History,* no. 19 (spring 1990): 35-37. See Allison Campbell, "Beatrice Brigden: The Formative Years of a Socialist Feminist, 1888-1932" (MA thesis, University of Manitoba, 1991).

Brisebois, Éphrem-A. (1850-1890) Police officer, politician. Born in Canada, he joined the Union army in 1865 and then fought with the Quebec volunteers of the Papal Zouaves in Italy. In 1873 he was appointed one of nine commanding officers of the NWMP. After training his division, he was promoted to inspector and was sent to Alberta, where he helped build Fort Macleod and then Fort Brisebois. He was not a popular commander, and he resigned from the force in 1876. He became active in Conservative politics in Quebec, and in 1880 he was appointed land titles registrar of the Little Saskatchewan District, based in Minnedosa, Manitoba. Here he was more successful, and in 1885 he was locally active against the North-West Rebellion. He died unemployed in Winnipeg. *DCB* XI, 111-12.

Brock, Jeffrey Hall (1850-1915) Financier. Born in Guelph, Canada, he was educated locally and at the High School of Montreal. After spending several years in various mercantile enterprises, he came to Winnipeg in 1879, entering into partnership with G.F. Carruthers in an insurance firm. In 1891 he founded, with 14 other businessmen, the Great-West Life Assurance Company, serving as its managing director from that date until his death. He was a warden at Holy Trinity Anglican Church. He died in California. *DCB* XIV, 146-47.

Brokovski, Edwin Frederick Thomas (1838-1916) Surveyor, journalist. Born in London, England, to Polish parents, he came to Canada in 1857 to teach school. He moved to Manitoba in 1871 as a surveyor, published a newspaper, the *Manitoba Gazette and Trade Review*, from 1872 to 1874, and served as a real estate agent. He covered the Lord Gordon Gordon case in 1873 as a journalist, making his reputation in the process. In 1875 he was the first representative of the Manitoba press to have a seat in the parliamentary press gallery in Ottawa. He helped organize the Manitoba Rifle Association and was an active volunteer fireman. Later he served as Dominion land agent in Battleford, Saskatchewan, where he died. *DCB* XIV, 147-48. There are papers at the PAM.

Brooker, Bertram (1888-1955) Writer, painter, musician. Born in Croydon, England, he came with his parents to Portage la Prairie in 1905. He moved to Toronto in 1921. He acquired a reputation as a writer, painter, musician, and poet. Brooker was a charter member of the Canadian Group of Painters, and he won the Governor General's Award for fiction in 1936 for *Think of the Earth*. See *Sounds Assembling: The Poetry of Bertram Brooker* (1980); Jennifer O. Sinclair, ed., *Bertram Brooker and Emergent Modernism* (1984).

Brooker, Joyce Margaret (McCulloch) (1921-1991) Musician. Born in Portage la Prairie, she was educated locally and served as secretary-manager of the Portage la Prairie Chamber of Commerce for many years. With her husband she led, and played piano in, the Brookers Bombshells, a leading dance band in southern Manitoba. She also helped found the Portage Music and Arts Festival. She died in Portage la Prairie.

Brooking, Robert (1813-1893) Missionary. Born near Tavistock, England, he attended Richmond Theological Institute, graduating in 1839, and was sent as a missionary to the Gold Coast of Africa. He withdrew from Africa because of illness and was sent to Upper Canada in 1847, then to Rupert's Land from 1854 to 1859, serving at Norway House and Oxford House. A skilled carpenter, he built many wooden structures while in the North. His papers are at the United Church Archives, Toronto. *DCB* XII, 127-28.

Broughall, George (1861-1927) Journalist, playwright. He came to Winnipeg to work on the *Manitoba Free Press*. He became secretary of the Manitoba Shorthand Writers' Association, and he served as an officer in the 90th Regiment during the North-West Rebellion. In 1885 he published *The 90th on Active Service, or, Campaigning in the North West: A Musical and Dramatic Burlesque in Two Acts*, which had played in the Princess Opera House in Winnipeg on 29 and 30 July of that year. He published *The Tearful and Tragical Tale of the Truly Troubador* in 1886. It too had been performed in the Princess Opera House, in September and October 1886. Broughall reputedly owned the first bicycle in Western Canada.

Brown, Bartley (1884-1939) Musician. Born in Toronto, he became well known as a boy soprano and soloist at St. James Cathedral. In 1904 he came to Winnipeg, where he taught singing, sang in church choirs and on the stage, acted in little theatre, and in later years performed on the radio. As an actor, he was best known for his role as Captain Hook in Barrie's *Peter Pan*. He was a soloist in a series of Winnipeg churches, including St. Luke's Anglican, First Baptist Church, Central Congregational Church, and Augustine United Church. From 1929 to 1939 he was choirmaster at First Federated Church.

Brown, Charles J. (1855-1926) Civil servant. Born in Kingston, Canada, he was a member of the 1872 Red River Expedition, and he subsequently joined his father, A.M. Brown, as a resident of Winnipeg. He succeeded his father as city clerk in 1878, serving as the city's returning officer for 42 years. In 1914, he was President of the American Municipalities Association.

Brown, Corydon Portlow (1848-1891) Surveyor, businessman, politician. Born in New Brunswick, he was educated in Fredericton as a civil engineer. He moved west in the early 1870s to work for the Dominion Lands Branch as a land surveyor. In 1873 he acquired land in Westbourne, Manitoba, and he soon became the region's major businessman. In 1874 he was elected from Westbourne to the Manitoba legislature as an independent Liberal, but he soon joined John Norquay. He served as provincial secretary in 1878-79 and as minister of public works from 1879 to 1886 in the Norquay Cabinet. He was one of a delegation appointed to go to Ottawa in 1883 "to procure from the Government of Canada a settlement of rights of the Province, as claimed by its Legislature." In his later years in office he was frequently attacked as a "boodle politician," a charge that eventually seemed to stick and made him unelectable after his victory in 1886. He died suddenly of pneumonia. *DCB* XII, 128-29.

Brown, David A. (1895-1990) Agronomist. Born in Scotland, he came with his family to the Deloraine area of Manitoba, graduated from high school there, and then attended the Manitoba Agricultural College. He began working at the Morden Experimental Farm in 1922, and in 1928 he went to the Brandon Experimental Farm, where he focussed on model agricultural stations and on the development of orderly crop-rotation systems, as well as the introduction of fertilizers and weed controls. He was an active Presbyterian layman. He was awarded an honorary life membership in the Manitoba Horticultural Association in 1962. Brown is a member of the Manitoba Agricultural Hall of Fame.

Brown, Edward (1865-1947) Broker, politician. Born in Gresham, Canada, and educated at St. Catharines, he was an early resident of Portage la Prairie and its mayor for six years. He moved to Winnipeg in 1909 to open Edward Brown and Company, financial brokers, which he headed until 1942. He led the Manitoba Liberal Association from 1905 to 1915 and became provincial treasurer from 1915 to 1922, serving as MLA for The Pas. He was later a Progressive.

Brown, (Francis) Roy (1896-1960) Pilot. Born in Stockton, Manitoba, he was educated in Winnipeg. In 1914 he was western Canadian cycling champion, and he joined the cycle corps in the Canadian Expeditionary Force. In 1916 he joined the Royal Flying Corps. Although he was a fighter pilot, he was not the Roy Brown who shot down the "Red Baron," a point he reiterated throughout his life. In 1927 he became a bush pilot with Western Canadian Airways, and he was one of the pilots who found a lost Arctic party in 1929. He had the first mail contract with Western Canada Airways in 1930. Later he founded Wings Limited, which was bought by CP Air in 1941. He subsequently became vice-president of Central Northern Airways. He was elected MLA for Rupert's Land as a Liberal-Progressive in 1953 and served as a spokesman for northern interests in the House.

Brown, John Hyslop (1860-1917) Lawyer, land registrar. Born in Woodstock, Canada, he attended the University of Toronto and moved to Winnipeg in 1881 to article in a law firm. He became deputy registrar of land titles in 1888 and district registrar in 1916. He was a leading real estate lawyer in Canada.

Brown, Philip (1836-1913) Merchant, immigration officer. He moved to Winnipeg from Montreal in the 1870s, establishing a clothing store at the corner of Water and Main. He later became an immigration officer. A leading Jewish layman, he helped found Shaarey Zedek Synagogue and was active in B'nai Brith.

Brown, William (1790-1827) Fur trader. Born near Glasgow, Scotland, he joined the HBC in 1811. From 1817 to 1819 he was head of the Manitoba District. He then served in the Athabasca and New Caledonia Districts.

Brown-Wilkinson, Eric (1888-c.1924) Soldier, lawyer, sportsman. Born in Bath, England, he was educated at Framlingham College and Nottingham University. He came to Manitoba in 1910 to work in the telegraph and maintenance department of the CPR, and enlisted in the Fort Garry Horse before the start of WWI. During the war he rose from sergeant major to captain. He completed his law study after the war and was called to the bar in 1919, specializing in veterans' cases. From 1920 to 1922 and in 1924 he was president of the Army and Navy Veterans' Association. He was also active in the Winnipeg Field Hockey Association and the Young Conservative Cricket Association.

Browne, Cecil ("Cec," b. 1894) Manitoba's "Athlete of the Century." Born in Winnipeg, he was educated at Isbister and Kelvin Schools. He was active in a number of sports, particularly hockey, track and field, soccer, and swimming. He began playing American football before WWI. He served in the Royal Winnipeg Flying Corps from 1917 until the end of the war. After the war, he played on three hockey teams that were Allan Cup finalists, played football for the Saskatchewan Roughriders, and played baseball for the Dominion Express team. In 1926 he became a charter member of the Chicago Black Hawks, but his contract was sold to the Seattle Eskimos, for whom he played from 1928 to 1930. He retired in 1930 and became a junior hockey coach during the 1930s. He was elected Manitoba's Athlete of the Century in 1970. He is a member of the Manitoba Sports Hall of Fame.

Bruce, John (1831-1893) Carpenter, Métis leader. A resident of St. Norbert from 1837, Bruce worked as a carpenter and legal practitioner on behalf of his countrymen, the Francophone Métis. In October 1869 he was elected president of the Métis National Committee that organized the resistance to Canada. A sick man, he resigned in December 1869 when the provisional government was formed. He later claimed that he was not happy with the direction the government was taking. Most contemporaries regarded him as merely a puppet of Riel, although one letter to a Montreal newspaper in December 1869 insisted that he had some talents, including an ability to speak English, French, and several Indian languages. In testimony during the 1874 trial of Ambroise Lépine,* Bruce acknowledged that he had been a mere figurehead in 1869, claiming that he had known very little about what was going on. Bruce served as commissioner of public works in the provisional government, and then disappeared into such obscurity that the date of his death went for many years unrecorded in the annals of the province. He died in Leroy, North Dakota. *DCB* XII, 131-33.

Bruce, Robert (1911-1981) Artist, illustrator. Born in Grandview, Manitoba, he grew up in Winnipeg. He was enrolled at the Winnipeg School of Art from 1928 to 1931. In the mid-1930s he departed for London, England, where he worked as a freelance illustrator. He returned to Canada in 1940. Shortly thereafter he became head of art at the *Winnipeg Free Press.* In 1943 he painted his first Winnipeg mural, and murals always were his most important work. He served as an official war artist during WWII although he never went abroad. After the war he studied in New York City, then taught art at the University of Buffalo from 1949 to 1955. He returned in 1955 to teach at the School of Art at the University of Manitoba, retiring in 1976. He died in Mexico.

Bruneau, François-Jacques (1809-1865) Métis leader. Born at Lac Vert (Saskatchewan), he came to Red River in 1822 and was educated at the École de Saint-Boniface. He intended to become a priest but decided to be a teacher, then moved into farming, where he became quite prosperous. He helped lead the Métis in the Sayer affair of 1849 and as a result

was nominated a member of the Council of Assiniboia in 1851. In 1850 he became a magistrate. He died of typhoid. *DCB* IX, 94-95.

Bryce, George (1844-1931) Professor, cleric, historian. A son of Scots, Bryce was educated at the University of Toronto. He later studied theology at Knox College before coming to Winnipeg in 1871. A year later he organized Knox Presbyterian Church as its first minister. He was active in higher education, founding Manitoba College and later assisting in the foundation of the University of Manitoba. He taught and administered in these institutions for many years. Bryce also served as the city's first school inspector in 1876. He was instrumental in founding the Manitoba Historical Society in 1875 and the Manitoba Historical and Scientific Society in 1879. Bryce's first historical work, *Manitoba: Its Infancy, Growth, and Present Condition* (1882), was in many ways promotional history. But he had obtained access to the extensive papers of the Selkirk family in Scotland, and much of the book became a careful study of Lord Selkirk* and the founding of Manitoba. In his later studies of the early settlers of Manitoba, as well as in his pioneering *A Short History of the Canadian People* (1887; rev. 1914), Bryce attempted to get beyond political and constitutional events to understand the dynamics of Canadian society. He was elected a fellow of the Royal Society of Canada in 1901 and served as its president in 1909. See Catherine Logan Macdonald, "George Bryce" (MA thesis, University of Manitoba, 1983). There are extensive papers at the University of Winnipeg.

Brydges, Charles John (1827-1889) Manager, land commissioner. Born in London, England, into a middle-class family, he worked for 10 years as a junior clerk in the London and South-Western Railway before his appointment as managing director of the Great Western Rail Road Company of Canada in 1852. Here he ran roughshod over an inexperienced board of directors, nearly bankrupting the line and precipitating an investigation into his management, which exonerated him in 1861. A year later, he left the Great Western to become general manager of the Grand Trunk Railway, where he remained until 1874, when he became land commissioner of the HBC. Brydges was responsible for a local rejuvenation of the fur-trading company and for moving its Canadian administrative offices to Winnipeg in 1880. He became associated with an aggressive HBC and with the expanding town of Winnipeg, which he successfully championed as the location for the CPR crossing of the Red River. Although greatly constrained by his opponents, including Donald Smith,* Brydges did succeed in making the land administration of the Company important and profitable. See Alan Wilson, "'In a Business Way': C.J. Brydges and the Hudson's Bay Company, 1879-89," in *The West and the Nation*, ed. Carl Berger and Ramsay Cook (1976), 114-39; J.E. Rea, ed., *The Letters of Charles John Brydges, 1883-1889* (1981). *DCB* XI, 121-25.

Buckingham, William (1832-1915) Journalist. Buckingham was born in Devon, England, and immigrated to Canada in 1857 to join the *Toronto Globe* as parliamentary reporter. In 1859 he and William Coldwell* brought a printing press to Red River by oxcart and established the *Nor'-Wester*. Buckingham returned east in 1861 to a distinguished career in journalism that included the post of official reporter to the Canadian delegation to the 1866 Confederation Conference in London. From 1863 to 1873 he was owner of the *Stratford Beacon*. A Liberal, he became Prime Minister Alexander Mackenzie's private secretary, then deputy minister of the interior.

Budd, Henry (1812-1875) Cleric. Budd was the son of an Indian and a Métisse. Educated in John West's* school, he became a clerk in the HBC around 1827 and served in the Columbia River area. Returning to Red River, he began teaching at the Upper Church (St. John's) parish school in 1837. In 1840 he was sent to Cumberland House District to teach and become a missionary, and in 1842 he moved to The Pas, where he established the Devon Mission. Budd was ordained a deacon in 1850, the first Aboriginal in North America to be admitted to the Church of England ministry. He was ordained a priest in 1853. He moved to Nipawin, Saskatchewan, and remained there until 1867, when he returned to The Pas. Budd was a big man, an eloquent preacher, and a first-rate farmer. See Katherine Pettipas, ed., *The Diary of the Reverend Henry Budd 1870-1875* (1974); Manitoba Department of Cultural Affairs and Historic Resources, *The Reverend Henry Budd* (1982). *DCB* X, 108-9.

Bulger, Captain Andrew (1789-1858) Soldier, colonial governor. Born in Newfoundland, Bulger became an ensign in the Newfoundland Regiment of Fencible Infantry in 1804. He became lieutenant two years later. He and the regiment (now the Royal Newfoundland Regiment) served in the Atlantic region and in Lower Canada before the War of 1812. Bulger was then ordered to serve under Major-General Isaac Brock on the Niagara Frontier, participating in most of the great battles in that military theatre. In 1814 he served in the West. In 1822 he was appointed for three years as secretary and registrar of Lord Selkirk's Red River settlement, with military responsibilities. He was also appointed governor *locum tenens* of Assiniboia. Arriving at Red River in June 1822, he quickly became disillusioned with "one of the most miserable countries on the face of the earth." He was particularly unhappy about the lack of military presence in the settlement and proper lines of authority, soon engaging in a running feud with HBC chief factor John Clarke* over the fur trade. Bulger advocated the introduction of a judicial system in Red River, the posting of troops, the legal entrance of settlers into the fur trade, a legal medium of exchange, and the necessity of a market for surplus grain. Without these things, he warned Andrew Colvile* in late 1822, "spend no more of Lord Selkirk's money upon Red River." He left Red River in ill health in August 1823, appreciated by the settlers more than by the Company. He subsequently went to Quebec in 1825 as a minor functionary, serving there without distinction until his death. See *An Autobiographical Sketch of the Services of the Late Captain Andrew Bulger of the Royal Newfoundland Fencible Regiment* (1865). *DCB* VIII, 111-13.

Bull, Manlius (1849-1929) Businessman, financier. Born in Smithfield, Canada, he came to Winnipeg from Brantford, Ontario, in 1882. Bull first went into the wholesale business but then established the Royal Crown Soap Company, which he sold to Lever Brothers in 1911. He was also active in a number of financial institutions. Bull was an avid golfer and gardener and a firm supporter of the City Beautiful movement.

Buller, Arthur Henry Reginald (1874-1944) Botanist. Born in Birmingham, England, Buller was educated at Queen's College, Taunton, and at several German universities. After a brief stay at the University of Birmingham, he came to the University of Manitoba as professor of botany, retiring in 1936. He was elected to the Royal Society of Canada in 1909, becoming its president in 1927. In 1929 he was awarded the Royal Society of Canada's Flavelle Medal, and in 1937 he was elected a fellow of the

Royal Society. His major work was *Researches in Fungi*, 7 vols. (1909-34). He wrote *Essays on Wheat* (1919) and *Practical Botany* (1929). Buller also wrote limericks, some of which were published in *Punch*. See R.H. Estey, "Arthur Buller: Pioneer Leader in Plant Pathology," *Annual Review of Phytopathology* 24 (1986): 17-25.

Bunn, John (1802?-1861) Surgeon, civil servant. The son of an HBC writer (clerk) and a Métisse, Bunn was born on Hudson Bay. A bright lad, he was sent to school in Edinburgh, and he then attended medical school at the University of Edinburgh for two years. In 1819 he returned to Moose Factory as a surgeon, unhappy that he had not completed his medical studies. In 1824 he moved to the Red River Settlement, establishing himself at Middlechurch and opening a private medical practice. He married into the influential Thomas family. In 1831-32 he attended the University of Edinburgh long enough to become a licentiate of the Royal College of Surgeons. He returned to Red River in 1832. After 1835 he served as a member of the Council of Assiniboia. He received an annual salary from this council in recompense for his medical work with the poor of the settlement. Bunn supported orderly administration and the development of local infrastructure, especially roads, and he was regarded by Governor Eden Colvile* as "the most sensible man in the Settlement." He served in a number of administrative and legal positions, including that of recorder of Rupert's Land from 1858 until his death. Bunn was always proud of his mixed-blood heritage and of the progress of Red River. In 1847 he won a prize for the best cheese in the settlement. He was a prominent Anglican layman. See Roy St. George Stubbs, *Four Recorders of Rupert's Land* (1967). *DCB* IX, 102-3. There are papers at the PAM.

Bunn, Thomas (1764-1853) Fur trader. Born in London, England, he worked as an "oil and colourman" before joining the HBC in 1797 as a "writer." He was soon posted to Osnaburgh House. He served at Brandon House as well, until he was posted to York Factory in 1803. He gradually rose in rank in the company service, becoming district master in 1818. In 1821 Nicholas Garry* promised him a retired share after 25 years' service on the understanding that he would retire to Red River. However, Bunn did not impress new governor George Simpson,* who suspected him of dishonesty, and he

soon headed for the settlement, arriving in November 1822. See Denis Bayley, *A Londoner in Rupert's Land: Thomas Bunn of the Hudson's Bay Company* (1969). Papers are at the PAM.

Bunn, Thomas (1830-1875) Civil servant, politician. Born in Red River, the son of Dr. John Bunn* and Catherine Thomas (a mixed-blood), Bunn was raised in the parish of St. Paul (Middlechurch) and educated at the Red River Academy. He settled in St. Andrew's and married first Isabella Clouston (1854) and later Rachel Harriott (1859). He began living at Mapleton in 1861. He served as clerk of the Council of Assiniboia and of the Quarterly Court from 1865 to 1869/70. In January 1868 he was appointed to the Council of Assiniboia. Bunn was a delegate to the November 1869 council from St. Clements. Although he spoke in favour of allowing Governor William McDougall* into the territory, like many of the English-speaking mixed-bloods he wanted decent terms from Canada, and subsequently he was usually regarded as a Riel supporter. Bunn chaired the open-air meeting of 19-20 January 1870 that heard from Donald A. Smith.* He was one of those appointed to the committee to arrange the subsequent elections to the Convention of Forty. An English delegate to that convention from St. Clements, he was made secretary of state in the provisional government, serving until 24 June 1870. Bunn survived the transition to a province without missing a step. He was called to the bar in 1871 and was clerk to the first General Quarterly Court, held in May 1871. He had already been returned as MPP from St. Clements in the first election of December 1870. *DCB* X, 111.

Burden, Dick (d. 1908) Turkish bath operator. Born in Ontario, he joined the circus at an early age. When the first circus came to Winnipeg, it stranded him in the city. He remained, appearing as a stage act and working as a bill-poster. His advertising business soon grew. Burden later opened Winnipeg's first Turkish baths, which flourished in the 1890s, at the Clarendon Hotel. He moved to Lapeer, Michigan, where he died.

Burdick, Richard (1834-1902) Store clerk. An American, Burdick clerked in the Winnipeg retail store of the HBC. He clashed with Louis Riel on 17 January 1870 when Riel tried to buy a pair of trousers from his store and had his payment refused by Burdick on the grounds that it represented money stolen from the HBC. At the Winnipeg election meeting on 22 January 1870, Burdick presented the resolutions that resulted in the election of Alfred Scott* as delegate to the Convention of Forty. He was briefly arrested by Riel on 29 March 1870. He and his wife and family left Red River for St. Paul aboard the steamboat on 5 May 1870, never to return.

Burgess, Helen (Spinks) (1920-1994) Publisher. Born in Newmarket, Ontario, after raising four children she worked for the Department of Indian Affairs and Northern Development in public relations, editing the magazine *North.* She came to Winnipeg in 1970 as assistant editor of *The Beaver,* and served as editor from 1972 to 1985. In 1977 she co-founded Watson & Dwyer Publishing Ltd., which specialized in books on Western Canadian and fur trade history, managing it until her death in Winnipeg.

Burman, William Alfred (1857-1909) Cleric, college administrator, teacher. Born in Yorkshire, England, he came to Manitoba at age 18 and was educated at St. John's College, being ordained as a deacon in 1879. He went to the Sioux reserve near Griswold, Manitoba, as a missionary, becoming fluent in Sioux. He served as first head of the Rupert's Land Industrial School in Middlechurch and helped build the St. Peter's mission on Selkirk Avenue in Winnipeg. In 1903 he became steward and bursar at St. John's College, adding these duties to his pre-existing ones of lecturing in botany and biblical literature. He examined in botany for the University of Manitoba for many years. There are papers at the Rupert's Land Archives and at the PAM.

Burnell, Colin H. (1880-1946) Farmer, politician. Born in Westbourne, Manitoba, he began farming in Oakville, Manitoba, in 1898. In 1904 he joined the Manitoba Grain Growers' Association. He was in charge of the Progressive Party campaign in Manitoba in the 1921 election and became president of the United Farmers of Manitoba in 1922. One of his major efforts was the organization of the Manitoba Wheat Pool in 1924. He became its first president, and he was also elected president of Manitoba Pool Elevators in 1925. A street in Winnipeg is named for him. He is a member of the Manitoba Agricultural Hall of Fame. See F. W. Hamilton, *Service at Cost: A History of Manitoba Pool Elevators* (1975).

Burns, Pat (1856-1937) Businessman, politician. Born in Oshawa, Canada, of Irish stock, Burns came to Manitoba in 1878, walking over 100 miles from Winnipeg to his new homestead near Minnedosa. He became involved in the cattle trade and moved to Calgary, where in 1890 he established the meat-packing firm of P. Burns and Company, Limited, which became one of the largest in the world. He sold his business in 1928 but kept his cattle ranches and his company directorships. He was appointed to the Canadian Senate in 1931. Burns was one of the founders of the Calgary Stampede. For a biography, see Grant MacEwan, *Pat Burns: Cattle King* (1979).

Burridge, James (1841-1912) Businessman, politician. Born in Exeter, England, he came to Hamilton in 1854. He moved to Winnipeg in 1879 to establish a branch of E. and C. Gurney Company, an iron foundry. In 1885 he created the Gurney Stove and Range Company, which he headed until 1899, when he founded the Burridge-Cooper Company. He was active in municipal politics and government, running for the Board of Control, serving as an alderman for Ward Five, and chairing the Public Works and Finance Committee. He was a founding member of Zion Church.

Burrows, (Charles) Acton (1853-1948) Journalist. Born in Bosbury, Hertfordshire, England, he came to Canada in 1873 and worked for the *Canadian Illustrated News.* In 1879 he came to Winnipeg and worked on a number of newspapers and the *Nor'West Farmer* until his move to Ottawa in 1898. He was also deputy minister of agriculture from 1882 to 1887.

Burrows, Theodore Arthur (1857-1929) Lawyer, surveyor, businessman, politician. Born in Ottawa, he came to Manitoba in 1875 to work as a surveyor. He then enrolled in Manitoba College to study law, soon leaving to join his uncle, Alfred Burrows, in real estate. He entered the lumber business in 1878 and soon moved to the Dauphin area, where he accumulated large timber holdings. In 1892 he was Dauphin's first (Liberal) MLA, and he remained in office until 1903. While in the legislature he was an active booster of a railway to Dauphin, and when it was built in 1896 by William Mackenzie* and Donald Mann* as the Lake Manitoba Railway and Canal Company, he became its land commissioner. This gave him inside knowledge of future development. He soon became one of Clifford Sifton's* political lieutenants in the province, and he remained so after his departure from politics. This gave Burrows further inside knowledge, and there were constant rumours and complaints of corruption. In 1900 he and his family moved to Winnipeg, eventually settling at 246 Roslyn Road. In 1903 he became Dauphin MP, and he served until 1908. He spent his last years in office fending off Tory charges of excessive corruption. In 1926 he was appointed lieutenant-governor of Manitoba. He was on the board of Wesley College, and he served as First Worshipful Master of Vermillion Lodge, A.F. and A.M., Dauphin. Burrows Avenue in Winnipeg is named after him. For a biography, see Deborah Welch, "T.A. Burrows, 1857-1929: Case Study of a Manitoba Businessman and Politician" (MA thesis, University of Manitoba, 1983). There are papers at the PAM.

Butler, William Francis (1838-1910) Soldier, traveller, author. Born in Ireland, he joined the 69th Foot and saw service around the Empire. When his career stalled in 1869, he dashed off to join the Wolseley Expedition and volunteered for intelligence service in Minnesota and Red River. At Red River he met Louis Riel, and then he joined up with Wolseley* at Fort Frances. He subsequently toured the West for Lieutenant-Governor Adams Archibald.* As a result of this tour he became an advocate for alternatives to the extermination of the Indians, greatly influencing the Macdonald government in its decision to organize the mounted police. This journey and his earlier one with Wolseley produced *The Great Lone Land* (1872). He later rejoined Wolseley and served in the major imperial campaigns of the late nineteenth century. It was he who persuaded Wolseley to employ Canadian voyageurs in the Sudan in 1884. In 1886 he was promoted to brigadier-general and made a knight commander of the Order of the Bath. He was promoted to major-general in 1892 and was commander of the British forces in South Africa in 1898 on the eve of war, soon resigning over the question of open conflict with the Boers, which he opposed. He died in Ireland. Butler published extensively, both fiction and travel accounts. He also produced a number of autobiographical accounts, most published posthumously by his family. They include: *From Sketchbook and Diary* (1909); *Sir William Butler: An Autobiography* (1911, edited by his daughter); and *An Autobiography, with Illustrations from Sketches by the Author* (1922, edited by his wife). The present whereabouts of the Butler papers is unknown. See also Leigh Maxwell, *The Ashanti Ring: Sir Garnet Wolseley's Campaigns, 1870-1882* (1885), and a biography by Edward Alexander McCourt, *Remember Butler: The Story of Sir William Butler* (1967). *DCB* XIII, 142-44.

Button, Thomas (d. 1634) Explorer. Born in Glamorganshire in Wales, he first served in the British navy at the time of the Armada. In 1612 he was sent to command the expedition to investigate what had happened to Henry Hudson,* although his instructions spoke in terms of scientific matters. The expedition penetrated Hudson Bay and wintered at the mouth of a river that Button named the Nelson River after one of his captains who died there. The following summer he sailed further around the Bay, naming Mansel Island in the process. Although he did not find the Northwest Passage, he was convinced until his death that it existed. See Miller Christy, ed., *The Voyages of Captain Luke Foxe of Hull, and Captain Thomas James of Bristol, in Search of a North-West Passage* (1894). For a biography, consult G.T. Clark, *Some Account of Sir Robert Mansel and Admiral Sir Thomas Button* (1883). *DCB* I, 144-45.

Cadham, Frederick Todd (1880-1961) Physician. Born in Winnipeg, he graduated from the University of Manitoba Medical College in 1905, having been introduced to medicine as a surgeon's assistant at the age of 12. He was on the teaching staff of the Medical College for 40 years, and directed the Manitoba Bacteriology Laboratory for 15 years.

Cadham, James Henry (1850-1907) Builder. Born in Canada to English parents, he came to Manitoba in 1870 and joined the Red River Volunteers. After his discharge in 1871 he became involved in the construction trade, designing and building many of Winnipeg's early buildings, including a number of warehouses. Among these was the Galt Building (now Artspace).

Cadotte, Joseph (fl. 1814-22) Interpreter. Possibly of Métis origin, he first appeared as a lieutenant in the Indian Department of Upper Canada in 1814, employed at Michilimackinac. In 1816 he was with the NWC and was a member of the party that murdered Owen Keveny.* He was at Fort Douglas when it was captured by Selkirk's forces in early 1817, and was set at liberty. He helped to lead the Métis against the Red River Settlement in 1817. He accompanied William Coltman* to Montreal later in the year and was eventually indicted for the murder of Keveny, but was never brought to trial. He later worked for the American Fur Company. *DCB* VI, 99-101.

Caldwell, William Bletterman (c. 1798-1882) Soldier, colonial official. A career army officer of unknown background, Caldwell was sent to Red River in 1848 in command of a small body of pensioners from the Chelsea Royal Hospital (the Chelsea pensioners) and as governor of Assiniboia, his salary paid by the HBC. He was not able to distance himself from the HBC, however, and he emerged from the Sayer affair with a reputation for weakness, particularly since he insisted he lacked the force to police the settlement. Criticism of Caldwell increased with the *Foss v. Pelly* case, which involved alleged marital indiscretions by Sarah McLeod,* the wife of chief factor John Ballenden,* with Captain Christopher Foss.* Caldwell, with the assistance of interested party Adam Thom,* presided at the trial. Some of the settlers, led by Alexander Ross,* petitioned for his dismissal, but he continued to serve until 1855. He got his revenge by testifying for the HBC and against the settlers in the parliamentary inquiry of 1857. He died in London. *DCB* XI, 138-39.

Cameron, Donald Roderick (1834-1921) Soldier, diplomat. He was born in Britain and was captain of the Royal Artillery. The son-in-law of Charles Tupper, he came to Red River with William McDougall* in 1869, hoping to command a version of the envisioned mounted police force. According to John O'Donnell,* he had "a fine gun" and shot after adjusting his monocle. With the Métis he had a reputation as a mannered fool, a typical English gent. He returned to Canada with McDougall, although the luggage belonging to him and his wife — which was held by the Métis — proved the occasion for a visit to the settlement by Sir Charles Tupper and a conversation with Louis Riel to secure its release. He translated Bishop Taché's* book on the Northwest (*Sketch of the North West*) into English in 1870. Cameron was later superintendent of the British section of the British-American boundary survey from 1872 to 1876, secretary of the Canadian delegation at the Paris Conference on Submarine Cables in 1883, and secretary to the Canadian Commission on Fisheries in Washington in 1887-88.

Cameron, Douglas Colin (1854-1921) Businessman, politician, sportsman. Born in Canada, he migrated to Manitoba in 1880, entering the lumber business and organizing the Rat Portage Lumber Company and later the Maple Leaf Flour Mills. His business interests included a heavy involvement in British Columbia forest enterprises. A Liberal, he represented Fort William and Lake of the Woods in the Ontario provincial legislature from 1902 to 1905 but was subsequently defeated in both the provincial and federal elections. In 1910 he was listed by the *Winnipeg Telegram* as one of Winnipeg's 19 millionaires. He was appointed lieutenant-governor of Manitoba in 1911, and he served until 1916. His stables won many honours at horse shows. He was made a knight commander of the Order of St. Michael and St. George in 1913. His letter-book 1911-12 is at the PAM.

Cameron, Duncan (c. 1764-1849) Fur trader, politician. Born in Glen Moriston, Scotland, Cameron went to New York with his parents in 1773 and joined a Loyalist regiment in 1780. In 1785 he came to Quebec and entered the fur trade in association with independent traders who were competing with the HBC northwest of Lake Nipigon. In 1795 he became a partner of the NWC, remaining in charge of the Nipigon Department until 1807, when he was sent to Lake Winnipeg. His clerks admired him very much. In 1814 he and Alexander Macdonell* were put in charge of the Red River Department, in direct confrontation with Lord Selkirk's colony. Cameron dressed in military uniform and insisted that he was "the chief of this Country." He and Macdonell convinced most of the Selkirk colonists to depart for Upper Canada in NWC canoes in 1815. A year later he was arrested by Colin Robertson* at Fort Gibraltar, sent to York Factory, and finally sent to England. He never stood trial for his actions, however, and after his return to Canada in 1820 he sued Robertson for false imprisonment. Cameron subsequently settled in Glengarry County, representing Glengarry in the House of Assembly from 1825 to 1828. *DCB* VII, 137-40.

Cameron, John Donald (1858-1923) Lawyer, politician, judge. Born in Woodstock, Canada, of Scottish ancestry, he was a brilliant student at the University of Toronto. Cameron came to Winnipeg in 1880. He was active in the Liberal Party and was MLA from South Winnipeg from 1892 to 1899. He served in the Greenway administration as provincial secretary and then as attorney general. He was appointed judge of the Court of King's Bench in 1908 and judge of the Court of Appeal in 1909. He had a reputation as the province's most literate judge. In 1919 he denied the first bail application of the eight leaders of the Winnipeg General Strike who were charged with seditious conspiracy. He died suddenly while visiting the United States.

Cameron, John Dugald (1777-1857) Fur trader. Probably born in Quebec, Cameron entered the fur trade with the NWC in 1794. He was known for his fluency in Ojibwa. In 1811 he was posted to Lake Winnipeg, and in 1813 he became a partner of the NWC. Two years later he transported most of the Selkirk colonists to Upper Canada. After the union of the NWC and HBC he headed the Columbia District until 1824, then moved to Rainy Lake and eventually to Fort La Cloche before his retirement in the mid-1840s. He formally married his Indian wife in 1833. Cameron was self-educated and read "almost every Book that ever came within his reach." *DCB* VIII, 121-22.

Cameron, Marie (fl. c. 1924) Physician, athlete. Born in Shoal Lake, Manitoba, she was educated at Brandon College and the University of Manitoba. She graduated from the latter institution in 1923, interned at the Winnipeg General Hospital, and, in 1924, opened a general practice. While in college she played on the Women's Hockey Club. She was also an active golfer and snowshoer.

Campbell, Alexander M. (1856-1910) Teacher, farmer, local politician. Born in Barrie, Canada, he came west in 1880, graduated from the University of Manitoba in 1882 with an honours degree in mental and moral philosophy, and received an MA in 1885. After service as a tutor in mathematics, he moved briefly to Edmonton and was principal of the city's first high school. He returned to Manitoba to farm at Stonewall and became one of the original members of the Livestock Commission of Manitoba. He also served as reeve of Woodlands municipality for many years.

Campbell, Archibald Glenlyon ("Glen," 1863-1917) Soldier, farmer, politician. Born at Fort Pelly in present-day Saskatchewan to Scottish parents, he was educated at Glasgow Academy and Merchiston Castle School. He eventually returned to the Gilbert Plains area of Manitoba and settled on ranching land. He served with the Boulton Scouts in 1885 and became a captain upon field promotion. He was elected Conservative MLA in 1903 and 1907, resigning in 1908 to run successfully as Dauphin MP. He was defeated in 1911 but was appointed chief inspector of Indian affairs in 1912, one of the few such officials who were fluent in Indian languages. He formed the 79th Battalion, Brandon, at the outbreak of WWI and rose to major. He later recruited the 107th Battalion as its lieutenant-colonel. This battalion was sent to France in 1917 and fought at Passchendaele. Campbell won the Distinguished Service Order in France and died there of kidney trouble.

Campbell, Arnold M. (1892-1963) Lawyer, satirist, judge. A fourth-generation descendant of Selkirk settlers, he graduated in arts at the University of Manitoba in 1918 and received his law degree while serving overseas with the 76th Battery of Canadian Field Artillery. Called to the bar in 1920, he was one of the creators of "The Diary of Harold Lex," a fictitious journal that ran in the Winnipeg newspapers for several years during the 1940s. He was elected president of the Manitoba Bar Association in 1942 and became a judge of Manitoba's Court of King's Bench in 1947. He died during surgery.

Campbell, Colin H. (1859-1914) Lawyer, politician. Born in Burlington, Canada, he attended the Toronto Law School. He was called to the Ontario bar in 1881, came to Winnipeg in 1882, and was called to the Manitoba bar. He became a QC in 1893 and was called to the bar of the North-West Territories. In 1899 he was elected as Conservative member for Morris and joined the Hugh John Macdonald*

Cabinet. He became attorney general in 1900 and held the post until 1911. He later served as minister of education and minister of public works. He retired from provincial politics in 1913. He chaired the University of Manitoba board of governors from 1897 to 1907 and was president of the YMCA. Campbell died in Winnipeg. His papers are at the PAM. *DCB* XIV, 173-76.

Campbell, Douglas Lloyd (1895-1995) Politician, provincial premier. Born in Flee Island, Manitoba, he was educated locally and at Brandon College. He ran successfully in 1922 as the United Farmers candidate for Lakeside in the Manitoba legislature and remained in office for more than 47 years. He was minister of agriculture under John Bracken* from 1936 to 1943 and under Stuart Garson* from 1943 to 1948. He succeeded Garson as premier late in 1948 and led a Liberal-Progressive coalition government with little opposition until shortly before his defeat by Duff Roblin's* Conservatives in 1958. A fiscal conservative, Campbell always balanced his budget. He was proud of the programs of rural electrification and highway improvement under his government. His response to the Manitoba flood of 1950 was cautious and was heavily criticized at the time for its failure to act in advance of federal assistance and its unwillingness to insist on more support from Ottawa. Campbell stepped down as Liberal party leader in 1961 and retired from politics in 1969. In retirement he continued to make public statements, opposing bilingualism, deficit financing, and government bureaucracy. His unpublished memoirs are held by the University of Manitoba history department. Personal correspondence 1936-50 and other papers are at the PAM. For a biography, see G. Molgat, *Campbell of Manitoba* (1961).

Campbell, George Huestis (1855-1928) Railroad and immigration agent, municipal politician. Born in Grand Village, Nova Scotia, he came west in 1879 to work for the CPR. He was the first CPR agent at Winnipeg in 1881, and later he managed the Winnipeg Electric Street Railway from 1892. He also served as Dominion immigration agent from 1880 to 1892. He was a city alderman. A keen curler, he was president of the Manitoba Curling Association in 1892-93 and a president of the Thistle Curling Club.

Campbell, Isaac (1853-1929) Lawyer. Born in Morpeth, Canada, he was educated at Osgoode Hall

Law School and was called to the bar in 1878. He came to Winnipeg in 1882. In 1888 he was elected MLA for South Winnipeg, serving to 1891 when he was defeated by Hugh John Macdonald;* he never ran for office again. In 1888 he became city solicitor of Winnipeg, a post he held until 1906. Because of his oratorical skills he was known as "the people's Isaac." He served as president of the Law Society from 1891 to 1898, and as vice-president of the Canadian Bar Association in 1914. His contemporaries regarded him as one of the leading lawyers of his generation.

Campbell, John Archibald (1872-1963) Schoolteacher, lawyer. Born in Ontario, he came to Winnipeg with his family in 1880 and was educated at Manitoba College. He taught school in Manitoba from 1890 to 1896, serving as principal of Boissevain School. He then articled in law, was called to the bar in 1899, and started up a practice in Dauphin. He was Liberal MLA from 1907 to 1910. He moved to The Pas in 1915 and was elected an MP in 1917. Campbell was a member of the Committee for Northern Manitoba at The Pas from 1916 to 1918 and 1921 to 1924. There are papers at the PAM.

Campbell, Minnie Julia Beatrice (Buck) (b. 1862) Teacher, volunteer worker. Born in Canada, she was educated at the Oakville College Institute and the Wesleyan Female College, Hamilton, and taught at the Ottawa Ladies' College before her marriage to Colin Campbell* of Winnipeg in 1884. She was one of the leading volunteer activists of Winnipeg, particularly active in the YWCA, the IODE, and the Empire Club. During WWI she served as chair of many war organizations.

Campbell, Robert (1808-1894) Sheep farmer, fur trader. Born in Perthshire, Scotland, he came to Canada in 1832 to take charge of the HBC sheep farm in St. James Parish, travelling to Kentucky to obtain breeding sheep. The venture failed and he became a fur trader. He married Eleonora Sterling of Perthshire, who came to Norway House for the marriage. Their children were dressed in tartans and raised with strong Scottish brogues, according to Walter Traill. After his retirement Campbell lived near Riding Mountain and was the first to import west Highland cattle into Manitoba. He was a corresponding member of the Manitoba Historical Society. His diaries are available on microfilm at the PAM. *DCB* XII, 155-56.

Camsell, Charles (1876-1958) Geologist. Born at Fort Liard, North-West Territories, he was educated at St. John's College School and the University of Manitoba (BA 1894) before continuing post-graduate studies at Queen's, Harvard, and MIT. A geologist, he soon joined the Geological Survey, becoming deputy minister of mines from 1920 to 1935 and commissioner of the Northwest Territories from 1935 to 1946. He directed the Dominion Fuel Board for many years and served on the National Research Council from 1921 to 1936. He was president of the Royal Society of Canada in 1930, and founded the Canadian Geographical Society in 1929, serving as president from 1929 to 1941. His autobiography, *Son of the North*, which took the story to 1920, was published in 1954. It includes an interesting account of student life at St. John's College School.

Carey, Daniel (1829-1890) Lawyer, journalist, poet. Born at Quebec City, he studied law and then took up journalism. He was active in Reform and Irish circles, and in 1873 headed west to become protonotary of the Court of Queen's Bench in Manitoba at a salary of 1,000 pounds per annum plus all fees collected up to 500 pounds, also combining the duties of librarian and interpreter. He was interpreter in the famous trial of Ambroise Lépine,* but ran into grief over the nature of the role of the protonotary and was forced to resign in 1878. He went into legal practice and became active in Catholic education. He published the first printed set of law reports in the Canadian west, *Judgments in the Queen's Bench, Manitoba, reported by Daniel Carey* (1875). He also composed a number of epic poems. He died in Winnipeg. *DCB*, XI, 151-2.

Carney, Thomas (1830?-1905) Politician, inventor. Born in Pennsylvania, he came to Manitoba in 1873, and in 1875 he founded the town of Emerson, which he served as mayor from 1880 to 1883 and as MLA from 1879 to 1883. During his time in Emerson he invented a mechanical coin changer or cash register, and in 1885 he moved back to the United States to join the National Cash Register Company. He died in Dayton, Ohio.

Carroll, John Benson ("Jack," 1921-1986) Politician. Born in The Pas, he attended local schools, was in the Canadian army, rising from private to lieutenant from 1942 to 1945, and attended the University of Manitoba from 1945 to 1948. In 1950 he took over the family hardware store in The Pas. Active in local political and community affairs, in 1958 he was first elected to represent The Pas in the provincial legislature as a Progressive Conservative. He remained in the house until 1969, serving briefly as provincial secretary in 1959, then holding in succession the portfolios of labour, welfare, and tourism and recreation. A student residence at Keewatin Community College in The Pas was named for him. There are extensive papers at the PAM.

Carruthers, George F. (1846-1918) Journalist, businessman, militia officer, municipal politician. Born in Toronto, he was educated at Upper Canada College and the University of Toronto. He served with the militia during the Fenian raids while working for the Grand Trunk Railway, and came to Manitoba in 1871 to work with Alexander Begg. He later became editor and proprietor of the *Manitoba Gazette* and, in 1874, managing director of the Canada West Fire Insurance Company in partnership with J.H. Brock.* He was active in militia affairs, and he organized the Winnipeg Infantry reserve militia. He was elected to City Council for Ward Six (north of the CPR tracks) in 1885 and later served from 1892 to 1994 and in 1900-1901. As a member of the City Council, he was instrumental in the passage of the Public Parks Act of Manitoba in 1892 (which, based on Ontario legislation, he is said to have drafted) and the subsequent creation of the Parks Board in 1893. He was president of the Manitoba Rifle Association and, in 1906, the Board of Trade, and was a life governor of the Winnipeg General Hospital.

Carruthers, James M. (1872-1947) Cheese-maker. Born in Quebec, he was educated at Huntington Academy and worked in the dairy business (especially cheese-making) after leaving school. He came west in 1900 to found the Crescent Creamery Company of Winnipeg and later became vice-president of the Dairy Corporation of Canada.

Carson, Jack (1910-1963) Actor. Born in Carman, Manitoba, he later moved to Milwaukee and attended Carleton College (Minnesota). He began his film career as a comic, shifted to playing sinister villains, and finally became best known as a Hollywood comedian. He was cast in a series of "second banana" roles, usually as the hero's buddy. He made over 70 films, including *Mildred Pierce* (1945) and *A Star is Born* (1954). In 1950 he co-hosted (with George Formby) the relief benefit concert for Manitoba flood victims held in May at Maple Leaf Gardens and broadcast to a network of nearly 600 stations around the world.

Carstens, Hugo Emil (1866-1941) Immigration agent, publisher. Born in Jever, Germany, he was educated in law. He came to Winnipeg in 1884, then homesteaded in Saskatchewan before becoming colonization agent of the Manitoba and Northwestern Railway. He later was federal immigration agent in Winnipeg. In 1896 he founded *Der Nordwesten*. He served as German consul for the Prairies from 1907 to 1914.

Carter, William H. (1874-1962) Builder, utilities officer. Born in Bismarck, Illinois, and educated in Danville, Illinois, he came to Winnipeg in 1900. He was the first president of the Winnipeg Builders Exchange in 1910 and was for many years a major builder in Winnipeg. In 1913 he became the first president of the amalgamated Board of Trade. In 1935 he was made vice-president of Winnipeg Electric, and he became president from 1940 to 1953. He served as chair of the Greater Winnipeg Transit Commission from 1953 to 1956. Carter was a governor of the Manitoba Jockey Club.

Cartier, George-Étienne (1814-1873) Lawyer, politician. Born in St. Antoine, Canada, and educated at the Collège de Montréal, Cartier was called to the bar in 1835. In 1837 he joined the Lower Canadian rebellion and spent some months in exile, although he was later allowed to resume his career. The leading French-Canadian spokesman for Confederation, he was Sir John A. Macdonald's right-hand man in Quebec until his death in 1873. Cartier was sympathetic to the Métis and to Louis Riel. He undoubtedly led Bishop Taché* and the 1870 delegates to Ottawa, notably Father Noel Ritchot,* to believe that he was totally committed to a general amnesty for the rebels, despite the execution of Thomas Scott.* Macdonald did not share these views but was incapacitated during most of the negotiations that produced the agreement with the rebel delegates that led to the Manitoba Act. Cartier appears to have felt that the public hostility in Ontario would die down more quickly than it did. In 1872 he was defeated in the general federal election, and he found a seat in the Provencher riding in Manitoba instead. Louis Riel himself was induced to give up his candidacy in the riding in Cartier's favour, and Cartier was elected by acclamation for a constituency he never visited. He died soon after in London. For a biography, see B.J. Young, *George-Étienne Cartier* (1981). *DCB* X, 142-52.

Cary, George Marcus (1795-1858) Soldier, farmer. Born in Ireland, he served in the British army. In 1836 he agreed to become manager of an experimental farm established by the HBC at the Red River Settlement. As with many an early figure in Red River, his credentials for the appointment are obscure. The farm failed in 1841, partly because the farming servants imported from England by the HBC proved useless, and partly because of opposition from the residents. According to one writer in the *Nor'-Wester,* "Capt. Cary exercised his agricultural talents in raising wheat, barley, potatoes and turnips — articles which everybody in Red River had for sale, and for which there was no market." Cary carried on farming on the property (adjacent to Upper Fort Garry) until 1847, when he moved to London, Canada. From 1837 to 1847 he was a member of the Council of Assiniboia and a justice of the peace. *DCB* VIII, 131-32. Scattered papers are at the PAM.

Casey, Lucille C. (1844-1902) Painter. Born in Mississippi to an important planter family, she accompanied her second husband, John Adolphus McArthur, to Winnipeg in 1884. She was a well-trained professional artist whose teaching and leadership were important to a nascent cultural community. In 1885 she contributed many works to the Agricultural and Industrial Exhibition. A year later she and her husband were active in founding the Winnipeg Art Society. From 1886 to 1888 she toured Europe and studied painting, even getting two works accepted by the Paris Salon. On her return to Winnipeg, she held an exhibition of her works that was extremely well attended, possibly because of the nude section. After 1891 she seldom resided in Winnipeg, having begun to gain Canadian acceptance of her work. Two of her paintings were exhibited at the Royal Canadian Academy's meeting in Montreal in 1893, and two at the World's Columbia Exposition in Chicago. Few examples of her painting survive, although the Winnipeg Art Gallery has several. She died at sea while returning to Canada after visiting Scotland. *DCB* XIII, 176-77.

Cass, Edward ("Eddie," b. 1893) Athlete. Born in Winnipeg, he was educated at St. Mary's Academy and attended Georgetown University in Washington, DC, where he played baseball. He served in the American army in WWI, then attended the College of Law at the University of Manitoba. He played for a number of Manitoba baseball teams, usually as a first baseman, and also coached. He was called to the bar in 1926, and he retired from baseball. In 1931 he helped start the Winnipeg High School Football League, and he was instrumental in the formation of an annual Catholic field day. He was involved in community affairs throughout his life. He is a member of the Manitoba Sports Hall of Fame.

Cassop, William Henry (1874-1949) Cleric. Born in England, he came to Winnipeg in 1884, was ordained an Anglican priest in 1910, and served parishes in Brandon and Edmonton. He was rector of a church in the Channel Islands during the Nazi occupation of WWII. He wrote *Winnipeg to London via Hudson Bay* (1936).

Cauchon, Joseph-Édouard (1816-1885) Journalist, politician. Born at Quebec City and educated at the Petit Séminaire de Québec, he was called to the bar but never practised law. He spent his early life as a journalist and politician, editing the *Journal de Québec* for most of the period between 1842 and 1875. He was an early confederationist, and he became first premier of Quebec after Confederation, before being appointed to the Senate. He changed parties and supported the Liberals in 1873. In 1877 he was appointed lieutenant-governor of Manitoba despite much criticism of his opportunism. While in office he speculated considerably in Winnipeg real estate, and like many others he was ruined in 1882. He retired to the Qu'Appelle Valley in 1884. *DCB* XI, 159-65.

Cavalier, Charles (1818-1891) Civil servant. Born in Ohio, he was the first "white settler" in Dakota Territory. Cavalier was appointed territorial librarian in 1848, then Pembina customs officer. He moved to Pembina in 1851. He was postmaster in Pembina in 1869-70, when he served as correspondent to the St. Paul newspapers about the Red River Rebellion. Cavalier, North Dakota, is named for him.

Chambers, John Hudson (1846-1924) Businessman. He was president of the Winnipeg-based Paulin-Chambers Ltd., established in 1882, which sponsored a number of local sports teams and manufactured Paulin's Chocolate Puffs. He died in Kitchener.

Champagne, Pierre (1832-1899) Farmer. A Métis of Ste. Anne des Chênes who was married to Marguerite Beauchamp (b. 1834), he was one of the guards detailed to execute Thomas Scott* in 1870.

Champion, George (1870-1946) Park planner, landscaper. Born in Frampton, Dorsetshire, England, he was employed at the Royal Gardens at Kew before coming to Canada in 1897. He moved to Winnipeg in 1907 to become superintendent of the Parks Board, retiring in 1935. Champion was responsible for the execution of the design of Assiniboine Park and for the design of Kildonan Park (1911), as well as for the creation of a number of smaller parks and municipal golf courses. From the beginning Champion envisioned an integrated park system linked with broad boulevards in the "City Beautiful" manner. He had some problems with the flatness of the landscape, although he designed the English Garden at Assiniboine Park. He was firmly opposed to commercial amusements in parks. He died in Toronto. See Catherine Macdonald, *A City at Leisure: An Illustrated History of Parks and Recreation Services in Winnipeg 1893-1993* (1995).

Champion, Henry Thomson (1847-1916) Soldier, banker. Born in Toronto and educated at Upper Canada College, he came west as a sergeant with the Wolseley Expedition and served for two years with the occupying forces. In 1879 he became a partner with William F. Alloway* in the banking firm of Alloway and Champion.

Chapman, Dr. Alva Burton (1863-1961) Physician. Born in Gananoque, Canada, he worked in the timber industry until he enrolled in Queen's University Medical School, graduating in 1899. On his way to British Columbia he stopped to visit in Reston, Manitoba, and remained to practise medicine there for the rest of his life. He was awarded the Victoria Cross in WWI.

Charette, Guillaume J. (1884-1952) Folklorist, historian. Born in St. Norbert, he attended the Grey Nuns' School and the Collège de Saint-Boniface, receiving his BA in 1910. He graduated from the Manitoba Law School in 1914. He worked in the immigration department for many years. President of the Union Nationale Métisse Saint-Joseph, he wrote often on Métis history and folklore. He was co-author of *Histoire de la nation métisse.*

A typescript of his biography of Louis Goulet is at the PAM.

Charitinoff, Moses (fl. 1915-1919) Journalist. He was editor of *Robotchny Narod* (Working People), a weekly paper published in Winnipeg in Russian and the organ of the Ukrainian Social Democratic Party. He had been tried in 1918 for possession of seditious literature but let off on a technicality, thanks to the defense of T.J. Murray. He was suspected in 1919 of receiving funds from Bolshevist organizations in the United States and was arrested on 17 June 1919. He was ordered deported by the federal government but was released after an appeal to Ottawa. At that point he disappears from the record.

Charles, John (b. c. 1784) Fur trader. Born in London, England, he joined the HBC as an apprentice in 1799. He spent most of his early career on the Churchill River and Reindeer Lake. In 1811 he became trader and second-in-command at Churchill, and in 1815 head of the New Churchill District. He was made a chief factor when the HBC and NWC merged in 1821, and from 1822 to 1824 he was in charge of the Nelson River District. Charles later served on the English River and in Athabasca. From 1836 to 1838 he commanded York Factory. He was a governor's councillor in 1815 and 1822 and a councillor of Rupert's Land from 1839. He lived in the Red River Settlement on a leave of absence from 1841 onward, officially retiring there in 1843. He was fluent in Cree and Chipewyan. George Simpson* described him as "a plain blunt Englishman, . . . a man of veracity and integrity, but not bright."

Chartrand, Gaspard (1876-1952) Métis leader. Born at the Waterhen, he settled with his family at Clear Lake in 1905. He served for several years with the HBC in Saskatchewan and worked to encourage Francophone settlement in the Egg Lake area of Saskatchewan. He moved to The Pas in 1926 as fur buyer for Revillon Frères, opening a fish business and a taxi service in 1927. He was a prominent Liberal organizer in the North.

Chase, R. Darwin (1905-1979) Co-op administrator, municipal politician. Born in Dauphin, he grew up there and was active in the Boys' Parliaments of the early 1920s. In 1935 he won an essay contest on civil administration in the City of Winnipeg. He subsequently worked with the National Grain Company and the Manitoba Provincial Elevator Pool until 1945, when he became field supervisor for Manitoba Co-operative Wholesale. In 1949, on the invitation of Premier Douglas Campbell,* he established a co-op-erative service branch for the Manitoba government and headed it for some years. He also helped found a National Association of Administrators of Co-op-eratives that worked to limit American influence in the Canadian co-operative movement. He moved to Fort Garry in 1948 and was its mayor from 1955 to 1959. In retirement he worked for the Canadian International Development Agency in Honduras. There are papers at the PAM.

Chenier, Felix (1843-1910) Lawyer, land official. Born in Canada, he came west in 1870 with the Wolseley Expedition and remained to be called to the bar in 1871. He was an MLA for Baie St. Paul from 1874 to 1878, and in 1885 he became examiner of titles in the Winnipeg Land Titles Office.

Cherniak, Joseph Alter (1885-1972) Lawyer, community leader. Born in Russia, he came to Manitoba in 1905. He was educated at St. John's College (BA, 1915) and Manitoba Law School (LLB, 1918). He practised as a lawyer in Winnipeg. Cherniak was one of the founders of the Jewish Radical School in 1914, renamed the I.L. Peretz School in 1915, which was among the first independent Jewish schools in North America. He founded the Jewish Welfare Fund and the Winnipeg League for Yiddish, among other community ventures.

Chester, Frank L. (1901-1966) Merchant, politician, athlete. Born in Winnipeg, he was educated in Winnipeg and Vancouver. He owned Chester's Hardware in Winnipeg. He was first elected to city council for Ward Three in 1946 and was elected Liberal MLA from Winnipeg North from 1950 to 1953. He served as chair of the farm loan board in Ottawa from 1954 to 1960. Chester played senior hockey and was president of the Kiwanis Club.

Chester, Philip (1896-1976) Business executive. Born in Derbyshire, England, he trained as an accountant and joined the HBC in 1923. He came to Winnipeg in 1924. He was appointed general manager of the HBC in 1930 and managing director in 1946. From 1940 to 1945 he served as the first civilian master-general of ordinance for the Canadian government. He also served on the Manitoba Flood Relief Committee in 1950.

Chevrier, Noah (1846-1911) Merchant, senator. Born in Canada, he came to Winnipeg in 1871 and headed a clothier and furrier establishment. He was appointed a senator in 1909.

Chipman, George F. (1882-1935) Journalist, horticulturalist. Born in the Annapolis Valley, he joined the *Grain Growers' Guide* and served as its editor from 1910 until his death. He operated an extensive fruit and vegetable breeding program at his Charleswood home and was convinced that horticulture was essential to a satisfying farm life on the Prairies. He wrote about horticulture in the pages of the *Guide* and in many pamphlets and special bulletins. One of his slogans was "The Million Dollar Apple." He received the Stevenson Memorial Gold Medal of the Manitoba Horticultural Society posthumously in 1938.

Chouart des Groseilliers, Médard (1618-c. 1690) Fur trader, explorer. Born in France, he came to Canada around 1641 and spent some time in the West. By the early 1650s he began investigating Hudson Bay, and he spent most of his time in the Upper Country trading furs with the Indians. In 1660 he and his brother-in-law Pierre Radisson* conducted a highly successful fur-trading expedition to Lake Superior, but upon their return to New France were thrown in jail by the authorities for trading without licences. The two men resolved to deal instead with the English or the Dutch in New York, and ended up in London in 1665, where they argued that the best way to gain access to the rich trade of the Bay was not overland but in large ships sailing directly to the heart of the continent. They convinced Charles II to grant a charter to the HBC, and began a complex period of changing allegiances while continuing to visit the Bay for trading purposes. Groseilliers was at the Bay in 1689, after which he returned to London. For a biography, see Grace Nute, *Caesars of the Wilderness* (1943, 1975). *DCB* I, 223-28.

Chown, Henry Bruce (1893-1986) Physician, medical researcher. Born in Winnipeg, he graduated from McGill University with a BSc in 1914. After service in the Canadian Forces overseas in WWI, where he won several decorations, he graduated from the University of Manitoba Medical School in 1922. Chown founded the Winnipeg RH Laboratory in 1944, serving as its director until 1972. His laboratory discovered the mechanism of RH haemolytic disease, its management, and its ultimate prevention, perhaps the most outstanding medical discovery ever made in Manitoba. In 1945 he carried out the first exchange transfusion of blood in Winnipeg. He was chair of pediatrics at the Children's Hospital from 1949 to 1959, and co-founded the RH Institute in 1969. He was awarded an honorary degree by the University of Manitoba in 1963. He died in Victoria. Chown's papers are at the University of Manitoba. See Patricia Saunderson, *Dr. Henry Chown* (1985).

Chrismas, W.E. (c. 1850-1923) Farmer, faith healer. Known in later years as "Father" Chrismas, he was born in London, England, and came to Canada in 1885. He farmed at Minnedosa, Manitoba, from 1889 to 1897, then at Oxbow, Saskatchewan. He gained repute as an evangelist and faith healer in Winnipeg from 1917 to his death. He was a striking figure with long flowing locks of hair down to his shoulders.

Christensen, Agnes (1886-1989) Volunteer worker. Born in Hjørring, Denmark, she moved to Winnipeg in 1907 and soon became involved in community service work. She served for years as president of the ladies' auxiliary of the Danish Lutheran Church. During WWII she placed Danish airmen in Winnipeg homes and organized knitting for troops overseas. As a result, she was honoured by the Danish government and the Canadian Red Cross. She died in Winnipeg.

Christie, Alexander (1792-1872) Fur trader. Reputedly born in Glasgow, Scotland, Christie joined the HBC in 1809, beginning his career in Moose Factory in the timber business. He advanced quickly, becoming chief factor in 1821. He headed Moose Factory from 1826 to 1830 and York Factory from 1830 to 1833. He became governor of Assiniboia until 1839, then again from 1844 to 1848. Christie's second term was taken up with attempting to enforce the HBC fur-trading monopoly. But he could not enforce his pretensions, and he opined to the Company that a military force was essential. One was sent in 1846 under Colonel John Folliot Crofton* and another in 1848 under Major William Bletterman Caldwell.* *DCB* X, 167-68.

Clare, Eva (1884-1961) Musician, teacher. Born at Neepawa, Manitoba, she studied piano in Berlin and New York. She made her London debut at Wigmore Hall to warm reviews. She subsequently performed in Toronto, New York, Vancouver, and other cities in the West. Clare taught in Regina before returning to Manitoba in 1918. In 1922 she was the first Canadian to play with the Minneapolis Symphony. She helped organize the Manitoba Music Teachers' Association, serving as first provincial president. She wrote *Musical Appreciation and the Studio Club* (1924; reprint, 1930). Her 1933 studio club was transformed into the "Wednesday Morning Musicale" concert series. In 1937 she became music director of the University of Manitoba, serving until her retirement in 1949. Eva Clare Hall at the University of Manitoba is named after her.

Clare, James Robert (1827-1867) Fur trader. Born in England, he was educated at the Royal Naval School in Camberwell and came to Moose Factory in 1845 as an apprentice clerk of the HBC. He served most of the next 20 years at York Factory and by 1858 was head of the post itself. He took charge of the Red River District in 1862 and stood in for Governor William McTavish* on several occasions. He died suddenly in London while on private business. *DCB* IX, 130-31.

Clark, Kelly (1935-1995) Visual artist, musician. Raised in St. Vital, he attended the University of Manitoba's School of Art from 1954 to 1958, won several prizes at Winnipeg shows, and received a Canada Council grant for travel in England in 1960. He returned to Winnipeg in 1963, refusing to exhibit at the Winnipeg Art Gallery as a matter of principle. He supported himself for some years in the 1960s as a folk singer, and made one record album with Capitol Records.. He later was graphics editor of *Omphalos,* Winnipeg's underground newspaper, and art director of *Canadian Dimension* magazine. He returned to painting in the mid-1970s, but never achieved popular success before his death from cancer. See George Swinton, et al., *Kelly Clark* (1998).

Clarke, Francis Ignatino (1849-1916) Lawyer, journalist. Born in Montreal, he came west in 1870, becoming a barrister and subsequently working as a journalist. He held several minor legal appointments while helping Alexander Begg* edit his *History of the North-West.* He left Winnipeg for British Columbia in 1899, serving in the years before his death in Victoria as secretary of the British Columbia Bureau of Information.

Clarke, Henry Joseph Hynes (1833-1889) Journalist, lawyer. Born in Donegal, Ireland, he came to Lower Canada at the age of three. He spent his early years as a journalist, criminal lawyer, and writer. Clarke came to Manitoba in November 1870 as an assistant to Lieutenant-Governor Adams Archibald* and soon became attorney general. He clashed with the lieutenant-governor over the issues of admission to the Manitoba bar and the establishment of courts, but continued to lead the government in the House of Assembly into the regime of Alexander Morris.* Although he was never formally premier, he is sometimes described as Manitoba's first. He was active in various political intrigues and court cases, including the trial of Lord Gordon Gordon's* kidnapper (who later beat him up in St. Paul). In 1885 he acted as counsel for a number of Louis Riel's followers. He was the author of *Sketch of the Life of Thomas D'Arcy McGee* (1868). See F. Ebbs-Canavan, "Manitoba's First Premier and Attorney-General Henry Joseph Clarke, Q.C., 1871-1874," *Manitoba History* 1, no. 3 (1946-49): 1-11. *DCB* XI, 192-94.

Clarke, John (1781-1852) Fur trader. Born in Montreal, Clarke joined the NWC in 1800. He quickly ended up in Athabasca, where by 1810 his conduct was regarded as "rather reprehensible." After a sojourn in Montreal, Clarke joined John Jacob Astor's Pacific Fur Company. He was in charge of the party that left New York in 1811 and arrived at Fort Astoria in May 1812. After the American traders sold out to the NWC in October 1813, Clarke rejoined the NWC. Then in 1815 he signed on with the HBC to head a new expedition to the Athabasca country. The HBC had enormous trouble in Athabasca, where Clarke was imprisoned early in 1817. Critics complained that his conduct left much to be desired and that his vanity was "inordinate." Clarke ended up as chief factor at Fort Garry in 1823, making himself much disliked by the colonists, for which he was criticized by the HBC's London Committee. Most of his last years in service were spent trying to gain recognition for his past contributions, but without much success. George Simpson* described him as wanting "of every principle or feeling allied to fair dealing, honour & integrity." *DCB* VIII, 158-59.

Clarke, Lionel Beaumaurice ("Nobby" or "Leo," 1892-1916) War hero. Born in Waterdown, Ontario, he was raised in England and came with his parents to Canada in 1903. He was educated at Argyle and Gladstone Schools in Winnipeg. As an acting corporal in 1916, Clarke single-handedly fought off an entire unit of Germans while a part of the Canadian position at Courcelette was secured. He was awarded the Victoria Cross for his bravery. Promoted to acting sergeant, he was killed in a trench cave-in a few months later.

Claxton, William Gordon ("Dozy," 1899-1967) WWI flying ace. Born in Gladstone, Manitoba, he reached the rank of captain in the RAF and at one point recorded 41 victories in 79 days. Between 4 July and 12 August 1918, he shot down 10 enemy airplanes and one kite balloon. He also developed new techniques of aerial photography. Shot down in 1918, he was taken prisoner by the Germans. After the war he went into journalism. He died in Toronto.

Clay, Charles (1906-1980) Missionary, teacher, author. Born in Winnipeg, he was educated in Washington State and Saskatchewan before entering Wesley College. A United Church missionary, he taught at Indian schools in northern Manitoba during the 1920s. He joined the *Winnipeg Free Press* in 1930, serving for some years as literary editor. He worked in Ottawa during WWII and in 1956 settled in Bewdley, Ontario, where he opened Clay Publishing Company, which produced journals and books for the popular market. In 1938 he published *Swampy Cree Legends*. He also wrote several other books for young people about Aboriginal subjects.

Clouston, Robert (c. 1793-1850) Fur trader. Born in the Orkney Islands, he joined the HBC in 1812, serving at York Factory, the Winnipeg District, Brandon House (1815-16), Swan River (1816-17), and Fort Hibernia (1817-18). He subsequently went to the Athabasca region, and he retired to Red River in 1828. He died at Red River.

Clubb, William R. (1884-1962) Politician, sportsman. Born in Morris, Manitoba, he served on the Morris municipal council before his election as Morris MLA as an Independent Farmer in 1920. He served in the Manitoba legislature from 1920 to 1940, including stints as public works minister and minister of labour. He was commissioner of the Manitoba liquor board from 1940 to 1956. He was an avid curler and flyer. There are papers at the PAM.

Coaffee, Cyril (1897-1945) Runner. Born in Winnipeg, he first came to prominence as an athlete in 1920, when he won the 100-yard-dash trials for the Canadian Olympic team but was initially left off the team for financial reasons. Winnipeggers raised the funds to send him to Antwerp. In 1922 he tied the world record in the 100-yard dash at 9.6 seconds. He was Canada's team captain at the 1924 Olympics, and he travelled internationally as a runner in the latter 1920s. Coaffee had an unusual running style caused by partial paralysis of his left arm, which gave him an extreme forward lean. He is a member of the Canadian Sports Hall of Fame and the Manitoba Sports Hall of Fame.

Coats, Darby R.F. (d. 1973) Radio pioneer. Born in England, he came to Canada in 1911. He served for many years as a wireless operator and was on a ship that was torpedoed in WWI. He worked for Canadian Marconi in 1920-21, then became manager-announcer of the Manitoba Telephone System radio station, CKY, in 1923. He later managed other stations in Saskatchewan. Known to many children as "Uncle Peter" from his children's radio shows, he was responsible for the supervision of Winnipeg's first television transmissions in 1933. He later worked for the Manitoba Telephone System in public relations.

Cochrane, Henry (c. 1834-1898) Cleric. A Protestant mixed-blood, Cochrane married Elizabeth Budd (b. 1844). He was ordained an Anglican cleric in 1859 and was the incumbent of St. Peter's from 1867 to 1874. In the 20 January 1870 meeting between the Red River settlers and Donald A. Smith,* Cochrane served as Indian translator. He was elected a delegate to the Convention of Forty from St. Peter's. He later served as a missionary and schoolteacher in the North. He died at Jackhead, Manitoba. *DCB* XII, 200-201.

Cockburn, John Wesley (1856-1924) Mechanical engineer, merchant, politician. Born in Thorold, Canada, and educated there, he worked as a mechanical engineer in Ontario before moving to Winnipeg in 1882 with the CPR. He subsequently opened general stores in Winnipeg and Boissevain, then moved into grocery retailing. He was elected alderman in 1891 and served as a member of the Winnipeg Board of Control for all but one year from 1907 to 1918. He was chair of the Winnipeg Police Commission.

Cocking, Matthew (1743-1799) Fur trader, explorer. Born in York, England, Cocking first came to York Fort in 1765 as a writer. In 1772 he went inland as a volunteer, travelling with the Natives for nearly a year. Upon his return, he provided detailed descriptions of life on the western prairie. He undertook several subsequent inland journeys before settling at Fort Severn in 1777 and then at York Fort in 1781. He retired to England in 1782, his service in providing information on the inland territory well appreciated by the HBC. *DCB* IV, 156-58.

Cockran, Rev. William (1796-1865) Cleric. Cockran was born in Northumberland, England, but was a Scot. Raised as a Presbyterian, he converted to Anglicanism and came to Red River in 1825 as a Church Missionary Society missionary. Both Cockran and his wife came from humble origins. His wife had been a servant maid and Cockran's speech was "broad and vulgar even as a scotchman." Nonetheless he was ideal for Red River because of his agricultural experience as an under-bailiff in Scotland. In the settlement, Cockran quickly turned to establishing a model farm as a means to attract the country-born to the church and the school associated with it. In 1829 he moved to the Lower Church (St. Andrew's), where he soon had another farm and school in operation. He even extended his work to the Saulteaux in 1831. Behind his operations was the intention of attracting Indians to Red River in order to evangelize them. In 1835 he joined the Council of Assiniboia. To his regret, he was unable to bring his aboriginal parishioners quickly to the degree of civilization he desired, and for a time he became slightly jaundiced. He was always a supporter of the HBC as an agent of civilization. He spent a year in Toronto in 1846-47 recovering his health before returning to Red River service. In later years he was often embattled, partly because of his support for Adam Thom* and governor William Caldwell,* partly because of his wife's involvement in the Ballenden scandal. He also came into conflict with the fledgling Presbyterian Church in Kildonan. In 1851 he moved to what became Portage la Prairie, where he worked with settlers and Natives alike beyond the boundaries of Assiniboia. See *A Brief Sketch of the Life and Labours of Archdeacon Cockran* (n.d.); and Raymond M. Beaumont, "The Rev. William Cockran: The Man and the Image," *Manitoba History,* 33 (spring 1997): 2-26. *DCB* IX, 134-37.

Codd, Donald (c. 1845-1896) Surveyor. Born in Norfolk, England, he came to Canada with his parents at an early age. He studied surveying under John Snow* and worked for Snow at Red River in 1869-70. He became John Dennis's* chief clerk at the Dominion Lands Office in 1871, and from 1873 to 1881 served as Dominion Lands commissioner in Winnipeg, where he was heavily criticized for his handling of Métis land claims. After 1882 he worked for the Great Northwest Railway. He wrote "Some Reminiscences of Fort Garry in 1869-70," published in *Great West Magazine* 13 (1899): 294-99. *DCB* XII, 203-4.

Colcleugh, Frederick William (1854-1907) Businessman, politician. Born in Canada, he studied law but entered business with his cousin in Selkirk, Manitoba. He served as Selkirk town councillor for many years and had two terms as mayor (1886, 1888-91). A Liberal, he was elected to the Manitoba legislature from St. Andrew's in 1888 and 1892.

Colcleugh, James (1841-1918) Pharmacist, politician. Born near Dundas, Canada, he trained as a pharmacist and was active in the Ontario militia against the Fenians. He came to Manitoba in 1875 to work on the CPR, becoming first superintendent of the telegraph line from Selkirk to Edmonton and the dispatcher of the first message to cross the Prairies. He was elected first mayor of Selkirk in 1882. In 1883 he opened a drugstore there, and in 1885 he established a Selkirk-Winnipeg telephone exchange. He spent several years in San Francisco but returned to Winnipeg in 1892. He died in Vancouver. His papers and diaries are in the PAM. *DCB* XIV, 228-29.

Coldwell, George R. (1858-1924) Lawyer, politician, athlete. Born in Darlingford, Canada, he was educated at Trinity College School and Trinity College, where he earned a BA in 1880. He was called to the Ontario bar but came to Winnipeg and then moved to Brandon, where he was a law partner of T. Mayne Daly.* He spent 20 years in municipal politics before joining the Conservative provincial Cabinet in 1907. He became minister of education in 1908. Coldwell was a noted rugby football and amateur soccer player.

Coldwell, William (1834-1907) Journalist. Born in London, England, he was educated in Dublin. Coldwell came to Canada in 1854 and worked on the *Toronto Leader*. He migrated to Red River with William Buckingham* in 1859 and founded the *Nor'-Wester*. He left the settlement in 1865 to work on the *Globe* until 1869, when he again came west to begin the *Red River Pioneer* with James Ross,* who was his brother-in-law. An excellent shorthand reporter, he served as English secretary to the 1870 Convention of Forty. In September 1870 he joined with Robert Cunningham* in publication of the *Manitoban,* which merged with the *Manitoba Free Press* in 1874. Soon afterward, he became an invalid. He died in Victoria. There are papers at the PAM.

Cole, Louise Olive (d. 1968) Dentist. Born in Cobourg, Ontario, she was educated at the University of Manitoba, Manitoba Dental College, and Northwestern University in Chicago, and she did postgraduate work at the Dewey School of Orthodontia in New York City. She was one of Winnipeg's pioneer women dentists, specializing in orthodontics. She was active in many Manitoba women's organizations.

Colen, Joseph (c. 1751-1818) Fur trader. Engaged by the HBC as a writer in 1785, Colen was subsequently appointed resident chief at York Factory and was active in organizing the first HBC expeditions to the Athabasca country. He was recalled in 1798, probably because of criticisms of his management. He offered Lord Selkirk* a favourable account of Red River in 1802, which helped influence Selkirk to persevere with his scheme of transplanting Highlanders to the region. *DCB* V, 194-95.

Collin, Louis Dona (b. 1882) Physician, athlete. Born in Quebec, he was educated at Ottawa University (where he played on a championship rugby team, 1904), Montreal University, and in Paris. He came to Winnipeg with his family as a child, graduated in medicine in 1911, and practised in Winnipeg before joining the Canadian Expeditionary Force in 1915. He received the Medaille d'Honneur en Vermeil from the French government. He returned to private practice in St. Boniface in 1919.

Collyer, Francis John (1865-1948) Farmer, livestock breeder, local politician. Born in Sussex, England, he came to Manitoba in 1882 to homestead in the Welwyn District. He became first secretary-treasurer of the Welwyn Farmers' Elevator Company, became a director of the Grain Growers' Grain Company in

1913 and served as director of the United Grain Growers 1916-1944. He was a member of the Canadian Council of Agriculture. A successful grain farmer, he also bred Aberdeen Angus and helped establish the Canadian Aberdeen Association. He was active in local government, being appointed a justice of the peace in 1894 and serving as chair of the board of the consolidated school at McAuley.

Colomb, Solomon (1886-1991) Aboriginal leader. Born on the Pukatawagan Reserve, he served as chief of the Mathis Colomb Indian Band from 1933 to 1958 and was instrumental in its acquisition of a sawmill. A native Cree speaker, he was a source of the old ways to his people and was regarded as the "spiritual grandfather" for the community. He died on the reserve.

Coltman, William Bachelor (d. 1826) Merchant. Born in England, Coltman came to Quebec in 1799 and soon established himself as a merchant. He was appointed to the Lower Canadian Executive Council in 1812. In 1816 he and John Fletcher were appointed as justices of the peace for the Indian territory of the Northwest by Governor Sherbrooke. Subsequently they were given a special commission to investigate the fur-trade war in the West, which had recently produced the Battle of Seven Oaks. Coltman's trading companies had supplied the fur trade, and both sides thought he would be sympathetic. Both Fletcher and Coltman headed west, but only Coltman carried on to Red River, where he arrested Lord Selkirk* and took thousands of pages of deposition. To Selkirk's chagrin, Coltman's subsequent 1818 report not only refused to support the legal position of the HBC in the dispute but sympathized with the NWC's position while condemning the use of violence by both sides. The report ("A General Statement and Report Relative to the Disturbances in the Indian Territories of British North America . . .," reprinted in G.B. Parliament, House of Commons Paper, 1819, 18, no. 584: 1-288) provides one of the best sources of documentation for the fur-trade war. Coltman later advocated the legislative union of Upper and Lower Canada. He died in London. *DCB* VI, 166-68.

Colvile, Andrew Wedderburn (d. 1856) Businessman. Born in England, he was a West India sugar merchant who became the brother-in-law of Lord Selkirk* in 1807 and was associated with Selkirk in

the HBC and the Red River Settlement. He became a member of the HBC managing committee in 1810. In 1813 he assumed the name Colvile by royal licence. He secured George Simpson* for the HBC, became a Selkirk trustee in 1820, and played a major role in the amalgamation of the HBC and NWC in 1821. He was deputy governor from 1839 to 1852.

Colvile, Eden (1819-1893) Colonial official. The son of Andrew Wedderburn Colvile,* he was educated at Eton and Cambridge. He came to Canada in 1844 to administer the seigneury of Beauharnois for the London Land Company. The HBC appointed him governor of Rupert's Land in 1850. He resided in Red River for less than a year, constantly embroiled in controversy, especially with recorder Adam Thom* and with the free traders. He became deputy governor of the HBC in 1871 and governor from 1880 to 1889. His letters (1849-52) were edited by W.L. Morton as *Eden Colvile's Letters 1849-52* (1956). He died in Devon. *DCB* XII, 206-7.

Comfort, Charles Fraser (1900-1994) Artist. Born in Cramond (Edinburgh), Scotland, he came to Winnipeg in 1912 and studied art at the Winnipeg School of Art. He began working for Brigden's commercial design studio in 1914, later describing it as the equivalent of "a fifteenth-century old master's studio." In 1918 and 1919 he won the Eaton's catalogue cover competition, and he moved to Toronto. He often exhibited with fellow Manitoba artists, especially Eric Bergman.* In 1923 he illustrated W.J. Healey's* *Women of Red River* along with Walter J. Phillips.* His best-known painting, a watercolour portrait of fellow artist Carl Schaefer as a generic unemployed *Young Canadian*, was done in 1932. Comfort shuttled between Winnipeg and Toronto, working sporadically at Brigden's until teaching at the Ontario College of Art from 1935 to 1938. In 1938 he began teaching at the University of Toronto, where he remained until 1960. He was an official wartime artist for the Canadian army from 1943 to 1946, president of the Royal Canadian Academy of Arts from 1957 to 1960, and director of the National Gallery of Canada from 1960 to 1965. He was best known for his large portraits and his murals. He was given the Order of Canada in 1972. Comfort died in Ottawa. See Margaret Gray, *Charles Comfort* (1976).

Conklin, Elias George (1845-1901) Real estate agent, politician. Born in Canada, he was educated at Paris Grammar School. He came west in 1874 and formed the real estate agency of Conklin and Fortune in 1880. He was often defeated as a candidate for the Manitoba legislature but did serve one term, from 1883 to 1886, as a Liberal representing Winnipeg North. He later served as clerk of the House from 1888 to 1900. He was an early president of the St. Andrew's Society.

Connolly, Suzanne ("La Sauvagesse," c. 1788-1862) Fur-trade wife. Born northwest of Lake Winnipeg, she was a young Cree who married a NWC fur trader, William Connolly, in 1803 "according to the custom of the country." Twenty-eight years later, she was "turned off" by Connolly, who married his second cousin in a Catholic church. After many tribulations she entered the Grey Nuns convent in Red River in 1841. After her death one of her sons sued the second wife for a share of the Connolly estate. The lower court found for the plaintiff, and so did the Court of Revision in 1869. The case was settled out of court before going to the Privy Council. *DCB* IX, 149-51.

Connor, **Ralph** See Gordon, Charles William.

Constantine, Charles (c. 1847-1912) Police officer. Born in England, he came to Canada as a boy. He served in the Wolseley Expedition, and he became deputy sheriff for Manitoba in 1873 and chief of the Manitoba Provincial Police in 1880. He served in the North-West Rebellion and in 1886 became an inspector of the NWMP, in charge of the Klondike detachment during the gold-rush years. He died in Long Beach, California. *DCB* XIV, 232-33.

Constantin-Weyer, Maurice (1881-1964) Author. Born in Bourbonne-les-Bains, France, he came to Canada in 1903 and settled at St. Claude, Manitoba. He returned to France to fight in WWI, where he was often wounded and decorated. After the peace he wrote 46 books, some 15 of which have Canadian content. He won the Prix Goncourt in 1928. He also wrote three plays and two movie scripts. *Towards the West* (1931) is a love story of two Métis. *La Bourrasque* (The Half-Breed), first published in 1925, is a fictionalized biography of Louis Riel; a Canadian version (revised rather than simply translated) appeared in 1930 as *A Martyr's Folly*. *La Bourrasque* involved its author in a lengthy controversy with the Métis community in Manitoba, in the course of which Donatien Frémont* accused Constantin-Weyer of abandoning his Métisse wife and three children in Manitoba before the war. Critics complained that he wrote only about stereotypical Métis, but also admitted that he described the western landscape well. He is easily the most prolific Francophone to have written fiction about the Canadian West. See Roger Motus, *Maurice Constantin-Weyer, écrivain de l'Ouest et du Grand Nord* (1982); Simone Knutson, "Constantin-Weyer's *La Bourrasque:* A Process in Mythification," in *Images of Louis Riel in Canadian Culture*, ed. Ramon Hathorn and Patrick Holland (1992), 257-78.

Cook, William Hemmings (c. 1766-1846) Fur trader. Born in London, he joined the HBC in 1786, advancing to command of the posts on the Nelson River in 1797, then of York Factory from 1809 to 1815. He retired to Red River in 1819 and became a councillor of the District of Assiniboia in 1839. George Simpson* found him a "most extraordinary mixture of generous eccentricity, Religion, Drunkenness and Misanthropy." *DCB* VII, 206-7.

Cooper, William (1860-1937) Cabinetmaker, teacher, industrial unionist. Born in Aberdeen, Scotland, he was a cabinetmaker who helped form the Aberdeen branch of the Social Democratic Foundation and served for 11 years as a member of the Aberdeen City Council. He came to Winnipeg in 1907. Besides writing extensively, he conducted classes at a Workers' University on Monday afternoons, influencing many, including James S. Woodsworth* and William Ivens.* He helped bring the philosophy of British industrial unionism to Canada and adapted it to Canadian conditions. In 1919 and 1920 he wrote regularly for the *OBU Bulletin*, producing much of its distinctive ideology.

Coppins, Frederick George (1889-1963) Military hero. Born in England, he moved to Winnipeg with his family. He served as a sergeant major in the Eighth Battalion of the Canadian Expeditionary Force. The winner of a Victoria Cross, he was the only surviving member of a party of five who had volunteered to destroy 24 enemy machine-gun nests. He not only succeeded but marched back with prisoners. In 1919 he enlisted as a special constable at the time of the Winnipeg General Strike and had two ribs broken in a melee on 10 June. He later moved to California and worked in the construction industry in Oakland.

He died in the U.S. Administration Hospital in Livermore, California.

Coquart, Claude-Godefroy (1706-1765) Missionary. Born at Melun, France, he came to Canada in 1739 and replaced Father Aulneau as the chaplain accompanying La Vérendrye in 1741. He remained at Michilimackinac until 1743, when he came to Fort La Reine (Portage la Prairie), thus becoming the first missionary to reach such a westerly point. But he was soon back on the St. Lawrence River. *DCB* III, 137.

Corbett, Griffith Owen (c. 1823-1909) Cleric, physician. Born near Minchinhampton, England, Corbett was one of those folk who have no biography before their arrival in North America. He came in 1851 and first entered the record when he was refused ordination by the bishop of Montreal. In 1852 he was sent to Rupert's Land, and he was ordained in 1853. He built Holy Trinity Church in Headingley in 1854, returned to England in 1855 to study medicine, and came back to Rupert's Land in 1857. He established the Red River Settlement's first printing press in 1858 so that he could publish arguments in favour of turning Red River into a Crown colony. He gained the support of the English-speaking mixed-bloods for his insistence on finding Red River a more regular place in the English colonial establishment. Corbett first got into trouble over his anti-Catholicism and dislike of Francophone Métis. Then in 1862 there were charges that he had attempted to induce an abortion upon his serving-girl. The trial in 1863 revealed that he had not only tried to abort the girl's child but had repeatedly committed adultery with her as well. His supporters insisted that the case had been fabricated by the HBC, and when petitions for his release failed, a mob led by schoolmaster James Stewart* forcibly freed him from jail on 20 April 1863. The subsequent arrest of Stewart led to Stewart's liberation by a similar mob. These cases are often used as illustrations of the lack of authority by the government of Assiniboia in its later years. In 1870, after returning to England, Corbett published more pamphlets advocating Crown colony status for Red River. Eventually reinstated as a cleric, he ran anew into charges about his morals. He died in Lingfield, England. Mrs. Corbett remained in Red River upon Corbett's return to Britain, subsequently moving to Swan Lake. See Frits Pannekoek, *A Snug Little Flock: The Social Origins of the Riel Resistance 1869-70* (1991). *DCB* XIII, 215-17.

Cornelius, Mary B. (Evans) (1864-1951) Osteopath. Born in Missouri, she married Dr. Charles Cornelius in 1887. She had received a BS from Oaklawn College in 1885, and studied at the American College of Osteopathy. She came to Winnipeg in 1907, becoming one of the first female osteopaths in the province. As well as practising osteopathy, she served as president of the Western Canada Christian Women's Board of Missions, and later as president of the Manitoba Women's Missionary Society of the Church of Christ (Disciples).

Cornish, Francis Evans (1831-1878) Lawyer, politician. Born in Canada, he was called to the bar in 1855 and held various municipal offices in London before moving west in 1872 to be one of the first lawyers called to the Manitoba bar. He was responsible for swearing out the warrant for the arrest of Ambroise Lépine* in 1873 for the murder of Thomas Scott. He was later awarded a share of the Ontario reward offered for the arrest of those responsible for the death of Scott.* He was mainly noted as a defence counsel, although in the Ambroise Lépine case he was a prosecuting attorney who summed up the prosecution's successful case for the jury. In 1874 he was elected first mayor of Winnipeg, and he was also elected to the Manitoba legislature as a "National" in 1874 for the riding of Poplar Point. In 1876 he was charged with stealing a poll book on election day. A branch of the Winnipeg Public Library is named after him. He died of cancer of the stomach. See R.S. Rannie, "Frank Cornish — The Man," *Manitoba History*, no. 9 (1985): 29-30; Keith Wilson, *Francis Evans Cornish* (1986). *DCB* X, 197-98.

Cotton, Almon James (1858-1942) Farmer, letter writer. Born in Port Hope, Canada, he moved to Treherne, Manitoba, in 1888, growing such successful wheat crops on rented land that he became known as the "Wheat King" of Manitoba. One year he shipped over 17,000 bushels of number one hard. Concerned about inheritances for his sons, he began acquiring land in the Swan River Valley in 1898 and moved there in 1901. Although he was an unsuccessful politician, having run once for the Manitoba legislature in the Valley as a prohibitionist candidate, he was active in local government. He served on the Harlington School Board and was Sunday school superintendent for the Methodist church in Kenville. He was also a member of the board of governors of the University of Manitoba from 1917 to 1934. Cotton wrote thousands of letters to immigrants over the years, answering their questions and boosting both Manitoba and the Swan River Valley. He died in Swan River. An ardent amateur photographer, he took many photographs that survive in family hands, as do most of his records and letter books. A selection of all these was published in 1985 as *The Wheat King*, edited by Wendy Owen. Cotton is a member of the Manitoba Agricultural Hall of Fame.

Coulter, Garnet (1882-1975) Municipal politician. Born in Dominion City, Manitoba, he came to Winnipeg in 1903 to article in law. He was called to the bar in 1907 and served overseas in WWI with the Canadian Forestry Corps as a transport officer. He resumed his legal career after demobilization, becoming KC in 1935. He served as a member of the Winnipeg School Board from 1924 to 1936 (chair, 1932-33) and in 1936 was elected as alderman from Ward Two. On city council he was an inveterate opponent of Mayor John Queen.* He ran successfully for mayor as an independent in 1942, and served until 1954. In the 1946 election, he received more than 62,000 votes. Mayor during the Manitoba flood of 1950, he was responsible for the creation of the Manitoba Flood Relief Fund. As mayor he was regarded as fair, but dull. After his defeat in 1954, he became chair of the Court of Revision.

Courchaine, Marie Thérèse (Goulet) ("Manie-Tobie," 1912-1970) Writer. Born in St. Boniface, she was educated at St. Adolphe Convent, St. Joseph's Academy, and the Manitoba Normal School. She taught in the public schools and in the Oblate schools for many years. She published in newspapers throughout her life, mainly under the *nom de plume* "Manie-Tobie." As well as poetry, she wrote about the Métis and their customs.

Coutlée, Louis William (1851-1917) Soldier, land registrar. An active militia soldier who served against the Fenians and in the North-West campaign of 1885, he organized the administration of justice eastward to the Lake of the Woods, created the municipal system of Manitoba under the Municipal Act of 1886, and in 1887 helped introduce the Torrens system of land titles registration in Manitoba. In 1895 he became assistant reporter of the Supreme Court of Canada and moved to Ottawa, where he died. *DCB* XIV, 243-44.

Cowan, James (1831-1910) Physician, politician. Born in Ireland, he graduated in medicine from Victoria University, Toronto, in 1861. He moved to Manitoba in 1871, settling in Portage la Prairie. He was active in land dealing throughout his career. He served as MLA from High Bluff from 1874 to 1881 and retired from his medical practice in 1894.

Cowan, William (1818-1902) Physician, fur trader, diarist. Born in Scotland, Cowan graduated in medicine from the University of Glasgow in 1843. He came to Red River in 1848 as doctor for the Chelsea pensioners, marrying Harriette Sinclair in 1852 and becoming a member of the Council of Assiniboia in 1853. He was appointed chief trader of the HBC in 1860, and in 1862 he was made second-in-command to William McTavish.* In 1867 he became chief officer of Fort Garry. Cowan, like McTavish, greeted the occupation of the fort by Louis Riel in 1869 with considerable equanimity, and he spent most of the winter of 1869-70 under house arrest. He continually maintained that the fort had insufficient force at its disposal to contest the occupation. The pro-Canadian forces always suspected collusion, however. He left the settlement only a few weeks behind Governor McTavish in the spring of 1870, moving to the United States for a few years before returning to Winnipeg in 1876 to practise medicine. In 1885 the Cowans moved to St. Paul, Minnesota. Cowan died there. His diary (on microfilm) is in the PAM. *DCB* XIII, 225-26.

Cowie, Isaac (1848-1917) Businessman, historian. Born in the Shetland Islands, he was educated at the University of Edinburgh and entered the HBC in 1867. In 1891 he was appointed secretary of the Edmonton Board of Trade, and he moved to Winnipeg in 1902. He was active in seeking land grants for white settlers who had resided in Rupert's Land before it joined Canada in 1870. He also wrote *The Company of Adventurers* (1913). His collection of Plains Cree material culture is housed in the Chicago Field Museum of Natural History.

Cowley, Abraham (1816-1887) Cleric. Born in Gloucestershire, England, he was admitted to the Church Missionary Society College in 1839, and in 1841, newly married, he set out with his wife for Red River via Montreal. Unable to get west from Montreal, the Cowleys returned to England to sail via Hudson Bay. Recorder Adam Thom* refused to recognize Bishop George Mountain's competence over Rupert's Land, and Cowley served as a missionary to the Native people at Fairford until the dispute was settled. He was ordained in 1844. His record with the Natives was mixed. He was good at teaching them farming but less successful in translating Christianity into terms they understood. He left Fairford in 1854 and served at the Indian Settlement (now Dynevor) until his death. He received an honorary DD from St. John's College in 1867. *DCB* XI, 208-9.

Cox, Frederick John Charles (1864-1939) Commercial traveller, municipal politician. Born in Huddersfield, Yorkshire, England, he was educated in Hamburg, Germany. He came to Winnipeg in 1881 and worked as a travelling dry-goods salesman. He spent a lifetime on the road, travelling across Canada 50 to 60 times in the course of his work. He was chosen head of the Order of United Commercial Travellers of America in 1918, and later became secretary of the Northwest Commercial Travellers Association. He was a city councillor from 1903 to 1907 and was president of the Imperial Immigration League.

Coy, Eric (b. 1913) Athlete. Born in the Winnipeg neighbourhood of Charleswood, he dominated Canadian field events from 1935 to 1954. He won his first Canadian championship in the javelin event in 1935. He added championships in the discus and shot put in 1938 and won medals at the 1938 British Empire Games. He was named Norton H. Crowe amateur athlete of the year in 1938. Coy was also a champion in snowshoe racing. He served in the RCAF in WWII and joined the Manitoba Telephone System in Winnipeg after demobilization. He established Canadian records during the 1948 Olympic trials. He was made a member of the Canadian Track and Field Hall of Fame in 1963 and is a member of the Canadian and Manitoba Sports Halls of Fame. An ice arena in Charleswood is named after him.

Coyne, James Bowes (1879-1965) Lawyer. Born in Ontario, he studied at Upper Canada College, the University of Toronto, and Osgoode Hall. He was called to the Manitoba bar in 1905. A Winnipeg lawyer and member of the law firm of Coyne, McVicar and Martin, he served as Crown counsel for many royal commissions. He was a prominent member of the 1919 Citizens' Committee of 1,000. He had

written in October 1918 that the Winnipeg Trades and Labor Council was dominated by "acknowledged Bolsheviki."

Crawford, Howard Leslie ("Krug," 1892-1959) Journalist, athlete. Born and educated in Brandon, he pitched his first pro baseball game for Brandon in the Western Canada League at the age of 16. He abandoned law school in 1915 and joined the 40th Battalion, Canadian Field Artillery. Upon demobilization he received his law degree from the Manitoba Law School in 1919, but instead of practising law he joined the *Brandon Sun* and spent 40 years in its employ, ending as managing editor.

Crawford, Mary Elizabeth (1876-1953) Physician. Born in Lancashire, England, she came to Ottawa (where her mother became principal of the Presbyterian Ladies College) and attended the Ottawa Normal School and the University of Toronto. She interned at the West Philadelphia Hospital for Women and Children. She came to Winnipeg in 1901, practising privately until she was appointed chief medical inspector of the public schools of Winnipeg. She served in this capacity from 1918 to 1941. She was a founder and first president of the University Women's Club and was president of the International Association of Women Physicians and the Women's Equity League.

Crawford, William (1847-1897) Surveyor, politician, farmer. Born in Canada, he came to Manitoba in 1871 as a young surveyor. By 1875 he was Dominion Lands surveyor, and in 1877 he was appointed as valuator of the CPR right-of-way. In 1883, after several failed efforts, he was elected from High Bluff and Poplar Point to the Manitoba legislature, and he sat until 1886. He later moved to Dauphin to farm, and he died there.

Creighton, Thomas (1874-1949) Prospector. Born in Dunedin, Ontario, he prospected in Manitoba for years before discovering in 1915 the ore base that became the Flin Flon mine. He later served as supervisor of exploration with Hudson Bay Mining and Smelting and was president of the HB Air Transport Company. He was a skilled tennis and badminton player. He died in Flin Flon.

Crerar, Thomas Alexander (1876-1975) Grain dealer, politician. Born in Huron County, Ontario, he came with his parents in 1881 to a homestead near Russell, Manitoba. Educated at Portage la Prairie Collegiate, he taught school, farmed on land obtained from the HBC, and managed a grain elevator. In 1907 he became a director of the Grain Growers' Grain Company, and was subsequently president until its merger with Alberta Farmers' Cooperative Elevator in 1917 to form United Grain Growers, of which he became president. He was appointed minister of agriculture in the Union government of 1917, responsible for the Wartime Food Control Board, but resigned in 1919 to protest high tariffs. He continued as president and general manager of United Grain Growers until 1929. He led the Farmers' Progressive Party in the 1921 election, representing the moderates who wanted reform of the existing party system rather than a totally new political structure. He refused to join Mackenzie King's government but also refused official Opposition status for the Progressives in 1921, and he resigned from the Progressive leadership in 1922. He joined the Liberal Cabinet as minister of railways and canals in 1929 but was defeated in the 1930 election. Crerar returned to the House in 1935 and became the leading member of the Liberal Cabinet until the end of WWII, serving from 1935 to 1945 as minister of mines and resources. He was also a member of the Cabinet war committee and Cabinet wheat committee from 1939 to 1945. He supported overseas conscription in 1944 and was appointed to the Senate in 1945, retiring in 1966. He was the first politician awarded the Companion of the Order of Canada. He was a member of the IOOF, serving as noble grand of the Russell lodge early in his career. He is a member of the Manitoba Agricultural Hall of Fame. See the biography by J.E. Rea, *T.A. Crerar: A Political Life* (1997).

Cressy, James Thomas (1859-1912) Schoolteacher. Born in Crofton, England, he apprenticed as a teacher and trained at York Diocese Training College. He became headmaster at St. Luke's Boys' School before setting off to see the world. He arrived in Brandon in 1888 and taught school in both Manitoba and the United States (Chicago) before becoming principal of the Ruthenian Training School in Brandon in 1905. He was an associate grand master of the Orange Order.

Criddle, Norman (1875-1933) Artist, entomologist. Born in England, he came to Manitoba with his family to homestead at Aweme. He was a talented artist who illustrated a number of agricultural books, collaborating with Dr. James Fletcher on *Farm Weeds of Canada* and *Fodder and Pasture Plants*. He developed the "Criddle Mixture" of poisons to counter the grasshopper menace in 1902 and was employed by the government to demonstrate its use to farmers. He became entomological field officer for Manitoba in 1913 and was appointed provincial entomologist in 1919. He was an expert on grasshoppers. He received an honorary diploma from the Manitoba Agricultural College and is a member of the Manitoba Agricultural Hall of Fame. See Alma Criddle, *Criddle-de-Diddle-Ensis: A Biographical History of the Criddles of Aweme, Manitoba Pioneers of the 1880's* (1973). Papers are at the PAM.

Criddle, Percy (1844-1918) Farmer, eccentric. Born in London, England, the son of a woman who was a well-known painter, he was educated at the University of Heidelberg and trained in music. Inept in business, he immigrated to Manitoba with his families (an English wife and a German mistress, plus two sets of children) in 1882, homesteading at Aweme. Criddle spent the remainder of his life farming in Manitoba, although a large number of children gradually enabled him to devote most of his time to more gentlemanly pursuits, such as organ playing, composing, and amateur science. For 35 years he was a self-conscious diarist, and his diary is one of the most revealing documents of the pioneering period in Manitoba. See the family biography by Alma Criddle noted above. Criddle's correspondence and diaries are in the PAM.

Criddle, Stuart (1877-1971) Farmer, gardener. Born in England, he immigrated with his family to Manitoba in 1882. He was educated at home, and he worked on the family farm. He enlisted in the 79th Regiment in 1916, returning to the farm in 1919. An active gardener, he developed one officially recognized strain of lily, *Lilium stuart criddlei*. He was appointed honorary game guardian in the 1930s, serving until his move to Sidney, British Columbia, in 1960.

Cripps, Eleanor Eliza See Kennedy, Eleanor E. (Cripps).

Crisp, Annie See Bond, Annie (Crisp).

Croft, James (1884-1968) Luthier. Born in Maidenhead, Berkshire, England, he came to Winnipeg in 1904 as an engineer. By 1915 he had moved into violin repairing, establishing an international reputation for his work. In 1926 he and his son opened Croft Music, which in 1927 became representative for W.E. Hill & Sons of London. The shop came to carry an extensive collection of musical instruments and classical sheet music. He retired in 1965 and died in Winnipeg.

Crofton, John Ffolliott (1800-1885) Soldier. Born in Dublin, Ireland, he was educated at Trinity College there. He served in the British army in Cape of Good Hope, India, and Aden before being sent as a lieutenant-colonel to command a detachment of troops in Red River in 1845. He and the troops arrived after the Oregon emergency for which they had been sent was settled, and he despised the local society as full of "vulgar and ill-bred folk." He left in 1847, subsequently defending the HBC against a petition of grievance presented by Alexander Kennedy Isbister* and then before the parliamentary inquiry of 1857. He was promoted to the rank of general in 1877 and died in London. *DCB* XI, 219-20. His diary 1846-47 is on microfilm at the PAM and in typescript at the Winnipeg Public Library.

Crossin, Albert L. (1868-1956) Chartered accountant. Born in Waterloo, Ontario, he moved to Winnipeg from Toronto to open a branch of the Toronto General Trust Corporation. He was a member of the Institute of Chartered Accountants. In 1918 he was a member of the Citizens' Committee of 100 that negotiated directly with the Winnipeg civic workers who were on strike. He was chair of the Citizens' Committee of 1,000 in 1919.

Crowe, George Reading (1852-1924) Grain dealer. Born in Old Barnes, Nova Scotia, he was educated in Clifton, Nova Scotia. He took a business course in Halifax and came to Winnipeg in 1879. He built the CPR around Kenora, Ontario. He was a leader of the Westminster Presbyterian Church and chair of the board of management of Manitoba College. From 1890 to 1920 he served as a grain trader. Crowe served on the Winnipeg City Council in 1885, 1912, and 1916. He was a founder of the Winnipeg Grain Exchange and was regarded as the dean of Winnipeg grain dealers.

Crowe, Harry Sherman (1922-1981) Educator. He was educated at United College (1942) and served

as a captain in the Canadian army during WWII. He finished a fifth year at the University of Manitoba (1947), and received an MA from the University of Toronto (1948) and Columbia University (1951). In 1950 he was hired as assistant professor of history at United College (now the University of Winnipeg). He was dismissed summarily by the College president, W.H. Lockhart,* in 1958, thus demonstrating the fragility of tenure at Canadian universities. The result was an invigoration of the Canadian Association of University Teachers to fight his case. From 1959 to 1966 Crowe served as director of research for the Canadian Brotherhood of Railway, Transport and General Workers, as research associate for the royal commission on bilingualism and biculturalism, and as press agent and political adviser to NDP leader Tommy Douglas. From 1966 he was professor and chair of history at Atkinson College, Toronto, stepping down as chair in 1969 to become dean from 1969 to 1974, and again from 1979 to 1981. See Canadian Association of University Teachers, "Report on the Crowe Case," *CAUT Bulletin,* 7:3 (1959).

Crummy, Eber (1861-1939) Cleric. Born in Frankville, Canada, he was educated at the University of Toronto and was ordained in 1887. He taught in Japan for eight years, returning to study philosophy at Queen's University. He came to Winnipeg in 1909 to become pastor of Grace Methodist Church, leaving for Vancouver in 1913. He returned to Winnipeg as principal of Wesley College from 1915 to 1917. He left Winnipeg again and returned in 1923 to serve as pastor of Maryland Methodist Church. He retired to Victoria in 1931 and died there.

Cumming, Cuthbert (1787-1870) Fur trader. Born in Banffshire, Scotland, Cumming joined the NWC as a clerk at Fort Dauphin in 1804. He remained at Swan River until 1828, surviving the merger of the NWC and HBC in 1821. He was promoted to chief trader in 1827, then transferred to the Montreal Department in 1828. He was not happy dealing with the timber trade and was pleased to return to the fur trade on the north shore of the Gulf of St. Lawrence in 1833 and then the north shore of Lake Superior in 1841. In 1843 he returned to Swan River, but he had difficulty adjusting to the new conditions in the fur trade and soon retired to Colborne in Canada. *DCB* IX, 169-70.

Cunningham, James (1823-1915) Politician. Born at Fort Churchill, he married a daughter of Alexander Ross* and moved to Kildonan, then to Headingley, and then Poplar Point. In 1870 he represented Headingley in the Manitoba legislature.

Cunningham, Patrick (c. 1789-1831) Early settler. Born in Calry, Sligo, Ireland, he joined the HBC as a labourer in 1812 and sailed aboard the *Robert Taylor* with Owen Keveny. He served in the East Winnipeg District in 1812-13 and in Swan River in 1813-14 before heading further west. He drowned in the Severn River.

Cunningham, Robert (1836-1874) Journalist, politician. Born in Ayrshire, Scotland, he was educated at Glasgow College and the University of London. Cunningham immigrated to Canada in 1868 and was sent west in 1869 as a special correspondent for the *Toronto Globe* and *Toronto Telegraph* to cover the Red River troubles. He was expelled from the settlement by Louis Riel shortly after his arrival, however. Nonetheless, after Manitoba became a province in 1870, Cunningham started the *Manitoban* with William Coldwell.* He was elected Liberal MP for Marquette in 1872, supported by Louis Riel. In Ottawa, Cunningham spoke consistently on behalf of the Métis community, supporting a general amnesty and the settlement of Manitoba land claims. He remained unenthusiastically with the Liberals after his re-election in 1874. Cunningham was appointed to the Council of the North-West Territories in 1874 but died suddenly in St. Paul, Minnesota, on his way back to Red River. *DCB* X, 210-11. His papers are at the PAM.

Currie, Andrew (1911-1990) Athlete, civil servant. Born in Brandon, he graduated from the University of Manitoba and taught at St. John's College School before serving overseas with the Royal Canadian Army Service Corps, being awarded the Order of the British Empire. A football player, he played for the Saskatchewan Roughriders in 1928 and competed in the Grey Cup in 1928, 1930, and 1933. He coached Daniel McIntyre Collegiate to four straight Winnipeg football championships after WWII. From 1957 to 1970 he was supervisor of officiating for the Western Conference of the CFL. After many years as director of physical education for Winnipeg (1951-57) and Manitoba (1957-61) and a period as director of parks for Greater Winnipeg (1961-71), he served as Manitoba deputy minister of urban affairs from 1971 to 1976. He died in Winnipeg.

Currie (Curry), Duncan Steele (1849-1925) Police officer, surveyor, financier. Born in Sydney, Nova Scotia, he was educated in private schools there. He joined the NWMP at an early age, coming to Winnipeg with the second contingent of Mounties in 1874. He worked on the Dominion survey until 1883. He then became the City of Winnipeg's auditor and comptroller, moving on to become a major organizer of complex financial and real estate transactions. In 1910 the *Winnipeg Telegram* listed him as one of the city's 19 millionaires. He retired to San Diego, California, in 1907 and died there.

Cyr, Joseph-Ernst (1854-1929) Teacher, journalist, politician. Cyr was a resident of St. Boniface, where he was a notary public. He was also police magistrate of St. Boniface, MLA for St. Boniface from 1883 to 1888, mayor of St. Boniface in 1885, MP for Provencher from 1904 to 1908, and superintendent of Dominion works for Manitoba in 1910.

Dafoe, Elizabeth (1900-1960) Librarian. The daughter of John W. Dafoe,* she was born in Montreal and moved to Winnipeg in 1901 with her family. She took her BA at the University of Manitoba in 1923 and studied library science in the United States at Columbia University and the University of Chicago. She became chief librarian at the University of Manitoba Library in 1937 and served until her death. She helped form both the Manitoba and the Canadian Library Associations and served as president of each. She was a member of the National Library Committee in 1948 and of the council of the American Library Association from 1949 to 1954. The main library at the University of Manitoba was named after her.

Dafoe, John Wesley (1866-1944) Journalist. Born in Combermere, Canada, Dafoe attended high school before beginning a journalistic career with the *Montreal Daily Star* in 1883. Converted to the merits of the Liberal Party, he edited the *Ottawa Journal* in 1885 and a year later joined the *Manitoba Free Press*. Following another sojourn in Montreal journalism, he returned to Winnipeg to edit Clifford Sifton's* *Free Press* in 1901, holding the position until his death. Dafoe made his newspaper the voice of Prairie Liberalism as well as an international newspaper of record. He combined an advocacy of western issues (lower tariffs, lower freight rates, provincial control of natural resources) with an international perspective that favoured the Commonwealth and the League of Nations. Dafoe helped found the Canadian Institute of International Affairs, and he was highly critical in the late 1930s of Mackenzie King's diffident foreign policy. He was a member of the Rowell-Sirois Commission on Dominion-provincial relations and from 1934 to 1944 was chancellor of the University of Manitoba. His books include *Laurier: A Study in Politics* (1922) and *Clifford Sifton in Relation to His Times* (1931). The best study is Ramsay Cook, *The Politics of J.W. Dafoe and the* Free Press (1963), but see also Murray Donnelly, *Dafoe of the* Free Press (1968). His papers are at the UML Archives and the PAM.

Dahl, Peter Martin (1869-1944) Publisher. Born in Truendalga, Norway, he moved to Sweden and then, in 1902, to Canada. In 1910 he founded *Norrona*, and later he took over the *Swedish Canada News*. Both were published in Winnipeg. He died in Winnipeg.

Dailley, Gordon Debenham ("Don," 1912-1989) Athlete, soldier. Born in Winnipeg, he graduated from the University of Manitoba and went to work in England, where he captained the British hockey team to the Olympic championship in 1936. He joined the Canadian army during WWII, rising to colonel by the time of his retirement in 1964. In 1968 he founded a Safari and Game Farm in Ontario, which nurtured over 700 species of wild animals. Dailley was active in Oxfam and various international-affairs organizations.

Dale, Arch(ie) (1882-1962) Cartoonist. Born in Aberdeen, Scotland, he began as a professional cartoonist at age 17, working on the *Glasgow News* and the *London Comic Cuts and Funny Wonders*. He came to Canada to homestead, but failed. He then joined the *Manitoba Free Press*. From 1921 to 1927 he worked in Chicago, but then he returned to the *Free Press* as staff cartoonist until his retirement in 1954. Dale's best work was done during the Depression. He was particularly hard on R.B. Bennett and William Aberhart. He seldom satirized W.L.M. King, whom he much admired.

Dallas, Alexander Grant (1816-1882) Colonial governor. Like James Douglas of British Columbia, Dallas was born in Berbice, Guyana. He went from there to Scotland with his family, spent some time in China, and in 1857 was sent by the HBC to investigate the Company's Western Department. Present during the Fraser River gold rush, Dallas fought with Douglas over land policy and was named by the HBC to succeed Douglas when he was appointed to the governorship of British Columbia on condition that he sever his ties with the Company. Douglas refused to give up his place with the HBC and had to be forced to transfer authority. In 1861 Dallas was appointed successor to Sir George Simpson,* and he arrived in Upper Fort Garry in May 1862. During his term as president of Council and governor-in-chief of Rupert's Land, he warned the Company of the need for better local government. He retired in 1864 to Scotland. He was the author of *San Juan, Alaska, and the North-West Country* (1873). See B.A. McKelvie, "Successor to Simpson," *The Beaver* (Sept. 1951): 41-45. *DCB* XI, 230-31.

Daly, Thomas Mayne (1852-1911) Lawyer, politician, judge. Born in Canada, his parents were prominent local figures. He was educated at Upper Canada College, was called to the bar of Ontario in 1876, and practised law in Stratford until he moved west to Brandon, Manitoba, in 1881, where he became the community's first legal practitioner. When the railroad arrived in 1882 to transform Brandon, he became its first mayor. He subsequently served as President of the Conservative Party of the Brandon electoral division and was elected to Parliament from the riding of Selkirk in 1887. He won again in 1891, beating Joseph Martin,* the author of the Manitoba School Act. A year later he became minister of the interior and superintendent-general of Indian Affairs,

his portfolio responsible for federal immigration and settlement. He strongly supported western settlement, and introduced in 1893 the North West Immigration Act. A supporter of Mackenzie Bowell, he was left out of the cabinet in the reshuffle that accompanied Charles Tupper's assumption of the prime minister's position in 1896. Rather than run in the 1896 election, he moved briefly to Rossland, B.C. He soon returned to Manitoba, settling in Winnipeg and becoming police magistrate in 1904. He wrote *The Canadian Spirit of the Northwest* (1907), *Canadian Criminal Procedure* (1911), and *The Magistrate's Manual* (1911). He ran for Parliament once more as Conservative candidate for Brandon in 1908, but lost to Clifford Sifton* and the Liberals by 69 votes. In 1909 he became Canada's first juvenile court judge. He was a prominent Anglican, a member of St. Luke's Church and of the advisory board of St. John's College. He died in Winnipeg. *DCB* XIV, 265-66.

Daman, Peter (1896-1953) Gardener. Born in Amsterdam, Holland, he came to Canada with his parents in 1910. He moved to Winnipeg in 1918, acquiring his own property on Frobisher Road in St. Vital, which he used as a market garden. He was very active in the Winnipeg Gardeners' Co-operative, helping during WWII to form the first marketing pool in Manitoba, which registered the "Peak of the Market" brand. He was a member of the Wartime Prices and Trade Board. He and his wife were named "Mr. and Mrs. Canada No. 6" in 1946 by the *Montreal Standard*. He also served as chair of the St. Vital school board.

Darrell, Hubert (c. 1875-1910) Trapper, explorer. Born in the south of England, he came to his elder brother's farm at Birtle, Manitoba, in 1891. In 1897 he went off to the Klondike, falling in love with the land and becoming an expert hunter and trapper, well known to local Native peoples and famous for his ability to survive in the wilderness. By 1901 the explorer David Hanbury had hired him as an assistant on a lengthy journey west of Hudson Bay. He returned to Birtle for a spell in 1902, marrying schoolteacher Agnes Dudley, who refused to follow him into the North. Distinguished Arctic explorers often praised him and tried to involve him in their expeditions. He sometimes joined and was often critical of their efforts. From 1906 to 1910 he was a special constable of the RNWMP. He disappeared while on an exploring and prospecting trip in 1910.

His journals and papers are in the Scott Polar Research Institute, Cambridge, England. *DCB* XIII, 238-40.

Darveau, Jean-Édouard (1816-1844) Cleric. Born at Quebec, he studied at the Petit Séminaire de Québec and subsequently became a sailor. He returned to Quebec in 1838 to study for the priesthood. Soon after his ordination he headed for Red River, where he learned Ojibwa with Father Belcourt.* Beginning in 1842 he made lengthy missionary trips into what is now northern Manitoba, meeting much opposition from rival Anglicans, especially Henry Budd.* He died in 1844, rumours circulating that he had been murdered by Indians who saw him as a *windigo. DCB* VII, 231-33.

Davidson, John (fl. c. 1850) Cook. An Orkneyman, Davidson was serving as mess steward (cook) at Fort Garry at the time of the Ballenden affair. He and his wife were included in the suit for defamation by Captain Christopher Foss* — to prevent their appearing as witnesses, Letitia Hargrave* claimed. The damages of £100 against the Davidsons awarded by the jury to Captain Foss were publicly forgiven by him.

Davidson, John Andrew (1852-1903) Merchant, politician, sportsman. Born in Thamesford, Canada, he came to Palestine (now Gladstone), Manitoba, in 1871, opening a store in 1873. He was secretary of the Palestine Baseball Club. He later moved to Beautiful Plains, where in partnership with Jonathan Joseph Hamilton he established the town of Neepawa, building a store, hotel, flour mill, and blacksmith shop to start it in business. They later added a real estate agency. Davidson was an early mayor and was president of Neepawa Mining as well as the Register Printing Company. He also helped establish the Neepawa Curling Club. He was elected to the Manitoba legislature as a Conservative from Dauphin in 1881 and re-elected in 1883. He was defeated in the Beautiful Plains riding in 1886 and 1887 but won it by a slender margin in 1892. In 1900 he became provincial treasurer and minister of agriculture and immigration despite not sitting in the Assembly, and he remained provincial treasurer until his death in Neepawa. A special train ran to Neepawa from Winnipeg for his funeral, conducted with full Masonic ritual. *DCB* XIII, 242-44.

Davidson, John Ralston ("Ral," 1870-1948) Physician, athlete. Born in St. Philippe d'Argenteuil,

Quebec, he moved with his family to Manitou, Manitoba, in 1878. He was educated at Manitoba College, where he received his BA in 1893, and the Manitoba Medical College, where he earned his MD in 1896. He was a keen athlete in track, soccer, lacrosse, hockey, and curling, and was named best all-round athlete at Manitoba College in 1892. After studying at Johns Hopkins University he returned to practise medicine in Winnipeg. He was appointed to the Faculty of Medicine in 1904, serving until 1933. Davidson was responsible for the development of a highly controversial treatment for cancer involving a high-vitamin diet, which was the subject of a House of Commons debate in 1944. His treatment was subsequently investigated by a four-man medical commission appointed by the province later in 1944, which discounted its efficacy. MLA Lewis St. George Stubbs* took up Davidson's case in the Manitoba legislature, lambasting the commission for its procedures. Davidson died in the St. Boniface Hospital. See Gurney Bishop, *Davidson of Manitoba* (1974).

Davies, Gwendda (1896-1988) Musician, teacher. Born Dorothy Owen in Wickham Market, England, she was an early gold medallist in advanced piano who subsequently performed at Queen's Hall in London. She came to Manitoba in 1923 to teach at Rupertsland College and decided to remain to teach piano. She studied with Nadia Boulanger in 1930. She accompanied many singers and choirs over the years and occasionally performed as soloist with musical aggregations such as the CBC Winnipeg Orchestra. She died in Winnipeg.

Davis, Angela Elizabeth (Pizzey) (1926-1994) Art historian. Born in London, England, she trained as a nurse at King's College Hospital before immigrating to Canada with her husband in 1951. She started painting while raising her family. She graduated from the University of Winnipeg in 1977, received an MA there in 1979, and was awarded a PhD in history from the University of Manitoba in 1987. In 1980 she co-founded the Osborne Gallery in Winnipeg. Davis wrote and taught extensively on Canadian art history. Her publications included *Art and Work: A Social History of Labour in the Canadian Graphic Art Industry to the 1940s* (1994) and several studies of Mary Riter Hamilton.*

Davis, Matilda (c. 1820-1873) Educator. Born in St. Andrews, Red River, she was educated in England before becoming a teacher at a young ladies' school begun in the settlement in 1840. The school was located in St. Andrews and was quite well attended through the 1850s. *DCB* X, 215.

Davis, Robert Atkinson (1841-1903) Teacher, hotelier, politician. Born in Dudswell, Canada, he attended St. Francis College and became a schoolteacher. He and his brother spent several years after the American Civil War in the American Rockies. In 1870 he came to Winnipeg, arriving on 10 May while the provisional government was still in control of the settlement. He bought George Emmerling's* hotel, renaming it Davis House. Its saloon became the social centre of the Ontario volunteers who came with the Wolseley Expedition, and Davis was able to expand his operations to include a barbershop, billiard parlour, and store. Davis soon became a spokesman for the newcomers in the village, who struggled with the HBC for its control. In 1873 he took the lead in drafting a bill to incorporate Winnipeg. Soon afterward he became a leader of the Patrons of Husbandry, using this group's influence to gain election to the Assembly in April 1874. He soon became provincial treasurer under Premier Marc-Amable Girard* and, in the unstable political situation of the time, assumed the premiership as leader of the Ontario faction in the House of Assembly. Fluent in French, he managed to persuade the French faction that he supported French rights, and his ministry did uphold the system of dual education and maintain legislation limiting speculation in Métis lands, despite pressure to do otherwise. He lobbied successfully for the route of the transcontinental railroad to pass through Winnipeg rather than Selkirk. His government was responsible for the abolition of the Legislative Council in 1875. It also negotiated better financial terms with Ottawa. Having in 1875 married an American resident of Illinois who did not move to Manitoba, Davis joined her and their child in the United States after his retreat from politics in 1878. The couple moved to Chicago in 1880, and Davis prospered in real estate speculation. His later years were marked by scandal. He was charged with breach of promise in 1890, and he publicly separated from his wife in 1896. He died in Phoenix, Arizona. *DCB* XIII, 253-56. Some papers are at the PAM.

Dawson, Simon James (1818-1902) Surveyor, engineer, politician. Born in Redhaven, Scotland, Dawson joined his family in Nepean Township, Canada, around 1840. He obtained government appointments through the influence of his brother William. He was appointed surveyor to the Hind Expedition in 1857. In the expedition's report, he dealt at length with the western route, proposing to use navigable waters in preparation for the railway. After Confederation he was placed in charge of constructing the Canadian-financed road from Lake Superior to Lake of the Woods, with the section from there to Fort Garry under the supervision of John Allan Snow;* this road is known as the "Dawson Road." In 1870 Dawson used 1,000 men to help expedite the passage of the Wolseley Expedition. Dawson and Wolseley* disagreed over the road under construction. The engineer wanted to await its imminent completion to move men and material, while Wolseley insisted that since it was not finished, he would have to use a more difficult water-route in order to guarantee the arrival of his troops in the summer of 1870. He continued his disagreement with Wolseley in his *Report on the Red River Expedition of 1870* (1871). As a consequence of the road-building, Dawson became involved in negotiations with the Saulteaux Indians of the Lake of the Woods. His concern over government policy toward the region led him into politics, and he represented northern Ontario in the Ontario legislature from 1875 to 1878 and then in the House of Commons from 1878 to 1891. He was suspected for his Catholicism, and by 1889 was being dismissed as an "old fossil." Moreover, his support for bilingualism for the North-West Territories, for Indian fishing rights, and for Aboriginal rights generally, were not well regarded by many of his constituents. He died unmarried in Ottawa. For a biography, consult Elizabeth Arthur, *Simon J. Dawson* (1987). See also Jack Manore, "Mr. Dawson's Road," *The Beaver* 71, no. 1 (February-March 1991): 6-11.

Deacon, Lawrence Sylvester (1911-1948) Murderer. Born in England, he came to Canada with his mother in 1919. During WWII he served with the Fort Garry Horse and was wounded in France. He was arrested in 1946 and charged with the murder of a Winnipeg taxi driver. The evidence was circumstantial, and Deacon insisted that he was innocent. After two trials and despite petitions for clemency signed by over 15,000 Manitobans, he was hanged at Headingley Jail on 16 April 1948. See W.E. Morriss, *Watch the Rope* (1996).

Deacon, Thomas Russ (1865-1955) Civil engineer, businessman, municipal politician. Born in Perth, Canada, he had an elementary education, then worked in the lumber camps of Northern Ontario, returning to school at the age of 20. He ultimately enrolled at the University of Toronto, graduating with a degree in civil engineering in 1891. Deacon moved in 1892 to Rat Portage (Kenora) as manager of the Ontario Gold Concessions for the district of Rainy River, also serving as managing director and consulting engineer for the Mikado Gold Mining Company. In 1902 he migrated to Winnipeg and founded Manitoba Bridge and Iron Works with H.B. Lyall. He was on the city council in 1906 when the Shoal Lake water supply was discussed, and he promoted Shoal Lake as a source of water for Winnipeg for years thereafter. In 1913 he was elected mayor of Winnipeg on a Shoal Lake platform and he implemented the scheme. He was re-elected mayor in 1914. Deacon was always hostile to trade unions. At one point he advised the city's unemployed to "hit the trail." He opposed any limitations on immigration. In 1917 he employed a private-detective agency to supply strikebreakers from Montreal, as well as an anti-picketing injunction and a suit for damages against one of the striking unions. His tactics as employer contributed to the Winnipeg General Strike. In November of 1919, after the strike, he introduced a "Work's Council" system of employee advisory boards into his shop to forestall unionization. Deacon was often employed by labour as the classic example of the anti-union, strikebreaking Winnipeg employer. He disappeared from the public eye after 1919. There is a clipping file at the PAM.

Dease, Peter Warren (1788-1863) Fur trader, explorer. Born at Mackinac (now Michigan), he joined the XY Company in 1801 and stayed on in the NWC after their amalgamation in 1804. He served in the Athabasca Department until 1824, when he was seconded to Sir John Franklin's* Arctic expeditions of 1824-27. In 1831 he took charge of the New Caledonia District, and in 1836 he was assigned to command the HBC's Arctic exploratory expedition. His second-in-command was Thomas Simpson,* who constantly complained that Dease was indolent. Nevertheless, the expedition filled in the gaps left by Franklin and others in the survey of the Northwest Passage. Dease married his fur-trade wife at Red River on 3 August 1840 and then retired to a farm near Montreal, where he lived contentedly until his death. *DCB* IX, 196-99.

Dease, William (1827-1913) Councillor. One of his descendants later claimed that Dease's grandfather was a native of Ireland and that his mother was a French-Canadian rather than a Métisse. Throughout his life Dease was a prominent Francophone Roman Catholic mixed-blood with connections in the Anglophone community. He lived at Pointe Coupée, near present-day Ste. Agathe. As a member of the Council of Assiniboia, Dease was one of the principal Métis opponents of Louis Riel in 1869-70. He was the leading spirit behind a meeting held at the courthouse in Winnipeg on 29 July that demanded Canadian recognition of Aboriginal rights, advocating the use of force if necessary. The Francophone Métis suspected that Dease was a henchman of John Schultz,* and he never had much following in the community. In the confusing events of February 1870, Riel made an attempt to arrest Dease, who was in communication with the dissidents of Portage la Prairie. After escaping through a window of his house, Dease agreed to subscribe to an oath of allegiance.

Decoigne, François (fl. 1798-1818) Fur trader. He was born in Quebec, and he operated near Slave Lake for some time. He moved to Fort Bas-la-Rivière (Fort Alexander in modern-day Manitoba) in 1806, before returning west. In 1816 he was hired by Colin Robertson* to help re-establish the HBC's Athabasca trade, at which assignment he was moderately successful. *DCB* V, 236-37.

De Jarlis, Andrew (1914-1975) Fiddler, bandleader. Born Joseph Patrice Éphreme Desjarlais near Woodridge, Manitoba, he moved to Winnipeg in 1934 and won his first fiddling contest in 1935. He performed regularly on CJRC with his "Red River Mates" from 1937 to 1948. In the 1960s he appeared on television with Don Messer. He won BMI's first Canadian annual award in 1969. During his career he made 25 LP records, which sold over half a million copies and contained 175 original compositions, including "Manitoba Golden Boy" and "Manitoba Waltz." De Jarlis was best known for his lilting waltzes.

de Jong, Klaas (1873-1959) Horticulturalist. Born in Holland, he came to Western Canada in 1893 and eventually settled on Lot 64 in Winnipeg, on the line between East and North Kildonan, where he began market gardening. He grew tomatoes, corn, and cauliflower, winning the North American Cauliflower

Crown in 1920. He won many prizes at fairs and exhibitions. See his autobiography, *Cauliflower Crown* (1973). There are family papers at the PAM.

Dejordy de Villebon, Charles-René (1715-1761) Soldier. Born in Îles Bouchard, New France, he was sent west as an ensign in 1749. He later became the last commandant of the *poste de l'Ouest*, serving from 1758 to 1760. He was killed in a shipwreck off Cape Breton Island in 1761. *DCB* III, 170-71.

Delbridge, Laurence (1916-1989) Safety administrator. Born in Winnipeg, he graduated from the University of Manitoba in arts and served with the Canadian Artillery and Signal Corps in WWII. In 1947 he moved to Nova Scotia to become manager of the Nova Scotia Safety Council. He was instrumental in the introduction of many safety reforms in Nova Scotia, including a drivers' education program for the schools and a mandatory seat belt law.

Delorme, Pierre (1831-1912) Métis farmer, politician. Born in St. Boniface, he farmed in St. Norbert. He sat for St. Norbert South in the Manitoba legislature from 1870 to 1874, simultaneously representing Provencher in Ottawa (1871-74). He was appointed a member of the North-West Council in 1873. He became minister of agriculture in the Norquay government in 1878 but soon resigned when the Francophones broke with the premier in 1879. He died at St. Adolphe. *DCB* XIV, 280-81.

Denig, Edwin Thompson (1812-c. 1862) Fur trader. Born in Philadelphia, he became an Indian scout and fur trader on the upper Missouri River, marrying a daughter of an Assiniboine chief. He was in charge of the American Fur Company's trading post at Fort Union for years. Around 1854 he migrated to Red River and began trading on White Horse Plain. Before his death he wrote a manuscript on the Crow Indians, published in 1950 as *Five Indian Tribes of the Upper Missouri* by the United States Bureau of American Ethnology.

Denison, Frederick Charles (1846-1896) Soldier. Born in Toronto, he was educated at Upper Canada College and called to the bar in 1870. Active in the militia, he was appointed orderly officer to Colonel Wolseley* in 1869, and he accompanied the invading party to Manitoba the following spring. He remained in Manitoba as aide-de-camp to Lieutenant-Governor Adams Archibald* in 1870-71, becoming friends with John Schultz* in the process. He returned to Toronto to practise law, and in 1884 was appointed commander of the Canadian boatmen who were being recruited for the Sudan. He served in the Sudan in 1884-85 and achieved some reputation as a hero. In 1887 he ran for Parliament. *DCB* XII, 243-46.

Dennis, John Stoughton (1820-1885) Land surveyor. Born in Kingston, Upper Canada, Dennis was educated at Victoria College. He then qualified as a land surveyor. In 1869 he was sent to Red River to survey lots. He met with considerable resistance from the Métis under Louis Riel and disbanded his survey on 9 December. He fled the colony two days later with Governor William McDougall,* having failed to raise much interest among "volunteers" to fight against the Métis on behalf of the Canadian government. In 1871 he became Canada's first surveyor general and head of the Dominion Lands Branch, and in 1878 deputy minister of the interior under Sir John A. Macdonald. He succeeded in establishing the 160-acre unit for homesteads rather than the 80-acre unit preferred by Macdonald. He resigned in 1881 and was made a Companion of the Order of St. Michael and St. George in 1882. See Colin Read, "The Red River Rebellion and J.S. Dennis, 'Lieutenant and Conservator of the Peace,'" *Manitoba History,* no. 3 (spring 1982): 11-20. *DCB* XI, 244-46.

De Salaberry, Charles d'Irumberry (1820-1882) Soldier. Born in Lower Canada, the son of the victor of the battle of Chateauguay (1813), he grew up in a family of private means and public service. In 1857 he served in the Hind Expedition to Red River, in the 1860s he held militia appointments, and in 1869 he was appointed a Canadian government emissary to Red River. He was chosen because he was one of the few French Canadians known to Ottawa who had any acquaintance with the settlement. He arrived in Pembina on Christmas Eve 1869 and in Red River in early January. But because Louis Riel insisted that his instructions did not empower him (or his colleague Father Thibeault) to negotiate a deal on behalf of Canada, the provisional government ignored him. His assurances that the Canadian government would pay the expenses of delegates to Ottawa to arrange a settlement were a useful if limited contribution. So too was his training of a boys' band in St. Boniface. He returned to Ottawa with Father Joseph-Noel Ritchot,* whom he introduced to George-Étienne Cartier* and Joseph Howe.* In later years he superintended woods and forests in the Montreal region. *DCB* XI, 441-42.

Desmarais, Francis (fl. c. 1867) Murderer. A mixed-blood connected with the Sioux, he was tried in 1867 for disembowelling a Saulteaux warrior in the HBC store at Red River. According to Walter Traill, who was present at the time, the warrior was sporting a scalping knife with a fresh Sioux scalp dangling from it. Desmarais came up behind him, seized the knife, and "cut him open to the waist so swiftly that [the] clerk did not see what had happened." Although found guilty of murder and sentenced to hang, he was eventually allowed to be transported out of the settlement.

Dexter, Alexander Grant (1896-1961) Journalist. Born in St. Andrews, he joined the *Free Press* in 1912 and served in Lord Strathcona's Horse from 1915 until he was invalided to England in 1917. He was an emphatic Liberal, completely loyal to the party. For many years (1923-44) he was parliamentary reporter in Ottawa for John Dafoe's* *Free Press*. During WWII he served as a private conduit for the government to Dafoe. He served as associate editor of the *Free Press* from 1946 to 1948, then as editor from 1948 to 1954. He received the Marie Moors Cabot Medal for journalism — the first Canadian so honoured — in 1946. See Allan Levine, "A Gentleman of the Fourth Estate," *The Beaver* 72, no. 6 (1992/1993): 17-23; Frederick W. Gibson and Barbara Robertson, eds., *Ottawa at War: The Grant Dexter Memoranda, 1939-1945* (1994). Some papers are at the PAM.

d'Iberville, Pierre Le Moyne See Iberville, Pierre Le Moyne, Sieur d'.

Dickens, Francis Jeffrey (1844-1886) Police officer. He was born in London, England, the son of Charles Dickens. After desultory employment in journalism he obtained a commission in the Bengal Mounted Police and served for years in India. In 1874, his inheritance dissipated, his sister got him an appointment with the NWMP. He first served at Dufferin, Manitoba, but then moved further west. He was not a very successful officer. He had a brief encounter with battle in the 1885 North-West Rebellion and left the force in 1886, dying shortly thereafter in the United States. See Vernon LaChance, ed., *Diary of Francis Dickens* (1930). *DCB* XI, 261-62.

Dickson, (Robert) Brian (1916-1998) Judge. Born in Yorkton, Saskatchewan, Dickson attended the University of Manitoba law school and in 1940 was called to the Manitoba bar. During WWII he served with the Royal Canadian Artillery, losing a leg. After the war he lectured in law at the University of Manitoba and practised law at the firm of Aikins and MacAuley until his appointment to the Manitoba Court of Queen's Bench in 1963. In 1950 he headed the Red Cross relief operation during the catastrophic flood. He served as chair of the University of Manitoba's board of governors in the mid-1960s. He joined the Manitoba Court of Appeal in 1967 and the Canadian Supreme Court in 1973, serving as chief justice from 1984 to 1990. In the 1970s he, Bora Laskin, and Wishart Spence were a liberal force on the Supreme Court, often called "LSD" by the press. Dickson was a supporter of individual and collective rights, both before and after the Charter of Rights of 1982. He chaired several royal commissions. In 1991 he became a Companion of the Order of Canada. He died near Ottawa.

Dickson, James (fl. 1835-37) Soldier of fortune. Dickson appeared out of nowhere at the end of 1835, having spent some time in Texas. George Simpson* described his face as "covered with huge whiskers and mustachios and seamed with sabre wounds." By 1836 he talked of creating an independent Indian state encompassing most of the western part of the continent. He recruited about 60 men around New York, and some Canadian leaders, many of whom had considerable experience in the fur trade. This expedition headed west for Red River, where it fizzled out under the confusion of Dickson's plans, leaving behind only a folk memory of potential "liberation." Dickson himself disappeared across the border in 1837. See Grace Nute, ed., "Documents Relating to James Dickson's Expedition," *Mississippi Valley Historical Review* 10 (1923-24): 173-81; "The Diary of Martin McLeod," *Minnesota Historical Bulletin* 4 (1921-22): 351-439; M.E. Arthur, "General Dickson and the Indian Liberating Army in the North," *Ontario History* 62 (1970): 151-62. *DCB* VII, 249-50.

DiCosimo, Silvio Jack (1908-1960) Boxer, restaurateur. Born in Winnipeg, he boxed professionally as a youth. He later founded DiCosimo's Chicken Inn in 1942, one of the first fast-food restaurants in the city and an important youth hangout. He was an active Catholic layman.

Dingwall, Donald Ross (1853-1913) Jeweller. Born in Scotland, he came to Canada as a young man and established a jewellery business in Winnipeg in 1882. He donated the Dingwall Trophy, the grand challenge prize of the Manitoba bonspiel.

Dixon, Frederick John (1881-1931) Gardener, politician, journalist. Born in Englefield, England, he apprenticed as a gardener and came in 1903 to Winnipeg, where he trained as a draftsman and worked for the Bemis Bag Company as an engraver. Although a social reformer, Dixon was highly critical of socialism because collective ownership would mean tyranny over the individual, whose rights he always held to be paramount. He was active in the direct legislation movement and the political equality movement, and was a supporter of Henry George. Dixon was elected to the Manitoba legislature in 1915 as a labour member for Centre Winnipeg, his platform including direct legislation (initiative, referendum, recall), home rule for Winnipeg, women's suffrage, public ownership of public utilities, opposition to subsidies for private enterprise, and a referendum on temperance. In the legislature, Dixon forced an investigation into the corrupt relationship between the construction firm that was erecting the Manitoba legislative building and the government of Sir Rodmond Roblin,* which led to Roblin's resignation as premier. Dixon became the first president of the Dominion Labor Party. A committed pacifist, in 1917 he addressed a meeting in Market Square, urging listeners to burn their registration cards and resist conscription. During the Winnipeg General Strike he published the *Western Star and Enlightener* after the *Strike Bulletin* was suppressed. Tried for seditious libel early in 1920, Dixon defended himself and was found innocent on all charges. He was elected to the Manitoba legislature as a labour candidate in 1920 and was chosen Independent Labor Party leader of the House. He retired in 1923 because of ill health and died of cancer. See Allen Mills, "Single Tax, Socialism and the Independent Labor Party of Manitoba: The Political Ideas of F.J. Dixon and S.J. Farmer," *Labour/Le Travail* 5 (spring 1980): 33-54; Duncan Norman Irvine, "Reform, War, and the Industrial Crisis in Manitoba: F.J. Dixon and the Framework of Consensus" (MA thesis, University of Manitoba, 1981); Harry and Mildred Gutkin, *Profiles in Dissent: The Shaping of Radical Thought in the Canadian West* (1997), 7-50. There are papers at the PAM.

Dobbs, Arthur (1689-1765) Colonial official. Born in County Antrim, Ireland, to Anglo-Irish parents, he entered the House of Commons of the Irish Parliament in 1727. While there, he investigated the political economy of Ireland, publishing his *Essay on the Trade and Improvement of Ireland* (1729). Around 1730 he became fascinated by the problem of the Northwest Passage, and a year later he laid his notes on all the voyages that had sought this passage before the HBC and the Admiralty. The result was an expedition led by Christopher Middleton,* which found nothing. Dobbs accused Middleton of falsification, and the two engaged in a pamphlet controversy for years. In 1744 Dobbs produced *An Account of the Countries Adjoining to Hudson's Bay,* which extolled the virtues of the region and criticized the HBC for its stewardship of it. In 1754 he was chosen governor of North Carolina, and he served with vigour until his death.

Doern, Russell ("Russ," 1935-1987) Politician. Born in Winnipeg, he was educated at Isaac Newton High School, United College, and the University of Manitoba. In 1955 he came second in Canada in the shot put and discus at the Junior Canadian Track and Field Competitions. From 1959 to 1966 he taught English and history in various Winnipeg high schools. In 1966 he was first elected to the Manitoba legislature as an NDP member for Elmwood, being re-elected in 1969, 1973, 1977, and 1981. In the House he served as Deputy Speaker in 1969-70, and he was minister of public works in the Schreyer government from 1972 to 1977. He resigned from the NDP in 1984 over his disagreement with the party's language policy. Doern published two books: *Wednesdays are Cabinet Days: A Personal History of the Schreyer Administration* (1981) and *The Battle over Bilingualism: The Manitoba Language Question 1983-1985* (1985). He committed suicide in Emerson, Manitoba. His papers (1965-86) are at the PAM.

Dolin, Mary Beth (Brugger) (1936-1985) Teacher, politician. Born in Fond du Lac, Wisconsin, Dolin was educated at Webster College (St. Louis, Missouri) before immigrating to Canada with her husband and family in 1968. She taught at Island Lake and Hodgson before moving to the Seven Oaks School Division in 1974 as a junior-high teacher of music and drama. She had been promoted to vice-principal at the time of her election as MLA for Kildonan in 1981. She served as minister of labour, minister of urban affairs, and minister responsible for the status of women in the NDP government from 1982 to 1985. She initiated pioneering reforms to pension legislation for women and reforms to labour legislation. Stricken with breast cancer at the start of her 1985 election campaign, she succumbed to the disease on 6 April 1985. Her papers (restricted access) are at the PAM. Dolin was known by other married names: Higgins (1957-66) and Andrus (1966-79). See the forthcoming biography by Jill Mayer.

Donkin, John George (1853-1890) Soldier. Born in Morpeth, England, he studied medicine and then tried journalism before joining the army. He immigrated to Manitoba in 1884 with no firm plans, soon joining the RNWMP, in which he served until 1888. He then returned to England and wrote about his experiences in *Trooper and Redskin in the Far North* (1889). He died in England from alcohol abuse shortly after the publication of his book. *DCB* XI, 266-67.

D'Orsonnens, Proteus (1781-c. 1834) Soldier. Born in Fribourg, Switzerland, D'Orsonnens joined the Regiment de Meuron in 1801, advancing to lieutenant in 1803 and to captain in 1814. He married in Montreal and returned there in 1817. He was hired by Lord Selkirk* to accompany Selkirk's party on the journey to Red River in 1816. Late that year he led a party of Meurons to Lac la Pluie. D'Orsonnens was praised by William Coltman* for successful exertions to prevent bloodshed on several occasions.

Douglas, Alexander J. (1874-1940) Health officer. Born in Erkfrid, Ontario, he attended McGill University and the University of Manitoba, receiving a medical education. He took up general practice in Winnipeg in 1899 and become the first full-time head of the Winnipeg Department of Health in 1900, serving for 40 years. Douglas was responsible for introducing many health services, including free vaccination for children, diphtheria immunization, and milk depots for babies' milk. Douglas faced several serious epidemics in his early years, including several smallpox outbreaks, and a major typhoid epidemic which saw 1,605 cases, and 138 deaths, in 1905 alone. Not surprisingly, he was an advocate of an improved water supply to prevent disease, especially typhoid, and he mounted a campaign for milk pasteurization.

Douglas, Charles S. (1852-1917) Journalist. Born in Wisconsin, he came in 1877 to Fort William, where he published a newspaper. A year later he moved to Emerson, where he established the *International* newspaper. He was American vice-consul at Emerson and was elected as Emerson representative to the Legislative Assembly of Manitoba in 1883 and 1886. He later became mayor of Vancouver, where he died.

Douglas, Jean (Wedderburn) (1786-1871) Administrator. A daughter of James Wedderburn of Ochiltree, she married Thomas Douglas, Fifth Earl of Selkirk,* in 1807 and accompanied him to Canada in 1815. Lady Selkirk stayed behind in Montreal to look after business and legal details after her husband returned to England in 1819 for the sake of his health. After his death she remained involved with affairs of the Red River Colony, spending much time in the 1820s attempting to facilitate the success of the Buffalo Wool Company.

Douglas, Margaret Ellen (d. 1950) Physician. Born in New Brunswick, she studied medicine at the Ontario Medical College for Women and the University of Toronto. In 1907 she became house physician in the New York Infirmary for Women and Children, and in 1909 she came to Winnipeg, where she became medical examiner for the Manitoba Government Telephone Company and attending physician to the Children's Aid Society. She organized the Women's Volunteer Reserve Corps in Winnipeg during WWI and was decorated several times. She served as treasurer of the University Women's Club of Winnipeg and was later president of the Canadian Federation of Business and Professional Clubs.

Douglas, Thomas, Fifth Earl of Selkirk (1771-1820) Philanthropist. The youngest son in a large Scottish aristocratic family, he was not expected to inherit the title. He pursued an education at the University of Edinburgh and travelled in Europe during the early years of the French Revolution. In 1799 he inherited not only his title but a large landed property which had been greatly enhanced in value through improvement. He turned his attention to experimental philanthropy, attempting to convince the British government to support his plan of settling rebellious Irish (later evicted Highlanders) in British North America. In 1803-4 he travelled to North America with a party of Highlanders whom he settled on Prince Edward Island; another group was sent to Upper Canada. These ventures led to his book *Observations on the Present State of the Highlands of Scotland* (1805), which advocated colonial settlement as a way of dealing with dispossessed agrarian peoples from the British Isles. Beginning in 1808 he and his family obtained effective control of the HBC, which Selkirk would later use as a basis for extending his colonization schemes. In 1811 the Company granted him 116,000 square miles in return for his commitment to found an agricultural settlement at Red River and to provide servants for the fur trade. The first party of settlers was sent in 1811, arriving at the Forks in 1812. Selkirk's settlement was plagued with difficulty from the outset. It was opposed by the rival NWC, which had the support of the administrations in Upper and Lower Canada as well as the ear of the British colonial secretary of the time, who had little enthusiasm for colonizing in distant parts. Selkirk lost all his credibility in 1816 when he personally led a private army into Fort William and purchased all the furs stored there from one of the NWC's partners. As well, he refused to honour Canadian warrants for his arrest. After visiting Red River in 1817, he returned to Canada via the United States and spent several years defending his position, without much success. By then dying of consumption (which had apparently been in remission during his years of activity), he returned to Britain in late 1818. He died at Pau, France, in 1820. As a product of the "Scottish Enlightenment," Selkirk always believed that it was possible to combine private self-interest with public-spirited enterprise. His critics in Britain and America were less certain. For a biography, see John Morgan Gray, *Lord Selkirk of Red River* (1963). See also J.M. Bumsted, ed., *The Papers of Lord Selkirk*, 2 vols. (1984, 1988). *DCB* V, 264-69.

Doupe, Joseph (1910-1966) Surgeon. Born in Winnipeg, he graduated from the University of Manitoba in 1934, then studied in England and, in 1936, became a member of the Royal College of Surgeons. Two years later he was appointed a fellow at the Banting Institute in Toronto. He served in the Royal Medical Corps during WWII, then became director of the medical research department of the University of Manitoba in 1946 and head of physiology in 1948. He was internationally noted for his research on nerve conduction. Family papers are at the PAM.

Drever, William (1800-1884) Merchant. Born in Kirkwall, Orkney Islands, Drever came to Hudson Bay in 1821. In 1843 he married Helen Rothney (d. 1866), who came to Red River as a governess to the Thom children in 1839, and before the marriage he became involved in Rothney's litigation with Adam Thom.* Drever was one of the earliest inhabitants of Winnipeg, settling in 1851 (some accounts say 1849). He owned a general goods store near the site of Portage and Main.

Drever, William (the Younger) (fl. 1870) Buffalo hunter. He was generally regarded by Louis Riel as a spy, and he helped some of Riel's prisoners escape from Fort Garry during the Red River Rebellion. He accompanied Captain William Butler* back to Fort Garry by steamer in the summer of 1870. Walter Traill described him as very dark-complexioned and endowed with Scottish traits and wisdom "to which he has added the plains crafts of his Indian and native friends."

Drewry, Edward L. ("E.L.," 1851-1940) Brewer. Born in London, England, he moved with his parents to St. Paul, Minnesota, in 1860. In 1875 he brought his family to Pembina, North Dakota and they settled in Winnipeg in May 1877. He took over the Herchmer and Batkin Brewery, which was idle, and operated it until he sold out in 1924. Along with the brewery he assumed possession of the home connected with it, Redwood, which had been built in 1857 by William Inkster.* He was a member of city council in 1883-84, and advocated the introduction of street lighting and fire alarms. He later served as Conservative member of legislature for North Winnipeg from 1886 to 1889, and as the first chair of the parks board from 1894 to 1899. For 40 years he was a member of the board of the Winnipeg General Hospital, and he was one of the founders of Rupert's Land Ladies' College.

Drummond, Louis Henry (1848-1929) Cleric, professor. Born in Montreal, he was the son of the attorney general of Lower Canada. He was ordained a Jesuit priest and came west in 1885 as professor of philosophy and rhetoric at the Collège de Saint-Boniface. An active writer, he produced "The Catholic Element in the Northwest" in 1887. He was also a poet and playwright. He was in Montreal from 1890 until 1892, when returned to St. Boniface as chair in philosophy, English, and classics. He was later editor of the *North West Review*. He resumed parish duties after 1908.

Druxman, George (1929-1999) Athlete. Born in Winnipeg, his parents moved to Portland, Oregon, when he was four years of age. He grew up in Portland, distinguishing himself as a high-school football and baseball player before attending the University of Portland, where he played football and received a BA in 1951. After military service during the Korean War, he became a member of the Winnipeg Blue Bombers in 1955, playing for nine years until 1964. He was an all-star centre five times, and played on Grey Cup championship teams from 1958 to 1962. He was inducted into the Blue Bomber Hall of Fame in 1991 and was voted YMHA Outstanding Jewish Athlete of the Last 40 Years in 1993. After his retirement from football, he owned and operated the Pembina Hotel in Winnipeg until 1989.

Dubienski, Ian Ventress (1921-1998) Lawyer, judge. Born in Winnipeg, he graduated from the University of Manitoba law school and was called to the bar in 1947. He became a QC and a provincial magistrate in 1961, rising to chief judge of the Provincial Judges' Court (Criminal Division). Active on many national and community boards, he was chair of the first Canadian Conference on Aboriginal Justice in 1973 and the National Congress on the Prevention of Crime in 1981. He researched and wrote on crime, justice, mental health, and Aboriginal issues. He was the author of *The Police Function in Canada* (1981).

Dubuc, Anne (Henault) (1850-1928) Volunteer worker. Born in Canada, she came to Manitoba in 1872 with her husband, Joseph. She was the first president of the women's auxiliary for the hospital and orphanage at St. Boniface and was active in volunteer work throughout her life.

Dubuc, Joseph (1840-1914) Journalist, politician, lawyer. Born in Ste. Martine, Canada, he worked in the United States before attending Montreal College (where he met Louis Riel) and McGill University. Shortly after his graduation from McGill in 1869 he came to Winnipeg, joining Riel's provisional government and engaging in journalism. He sat in the first Manitoba legislature for St. Norbert and subsequently served briefly as attorney general and as Speaker. He was appointed to the Council of the North-West

Territories in 1872. He served as one of the defence counsel in the trial of Ambroise Lépine* in 1873-74. In 1878 he was elected as a Conservative from Provencher to the House of Commons. A year later he was appointed to the Manitoba Court of Queen's Bench, becoming chief justice in 1903 and retiring in 1909. He suffered heavy financial losses from land speculation after 1880. In 1912 he was the first French Canadian from Western Canada to be knighted. He died in St. Boniface. His papers are at the Archives of the Archbishop of Saint-Boniface and at the PAM. For a biography, consult Maureen McAlduff, "Joseph Dubuc: Roles and Views of a French Canadian in Early Manitoba" (MA thesis, University of Ottawa, 1967) and E. Lecompte, *Un Grand Chrétien, Sir Joseph Dubuc, 1840-1914* (1923). See also Sir Joseph Dubuc, *Autobiographie et lettres* (1888). *DCB* XIV, 313-14.

Dudley, Margaret (c. 1898-1980) Botanist, civil servant. Born near Birtle, Manitoba, she was educated at the University of Manitoba (where she earned her MSc in 1932, graduating magna cum laude) and the University of Minnesota (where she received her PhD in botany in 1935). She lectured in botany at the University of Manitoba and Brandon University, and in 1944 joined the Correspondence Branch of the Manitoba Department of Education, from which she retired in 1962. Her herbarium plants formed the basis of the collection at the Plant Sciences Building of the University of Manitoba. Papers are at the PAM.

Duffin, Simon (1843-1900) Photographer. Born in Ireland, he came to Canada at an early age. In 1872 he arrived in Manitoba, where he ran a photography business until 1888, when he became a wholesale photo supplier. *DCB* XII, 275.

Dufrost de la Jemerais, Christophe (1708-1736) Fur trader. Born in Varennes, New France, he entered the army at an early age. In 1731 he accompanied his uncle La Vérendrye* on his expedition to the "western sea," and in 1733 he reached a point near Lake Winnipeg with his cousin Gaultier.* He was sent to the Mandans on the Missouri River in 1735. In 1736 he died at Fort Maurepas on the Rivière Rouge. *DCB* II, 201-2.

Dugas, Georges (1833-1928) Cleric, historian. Born at St. Jacques de l'Achigan in Canada, Dugas was educated at Assomption College and ordained in 1862. He served as a missionary in Red River/ Manitoba from 1866 to 1888, thereafter moving to Ste. Anne des Plaines, Quebec. Dugas regarded himself as an expert on the prairie West and an eyewitness to the Red River Rebellion of 1869, about which he wrote often from the Métis perspective. His major works are *Mgr Provencher et les missions de la rivière Rouge* (1889), *L'Ouest canadien* (1896; English ed., 1905), and *L'Histoire de l'Ouest canadien de 1822 à 1869* (1906).

Dumont, Gabriel (1837-1906) Buffalo hunter, rebel, showman. Born in Red River to a leading Métis family, by the 1860s he was an important buffalo hunter whose operations were based at Fort Carlton in modern-day Saskatchewan. In 1863 he was elected leader of the hunt. Despite his later assertions, there is no contemporary evidence that he assisted Louis Riel in Red River in 1869-70. By the 1870s Dumont was an influential Métis leader in the North-West Territories, elected "president" of a body of Métis who met at St. Laurent to provide local administration for the region. Dumont took the lead in 1884 in organizing Métis resistance to the Canadian government, and he advocated the invitation to Louis Riel to lead his people. There is little evidence to support his later arguments that he wanted to be more militarily aggressive than Riel. He was wounded in late March 1885 at Duck Lake, the scene of a major Métis victory that resulted in the death of Gabriel's brother and several kinsmen. Dumont led his outnumbered Métis to another minor victory at Fish Creek, but the Canadians soon captured Batoche. Dumont headed for the United States, where he was briefly held in custody before being released. Despite his inclusion in the 1886 amnesty, Dumont joined Buffalo Bill Cody's Wild West Show as a trick-shot performer. On tour in the East, he became lionized by French Canadians as a symbol of Métis resistance, but on subsequent lecture tours he shocked audiences with his anti-clerical attitudes and criticisms. His last years were spent in obscurity. The major biography is by George Woodcock, *Gabriel Dumont: The Métis Chief and His Lost World* (1975). For an autobiography, see also Michael Barnholden, trans., *Gabriel Dumont Speaks* (1993). *DCB* XIII, 302-7.

Dumoulin, Sévère-Joseph-Nicholas (1793-1853) Cleric. Born in Lower Canada, he was ordained as a priest in 1817. A year later he and Joseph-Norbert Provencher* were sent west to minister to the settlers at Red River and especially to be missionaries to the Aboriginal population of the region. Unlike his colleagues, Dumoulin thought missionary activity among the Natives would be simplified by gathering them together into villages, and his first attempt was at Pembina, which was a success. He was recalled in 1823 because the community was south of the international boundary, and he returned east. In Lower Canada he continued to raise money for western missions and published *Notice sur les missions de la rivière Rouge* (1824). His correspondence from Red River was edited and published by G.L. Nute in *Documents Relating to Northwest Missions, 1815-1827* (1942). His papers are at the Archives of the Archbishopric of Quebec. See also J.-E. Champagne, *Les Missions catholiques dans l'Ouest canadien (1817-75)* (1949). *DCB* VIII, 249-51.

Dunbar, R.H. ("Bob," b. 1860) Curler, bartender. Born in Pictou, Nova Scotia, he came to Winnipeg in the 1870s. An outstanding athlete, he began curling before 1890. He worked as a bartender at a hotel near the Thistle Club, where he curled. He became the leading curler in Western Canada before he left for St. Paul, Minnesota, in 1905, and he was very influential for his innovations in strategy (the "takeout") and body mechanics.

Duncan, David Merritt (1870-1951) Educator. Born in Evanston, Illinois, he was educated at Galt Collegiate and the University of Toronto, earning his BA in 1894. In 1895 he was appointed classics master at Winnipeg Collegiate, and he became registrar at the University of Manitoba in 1908. In 1912 he was the first principal of Kelvin Technical High School. During WWI he served overseas with the 43rd Cameron Highlanders. He was a leading figure in the founding of the Community Chest in 1923. He served as superintendent of Winnipeg schools from 1928 to 1934. He died in Winnipeg.

Duncan, Donald Albert (1916-1944) War hero. Born in Winnipeg, he was educated at the University of Manitoba. He became a lieutenant in the Winnipeg Light Infantry in WWII, and was killed in France in 1944. A collection of his writings, much admired at the time, was published as *Some Letters and Other Writings of Donald Albert Duncan* (1945).

Durkin, Douglas Leader (1884-1968) University professor, author. Born in Ontario, he accompanied his family to Swan River, Manitoba. He received a BA at the University of Manitoba in 1908, then taught at Carman before going to teach at Brandon College and then, from 1915 to 1922, the University of Manitoba. He and Martha Ostenso* began living and working together in the early 1920s in New York. Much of the work published under her name is now regarded as being co-authored by Durkin. He wrote several novels set in Manitoba: *The Heart of Cherry McBain* (1919), *The Lobstick Trail: A Romance of Northern Manitoba* (1921), and *The Magpie* (1923). See David Arnason, "The Development of Prairie Realism" (PhD diss., University of New Brunswick, 1980).

Duthie, James (1885-1932) Farmer, livestock breeder, local politician. Born in Aberdeenshire, he came to Canada in 1880, attending the Ontario Agricultural College before moving to Hartney, Manitoba. He farmed two sections of land, one for wheat and the other for stock raising, usually running a herd of 75 Shorthorns. He received an agricultural diploma from the Manitoba Agricultural College and served on its advisory board. He was president of the Manitoba Cattle Breeders' Association, first president of the Hartney Agricultural Society, a municipal councillor and a school trustee. He is a member of the Manitoba Agricultural Hall of Fame.

DuVal, Frederick Beal (1847-1928) Cleric, social reformer. Born in Maryland, he graduated from Princeton with gold medals and prizes. He then attended a theological seminary and ministered to churches in Delaware and Ohio. In 1888 he was offered an appointment at Knox Presbyterian Church in Winnipeg, which he accepted. DuVal quickly became a leader of the national Presbyterians, eventually serving as moderator of the Presbyterian Church of Canada. He was also a staunch anti-Catholic and fervent social reformer. His principal causes were prohibition and vice. In 1903 he spearheaded a major church attack in Winnipeg on prostitution, helping the reform candidate, Thomas Sharpe,* to easily win the mayoralty election of that year. For years DuVal advocated more active law enforcement by the city police, without much visible success. See James H. Gray, *Red Lights on the Prairies* (1971).

Du Val, Paul (1893-1970) Soldier, lawyer, judge. Born in Winnipeg, he attended Central Collegiate and the University of Manitoba. He joined the Fort Garry Horse in 1914, became a second lieutenant and transferred to the Royal Flying Corps in 1917, where he was several times decorated. He graduated from University of Manitoba law school in 1921. He was president of the Manitoba Bar Association in 1944, and was appointed to the Court of Queen's Bench in 1951. From 1951 to 1956 he was chair of the University of Manitoba board of governors.

Dysart, Andrew Knox (1875-1952) Lawyer, judge. Born in Cocagne, New Brunswick, he graduated from St. Joseph's University in Memracook in 1900 and then received an LLB from Harvard. He attended Oxford and was admitted to the New Brunswick bar in 1905. He came to Winnipeg in 1906, starting the law firm of Dysart and Dysart in 1909. In 1921 he was appointed to the Court of Queen's Bench. He was the judge who sentenced Earle "Strangler" Nelson* to death. He served on many royal commissions and held an ad hoc appointment to the Canadian Supreme Court in 1935. He was chancellor of the University of Manitoba from 1934 until his death.

Dysart, Arthur Long (1886-1964) Lawyer, poet. Born in Cocagne, New Brunswick, he was a graduate of the University of New Brunswick. He worked for the *Ottawa Journal* and came to Winnipeg in 1906 to study law, becoming a partner with his brother Andrew* in the firm of Dysart and Dysart. He wrote poetry and was an expert on Robert Burns. He practised law in Winnipeg until his death. A poetry manuscript is at the PAM.

Earl, Leonard (1881-1968) Lawyer, journalist. Little is known of his early life. He was a law graduate of Wesley College, with the Governor General's Medal for highest standing. After practising law in Manitoba he turned to journalism, writing for the *Winnipeg Telegram* as early as 1908. He covered the Manitoba legislature and the House of Commons for the *Winnipeg Tribune* until his retirement in 1955. He then became a stringer for the *Financial Post* and other eastern journals. He was honorary life president of the Manitoba Press Gallery. Papers are at the PAM.

Eckhardt, Ferdinand (1902-1995) Gallery director. Born in Vienna, he studied at the University of Vienna and obtained a doctorate in art history. He moved to Berlin in 1929 as a freelance writer and worked for several years in the advertising department at Bayer IG-Farben. He was in the German army from 1942 to 1945. After WWII he developed a division of art education for the Austrian government, and in 1953 he immigrated to Canada as director of the Winnipeg Art Gallery, a post he held until his retirement in 1974. He worked hard to obtain a new building, which was finally completed in 1971. After his retirement he devoted most of his time to memorializing the career of his wife, Sonia, founding the Eckhardt-Gramatté National Music Competition for the Performance of Canadian Music in 1976 and completing her biography in 1977. In 1983 he founded the Eckhardt-Gramatté Foundation, through which the arts in Canada have been supported.

Eckhardt-Gramatté, Sophie-Carmen (Fridman) ("Sonia," 1899-1974) Musician, composer. She was born in Moscow to a musical mother, but there is some question of her paternity. She was sent as an infant to a Tolstoyan colony in the Cotswolds in England and was reunited with her mother in 1904 in Paris, where she proved a piano (and later violin) prodigy. She began a solo career at the age of 11. In 1914 she and her family moved to Berlin, where she gradually moved to composition. In 1920 she married the German painter Walter Gramatté. After moving to Spain in 1924 she worked with Pablo Casals, but she postponed her own career because of the illness of her husband, who died in 1929 of tuberculosis. She resumed performing in 1929-30 but soon gave this up in favour of composition. She married the Austrian art historian Ferdinand Eckhardt* in 1934 and moved to Vienna in 1939. When her husband became director of the Winnipeg Art Gallery in 1953, she moved to Manitoba, where she received many commissions and wrote many compositions. A contemporary described her as "friendly, volatile, restless, quick-witted, quick-tempered and altogether alive." Her compositions became simultaneously more abstract and more tempestuous over the decades. She developed her own methods for teaching and performing on both the piano and the violin. Others carried through with her plans for a competition for young artists playing contemporary composers, which was named after her. She died in Stuttgart after a fall. She was easily the most important Canadian female composer, and arguably the most important Canadian composer, of her time. See Ferdinand Eckhardt, *Music from Within* (1985); Glen B. Carruthers, "The Career and Compositions of S.C. Eckhardt-Gramatté" (MA thesis, Carleton University, 1981). The vast bulk of her compositions were published as *S.C. Eckhardt-Gramatté: Selected Works*, 23 vols. (1980-84).

Ellice, Edward (1783-1863) Merchant, politician. Born in London, England, to a Scottish merchant family that was active in the Quebec trade, he attended Winchester and graduated from Marischal College, Aberdeen, in 1800. He became head of the family business, which was international but based in North America, upon his father's death in 1805. He was known as "Bear" or "The Bear." Since one of his firms (Phyn, Ellice and Company) was a principal London agent and supplier of the NWC, Ellice tried in 1804 to buy out the HBC. When he was unsuccessful he pressed for the amalgamation of the two great fur companies, which was finally achieved in 1821. He was the lone major figure of the NWC who remained active in the affairs of the new HBC. Ellice had connections in high corners of the government — his first wife was Lady Hannah Althea Grey, sister of Earl Grey — which he used to benefit the HBC over the years in a variety of ways. It was his interest that helped protect the HBC in the parliamentary inquiry of 1857. He sold out with the transfer of the Company to Edward Watkin's people in 1863. Ellice was the author of *The Communications of Mercator, upon the Contest between the Earl of Selkirk, and the Hudson's Bay Company, on One Side, and the North West Company, on the Other* (1817) and *Continuation of the Communications of Mercator* (1817). Letters from Prosper Mérimée to him (1857-63) were published as *Lettres à Edward Ellice*, ed. Marianne Carmalhan (1963). *DCB* IX, 233-39. A Winnipeg street and a Manitoba rural municipality are named after him.

Elliott, Martha Jane (1867-1956) Women's activist. Born in Collingwood Township, Ontario, she began teaching at age 15. She came to Manitoba in 1890, took a teaching course in Brandon, and taught in rural Manitoba before marrying in 1894. During WWI she organized three branches of the Red Cross Society, and she was a founding member of the United Farm Women of Manitoba in 1918, becoming a board member and placed in charge of youth. She was a popular platform speaker on behalf of farm women, arguing for improved medical and nursing facilities as well as equal rights to the homestead. She was elected president of the United Farm Women of Manitoba in 1923. She is a member of the Manitoba Agricultural Hall of Fame.

Ellis, Frank H. (b. 1896) Bus driver, aviation expert. Born in Nottingham, England, he came to Canada in 1912. In 1920 he flew as a mechanic on the first airplane flight north of the 53rd parallel. He became a bus driver in 1925, an occupation he pursued until his retirement. In 1954 he published *Canada's Flying Heritage,* a pioneer history of Canadian aviation, and in 1959 he produced *In Canadian Skies.*

Ellis, Joseph Henry (1890-1973) Professor. Born in Coventry, England, he came to Manitoba as a youth, receiving his BSA from the Manitoba Agricultural College and his MSc from the University of Minnesota. He was appointed to the Field Husbandry Department of the Manitoba Agricultural College in 1918 and became head of its Soils Department in 1927. He began the soil survey of Manitoba, publishing *The Soils of Manitoba* in 1938. He also wrote *The Land for Thine Inheritance* (1941). Regarded as a dynamic teacher, he was awarded an honorary doctorate by the University of Manitoba. He is a member of the Manitoba Agricultural Hall of Fame. There are extensive research papers at the University of Manitoba.

Emerson, William J. (1913-1970) Horticulturalist. Born in Winnipeg, he began gardening at an early age, working in a number of places before joining the Province of Manitoba, on loan to the lieutenant-governor as gardener and florist at Government House. He worked there from 1947 until his retirement in 1979. He was active in scouting and was a member and officer of the St. John Ambulance Society for 38 years. He was awarded the Manitoba Horticultural Association Meritorious Service Award in 1976. He died in Kingston, Ontario.

Emmerling, George (fl. 1860-71) Hotelier. Known as "Dutch George," Emmerling came to Red River in 1860 and opened a hotel on Main Street. He ran the major hotel establishment in the village during the Red River Rebellion. It had a substantial liquor cupboard and two pool tables. He left in May 1871, selling out to John Davis.*

Emmett, Arthur Coates (1872-1959) Journalist, lobbyist. Born in England, he came to Canada in 1902 to farm at Brandon. He moved to Winnipeg in 1904, helping to found the Winnipeg Automobile Club that same year. He became secretary of the Winnipeg Automobile Club and later of the Manitoba Motor League, also serving as automotive editor for the *Manitoba Free Press* for many years. Beginning in 1913, he compiled road guides for Manitoba. In 1921 he advocated a provincial trunk highway system, and he continued to lobby for better roads throughout his lengthy career. He was credited with introducing to Canada the system of numbering highways. See Karen Nicholson, "A.C. Emmett and the Development of Good Roads in Manitoba," *Manitoba History,* no. 27 (spring 1994): 15-19. There is a scrapbook at the PAM.

English, Thomas (1846-1916) Police officer. Born in London Township, Canada, he worked as a police officer in Ontario before joining the Winnipeg police force in 1882, becoming sergeant a year later. In 1886 he refused to testify in an investigation over police corruption involving bawdy houses and was dismissed by the police commissioners. He became a city licence inspector until he was appointed Calgary police chief in 1891, serving until 1909. He died in Vancouver. *DCB* XIV, 343-44.

Erasmus, Peter (1833-1931) Guide and interpreter. Born in Kildonan, he worked for the missionaries Henry Steinhauer and George McDougall in the North. He also served as a guide for the Palliser expedition in 1858-59, working the scientific instruments for Dr. James Hector* in the Rocky Mountains. In August, 1859 he left the expedition to search for gold, for which he later apologized to Hector. He was interpreter at the signing of Treaty Six in 1876, and was still working as a Cree interpreter in 1913.

Ermatinger, Francis (1798-1858) Fur trader. Born in Lisbon, Portugal, he joined the HBC in 1818. From 1825 to 1846 he served in the Columbia District, and later he served at York Factory after he was made a chief factor in 1842. He died at St. Thomas, Canada. See Lois Halliday McDonald, ed., *Fur Trade Letters of Francis Ermatinger, 1818-53* (1980).

Éschambault, Antoine d' (1896-1960) Cleric, historian. Born in Manitoba, he was ordained a priest in 1921. He was secretary to the archbishop of St. Boniface from 1924 to 1934 and chancellor of the archdiocese from 1934 to 1966. He was for many years president of the St. Boniface Historical Society. He published *Essais historiques* (1961) and *Petite Histoire du voyageur* (1971).

Esplin, Charles (1834-1905) Engineer, inventor. Born in Arbroath, Scotland, he came to Canada in 1846 with his family. Educated at McGill, he became an engineer, specializing in sawmills and grain mills. He came to Winnipeg in 1878, then moved to Minneapolis in 1882. There he designed a number of sawmill and gristmill improvements and took out patents on them. After a sojourn on the Pacific coast, he returned to Winnipeg in 1897 and soon set up as a consulting engineer, installing the first electrical lighting plant in the city and perhaps the first asphalt plant and the first water-softening plant. *DCB* XIII, 322.

Evans, Edward Gurney Vaux (1907-1987) Politician. Born in Winnipeg, he was educated at Ridley College and the University of Manitoba. He served with the Royal Winnipeg Rifles in WWII, receiving the Order of the British Empire and retiring as lieutenant-colonel. He represented Fort Rouge in the provincial legislature as a Progressive-Conservative from 1953 to 1969, serving as minister of industry and commerce (1958-66), minister of mines and natural resources (1958-59, 1966-67), provincial secretary (1959-63), and finance minister (1966-69). He was executive director of the Carswell-Shaw Commission which calculated flood damages to Manitoba in 1950, and was executive director of the Red River Valley Board after the 1950 flood. He also served as chair of the Civil Service Commission of Manitoba. There are papers at the PAM.

Evans, James (1801-1846) Cleric, linguist. Born in Kingston-upon-Hull, England, Evans came to Canada after his parents and began teaching. Around 1825 he experienced a crisis conversion at a Methodist camp meeting, and by 1828 he was teaching at the Rice Lake school for Indian children. A facility for language enabled him to become an expert in Ojibwa, and he began preparing a dictionary of the language. In 1831 he became a probationer in the Methodist Episcopal Church. His Ojibwa syllabary was refused for publication in Toronto in 1836, and he had it published in New York in 1837. In 1840

George Simpson,* anxious to limit the activities of Roman Catholic and Anglican missionaries, agreed with the Wesleyan Methodist Missionary Society to allow three of that denomination in the Northwest. Evans was quickly posted to Norway House, where he began working on a Cree syllabary and criticisms of the HBC. In 1844 a gun he was handling accidentally discharged and killed Thomas Hassall,* an Aboriginal member of his party. Contemporaries blamed the accident for a change in Evans's personality, and there were subsequent rumours of sexual abuse of young Indian girls that were never proven. He died of a heart attack in London. His major work was *The Speller and Interpreter, in Indian and English, for the Use of the Mission Schools, and Such As May Desire to Obtain a Knowledge of the Ojibway Tongue* (1837). For a biography, see E.R. Young, *The Apostle of the North, Rev. James Evans* (1900). *DCB* VII, 275-78.

Evans, Mary Irene Gurney (fl. c. 1907) Musician. A gifted pianist, she founded the Women's Musical Club of Toronto and in 1907 became first president of the Women's Canadian Club of Winnipeg. She was also president of the Women's Musical Club of Winnipeg, and a promoter of the CNIB. The wife of William Sanford Evans,* she died in Winnipeg.

Evans, William Sanford (1869-1949) Journalist, politician, historian. Born in Spencerville, Ontario, Evans entered journalism and became editor of the *Winnipeg Telegram* in 1901. He was mayor of Winnipeg from 1905 to 1911. Leaving journalism, he became an investment broker and in 1921 founded Sanford Evans Statistical Services. He sat for Winnipeg in the Manitoba legislature from 1922 to 1935, and from 1935 to 1936 he led the Conservative Opposition in the House. He wrote *The Canadian Contingents and Canadian Imperialism* (1901). See Wade Henry, "W. Sanford Evans and the Canadian Club of Winnipeg, 1904-1919," *Manitoba History,* no. 27 (spring 1994): 2-8. Extensive papers are at the PAM.

Ewart, John Skirving (1849-1933) Lawyer, Canadian nationalist. Born in Toronto, Ewart went to school at Upper Canada College and Osgoode Hall. He practised law in Toronto before moving to Winnipeg in 1882. In Manitoba he became involved in the Manitoba School Question on behalf of the Roman Catholic minority, arguing the case before the Supreme Court and the Privy Council. As a result of this and other experience, he became a specialist in constitutional law, moving to Ottawa and undertaking only cases before the highest courts of appeal. After 1900 Ewart became an ardent Canadian sovereigntist, insisting that full Canadian independence from Great Britain was necessary in order for the nation to fulfill its destiny. His most important books were *The Kingdom Papers* (1911-1914) and *The Independence Papers* (1925-1930). See the unpublished thesis by Douglas L. Cole. There are papers at the PAM.

Ewart, Mary (fl. c. 1911) Artist. Born in the United States, she studied at the Pennsylvania Academy of Art and with several prominent artists. She was president of the Western Arts Association and a member of the Arts Club of Winnipeg. In 1911 she established a Free Art School in Winnipeg, and a year later she advocated in the press the establishment of an art gallery and professional art school in the city. She pledged $100 toward the establishment of an art gallery.

Eyden, Jean (1889-1990) Artist. Born in Lancashire, England, she studied at the Liverpool School of Art before coming to Canada in 1921. She became a member of the Winnipeg Sketch Club in 1924, and from that year until 1928 she was enrolled at the Winnipeg School of Art. She became a member of the Manitoba Society of Artists in 1943. She overcame many physical handicaps, including partial blindness and partial deafness. Over the years she produced and exhibited (most recently in 1982) many watercolour landscapes of local scenes.

Eylands, Valdimir Jónason (1910-1983) Cleric. Born in Hunavatnssyla in northwestern Iceland, he was educated at the Lutheran Theological Seminary in St. Paul, Minnesota. He was ordained in 1925, then took a BA at Concordia College. After pastoral service in North Dakota and Washington state, he came to the First Lutheran Church in Winnipeg in 1938, serving until 1968. He baptized 1,410 children, conducted 1,066 funerals, and celebrated 844 weddings. In 1945 he published *Lutherans in Canada* as well as *Iceland's Thousand Years,* a series of popular lectures in Icelandic history. He was awarded the Grand Cross of the Order of the Falcon by the Icelandic government, and he received an honorary doctorate from United College in 1953. His autobiography was published in 1981 in Iceland.

Fafard, Théogène (1855-1890) Physician, pharmacist. Born in Canada, he studied at the Collège de Montréal and then the Montreal School of Medicine and Surgery, subsequently practising medicine in Montreal. He came to Manitoba in 1878 and quickly became associated with the Hôpital de Saint-Boniface. He was a director of the Manitoba Colonisation Society but was not successful in his political endeavours. In 1880 he became coroner for Manitoba, and he opened a pharmacy in 1882 with his brother Abel. In 1884 he helped incorporate the private Manitoba Medical College and became a professor of botany there. *DCB* XI, 306-7.

Fahey, James A. (c. 1849-1888) Journalist. Born in Canada, he served as a journalist in Ontario and California before spending a brief spell in 1881-82 as editor of the *Winnipeg Sun*. He returned to Toronto and died there. *DCB* XI, 307-8.

Fahrni, Gordon (1887-1995) Surgeon. Born in Gladstone, Manitoba, he grew up on a farm. He studied at Wesley College in Winnipeg from 1904 to 1906, then entered the new five-year course at the Medical School, graduating in 1911. After military service during WWI he became a surgeon, specializing in thyroidectomy. He was president of the Manitoba Medical Association in 1923 and of the Canadian Medical Association from 1940 to 1942. He served as a field surgeon during WWII and was in charge of medical services during the 1950 Manitoba flood.

He was appointed to the Order of Canada in 1987. Fahrni was a well-known and outspoken critic of "socialistic encroachment on health care." He was chair of the Music Committee of St. Andrew's United Church for many years. He moved from Winnipeg to Vancouver in 1951 and retired in 1965. His autobiography was published as *Prairie Surgeon* in 1975.

Falcon, Pierre (1783-1876) Poet. Born at Elbow Fort in what is now the province of Manitoba, the son of a NWC employee and a Cree woman, Falcon was educated in Quebec. He returned to Red River in 1806, and in 1812 he married a sister of Cuthbert Grant.* He accompanied Grant to Seven Oaks in 1816. Falcon subsequently helped Grant found Grantown (St. François Xavier) and became a distinguished citizen there. He was also a folk poet who wrote mocking songs about local events, such as Seven Oaks ("La Chanson de la Grenouillère"), Lord Selkirk's* capture of Fort William ("Le Lord Selkirk au Fort William") and the expedition of General James Dickson* ("Le General Dickson"). He described himself as "poète du canton" and was later known as "le barde des plaines." See Margaret MacLeod, "Bard of the Prairies," *The Beaver* (spring 1956): 19-23; Manitoba Historic Resources Branch, *Pierre Falcon* (1984). *DCB* X, 276-77.

Fanshaw, Herbert Valentine (1878-1940) Artist. Born in Sheffield, England, he attended the Sheffield Technical School of Art, the Royal College of Art in

London, and the Académie Royale des Beaux Arts in Antwerp. He emigrated to Portland, Oregon, to teach art, but soon moved to Winnipeg, where in 1913 he was appointed director of the Art Department at Kelvin Technical High School. Fanshaw was noted as a teacher and as an exhibiting artist. He was a member of the Winnipeg School of Art's Art Committee from 1926 to 1938. One of his favourite media was the colour block print.

Faraud, Henri (1824-1890) Missionary. He came from Montreal to St. Boniface in 1846 to assist Bishop Provencher and was ordained an Oblate in 1847. After studying Indian languages and customs, he became a missionary at Athabasca and, in 1862, its first bishop. He returned to St. Boniface in 1889 and died there soon after. He published *Dix-huit Ans chez les sauvages: Voyages etmissions . . . dans l'extrême nord de l'Amérique Britannique* (1866). Other writings are at the Oblate Archives, Ottawa. *DCB* XI, 310-11.

Farmer, Seymour James (1878-1951) Politician. Born in Cardiff, Wales, Farmer came to Canada in 1900. He was employed at the Winnipeg Grain Exchange from 1913 to 1927, clerking at the International Elevator Corporation in 1919. He supported direct legislation and a single tax, and was an ardent pacifist. Farmer was active in the founding of the Labour Church in 1918, and was chair of the Dominion Labor Party in Manitoba that same year. He was one of the founders of the Independent Labor Party in 1921, and was elected mayor of Winnipeg in 1922-23. He was subsequently a CCF MLA and was leader of the Manitoba CCF from 1935 to 1949. He was minister of labour in the coalition government of WWII, resigning in 1942 when John Bracken* became national leader of the Conservative Party. Farmer won six elections as an ILP and CCF candidate, the last in 1945.

Farquharson, James (c. 1819-1874) House painter, agitator. Born in Scotland, he immigrated to Newfoundland in 1846 and became a house painter. He subsequently moved to Demerara and then ended up in Red River in 1862 on his way to British Columbia. He helped paint the St. Boniface Cathedral in 1867, about the time his daughter Agnes married John C. Schultz.* Farquharson then headed off as a trader in the West. In 1870 he was briefly imprisoned by Louis Riel, who refused to accept his oath to keep the peace because he was alleged to have twice broken it already. In August of 1870 he tried to publish a reward for the capture of Riel and his associates, and he was involved in the death of Elzéar Goulet* shortly after, as well as a number of election riots in the early 1870s. In his later years he was known as "Old Depravity," described by Lieutenant-governor Adams Archibald* as "a well known blackguard who has been in every row since I came here." See Allen Ronaghan, "James Farquharson: Agent and Agitator," *Manitoba History* 17 (spring 1989): 12-16.

Farrally, Betty (1915-1989) Dancer and dance administrator. Born in Bradford, England, she was educated at Harrogate Ladies College and came to Canada in 1938 with her friend Gweneth Lloyd.* The two founded the dance company that became the Royal Winnipeg Ballet. Farrally served as director of the Royal Winnipeg Ballet from 1955 to 1957 and later moved to Kelowna, where she taught dance. She died in Kelowna.

Federenko, Savva (fl. 1905-1910) Exiled revolutionary. A Russian revolutionary of 1905, he escaped to Winnipeg in mid-July 1910. A few days later he was arrested and charged with murder and arson under the 1886 extradition treaty between Russia and Canada. Various labour and socialist leaders spoke out on his behalf, but he was summarily convicted in a court presided over by Chief Justice T.G. Mathers* in October 1910. Both the *Manitoba Free Press* and the *Winnipeg Tribune* editorialized on his behalf, and at a Walker Theatre rally on 20 November 1910, a non-partisan group which included Rev. C.W. Gordon* (the novelist Ralph Connor) resolved that extradition should be refused if there was a political motive behind Russia's request for it. On 23 November 1910, a court under Mr. Justice Hugh Robson* ruled that Federenko's crime was political. He was eventually given his unconditional release and departed Winnipeg for places unknown.

Ferguson, Alexander Hugh (1853-1911) Physician, educator. Born in Canada, he was educated at Manitoba College and the Trinity School of Medicine in Toronto, later studying in New York, Glasgow, London, and Berlin (the Koch Laboratory). He returned to Winnipeg in 1881 to practise, becoming a founder of the Manitoba Medical College and one of its first professors. In 1893 he was offered the chair of surgery in the Postgraduate Medical School in Chicago, which he accepted. He died in that city.

He was the author of *The Technic of Modern Operations for Hernia* (1907).

Ferguson, Colin Campbell (1921-1991) Surgeon, educator. Born in Winnipeg, he was educated at Ravenscourt School and the University of Manitoba Medical School (1944). He served in the Canadian navy as surgeon-lieutenant commander. He did graduate work in surgery at McGill University, then held appointments at the Children's Medical Center, Boston, and as Fellow in Surgery at Harvard University. He was appointed head of Surgery at the University of Manitoba in 1953, serving until 1969. He remained professor of surgery until 1986. He was active on the boards of St. John's-Ravenscourt and Balmoral Hall schools. He published extensively in pediatric surgery and vascular surgery, and was the author of *One Hundred Years of Surgery, 1883-1983: Professors of Surgery, University of Manitoba* (1983).

Ferguson, John ("Ion," 1909-1998) Motion picture executive. Born in Glasgow, Scotland, he came to Winnipeg in 1910. He began as a film projectionist for silent films in 1926, working his way up through the sound era to become district supervisor of theatres for Famous Players for the Prairie region and northwestern Ontario in 1954. He retired in 1973 to operate the Delta Drive-In Theatre in Portage la Prairie, which he did until 1992.

Ferguson, William Graham (1896-1964) Lawyer, judge. Born in Winnipeg, he attended Machray and Alexander public schools, then Central Collegiate. He served in the 184th Canadian Infantry Battalion and saw action at Vimy Ridge in 1917 before transferring to the Royal Flying Corps. He was called to the bar in 1921. He practised law in Minnedosa from 1925 to 1960, before his appointment to the Manitoba Court of Queen's Bench.

Ferns, Stanley Joseph (b. 1888) Civil servant. Born in London, Ontario, he came west temporarily in 1905 with a harvest excursion. He moved to Calgary in 1910 and worked at a series of jobs, including assistant janitor at a school, until becoming manager of a CPR demonstration poultry farm in Strathmore, Alberta, in 1917. From 1923 to 1928 he worked as an itinerant poultry inspector for the Dominion Department of Agriculture. He moved to Winnipeg in 1929 to work as a federal employee with the poultry industry in Manitoba, which he did until 1954. In 1956 he joined the Manitoba Turkey Association as secretary-manager, and he served there until 1964. His autobiography, written with his son H.S. Ferns, was published in 1978 as *Eighty-Five Years in Canada*.

Fetherstonhaugh, Edward Phillips (1879-1959) Educator. Fetherstonhaugh (pronounced "Fanshaw") was born in Montreal. He was educated at McGill University and lectured at McGill before moving to Manitoba in 1907 to work for Westinghouse. In 1909 he was appointed professor of electrical engineering at the University of Manitoba. He served as a major in the Canadian Engineers during WWI, and later as commanding officer of the Canadian Officers in Training Corps (COTC) at the University of Manitoba from 1924 to 1930. In 1921 he became dean of engineering, retiring in 1945. He was a member of the National Research Council from 1936 to 1945, and its president in 1945. An engineering building at the University of Manitoba is named for him.

Fetherstonhaugh, Margaret Adele (Bain) (d. 1975) Musician, volunteer. Born in Montreal, she came to Winnipeg where she married E.P. Fetherstonhaugh* in 1925. She took an active role in musical affairs in Winnipeg, serving for many years as president of the Women's Musical Club. She was also involved in the Wednesday Morning Musicale (1937-73), the Eva Clare Studio Club (1923-29), and the Manitoba Music Festival (1966-74), where she often played piano as an accompanist. For 25 years, she was president of the Altar Guild of All Saints Church. She was named the Volunteer of the Year in 1972. There are papers at the PAM.

Fidler, Peter (1769-1822) Fur trader, surveyor. Born in Bolsover, England, Fidler joined the HBC in 1788. As someone with both education and steadiness, he soon advanced in the Company service. He was sent inland, and in 1790 was taught surveying and astronomy by Philip Turnor,* whom he was probably intended to succeed. Fidler accompanied Turnor to the Athabasca region in 1790-92, and did well. He subsequently went on a number of surveying and trading expeditions, constantly experiencing trouble with the NWC but providing the HBC with much useful information. By 1810 the intimidation led Fidler to request a year's furlough in England, and he returned in 1812 to be transferred to Red River. When Miles Macdonell* became incapacitated in 1815, Fidler was in command when a capitulation had to be signed, and he led the loyal settlers north to be met by Colin Robertson.* In 1816 he was in Brandon House when the post was plundered. He returned to the fur trade in 1817. By 1821 he had suffered a stroke, and he died shortly thereafter, leaving behind 11 children. Fidler was simultaneously pedantic and diffident. He was not regarded as a great leader, although he was a highly competent surveyor. He is a member of the Manitoba Agricultural Hall of Fame. See J.G. MacGregor, *Peter Fidler: Canada's Forgotten Surveyor, 1769-1822* (1966). *DCB* VI, 249-52.

Finkelstein, Moses (1873-1939) Furrier. Born in Russia, he was educated in Winnipeg. A furrier, he was the proprietor of the North West Fur Company. From 1905 to 1906 he was a Winnipeg alderman. Finkelstein was a leading Jewish layman in the city.

Finlayson, Duncan (c. 1795-1862) Fur trader. Born in Scotland, he joined the HBC in 1815 and served at Red River in 1819-20. He became a clerk at Fort Garry in 1826 and chief trader in 1828. In 1831 he was transferred to Fort Vancouver. He became governor of Assiniboia and councillor of Rupert's Land, based at Fort Garry, in 1839, shortly after his marriage in Scotland to George Simpson's* sister-in-law, who joined him in 1840. In 1844 he moved to Lachine as company agent, a posting that really meant he was assisting George Simpson. Finlayson was noted for his upstanding personal conduct and concern for Native peoples. He retired in 1859. *DCB* IX, 260-61.

Fisher, James (1840-1927) Lawyer, politician. Born in Perthshire, Scotland, he immigrated to Canada at a young age. Fisher was educated at the University of Toronto. He practised law in Stratford, Ontario, and in 1883 was called to the bar in Manitoba. He sat for Russell in the Manitoba legislature from 1888 to 1899. Fisher's was one of the loudest voices calling for the construction of the Hudson Bay Railway to Churchill.

Fisher, Randolph Murray (1886-1965) Civil servant. Born on a homestead west of Portage la Prairie, he was educated at Poplar Bluff and at Portage Collegiate. He attended Queen's University and was university medallist in political economy, as well as the first athletic stick. He was called to the bar in 1914, and he served in the Canadian Tank Battalion of the Canadian Expeditionary Force. He practised law until 1928, when he was appointed legislative

counsel. A year later he became deputy minister of municipal affairs and deputy provincial secretary, jobs he held until his retirement in 1958. He received an honorary degree from the University of Manitoba in 1952. He was treasurer and president of the Committee on Uniformity of Legislation in Canada from 1930 to 1946. He and his wife both suffered fatal heart attacks in their home on the same evening.

Fitzgerald, Lionel Lemoine (1890-1956) Painter. Born in Winnipeg, he spent his entire life there except for brief periods of art training in the United States and Montreal. He began exhibiting in 1911 and left a real estate job to work as an artist in 1912. He taught at the Winnipeg School of Art from 1924 to 1949 and was its principal from 1929 to 1947. At an early age he moved to pointillism ("little strokes or spots of pigment," he called it), particularly for landscapes, and he was much influenced by Cézanne and Seurat. In 1932 he was asked to join the Group of Seven. During the 1930s he was very impressed by the Bauhaus movement, which influenced his educational philosophy at the School of Art. After his retirement in 1949 he shifted entirely to abstractionism. The University of Manitoba awarded him an honorary LLD in 1952. He was often linked with Bertram Brooker.* See, for example, Carole Francis Luff, *Progress Passing through the Spirit: The Modernist Vision of Bertram Brooker and Lionel Lemoine Fitzgerald* (1980). See also Winnipeg Art Gallery, *Lionel Lemoine Fitzgerald: The Development of an Artist* (1978).

Fleming, Alexander (1841-1897) Physician. Born in Scotland, he was educated at the Glasgow School of Medicine and at Harvard University. He practised medicine in Sackville, New Brunswick, for 10 years before coming to Brandon in 1882 as the city's first medical director. He was president of the Manitoba and Northwest Farmers' Union, and he helped found Brandon General Hospital in 1891, becoming a member of its staff.

Fleming, Sandford (1827-1915) Engineer. Born in Fifeshire, Scotland, Fleming studied engineering in Scotland and immigrated to Canada in 1845, subsequently working for the Northern Railway. He served as chief engineer of the Intercolonial Railway while it was under construction. He was then appointed engineer-in-chief for the surveys of the CPR, providing the surveys on which that railroad's route was based. In 1879 he investigated early flooding in

Manitoba in order to decide where to place bridges across the Red River. In 1880 he retired to do scientific work. He developed, among other things, daylight saving time and the 24-hour method of reckoning time. He also worked on cable communication. Knighted in 1877, he was an ardent imperialist who served as president of the Royal Society in 1888. His major publications include *A Railway to the Pacific through British Territory* (1858). The best biography is H. MacLean, *Man of Steel: The Story of Sir Sandford Fleming* (1969).

Fletcher, Robert (1871-1963) Civil servant. Born in Ontario, he was educated at Trinity University in Toronto, the Model School at St. Thomas, and, after coming to Manitoba in 1893, the normal school in Winnipeg. He taught school in various places, including St. John's College. He entered the Manitoba Department of Education in 1903. In 1908 he was appointed deputy minister of education for Manitoba, and he served until 1939. He was a major advocate of school consolidation. He was active on the Winnipeg Playground Commission and served as chair of the Winnipeg Public Parks Board from 1922 to 1924. He was a major advocate of school consolidation and also sat on the board of St. John's-Ravenscourt School. There are papers at the PAM.

Flett, George (1775-1850) Fur trader. Born in Firth, Scotland, he joined the HBC as a labourer in 1796, contracting to work for five years at six pounds per annum. After many years' service at Moose Lake, where he was master from 1812 to 1822, he retired to the Red River Settlement in 1823. George Simpson* described him as "a faithful interested old Servant, deficient in Education but a good trader."

Flett, John (1784-1865) Settler. Born in the Orkney Islands, he came to Red River around 1817. He was granted Lot 24 (now the Kildonan Park Golf Course) by Lord Selkirk, and spent the remainder of his life there farming. In 1847 a school was opened in his home. He died in Kildonan.

Flye, Thomas (1874-1943) Labour leader. Born in Dowlais, Wales, he worked as a blacksmith and steeplejack before coming to Canada in 1910. Flye was a foreman at Dominion Bridge during WWI, then a blacksmith at the CPR. Originally carrying over his Labour affiliations from Britain and becoming a member of the Independent Labor Party, he later broke with that party and ran as an independent. Flye was a member of the Central Strike Committee in the Winnipeg General Strike of 1919. He was also a member of Winnipeg City Council from 1921.

Fonseca, William Gomez da (1823-1905) Merchant. Born in the Danish West Indies, perhaps of Creole background, Fonseca migrated to New York, where he became an American citizen, then moved to Minnesota and in 1860 to Winnipeg. He had a shop in a building owned by his father-in-law, Thomas Logan. He lectured on the West Indies and was regarded highly enough to be considered for the post of American consul that went to Oscar Malmros.* In 1869 he was carting and freighting. He was arrested by Louis Riel on 13 December and released two days later upon the surrender of his American citizenship papers. He later became a prominent Winnipeg businessman, land speculator, and local politician, serving six terms as alderman for the North Ward. His property included most of Point Douglas. He was a vestryman at St. John's Cathedral for 36 years. He wrote *On the St. Paul Trail in the Sixties* (1900). For a biography, see Albert G. Fonseca, *From Palms to Maples* (1992). *DCB* XIII, 350-51. There are papers at the PAM.

Foote, Lewis Benjamin ("L.B.," 1873-1957) Photographer. Born in Foote's Cove, Newfoundland, he worked on the *Summerside Journal* (Prince Edward Island), where he discovered his flair for photography. He moved to Halifax and then to Winnipeg in 1902, where he became a professional photographer. For more than 50 years his photographs chronicled the development of the city. His most famous work was done in 1919 during the Winnipeg General Strike, but he was also the official photographer to the Winnipeg coroner. There are papers and photographs at the PAM. See Doug Smith and Michael Olito, eds., *The Best Possible Face: L.B. Foote's Winnipeg* (1985).

Forest, George (1924-1990) Language rights activist. Born in St. Boniface, he founded the Agence d'Assurances Forest Limitée in 1948 and operated it throughout his life. He engaged in a long battle to restore French as an official language in Manitoba, winning a famous court case in the Canadian Supreme Court over a unilingual parking ticket in 1979. He was co-founder of the Festival du Voyageur in

1970. He died of a heart attack at a Festival dinner in St. Boniface.

Forest, Grant (b. c. 1794) Fur trader. Born in Montreal, he arrived in Red River in 1820 with a load of trade goods, which he was not allowed to trade for furs. In 1821 he went with Robert Dickson* to Prairie du Chien to meet a herd of American cattle. He was an accountant at Fort Douglas in 1824 when he married Mary Allez, a Guernsey native hired as schoolmistress for the Red River Settlement. He clerked at Lake of Two Mountains in 1827.

Forke, Robert (1860-1934) Politician. Born in Scotland, he came to Manitoba in 1882 and farmed at Pipestone, where he served as reeve from 1892 to 1915. During WWI he was a member of the Manitoba Public Welfare Committee and of the Returned Soldiers Committe. In 1921 he was elected to the House of Commons as a Progressive. He was appointed House leader of the party in 1922, and he succeeded Thomas Crerar* as Progressive leader. He served as minister of immigration and colonization in the Liberal government in Ottawa from 1926 to 1929 and then was appointed to the Canadian Senate. He died in Winnipeg. See W.L. Morton, *The Progressive Party of Canada* (1950).

Forkin, Martin, Jr. ("Joe," 1899-1962) Radical. Born in England, he came with his family to Brandon in 1912. He became secretary-treasurer of the Brandon unit of the Provincial Employment Association in 1922 and the secretary of the Brandon Unemployed Workers' Council in 1927; both organizations were associated with the Communist Party. He ran as a Communist candidate in North Winnipeg in 1930 and organized mine workers in Saskatchewan in 1931. Two years later he ran for mayor of Winnipeg on the Winnipeg Workers' Election Conference ticket against John Queen,* receiving 4,745 votes. Forkin was finally elected to office in 1934 as alderman in Ward Three, serving until 1940. He was re-elected to Winnipeg City Council in 1942, and remained a councillor until his death. See Errol Black, "Brandon's Revolutionary Forkins," *Prairie Forum* 20, no. 2 (1995): 255-79.

Forrester, Gladys (1914-1998) Dancer. Born in Winnipeg, she studied dancing of all kinds from an early age, winning the Highland dance championship for Western Canada in 1921. She studied ballet in New York, and she operated a dancing school in Winnipeg from 1936 to 1941. She danced in the first two seasons of the company created by Betty Farrally* and Gweneth Lloyd* and became an exponent of the Royal Academy of Dancing method of teaching. In 1948 she was one of the dancing corps in the film *The Red Shoes*. That same year she moved with her husband to Toronto, where she taught dance and did choreography until her death. She helped to introduce jazz dance to Canada in the 1950s.

Fortinay (Fortney), George (1846-1925) Steamboat captain. Born in Canada, he came to Red River with the Canadian road crew. He was one of the workmen who threatened John Snow* with physical violence at Oak Point in October 1869, for which he was fined at the November General Quarterly Court. A month later, he was a member of the party inside John Schultz's* house that surrendered to Louis Riel. He was subsequently imprisoned at Fort Garry for 71 days. Fortinay later became a pioneer Red River steamboat captain. In the 1890s he ran steamboats to Skagway and the Yukon. Although nearly 70, he enlisted and served overseas in the 100th Battalion during WWI.

Fortune, Mark (1847-1912) Businessman. Born in Wentworth, Canada, he went to California as a youth. In 1871 he came to Winnipeg and began speculating in real estate, especially along the Assiniboine River. He served as a city councillor and a trustee of Knox United Church. In 1911 he built a huge mansion at 393 Wellington Crescent. He died in the sinking of the *Titanic*. His death is marked by a plaque in Winnipeg City Hall.

Foss, Christopher Vaughan (fl. 1834-52) Soldier. Foss was an ensign in the Second West India Regiment of Foot in 1834 and was a lieutenant in 1838. In 1839 he transferred to the 18th (Royal Irish) Regiment of Foot, and he sold out his commission in 1842. He came to Red River as a staff officer of the Chelsea pensioners. Rumour spread that he had become too friendly with the wife of HBC chief factor John Ballenden.* After consulting with recorder Adam Thom,* Foss started a suit for defamatory conspiracy against chief trader Augustus Edward Pelly and his wife, as well as mess steward John Davidson* and his wife. The trial opened on 16 July 1850, with Foss declaring that he sought to clear Mrs. Ballenden's reputation. After an uproarious trial, the jury found the defendants guilty and awarded the plaintiff damages. Critics of Thom used the case as an illustration of the problems besetting his court. Ironically enough, Thom later found evidence that Captain Foss and Mrs. Ballenden were still intimately involved. Foss subsequently held an appointment as a staff officer of pensioners in Western Australia in 1852.

Foster, Harold (1892-1982) Cartoonist. Born in Halifax, he came to Winnipeg in 1911 and worked for Brigden's until 1921, when he moved on to Chicago. His work at Brigden's was mainly on the Eaton's catalogue, where he specialized in buttons, bloomer lace, women's lingerie, and toys. In 1929 the publishers Grosset and Dunlop chose Foster to illustrate Edgar Rice Burroughs' book *Tarzan of the Apes*. Foster began drawing Tarzan as a comic strip in 1931, and in 1937 he created "Prince Valiant," a comic strip set in the early Middle Ages, with authentic costumes and settings. He died in Florida.

Foucher, Médéric (1838-1909) Francophone leader. Born in Saint-Jacques-de-l'Achigan, Canada, he studied at Holy Cross College in Worcester, Massachusetts, from 1857 to 1859 before returning to his home town, where he kept a store and became a local leader. In the early 1870s he moved to St. Boniface, where he was active in the circle of Francophones who were struggling to maintain the French presence in the province. He moved back to Quebec in 1877 as a newspaper translator in Montreal and then returned to Saint-Jacques-de-l'Achigan to become a pioneer tobacco farmer. *DCB* XIII, 354-55.

Fowler, Frank Oliver (1861-1945) Municipal politician. Born in Wingham, Canada, he came to Manitoba in 1881. Fowler became a leading grain dealer, secretary of the North West Grain Dealers' Association, and manager of the Winnipeg Grain and Product Exchange Clearing Association. He was elected to the Manitoba legislature from South Brandon in 1897, serving until 1903. Beginning in 1908, he served as a Winnipeg city councillor. In 1918 he introduced a motion denying all civic employees the right to strike, which narrowly passed Council by a vote of nine to eight. On 26 May 1919 he co-introduced a motion prohibiting firemen from belonging to any union affiliated with an organization that could give it commands contradictory to Council's orders. It passed by a vote of nine to five. He was later mayor of Winnipeg, elected by acclamation in 1922.

Foxe, Luke (1586-1635) Sailor, explorer. Born in Yorkshire, England, he became an experienced sailor who was fascinated with the Arctic and the possibility of a Northwest Passage. In 1629 he succeeded in gaining support for an exploratory voyage, which left London in 1631 and returned there that same year. Foxe discovered little of importance. He recounted his story in a work titled *North-West Fox* (1635), which began by reviewing the work of his predecessors and which was regarded by some commentators as "quaint" and "amusing." He did manage to resurrect Thomas Button's* major voyage to Hudson Bay, which had been forgotten for many years. See Miller Christy, *The Voyages of Captain Luke Foxe of Hull* (1899). *DCB* I, 311-12.

Franklin, George Edmund (1910-1990) Environmentalist. Born near Deloraine, Manitoba, he received his diploma in agriculture from the University of Manitoba. His farm was a combined grain and cattle operation, and he was a pioneer agricultural environmentalist, concerned with soil depletion and erosion. He stopped ploughing in 1938 and participated in the "zero tillage" movement of the 1970s. He was also part of the movement against chemicals. He was active in agricultural organizations and several times was a member of international missions. He is a member of the Manitoba Agricultural Hall of Fame.

Franklin, Sir John (1786-1847) Explorer. Born in Lincolnshire, England, he first commanded an expedition to explore the Arctic coast of North America and find a Northwest Passage in 1819. On his second expedition (1825-27) he travelled to and from the Arctic via Lake Winnipeg, describing the terrain in his *Narrative of the Second Expedition to the Shores of the Polar Sea, 1825, 1826, 1827* (1828). After serving as lieutenant-governor of Van Diemen's Land (Tasmania) from 1836 to 1843, he went back to the Arctic for a third expedition in 1845, but did not return. Nearly 30 expeditions were sent to find him, motivated by the mystery of his disappearance and rewards set afoot by his wife. John Rae* brought back Eskimo stories of his death in 1852. In 1859 the expedition of Francis McClintock found remains and two brief written records that noted Franklin's death. Franklin was a brave and charming man but not particularly skilful as an explorer. He was more important for the work done during attempts to find him than for his own expeditions. See G.F. Lamb, *Franklin — Happy Voyager* (1956); Roderick Owen, *The Fate of Franklin* (1978). *DCB* VII, 323-26.

Fraser, James (1790-1862) Settler. Born in Ulva, Scotland, he came to Red River to help manage Hayfield Farm under the stewardship of William Laidlaw.* By 1830 he was farming on Lot 15. The home he built there now stands preserved in Lower Fort Garry. In 1851 he was chosen one of the six elders of the newly opened Kildonan Presbyterian Church. He is buried in St. John's Cemetery, Winnipeg.

Fraser, John Arthur (1817-1897) Pioneer. Born in Kildonan, he was locally educated. His marriage to Jane Matheson was the first among Anglophones born in Red River, and on their golden anniversary Countess Selkirk sent them an engraved teapot. Fraser was a successful farmer. *DCB* XII, 335-38.

Fraser, William (1832-1909) Farmer, local politician. A Kildonan resident of Scottish origin, he was educated at Pritchard's School and St. John's School and Academy. He was appointed road superintendent of the Middle Section of Assiniboia in 1863 at a salary of £15 per annum. Fraser was active in the Kildonan Presbyterian Church from the time of its founding, serving as church treasurer for over 40 years. He was a member of the Council of Assiniboia from 1868 to 1870 and later of the North-West Territorial Council. He was also active in the foundation of Manitoba College and was reeve of Kildonan 12 times.

Frasse de Plainval, Louis, a.k.a. Louis Nathal (1841-1890) Police chief, theatrical entrepreneur. Born in France, he enlisted in the Quebec Rifles in 1870 for the Wolseley Expedition. In Manitoba he became well known for his theatricals. He was appointed assistant chief (1870), then chief (1872), of the Manitoba Constabulary, the provincial police force. He left for the United States in 1873 to begin a theatrical career and reappeared briefly in Winnipeg in 1879 as Louis Nathal, head of the Nathal Comic Opera Company, which performed such works as *The Chimes of Normandy*. He was also a successful playwright. He married the soprano Louise Lester. See "Louis Frasse: Comte de Plainval: Manitoba's Second Police Chief" in the Manitoba Legislative Library. *DCB* XI, 325-26.

Fredrickson, Frank (1895-1979) Hockey star. Born in Winnipeg, he attended Kelvin Technical Institute and Central Collegiate before enrolling at the University of Manitoba law school, where he captained the hockey team. He served in the 196th Battalion in WWI, then captained the 1920 Allan Cup team that won Canada's first hockey gold medal in the 1920 Olympics at Antwerp. He played for Lester Patrick in the Pacific Hockey League in the early 1920s and then joined the Detroit team of the NHL in 1926. He was sold to Boston, and he finished his career with Pittsburgh, where he was the league's first playing coach. He coached hockey and lacrosse after his retirement. He was elected to the Canadian Hockey Hall of Fame in 1958 and is a member of the Manitoba Sports Hall of Fame.

Freedman, Max (1914-1980) Journalist. Born in Winnipeg's North End, he was the brother of Samuel Freedman.* Their family could not afford to send Max to university. Instead, he spent four years reading as many books as he could in the University of Manitoba library, and he would later claim to be a "graduate" of the University of Manitoba library. He began his journalistic career with the *Edmonton Bulletin* (having been recommended for the job by Winnipeg's three chief librarians) and then served during WWII in the engineers and as education officer with the Canadian Legion. After the war he worked briefly on London's Fleet Street, and in 1946 joined the *Winnipeg Free Press* as Ottawa correspondent. In 1949 he became the *Free Press's* correspondent in Washington, then in 1952 served in Winnipeg as its senior editorial writer. In 1953 he returned to Washington as correspondent for the *Manchester Guardian*, and he added work for the *Free Press* to his portfolio in 1954. His syndicated column for the *Chicago Daily News* was carried by more than 100 newspapers and his advice sought by many politicians, including those on John F. Kennedy's staff. He retired in ill health in 1967.

Freedman, Samuel (1908-1993) Lawyer, judge. Born in Russia, he came to Manitoba with his parents at the age of three and was educated at Aberdeen School, St. John's Technical High School, and the University of Manitoba, graduating in honours classics in 1929, when he entered University of Manitoba law school. He articled with Steinkopf and Lawrence. As a law student and afterwards he was an accomplished debater, winning the McGoun Cup in 1930 with W.L. Morton* as his partner. He served four years as editor of the *Manitoba Bar News* and was president of the Manitoba Bar Association in 1951-52. He was appointed to the Court of King's Bench in 1952 and elevated to the Manitoba Court of Appeal in 1960; he was acting chief justice in 1966-67 and became chief justice in 1971, retiring in 1983. He served as chair of a commission investigating railroad labour troubles in 1954-55. He was chancellor of the University of Manitoba from 1959 to 1968. Freedman was extremely active in the Jewish community throughout his career. There are papers at the PAM. See Cameron Harvey, ed., *Chief Justice Samuel Freedman: A Great Canadian Judge* (1983).

Freer, James S. (1855-1937) Filmmaker. Born in England, he immigrated to Canada in 1888, after a career as a journalist in Bristol, and settled in the Brandon Hills. He obtained an Edison combination movie camera-projector in 1897 and began making films. Arguably Canada's first moviemaker, he toured England in 1898 under the auspices of the CPR with a film lecture series titled "Ten Years in Manitoba." Freer also filmed English scenes to show to homesick Manitobans. A less successful tour followed in 1902 under the auspices of the federal government. Freer relocated to Eriksdale in 1901. He moved to Winnipeg in 1917 to become staff editor for the *Manitoba Free Press*.

Frémont, Donatien (1881-1967) Journalist, historian, author. Born in Erbray, France, he was educated at Nantes and came to Canada in 1904. After working in farming and journalism in Saskatchewan, he edited *La Liberté* in Winnipeg from 1923 to 1941. He worked for the Wartime Information Board from 1941 to 1947 and edited *Le Canada* from 1947 to 1952. He was a fellow of the Royal Society of Canada. Frémont wrote extensively on the early history of the Canadian West. Among his works were *Mgr Provencher et son temps* (1935), *Les Secrétaires de Riel* (1953), and *Les Français dans l'Ouest canadien* (1959). See Hélène Chaput, *Donatien Frémont, journaliste de l'Ouest canadien* (1977).

Friesen, David K. (1910-1991) Printing executive. Born in Altona, Manitoba, he was educated at the Mennonite Educational Institute. He joined D.W. Friesen and Sons, building it into a national printing establishment before his retirement in 1985. He was mayor of Altona from 1970 to 1975 and was active in many community organizations.

Friesen, Victor (fl. 1926-56) Artist. Born in Ukraine, he came to Canada in 1924, originally settling in Waterloo, Ontario. He arrived in Winnipeg in 1926 to work at Brigden's. From 1929 to 1934 he attended the Winnipeg School of Art, where he won scholarships and prizes. Although he exhibited often, he worked chiefly as a commercial artist, after 1956 in his own firm.

Fullartine, John (c. 1652-1738) HBC governor. Probably born in Edinburgh, Scotland, he first joined the HBC in 1683 as one of its first Scots employees. He was captured by the French in 1689 and was held until 1692, when he was released from La Rochelle. He became deputy to James Knight* in 1694 and was left in command by Knight in 1697, although his appointment was not confirmed. He finally received a commission as governor and chief commander of Albany River, Moose River, and Rupert River in 1702, subsequently contending with Anthony Beale* for the primacy of command. In 1709 he fought off a French attack at Albany Fort. He retired from Rupert's Land in 1711 and was elected to the General Court that same year, serving faithfully until his death. *DCB* II, 231-33.

Fullerton, Charles Percy (1870-1938) Lawyer, judge. Born in Amherst, Nova Scotia, Fullerton was educated at Dalhousie University. After legal work in Nova Scotia, he was called to the Manitoba bar in 1906. In 1917 he was appointed a justice of the Court of Appeal of the Supreme Court of Manitoba, and he served until 1931, when he became chief commissioner of the Board of Railway Commissioners for Canada. In 1934 he was appointed chair of the board of trustees of the CNR.

Funk, Johann (1836-1917) Cleric. Born near Mariupol, Ukraine, he was baptized in 1857. He came to Canada in 1874 with others of his community, arriving at Altbergthal, Manitoba. He was ordained in 1877 and then became bishop of the Bergthaler Mennonite Church. He helped organize the Mennonite Educational Institute, which began in 1889 over the objections of many who feared that higher education was inimical to tradition. The institute caused a schism in the church, and Funk remained with the minority group, eventually resigning in 1911. He died in Altbergthal. There are papers at the Mennonite Heritage Centre Archives in Winnipeg. See M.D. Jeffery, ed., *Aeltester Johann Funk: A Family Tree with Notes on His Life and Work* (1980). *DCB* XIV, 379.

Gaboury, Marie-Anne (c. 1782-1875) Pioneer. Born in Trois-Rivières, she married Jean-Baptiste Lagimodière* in 1806 and insisted on accompanying him back to the Northwest, where he was employed at Pembina by the HBC. She gave birth there to a daughter, Reine, reputed to be the first white woman born in the West. The Lagimodières were probably the first European family to settle in Western Canada. In 1818 they moved to St. Boniface, where Marie-Anne lived until her death. She was Louis Riel's grandmother. Legends about her courage are common among Franco-Manitobans. See George Dugas, *La PremièreCanadienned uNord-Ouest*(1883).*DCB*X,296-97.

Gaddy, William (b. 1815) Farmer. A mixed-blood farmer who had settled in Portage la Prairie, he was captured as a spy by Louis Riel in February 1870. According to Riel, he had been a courier for friends of John Schultz,* the leader of the Canadian Party, and the Métis had demanded his execution on the spot. He was led to one of the bastions of Fort Garry to be executed by A.D. Lépine* and Elzéar Goulet,* but was allowed to escape.

Gale, Samuel (1783-1865) Lawyer. Born in Florida, he moved to Canada with his Loyalist parents, and was called to the bar on 8 March 1807. Gale became Lord Selkirk's* Canadian lawyer in 1815 and accompanied Selkirk west in 1817. In 1818 and 1819 he helped manage the many trials in the Canadas that resulted from the fur-trade wars. He published *Notices on the Claims of the Hudson's BayCompany and the Conduct of Its Adversaries*(1817) and was rumoured to be involved in other writings that defended Selkirk's name. He became a judge of the Court of King's Bench in Montreal in 1834 and survived pressures for his dismissal in 1835. During the Rebellion of 1837 he suspended habeas corpus. *DCB*IX, 296-97.

Galt, Alexander Casimir (1853-1936) Judge. Born in Toronto to a distinguished family, he was the son of A.T. Galt, a Father of Confederation. He graduated from the University of Toronto in 1873. He moved to Rossland, British Columbia, and then in 1896 to Winnipeg. He was appointed to the Court of King's Bench in 1911, and served on several royal commissions. He presided controversially at the 1919 trial of F.W. Dixon,* one of the leaders of the Winnipeg General Strike, where he made little effort to hide his opinion that the plaintiff was guilty, especially in his summation to the jury. He retired in 1933.

Galt, George Frederick (1855-1928) Merchant, sportsman. Born in Toronto, he was educated at Galt Collegiate Institute. He came west in 1882 to found the wholesale house of G.F. and J. Galt. That same year he founded the Winnipeg Rowing Club, which he led to prominence. In 1888 he was president of the Board of Trade. He was later president of the Winnipeg General Hospital and the Manitoba Red Cross Society.

Gardner, Charlie ("Chuck," 1904-1934) Hockey goalie. Born in Edinburgh, Scotland, he came with his family to Winnipeg in 1911. He played for the Winnipeg Maroons in 1926-27 and was signed by the Chicago Black Hawks, playing in goal for them until his death. He won the Vezina Trophy as best goalie in 1932, and in 1933 allowed only 83 goals in 48 games, 10 of them shutouts. Although suffering from tonsillitis, he insisted on playing in the 1934 Stanley Cup finals, which Chicago won. Upon his return to Winnipeg after the victory, he died in St. Boniface Hospital. Gardner had a lifetime goals-allowed average of 2.02 in the NHL, which dropped to 1.37 in playoff games. He was elected to the Hockey Hall of Fame in 1945 and the Canadian Hockey Hall of Fame in 1957, and is a member of the Manitoba Sports Hall of Fame.

Garrett, Charles (b. 1818) Hotelier. Probably from Simcoe, he was a Winnipeg hotelkeeper and critic of the HBC. He was one of those taken prisoner by Louis Riel in the surrender of John Schultz's* house in December 1869. He was incarcerated for 66 days and was forced by the provisional government to leave the country after his release.

Garrioch, Alfred Campbell (1849-1934) Cleric, author. Born in Kildonan of mixed-blood origin, Garrioch studied theology at St. John's College during the Red River Rebellion of 1869-70. He negotiated with Riel for safe passage for his brother, one of the Portage la Prairie party that attempted to free prisoners in February 1870 and ended up prisoners of the Métis. He was later ordained as an Anglican priest, serving in Peace River and then in Manitoba. While in England in 1885 he published several translations into the Beaver language, as well as an English-Beaver and Cree dictionary. After retiring in 1905, he wrote a number of autobiographical works, including *First Furrows* (1923) and *The Correction Line* (1933).

Garrioch, Peter (1811-1888) Free trader. Educated at Kenyon College (1838-39), he worked as a schoolteacher, then moved into trade with the United States through St. Peter's in the 1840s. He was ordered in 1845 to pay duty on his imported goods, and was active in the free trade agitation of the 1840s. In the 1860s he had moved into the buffalo robe trade. See his "Journal of Peter Garrioch, Red River, 1843-47" in the UML Archives. There are also papers at the PAM.

Garrioch, William (b. 1787) Fur trader, schoolmaster. Born in Stromness, Orkney Islands, he joined the HBC in 1807 as a potential schoolmaster. For most of his years with the Company he worked in the fur trade. He retired in 1822 to Image Plain to reside next to his father-in-law, William Hemmings Cook.* In 1823 he taught school in the Red River Settlement under the supervision of Rev. John West,* and by 1825 he was a schoolmaster for the Church Missionary Society.

Garry, Nicholas (c. 1782-1856) Fur-trade governor. Born in England, he was probably the illegitimate son of a wealthy London merchant who financed his upbringing. He learned to speak German, French, and Russian well, and apparently was active in the Baltic trade before joining the HBC London Committee in 1817. After the merger of the HBC and NWC in 1821, Garry volunteered to travel to British North America to explain the agreement to the wintering partners. Appointed president of the Council of the Northern Department, he left London on 29 March 1821 and kept a detailed diary of his journey. He wrote more about the people he contacted than about the business he conducted, however. In the West he travelled with Simon* and William McGillivray,* who appear to have dominated affairs much of the time. But it was Garry who placed George Simpson* at the head of the Northern Department. In 1822 he became deputy governor of the HBC, serving until 1835, when he was declared of unsound mind. For his diary, see Francis N.A. Garry, ed., "Diary of Nicholas Garry, Deputy-Governor of the Hudson's Bay Company from 1822-1835," Royal Society of Canada *Transactions*, 2nd ser., 6 (1900), sect. II: 73-204. *DCB* VIII, 314-15.

Garson, Stuart Sinclair (1898-1977) Premier. Born in St. Catharines, Ontario, he came to Manitoba with his parents in 1901. He received an LLB from the University of Manitoba in 1918 and was called to the bar a year later. He practised law in Ashern from 1919 to 1928. In 1927 he was elected to the Manitoba legislature, and he became provincial treasurer in 1936. Concerned with the need for new financial arrangements for the province with the federal government, he advocated a federal royal commission to resolve the constitutional and financial impasse. In 1941 he added the telephone ministry and the Manitoba Power Commission to his portfolios. When John Bracken* entered federal politics in 1943,

Garson succeeded him as premier. Garson remained as provincial treasurer and also became minister for Dominion-provincial relations. He ran a budget surplus, while concentrating on rural highway construction and rural electrification. In 1948 he moved to the federal scene to become minister of justice and attorney general in the St. Laurent Cabinet. Two years later he became solicitor general and chair of the Continuing Committee on Constitutional Amendment. He was defeated in the 1957 election, and he stepped down from politics to practise law. He became a Companion of the Order of Canada in 1971. See Mark E. Vajcner, "Stuart Garson and the Manitoba Progressive Coalition," *Manitoba History,* no. 26 (autumn 1993): 29-35.

Garson, William C.W. (1856-1911) Politician. Born in the Orkney Islands, Scotland, he came to Canada in 1857. He was an Ontario MPP from 1886 to 1890, and he moved to Winnipeg in 1901. He founded the Garson Quarries in Tyndall. He was a member of Winnipeg's first Board of Control and was regarded as a superb platform orator. He died in Calgary.

Gasté, Marie-Joseph-Eugène-Alphonse (1830-1919) Missionary priest. Born in Andouillé, France, he was ordained a priest in 1855 and came to British North America in 1860 to join the Oblates in Rupert's Land. He spent 40 years as a missionary at St. Pierre, near the HBC fur-trading post of Lac-du-Brochet House on Reindeer Lake. He opened schools and spread his mission widely in the region. He ended his career as superior of the Oblates at Prince Albert. He returned to France in 1908. *DCB* XIV, 392-93.

Gaultier de la Vérendrye, Jean-Baptiste See La Vérendrye, Jean Baptiste Gaultier de.

Gaultier de la Vérendrye, de Boumois, Pierre See La Vérendrye, Pierre Gaultier de Boumois.

Gaultier de la Vérendrye, Louis-Joseph See La Vérendrye, Louis-Joseph.

Gaultier de Varennes de la Vérendrye, Pierre See La Vérendrye, Pierre Gaultier de Varennes.

Gauvin, Marshall Jerome (1881-1978) Freethinker. Born near Moncton, New Brunswick, to Acadian parents, he worked for the CNR while educating himself to be a public lecturer on freethinking. He toured North America for 14 years before settling in Winnipeg in 1926 at the invitation of the One Big Union. He lectured weekly from 1926 to 1940 at various theatres in the city. After he retired he worked at MacDonald Aircraft during WWII. He was the author of *Fundamentals of Free Thought* (1923). His papers are in the UML Archives, as is his extensive library of esoteric thought.

Gay, Norbert (fl. 1870) Adventurer. A Frenchman who arrived in Red River mysteriously in January 1870, he claimed to be a correspondent for a Paris newspaper. It was rumoured that he was a spy, but no one was certain for whom he was spying. Known as "Captain Gay," he became a loyal Riel supporter and attempted to instill European cavalry tactics into Riel's few remaining armed horsemen in the spring of 1870. Gay was a member of the party of horsemen led by Riel that made the final reconnoitre of the Wolseley encampment before the expedition officially arrived at the Forks.

Gebhardt, C. Keith (1899-1982) Artist. Born in Cheboygan, Michigan, he studied at the University of Michigan and the Art School of the Art Institute of Chicago. His first professional appointment was as principal of the Winnipeg School of Art in 1924. During his years in Winnipeg he exhibited often and was active in the community, particularly in set design for local theatre. He left Winnipeg in 1929 to tour Europe and did not return, going instead to Chicago for graduate work. In 1932 he joined the staff of the Milwaukee Public Museum of Natural History, where he found his true métier producing dioramas, models, and exhibits. He died in Milwaukee. See Marilyn Baker, *The Winnipeg School of Art: The Early Years* (1984).

Gee, Fred M. (1882-1946) Musician, impresario. Born in Cardiff, Wales, he immigrated to Winnipeg in 1902 and worked as a piano accompanist and organist. He joined the staff of the Winnipeg College of Music in 1903 and served as a church organist for years. He was also a faculty member of the Imperial Academy of Arts and Music. He was organist for the Winnipeg Oratorio Society from 1908 to 1928. In 1927 he became a full-time concert impresario, and he promoted the "Celebrity Series" of recitals across Canada in the 1930s. He died in Winnipeg. The "Celebrity Series" papers are at the PAM.

Gerrie, Robert (1830-1908) Merchant, land specu-lator. Born in Aberdeenshire, Scotland, he immigrated to Dundas, Upper Canada, at an early age. During the American Civil War he served with the Union Army as a veterinarian, stationed in Chicago. After the war he established a tobacco company in Montreal with his half-brother. In 1871 he headed for Duluth, Minnesota, and he arrived in Winnipeg with a load of furniture ("a better class of house furnishings") in 1873 to open the first furniture store in the West. He later went into business with his brother-in-law, Robert Bathgate. He was an active land speculator during the boom of the early 1880s. His real estate holdings included most of Princess Street, and he constructed the Grand Union Hotel, the Gerrie Block, and the Palace Stables. His health declined following a street assault in 1889 in which he lost an eye, but he helped open the West End in the early years of the twentieth century and was known as the "father of the Winnipeg Boom." He died in Winnipeg. *DCB* XIII, 379-80.

Geyer, George (fl. 1672-97) HBC fort governor. Known only for his service in the HBC, Geyer was governor of York Fort from 1686 to 1690. His term saw an attempt to settle at Churchill River and the first inland expedition of Henry Kelsey. *DCB* I, 328-29.

Gibbons, Lillian (1906-1996) Journalist, author. Born in Winnipeg, she was educated at the University of Manitoba. She was an early female gold med-allist in history (1928), and she received her MA in history in the 1930s. She worked for the *Winnipeg Tribune* from 1932 to 1972. Gibbons lived in the same bed-sitter in the downtown area of Winnipeg for 58 years. In 1969 she published *My Love Affair with Louis Riel*. Her book *Stories Houses Tell* (1978), produced for the Junior League of Winnipeg, was a best-seller. She died while cruising on the Amazon River in Bra-zil, having blithely informed her fellow passengers earlier that if she died on the boat, her body was to be thrown overboard immediately.

Gibson, Alexander (1883-1956) Surgeon. Born in Edinburgh, he graduated from the University of Edinburgh and demonstrated in surgery there. He became a Fellow of the Royal College of Surgeons in 1913, the year he came to Winnipeg to become professor of anatomy at the University of Manitoba Medical School. In the early 1940s he introduced and perfected the vitallum cup hip operation for arthritis sufferers. He published extensively in ana-tomical and orthopaedic subjects. During WWII he ran the Canadian Red Cross unit in Scotland.

Gibson, Reginald M. ("Reg," 1932-1998) Enter-tainer. Born in Carman, Manitoba, he began singing publicly at the age of four as "Little Reggie Gibson, the yodelling cowboy." He sang at fairs and rodeos, and was a popular radio and television performer of country music between 1949 and 1976, mainly on the CBC. He toured the Middle East to entertain troops in 1966-67. He was president of the Manitoba Cutting Horse Association and was Manitoba cham-pion from 1965 to 1967 on his horse Deacon Joe. He served as president of ACTRA from 1971 to 1973 and received its president's award for distin-guished service in 1989.

Gibson, Ronald Wilson (1903-1993) Musician. Born in Maidstone, Kent, England, he moved with his family to Morden, Manitoba, in 1913, where he began taking music lessons. The family moved to Winnipeg in 1918, where he studied organ. He was church organist at several Winnipeg churches over the years, including Holy Trinity from 1934 to 1987. He also conducted the Winnipeg Choral and Orches-tral Society (1927-29), and the Manitoba Schools Or-chestra (1935-40). He served with the RCAF during WWII, then studied in England (1946-49) before returning to direct the University of Manitoba School of Music until 1963. He retired in 1968 to turn to a career as a composer; he also wrote music reviews for the *Winnipeg Free Press*. He is a member of the Order of the Buffalo Hunt.

Gill, Edward Anthony Wharton (1859-1944) Cleric, author. Born in Scraptoft, Leicestershire, Eng-land, and educated at Loughborough Grammar School, Gill attended the University of London and then taught school at Market Drayton and in the Dan-ish West Indies before immigrating to Canada in 1884. He completed his education at the University of Manitoba in 1889 and was ordained a priest, serv-ing at Minnedosa from 1889 to 1919. He became pro-fessor of pastoral theology at St. John's College, Winnipeg, in 1920. He wrote two novels, *Love in Manitoba* (1911) and *An Irishman's Luck* (1914), as well as the semi-autobiographical *A Manitoba Chore Boy* (1912).

Gillam, Benjamin (1662/3-1706) Mariner. He ac-companied his father, Zachariah Gillam, on *The*

Bachelor's Delight to Nelson River in 1682, survived the shipwreck of the *Prince Rupert* that killed his father, and was captured by the French. Upon his return to New England he was imprisoned for interloping, but he was exonerated. *DCB* II, 247.

Gillam, Zachariah (1636-1682) Mariner. Born in Boston, he became involved in Hudson Bay through the support given by New England to Radisson and Groseilliers, and he served as captain of the *Nonsuch* on its 1668-69 voyage. He was subsequently dismissed by the HBC for private trading, but rejoined the Company in 1682 in command of the *Prince Rupert*, which was lost at sea in October 1682. His family remained in Boston. Gillam, Manitoba, is named after him. See G.A. Moriarity, "Captains Gillam and Sanford of the Hudson's Bay Company," *Genealogists' Magazine* 10 (1947-50): 568-71. *DCB* I, 337-38.

Ginter, Benjamin George (1923-1982) Brewer. Born in Swan River, Manitoba, he left school at age 13 and wandered the country working on farms and construction. In 1949 he established a construction firm in Prince George, British Columbia, which won many highway contracts from the Social Credit government. Ginter's firm also specialized in pulp-mill cleaning. In 1962 he bought the Caribou Brewing Company, changing the name to Tartan Brewing and putting his own name and picture on its most popular beer, "Uncle Ben's." He marketed the first canned beer in British Columbia in 1966. Ginter died in Richmond, British Columbia.

Girard, Marc-Amable (1822-1892) Premier. Born in Varennes, Canada, he was educated at the Collège de Saint-Hyacinthe. A protégé of Sir George-Étienne Cartier, Girard was brought to Manitoba in 1870 by Archbishop Taché to provide a French-Canadian presence in the new province and especially to help protect the guarantees made to the Francophones in the Manitoba Act. A Conservative, he was elected to represent St. Boniface in the legislature from 1870 to 1878 and from 1879 to 1883. He briefly served as premier in 1874. He also was a member of the Canadian Senate from 1871 and was senior member of the Council of the North-West Territories from 1872. He chaired a Senate Select Committee that studied the route of the CPR in 1877. From 1879 to 1883 he served in the Norquay government as provincial secretary and then as minister of agriculture. A personable man, he did not provide strong leadership,

and he gradually faded from the public scene. He was, however, the first president of the Société Saint-Jean-Baptiste of Manitoba. *DCB* XII, 369-73.

Giroux, Louis-Raymond (1841-1911) Cleric. A college chum of Louis Riel, he came to Red River in 1868 and served as priest at the Roman Catholic cathedral and at Ste. Anne des Chênes. He served as chaplain to Riel's forces at Fort Garry during the Red River Rebellion of 1869-70. He was later professor and rector of the Collège de Saint-Boniface. He died at Ste. Anne des Chênes.

Gladman, George (1800-1863) Fur trader, explorer. Born at New Brunswick House in present-day Ontario, the son of a fur trader and an Indian woman, he joined the HBC in 1814 and served at Moose Factory from 1819 to 1834. He became a chief trader in 1836 and served at York Factory, Norway House (1836-41), Upper Fort Garry, and Oxford House before retiring to Port Hope, Canada. In 1857 he was called out of retirement to head a scientific expedition to explore the possibility of a route to Red River from Ontario. His associates, Henry Youle Hind* and Simon James Dawson,* were highly critical of his leadership, and he withdrew from the expedition in 1858. *DCB* IX, 319-20.

Gladstone, Joseph Benjamin (1904-1990) Social activist, journalist. Born in Panevezys, Lithuania, he came to Brandon in 1908 and moved to Winnipeg after high school. He worked for years for the One Big Union and was associate editor of *The Commonwealth,* a CCF publication. He was a pioneer in the health food industry, and he edited *Healthful Living Digest* from 1955 to 1975. He retired to British Columbia in 1975 but died in Winnipeg.

Glass, David (1829-1906) Lawyer, politician. Born in Upper Canada of Irish descent, he joined the California gold rush in 1849, then entered the law and was called to the bar in 1864. He was an important municipal politician in London, Canada, serving as mayor in 1858 and 1864. Initially a supporter of John A. Macdonald when elected MP for Middlesex in 1872, Glass broke with the prime minister over the Pacific Scandal and was defeated for Parliament in the elections of 1874 and 1878. He came to Manitoba in 1882 and became solicitor for the City of Winnipeg. In 1886 he was elected to the Manitoba legislature from St. Clement's, and he served as

Speaker from 1887 to 1888, when he retired because of ill health.

Godfrey, Alvin K. (1871-1951) Businessman. Born in St. Louis, Missouri, he became a naturalized Canadian citizen in 1913. Godfrey was educated at the University of Minnesota before coming to Winnipeg, where he organized the Canadian Electric Company and Monarch Lumber. He was a prominent member of the Citizens' Committee of 1,000 during the Winnipeg General Strike of 1919.

Gollmer, Nancy Joan Carr (1929-1991) Militia officer. Born in Winnipeg, she graduated in arts from United College in 1949, then joined the militia in 1954. In 1957 she was made an officer, and after 1965 she was part of the Fort Garry Horse militia regiment. In 1971 she was one of the first women to attend the Militia Officers Staff College, and she became the first militia lieutenant-colonel in Canada in 1975. She commanded NLCC Lord Selkirk in Winnipeg from 1980 to 1986.

Good, J.W. (1858-1926) Physician. Born in Kincardine, Canada, he was educated in medicine in Toronto. He came to Winnipeg in 1880, becoming dean of the faculty at Manitoba Medical College. In 1898 he went to the Klondike, where he served as the first health officer of Dawson City in 1898-99. He then practised medicine in Winnipeg from 1899 to 1920, the first Winnipeg doctor specializing in eye, ear, nose, and throat problems. He was noted as a local eccentric. He retired to Vancouver in 1920, where he died. He left an estate worth $500,000. See the unpublished memoir by J.W. Montgomery, "J.W. Good, the Most Unforgettable Character I Have Known," Manitoba Legislative Library.

Good, Mary Ann (Kirton) (b. 1841) Amateur landscaper. Born in Red River, she brought home a maple sapling in 1857 and planted it near her house. She continued the practice of planting trees, including elms and maples, after she and her husband moved in 1860 to the banks of the Assiniboine River in what is now the Wolseley district of Winnipeg. They built a house on the corner of Newman and Wolseley. She was reputed to have planted the famous "Wolseley Elm." See W.J. Healey, *Women of Red River* (1923), 101-6.

Goodeve, Charles (1904-1980) Scientist. Born in Neepawa, Manitoba, he attended the University of Manitoba and University College, London. In 1940 he developed a method of rendering ships immune to magnetic mines, and as commander of a Royal Navy research unit he made other technological breakthroughs. He headed the British Iron and Steel Research Association from 1945 to 1969. Goodeve worked to promote Anglo-Canadian scientific cooperation. He was knighted in 1946.

Gordon, Charles William, a.k.a. Ralph Connor (1860-1937) Cleric, author. Born in Glengarry County, Canada, the son of a Presbyterian minister, he graduated from the University of Toronto and also studied at Knox College and the University of Edinburgh. He was ordained to the Presbyterian ministry in 1890. After some missionary years in Western Canada, Gordon accepted the pulpit at St. Stephen's Church in Winnipeg. He was an active social gospeller and advocate of temperance, and he became senior Protestant chaplain to the Canadian forces during WWI. As Ralph Connor, he was a prolific and popular novelist of the day. Many of his early novels drew on his missionary experience, as he wrote with vigour about a muscular Christianity that always triumphed in the end. Much of his work concentrated on the Western Canadian frontier, with good confronting evil in the plots. His best-known books — *The Man from Glengarry, Glengarry School Days,* and *The Foreigner*— have different themes, the last dealing with the assimilation of a new immigrant to Canada, the first two with growing up in Ontario. But all three are concerned with young men and their development. In the years before WWI, Ralph Connor was one of the world's best-selling writers, and his work never ceased to find an audience during his lifetime. Scholars study him today less for his craftsmanship than for his attitudes, many of which were quite typical of much of middle-class Anglophone Canada. An ardent imperialist, he was an enthusiastic patriot in WWI, and undertook many fundraising and speaking tours during the conflict. He was also an early enthusiastic cottager at Lake of the Woods. His autobiography was published as *Postscript to Adventure* (1938). His papers are at the UML Archives.

Gordon, (John) King (1900-1989) Activist, author. Born in Winnipeg, he was educated locally, and graduated from the University of Manitoba in 1920.

He was a Rhodes scholar at Oxford in 1920-21. He later studied theology at what became United College, graduating in 1927, and did graduate work at Oxford and the Union Theological Seminary. He served as a United Church minister in Manitoba and then as professor of Christian ethics at the Union Theological Seminary in Montreal from 1931 until 1935, when he was dismissed for his left-wing opinions. In the 1930s and 1940s he was active in the CCF and the League for Social Reconstruction. He served as a book and magazine editor (managing *The Nation* magazine from 1944 to 1947) and was UN correspondent for the CBC from 1947 until 1950, when he became human rights and information officer for the UN. He held that post until 1962. He served with several UN social and cultural agencies in a variety of places, including Korea and the Congo. After retirement he wrote and lectured extensively on social and international issues. The author of *The UN in the Congo* (1962) and *The New International Economic Order* (1976), he was awarded an honorary degree from the University of Manitoba in 1983. He was awarded the Order of Canada in 1977 and the Pearson Peace Medal in 1980. His papers are at the NAC.

Gordon, "Lord" Gordon, a.k.a. Hon. Mr. Herbert Hamilton and numerous other aliases (c. 1840s-1874) Confidence trickster. He left Britain in early 1870 after impersonating a Scottish peer in order to buy a shooting estate. In 1871 he emerged in Minnesota, then in 1872 in New York, where he briefly took in Jay Gould for a reported million dollars. Later in 1872 he settled in Winnipeg, posing as a British gentleman until he was kidnapped in early July 1873 by a band of bounty hunters who attempted to take him into the United States to collect a reward offered by Gould. They failed and were arrested in Winnipeg. In the course of the subsequent legal proceedings, which became an international incident leading to desperate messages in code from Canadian prime minister Sir John A. Macdonald, Gordon was fully exposed. At a boarding house in Headingley in 1874, when police tried to arrest him for extradition to New York, he shot himself in the head. See J.L. Johnston, "Lord Gordon Gordon," *HSSM Papers*, 3rd series, no. 7 (1952), 7-20. *DCB* V, 307-08 and David Samuels, "The Confidence Man," *The New Yorker*, 26 April & 3 May, 1999, 150-61. There are papers at the PAM.

Gordon, Ruth ("Fee," 1908-1998) Musician. Born in Winnipeg, the daughter of Charles W. and Helen

Gordon, she graduated from the University of Manitoba in 1928 with a BA in classics. She became actively involved with the Winnipeg music community as an accompanist, playing for the Winnipeg Ballet, the Manitoba Music Festival, and the CBC Radio School Broadcasts (with which she was associated for 30 years). Gordon was also a part of Winnipeg's amateur theatre.

Gotlieb, Sarah ("Sally," 1899-1998) Zionist leader. Probably born in Skala, Galicia, she emigrated with her parents to Philadelphia. She moved to Winnipeg with her family as a child and graduated from St. John's High School. She became active in the Ezra Chapter of Hadassah, was elected its president in 1922, and in 1932 became president of the Winnipeg Hadassah Council. In 1934 she was voted western vice-president of Hadassah, and she served until 1951. During WWII she was chair of Hadassah Youth Aliyah and was known locally as "the woman who led everything." From 1951 to 1955 she served as national president of Canadian Hadassah. She was also active in the Women's International Zionist Organization (WIZO) and was its first representative to UNESCO. She declined the presidency of World WIZO because her husband refused to leave Winnipeg.

Goulet, Elzéar (1836-1870) Métis leader. Born in St. Boniface, he was educated there. A member of the military tribunal that condemned Thomas Scott,* in September 1870 he was attacked by a mob of Canadian volunteers from the Wolseley Expedition, who forced him with stones to the river, where he drowned. His recovered body indicated he had been struck in the head with a stone. Goulet was apparently an American citizen, a result of his serving as a mail carrier from Pembina to Upper Fort Garry from 1860 to 1869. *DCB* IX, 329-30.

Goulet, Roger (b. 1867) Educator. Born in Red River, he was educated at the Collège de Saint-Boniface. He received his BA from the University of Manitoba in 1891 and his MA in 1895. In 1900 he was appointed inspector of bilingual schools in the province and principal of the St. Boniface Normal School. In 1909 he became president of the Union Nationale Métisse. He was a member of the Société Historique de Saint-Boniface and Bon Parler Français.

Gow, George F. (1835-1911) Hotelier. Born in England, he came to Canada from Ireland, where he had grown up. He was appointed Indian agent at Winnipeg in 1878 by the Macdonald government, but he soon resigned to become proprietor of the Morris House in Morris, which he ran for 15 years while farming in the area. He then moved to Estevan, Saskatchewan, before returning to Winnipeg to operate a real estate and insurance business.

Gowanlock, Ab (1900-1988) Curler. He began curling at Glenboro, Manitoba, at an early age, later skipping teams that were nationally successful. Employed by the Department of Highways, he moved to Dauphin in the 1940s. He skipped two of the three rinks from outside Greater Winnipeg that represented Manitoba at the Brier between 1927 and 1957, winning both times (1938 and 1953).

Gowler, Oliver (1812-1866) Farmer. He was born in Lincolnshire, England. In 1836 he and his wife came to Red River, where Gowler was to run the HBC experimental farm. The venture soon failed, and Gowler began his own farm at Kildonan, moving to higher ground on the Assiniboine River in Headingley after the flood of 1852. Gowler's success at farming was written about in the *Nor'-Wester*, and at considerable length by Henry Youle Hind* in his 1860 report on the Canadian Red River Exploring Expedition of 1857. According to Hind, Gowler farmed fifty acres in white and green crops. His turnips, potatoes, and melons were superior, although his homegrown tobacco was "dreadfully strong." In 1859 he realized 700 bushels of wheat, 350 of barley, 480 of oats, and 2,100 of potatoes. These yields, Hind insisted, meant that Red River was "one of the best agricultural countries on the face of the globe."

Graham, Andrew (c. 1730s-1815) Fur trader, natural scientist. Born in Scotland, he joined the HBC in 1749. He served as master of Fort Severn, acting chief of York Factory, and, in 1774-75, chief factor of Fort Prince of Wales. He retired to Edinburgh in 1775. He wrote an elaborate series of manuscript "Observations" beginning in the 1760s, mainly about natural history and Company trading methods, which were eventually published as *Andrew Graham's Observations on Hudson Bay, 1767-91* (1969). In the eighteenth century much of his scientific work was improperly appropriated by Thomas Hutchins, who used it to gain a reputation as a natural scientist. *DCB* V, 362-63.

Graham, George Edward (1873-1912) *Titanic* victim. Born near St. Mary's, Ontario, he worked as a hardware clerk before obtaining employment with Eaton's department store. In 1906 he was sent by Eaton's to its new store in Winnipeg to head its crockery and china section. He died in the sinking of the *Titanic* in 1912. There is a commemorative plaque in his memory in Winnipeg City Hall, and a street was named in his honour.

Grahame, James Allan (1825-1905) Fur trader. Born in Edinburgh, Scotland, he attended Edinburgh Academy and joined the HBC as an apprentice clerk in 1843. He learned the fur business at York Factory and Upper Fort Garry, and then was sent to the Columbia District, where he spent many years, rising to chief trader in 1854 and head of the Oregon Department in 1858. He was responsible for the transfer of Fort Vancouver to the Americans in 1860, and moved everything he could to Fort Victoria. In 1861 he was transferred to the Northern Department. He served as head of Lower Fort Garry in 1861-62 and of Norway House from 1862 until 1867, when he was returned to the Western Department. In 1870 he and Roderick Finlayson became heads of the department; he was responsible for the coastal operations, and he took over sole command in 1872. That same year he became subcommissioner of the HBC, serving in that post until 1874, when he succeeded Donald A. Smith* as chief commissioner of the Company in North America. Grahame led the HBC into transportation and retailing but without much enthusiasm, and he was criticized in the early 1880s for being "much behind the times." His letter of resignation of 1883 was accepted in 1884. After retirement he moved first to Montreal and then, in 1887, to Victoria, where his wife's relatives were part of the British Columbia elite. He died in Victoria. *DCB* XIII, 398-400.

Grandin, Vital Justin (1829-1902) Missionary. Born in France, he entered a seminary despite a speech impediment. He was finally ordained by the Oblates in 1854. He volunteered for service in the Canadian West and arrived at St. Boniface that same year. He was soon sent into the field among the Natives, totally lacking in advance preparation. In 1859 he became coadjutor bishop of St. Boniface, based in the Mackenzie Basin. The community of St. Vital, founded in 1860, was named after him. He accompanied A.A. Taché* to Rome and France in 1867, and in 1871 became the first bishop of Saint Albert. He protested the treatment of the Métis in the 1880s, and later objected to the provincial government policy toward Catholic schools. See B. Owens and C. Roberto, eds., *The Diaries of Bishop Vital Grandin* (1989), and, for a biography, P.-E. Breton, *Vital Grandin, o.m.i.* (1960).

Grandmaison, Nicholas de (1892-1978) Artist. Born in Russia, he served in the Russian army and was a German prisoner of war. He ended up in England after WWI but, uncertain of his immigrant status there, he came to Canada. In Winnipeg, he found work at Brigden's, and he was enrolled at the Winnipeg School of Art from 1923 to 1926 and 1928 to 1929. Travels outside Winnipeg led him to become fascinated with Indians. A successful career as a portrait artist and commercial illustrator in Winnipeg was ended by the Depression. By 1931 he was in Calgary as a staff member of the Technical School. Throughout the remainder of his life he specialized in portraits of Indians. He entered the Royal Canadian Academy in 1942 and received the Order of Canada in 1972. See Hugh A. Dempsey, *History i n Their Blood: The Indian Portraits of Nicholas de Grandmaison* (1982).

Grant, Cuthbert (d. 1799) Fur trader. He was probably the son of David Grant of Strathspey, Scotland. First observed in the West in 1785, Cuthbert Grant was active in the Great Slave Lake and Athabasca regions before locating in the upper Assiniboine district at River Tremblante. He became a partner of the HBC in 1795. *DCB* IV, 310.

Grant, Cuthbert James (c. 1796-1854) Métis leader. A mixed-blood son of Cuthbert Grant,* he was born in Rupert's Land and was educated in Montreal. He returned west in time to lead the "bois-brûlés" against the Selkirk settlers in 1815 and 1816. He was the military captain of the Métis in the Seven Oaks affair. Arrested in 1817 and sent east, he was later released on bail and was never tried. He jumped bail and returned to the West in 1818. He served briefly with the HBC but then settled at White Horse Plain, where he became known as the "Warden of the Plains," an official title given him by the HBC in 1824 (with an accompanying annual salary of £200). Grant became the leader of the Métis at White Horse Plain and eventually the most respected Métis in the settlement. In later years Grant was a friend both of

Red River and of the HBC. From 1835 until his death he was a member of the Council of Assiniboia and a justice of the peace for the Fourth District of Assiniboia. He sat on the bench in the notorious *Foss v. Pelly* case of 1850. For a biography, see M.A. MacLeod and W.L. Morton, *Cuthbert Grant of Grantown* (1963). *DCB* VIII, 341-44.

Grant, Peter (c. 1764-1848) Fur trader. Born in Scotland, he entered the NWC in 1784 and was posted to the Lower Red River. In 1797 he became a full partner with control of the Lac La Pluie Department. In 1804 he wrote a study of the Saulteaux Indians which was highly regarded by later scholars. He settled in Lower Canada in 1805, moving to Lachine in 1820, where he died. He joined the Beaver Club in 1807. See his "The Saulteaux Indians about 1804," in *Les Bourgeois de la Compagnie du Nord-Ouest*, ed. L.-F. Masson, vol. 2, 303-66. *DCB* VII, 356-57.

Gray, Charles Frederick (1879-1954) Municipal politician. Born in London, England, he was a consulting electrical engineer with no apparent links to Winnipeg's commercial elite before his election to the Board of Control in 1917. He lived in Elm Park. During the 1918 municipal workers' strike, he began by favouring a compromise with the unions and ended up supporting the resolution denying to all civic employees the right to strike. He ran for mayor in 1918 on a platform of honest government, and was mayor during the Winnipeg General Strike in 1919. He was gradually persuaded that the strike was Bolshevism run rampant. He supported the efforts of city council to force its employees back to work through "yellow dog" tactics, and issued public proclamations against street demonstrations. On 5 June he ordered the use of special constables. On "Black Friday" (20 June) when he was told the specials could not control the crowds, he personally drove to NWMP headquarters to request the Mounties to intervene. He subsequently read the riot act to the demonstrators at city hall. In 1941 he moved to Ashland, British Columbia, where he operated a salt mine. He died in Victoria.

Gray, Claude W. (c. 1880-1937) Sculptor. Born in London, England, he immigrated to Manitoba in 1902 and won a gold medal that year for displays at the Winnipeg Industrial Fair. Before WWI he worked for photographic studios, probably as a colour retoucher, and (from 1910) for the CPR in the drafting department. He enlisted in the army, and after de-mobilization he set up a studio across the street from the Winnipeg School of Art. He worked in many media, although he became most interested in sculpture, winning some national attention but little financial reward.

Gray, James H. (1906-1998) Historian, journalist. Born in Whitemouth, Manitoba, and brought up in Winnipeg, he attended Kelvin High School, leaving it after Grade Nine to work in the Winnipeg Grain Exchange. He spent the Great Depression on relief until he became a reporter for the *Winnipeg Free Press* in 1935, working in the Ottawa press gallery until 1947, when he lost his job over his treatment of Canadian trade policy. Gray later worked as a journalist in many parts of Canada, editing the *Farm and Ranch Review* and the *Western Oil Examiner*. He took early retirement in 1963 to complete the manuscript of *The Winter Years* (1966), which had been rejected by Macmillan nearly 20 years earlier. He subsequently wrote a series of autobiographical social histories of the Canadian Prairies, including *The Boy from Winnipeg* (1970) and *The Roar of the Twenties* (1975). Other historical works included *Men against the Desert* (1967), *Red Lights on the Prairies* (1971), and *Booze* (1972). Gray was at his best when he had some personal stake in the narrative, although his prose was always lucid. He won the Pierre Berton Award from Canada's National History Society for distinguished achievement in popularizing Canadian history. He died in Calgary.

Green, Verna Merle Christina (Feely) (1908-1999) Community leader. Born in Winnipeg, she resided in River Heights as a child and was educated at Mulvey School, Kelvin High School, and the University of Manitoba. She taught school until moving to Edmonton in 1934. She and her husband then moved to Minnedosa and operated a local five-and-dime store from 1941 to 1967. For many years she wrote annual Santa letters to local children from Box No. 1, Snow Flake Lane. She was honoured often for this service and was awarded the Order of the Buffalo Hunt in 1980. Green died in Minnedosa.

Greenfield, Joseph (1845-1910) Architect. Born in England, he came to Toronto to practise as an architect and later moved to Winnipeg. He became superintendent of public works for the federal government in 1903. Among his buildings were: the Cornelius Building at 120 King Street (1876), 148-150 Alexander Avenue (1884), the Ryan Block on Main Street (1903), and Benard House (1903).

Greenway, John Franklin (1865-1930) Civil servant. Born in Exeter, Ontario, he came to Crystal City, Manitoba, where he operated as a grain dealer. He moved to Winnipeg in 1915 to be assistant deputy minister of education, serving until his death. He was a nephew of Thomas Greenway.*

Greenway, Thomas (1838-1908) Premier. Born in Kilhampton, England, he immigrated with his parents to Canada in 1846. He fought his first election campaign in Ontario in 1872 as a federal Conservative, employing Pacific Scandal money. In 1875 he finally won by acclamation. In 1876 he broke with the Tories and joined the Liberal caucus. Two years later, having bought a farm of 800 acres, he led a party of settlers (the Rock Lake Colonization Company) to Manitoba, where they settled around Crystal City in the southwestern part of the province. In 1879 he was elected to the Legislative Assembly from the Mountain riding. He ran as a Provincial Rights candidate in 1883 and became legislative leader of the Opposition to the Norquay Conservatives. Finally in 1888 he led the Liberals to victory at the polls. Greenway became associated with 1890 legislation that eliminated the dual system of Protestant-Catholic schools which had prevailed since 1870. Instead it created a non-denominational public school system supported by public funds, and denied funding to Catholic schools. Many scholars claim that the support for public schools in Manitoba was less a reflection of anti-Catholicism than of a desire for a province totally assimilated to Ontario values. In any event, Greenway's Liberals won a decisive victory at the polls in July 1892 and continued to use the schools business to great effect, refusing to give in to threats of federal remedial legislation and in general opposing Ottawa. A greater electoral victory for Greenway ensued in early 1896. After the election of the Laurier Liberals in Ottawa in 1896, a compromise (the "Laurier-Greenway" Compromise) was reached, permitting religious instruction and the teaching of languages other than English in the public schools. But Greenway did not concede the basic principle. Nevertheless, public opinion was not enthusiastic about the compromise, and the Laurier government did not provide Manitoba with significantly better financial arrangements. The failure of the provincial government to acquire additional railroads quickly enough was a mark against it. Greenway's Liberals lost the 1899 election despite receiving almost half the popular vote. After several years of lacklustre leadership of the Opposition, Greenway ran federally and won in 1904. In 1908 he died in Ottawa before he could take up an appointment on the Board of Railway Commissioners. See Manitoba Historic Resources Branch, *Thomas Greenway* (1984); Joseph Hilts, *The Political Career of Thomas Greenway* (1974); Keith Wilson, *Thomas Greenway* (1985). Greenway is a member of the Manitoba Agricultural Hall of Fame. *DCB* XIII, 416-23. There are extensive papers at the PAM.

Grey Owl, a.k.a. Archibald Stansfeld Belaney (1888-1938) Author, environmentalist. Born in England, he came to Canada at an early age and adopted Aboriginal ways. After service in the Canadian forces during WWI, he was adopted by the Ojibwa in 1920. He passed as an Indian, claiming to be the "half-breed" son of an Apache mother. In 1931 he lived and worked in Riding Mountain National Park, Manitoba, engaged in the conservation of wildlife. He moved on to Prince Albert National Park in Saskatchewan, which served as the arena for most of his best-known work. In the 1930s he became a leading lecturer and writer on conservation, in the process celebrating the lifestyle of the Aboriginal people of North America. His most important works were *Men of the Last Frontier* (1931) and *Pilgrims of the Wild* (1934). See Lovat Dickson, *Half-breed: The Story of Grey Owl* (1939); Anahareo [his wife], *Devil in Deerskins: My Life with Grey Owl* (1972); Donald B. Smith, *From the Land of Shadows: The Making of Grey Owl* (1990).

Groseilliers, Médard Chouart des See Chouart des Groseilliers, Médard.

Grove, Frederick Philip (1879-1948) Author. Born Felix Paul Greve in Prussia, he lived a wandering life and privately published several books (including *Fanny Essler* and *Mauermeister Ihles Haus*, as well as a collection of poetry entitled *Wanderungen*) after being convicted of fraud in 1903 and imprisoned for a year. Upon his release he was unable to make a living with his pen, and he fell ever deeper into debt. He first fled to Sweden and then in 1909 to North America, ending up in Manitoba via North Dakota as schoolteacher Fred Grove. His knowledge of German led to his appointment to teach at Kronsfeld School in the Mennonite village of Haskett near Winkler. After attending normal school, he became principal of the intermediate school at Winkler, then moved to Virden and in 1916 to Gladstone, where he became principal of the high school. Two years later he moved to a small rural school near Falmouth. The bushland country of this area northeast of Gladstone was an environment that appealed to Grove, and it became the setting of his finest novels as well as the basis of *Over Prairie Trails* (1922) and *The Turn of the Year* (1923). In 1923 he retired to devote himself to writing, and he published his first Canadian novel, *Settlers of the Marsh*, in 1925. The partly autobiographical *A Search for America* came in 1927, and *Our Daily Bread* in 1928. Grove continued to be plagued by lack of material success, although he was becoming increasingly recognized as a major writer. He failed in publishing, then as a dairy farmer, and his family was supported by his wife's teaching through most of the Depression. He continued to write until his death, to increasing Canadian recognition for his unsparing depiction of Prairie reality. His later fiction included *The Yoke of Life* (1930), *Fruits of the Earth* (1933), *Two Generations* (1939, set in Ontario), *The Master of the Mill* (1944, also set in Ontario), and *Consider Her Ways* (1947). His autobiography, *In Search of Myself* (1946), won the Governor General's Award in 1947. The title was ironic, and the work should probably be regarded as fiction much like the novels, since it created a Swedish aristocratic background for Grove that was quite untrue and that muddied accounts of his life until Douglas Spettigue published *F.P.G.: The European Years* (1973), setting the record straight. Grove's prose in English was always somewhat awkward and ponderous. One of his favourite themes was that of the harsh patriarch, another the oppressed younger woman seeking autonomy, and a third the older male failure seeking to understand his life. Grove has long attracted both critical and biographical attention from Canadian scholars. Desmond Pacey's *Frederick Philip Grove* appeared in 1945, Ronald Sutherland's *Frederick Philip Grove* in 1969, and Margaret Stobie's *Frederick Philip Grove* in 1973. His *Letters* were edited by Pacey and appeared in 1976. The Grove papers and D.O. Spettigue's papers on Grove are at the UML Archives.

Grymington, Michael (d. 1710) Mariner. He joined the HBC as a seaman in 1680 and achieved his first command in 1685. He was captured by the French in 1688 and did not return to London until 1689. He sailed as first mate on the *Royal Hudson's Bay* in 1689, helping its captain, Leonard Edgecomb, fend off the French at sea off the Scilly Islands. He was rewarded with the command of the *Dering* that same year, and he continued to captain HBC vessels for the remainder of his life, usually stationed at York Fort. He was regarded as a highly skilled navigator. *DCB* II, 265-67.

Guest, Marie Olivia (Hewson) (1880-1966) Artist. Born in Oxham, Nova Scotia, she attended Mount Allison College and studied art in Boston and New York. She later attended the Yellow Door School in London, England, and from 1917 to 1919 taught painting and crafts at Mount Allison College. She married Benson Guest and moved to Winnipeg in 1919. She began exhibiting again in 1927, becoming one of Winnipeg's major female painters until the 1940s. A retrospective exhibition of her work was held in 1991. See the exhibition catalogue, *A Winnipeg History: The Art of Marie Guest, 1880-1966* (1991), and Claudine Majzels, "Constructing the Woman Artist: Marie Hewson Guest in Winnipeg," *Manitoba History*, no. 29 (spring 1995): 2-10.

Guiboche, Louis (c. 1785-c.1859) Fur trader. Born in Rupert's Land, he was a Métis who was employed as interpreter by the NWC in 1804. He joined the HBC in 1810 and served in the Athabasca country until settling in Red River in the early 1820s. For several years he carried goods between the settlement and York Factory, and then, with Cuthbert Grant,* he did independent trading (with HBC approval) in the Qu'Appelle region, retiring as postmaster in 1831. Although he held property on the Assiniboine River, he eventually possessed only his lot at St. Boniface, where he resided. *DCB* VIII, 349.

Gunn, Donald (1797-1878) Farmer, schoolmaster, author. Born in Halkirk, Caithness, Scotland, he entered the employ of the HBC in 1813, serving at York Factory, Fort Severn, and Oxford House. Gunn criticized both the Company and Lord Selkirk, later writing as if he had been a Selkirk settler. In 1823 he settled at Red River in "Little Britain" (St. Andrews Parish) as a farmer. He also served for years as a justice of the petty court, and he was foreman of the jury in the Sayer trial of 1849. A prominent Presbyterian, he taught for 18 years in the Church Missionary Society parish school before the establishment of a Presbyterian church in Red River, and served as the settlement's librarian for years. He became a member of the Council of the Institute of Rupert's Land in 1862, and he was a meteorological correspondent of the Smithsonian Institution, later collecting specimens for its museum. Gunn was chosen as a delegate to the November 1869 council from St. Andrews, and English delegate to the 1870 Convention of Forty from the same community. He was later appointed to the Legislative Council of Manitoba, serving from 1871 to 1876. He supported the council's abolition. His *History of Manitoba* was completed by his nephew Charles Tuttle* and published in 1880. It displays an anti-Selkirk and anti-HBC, as well as an anti-clerical, bias. *DCB* X, 324-25.

Gunn, George (fl. 1869-70) Farmer. A Scots mixed-blood, he was a Poplar Point merchant and farmer. He was a delegate to the November 1869 council from Ste. Anne's. Subsequently, he was chosen councillor to the new provisional government from Ste. Anne's on 28 February 1870 because he might have refused to serve if selected informally. A Red River Rebellion claimant, he was awarded nothing in compensation.

Guttormsson, Guttormur Jónsson (1878-1966) Author. Born in Icelandic River (Riverton), Manitoba, he had little formal education. He spent most of his life, apart from a brief stint as a storekeeper, farming in Icelandic River. He wrote poetry and plays in Icelandic and was revered in Iceland as a major literary voice, being honoured by the Icelandic government in 1939. He was also a prominent local bandsman of his day. He published three volumes of verse in Icelandic: *John of the East Fjords and Various Poems* (1909), *A Farmer's Daughter* (1920), and *Jest and Ernest* (1930). *Ten Plays* was published in Reykjavík in 1930. The plays are regarded as not stageable because the author knew nothing about stagecraft, having seen no more than one or two plays performed in his lifetime. He was regarded as a great platform performer, however, particularly when reciting his poetry. A volume of his work in English was published as *English Translations of Icelandic Poems* (1993). See Roy St. George Stubbs, *In Search of a Poet* (1975).

Hagel, Nathaniel Francis (b. 1846) Criminal lawyer. Born in Oxford, Canada, he was educated at Ingersoll and Woodstock before articling for the law. He came to Winnipeg in 1881, becoming the province's best-known criminal lawyer of his day. Between 1898 and 1905 he practised in British Columbia and the Yukon Territory. A Conservative, he unsuccessfully contested provincial seats several times. *DCB* XIV, 443.

Haggart, Alexander (1848-1927) Lawyer, judge, politician. Born in Peterborough, Canada, he attended Victoria University in Cobourg and was called to the Ontario bar in 1878. He came to Winnipeg in 1880 and became the law partner of Hugh John Macdonald* and A.C. Killam.* He was a member of the Winnipeg School Board, and ran successfully for Parliament as a Tory in 1908. He was re-elected in 1917. He served as president of the Law Society from 1906 to 1910, and on the Manitoba Court of Appeal from 1912 to 1920. He was a Mason and a member of the Congregational Church. Haggart was also a proud Scotsman.

Haig, James Campbell (1910-1980) Senator. Born in Winnipeg, he graduated from the University of Manitoba in 1934. A highly successful corporate lawyer, he served as chair of the Winnipeg School Board and as a member of the Board of Regents of United College. He was also director and secretary of CJAY-TV and president of the Canadian

Council of Crippled Children (1959-60). A Progressive-Conservative, he was appointed to the Canadian Senate in 1962, retiring in 1977. He lived on Wellington Crescent.

Haig, Kennethe McMahon (c. 1886-1977) Journalist, author. She graduated from the University of Manitoba in arts and worked for the *Free Press* as a reporter and editorial writer for most of her life. Her columns appeared under the byline "Ailison Craig." She was president of the Canadian Women's Press Club. Haig was the author of a biography of Cora Hind (1946) and several other biographical works, as well as *Precedent to Precedent: The Development of Civil Rights, Great Britain and Canada* (1956).

Haldane, John (c. 1775-1857) Fur trader. Born in Scotland, he entered the fur trade in 1798, probably with the XY Company. He joined the NWC in 1804 and was a leader of the wintering partners in their struggles with the Montreal and London merchants from 1816 to 1821. He became a chief factor when the HBC and NWC merged in 1821, in charge of the Columbia District. Haldane disagreed with George Simpson* and resigned in 1826 to return to Scotland. *DCB* VIII, 350-51.

Hales, Benjamin Jones (1869-1945) Educator. Born in Peterborough, Ontario, he was educated at the University of Toronto. He served as a teacher in Manitoba and Saskatchewan before joining the staff of the first normal school in Brandon in 1907; he was its principal from 1913 to 1938. He served as a Brandon alderman from 1920 to 1923 and was chair of the Parks Board for 19 years. His books on trees and wildflowers became standard school texts. His natural history collection is in the B.J. Hales Museum at Brandon University. He died in Brandon. See Manitoba Culture, Heritage and Recreation, Historic Resources Branch, *Brandon Normal School* (n.d.).

Halkett, John (1768-1852) Colonial official, businessman. Born in Pitfirrane, Scotland, his father assumed the name of Halkett when he became baronet of Pitfirrane in 1779. John attended St. Andrew's and was admitted to the bar in Edinburgh in 1789. He served as secretary to his cousin Baron Loughborough, who was Chancellor of Exchequer (1797-1801), and then held a series of colonial appointments, first as governor of the Bahamas (1801-3) and then as governor of Tobago (1803). He subsequently became first chief commissioner of West Indian accounts. Halkett and his cousins became interested in the HBC in 1808 and he became a member of the London Committee in November 1811. In 1815 he married his cousin, Lady Katherine Douglas, sister of Lord Selkirk.* Between 1815 and 1820 Halkett engaged in damage control on behalf of Selkirk, writing a number of printed pamphlets and private letters to the colonial secretary defending Selkirk's conduct in North America. He was not successful, either in convincing the public or the British government of the propriety of Selkirk's cause. In 1821 Halkett, as an executor to the Selkirk estate, travelled to North America to deal with business affairs, keeping a journal of his experiences. In Montreal he was threatened on several occasions with violence, including a horsewhipping, and was actually attacked with a whip. Halkett responded by shooting his assailant. In 1822 he travelled by canoe with Andrew Bulger* to Red River, where he assured demoralized settlers that the estate would honour Selkirk's promises. He also chaired a meeting of the HBC Northern Department council that passed resolutions about education and land-granting to mixed-bloods at the settlement. Halkett's most important Selkirk pamphlet was *Statement respecting the Earl of Selkirk's Settlement upon the Red River* (1817, expanded edition 1817). He also published his *Correspondence* with Lord Bathurst, 1817-19 (1819). He later published *Historical Notes Respecting the Indians of North America with Remarks on the Attempts Made to Convert and Civilize Them* in 1825. This work was based on a reading of extensive secondary literature and recommended a more sympathetic policy toward the Aboriginal peoples of British North America. *DCB* VIII, 351-53.

Hall, Elmer E. (b. 1865) Banker, businessman. Born in Nashua, Iowa, he grew up as a farm boy before taking employment at a bank in Iowa. He rose through the ranks to cashier and then president of the First National Bank of Hartley. He began investing in land in Western Canada in 1902 and moved to Saskatchewan in 1906 to open a general banking business, which became the Hall Company Limited, with its head office in Winnipeg, where he came to reside. He also founded the Central Grain Company, Limited, and was president of the Security National Insurance Company of Canada, Limited, which operated a large line of grain elevators. His Sheldon Farm Company, Limited, operated a 7,680-acre farm near Hanley, Saskatchewan. He was proud of his status as a naturalized Canadian, and belonged to the St. Charles Country Club and the Winnipeg Golf Club.

Hall, Frederick William (1885-1915) War hero. Born in Kilkenny, Ireland, he served with the Second Scottish Rifles before moving to Pine Street (now Valour Road), Winnipeg. In September 1914 he enlisted in the Royal Winnipeg Rifles. He was killed at Ypres in 1915 while carrying a wounded soldier on his back, and was awarded the Victoria Cross for bravery.

Hall, William B. (1833-1902) Nurseryman. Born in Fort Erie, Upper Canada, he came to Red River in 1858 and settled at Headingley a year later, where he farmed. His house in Headingley was called The Hermitage. Hall organized the first provincial agricultural exhibition in 1871. He became Manitoba's first professional nurseryman.

Halldorson, Elin Salome (1888-1970) Teacher, politician. Born in Lundar, Manitoba, she was educated at Wesley College and taught Latin, French, and German at the Jón Bjarnason Academy in Winnipeg from 1918 to 1938, subsequently teaching at Morden, Treherne, and Balmoral Hall School. She was a Social Credit member of the Manitoba legislature from 1938 to 1943, one of the first women elected to the legislature in the province.

Hallett, William (1824-c. 1874) Farmer. A Protestant mixed-blood from St. James, he was described by the poet Charles Mair* as a leader of the "English Plains Hunt." Others called him a "Scotch half-breed." Along with John Bourke,* he helped free James Stewart* from jail in 1863. He signed the *Nor'-Wester* ad of 24 July 1869 calling for a meeting to deal with Canada. He was employed in 1869 as guide and interpreter for one of the John Dennis* survey parties, helping Dennis evade Métis patrols. He was taken prisoner by Louis Riel, and he engaged in a word-slinging match with Riel the night John Schultz* and others escaped from Fort Garry. He ended up in irons and was bailed out for $450 on 12 February 1870. He was subsequently compensated for lost property and imprisonment. According to testimony at the Ambroise Lépine* trial in 1874, his health was broken by the confinement and he committed suicide.

Hallgrimsson, Fridrik (1872-c. 1925) Cleric. Born in Iceland, he was educated at Reykjavíc College before graduating in theology from the University of Copenhagen, Denmark, in 1897. He came to Manitoba in 1903 and spent over 20 years serving rural pastorates (Baldur, Glenboro) before returning to Iceland in 1925 to become associated with the Reykjavíc Cathedral.

Halpenny, Jasper (b. 1869) Physician, professor. Born in Ontario, he came with his family to Manitoba in 1880. He was educated in Neepawa, at the University of Manitoba, and at Johns Hopkins University. He taught school in MacGregor before opening a medical practice in Winnipeg in 1891. He subsequently became professor of surgery and director of the Department of Surgery at the University of Manitoba. He was the author of *How to Be Healthy* (1911).

Halter, G. Sydney ("Syd," 1905-1990) Sports executive. Born in Winnipeg, he graduated in arts and law from the University of Manitoba, then practised law in Winnipeg. He was president of the Amateur Athletic Union of Canada from 1938 to 1946. He served as an executive of the Winnipeg Football Club for years, becoming commissioner of the Western Interprovincial Football Union from 1953 to 1957 and then commissioner of the Canadian Football League from 1958 to 1967. Halter was chair of the Manitoba Horse Racing Commission (1965-71 and 1978-81). He is a member of the Canadian Football Hall of Fame and the Manitoba Sports Hall of Fame. He was named an Officer of the Order of Canada in 1977.

Ham, (Catherine) Penny (1946-1993) Author, historian. She was born Penny Emisch at Plumas, Manitoba. She attended Brandon University and taught briefly at Sidney and Carberry. She later wrote regular columns for the *Brandon Sun*. Her books include *Place Names of Manitoba* (1980), *The History of the Manitoba Agricultural Museum* (1981), and a posthumously published collection of her columns, *A Celebration of Rural Manitoba* (1993).

Ham, George Henry (1847-1926) Journalist, author. Born in Trenton, Canada, he came to Winnipeg in 1875, becoming a journalist, member of the city council, and registrar of titles. In 1891 he was appointed advertising manager of the CPR and moved to Montreal. He helped form the Canadian Women's Press Club during a train journey to the World's Fair in St. Louis in 1904, and was made an honorary member of the club. He was the author of *The New West* (1888). His autobiography appeared as *Reminiscences of a Raconteur* (1921). He died in Montreal.

Hamerton, Robert (1911-1990) Athlete. Born in Winnipeg, he attended city schools. He was a member of the Canadian Olympic swimming team in 1936, and he held many Canadian records. He also swam competitively as a senior and coached swimming for many years. He was employed at the Winnipeg Grain Exchange. He is a member of the Manitoba Sports Hall of Fame.

Hamilton, Alice (1913-1991) Educator. Born in Bedford, Nova Scotia, she graduated in arts from Dalhousie and received a PhD from the University of London. After teaching at Dalhousie and Union Theological Seminary she came to United College in 1959, teaching there until her retirement in 1979. She was a specialist in the works of Chaucer, Samuel Beckett, and John Updike

Hamilton, Charles Edward (fl. 1881-1888) Lawyer, politician. He came to Winnipeg from St. Catharines, Ontario, in 1881 to practise law. He ran for mayor on the citizen's ticket in 1884 and won. In 1885 he was Conservative MLA from South Winnipeg, then from Shoal Lake in 1886. From 1885

to 1888 he was attorney-general of Manitoba, his chief accomplishment being the introduction of the Torrens title bill which reformed the Manitoba land registry. He left for St. Paul, Minnesota, in 1888.

Hamilton, Daniel Salmon (d. 1929) Cleric, social worker, sportsman. Born in Ontario, he attended McGill University (where he played on a championship rugby team) and Canada Congregational College before taking postgraduate work at the Chicago Theological Seminary. He did practical social settlement work in Chicago before assuming pastorates of churches in Forest, Ontario, in Montreal, and in London, Ontario. He became associate pastor of the Central Congregational Church in Winnipeg. He was active in the Church Union movement for many years. Beginning in 1915 he concentrated on social welfare work, becoming chief inspector of the Child Welfare Division, Department of Public Welfare. He was an ardent temperance reformer.

Hamilton, George A.M. (1901-1976) Soldier, theatrical producer. Born in Belfast, Ireland, he came to Canada in 1912. He served with the Winnipeg Rifles (90th Infantry Battalion) in WWI. For 50 years he produced grandstand shows for western Canadian fairs and exhibitions.

Hamilton, Mary (Riter) (1873-1954) Painter. Born in Teeswater, Ontario, she came to Clearwater, Manitoba, with her family at an early age. When she married Charles W. Hamilton in 1889 she moved to Port Arthur, where her husband was a leading merchant. He died in 1893, leaving her independently wealthy. She moved to Winnipeg and began painting china in 1894. Hamilton went to Europe in 1901 to study art, and for the most part she remained in Paris until 1911, occasionally returning to Canada. By 1905 some of her painting was exhibited at the Paris Salon. She returned to Winnipeg in 1911 to mount a major exhibition of her work. After WWI she obtained a publisher's commission to "reproduce the battlefields in paint," and she remained abroad until 1922, producing over 300 paintings and innumerable sketches. Her work was exhibited in Paris in 1922 and in London in 1923. She subsequently donated most of the war paintings to the Public Archives of Canada. In 1929 she moved to Vancouver, where she taught art for many years. She died there. Posthumous exhibitions of her battlefield art were mounted in Victoria in 1978 and at the University

of Winnipeg in 1989. See Angela Davis, "Mary Riter Hamilton: An Artist in No-Man's Land," *The Beaver* 69, no. 5 (1989): 6-16.

Hamilton, Robert (1842-1911) Merchant, politician. Born in Canada, he came to Emerson in 1882, where he was a contractor and hardware merchant. He served five terms as mayor of Emerson, resigning to become immigration inspector in 1910.

Hamilton, Thomas Glendinning (1873-1935) Physician, politician. Born in Agincourt, Ontario, he was brought to Saskatoon by his parents at age 10, moving to Winnipeg in 1891. He was educated at Winnipeg Collegiate Institute and the University of Manitoba Medical School. He served as a Winnipeg School Board trustee from 1905 to 1915. Hamilton was elected as the MLA for Elmwood in 1915, and was active in much reform legislation of the Norris government, including mother's allowances. He was chosen president of the Manitoba Medical Association (1921-22) and was president of the University of Manitoba alumni in 1921. Around 1921, he began psychic research, and many visitors to the city, including Arthur Conan Doyle, attended his seances. His psychic research included attempts to photograph "ectoplasms" emanating out of mediums. He founded the Winnipeg Society for Psychic Research in 1931. After his death, Hamilton's son published the records of some of his experiments as *Intention and Survival* (1942). His extensive papers, including the photographs from his experiments, are at the UML Archives.

Handscomb, Charles W. (1867-1906) Journalist, musician, playwright. Born in England, he moved to Winnipeg in 1879 and worked as a journalist with the *Winnipeg Times* and the *Manitoba Free Press*. He was noted for his fine tenor voice and spent some time in the United States on the stage. Upon his return to Winnipeg he became editor and proprietor of the magazine *Town Topics*. He was one of Winnipeg's first playwrights, authoring a play entitled *Boom Times* in the early 1880s.

Hardisty, Richard (1832-1889) Fur trader, senator. Born at Moose Factory of mixed-blood ancestry, he was educated at Red River Academy. He served in the HBC from 1847, and became chief factor in 1867 and inspecting chief factor in 1887. While on leave in 1869-70 he came to Upper Fort Garry with his brother-in-law Donald Smith* and was put under house arrest by Louis Riel. He served in the Canadian Senate in 1888-89. He died in Winnipeg from injuries suffered in a horse and buggy accident in the North-West Territories.

Hargrave, James (1798-1865) Fur trader. Born in Hawick, Scotland, he attended Fysshe's Academy in Galashiels before persuading his family to immigrate to Canada. Hargrave joined the NWC, serving as apprentice clerk at Sault Ste. Marie. He continued with the company after its union with the HBC, and after several years on the lower Red River he was posted permanently to York Factory, which he operated with singular efficiency. Promotion was held back by his failure to learn Native languages and by his general reputation for being ill-tempered. His marriage to Letitia MacTavish* in 1840 brought a major improvement to his life. In 1844 he was finally promoted to chief factor. After a year in Scotland, he returned to York Factory until 1851, when he was posted to the Sault. His wife and youngest child died there in 1854. In ill health through most of his years in British North America, he retired in 1859, eventually settling on a property in Brockville, Canada. Hargrave was a prolific letter writer whose correspondence reveals much about life in the fur-trade region in the period. A selection of his letters, edited by George Glazebrook, was published as *The Hargrave Correspondence 1821-1843* by the Champlain Society in 1938. *DCB* IX, 364-66.

Hargrave, Joseph James (1841-1891) Fur trader, historian. The son of James* and Letitia Hargrave* and nephew of William McTavish,* he was born at York Factory. Little "Beppo," as he was affectionately known, was sent to school in Scotland at an early age, not returning to the West until 1861, when he entered HBC service. In 1869-70 he was private secretary to Governor William McTavish and was thus perfectly placed to produce a pseudonymous series of letters on the Red River Rebellion, published in the *Montreal Herald* under the name "Red River." These letters were critical of Louis Riel but generally supported the Métis in their efforts to negotiate terms with Canada, thus reflecting the position of HBC officials at the time. Walter Traill wrote of Hargrave in 1866 that he walked two miles around Fort Garry every evening. According to A.C. Garrioch,* Hargrave was one of three or four Winnipeggers present who cheered when the

Wolseley Expedition raised the flag at Fort Garry in 1870. In 1871 Hargrave published *Red River*, based on his father's papers and his own recollections of the 1860s, but this work did not include the Rebellion letters, which he intended to publish as a separate supplement. He never did. *Red River* was a gossipy book, full of juicy scandal. Its major thesis was the breakdown of authority in the settlement, which made the Rebellion of 1869-70 (never mentioned) perfectly comprehensible. Hargrave was promoted to chief trader in 1879, and he retired to Montreal 10 years later, where he died. *DCB* XII, 408-9.

Hargrave, Letitia (MacTavish) (1813-1854) Letter writer. Born in Edinburgh, Scotland, she was courted in 1837 at her home near Campbeltown by chief trader James Hargrave,* who eventually proposed to her by mail. The couple were married in 1840 and, complete with a piano, sailed for York Factory in June of that year. Like many women in her position, her first reaction upon her arrival was "to turn my back to the company & cry myself sick." But she soon recovered her natural ebullience and used letters to her family (edited by M.A. MacLeod and published by the Champlain Society in 1947 as *The Letters of Letitia Hargrave*) as therapy. The letters offer a unique European female perspective on life in the trading posts and constitute her main claim to fame. At the same time, the letters demonstrate that Hargrave, the only white woman at York Factory for most of her stay there, was extremely privileged. She had a personal maid and was often indulged by her husband, who added a nursery to their house, for example. She bore three children at York Factory, two of whom survived. In constant ill health, she returned to Scotland in 1846, then came back to York Factory in 1847. She gave birth to two more children before Hargrave was transferred to Sault Ste. Marie in 1851. She died of cholera at the Sault. *DCB* VIII, 589-90.

Harkness, David Bruce (1878-1949) Cleric, judge. Born in Ontario, he was educated at McMaster University and came to Emerson as a Baptist minister. He was the first editor of *Western Outlook,* the official journal of the Baptist Convention of Western Canada, and became the first judge of the Winnipeg juvenile court. He helped draft the Manitoba Child Welfare Act and the Winnipeg Juvenile Delinquency Act. He was active in the early Community Chest of Winnipeg. In 1925 he moved to Toronto, where he helped establish the city's welfare department and headed its unemployment and relief department. He died in Burlington, Ontario.

Harmon, Daniel Williams (1778-1843) Fur trader. Born in Bennington, Vermont, he joined the NWC in 1800 and spent five years at Swan River and the upper Assiniboine. He later became a wintering partner in Athabasca and New Caledonia. He retired from the fur trade in 1821, moving first to Vermont and then in 1842 to Canada, where he died in poverty. He was the author of *A Journal of Voyages and Travels in the Interior of North America* (1820), a heavily edited edition of his manuscript journal that was replaced in 1957 by *Sixteen Years in the Indian Country: The Journal of Daniel Williams Harmon, 1800-1816*, ed. W. Kaye Lamb. See John Spargo, *Two Bennington-Born Explorers and Makers of Modern Canada* (1950). *DCB* VII, 385-86.

Harper, John Joseph (1951-1988) Aboriginal leader. He was executive director of the Island Lake Tribal Council in 1988, when he and a Winnipeg police constable scuffled after he was mistakenly taken for a young car thief. Harper was killed by the officer's pistol. The policeman was exonerated, but the case became symbolic for Indian leaders as an illustration of police abuse and helped lead to the Manitoba Aboriginal Justice Inquiry.

Harriott, John Edward (1797-1866) Fur trader. Born in London, England, he joined the HBC in 1809. He spent most of his active career in the Saskatchewan District and the Columbia District, becoming chief trader in 1829 and chief factor in 1846. He had little formal education but was very good with Native languages. He retired to Red River in 1855 and built Hawthorne Lodge near what is now Lockport. He died in Montreal.

Harris, John Walter (1845-1926) Mathematician, surveyor, sportsman. Born in Kemptville, Canada, he was a brilliant mathematician who worked as a mathematics reformer, introducing the "Lightning Calculator" System to schools in the Midwestern United States from 1869 to 1871. He came to Winnipeg in 1873 and was Dominion Land surveyor from then until 1879, when he resigned to practise privately. In 1879 he was the first assessor of Winnipeg. He was appointed city surveyor in 1882, and he conducted a major survey of the city from

1890 to 1894. He was an ardent baseball fan who introduced the game to Winnipeg and was the first president of the Winnipeg Baseball Club. His diary is at the PAM.

Harrison, David Howard (1843-1905) Physician, rancher, politician. Born in London Township, Canada, he graduated in medicine from McGill College and opened a practice in St. Mary's, Perth County. In 1882 he moved to Newdale, Manitoba, to become a rancher. Within months he was the Conservative candidate for Minnedosa in the provincial election, and he struck up a friendship with Premier John Norquay. He briefly held a series of Cabinet posts in 1886 and 1887. Later he broke with Norquay over the government's railroad intrigue, becoming premier himself on Boxing Day 1887 and serving for one month. Divisions in the party remained through 1888, and Harrison refused to implement a compromise on railways worked out in Ottawa (whereby the province would cease hostile legislation and the CPR would lose its monopoly in 1891). He resigned in January 1888 and pursued various business interests, first in Neepawa and then, after 1900, in Vancouver.

Harrison, Thomas Auguste (1837-1907) Politician. A French delegate to the 1870 Convention of Forty from Oak Point, he voted on 5 February against Riel's motion that the HBC be left out of the transfer arrangements of the territory, which should be negotiated between Canada and the people of Red River. Riel responded by calling him and delegates Nolin and Klyne "traitors." Harrison later suggested that the provisional government plan a bonfire and guard of honour to welcome the Wolseley Expedition.

Harrison, Thomas James (1885-1964) Agronomist, professor. Born in Graysville, Manitoba, he was the first student to enrol in the Manitoba Agricultural College. After graduation he taught field husbandry there until 1913, when he became superintendent of the Dominion experimental farm in Indian Head, Saskatchewan. He came back to the college in 1915 to become professor of field husbandry. His research on crossbreeding and high-yield barley was important for the malting industry. He helped found the Manitoba Agronomists Conference in 1920 and became assistant commissioner for Manitoba with the Board of Grain Commissioners in 1925. He also served as president of the Canadian Seed

Growers Association. In 1932 he became chair of the National Barley Committee and was instrumental in founding the Barley Improvement Institute. He was a member of the Winnipeg Kiwanis Club and was responsible for a public-speaking contest open to members of boys' and girls' clubs of the province. He was elected to the Agricultural Institute of Canada and the Royal Academy. In 1951 the University of Manitoba gave him an honorary LLD. He is a member of the Manitoba Agricultural Hall of Fame.

Harrower, James (1833-1892) Politician. Born in Upper Canada of Scottish descent, he worked his way across the continent to Oregon and Vancouver Island before settling in St. Paul Parish, Manitoba, in 1880. He later moved to Strathclair, and he served as MLA for Shoal Lake from 1888 to 1891.

Hart, Thomas (1835-1912) Professor, historian. Born in Paisley, Scotland, he immigrated to Canada with his family in 1842. He graduated from Queen's University in 1860 (subsequently receiving his MA in 1868 and BD in 1880) and taught school in Perth, Ontario, before coming to Manitoba in 1872 to teach at Manitoba College. He became a professor there in 1874 and was one of the founders of the University of Manitoba in 1877, active on a number of boards associated with it. He was a member of the Protestant section of the Provincial Board of Education from 1878 to 1890. He helped found the Historical and Scientific Society of Manitoba and served as its president in 1887. As well as teaching classical languages and literature until his retirement in 1909, he was active in Indian missions, serving as moderator of the synod of the Presbyterian Church in Manitoba and the North-West Territories from 1880 to 1890. See his *Mission Work among the Indians of the North-West, A Sermon* (1890). *DCB* XIV, 457-58.

Harvey, J.G. (1840-1923) Carriage maker, municipal politician, sportsman. Born in Lanark County, Upper Canada, he came west to Manitoba in 1872. In 1875 he purchased a flour and feed business in Winnipeg, later adding a carriage shop. He was elected to city council in 1883, and again in 1888 for 10 consecutive years. He then served on the Board of Control. He was an ardent curler and lawn bowler in later years.

Hassall, Thomas (c. 1811-1846) Interpreter. Born near Churchill to Chipewyan parents, he was sent to Red River for education at the mission school and renamed after a Welsh friend of David Jones.* In 1831 he joined the HBC and in 1833 was employed as an interpreter by the arctic expedition of George Back,* who reported that Hassall had some trouble speaking his native tongue. In 1840 he joined the Methodist mission at Norway House, soon becoming an interpreter and schoolmaster. James Evans reported favourably upon him in 1844, noting that he spoke "English well, French tolerably well, Cree fluently, and Chippewayan (not Ojibaway, but an entirely different language)." Evans licensed him as a "Local Preacher," the first Native so dealt with by the Methodists in the Northwest. Not long after, Evans accidentally shot and killed him while attempting to shoot some ducks from their canoe. *DCB* VII, 390.

Hatch, Lloyd Montgomery (1914-1989) Sheep and cattle breeder. Born south of Oak Lake, Manitoba, he ran a mixed farming operation there named Pleasant Dawn Farms, specializing in Suffolk sheep and polled Shorthorn cattle. In 1956 he was dubbed "Manitoba Ace Sheepman." His animals received many awards on the show circuit over the years. He won the Premier Breed Award in 1971 at Regina and the "Builders of the Breed" award from the Shorthorn world organization. He was active in local government and in Ducks Unlimited. He is a member of the Manitoba Agricultural Hall of Fame.

Hatskin, Benjamin (1917-1990) Sports executive. Born in Winnipeg, he attended the University of Oklahoma and played professional football for the Winnipeg Blue Bombers. He became a real estate developer and was a co-founder of both the Winnipeg Jets and the World Hockey Association. He served as chair of the WHA from 1975 to 1979 and merged it with the NHL. He died in Winnipeg.

Haukaness (Haukness), Lars (1863-1929) Artist, cartoonist, teacher. Born in Hardanger, Norway, he studied at the Royal Academy of Norway. He emigrated to Chicago around 1888 and travelled extensively outside the city, sketching the countryside. Landscape was his forte, although he was also a cartoonist for Norwegian-American newspapers. He first exhibited in Winnipeg in 1920, and by 1923 had moved to the city and joined the staff of the Winnipeg School of Art. Unsuccessful in his application to replace Franz Johnston* as head of the school, he moved to Calgary and helped found the art department at the Technical School. He died on a sketching expedition to Lake Louise.

Hawkins, Robert (1879-1962) Magistrate, politician. Born in Somerset, England, he came to Canada in 1904 and to Dauphin in 1905. He joined a local insurance firm and took it over in 1914. He served as police magistrate and juvenile court justice until he ran for the legislature as a Liberal Progressive in 1932. He represented Dauphin in the legislature for 17 years. He was appointed Speaker in 1937 and was reappointed in 1941 and 1945. His correspondence while Speaker of the legislature is in the PAM.

Hay, Edward Henry George Gunson (1832-1918) Miller, politician, civil servant. Born in England, he was a miller in St. Andrews from 1863 to 1881. He supported the election of English delegates to the November 1869 council meeting, and was elected a councillor to the provisional government from St. Andrews on 19 February 1870. He subsequently served as a member of the Legislative Assembly (as Liberal member from St. Andrews South from 1870 to 1874 and from St. Clements in 1879) and the Executive Council of Manitoba. He moved to Portage la Prairie and opened a foundry, which remained in operation until 1893. In 1889 he was appointed police magistrate and in 1900 was made clerk of works at St. Andrews Lock. He retired in 1911 and died at Lockport. His papers and correspondence are in the PAM.

Hay, William (1866-1947) Engineer. Born in St. Andrews, the son of E.H.G.G. Hay,* he attended Old St. Andrews School. A mechanical engineer, he headed north in the Klondike Gold Rush and remained in the North on the Mackenzie River for many years as a steam engineer for the HBC. He later was locks superintendent at Lockport. His papers are in the PAM.

Hayes, Kate (Simpson) (1857-1945) Journalist, author. Born in Dalhousie, Nova Scotia, she came west in 1879 with two children. She was librarian of the North-West Territories legislature from 1891 to 1898. She joined the *Manitoba Free Press* in 1899 and started its first women's page, working for the newspaper for many years. She was a co-founder of the Canadian Women's Press Club. She wrote a number of books, many under the pseudonym of Mary

Markwell. Her publications included *Prairie Pot-pourri* (1895), a serial entitled "The Taras Pioneer of the West," and *Derby Day in the Yukon*. She died in Victoria.

H'damani (c. 1831-1912) Santee Sioux chief. Born on the upper Minnesota River, after the 1862 Sioux uprising in Minnesota he led a small band to the Turtle Mountain region of present-day Manitoba, where he intended to live peaceably. He refused to move from this location, and in 1886 the government created the tiny Turtle Mountain Indian Reserve to accommodate him and his people. The government eventually closed down the reserve in 1909 by manipulating the votes of its inhabitants. H'damani died shortly thereafter near Pipestone. *DCB* XIV, 464-65.

Healy, William James (1867-1950) Journalist, librarian, historian. Born in Belleville, Canada, he received a BA from the University of Toronto in 1890. He worked for the *Toronto Telegram* before becoming Ottawa correspondent for the *Daily Mail* (1891-95) and secretary of the Parliamentary Press Gallery (1892-95). He was a co-owner of the *Brockville Times* from 1895 until 1899, when he was appointed associate editor of the *Manitoba Free Press*. From 1911 to 1920 he served as Western Canadian correspondent of the Commercial Intelligence Branch of the British Board of Trade Department. He was chief associate editor of the *Grain Growers' Guide* from 1918 to 1920. In 1920 he became provincial librarian of Manitoba. He compiled *Pioneers and Prominent People of Manitoba* (1925). Healy served on the provincial diamond jubilee committee in 1930. He produced two works of history, *Women of Red River* (1923) and *Winnipeg's Early Days* (1927), as well as a biography of Sir John Thompson (1894). His papers and correspondence are in the PAM.

Heaps, Abraham Albert (1885-1954) Politician. Born in Leeds, England, of Polish-Jewish descent, he came to Canada in 1910 and to Winnipeg in 1911. He was a member of the Social Democratic Party and a pacifist, opposing conscription in 1917 with F.J. Dixon* and John Queen.* During the Winnipeg General Strike of 1919 he supervised the commissariat for the strike committee, and in council advocated banning all parades. He was arrested on 17 June 1919, and he conducted his own defence against charges of seditious libel. He was found innocent on all counts on 28 March 1920, after a masterful address to the jury. He then started an insurance agency for Great-West Life Incorporated, from which he resigned in 1925 when he was elected to the House of Commons from Winnipeg North. He later became a CCF MP. In 1926 he confronted Arthur Meighen* in the House over government policy at the time of the Winnipeg General Strike. Heaps was on friendly terms with R.B. Bennett and Mackenzie King but was cordially hated by Meighen and Tim Buck, the leader of the Communist Party of Canada. He served in the Commons as an unofficial critic on economic policy until 1940, when he retired. See Harry and Mildred Gutkin, *Profiles in Dissent: The Shaping of Radical Thought in the Canadian West* (1997), 299-342; Leo Heaps, *The Rebel in the House: The Life and Times of A.A. Heaps, M.P.* (1970).

Hearne, Samuel (1745-1792) Fur trader, explorer. Born in London, England, he served in the Royal Navy before joining the HBC as a mate on the sloop *Churchill*. Hearne was soon singled out as an explorer, and beginning in 1769 he made a series of attempts to reach the Coppermine River by an overland route. After several abortive efforts, Hearne accompanied the guide Matonabbee* and his family on a lengthy journey to the North, becoming the first European to reach the Arctic Ocean overland from North America and the first to cross Great Slave Lake. He returned on 30 June 1772 and sent his journals back to England. In 1776 he was appointed head of Fort Prince of Wales at Churchill, and he surrendered it to the French in 1782. By 1787 he was ready to retire. He spent his last years in London working on his journals and maps. His *A Journey from Prince of Wales's Fort, in Hudson's Bay, to the Northern Ocean* was published in 1795 in London, going through several editions and translation into German, Dutch, and French. For a biography, see Gordon Speck, *Samuel Hearne and the Northwest Passage* (1963). *DCB* IV, 339-42.

Hector, James (1834-1907) Physician, explorer, geologist. Born in Edinburgh, Scotland, he attended Edinburgh Academy and the University of Edinburgh, graduating in medicine in 1856. A year later he was appointed to the Palliser Expedition as its physician. He spent four years in western North America, his activities and findings reported in *On the Physical Features of the Central Part of British North America* (1861) and *On the Geology of the Country between Lake Superior and the Pacific Ocean* (1861). Captain John Palliser* remarked especially on Hector's medical ministrations to the Blackfoot. After his

return to Scotland he was appointed as government geologist in New Zealand, later becoming chancellor of New Zealand University. He was made a knight commander of the Order of St. Michael and St. George in 1887.

Heeney, Arnold (1902-1970) Teacher, civil servant, diplomat. Born in Montreal, the son of William B.A.* and Eva Heeney,* he was educated at the University of Manitoba, and he taught at St. John's College School before receiving a Rhodes scholarship to Oxford. According to school legend, he tore up his discipline book in front of the boys at St. John's upon receiving the telegram about the Rhodes scholarship. After practising law in Montreal, he became Mackenzie King's principal secretary in 1938, and in 1940 became clerk of the Privy Council and secretary of the Cabinet. He was perhaps the most important civil servant in Ottawa during WWII because of his co-ordination of the Cabinet War Committee. He was appointed undersecretary of state for external affairs in 1949, subsequently serving as ambassador to NATO and the United States. He also served as chair of the Civil Service Commission and Canadian head of the International Joint Commission. His autobiography was published as *The Things That Are Caesar's: Memoirs of a Canadian Public Servant* (1972). See also Brian Masschaele, *Memoirs and Minutes: The Cabinet War Committee and the Establishment of the Canadian Cabinet* (1996).

Heeney, William Bertal A. (1872-1955) Cleric, historian. Born in Danford Lake, Quebec, he was educated at McGill (BA, 1899) and had degrees from St. John's College. He became rector of St. Luke's Church, Winnipeg, in 1909, serving until his retirement in 1943, when he moved to Montreal. He wrote a number of novels for children, such as *Pickanock: A Tale of Settlement Days in Older Canada* (1912), and was an active historian of the early Anglican Church in Western Canada. See his *John West and His Red River Mission* (1920), *The Founding of Rupert's Land and Its First Bishop* (1929), and *Our Church in Rupert's Land* (1933). He also compiled *Leaders of the Canadian Church* (1918) and *Centenary Addresses and Sermons* (1922), as well as writing *I Walk with a Bishop* (1939). His papers are in the PAM and the Rupert's Land Archives.

Henday, Anthony (fl. 1748-62) Fur trader, explorer. Born on the Isle of Wight, he had been outlawed as a smuggler before joining the HBC in 1750. He began travelling with the Plains Cree into the interior in 1754. His journal entries are too vague to permit accurate identification of his route, which probably took him to the Rocky Mountains (although they are not mentioned). He returned to York Fort almost a full year later. His accounts of Indians riding horses were greeted with particular derision. He made several subsequent, less well documented journeys, but quit the Company in 1762 when he was not promoted. A journal of 1754-55 was published as *The Journal of Anthony Hendry* (1973). See J.G. MacGregor, *Behold the Shining Mountains: Being an Account of the Travels of Anthony Henday, 1754-55, the First White Man to Enter Alberta* (1954); Glyndwr Williams, "The Puzzle of Anthony Henday's Journal, 1754-55," *The Beaver* (winter 1978): 40-56. *DCB* III, 285-87.

Henderson, John (b. 1841) Farmer. Born in Kildonan, he farmed on the east side of the Red River until his retirement. During the 1860s he was active in freighting to St. Paul. He frequently boasted about the prices he received for his land when he sold it at the end of the century. He was a life member of the Lord Selkirk Association of Rupert's Land. There are extensive papers in the PAM.

Henry, Alexander (the Younger) (d. 1814) Fur trader. The nephew of Alexander Henry the Elder, he had other relations in the fur trade. He is best known for his journal, begun in 1799 on the Whitemud River in what is now Manitoba. In the employment of the NWC, Henry operated in the Red River/Pembina area until he moved to the Saskatchewan River in 1808. He kept moving west, and in 1813 helped establish NWC trade at the mouth of the Columbia River. He drowned there in 1814. A journal covering the years 1799 to 1814 was edited by Elliott Coues as *New Light on the Early History of the Greater Northwest*, 3 vols. (1897). *DCB* V, 418-19.

Henry, Robert (1778-1859) Fur trader. Born in Albany, New York, he was one of a number of Americans who entered the Montreal fur trade. For many years he traded on the Churchill River for the NWC. In 1816 he led a band of Indians from Fort William to Red River and was involved in attacks on the HBC at Fort Athabasca. He retired from the fur trade in 1817 and settled in Cobourg, Upper Canada, where in 1839 a bank in which he was employed was attacked by a band of "Patriots" based in the United States. He died in Cobourg. *DCB* VIII, 390-91.

Henry, William (c. 1783-c. 1864) Fur trader. The eldest son of Alexander Henry the Elder (d. 1824), he joined the NWC in 1801, serving in Red River from 1801 to 1809. He then was posted further west, ending up in the Columbia Department in 1812 and moving to Fort William in 1816. He survived the 1821 merger of the NWC and HBC with an appointment, but retired to Canada in 1823, where he became a surveyor and civil engineer. He eventually settled in Newmarket, Canada, where he died.

Herchmer, Lawrence William (1840-1905) Indian agent, police officer. Born in Shipton-on-Cherwell, England, he was descended from United Empire Loyalists. He was educated in Henley-on-Thames, Trinity College (Toronto), and the Royal Military Academy (Woolwich). He became supply officer to the 1872 boundary commission, and in 1874 opened a brewery in Winnipeg. In 1876 he was appointed Indian agent at Birtle, Manitoba, and he was successful enough to become inspector of Indian agencies for the North-West Territories in 1885. A year later he became commissioner of the NWMP. By 1890 there were accusations against him of wrongdoing, but nothing was ever proved. He volunteered for service in the Boer War in South Africa in 1900, where he became embroiled in further controversy. He died in Vancouver. See William Beahan and Stan Horrall, *Red Coats on the Prairies: The North-West Mounted Police, 1886-1900* (1998). *DCB* XIV, 482-85.

Herklots, Hugh Gerald Gibson (1903-1971) Cleric, author, historian. An Anglican theologian and church historian, he taught at St. John's College, Winnipeg, in the 1930s. His memoirs of these years were published as *The First Winter: A Canadian Chronicle* (1935). He also wrote *Paper Aeroplanes: A Book of Essays* (1931) and *Pioneer Days in the Western Church: The Early History of the Anglican Province of Rupert's Land* (1933).

Herron, Shaun (1912-1989) Journalist, author. Born in Carrickfergus, Northern Ireland, he studied at Queen's University Belfast and at Princeton before fighting in the Spanish Civil War. He served as a United Church minister in Weyburn, Saskatchewan, in the 1950s and was an editorial writer for the *Winnipeg Free Press* from 1965 to 1976. In later years he wrote a number of novels, such as *The Whore-Mother* (1973) and *Bird in Last Year's Nest* (1974), as well as a series of nine spy thrillers featuring a protagonist named only "Miro." *Miro* won an award from the Mystery Writers of America in 1969. His thrillers were best-sellers (one sold 15,000 copies during the first month of publication in 1970) and won many awards. He died in Port Hope, Ontario.

Hershfield, Leible (1909-1999) Athlete. Born in Zhitomer, Russia, he moved to Winnipeg with his family in 1910. A natural athlete, he played most sports well and excelled at several, including track and field, soccer, and softball. He played softball for the YMHA teams from the age of 15, and later boasted that for 27 years he had played centre field without a glove. Spending most of his working life with the YMHA, he taught hundreds of children and adults how to swim. In 1969 he was selected Jewish athlete of the half-century, and in 1981 was inducted into the Manitoba Sports Hall of Fame. A sports columnist in later years for the *Jewish Post*, he wrote a survey of Jewish sports in Winnipeg entitled *The Jewish Athlete: A Nostalgic View* (1980).

Hespeler, Wilhelm (1830-1921) Merchant, immigration agent, politician. Born in Baden, Germany, he was educated at the Institute at Karlsruhe. He came to Canada in 1850 and became a merchant in Ontario. In the late 1860s and early 1870s he visited Germany and Ukraine to recruit Mennonites for the Canadian Prairies. He moved to Manitoba, where he was a Dominion immigration agent from 1870 to 1882 and consul for Germany from 1883 to 1909. Although not a Mennonite himself, in 1873 he tried to settle a party of Mennonites in southern Manitoba, but they went on to the Dakotas. He finally succeeded in attracting Mennonite families in 1874, and he is often regarded as the founder of German Mennonite settlements in southern Manitoba. He was MLA for Rosenfeld from 1899 to 1903 as an independent Conservative, and was Speaker of the House for the same period. He was given the Order of the Red Eagle by the German emperor in 1903. A Winnipeg street is named for him. He died in Vancouver.

Hettle, John (1842-1897) Merchant, politician. Born in England, he immigrated with his family to Canada in 1857. He came west to Boissevain, Manitoba, to become an agricultural implement agent. After local service as a municipal councillor and school board

officer, he was elected Liberal MLA for Turtle Mountain in 1888, 1892, and 1896.

Heubach, Fred (c. 1859-1914) Real estate developer. Born in Ottawa, he came to Winnipeg in 1879 and served until 1893 as private secretary to C.J. Brydges,* the HBC land commissioner. He then became manager of the Winnipeg Industrial Exhibition, and in 1902 went into partnership as a real estate developer with W.J. Christie. In 1907 he formed Heubach, Finkelstein, and Heubach, a real estate and financial firm that helped develop the Tuxedo and Norwood neighbourhoods of Winnipeg. He became mayor of Tuxedo at its incorporation in 1913.

Heurter, Frederick Damien (fl. 1816-21) Soldier. Born in Switzerland, he was a sergeant in the De Meuron regiment that disbanded in Canada in 1816 when he was recruited by the NWC for service at Red River. Accompanying the Nor'Wester brigades west in the summer of 1816, he witnessed the aftermath of the Battle of Seven Oaks. Appalled by the brutality of the NWC, he defected to the HBC in the spring of 1817, and his narrative of his experiences was published as *Narratives of John Pritchard, Pierre Chrysologue Pambrun, and Frederick Damien Heurter, Respecting the Aggressions of the North-West Company, against the Earl of Selkirk's Settlement upon Red River* (1819). He later returned to Switzerland to recruit settlers for the Red River Settlement.

Hicks, Anna (Kennedy) (1896-1982) Home economist. Born in Flint, Michigan, she came to Winnipeg in childhood and graduated from the Manitoba Agricultural College in 1920 as a home economist. She did graduate work at Columbia University and returned to Winnipeg to teach household arts at the Manitoba School for the Deaf and at Earl Grey School. In 1926 she married and moved to a farm in Souris, and she joined the Women's Institute in 1927. She was also active in the United Church and was appointed a member of the Rural Electrification Commission. For many years she was a director of the Souris and Glenwood Agricultural Society. A member of the Golden Age Club, she helped plan Victoria Park Lodge in Souris. She is a member of the Manitoba Agricultural Hall of Fame.

Hiebert, Paul Gerhardt (1892-1987) Professor, poet. Born in Pilot Mound, Manitoba, and raised in Altona, Hiebert graduated from the University of

Manitoba (honours philosophy), and received an MA from the University of Toronto in Gothic and Teutonic philology and a PhD from McGill University in physics and chemistry. Professor of chemistry at the University of Manitoba, he was also the author of the parodic poetry of Sarah Binks, "the Sweet Songstress of Saskatchewan," first published in 1947 in a "biography" entitled *Sarah Binks.* "Sarah" writes deliberately awful poetry, which does offer a nostalgic view of the pre-Depression prairie West in which so many Canadians grew up. Hiebert also wrote a number of other works of fiction, non-fiction, and poetry. His papers are at the UML Archives.

Hildes, John A. ("Jack," 1918-1984) Physician. Born in Toronto, he grew up in Northern Ontario and graduated from the University of Toronto in 1940. He served with the army medical corps during WWII. He returned to Canada in 1949 to join the University of Manitoba physiology department. He became director of Winnipeg Municipal Hospitals in 1951, where he was noted for his work during the 1953 polio epidemic. In 1970 he established the Northern Medical Unit at the University of Manitoba. He was named to the Order of Canada in 1979. He died in Winnipeg. His publications include *The Circumpolar People: Health and Physiological Adaptations* (1966).

Hill, James Jerome (1838-1916) Entrepreneur. Born near Guelph, Upper Canada, he worked on the Mississippi River as a clerk, and in 1867 joined the St. Paul and Pacific Railway Company as an agent. In 1872 he went into partnership with Norman Kittson* in the Red River Transportation Company, operating steamboats on the Red. He bought the St. Paul and Pacific Railway with Kittson, Donald A. Smith,* and George Stephen in 1878, reorganizing the company in 1879 to become the St. Paul, Minneapolis and Manitoba Railway. Hill helped underwrite the CPR and was an original director of the company from 1880 to 1883. He also recommended William Van Horne as chief engineer of the railroad. Hill acquired one of the great fortunes of the "robber baron" era in the United States, based upon his control of the Great Northern Railway Company. He wrote *Highways of Progress* (1910). See Albro Martin, *James J. Hill and the Opening of the Northwest* (1976).

Hill, Robert Brown (1843-1900) Carriage maker, journalist, historian. Born in Scotland, he worked in Glasgow before immigrating to Portage la Prairie in the 1870s. By trade a carriage maker, he became a journalist. He wrote *Manitoba: History of Its Early Settlement, Development and Resources* (1890).

Hillier, William (fl. 1811-14) Agent. He was employed by the HBC in 1811 to train and lead a party of men who would be able to confront the NWC when it became too aggressive. He sailed for York Factory with Miles Macdonell* in 1811 and accompanied him to Red River in 1812, where he acted as agent for Lord Selkirk* at East Winnipeg for several years. He left the Company upon the expiration of his three-year contract, claiming he had not been properly supported. Colin Robertson* thought him too friendly with the Nor'Westers.

Hime, Humphrey Lloyd (1833-1903) Pioneer photographer. Born in Ireland, he was the photographer and surveyor for the second year of the Canadian expedition to Red River led by Henry Youle Hind* in 1858. His photographs, including the first of the Red River Settlement, were published in 1860. He later moved into business, becoming president of the Toronto Stock Exchange. See H.L. Hime and Richard J. Huyda, *Camera in the Interior, 1858* (1976).

Hind, Ella Cora (1861-1942) Teacher, journalist, feminist reformer. Born in Toronto, Hind came west in 1882 to become a teacher, but her credentials were inadequate and she ended up as a typist in a law office. In 1893 she opened her own typing bureau and first published in the *Manitoba Free Press.* Two years later she became western correspondent for eastern newspapers. In 1901 she was hired as agricultural reporter for the *Manitoba Free Press,* where she became a noted journalist famed for her crop estimates, which usually contained less than a one percent margin of error. Hind was also involved in reform and women's issues. She was a member of the Woman's Christian Temperance Union, wrote newspaper pieces on living and working conditions in Winnipeg, and in 1894 helped found the Manitoba Equal Franchise Club. She was involved in the Women's Institutes movement and in 1912 was a founding member of the Political Equality League. Like many reformers of her generation, she feared the influx of non-British "foreigners." She wrote *Red River Jottings* (1905). Her account of agricultural conditions around the world, based on extensive travel, appeared in 1939 as *My Travels and Findings.* She was awarded an honorary LLD from the University of Manitoba and in

1935 was made an honorary life member of the University Women's Club. In later years she put much of her energy into the Red Cross. She is a member of the Manitoba Agricultural Hall of Fame. Some of her papers are in the UML Archives; some are in the PAM. See Kennethe M. Haig, *Brave Harvest: The Life Story of E. Cora Hind, LLD* (1945); Carlotta Hacker, *E. Cora Hind* (1979).

Hind, Henry Youle (1823-1908) Professor, geologist, explorer. Born in Nottingham, England, he was educated at Leipzig and Cambridge. He immigrated to North America in 1846 and settled in Toronto a year later as a schoolmaster at the new normal school. In 1851 he became a member of the Canadian Institute, and in 1852 became first editor of the *Canadian Journal: Repertory of Industry, Science and Art*, Canada's first scientific journal. He became professor of chemistry at Trinity College in 1851, and thereafter became increasingly interested in geology. In 1857 he was appointed as geologist and naturalist to a party sponsored by the Canadian legislature to survey the Northwest under the titular leadership of George Gladman.* In fact, Hind became the expedition's leader. His observations on the region — published for popular consumption in 1860 as *Narrative of the Canadian Red River Exploring Expedition of 1857* — proved poor geology but first-rate travel literature and propaganda on the value of the West. He died in Windsor, Nova Scotia. See W.L. Morton, *Henry Youle Hind, 1823-1908* (1980). *DCB* XIII, 471-74.

Hind, William George Richardson (1833-1889) Artist, explorer. Born in Nottingham, England, he was the younger brother of Henry Youle Hind.* In 1861-62 he joined an overland party heading by Red River cart from Upper Fort Garry to the Cariboo, sketching all along the way. He returned to Winnipeg in 1869 and again sketched and painted. His painting of a Red River cart has been reproduced often. He spent his later years in New Brunswick. *DCB* XI, 416-18.

Hirsch, John (1930-1989) Theatrical director. Born in Siofok, Hungary, he immigrated to Canada in 1947 and attended the University of Manitoba. He began his career with a puppet theatre, but in 1957 he and Tom Hendry founded Theatre 77, which in 1958 was combined with the Manitoba Little Theatre to produce the Manitoba Theatre Centre. Hirsch became its first artistic director. The MTC served as

the model for regional theatre in Canada. Hirsch co-directed the Stratford Festival from 1967 to 1969 and was head of television drama at the CBC from 1976 to 1979. In 1980 he became artistic director at Stratford, Ontario. He often directed abroad, and he won several important awards. He died in Toronto of a complication resulting from AIDS.

Hislop, Charles (1841-1919) Labour leader, politician. Born in Edinburgh, Scotland, he arrived in Winnipeg in 1882. For many years he operated Hislop's Employment Bureau. A leading labour figure associated with the Trades and Labor Council, he was elected alderman for Ward Four in 1896, the first successful labour politician in the city.

Hodge, F. Andrew (1922-1985) Veterinarian. Born in Teulon, Manitoba, he graduated from the University of Manitoba as a gold medallist and joined the RCAF. After WWII he attended the Ontario Veterinary College and won a second gold medal, becoming the only double-gold-medal winner to practise veterinary medicine in Manitoba. He moved to Hamiota in 1949. He became president of the Manitoba Veterinary Medicine Association and established the Hamiota and District Veterinary Clinic. He was active in community affairs. He is a member of the Manitoba Agricultural Hall of Fame.

Hollands, Ward (1883-1953) Lawyer. Born in Chisholm, North Dakota, he came to Beaudry, Manitoba, in 1900, later articling as a law student. He became a member of the firm of Bonnar, Trueman, Hollands, and Robinson, and helped defend the arrested leaders of the Winnipeg General Strike in 1919-20.

Holmes, Francis J.S. (1909-1991) Filmmaker. He was influenced by Robert Flaherty (*Nanook of the North*, 1922) and began filming in northern Manitoba at an early age, making his first commercial motion picture when he was 16. He was among Western Canada's most important commercial photographers, specializing in films for agricultural companies and making a decent living as a filmmaker. He had a mobile studio and often produced his films single-handedly, even composing the background music. Among his films were *Beyond the Steel* (1953), an account of the move of the town of Sherridon to Lynn Lake between 1950 and 1953, and *Each Year They Come* (1958), a story about waterfowl conservation made for Ducks Unlimited. The latter film won several awards. His papers, including film scripts, are at the PAM.

Hooker, Marion (Nelson) (1866-1946) Artist. Born in Richmond, Virginia, she came to St. Catharines, Ontario, with her parents at an early age. Educated locally, she pieced together an art education over the years, studying in Toronto, Buffalo, and New York City. In 1902 she toured Europe, thanks to a small inheritance. Her exhibition record expanded in the early years of the century. In 1907 she married Selkirk businessman Frank Hooker, a widower with six children who had been married to her best friend, and moved to Selkirk, Manitoba. She continued painting in Selkirk, shifting to Manitoba subjects. She also founded the Selkirk Art Club (1923) and the Dickens Club. A devout Anglican, she often painted Anglican churches. She left Selkirk after the death of her husband and died in St. Catharines. See Mary Jo Hughes, *Marion Nelson Hooker: Two Lives — One Passion* (1999).

Hoop, W.H. ("Bill," b. 1876) Labour leader, politician. Born in Durham County, England, Hoop was a steelworker in London and then a postal worker in Winnipeg after his arrival there in 1893. He was an "impossibilist" member of the Socialist Party, and he helped organize the party in Winnipeg in 1906. His political views later moderated. He was a supporter of the revised Direct Legislation League. In the 1912 municipal election Hoop ran for alderman in Ward Four, declaring, "Race-protection, race-progression, and race-perfection are the ideals of my religion, and if elected I will put them in practice." During WWI he was an ardent conscriptionist. In 1919 he was organizer of the retail clerks and a moderate member of the Trades and Labor Council.

Hooper, Samuel (1851-1911) Stonemason, architect. Born in Devon, England, he came to Canada in 1869 and trained in stone carving and monument work. He migrated to Winnipeg in 1881 and was employed as a monument designer and builder, his works including the Red River Rebellion monument at the city hall and the Seven Oaks monument. He subsequently studied architecture in England, and he began practising in Winnipeg toward the end of the century. He was the architect of the Exchange Building (1898), as well as the Agricultural College, the normal school, and the Carnegie Library. He

became provincial architect of Manitoba in 1904. He died in London, England, but was buried in Winnipeg. *DCB* XIV, 505-6.

Horch, Benjamin (1907-1992) Musician. Born in Russia, he moved with his family to Canada in 1909. He served as choir director of the Winnipeg Bible Institute from 1932 to 1938, studied music in Los Angeles, and returned to become music director of Mennonite Brethren Bible College from 1943 to 1955. He was a co-founder of the Mennonite Symphony Orchestra, and he helped edit the Mennonite *Gesangbuch,* published in 1952. Horch is regarded as one of the founders of Mennonite music in Manitoba. He retired in 1972.

Horner, Ralph (1848-1926) Musician, composer. Born in Monmouthshire, England, he was educated at the Leipsic Conservatorium of Music. He began his career in Peckham, where he served as conductor of the Peckham Choral Society and the English Opera Company. In 1888 he moved to Nottingham, where he conducted the Nottingham Amateur Orchestral Society, the Nottingham Operatic Society, and the Nottingham Philharmonic Choir, and served as lecturer in music at Nottingham University. He received a bachelor of music degree at Durham University in 1893 and became doctor of music in 1898. He went to New York in 1906 and moved to Winnipeg in 1909 to direct the Imperial Academy of Music and Arts. Horner was one of Winnipeg's first successful composers, having composed a number of operas, including *Confucius* (1888), six operettas, more than 100 songs, several sacred cantatas, and many piano pieces. The manuscript for one opera survives in the Boston Public Library, and manuscripts for a number of songs are in the British Museum. He is not to be confused with Ralph Horner of Toronto, who also wrote religious music.

Horwood, Victor William (1878-1939) Architect. Born in Frome, Somersetshire, England, he came with his family to Ontario in 1884. He studied architecture in Ottawa and Minneapolis. He began his career as an architect in Ottawa, coming to Winnipeg in 1904. In 1914 he wrote a history of the Manitoba Architects Association. He was appointed provincial architect, and he designed the legislative building and the law courts. He became a central figure in the royal commission hearing into corruption during the legislative building construction. His story differed from that of other witnesses, but the commission chose to believe him. He was an active snowshoer and was captain in the militia in 1911. His papers are in the PAM.

Howard, Thomas (1845-1903) Soldier, politician. Born in Canada, he came to Manitoba as a captain with the Wolseley Expedition in 1870 and rapidly integrated into the community. He was elected as MLA from St. Peter's in the first provincial election, serving in the government as minister of agriculture, minister of public works, provincial secretary, and provincial treasurer. He was re-elected in 1874 and sat in the House until 1878. He was secretary of the Board of Health for Manitoba and the North-West Territories and was a charter member of the Manitoba Club. He was murdered in San Francisco.

Howden, James Henry (1860-1938) Lawyer, politician. Born in Canada, he came to Winnipeg and articled in law, being called to the bar in 1887. In 1892 he moved to Neepawa, where he served as mayor for many years. He was elected as a Conservative to the Manitoba legislature for three terms beginning in 1903 and ending in 1915, serving as minister of telephones, provincial secretary, and attorney general. He died suddenly at a family reunion at Wasagaming.

Howe, Joseph (1804-1873) Journalist, politician. Nova Scotia's leading newspaper editor and politician, Howe opposed Confederation in 1866 and was elected to Parliament in 1867 as an anti-unionist. When it became clear that the confederation would not be dissolved, he joined the government as secretary of state. Part of his portfolio was the transfer of Red River to Canada. Howe therefore visited the settlement on a fact-finding trip in October 1869. He insisted he was the first Canadian to read the official records of Assiniboia, which he found most interesting. Howe's visit exposed the abysmal ignorance of, and lack of interest in, the settlement on the part of most members of the government. William McDougall* later charged him with encouraging the Red River Rebellion, an accusation that Howe vehemently denied. See the biography by J. Murray Beck, *Joseph Howe* (1982-83). *DCB* X, 362-70.

Howell, Hector Mansfield (1842-1918) Lawyer, judge. Born in Thurlow Township, Canada, he was educated at Belleville Seminary and Osgoode Hall. He was called to the bar in 1871, and migrated to Winnipeg in 1879. Although he was a supporter of Sir John A. Macdonald, he became disenchanted with the Macdonald government's neglect of the West. An increasingly well known criminal lawyer, in 1890 he defended Liberal attorney general Joseph E. Martin* in a famous libel trial involving the editor of the *Manitoba Free Press,* William Luxton.* The Manitoba School Question led him to become a Liberal, and he was appointed chief justice of the Court of Appeal in 1906. He was president of the Law Society of Manitoba in 1904. He died in Winnipeg. *DCB* XIV, 509-11.

Howse, Joseph (1775-1852) Fur trader, explorer, linguist. Born in Cirencester, England, he joined the HBC in 1795 with a reputation for linguistic ability. At the Bay he soon learned Cree, and he spent a number of years engaged in the fur trade before heading into the Rocky Mountains for the HBC in 1809, ending up at Rocky Mountain House. In 1810 he recorded crossing the Continental Divide and explored widely in a country never previously visited by Europeans. He went to England in 1812, and on his return led a party on snowshoes from York Factory to Vermilion River, returning by dogsled and horseback. He was arrested by the NWC in 1814, and in 1815 he retired from the fur trade to Cirencester, where he worked as a gentleman-scholar on his Cree grammar until its eventual publication in 1844 as *Grammar of the Cree Language, with Which Is Combined an Analysis of the Chippeway Dialect.* He was made a fellow of the Royal Geographical Society in 1837. *DCB* VIII, 411-14.

Hryhorczuk, Nicholas Apoluner (1888-1979) Politician. Born in Buchachky, Western Ukraine, he came to Canada with his family in 1897, settling north of Gilbert Plains, Manitoba. He moved to Ethelbert in 1911 and opened a business, which he operated until his retirement in 1978. He was elected an Independent MLA in 1920 and then served as a Liberal until 1945. He was the first person of Ukrainian descent to become an MLA in Manitoba. Hryhorczuk was an active supporter of Ukrainian culture in Canada.

Hubble, Filmer Edwin (1904-1969) Musician. Born in Dulwich, England, he was educated at St. Olan and St. Saviour's Grammar School, London.

He came to Winnipeg in 1921 to be assistant organist at Holy Trinity Anglican Church. From 1943 until his death he was organist at St. Stephen's Broadway United Church. Hubble conducted many choral groups and was a regular music festival adjudicator. He also conducted the University of Manitoba Symphony Orchestra.

Hudson, Albert Bellock (1875-1947) Lawyer, politician, judge. Born in Ontario, he was educated in Winnipeg and called to the bar in 1899. In 1914 he was elected MLA from Winnipeg South, and he served until 1920. From 1915 to 1917 he was attorney general of Manitoba. In 1921 he was elected an MP for South Winnipeg, serving until 1925. He was a judge of the Supreme Court of Canada from 1936 to 1947.

Hudson, Gordon (1894-1959) Curler. Born in Kenora, Ontario, he first played lead in the Manitoba Curling Association bonspiel in 1909. In 1914 he skipped the "Hudson Kid" rink, which was a sensation in that year's bonspiel. He fought in WWI, joined the Strathcona Curling Club in 1919, and won bonspiels in 1922, 1923, 1928, and 1941. He also skipped the Strathcona rink that won the Canadian championships in 1928 and 1929. He served the Strathcona club as president from 1925 to 1927 and was subsequently its secretary. In 1949 he was president of the Dominion Curling Association. Called "the greatest curler of them all," he was elected to the Canadian Curling Hall of Fame in 1974 and the Manitoba Sports Hall of Fame in 1985.

Hudson, Henry (d. 1611) Explorer. One of those figures who emerge from the darkness of obscurity with an international reputation already made, Hudson first entered the record as an employee of the English Muscovy Company in 1607, hired to find a short route to China over the North Pole. He failed in this, as in a 1608 search for a Northeast Passage through the Russian Arctic. The Dutch hired him in 1609 for another search for the Northeast Passage, but a recalcitrant crew forced him to head west instead, where he ascended the Hudson River. On his return he was hired by the English for a venture aboard the *Discovery* to find a Northwest Passage. Again he had, from the beginning, a difficult crew, which, after a year's sailing and wintering in Hudson Bay in conditions of great privation, mutinied and set Hudson and a few others adrift on a shallop. They

were never heard from again. The ringleaders of the mutiny were never punished for this crime. A few were eventually arraigned for murder but acquitted. Despite his nautical achievements, Hudson was obviously not a good leader of men. See G.M. Asher, ed., *Henry Hudson, the Navigator: The Original Documents in Which His Career Is Recorded, Collected, Partly Translated, and Annotated* (1860). *DCB* I, 374-79.

Hugg, Jabez Bowen (b. 1872) Lawyer, law examiner. Born in Ontario, he was educated at Orillia High School and came to Manitoba in 1890, attending the University of Manitoba (BA, 1895; first scholarship and medal winner in pure mathematics). He studied law with Sir James Aikins* and was called to the bar in 1906. A resident of Winnipeg, he was counsel for the Prairie Provinces Branch of the Canadian Manufacturers' Association and member of the law firm of Hugg and Johnston. Hugg served as lecturer and examiner at the Manitoba Law School from 1915 to 1918. In the April 1919 issue of *Industrial Canada* he called for the government to "assert the authority of the state and. . . suppress all unlawfulness no matter by whom committed." With H.A. Robson* he co-authored several important law texts, including *Cases on Municipal Law* (1915 and 1920).

Hunt, Frank Larned (1825-1903) Lawyer. Born in Michigan, he came to Red River in 1860 after some sort of domestic crisis and practised law for several years. He was the first qualified lawyer in the settlement. He was part of the defence team in the trial of G.O. Corbett,* but he played only a minor role in the courtroom. In later life he moved to Poplar Point and wrote poetry and prose, the former published in the *Manitoba Free Press* and the latter covering subjects such as family history and folklore. He was the author of *Britain's Own Utopia* (1902), which argued that the Red River Settlement had enjoyed an Edenic society.

Hunt, Isabel Ross (MacLean) (1894-1990) Lawyer. Born in Deloraine, Manitoba, she grew up in Winnipeg, graduated in law from the University of Manitoba, and was called to the bar in 1916. She practised law in Grandview, married in 1919, and resumed her practice in Winnipeg in 1923 when her husband died. For many years she worked in the legal department of the City of Winnipeg, and she was named QC in 1953, the first woman in the province so honoured. She died in Toronto.

Hunter, Alexander Jardine (d. 1940) Medical missionary. Born in western Ontario, he attended the University of Toronto medical school and Knox College, Toronto, graduating in 1899. He became a medical missionary for the Presbyterian Home Missionary Society, setting up operations in Teulon, Manitoba, in 1902. He learned Ukrainian and translated Ukrainian stories and poems into English, including the poetry of Taras Shevchenko, notably Shevchenko's *Kozbar* (1922). He studied insects, and a fly (*Chilosia hunteri*) was named for him. He wrote *The Work among the Ukrainians* (c. 1922). His autobiography, *A Friendly Adventure: The Story of the United Church Mission among New Canadians at Teulon, Manitoba*, was published in 1929. He was made an Officer of the Order of the British Empire in 1935. He died in Teulon.

Hunter, James (1817-1882) Cleric, linguist. Born in Barnstaple, England, he came to Rupert's Land as a Church of England priest in 1844. He was first posted to Cumberland Station at The Pas on the Saskatchewan River. He began translating religious literature into Cree from an early period of his ministry. His wife died in Cumberland in 1847, and he married Jean Ross, the daughter of the head of the trading post, who was fluent in Cree. He served temporarily at St. Andrews before going with his wife to England in 1854 to oversee the publication of many of their translations, including the Bible and Book of Common Prayer. Hunter moved to St. Andrews permanently (1855-65) and was involved in 1862-63 with the trial of Rev. Griffith Owen Corbett,* being accused (apparently falsely) of moral turpitude himself. The libel may have cost him the bishopric in 1864. He later became vicar of St. Matthew's Church Bayswater in London. One of the pioneer students of the Cree language, he died in London. He was the author of *A Lecture on the Grammatical Construction of the Cree Language* (1875). *DCB* XI, 436-37.

Hutchings, Elisha Frederick (1855-1930) Saddle maker, merchant, financier, politician. Born in Newboro, Canada, he was apprenticed to a saddle maker. He came to Winnipeg in 1876. In 1877 he bought a junior partnership in Stabler and Caswell, harness makers. A year later he established the Great West Saddlery Company, which he built into a major operation by 1900. He was also active in building supplies, insurance, and loan companies. He served four terms on city council. In 1910 the *Winnipeg*

Telegram described him as one of the city's 19 millionaires. He collected war trophies and memorabilia.

Hutchins, Thomas (d. 1790) HBC chief factor, naturalist. He first joined the HBC in 1766 as a surgeon at York Fort. In 1771 he observed and reported on an eclipse of the sun, and in 1776 published his findings on the congealment of mercury by cold. Later experiments gained him the Royal Society's Copley Medal in 1783. After his retirement from the field he become corresponding secretary of the HBC. Much of the natural history attributed to him was actually written by Andrew Graham.* See Glyndwr Williams, "Andrew Graham and Thomas Hutchins: Collaboration and Plagiarism in 18th-Century Natural History," *The Beaver* (spring 1978): 4-14. *DCB* IV, 377-78.

Hutton, George F. (1922-1976) Farmer, politician. Born in Winnipeg, he was educated at Daniel McIntyre Collegiate, St. John's College, and United College, graduating with a BA in 1950. He farmed 800 acres at Rosser. Elected president of the provincial Progressive Conservative Association in 1958, he was subsequently appointed minister of agriculture and conservation. He was largely responsible for piloting the Winnipeg Floodway legislation through the legislature in 1962. He later served in Africa and India with the Food and Agriculture Organization of the UN.

Hyman, Marcus (1883-1938) Lawyer, politician. Born near Vilna, Poland, he emigrated to London, England, in 1895, was educated at Oxford and went to India as a private tutor to a young prince in 1907. He came to Winnipeg in 1913. During WWI he was president of the Western Canada Jewish Relief. He was the lawyer appointed by the Winnipeg Trades and Labor Council to defend radical aliens before the Board of Inquiry after the 1919 General Strike, and was able to have the deportation orders of five of the strike leaders reversed. Hyman later taught law at the Manitoba Law School. Hyman was associated with the Independent Labor Party while serving as an MLA.

Hyman, Walton (fl. 1869-74) Tanner. A Canadian from London, Ontario, who settled in Red River in the summer of 1869, Hyman opened a tannery at Stinking River. (His father was a leading Canadian entrepreneur who had begun as a tanner.) According to later accounts, Hyman was a spy for John Schultz,* the leader of the Canadian Party. On 22 October 1869 he made an affidavit about the proposed Métis resistance, and he later joined the party in Schultz's house that surrendered to Louis Riel in December. He tried to escape in January 1870, was recaptured, and was eventually released. His feet were frozen during the abortive escape, and he was removed from Fort Garry in a sleigh. He opened a boot and shoe shop in Winnipeg in December 1870. In 1874 he built a small steamboat and operated it on the Assiniboine and Red Rivers. That same year he lost his right arm in a shooting accident and received the first patent granted to a Manitoban (for a pipe wrench). He may have been Winnipeg's first Jewish resident.

Iberville, Pierre Le Moyne, Sieur d' (1661-1706) Soldier. Born in Montreal, he was apparently trained by his father as a seaman. In 1686 he participated in a Canadian expedition against the HBC, journeying overland to Hudson Bay by a chain of waterways that was extremely perilous. The French remained in the Bay for the next few years, d'Iberville's handful of men continually defeating their more numerous English counterparts. D'Iberville returned to Canada in 1690 to take part in a French guerrilla raid on New York, then returned to the Bay in July 1690 for another series of campaigns against the English, punctuated by occasional forays into other regions. In 1697 his ship the *Pelican* single-handedly defeated three English warships at the mouth of the Nelson River, thus sealing the fate of the English on the Bay. When d'Iberville left Hudson Bay in 1697, he could hardly know that he would never return or that New France would be unable to retain his conquests. He spent his last years involved in Louisiana and then the Caribbean, much of the time fending off charges of corruption. See Guy Frégault, *Iberville le conquérant* (1944); Nellis M. Crouse, *Lemoyne d'Iberville: Soldier of New France* (1954). *DCB* II, 390-401.

Ingersoll, William Ernest ("Will," 1879-1968) Author and journalist. Born in Shoal Lake, Manitoba, he joined the *Free Press* as a reporter in 1908 and served as church editor from 1935 to 1960. He had a short story in the first anthology of Canadian writing, published in 1929. He had previously published *Daisy Herself* (1918) and *The Road That Led Home; A Romance of Plow-land* (1918). A follower of boxing, he began collecting Elvis Presley records at the age of 80. He died in Winnipeg.

Inkster, Colin (1843-1934) Sheriff. Born at Seven Oaks, he worked as a boy on the farm belonging to his father, John Inkster.* He attended St. John's College until 1863 and then freighted between Minnesota and Red River from 1863 to 1870. He met Bishop Robert Machray* in Minnesota in 1864. In 1871 he became a member of the Manitoba Legislative Council, serving until 1876 and becoming minister of agriculture and president of the council in 1874. He cast the deciding vote for abolition of the council in 1876. Upon the council's abolition, he was made high sheriff of Manitoba, a post he held until the province was divided into three judicial districts in 1881, at which time he became sheriff of the eastern judicial district, which he served until 1928. An Anglican, he was rector's warden of St. John's Cathedral for over 50 years. In later years Inkster was always prepared to reminisce about the "early days." A boulevard in Winnipeg is named for him.

Inkster, John (1799-1874) Stonemason, farmer. Born in the Orkney Islands, he came to the West in 1819 as a stonemason for the HBC. He soon left the Company and began farming along the Red River, not far from Seven Oaks. He later became a trader and merchant. He also taught in the Kildonan School organized in 1849 by the Scottish Presbyterian settlers, although he was an active Anglican and served as rector's warden of St. John's Cathedral. He was magistrate of the Lower District from 1850 to 1858. In 1856 he became president of the Steam Mill Company. He was a member of the Council of Assiniboia from 1857 to 1868 and was a member of the November 1869 council (although he did not attend). His house, constructed in Seven Oaks near his store between 1851 and 1853, was lived in continuously by the Inkster family until 1954, and is now a museum. He was known as "Orkney Johnny." He is buried in St. John's Cemetery. There are papers in the NAC and the PAM. *DCB* X, 376-77.

Inkster, William (1836-1868) Mixed-blood leader. Born in Red River, he was educated at St. John's Parochial School and St. John's College, and then became a teacher. He was a charter member of the Masonic lodge at Fort Garry, and he became its junior warden. He was appointed to the Council of Assiniboia in 1868.

Ironside, Robert (1854-1910) Cattleman. Born in Canada to Presbyterian Scots, he came to Manitou, Manitoba, in 1883 as an agent for agricultural implements. He soon opened his own business in Manitou and gradually added livestock dealings to his lumber and grain interests. He built the first grain elevator in Manitou. In 1890 he and James Thomas Gordon sent a large shipment of steers to Montreal, and they soon sent others to the United Kingdom. By 1897 Gordon, Ironside, and Fares was the largest livestock-exporting house in Canada, shipping 50,000 head of cattle to England in 1900 alone. They also had an abattoir in Winnipeg. Ironside was elected Liberal MLA from Manitou in 1892. He withdrew from contesting the federal riding of Lisgar in 1896 rather than compete with his business partner, who was the Conservative candidate. He later moved to Montreal, where he died, but he always remained associated with Manitoba. *DCB* XIII, 498-99.

Irvine, Acheson Gosford (1837-1916) Police officer. Born in Lower Canada, he served as a major in the Second Battalion of the Quebec Rifles during the Wolseley Expedition. He remained in Manitoba in command of a rifle battalion, retiring as lieutenant-colonel in 1875 to become assistant commissioner of the NWMP. In 1880 he became commissioner.

He commanded the police during the North-West Rebellion of 1885 and retired from the NWMP in 1886. In 1892 he became warden of the Stony Mountain penitentiary. He died in Quebec City.

Irvine, William (1885-1962) Politician. Born in Gletness, Shetland Islands, he came to Canada in 1908. He studied in Winnipeg at Wesley and Manitoba Colleges. Ordained in the United Church and later moving to the Unitarian Church, he represented various Calgary ridings as Labor and later CCF member of the House of Commons (1921-35, 1945-49). He was the author of *The Farmer in Politics* (1920), *Co-operative Government* (1929), and *The Forces of Reconstruction* (1934). In 1935 a play he had written, *The Brains We Trust*, was performed in Toronto. See Anthony Mardiros, *William Irvine: The Life of a Prairie Radical* (1979).

Isaacs, Leonard (1909-1997) Musician. Born in Manchester, England, he was educated at the Royal College of Music and in Paris, where he studied with Alfred Cortot. He worked with the English Light Opera Orchestra before joining the BBC in 1936. He was in charge of musical programs for the BBC from 1957 until 1963, when he became founding director of the University of Manitoba's School of Music. He retired in 1973 and remained in Winnipeg until his death. In his later years he was most noted for his letters to the press, although he performed publicly on the piano until the end. There are papers at the PAM.

Isbister, Alexander Kennedy (1822-1883) Educator, Native rights reformer. Born at Cumberland House in present-day Saskatchewan, he was the son of an Orkney clerk of the HBC and a mixed-blood daughter of Alexander Kennedy and his Cree wife Aggathas. He was originally schooled in the Orkney Islands, but he returned to Rupert's Land to attend Red River Academy (1833-37). He entered HBC service in 1838 but was unhappy with the lack of advancement granted to mixed-bloods. Isbister resigned in 1841 and left for Great Britain in 1842. He attended King's College (Aberdeen) for two years and the University of Edinburgh for one year. He joined the staff of East Islington Proprietary School in 1849, was headmaster in 1851, and moved to a series of more prestigious headmaster appointments (Jews' College, 1855; Stationers' Company School, 1858). He became active with the College of Preceptors that oversaw the English teaching profession. He edited its magazine, the *Educational Times*, and was dean after 1872. He was a prolific author of school textbooks. Isbister received an MA from the University of Edinburgh in 1858 and an LLB from the University of London in 1866. Not surprisingly, he fought hard and long on behalf of his mixed-blood countrymen, whom he regarded as being under the tyranny of the HBC. In 1847 he presented to the Colonial Office a petition from 1,000 of the Red River Settlement's inhabitants for status as a recognized colony, and he was an active lobbyist on behalf of the settlement with the public and the British authorities. He also wrote *A Proposal for a New Penal Settlement in the Uninhabited Districts of British North America* (1850) and, with A.W. Chesson, *The Red River Insurrection: Three Letters and a Narrative of Events* (1870). In 1857 Isbister testified before the parliamentary inquiry investigating the charter of the HBC. He endowed a schools prize for Red River in 1867 (now awarded by St. John's College) and a trust fund for scholars ($100,000, first awarded in 1885) at the University of Manitoba. In addition, he left his extensive collection of nearly 5,000 books to the University of Manitoba. Regrettably, most were lost in a fire in 1898. He died in England. For a biography, see Barry Cooper, *Alexander Kennedy Isbister: A Respectable Critic of the Honourable Company* (1988). *DCB* XI, 445-46.

Isbister, Joseph (c. 1710-1771) Fur trader. Probably from Stromness, Orkney Islands, he was apprenticed to Christopher Middleton* of the HBC in 1726. By 1740 he was master of a sloop, and soon he became head of Albany Fort. Isbister defied the London Committee of the HBC and established a trading post inland from Hudson Bay (Henley House) in 1743. He retired from Albany because of ill health in 1747 but soon became head of Fort Prince of Wales at Churchill. In 1752 he returned to Albany. While at Albany in the 1740s he had attempted to enforce committee instructions about drinking and Native women at posts, often using brute force in the process. His prohibition against all Native women except his own was decidedly unpopular. In 1755 he executed several Natives for the destruction of Fort Henley, and he was recalled soon after. He settled with his family in Quebec City in 1760. *DCB* IV, 380-81.

Isbister, William (fl. 1739-51) Fur trader. He first appears in the historical record as a sailor for the HBC in 1739, and he became master of Henley House in 1743. He had trouble with the isolation of the Bay and turned increasingly to alcohol. By 1751 he returned to England, one step ahead of a recall for general "sottishness and ill Conduct." *DCB* III, 300-301.

Isham, Charles Thomas (1755-1814) Fur trader. Born at York Factory, the son of James Isham* and a Native woman, he was sent to England to be educated. He entered apprenticeship to the HBC in 1766, and by 1774 was sent inland. He was trading at Cumberland House by 1775-76. He was one of the few inlanders with any skills at canoeing, and he worked as canoeman and interpreter through the 1780s. In 1790 he became master at Swan River, the first Hudson Bay native to rise from the ranks into even a minor officership. In 1812 he served as interpreter for Miles Macdonell* at Red River. *DCB* V, 450-51.

Isham, James (c. 1716-1761) Fur trader. Born in Holborn, London, England, he first joined the HBC in 1732 as a writer. With occasional visits home, he remained at the Bay until his death. He became head of York Factory in 1737 and, as well as becoming intimately knowledgeable about the fur trade, he managed to send unusual bird specimens to London, which were employed by the naturalist George Edwards in his *Natural History of Uncommon Birds* (1750). In 1741 he was transferred to Churchill. In ill health, he went to England in 1745 with a collection of manuscript writings on the fur trade and the Bay, including an early vocabulary of Cree. Isham became involved in the controversy initiated by Arthur Dobbs,* because he had been friendly with Christopher Middleton* while at the Bay in 1741. He ended up at Flamborough House in 1750, where he served until 1761. Isham did not publish his work, and he remained known mainly through the writings of others until the publication of *James Isham's Observations on Hudson Bay, 1743*, ed. E.E. Rich (1949). *DCB* III, 301-4.

Ivens, William J. ("Bill," 1878-1958) Strike leader, politician. Born in Barford, Warwickshire, England, he came to Canada in 1896. Originally he worked as a market gardener, but he attended the University of Manitoba as a Methodist ministerial candidate and became Methodist minister at McDougal Church, Winnipeg. An active social gospeller, Ivens broke with the church over his pacifism during WWI and was expelled from the ministry for his refusal to accept church authority. He thereupon founded the Labour Church and in 1918 became editor of the labour newspaper the *Western Daily News.* During the Winnipeg General Strike he edited the daily strike bulletin, and he was arrested on 17 June by the federal authorities. His address to the jury in his trial lasted 14 hours. He was found guilty of seditious conspiracy by a jury on 28 March 1920 and sentenced to one year in prison. Before his trial, he had been charged with contempt of court for statements he had made regarding the trial of R.B. Russell.* He was elected to the Manitoba legislature in 1920 and re-elected in 1922 and 1927. He was active in the Anti-Vaccination League. He took a correspondence course with an American chiropractic college and set up a successful practice in 1925. He was defeated in the 1933 federal election and never held public office again. Ivens died in Chula Vista, California. See Michael Butt, "'To Each According to His Need, and from Each according to his Ability. Why cannot the world see this?': The Politics of William Ivens, 1916-1936" (MA thesis, University of Winnipeg, 1993); Harry and Mildred Gutkin, *Profiles in Dissent: The Shaping of Radical Thought in the Canadian West* (1997), 51-92.

Jackson, Vincent William (1876-1953) Botanist. Born in South Grimsby, Ontario, he was educated in Ontario schools. He served on the staff of the Ontario Agricultural College in Guelph until 1906, then served as director of New Zealand's Agricultural Education Department until 1910. He taught in Toronto briefly before becoming director of biology and botany at the Manitoba Agricultural College from 1913 until 1930, when he was appointed professor of biology at the University of Manitoba. He retired in 1940. Jackson offered a series of weekly radio programs on nature until 1942. He was the author of *A Manual of Vertebrates of Manitoba* (1934). He died in Hamilton, Ontario.

Jacob, Robert (1879-1944) Lawyer, sportsman. Born in Baltensborough, Somersetshire, England, he came to Gladstone, Manitoba in 1892. He was educated there and at St. John's College (class of 1901). He was proud that he had worked his way through school. Jacob then articled to a Gladstone lawyer, Thomas Morton, and later practised law in Winnipeg. He was a member of the Winnipeg School Board, was an Independent MLA from North Winnipeg from 1922 to 1928, serving for a time as provincial attorney general, and was chair of the unemployment advisory board. He was a footballer, a golfer (president of the Canadian Golf Association), and a lawn bowler (founder of the Manitoba Lawn Bowling Association). He was also a curler, serving two terms as president of the Manitoba Curling Association.

James, Charles (1854-1911) Livery operator. Born in Ireland, he came to Canada in 1870 and to Winnipeg a few years later. He worked first as a horse driver and later as proprietor of his own livery company. He was noted for his "bridal coach" and was known as "Dublin Dan."

James, Thomas (c. 1593-c. 1635) Explorer. Probably born in Bristol, England, he apparently represented that city as a lawyer in a venture to search for a Northwest Passage and ended up in charge of the expedition. James sailed from Bristol on 3 May 1631 aboard the *Henrietta Maria* with a crew of 22, none of whom had any northern experience. After exploring the south coast of Hudson Bay, James deliberately wintered off Charlton Island, sinking his ship to preserve it from storms. Some of his crew died of scurvy, although most survived by eating green plants found along the shore. James took careful observations, especially of the effects of low temperatures. In the spring the crew refloated the ship and engaged in further exploration before returning to Bristol on 22 October 1632. James's account of the journey was published as *The Strange and Dangerous Voyage of Captaine Thomas James, in His Intended Discovery of the Northwest Passage into the South Sea wherein the Miseries Indured, Both Going, Wintering, Returning; and the Rarities Observed, Both Philosophicall and Mathematicall, Are Related in This Journall of It* (1633). It was a literary triumph. James concluded that no Northwest Passage existed south of 66° North, and this and his account of his sufferings further deflected English Arctic exploration throughout the seventeenth century. James Bay is named for him. *DCB* I, 384-85.

James, Thomas William (b. 1883) Bandmaster. He was born in Umballa, India. His father was a schoolmaster and bandleader. James came to Winnipeg in 1911 to become assistant musical director of the 106th Regiment Light Infantry Band. He joined the Canadian Expeditionary Force in August 1915, organizing the first Canadian Band with his division. After WWI he returned to Canada to form the Great War Veterans' Association Band, which toured widely in North America and Europe, and he became director of music of the Princess Patricia Band, based in Winnipeg.

Jameson, Richard Willis (1851-1899) Municipal politician. He was born in South Africa and educated in England (BA, King's College London, Trinity College Cambridge). He came to Canada in 1876 and to Winnipeg in 1881, and was admitted to the bar in 1882. Jameson became a municipal official of the City of Winnipeg, an alderman from 1892 to 1895, and eventually mayor in 1896. He was elected as a Liberal in a by-election for the House of Commons seat from Winnipeg in 1897. He was known as a fine public speaker. *DCB* XII, 468.

Jarvis, Edward (d. c. 1800) Fur trader, interpreter. First employed by the HBC in 1771, he became fluent in Cree and thus became a leader of mapping expeditions of the 1770s. Of a weak constitution, he was ill-suited to the field, but he advocated inland expansion. He retired in ill health in 1797. *DCB* IV, 390-91.

Jérémie, Nicolas (dit Lamontagne) (1669-1732) Fur trader. Born at Quebec, he served the Compagnie du Nord at Hudson Bay from 1694 to 1714. In his early years he often worked with Pierre Le Moyne d'Iberville. He wrote "Relation du Détroit et de la baie d'Hudson" (1720), which was translated and edited by R. Douglas and J.N. Wallace as *Twenty Years of York Factory 1694-1714* (1926). As an author, Jérémie emphasized only what he had examined in person, and he included landscape, flora, and fauna, as well as a history and eyewitness account of the French presence on the Bay. *DCB* II, 296-300.

Jobin, Francis Laurence ("Bud," 1914-1995) Lieutenant-governor, politician. Born in Winnipeg,

he was educated at St. Mary's School, St. Paul's College, and the University of Saskatchewan. He moved to Flin Flon in 1935, working for the Hudson Bay Mining and Smelting Company until the late 1960s. He was first elected a Liberal MLA from The Pas constituency in 1950, serving as minister of industry and commerce from 1956 to 1958. He ran unsuccessfully for Parliament in 1962, was a member of the Flin Flon municipal council from 1966 to 1974 and was mayor in 1974. He subsequently served as lieutenant-governor of Manitoba from 1976 to 1980.

Johns, Ethel (1870-1968) Nurse. Born in Meonstoke, England, of Welsh parentage, she came with her parents to the Wabigoon district in 1888. She graduated from the Winnipeg General Hospital in 1902 and served it in many nursing capacities for many years. She was editor of the *Canadian Nurse* and wrote often on medical and nursing problems. See Margaret M. Street, *Watch-Fires on the Mountains: The Life and Writings of Ethel Johns* (1974).

Johns, Richard J. ("Dickie," 1889-1970) Labour leader. Born in Cornwall, England, he came to Canada in 1912 via Denver, Colorado. In 1917 he urged a general strike against conscription and national registration. In 1919 he was a machinist for the CPR, a member of the Social Democratic Party, and a leader of the One Big Union (OBU). He had been a delegate to the Calgary Convention of 1919 that had established the OBU. He was in Montreal at sittings of the National Railway Board as the elected representative of the machinists when a warrant charging him with seditious conspiracy was issued for his arrest on 17 June 1919. He was found guilty by a jury on 28 March 1920 and was sentenced to one year in prison. He subsequently became an industrial arts teacher, served as night-school principal at St. John's High School, and was eventually appointed director of technical education by the Province of Ontario. He became principal of the Manitoba Technical and Vocational Training Institute in 1951 and retired in 1953. He eventually moved to Victoria, where he died. See Harry and Mildred Gutkin, *Profiles in Dissent: The Shaping of Radical Thought in the Canadian West* (1997), 204-12.

Johnson, Albert C. (b. 1867) Consul. Born in Iceland, he came to Winnipeg in 1887, and entered the real-estate business in 1912. Fluent in Danish, Swedish, Norwegian, Icelandic, and English, in 1924 he was appointed consul in Winnipeg for the Danish and Icelandic governments.

Johnson, Francis Godschall (1817-1894) Judge. Born in Bedfordshire, England, to a military family, he was educated in France and Belgium before coming to Canada. He was called to the bar of Lower Canada on 22 November 1839, and he subsequently served on the commission in charge of revising the statutes of Lower Canada. He opposed the Rebellion Losses Bill (which cost him his QC for a few years) and in October 1849 signed an Annexation Manifesto that called for union with the United States. In 1854 he was appointed recorder of Rupert's Land by the HBC, chiefly because of his fluent bilingualism. He also became assessor and legal adviser to the governor of Assiniboia and to the HBC. On 29 July 1855 he was named assistant governor of Assiniboia, and on 26 November 1855 he was appointed governor. He held that post until 1858. While recorder, his major action was to release Andrew G.B. Bannatyne,* who had been arrested by chief factor George Barnston* in 1857 for defiance of HBC trade regulations. In 1858 he returned to his law practice in Lower Canada. He appeared for the Crown in the case against Confederate soldiers who had raided St. Albans, Vermont, from Canada. Following the establishment of the province of Manitoba in 1870, Johnson agreed to resume as recorder for one year, and held his first sitting of the court on 17 November 1870, when it heard cases against three Fenian supporters arrested at the border. Johnson also chaired the commission that considered and awarded compensation for Red River Rebellion losses, hearing the claims in 1871 and completing the awards in 1872. He was appointed lieutenant-governor of Manitoba to succeed Adams Archibald,* but his appointment was revoked before he arrived, and he agreed to act as judge of the General Quarterly Court for one term. He was appointed chief justice of the Superior Court in 1889 and was awarded a knighthood shortly thereafter. See Roy St. George Stubbs, *Four Recorders of Rupert's Land* (1967). *DCB* XII, 476-78.

Johnson, George (1920-1995) Physician, politician. Born in Winnipeg, he attended local schools and the University of Manitoba (BSc 1941). He served in the Royal Navy from 1941 to 1945 in the North Sea. In 1950 he graduated from University of Manitoba Medical School and set up in practice at Gimli. Elected to the legislature in 1958, he entered the

Cabinet immediately and served there under Premiers Roblin and Weir. He was the minister of health responsible for bringing the early stages of Medicare to Manitoba. He was awarded the Order of Canada in 1986. In the same year, he was appointed lieutenant-governor of Manitoba, serving to 1991. His papers are at the PAM.

Johnson, Thomas (d. 1869) Murder victim. In December 1869 he was found outside his door in Winnipeg, apparently frozen to death, but it turned out he had been shot in a drinking quarrel the previous night. This was one of the few recorded murders in the history of the Red River Settlement. His murderer, although known to authorities, was never apprehended because the culprit hastily left the settlement.

Johnson, Thomas Herman (1870-1927) Politician. Born in Iceland, he moved to Manitoba with his family in 1878, first to Gimli and then to Winnipeg. He sold newspapers to finance his education. He obtained a teaching certificate in 1888 and entered law studies in 1895, being admitted to the bar in 1900. He became chief legal counsel for both Lord Strathcona* and the HBC. A Liberal, he was elected Winnipeg MLA in 1907, and he served as Centre Winnipeg MLA from 1914 to 1922. He became the right-hand man of Premier Tobias Norris* and entered the Norris Cabinet, where he promoted welfare legislation, prison reform, and workmen's compensation. He retired in 1922 in ill health.

Johnston, Franz H. ("Frank," 1888-1949) Artist. The son of Irish immigrants in Toronto, Johnston joined Grip Limited in 1907 and subsequently studied art in both Toronto and the United States. He was an official war artist in 1917-18, painting scenes in training camps, and for his work was granted associate status in the Royal Canadian Academy. He subsequently became a member of the Group of Seven, which he left in 1924. From 1921 to 1924 he served as principal and teacher at the Winnipeg School of Art, and then he taught at the Ontario College of Art. He moved to full-time painting in 1930, although he also opened a summer school of painting in the Ontario wilderness. After the 1920s, Johnston was less popular with the critics and the art establishment than he was with the public, who seemed to appreciate his Canadian scenes and bought them on a regular basis.

Johnstone, Robert Cuthbert (1857-1934) Cleric, author. Born in Scotland, probably in Edinburgh, he was ordained in the Anglican Church in 1880. In 1895, during a bout of amnesia incurred in Scotland, he came to Manitoba to visit a friend, and remained. He was reference librarian at the Winnipeg Public Library from 1914 to 1924. He lectured at St. John's College from 1919 to 1927 and became vicar of St. Aidan's Church in 1931. As "Alan Gray" he published a number of books, including *The White Rose of Darvel* (a historical novel, 1916) and two volumes of memoirs, *The Gentle Persuasion* (1918) and *Memories* (1923).

Jonasson, Einar (1887-1935) Municipal politician. Born in Mountain, North Dakota, he was educated at Vernon, British Columbia, and Gimli, Manitoba. He served as first clerk of Gimli village from 1908 to 1920 and was secretary-treasurer of the rural municipality. He was mayor of Gimli from 1923 to 1925 and was president of the Gimli Athletic Association. In 1930 he was elected MLA for Gimli. He served on the provincial fisheries commission.

Jonasson, Eric Leonard (1948-1998) Genealogist. Born in Winnipeg, he graduated from Winnipeg Technical Vocational High School in 1968 and attended the University of Minnesota. After establishing a mapping firm in Winnipeg, he became involved in family history. He wrote *Tracing Your Icelandic Family Tree,* organized the Manitoba Genealogical Society in 1976, and wrote *The Canadian Genealogical Handbook* (1978). Jonasson formed Wheatfield Press in 1975 to publish his work. He served as a St. James-Assiniboia school trustee from 1986 to 1998 and as president of the Canadian School Boards Association in 1996.

Jonasson, Sigtryggur (1852-1942) Immigration agent. Born in Iceland and educated at home, he came to Canada in 1872 and prospered. He was appointed an immigration agent by the Ontario government in 1874, to guide a large contingent of Icelanders to Kinmount. The settlement did not do well. That same year Rev. John Taylor suggested that the Canadian government establish an Icelandic settlement in Manitoba, and Jonasson became associated with the venture. People from Kinmount came west to the site of present-day Gimli in 1875, and Jonasson went to Iceland to recruit another 1,200 settlers. He helped produce a constitution and legal code for the

new settlement and soon had a newspaper, *Framfari,* (Progress) under way. Jonasson bought a steamer in 1879 to provide transportation to the region, and was active in other business ventures that provided employment for the settlers. He moved to Selkirk in 1880 and was elected Liberal MLA for St. Andrews in 1896. He served as homestead inspector for the Interlake District from 1901 to 1906. In later years he lived quietly on his homestead. In 1930 he represented Canada at the celebrations of the millennium of the founding of Iceland's Parliament. He was the author of *The Early Icelandic Settlements in Canada* (1901).

Jones, David Thomas (1796-1844) Cleric. Born in Wales, he studied at Lampeter Seminary and became a missionary candidate of the Church Missionary Society. He was ordained a deacon in December 1822 and a priest in April 1823, when he left for Red River as John West's* temporary replacement. A low churchman, he got on well with the settlers. He refused to baptize Native people without religious preparation, however. He returned to Wales in 1828-29 and married. Upon his return he established a boarding school at Upper Church, which became known as Red River Academy. He was appointed to the Council of Assiniboia in 1835. He left the settlement in 1838 after the death of his wife, subsequently serving as professor of Welsh at St. David's College in Wales. At the time of his death he was rector at Llangoedmor. See Thomas F. Bredin, "The Reverend David Jones: Missionary at Red River," *The Beaver* (autumn 1981): 47-52. *DCB* VII, 454-55.

Jones, James Robert (c. 1852-1916) Physician. Born in Canada, he was educated at the Toronto School of Medicine, where he received his MD in 1878. He studied in England and returned to Manitoba to practise. He helped found the Manitoba Medical College in 1883, becoming initial professor of internal medicine. He was president of the College of Physicians and Surgeons and was acting dean of the Medical College from 1898 to 1901. A member of the board of governors of the University of Manitoba, he also served as a federal immigration officer. He died in St. Paul, Minnesota.

Jones, Lyman Melvin (1843-1917) Politician. Born in Canada, he came west in 1879 as western manager of A. Harris, Son and Company, the farm implement manufacturers. He soon became active in

Winnipeg politics, being elected alderman in 1881. He was chair of the city's finance committee and in 1887 and 1888 was mayor. In 1888 he joined the Thomas Greenway* government as provincial treasurer, winning a seat in Shoal Lake as a Liberal in a by-election. He subsequently represented North Winnipeg. He negotiated the provincial loan to build a railway line between Winnipeg and Brandon. In 1889 he left politics, and in 1891 he moved to Toronto to become director and general manager of Massey-Harris. He was elevated to president and general manager in 1903. Called to the Senate in 1901, he was made a knight commander of the Order of St. Michael and St. George in 1911. He died in Toronto. *DCB* XIV, 545-46.

Joseph, Herbert (1887-1965) Artist. Born in London, England, he immigrated to Winnipeg in 1904 and worked as an architectural draftsman. He studied at the Winnipeg School of Art in 1913-14 but enlisted in the engineering corps during WWI, returning to Winnipeg in 1919 with sketches of the devastation. He left Winnipeg in 1923, ending up in Chicago, but he continued to have local contacts that led, for example, to his illustrations for J.J. Gunn's *Echoes of the Red* (1930).

Juba, Stephen (1914-1993) Municipal politician. Born in Winnipeg, he was educated at United College. He founded Keystone Supply, a wholesale firm, in 1944. He was elected as an Independent MLA in 1953 and was elected mayor of Winnipeg in 1956, driving to City Hall in his bright yellow Cadillac. Juba came out of Winnipeg's multi-ethnic North End, and his election as mayor symbolized the end of WASP domination of city politics. Known as a quick wit, he had few avocations besides politics. Juba was a populist who supported development and lower taxes. In 1959 he introduced the three-digit emergency phone number into North America. He worked hard to get the Pan Am Games for Winnipeg in 1967. He also sabotaged the concept of cabinet government intended for Unicity, forcing the continuation of the mayor as a strong executive independent of the city council. He retired as mayor in 1977. He died at Petersfield. See Michael Czuboka, *Juba* (1986).

Jurriens, Henny (1949-1989) Dancer. Born at Arnheim, Netherlands, he joined the Royal Winnipeg Ballet in 1986 as a principal dancer. He was noted for his artistry and the range of his repertoire. He retired from the stage in 1988 to succeed Arnold Spohr as RWB artistic director. A few months later he was killed in a car crash in rural Manitoba.

Jury, Helen See Armstrong, Helen (Jury).

Jutras, Norbert (1856-1929) Cleric. Born in Canada, he studied at Nicolet Seminary and in 1880 came to Manitoba. He was ordained to the priesthood in 1882. He began his ministry at St. Pie and in 1889 moved to Letellier, where he became known as the "Apostle of Mixed Farming." He wrote in French on agricultural reform for many years, especially in the French-language journals of the province. He was a staunch advocate of modern machinery. He is a member of the Manitoba Agricultural Hall of Fame.

Kahanovitch, Israel Isaac (1872-1945) Cleric. Born in Poland, he was educated at Grodno Yeshiva College and Slbodka Shovno College. After serving as rabbi at Suvaeki, he went to the United States in 1905 to become rabbi at Scranton, Pennsylvania. An active Zionist, he was called to Winnipeg in 1906 to become chief rabbi. He organized kosher slaughterhouses and founded both the United Charity and the Hebrew School, thus awakening the spirit of the Jewish community in Winnipeg. He later became great rabbi for Western Canada.

Kane, Paul (1810-1877) Artist. An Irish-born artist who spent much time in Toronto before touring the Canadian West from 1845 to 1848, he went to a number of HBC posts, to Oregon, to New Caledonia, and to Vancouver Island, with a commission from Sir George Simpson* for a series of paintings of Native life. He made hundreds of sketches, from which he derived 100 large canvases of a way of life on the edge of extinction, which offer much of our best visual record of the early West. Kane also wrote *Wanderings of an Artist among the Indians of North America* (1859), distinguished for its sparse narrative and translated into numerous languages. For a biography, see A.H. Robson, *Paul Kane* (1938). The originals of Kane's paintings are in Ottawa, Toronto, and Orange, Texas, but his collection of Indian artifacts is in the Manitoba Museum of Man and Nature. *DCB* X, 389-94.

Kapeyakwaskonam ("One Arrow, Une Fleche") c.1815-1886) Cree chief. Chief of a band of Willow Crees who hunted in the Cypress Hills, he was arrested on a charge of treason-felony during the North-West Rebellion. After an unsatisfactory trial, in which he spoke to defend himself only after a verdict of guilty had been given, he was sentenced to three years in Stony Mountain Penitentiary. During his imprisonment he was converted to Catholicism, and when he was released because of ill health in April 1886 he was taken to the archbishop's palace in St Boniface, where he died a few weeks later. *DCB* XI, 461-62.

Kauffman, Ulric (1785-1863) Pioneer. Born in Switzerland, he was one of the De Meuron regiment that disbanded in York in 1815 and was among those recruited by Lord Selkirk to defend the Red River Colony. Unlike most of his compatriots, he remained in Red River after the 1826 flood, settling on Lot 64 in Kildonan.

Kaufman, Walter (1907-1984) Musician, composer. Born in Karlsbad, Bohemia, he was educated at Prague University and the Hochschule fuer Musik, Berlin. He was musical director of the All-India Radio Bombay orchestra from 1938 to 1946, and came to Canada in 1947, first to Halifax, then to Winnipeg from 1948 to 1956. He was the first conductor of the newly formed Winnipeg Symphony Orchestra, directed the Winnipeg Philharmonic Choir from 1949 to 1953, and revived the Winnipeg Male Voice Choir in 1950. He was also an active composer. He conducted the premiere of his opera "Bashmachkin" on CBC in 1952, had two ballet scores choreographed by the RWB in 1948 and 1949, and wrote a "Coronation Cantata"which was performed on CBC in 1953. He joined the music faculty of Indiana University in 1957.

Kavanagh, François (b. 1833) Cleric, educator. Of Irish descent, he was trained in a Montreal seminary and came to St. Boniface after his reception into Holy Orders in 1866. He was soon sent to St. François Xavier Parish to assist Father Thibault, and he was active in establishing schools within the parish. In late 1869 he was shot in the back while riding, but he recovered. He remained at St. François Xavier throughout his active career.

Kean, Arthur David (1882-1961) Film producer. Born in Emerson, Manitoba, he moved with his family to Texas and then to British Columbia. He became a champion rodeo competitor, and he gradually combined rodeo advertisement with motion picture production. He produced many films for the Canadian government during WWI. In 1924 he began filming R.G. MacBeth's* *Policing the Plains,* which was finally released in 1927 to mixed reviews. This lack of success ended his motion picture career, and he turned to radio work, specializing in the Old West. Few of Kean's films have survived. See Dennis J. Duffy and David Mattison, "A.D. Kean: Canada's Cowboy Movie-Maker," *The Beaver* 69, no. 1 (1989): 28-41.

Keeper, Joseph B. (1886-1971) Long-distance runner, war hero. Born in Walker Lake, Manitoba, he was sent to the Brandon Indian Residential School, remaining there from 1899 to 1909. He ran his first race in 1909 in Brandon, then moved to Winnipeg in 1910 and became a member of the North End Athletic Club. That year he won a seven-mile road race, and he set a Canadian 10-mile record at Fort William in 1911. He was named to the Canadian Olympic team in 1912. Keeper joined the army in 1916 and won the Military Medal for bravery at Cambrai in 1917. After the war he returned to the North and worked for the HBC at Norway House. He is a member of the Manitoba Sports Hall of Fame.

Keeseekoowenin, a.k.a. Moses Burns (1818-1906) Native leader. Born in the Bow River region of what is now Alberta, he moved with his family and band to the Riding Mountain region of present-day Manitoba in 1822. In 1871 the band signed Treaty Two with the federal government, and, as a result, they moved their reserve to a place near Elphinstone in 1875. Keeseekoowenin was regarded by the government as chief. The band had accepted the mission of Presbyterian George Flett,* and the chief was baptized as Moses Burns, although a remote branch of the band at Clear Lake remained Catholic. Keeseekoowenin successfully blended Christian values with Native beliefs and traditional rituals. He died near Elphinstone. *DCB* XIII, 537-38.

Keith, George (1779-1859) Fur trader. Born in Scotland, he came to America to join Forsyth, Richardson and Company (or the XY Company) as an apprentice fur trader, serving in the Athabasca country. He remained there for many years, and as head of the NWC's Athabasca Department in 1817 led the local struggle against the HBC. After the merger of the NWC and HBC he became a chief factor, first at English River and later at Michipicoten. He was appointed a councillor of Rupert's Land in 1839. He and his mixed-blood wife retired with their family to Scotland in 1844. He died in Aberdeen. His papers are at the Aberdeen University Library. *DCB* VIII, 453-54.

Kelly, Andrew (1852-1930) Miller, insurance executive. Born in Ailsa Craig, Canada, he farmed in Ontario before entering the grain business. In 1881 he came to Manitoba and opened a flour mill at Brandon. He was elected mayor of Brandon in 1899 and 1901. In 1905 his mill became part of the newly organized Western Canada Flour Mills, which prospered under his direction. He was an original founder of Great-West Life. Kelly was a keen baseball and lacrosse player.

Kelly, Thomas (1855-1939) Builder. Born in Roscommon, Ireland, he went to the United States in 1864 and was educated at Oneida, New York. He came to Winnipeg to start Kelly Brothers Construction, and became one of the city's major builders. When his firm constructed the Manitoba legislative building he was accused of corruption. He retired to Beverly Hills, California, in 1924 and died there.

Kelsey, Henry (c. 1667-1724) Fur trader, explorer. Probably born in East Greenwich, England, he was apprenticed to the HBC in 1684 and posted to the Nelson River. He quickly achieved a reputation as "a very active Lad, Delighting much in Indians Company." In 1689 he was sent to Churchill River, and he kept his first journal of the endeavour, which included an unsuccessful overland march. A year later, under orders from the Company, he began his expedition from York Fort "to call, encourage, and invite the remoter Indians to a Trade with us." The journal he kept of this expedition is one of the most famous and controversial in the literature of western exploration. It was published in 1929 by A.G. Doughty and Chester Martin as *The Kelsey Papers*. The notoriety is a result of the journal being written partly in rhyme. The controversy revolves around Kelsey's route, particularly how far north and west he got. Whatever his actual route, he was the first European to travel extensively west and north of the Bottom of the Bay, and the first to record descriptions of many things, including buffalo and grizzly bears. Kelsey remained at the Bay almost continuously until 1722, one of the most enigmatic of the early European figures of the region. He was well known for his expertise in Native languages, and he made several subsequent forays into the North. *DCB* II, 307-15.

Kennedy, Alexander (c. 1781-1832) Fur trader. Born in the Orkney Islands, he joined the HBC in 1798 as a writer. He served at York Factory before becoming master of Cumberland House from 1804 to 1806. In 1808 he went to Swan River, before becoming master of Brandon House in 1811-12. He returned to head the Swan River District in 1812-13 and was the head of Norway House in 1820-21. He returned to Cumberland House in 1821. He was a governor's councillor from 1822. In 1830 he retired with his family to the Red River Settlement, but he subsequently died of typhus fever in London. There are papers at the PAM.

Kennedy, Eleanor E. (Cripps) (1825-1913) Artist. The wife of Captain William Kennedy,* she was born in London and came to Manitoba with her husband. She was well known among contemporaries for her paintings and her singing. A notebook of her botanical paintings is in the Manitoba Museum of Man and Nature. She taught music in St. Andrews and was the organist at St. Andrews on the Red. During hard times for the family in the 1860s she ran a fashion shop from the Kennedy home. She

possessed one of the first pianos in the province. In 1870 she complained she was being falsely accused of being a supporter of Louis Riel. She was known as "the Duchess" and died in Virden. There are papers at the PAM. *DCB* XIV, 251-53.

Kennedy, Ella MacTavish (1887-1953) Probation officer. Born in Port Hawkesbury, Nova Scotia, she was educated at Pictou Academy and came to Winnipeg in 1906 to complete her education at Winnipeg Business College. She worked as a schoolteacher, a stenographer, and an investigator and supervisor for mother's allowances. She was appointed to the juvenile court as the only probation officer in the province in 1919. In 1921 she was secretary of the Manitoba Civil Servants' Association. She helped found the Big Sisters' Association of Winnipeg and was secretary of the Royal Templars of Temperance. She retired to Vancouver in 1951 and died there.

Kennedy, John Wesley (1845-1910) Pioneer. Born in Peterborough, Canada, he was a professional soldier (beginning as a bugler) who came to Winnipeg about 1880 and became part of the home guard. In 1885 he recruited a company for the North-West Rebellion. He later operated a decorating business with his brothers. He was a supporter of the temperance movement. In later years he worked as a clerk in the Land Titles Office. He built a house at 965 Portage Avenue in 1902.

Kennedy, William (1814-1890) Fur trader, explorer. Born at Cumberland House in present-day Saskatchewan to the Cree wife of an HBC chief factor, Kennedy was educated in Scotland before joining the HBC in 1833, spending a number of years in the Ottawa Valley and Labrador. He resigned from the Company in 1846 because he objected to its liquor policy, and subsequently served as commander of Lady Franklin's second privately financed expedition to find her husband. He insisted on proper equipment (including Native outer-garments), and although he did not find Franklin, he expanded geographical knowledge of the Arctic and returned his crew to England without loss of life. He led a second expedition financed by Lady Franklin in 1853, but jailed its crew in Chile after a mutiny. Kennedy returned to Canada in 1856 and was one of the proponents of Canadian annexation of Rupert's Land. He travelled overland from Toronto to Red River in the winter of 1857 to prove that it could be done, whatever the weather. In the Red River Settlement he got 575 signatures to a petition requesting union with Canada. A year later he carried the first mail from Toronto to Red River. In 1860 Kennedy settled at the Maples in St. Andrews. He was not very active at the time of the Red River Rebellion in 1869-70, although at a parish meeting in St. Andrews in October 1869 he opposed welcoming Governor William McDougall* into the settlement, saying he was suspicious of the man's character and background. Kennedy on this occasion called for Confederation "on equal terms with other provinces." He was a founding member of the Historical and Scientific Society of Manitoba and an advocate in the 1880s of a railway to the Bay. Kennedy was the author of *A Short Narrative of the Second Voyage of the Prince Albert in Search of Sir John Franklin* (1853). For a biography, see Manitoba Board of Historic Resources, *William Kennedy* (1982). There are papers at the PAM. *DCB* XI, 470-71.

Kennedy, William Nassau (1839-1885) Soldier. Born in Upper Canada, he worked as a house painter before joining the Peterborough Rifles as a private in 1857. He progressed through the ranks, and as Captain Kennedy he received the appointment allotted to the 57th Battalion for an officer to participate in the Wolseley Expedition. He served as a lieutenant in the Ontario Rifles and elected to stay in Manitoba. During the 1871 Fenian crisis he raised a temporary volunteer unit, and he became commander of another that was founded later. He served in a number of appointive clerical positions for the government and became an active promoter of railway companies. He founded the Winnipeg Philharmonic Society in 1880. In 1883 he organized the 90th Winnipeg Rifles under his command to protect the West, and shortly thereafter was allowed to proceed to the Nile River with a force of 100 Manitoba volunteers he had raised to support the British expedition of Lord Kitchener. Many of these men lacked the voyageur experience Kennedy had been instructed to emphasize, and they proved indifferent boatmen on the Sudan. In Egypt he benefited from his earlier service with General Garnet Wolseley* and his experience in manoeuvring in militia politics, ending up as paymaster. He died in London of smallpox. See C.P. Stacey, ed., *Records of the Nile Voyageurs, 1884-1885* (1959); Roy MacLaren, *Canadians on the Nile, 1882-1898* (1978). There are papers at the PAM. *DCB* XI, 471-73.

Kenner, Henry (1832-1916) Cleric. Born in Tresmere, Cornwall, England, he was educated at a Bible college in North Devon and was ordained in 1855. He served many Methodist churches in England before coming to Canada in 1861 and to Manitoba in 1882. He moved to Winnipeg in 1889. He celebrated his sixtieth anniversary as an ordained minister before his death in Winnipeg. There are papers (including a diary) at the University of Winnipeg.

Kenrick, Edgar Boteler (1863-1905) Educator. Born in Kent, England, he came to Canada in 1879 and was educated at Upper Canada College and at University College, Toronto (BSc, first-class honours, 1884). After working in Ottawa he became professor of natural science at St. John's College and later the University of Manitoba. He joined the CPR as a chemist in 1904. He is reputed to have owned the first automobile in Winnipeg.

Ketchen, A.P. (1866-1908) Journalist. Born in Canada, he worked for the Ontario Department of Agriculture before attending the Ontario Agricultural College, where he received his BSA in 1903. In 1904 he became editor-in-chief of the *Nor'West Farmer,* based in Winnipeg. His specialty was livestock judging. He was appointed deputy commissioner of agriculture for Saskatchewan in 1908.

Ketchen, Huntley Dudley Brodie (1872-1959) Soldier. Born in India and educated at Sandhurst, England, Ketchen came to Winnipeg in 1894. He served as a lieutenant in the Boer War, then as brigadier-general of the Sixth Canadian Infantry from 1915 to 1917. He was relieved of active command after a military fiasco at St. Eloi (Flanders) in 1915. At the time of his death he was a major-general. After WWI he was appointed commanding officer of the military district in which Winnipeg was located, serving from 1919 until 1929, when he retired. Ketchen was thus in charge of the military during the Winnipeg General Strike. As district commander, he followed orders from Ottawa and in general restrained his troops from confrontations with the civilian population. He also favoured use of the War Measures Act to deal with post-war problems of the cost of living by appointing a prices board to investigate complaints and with power to prosecute. He met daily with local officials about the strike and was one of the chief advisers to government. He opposed bail for the arrested strike leaders in 1919 on the grounds that the militia would be unhappy with such an action.

Keveny, Owen (d. 1816) Murder victim. A native of Sligo, Ireland, he was employed by Lord Selkirk* as second-in-command to Miles Macdonell* at Red River, and he led the second party of Selkirk settlers to the settlement in 1812. He was regarded by his men as a harsh disciplinarian, and he nearly left the region on several occasions. Employed by Selkirk to lead a party from Fort Albany to Red River in 1816, Keveny was arrested at Bas-de-la-Rivière (Fort Alexander) under a warrant issued by a NWC magistrate and was eventually murdered by two employees of the NWC in September 1816. One of his killers was convicted of the crime, the only guilty verdict rendered in the complex court battles over Red River that occurred in the Canadas from 1817 to 1819. *DCB* V, 465-66.

Kilgour, James Frederick (1874-1931) Lawyer, judge. Born in Hillsburg, Ontario, he attended Osgoode Hall. He came to Brandon and was called to the bar in 1902. He headed a Brandon law firm from 1901 to 1927, and then was appointed to the Court of King's Bench. He was active in the Boy Scouts' movement and was president of the Brandon Children's Aid Society.

Killam, Albert Clements (1849-1908) Lawyer, judge. Born in Yarmouth, Nova Scotia, he attended the University of Toronto, graduating in 1872 as the Prince of Wales medallist with silver medals in mathematics and modern language. Admitted to the bar in 1876, he practised in Windsor, Ontario, before moving to Winnipeg in 1879. In Manitoba, he was soon an examiner of the Law Society and a QC (1884). In 1883 he ran for the Legislative Assembly as a Provincial Rights candidate against Charles Tuttle* in Winnipeg South, defeating him by 63 votes. He was appointed to the Manitoba Court of Queen's Bench early in 1885. One of his first cases was the appeal of Louis Riel, which led to a concurrence in the judgment against the Métis leader. In 1890 he upheld the provincial government in its effort to establish a single public school system, a decision ultimately upheld by the Privy Council. He was elevated to chief justice in 1899 and to the Supreme Court of Canada — the first western judge appointed — in 1903. Early in 1905 he became chief commis-

sioner of the Board of Railway Commissioners. He died in Ottawa. *DCB* XIII, 542-44.

King, George (d. 1925) Journalist. Born in Canada, he was editor of the *Oakville Star* before coming to Manitoba and working on both the *Winnipeg Sun* and *Manitoba Free Press*. In 1899 he became editor of the *Dauphin Press,* which was controlled by T.H. Burrows and D.B. Hanna. In 1911 he and his son founded the *Dauphin Herald,* and in 1914 they merged it with the *Press* into the *Dauphin Herald and Press.* King was first president of the Dauphin General Hospital and was mayor of Dauphin from 1901 to 1903.

King, John Mark (1829-1899) Cleric, educator. Born in Roxburghshire, Scotland, he received his education at the University of Edinburgh (MA, 1856), the University of Halle in Germany, and later Knox College Toronto (DD, 1882). He went to the United States in 1856 to minister to a congregation in Columbus, Ohio, and in 1863 was appointed pastor of St. James Square Church in Toronto. In 1883 he became principal of Manitoba College and moderator of the Presbyterian Church in Canada. He took Manitoba College out of debt and began building an endowment. One of his daughters married Rev. C.W. Gordon.* He wrote *The Characteristics of Scottish Religious Life and Their Causes* (1882) and *A Critical Study of "In Memoriam"* (1898). Microfilm of some of his papers is at the University of Winnipeg. *DCB* XII, 489-91.

King, William See Peguis.

Kirchhoffer, John Nesbitt (1848-1914) Pioneer, politician. Born in Ballyromney, County Cork, Ireland, he was educated at Marlborough College, Wiltshire, and came to Canada in 1864. He took part in the Fenian troubles as militia ensign and later captain of the 46th Battalion. He was called to the bar in 1871, and he practised in Port Hope before moving to Manitoba in 1883, where he founded the Plum Creek settlement and the town of Souris. He served as reeve of the Municipality of Glenwood in 1885-86 and as mayor of Souris. He was an active member of agricultural societies and was Conservative MLA from West Brandon from 1886 to 1888. On several occasions he captained Canadian international cricket teams. In 1892 he was appointed to the Canadian Senate, and he served until his death.

Kirk, Jessie (fl. 1919-1934) Politician. Kirk ran as a labour candidate in the 1919 municipal elections for the Winnipeg School Board. She had lost her job as a schoolteacher for her labour activities. She lost in 1919, but was elected to the municipal council in 1920. She withdrew from the 1920 provincial election in favour of male strike leaders. She was elected to the executive committee of the Dominion Labour Party in March 1920 as one of two female representatives. In 1921 she became the first woman elected to the Winnipeg city council. She subsequently ran for city council in 1922, 1926, and 1934.

Kirkconnell, Watson (1895-1977) Educator, linguist. Born in Port Hope, Ontario, he was educated at the Collegiate Institute in Lindsay, Queen's University, the Toronto Conservatory of Music, and Lincoln College, Oxford. He was professor of English at Wesley College in Winnipeg from 1922 to 1930 and head of the classics department there from 1930 to 1940. He then led the federal government's "Nationalities Branch" (which became the Citizenship Bureau) during WWII. He also headed the Humanities Research Council in 1943 and the Baptist Federation of Canada in 1944. After a period at McMaster University, he became president of Acadia University from 1948 to 1964. He wrote 40 books and 600 articles, as well as innumerable translations from some of the 50 languages with which he was familiar. He was particularly important in translating Ukrainian and Icelandic poets into English. His memoir of his father was published as *A Canadian Headmaster* in 1935, and his own memoirs, *A Slice of Canada,* appeared in 1967. He was awarded the Order of Canada in 1969. See J.R.C. Perkin, ed., *The Undoing of Babel: Watson Kirkconnell, the Man and His Work* (1975) and Perkin's *Morning in His Heart: The Life and Writings of Watson Kirkconnell* (1986).

Kirton, Mary Ann See Good, Mary Ann (Kirton).

Kittson, Alexander (1853-1883) Politician. The son of Norman* and Elise Kittson,* he was born in North Pembina and educated at St. Boniface College. He was elected a Liberal-Conservative MLA in 1879 for Ste. Agathe, and served until his death.

Kittson, Norman Wolfred (1814-1888) Fur trader, entrepreneur. Born in Lower Canada, Kittson joined the American Fur Company in 1830, eventually becoming head of that company's operations in North Dakota and working out of Pembina. Kittson's fur-trading activities were based in part on receiving furs from Métis free traders to the north, and he helped contribute to the arrival of free trade in Red River in 1849. Kittson served on the Minnesota Territorial Legislative Council from 1852 to 1855. In 1854 he moved from Pembina to St. Paul, where he became a major businessman (in real estate and commercial operations) and was city mayor in 1858-59. Beginning in 1856 he began investing in the Red River Settlement, opening steamboat transportation on the Red River in 1858-59. After Manitoba became a province, Kittson and James Jerome Hill* capitalized the Red River Transportation Company to run five steamboats on the Red. Kittson was one of several partners who in 1879 bought the St. Paul and Pacific Railway and reorganized it as the St. Paul, Minneapolis and Manitoba Railway, connecting St. Paul and St. Boniface. Appropriately, he died on board a train in 1888. See C.W. Rife, "Norman W. Kittson, a Fur-Trader at Pembina," *Minnesota History* 6 (1925): 225-52. *DCB* XI, 476-77.

Knight, James (1640-c. 1720) Fur trader. Born in England, Knight joined the HBC in 1676 as a carpenter. He was appointed chief factor at Albany Fort in 1682 and subsequently deputy governor. He was energetic if unpolished, and it was rumoured that he was too friendly with the New England traders in the Bay. He was charged with private trading in 1685 and released from service in 1687 after a hearing. A few years later, in 1692, a Captain James Knight of London, "Merchant," was given royal letters patent naming him governor and commander-in-chief at the Bay. Given French depredations, it is not surprising that he was to act militantly and recover any territory lost to the French. He sailed with four ships. Knight tilted to a standoff with Pierre Le Moyne d'Iberville* in the mid-1690s. He returned to London in 1700, remaining there on the HBC's governing committee until 1714, when he was sent back to the Bay with Henry Kelsey* to receive the French surrender of forts agreed to at the Treaty of Utrecht. Knight remained to guide the HBC into the postwar era, opening a post on the Churchill River and sending out several exploration parties. He himself led one voyage north of 64° in 1719, from which he never returned; the ships were apparently wrecked in a cove on Marble Island. Some of the survivors — according to later Eskimo testimony — lived until 1721. A journal kept by Knight in 1717 has been edited by J.F. Kenney and published as *The Founding of Churchill* (1932). *DCB* II, 319-20.

Knowles, Stanley (1908-1997) Politician. Born in Los Angeles to Canadian parents, he returned to Canada to study at Brandon College (BA, 1930), United College, and the University of Manitoba (where he majored in economics and philosophy). First elected a Winnipeg alderman in 1941, he was elected to the federal House of Commons from Winnipeg North Centre as successor to J.S. Woodsworth* in 1942. He subsequently won 12 elections to Parliament, losing only in the 1958 Diefenbaker sweep. Knowles helped found the NDP out of the shards of the CCF, having chaired the National Committee for a New Party from 1958 to 1961. He wrote *The New Party* (1961). He was noted for his mastery of the procedural rules of the House of Commons and was made an honorary officer of the House in 1984 so that he could sit at the clerk's table. An ordained United Church minister, he often celebrated weddings, christenings, and funerals while not engaged in parliamentary duties. See the biography by Susan Mann Trofimenkoff, *Stanley Knowles: The Man from Winnipeg North Centre* (1982), and G. Gerald Harrop, *Advocate of Compassion: Stanley Knowles in the Political Process* (1984).

Knudson, George Alfred Christian (1937-1989) Golfer. Born in Winnipeg, he began playing golf at the St. Charles Golf and Country Club. He turned professional in 1961 and won eight PGA victories before his retirement in 1972. He and Al Balding won the World Cup for Canada in 1968. He was a fairway specialist but an indifferent putter. He later worked as a club pro in Toronto. He was a member of the Canadian Golf Hall of Fame and was awarded the Order of Canada. He died in Toronto.

Konantz, Margaret MacTavish (Rogers) (1899-1967) Politician. Born in Winnipeg, she was educated at Bishop Strachan School and Miss Spence's School. Daughter of Edith Rogers,* the first Manitoba female MLA, Konantz kept a vow to her husband to remain out of public life that ended only with his death in 1954. By 1959 she was national vice-president of UNICEF and in 1961 became national vice-president of the UN Association. She first ran for Parliament in 1962, and became Manitoba's first female MP in 1963, when she was elected to represent Winnipeg South. Her papers are at the UML Archives and the PAM.

Konrad, John (1899-1962) Musician. Born in Halbstadt, Ukraine, he studied violin in Russia and came to Winkler in 1926, then to Winnipeg in 1931. He served as choirmaster of many churches and taught at the Bornoff School of Music. He was the first head of the music department at the Canadian Mennonite Bible College and in 1941 became head of the Bornoff School, changing its name to the Konrad Conservatory of Music in 1950. The Konrad Conservatory's student body in the late 1950s — 350 pupils — was the largest in Canada and included many subsequently distinguished musicians. Konrad was regarded as too worldly a musician by many Mennonites.

Koreichuk, Tymofei (1879-1919) Labour organizer. Born in Bukovyna (Ukraine), he was an active socialist organizer there until he immigrated to Canada in 1913. He soon became involved with the Federation of Ukrainian Social Democrats, moving in 1914 to Winnipeg to serve as its western organizer. He briefly ran a bookstore in Winnipeg's North End in 1916. Koreichuk was a highly experienced labour organizer whose work was limited only by his ill health. He later settled near Vegreville, Alberta. He was arrested for making seditious speeches and interned at a camp near Vernon, British Columbia, in 1919, where he died of tuberculosis. *DCB* XIV, 562-63.

Korol, Taras ("Ted," 1918-1998) Theatrical designer. Born in the Winnipeg suburb of East Kildonan, he became involved with the theatre at an early age and began designing sets and costumes for local productions in the early 1940s. He worked for all Winnipeg theatrical groups, including John Hirsch's Manitoba Theatre Centre. The Korol Studio at the renovated Pantages Playhouse Theatre was named for him and his wife in 1995.

Koster, Wally (1923-1975) Musician. Born in Winnipeg, he became a band singer in 1939. After WWII he was trombonist and chief male vocalist with the Mart Kenny Band from 1949 to 1952. He later starred in CBC-TV's *Cross Canada Hit Parade* and sang in musicals at Rainbow Stage in the 1950s. He made several LP recordings. He died in Winnipeg.

Krafchenko, John ("Bloody Jack," 1881-1914) Outlaw. Born in Romania in 1881, he came to Canada with his parents aged seven and settled in Plum Coulee, Manitoba. He was constantly in trouble as a child. He later fought as a boxer. He was arrested for passing bad cheques in 1902, robbed a bank in 1906, and robbed another bank at Plum Coulee in 1913, killing the manager. He was arrested in Winnipeg in December 1913, escaping from the Winnipeg police station and setting off a major manhunt. He was recaptured on 18 January 1914, and was hanged on 9 July 1914. He is the subject of a long poem by Dennis Cooley, *Bloody Jack* (1984).

Kristjanson, Jonina Thorunn (1906-1979) Musician. Born in Winnipeg, she was an accomplished pianist who taught music at Elm Creek. She later taught piano in Winnipeg and was an active accompanist at the Winnipeg Music Festival, the Icelandic Festival, and the British Wives Club of Winnipeg.

Kristofferson, Kristine (1914-1997) Author. Born in Gimli, she attended Gimli Public School and Winnipeg Normal School. She taught in Gimli from 1938 to 1947, retired from teaching to raise a family, and returned to teaching in 1962. Her novel *Tanya* was written "between the ironing board and the kitchen stove." Set in the Interlake region of Manitoba, it was submitted for the Ryerson fiction contest. Although it did not win, Ryerson encouraged her to revise it for publication and it appeared in 1951. She continued to write and to translate, but the promised second novel, "Jorunn," was never published. Her papers are at the UML Archives.

Kroeker, Abram Arthur (1892-1981) Farmer. Born in Winkler, Manitoba, he was active in business before buying a farm in 1928 to allow his family to experience that way of life. He was a pioneer reformer in the Mennonite communities, using chemical fertilizer and developing a new technique of corn drying. He introduced new crops into Mennonite farming, such as sunflowers, potatoes, and sugar beets. He is a member of the Manitoba Agricultural Hall of Fame.

Kurelek, William (1927-1977) Artist. Born in Edmonton, he moved with his parents to Stonewall, Manitoba, at an early age and grew up there. He attended the University of Manitoba, graduating in arts in 1949. He then attended the Ontario College of Art. He travelled the world and then began serious painting after admitting himself to a London mental institution. Having converted to Catholicism, he returned to Toronto in 1959. His autobiography, *Someone with Me,* appeared in 1980. His paintings illustrated many books, in some cases his own texts. He often painted scenes of his Manitoba childhood, such as those in *A Prairie Boy's Winter.* See Patricia Morley, *Kurelek: A Biography* (1986); Michael Ewanchuk, *William Kurelek, the Suffering Genius* (1995).

Kurth, Burton Lowell (b. 1890) Musician. Born and educated in Buffalo, New York, he came to Winnipeg in 1909 to teach music. He established the St. Cecilia's Ladies' Choir in 1921, was president of the Music Teachers' Association in 1924, conducted the Selkirk Choral Union, and was organist at a number of Winnipeg churches, including Broadway Baptist Church. His studio was in the Birks Building. Kurth moved to Vancouver in 1927. He wrote and published many books of songs, including *Little Songs for Young People* (1943) and *Sensitive Singing* (1973), advising young singers on the use of the voice.

Kurth, Olive (Quast) (fl. 1909-1927) Musician. One of the city's best-known contraltos, she studied in New York and Chicago and sang with the American Opera Company in Chicago. She often sang at the Broadway Baptist Church in Winnipeg, where her husband Burton Kurth* was organist.

Kvaran, Einar (1859-1938) Journalist, poet. Born at Goodelir, Skagafjaroarsysla, Iceland, a son of the manse, he graduated from the College of Iceland in 1881, and in 1882 became a doctoral candidate in economics at the University of Copenhagen. He came to Canada in 1885 and worked as a journalist in Winnipeg for 10 years. He edited two weeklies, *Heimskringla* and *Lögberg.* He began publishing his poetry and fiction in these papers. He was active in Liberal politics while in Canada. His well-known story "Vonir" was published in 1890.

Laflèche, Louis-François Richer (1818-1898) Missionary. Born in Ste. Anne de la Pérade, Lower Canada, he was educated at the Collège de Nicolet and ordained in 1844. He translated the laws of Red River into French in 1851. He served as a western missionary to the buffalo hunters from 1844 to 1856 and then returned to the Collège de Nicolet as a professor. He became vicar general and later bishop of Trois-Rivières. *DCB* XII, 506-12.

La France, Joseph (c. 1707-c. 1740s) Explorer. Born at Michilimackinac to a French fur trader and an Ojibwa woman, he was taken to Quebec and educated in French. To avoid arrest as an unlicensed trader, he headed west to Hudson Bay in 1739, arriving in 1742. He was sent to England, where he met Arthur Dobbs, to whom he recounted his journey via a water route between Lake Superior and Hudson Bay. At the time, his adventures were discounted. *DCB* III, 341-42.

Lagimodière (Lagimonière), Jean-Baptiste (c. 1777-1855) Trader. Born in Quebec, he joined the NWC in 1800, serving in the West until 1806, when he returned home to marry Marie-Anne Gaboury.* The couple moved to Pembina and later to Cumberland House. He worked for Miles Macdonell* as a buffalo hunter in 1812-13, and in the winter of 1815-16 he made a legendary journey overland from Red River to Montreal, mainly on snowshoes, to bring Lord Selkirk* news of the attacks on the Red River settlement. He was rewarded by Selkirk with a grant of land at present-day St. Boniface. On his return he was captured by the NWC but was released. He served as an HBC voyageur and messenger for many years, and later became a farmer. He was the grandfather of Louis Riel. A boulevard in Winnipeg is named for him. See Robert Gosman, *The Riel and Lagimodière Families in Métis Society, 1840-1860* (1977). *DCB* VIII, 481-82.

Lagimodière (Lagimonière), Marie-Anne See Gaboury, Marie-Anne.

Laidlaw, William (fl. 1816-22) Farm manager. The son of a Scottish farmer, he was recruited by Lord Selkirk in 1815 to manage the home farm at Red River (Hay Field) for a share of profits. He accompanied Selkirk to Fort William in 1816, became involved in the arrests of Nor'Westers there, and came with the invading party to Fort Douglas in January 1817. He was unable to make a profit farming in Red River. He faced the ravages of grasshoppers and drought, and complained constantly of the lack of tools and experienced manpower. After a considerable battle with the Selkirk estate over his contract, he left the settlement for the United States in 1822. Laidlaw later, in 1827, became a partner in the American Fur Company.

Lamb, Thomas ("Tom," 1898-1969) Aviator. Born in Grand Rapids, Manitoba, he was educated by his father, an English ex-Guardsman. He was a mechanic on flying boats in 1921-22, and he hauled the first whitefish from Manitoba to market by air in 1932. He became Manitoba's first flying trapper and the founder of Lamb Air. He received an honorary law degree from the University of Manitoba in 1968. He was sometimes called "Mr. North." His "Reminiscences of Grand Rapids and The Pas, 1892-1967," as well as his papers, are in the PAM.

Lamont, Francis Bastin ("Frank," 1933-1998) Lawyer. Born in Winnipeg, he was raised in Headingley and later attended Laura Secord School and Gordon Bell High School before attending the University of Manitoba (BA, 1953). He started rowing in 1953 and won a Rhodes Scholarship in 1956, later rowing for Oxford. He joined James Richardson and Sons in 1963, first as a one-man legal department and eventually as chief executive officer. He was active on the boards of community cultural organizations (Rainbow Stage, Winnipeg Symphony, YMCA) as well as in the Liberal Party. In later years he often consulted abroad for the Canadian International Development Agency. He is buried in Headingley.

Lamont, Joseph Laurie (b. 1891) Physician. Born in Treherne, Manitoba, he was educated at Winnipeg Collegiate and the University of Manitoba (BA, science medal winner, 1911). He was appointed to the chemistry department at the University of Manitoba before enrolling in medical school in Edinburgh in 1913. Following completion of his course he served in the Royal Navy, and in 1919 he returned to Treherne to take over his father's practice.

Lang, Byllee Fay (1908-1966) Artist. Born in Alberta, she was the daughter of a rancher. She studied at the Winnipeg School of Art from 1926 to 1930, before moving on to the Ontario College of Art in Toronto. She later studied in Europe. Lang returned to Winnipeg when her husband joined the Spanish Red Cross during the Spanish Civil War, and taught sculpture at the Winnipeg School of Art from 1940 to 1943. She also operated a private school of sculpture and completed a number of portraits in stone. She became convenor of the Manitoba Regional Group of the Federation of Canadian Artists in 1942, commenting, "The isolation of artists in western Canada has been practically a disease." In 1945 she again left Winnipeg, first for Montreal and then for Bermuda, where she settled.

Langevin, Louis-Philippe-Adélard (1855-1915) Cleric. Born in Canada, he was educated at Montreal College, the Sulpician Grand Seminary, and St. Mary's College. He joined the Oblates in 1881 and was ordained a priest in 1882. He taught at the University of Ottawa until he was invited to Manitoba in 1893 to become head of the Oblate Order in the West. A year later he was appointed rector of St. Mary's Church, Winnipeg, and in 1895 he succeeded Archbishop Taché* at the See of St. Boniface. Inevitably, he was involved in the Manitoba School Question, and he helped found the Société Historique de Saint-Boniface in 1903. He was a great supporter of French settlement in Western Canada. In 1911 he published a religious analysis of the Diocese of St. Boniface, *Mémoire confidentiel sur la situation religieuse . . . de Saint-Boniface*. He died in Montreal. *DCB* XIV, 597-601.

LaPérouse, Jean-François de Galaup, Comte de (1741-1788) Naval officer, explorer. Born in Albi, France, he was a career naval officer who was promoted to captain in 1780, soon receiving command of the frigate *Astrée*, with which he achieved great military success in 1781. In 1782 he took command of the *Sceptre* and brought it, along with two other ships of a dispersed French fleet, to Hudson Bay. On 9 August he accepted the surrender of Samuel Hearne at Fort Prince of Wales, and two weeks later had equal success at York Factory. He treated his prisoners with considerable kindness and lost not a single man under his command in this military mission. He was appointed in 1785 by the king of France to command an expedition to the west coast of America. He sailed around Cape Horn and arrived in Kamchatka on 7 September 1786. He then sailed into the central Pacific, disappearing in 1788. Wreckage of his ships was discovered later. See John Dunmore, *French Explorers in the Pacific,* 2 vols. (1965-69); Paul Fleuriot de Langle, *La Tragique Expédition de LaPérouse et Langle* (1954). *DCB* IV, 282-83.

Larcombe, Samuel (1851-1937) Horticulturalist. Born in Axminister, Devonshire, England, he came to Birtle, Manitoba, in 1889, renting a farm he later bought. A gifted gardener, he attempted to prove that every vegetable grown in England could be produced in Manitoba, employing intensive cultivation and hybridization in the process. He entered competitions in Eastern Canada after 1903, under the auspices of the CPR. Just before WWI, he began growing grains, in 1917 producing a rust-resistant strain he called "Axminister." At a 1917 international exhibition in Peoria, Illinois, he won the world's championship for his wheat (gaining 99 out of 100 marks in the judging), as well as 26 other prizes, and became one of Manitoba's many "Wheat Kings." At Kansas City in 1919 he showed 382 different varieties of vegetables. He is a member of the Manitoba Agricultural Hall of Fame. See Robert Harvey, *Pioneers of Manitoba,* 21-23.

LaRivière, Alphonse Alfred Clermont (1841-1925) Politician. Born in Montreal, he was educated at Jacques Cartier Normal School and St. Mary's College. He was appointed captain of the military district of Manitoba in 1871 and also appointed to the Dominion Lands Office, where he served until 1875. He founded the Manitoba St. Jean Baptiste Society in 1872, serving as president in 1875. He was appointed justice of the peace for Selkirk in 1874 and was elected St. Boniface MLA in 1878 and 1879. He served as provincial secretary in 1881. He was MP for Provencher from 1889 to 1904 and senator from 1911 to 1917.

Larocque, François Antoine (1782-1869) Fur trader. He joined the XY Company as a clerk in 1801 and was stationed on the Red River for a time. He retired in 1815 to St. Hyacinthe, Lower Canada. His journal was published as *Journal of Larocque from the Assiniboine to the Yellowstone, 1805,* ed. L.J. Burpee (1910).

Laurence, Margaret (1926-1987) Author. Born in Neepawa, Manitoba, as Jean Margaret ("Peggy") Wemyss, she graduated in honours English from United College, Winnipeg, in 1947. She married a hydraulic engineer and moved to England and then to Africa (Somaliland and Ghana), which served as the setting for most of her first published writing. Her African experience produced *A Tree for Poverty* (1954), *The Tomorrow-Tamer* (1963), and her first novel, *This Side Jordan,* which was set in Ghana (1960). She also published *Long Drums and Cannons* (1968), a study of Nigerian writing. She returned to Vancouver in 1957, then moved to England for several years. She and her husband were divorced in 1969, and in 1974 she moved to Lakefield, Ontario. Her major work is a four-volume set of "Manawaka" novels: *The Stone Angel* (1964), *A Jest of God* (1966), *The Fire-Dwellers* (1969), and *The Diviners* (1974). These novels are often compared with William Faulkner's work in their creation of a rich and satisfying fictional place, and of characters who obviously belong within it and nowhere else. The books are about memory, ancestry, and the passage of time. Consult Clara Thomas, *The Manawaka World of Margaret Laurence* (1975). Laurence also wrote a number of children's books and stories. She has often been regarded as Canada's outstanding novelist. She published memoirs of her African years as *The Prophet's Camel Bell* in 1963. See also Susan J. Warwick, *Margaret Laurence: An Annotated Bibliography* (1979). The authorized biography is *The Life of Margaret Laurence* by James King (1997).

Laurie, Patrick Gammie (1833-1903) Journalist. Born in New Pitsligo, Scotland, he came with his family to Toronto in 1842, soon moving to Cobourg and then to several other Ontario cities. In 1855 he bought the *Owen Sound Times.* He sold it in 1859 when John Schultz* convinced him of the need for a newspaper in Red River. He had reached Windsor on his way west when he heard that the *Nor'-Wester* had already begun operation. So he stopped in Windsor, and bought the *Essex Record* in 1861. He finally left for Red River in 1869 and worked for the *Nor'-Wester.* He was expelled from the settlement in November 1869 for refusing to print a proclamation of the provisional government. He returned in 1870, just after the Wolseley Expedition, and worked for a variety of Winnipeg newspapers. In 1878 he went to Battleford to begin the *Saskatchewan Herald,* which became one of the leading boosters of Western Canada. He remained its editor until his death. Laurie was an Anglo-Canadian imperialist who saw no place in the West for Native people and French Canadians. He opposed block settlement because it prevented the fusion of newcomers of several backgrounds into a "homogeneous whole." The North-West Rebellion of 1885 drove him up the wall, and he was an ardent critic of Riel and his supporters. In his later years he opposed the New Immigration. He died in Battleford. See Walter Hildebrandt, "P.G. Laurie of Battleford: The Aspirations of a Western Enthusiast," *Prairie Forum* 8 (1983): 157-78. His memoir of 1869-70 in Red River, written in 1902, is at the PAM. *DCB* XIII, 577-80.

Laut, Agnes Christina (1871-1936) Author. Born in Ontario, she came to Manitoba with her family at an early age and attended the University of Manitoba. She served as an editorial writer with the *Manitoba Free Press* from 1895 to 1897, and later moved to the

United States, where she made a career as an author and journalist. She wrote for many of the leading American journals, including the *Saturday Evening Post* and *Colliers*. Many of her 22 books dealt with Canadian themes. Among her works are *Lords of the North* (1900), *Heralds of Empire* (1902), *Vikings of the Pacific* (1905), and *Pioneers of the Pacific Coast* (1915). She also wrote a general history, *The Conquest of the Great Northwest* (2 vols., 1908). Laut died in New York.

La Vérendrye, Jean Baptiste Gaultier de (1713-1736) Explorer. Born on Île Dupas, Canada, he was commissioned a cadet in 1731, and he became a member of the contingent sent west under his father's command. He wintered at Rainy Lake and in 1733 built a fort on the Winnipeg River. He accompanied his father to Fort Saint-Pierre (at Rainy Lake) to meet with warring Crees and Monsonis. He left his father to accompany the Aboriginals on the warpath against the Sioux, but later left that expedition and built Fort Maurepas on the Red River north of present-day Selkirk. He wintered at Fort Saint-Charles (Lake of the Woods) in 1735-36. He and a number of companions were killed by Indians on a small island on Lake of the Woods. He is often regarded as the founder of the province of Manitoba. *DCB* II, 238-40.

La Vérendrye, Louis-Joseph Gaultier de (1717-1761) Explorer. Born at Île aux Vaches, Canada, he was sent to Quebec by his father, to learn mathematics and drawing in preparation for exploration. He was sent west in 1735 and was probably responsible for the La Vérendrye map of the West drawn in 1737. He travelled as far south as the Missouri River in 1737-38, and in 1739 was sent by his father to explore the region west of Lake Winnipeg. He assumed command of Fort Saint-Charles (Lake of the Woods) in 1740 and then spent the winter of 1741-42 at Fort la Reine (Portage la Prairie). In April 1742 he headed west with a party of Indians, reaching far enough in that direction to see the mountains. On his return trip east, he buried a lead plaque near present-day Pierre, South Dakota, in March 1743. He remained in the West when his father retired, but was eventually shut out of the West by the group headed by Intendant Bigot in 1750. Louis-Joseph returned to the western fur trade in 1752. He was dispatched with Indian allies in July 1759 to aid in the defence of Lake Champlain, and he died on a voyage to France in 1761. See L.J. Burpee, *The Search for the*

Western Sea (1908); Antoine Champagne, *Les La Vérendrye: Nouvelles Études sur les La Vérendrye* (1971). *DCB* III, 241-44.

La Vérendrye, Pierre Gaultier de Boumois (1714-1755) Soldier. Born at Île aux Vaches, Canada, he served in the army as a cadet before joining his father in the West in 1731. He spent the winter of 1740-41 at Fort la Reine on the Assiniboine River and went from there south into present-day Nebraska. He then returned to Fort la Reine. He was in Montreal in 1745, fought in New England, and returned west to Michilimackinac in 1747. After some time in New France, he spent the years 1752-55 at Fort Beausejour in New Brunswick. He died in Canada. *DCB* III, 244-45.

La Vérendrye, Pierre Gaultier de Varennes (Sieur de) (1685-1749) Explorer. Born in Trois-Rivières, Canada, he was briefly a student at the seminary of Quebec before entering the military. He served in the French army from 1708 to 1712 but could not afford the social obligations, so he returned to Canada, where he became a farmer-cum-fur trader. In 1726 he joined his brother Jacques-René in the western fur trade north of Lake Superior, soon beginning a quest for the "western sea," which by all contemporary accounts lay not far to the west of the border lakes. His plan was to establish French posts further west — not coincidentally, in rich fur-trading country — from which the western sea could be easily reached. He and three sons set out in 1731 to execute this design. The extent to which he was ever seriously committed to the idea of the western sea is open to question. In 1731 he declared to the intendant of New France that he sought "to carry the name and arms of His Majesty into a vast stretch of countries hitherto unknown, to enlarge the colony and increase its commerce." The La Vérendryes built Fort Saint-Charles at Lake of the Woods in 1732. La Vérendrye succeeded in obtaining more government support at this point, chiefly in the form of fur-trading monopolies in the West. The next years were spent discovering that the Missouri River was not the "river of the west" but rather flowed southeast to the Gulf of Mexico, and getting some notion of the complexity of the Winnipeg River and Manitoba lakes system. At the same time, of course, La Vérendrye was collecting large numbers of furs and Indian slaves. By 1737 he was made to realize by the government of New France that results were required, and he made a real push onto the prairies, establishing Fort la Reine at present-day Portage la Prairie in 1738 and moving on to Mandan country in western North Dakota. In 1741 he received another monopoly over the new territory he had opened up, and he returned to Fort la Reine. Over the next few years more posts were built in Cree territory, mainly for trade. The government in New France suspected his motives by now, however, and he resigned effective in 1744, settling down in Montreal. His last years were spent in relative penury. He never discovered his ocean, but he had certainly increased the influence of the French in the central lake and prairie region of North America. *Journals and Letters of La Vérendrye* have been edited by L.J. Burpee (1927). For a biography, see N.M. Crouse, *La Vérendrye, Fur Trader and Explorer* (1956). Consult also Antoine Champagne, *Les La Vérendrye et le poste de l'Ouest* (1968). *DCB* III, 246-54.

Lavoie, Théophile (1836-1908) Educator, cleric. Born in Kamouraska, Lower Canada, he studied law at Université Laval in 1857-58, before entering the Oblate Order. He was ordained in France in 1864, and he returned to Canada as director of studies at the Collège d'Ottawa, where he found bilingualism awkward. He attempted to oppose the English group at the college and found himself transferred to Manitoba in 1870, where he became director of the Collège de Saint-Boniface. His term saw the college incorporate and become part of the foundation of the University of Manitoba. But the Oblate presence could not be sustained at the college, and Lavoie became a parish priest in Winnipeg before being sent to various parishes in the United States. He ended up at the Collège d'Ottawa, where he now supported bilingualism. He died in Montreal. *DCB* XIII, 585-86.

Lawler, Patrick (1835-1905) Police sergeant. Born in County Clare, Ireland, he joined the 31st City of London Regiment in 1849, serving in the Crimea, Malta, India, and China. He came to Winnipeg in 1874 and worked as a police sergeant before his appointment as governor of the provincial jail, a post he held until his death. He served in the North-West Rebellion of 1885.

Lawrence, George (1855-1924) Politician. Born in Canada to Irish parents, he came to Manitoba in 1878, homesteading for a time at Rock Lake before opening a branch of the Massey Manufacturing Company in Killarney in 1886. He ran as a Conservative in the 1892 provincial election and was defeated, but was successful in 1899, 1903, 1907, and 1910. He joined the Cabinet as minister of agriculture in 1911.

Lawrence, William Blake (1870-1918) Theatre manager. Born in Gainesville, New York, and raised in Detroit, he worked his way up to become manager of the Detroit Opera House. In 1906 the American company of Drew and Campbell acquired the Winnipeg Theatre and dispatched Lawrence to Manitoba as its manager. He brought a theatrical stock company with him (renamed the Winnipeg Stock Company), and soon leased the Grand Theatre and the Dominion Theatre. By 1910 he was a major figure on the Winnipeg theatrical scene, becoming manager of the Walker Theatre as well as others. Soon afterward he joined up with Alexander Pantages, and he managed the Pantages Theatre upon its opening in 1914. Lawrence was local agent for a number of leading theatrical circuits as well as manager of several local stock companies. He was a key figure in live theatre in Winnipeg for a decade, until he suffered a stroke in 1916. He died in Winnipeg but was buried in Detroit. *DCB* XIV, 629-30.

Lawson, May (1901-1965) Musician. Born in Scotland, she moved to Winnipeg with her family in 1914 and studied singing there, in Toronto, and in New York. She was a soloist at St. Luke's Anglican Church from 1923 to 1926 and then at Knox United Church for many years (1926-46). A contralto, she sang in oratorio and in light opera and was frequently heard on CBC Radio. She often sang Scottish traditional songs to great effect. After years as a private teacher, she spent her last years (1958-65) teaching at the Canadian Mennonite Bible College. She helped her brother James Terry Lawson produce the manual *Full-throated Ease: A Concise Guide to Easy Singing* (1955).

Leacock, Edward Philip (1853-1927) Confidence man. Born on the Isle of Wight, he claimed he had been educated at the University of Geneva (receiving a BA in 1873) before joining his family and nephew Stephen in Canada. He acquired some connection with former Manitoba lieutenant-governor Alexander Morris* and arrived in Winnipeg in June 1879. From the beginning, Leacock was a promoter par excellence, a director and officer of the Westbourne and North West Railway Company, the

Manitoba Drainage Company, and the Canadian Pacific Express Company. He was also a founding member and secretary of the Selkirk Club. He constructed a large brick home on a river lot in Kildonan. Leacock entered provincial politics in 1882 as a Conservative in a by-election in Birtle, where he subsequently built another house known as "the Castle." He served as chair of the caucus, but in 1887 broke ranks with the Norquay government, and he was defeated in the election of 1888. He served as central organizer (with C.A. Burrows*) for the Tories in the 1891 federal election. He was under a financial cloud for many years, and he returned to England in 1894, where he resided in Maldon as "Colonel Leacock," a retired colonel of the NWMP. He published *Hudson's Bay Route: A Lecture* (1883), and he features in several sketches written by his nephew Stephen Leacock.

Leah, Vince (1913-1993) Journalist. Born in Winnipeg, he contracted polio at age eight. He was educated at Ralph Brown and Isaac Newton Schools. He joined the *Winnipeg Tribune* in 1930 and was a sportswriter there for 50 years. He coached hockey and other sports, especially soccer, and was a constant booster of community sports. Leah became a columnist for the *Winnipeg Free Press* in 1980 and also wrote for *Seniors Today*. Three Winnipeg streets and a recreation centre have been named for him. He is a member of the Manitoba Sports Hall of Fame. He wrote several books, including *Pages from the Past* (1975).

Le Blanc, Pierre (1782-1838) Craftsman. Born in Montreal, he joined the NWC in 1810 and continued with the HBC after the two companies merged in 1821. A useful craftsman, he helped build Upper Fort Garry in the 1830s. In 1838 he guided two English botanists on a scientific expedition.

Lecourt, Joseph-Pierre-Michel (1824-1913) Architect. Born at Quebec, he was educated at the Séminaire de Nicolet from 1840 to 1844, and then studied with Frederick Hacker as an architect. By 1852 he was designing buildings for the province of Canada, turning from the neo-classicism of his teacher to a neo-renaissance style. He came to Manitoba in 1873 as supervising architect for the Department of Public Works. Here he designed many federal buildings, including the post office and customs house (1873) and the lieutenant-governor's

residence (1880). He returned to Ottawa in the 1880s. *DCB* XIV, 635-37.

Lee, Fong Kwong, a.k.a. George Lee (1906-1992) Restaurateur. Born in Toisan, China, he joined his father in Winnipeg in 1920. He established George's Taxi in 1936 and then joined his family in the Nanking Restaurant in 1940. He was known as the host of Chinatown and was active in Chinese causes. He was one of the first Chinese Canadians in Winnipeg to receive a community service award.

Lefroy, John Henry (1817-1890) Explorer. Born in Hampshire, England, and educated at the Royal Military Academy in Woolwich, he took up the superintendency of the Toronto observatory in 1842. A few months later, in May 1843, he left on an expedition to locate the magnetic north pole. The journey of 5,000 miles took him across the Northwest before he returned to Toronto late in 1844. He came back to Manitoba several times in later life. He received the Companion of the Order of the Bath in 1871 and was made a knight commander of the Order of St. Michael and St. George in 1877. He died in Cornwall, England. His *Autobiography* was published in 1895. See also his *Diary of a Magnetic Survey of a Portion of the Dominion of Canada, Chiefly in the North-Western Territories: Executed in the Years 1842-1844* (1883), and G.F.G. Stanley, ed., *In Search of the Magnetic North: A Soldier-Surveyor's Letters from the North-West, 1843-44* (1955). *DCB* XI, 508-10.

Leggo, William (1822-1888) Lawyer. Born in Perth, Upper Canada, he studied law at Brockville, was called to the Ontario bar in 1870, and was master of Chancery in Hamilton until 1876. After four years in Ottawa he came to Winnipeg to be Manitoba master of Chancery, a post he held until his death. He was a frequent contributor to journals such as the *Scottish Review*. He wrote *Forms and Precedents of Pleadings and Proceedings in the Court of Chancery for Ontario* (1872) and *The History of the Administration of the Right Honorable Frederick Temple, Earl of Dufferin* (1878).

LeGoff, Christine (1915-1994) Designer. Born in St. Boniface, she became a noted Winnipeg fashion artist and costume designer, often working for Le Cercle Molière. She received the Canadian Drama Award in 1962.

LeGoff, Pauline (Boutal) See Boutal, Pauline (LeGoff)

Leishman, Ken ("The Flying Bandit," 1931-1980) Bank robber. Born in Holland, Manitoba, he moved to Winnipeg in 1947 and was first convicted of theft in 1950. When he got out of prison he became fascinated with airplanes and learned to fly. He was imprisoned again for a bank robbery in Toronto in 1957, in which he flew to Toronto and back to Winnipeg with $10,000. He was released in 1961 on parole. In 1966 he managed to hijack $383,497 worth of gold from the Winnipeg airport. Imprisoned again, he escaped from Headingley Jail and stole an airplane, becoming known as the "Flying Bandit." He and his accomplices were arrested in a shootout in Gary, Indiana. After his release from prison, Leishman moved to Red Lake, Ontario, in 1975 to manage Tomahawk Airlines, even becoming mayor of the community. He disappeared while on a mercy flight in 1979 and was declared officially dead in 1980. Leishman's exploits caught the fancy of the public, and he became something of a "Robin Hood" figure. See Heather Robertson, *The Flying Bandit* (1981).

Leith, James (1777-1838) Fur trader. Born in Scotland to wealthy parents, he was a NWC wintering partner by 1799. He spent one winter at Red River and three at Rainy Lake. Leith was one of the NWC partners who went to Red River in 1816 to hand out presents to the Métis who had been involved in the Battle of Seven Oaks, and he was present in the colony again in 1817 when William Coltman* was there to conduct his investigation into the fur-trade war. He became a chief factor after the merger of the NWC and HBC, spending most of the remainder of his career in the Athabasca country and at Cumberland House. He gave his half of Colquoich, a 1,000-acre landed property, to his brother in 1830. He left half his estate in trust for "establishing, propagating and extending the Christian protestant Religion in, & amongst the native aboriginal Indians in ... the Hudson's Bay Territory." There is no corroboration of the story, later known as "Leith's noble revenge," that he so acted because Indians had murdered his family at The Pas. See E.R. Bagley, "James Leith Takes His Revenge," *The Beaver* (June 1943): 36-37. The estate spent several years in the Court of Chancery, but the Diocese of Rupert's Land received £15,000 in 1848, and the estate became properly administered in 1849. There is a portrait at the PAM. *DCB* VII, 498-99.

Lemiez, Armand (1894-1984) Farmer, artist. Born in Belgium, he came to Canada in 1911 and homesteaded at Grahamdale, Manitoba, where he built a small house. He spent a lifetime painting in oil and creating life-sized sculptures, which he displayed in his house and happily showed to visitors.

Le Moyne d'Iberville et d'Ardillières, Pierre See Iberville, Pierre Le Moyne, Sieur d'.

Le Moyne de Martigny et de La Trinité, Jean Baptiste See Martigny et de La Trinité, Jean Baptiste, le Moyne de.

Lépine, Ambroise (1840-1923) Métis leader. Born in St. Vital, he was the son of a French-Canadian father and a Métisse. From the beginning of the Red River Rebellion, he was Louis Riel's military lieutenant and chief enforcer. He led the armed party that ordered Governor William McDougall* out of the settlement in October 1869. He was prominent in the surrenders of the John Schultz* party in December 1869 and of the Charles Boulton* party in February 1870. His appearance in 1870 was described by Roderick MacBeth:* "a man of magnificent physique, standing fully six feet three and built in splendid proportion, straight as an arrow, with hair of raven blackness, large aquiline nose and eyes of piercing brilliance; a man of prodigious strength, a skilled roughrider. ..." He was subsequently arrested and tried for the murder of Thomas Scott* in 1874. He was found guilty by a jury, but was granted an amnesty by the Governor-General of Canada with the provision that he lose his civil rights. See Manitoba Historic Resources Branch, *Ambroise-Didyme Lépine* (1985) and J.M. Bumsted, "The Trial of Ambroise Lépine: Murder, Politics, and the Public Memory," *The Beaver* 77, no. 2 (April-May 1997): 9-19.

Lépine, Jean-Baptiste (fl. 1869-71) Métis leader. A brother of Ambroise,* in 1869 he policed Red River looking for suspicious strangers. In March 1870 he was a member of the council that condemned Thomas Scott;* he voted against the death penalty. At the time of the Fenian threats in 1871, he had gone with André Nault* to meet with William O'Donoghue* at the border and then reported on O'Donoghue's plans to the Manitoba Métis. He disappeared from view soon after. *DCB* X, 439.

Le Sueur, Amelia See Yeomans, Amelia (Le Sueur).

Letendre, François-Xavier (c. 1841-1901) Métis leader. Born in St. Boniface, he moved permanently to the North-West Territories in 1872, founding the village of Batoche. A successful merchant, he initially supported Métis complaints against the federal government but in 1885 disassociated himself from Louis Riel and the militants. He received $19,000 in compensation for losses from the Battle of Batoche. After the uprising he continued to petition for Métis rights, without much success. *DCB* XIII, 595-96.

Lewes (Lewis), John Lee (1791-c. 1860) Fur trader. Born in Southwark, England, he joined the HBC in 1807 and served at Churchill Factory and Nelson House before going to the Athabasca District in 1814. After the merger of the HBC and NWC, he became a chief trader in the Columbia Department. In 1827 he was appointed to Moose Factory, and in 1830 was put in charge of the Island Lake District, where he supervised the construction of the winter road from York Factory to Lake Winnipeg. He became a councillor of Rupert's Land in 1839. He retired in 1853 to St. Andrews.

Little, Olive (1918-1997) Athlete. Born at Poplar Point, Manitoba, she was educated at a teacher's college. She pitched for the CUAC Blues and the Moose Jaw Royals women's baseball teams in seasons in which both teams won provincial championships. She turned professional in 1940, and played for the Rockford (Illinois) Peaches during the war years when women's baseball was so popular. She was a league all-star and pitched a number of no-hit games. She also pitched softball, and was elected to the Canadian Softball Hall of Fame in 1983 and the Manitoba Sports Hall of Fame in 1985.

Livesay, Dorothy (1909-1996) Poet. Arguably the most distinguished poet native to Manitoba, she was born in Winnipeg during a blinding snowstorm. Her journalist father joined the Canadian Press in 1920 and took his family to Toronto. She was educated at Glen Mawr School for Girls; Trinity College, the University of Toronto; and the Sorbonne. She published her first book of poems, *Green Pitcher,* at age 18. From early life she was a feminist and a socialist. She joined the Communist Party in 1932 and was an organizer for the party during the Depression, while employed as a social worker in New Jersey and in Montreal. She continually published poetry, winning the Governor General's Award for poetry in 1944 (*Day and Night*) and 1947 (*Poems for People*). She married Duncan Campbell Macnair in 1937 and raised two children in Vancouver, then spent several years in Zambia with UNESCO in the early 1960s, and began a new career in poetry with *The Unquiet Bed* (1967) and *Plainsongs* (1969). She was the author of many volumes of poetry written in many different styles. She founded the poetry magazine *CVII* in 1975. British Columbia's major poetry prize is named in her honour. In later years she wintered in the Gulf Islands and summered at Lake Winnipeg. A fictionalized volume of her Winnipeg reminiscences was published in 1973 as *Beginnings: A Winnipeg Childhood*. She died in Victoria. Her papers are at the UML Archives and the PAM.

Livingstone, Donald (b. 1791) Settler, boat builder. Born in Islay, Scotland, he came to Red River with Owen Keveny* in 1812. He worked as a boatwright in the settlement and was assigned Lot 37 by Lord Selkirk* in 1817. He was appointed one of the settlement's first constables that same year. He and his family left Red River for Cedar Grove, Iowa, in 1840.

Lloyd, Cecil Richard Francis (1884-1938) Author. Born in Hertsfordshire, England, he was educated at Queen's University and London University. He was a Winnipeg businessman from 1917 to 1930, until becoming a freelance writer. He published a number of volumes of essays and poetry, including *Landfall: Collected Poems* (1935). He died in Winnipeg. See Watson Kirkconnell, ed., *Rest, Perturbèd Spirit: Being the Life of Cecil Francis Lloyd, 1884-1938, Presented in a Cento of Excerpts from His Letters* (1974).

Lloyd, Gweneth (1901-1993) Choreographer and dance producer. Born in England, she came to Canada in 1938 with Betty Farrally.* They founded the Canadian School of Ballet and the Winnipeg Ballet Club in 1939. Lloyd transformed the Winnipeg Ballet into the Royal Winnipeg Ballet, receiving the Queen's patronage in 1953. She produced 35 original ballets for the Royal Winnipeg Ballet before her retirement from the company in 1955. She moved to Kelowna, British Columbia, with Farrally in 1957 and co-founded the Canadian School of Ballet in Kelowna in 1962. She directed the Banff Centre School of Fine Arts from 1946 to 1965. She died in Kelowna.

Lockhart, Wilfred Cornet (1906-1991) Educator. Born in Ontario, he was educated at the University of Toronto and the University of Edinburgh (PhD, 1936). Returning to Canada, he worked at many jobs and served as minister at a number of United Churches. In 1955 he was appointed principal of United College, serving until 1967, when it became the University of Winnipeg. He was first president and vice-chancellor of the University of Winnipeg from 1967 to 1971. In 1958 Lockhart touched off the "Crowe Case," the best-known academic freedom case in Canada, when he fired Professor Harry Crowe* for writing a "disrespectful and irreligious" private letter which was sent to Lockhart by mistake; the fallout continued for years. He later served as moderator of the United Church (1966-68). A building at the University of Winnipeg is named after him. He retired to Toronto and died there. He was the author of *In Such an Age: Younger Voices in the Canadian Church* (1951).

Lodge, Rupert C. (1886-1961) Philosopher. Born in England, he spent most of a distinguished academic career (1920-47) at the University of Manitoba. Arguably the best-known modern philosopher to work in Canada, Lodge was the author of a number of important works, including *An Introduction to Modern Logic* (1920), *The Questioning Mind* (1937), *The Philosophy of Education* (1937), and *The Great Thinkers* (1949). His strength was his ability to communicate philosophical ideas free from jargon. Marshall McLuhan,* who was Lodge's student in the early 1930s, regarded him as the only professor at the University of Manitoba of real intellectual stature.

Logan, Alexander (1841-1894) Landowner, municipal politician. Born at Fort Douglas, the son of Robert* and Sarah Logan,* he attended St. John's College. His house was located on the banks of the Red River, at the foot of the present Logan Avenue, which was named after the family. He inherited large quantities of Winnipeg real estate. He served as Winnipeg alderman for many years, and was mayor of Winnipeg in 1879-80, 1882, and 1884. It became a tradition for every prominent Winnipegger to call on the Logans on Christmas Day. See A.F.T. Artibise, "Mayor Alexander Logan of Winnipeg," *The Beaver* (spring 1874): 4-12. *DCB* XII, 568-69.

Logan, Robert (1773-1866) Fur trader. Probably born in Scotland, the son of a West Indian planter who moved to Montreal in the 1780s, he was fluently bilingual in French and English, and he entered the NWC in 1801. He did not progress in the company's service, and in Montreal in 1814 was persuaded to join the HBC. In 1819, at Lord Selkirk's* request, Logan came to the Red River Settlement as his agent, and remained. George Simpson* wrote in 1822, "Logan is the best settler about the place without exception." In 1825 Logan purchased property on the Red River from the Selkirk estate and built a house at the foot of present-day Logan Avenue. He ran the settlement's first gristmill and engaged in various forms of trade. He was a councillor of Assiniboia from 1823 to 1839, justice of the peace in 1835, chair of the Board of Public Works in 1844, and a magistrate in 1850. Although he had previously attended the Anglican Church, he was active in obtaining a Presbyterian minister for the Settlement in 1851. See Ross Mitchell, "Robert Logan of Red River, 1775-1866," *Manitoba Pageant* 13, no. 2 (1967-68): 19-23. Logan's papers are in the PAM. *DCB* IX, 472-73.

Logan, Robert Fulton (d. 1941) Artist. Born on a farm near Lauder, Manitoba, he left to study art in Paris at age 16. He subsequently studied at the Boston School of the Museum of Fine Arts, and instructed in art in Hartford, Connecticut. He was a painter and a specialist in copper etchings.

Long, Victor (1864-1938) Artist. Born in Toronto, he studied in Paris and resided for many years in Winnipeg, making a living by painting portraits. He painted many early mayors and other politicians. He moved to Vancouver in 1923. His correspondence relating to Manitoba political portraits (1915-27) is in the PAM.

Longmoor, Robert (fl. 1771-1812) Fur trader. Probably born in Edinburgh, Scotland, he joined the HBC in 1771. He moved inland in 1774 and helped establish the trading posts on the Saskatchewan River. From 1787 to 1792 Longmoor was second-in-command at Churchill, and in 1793 he became superintendent at York. He later acted as master of the Swan River District, and he retired in 1810. He died on his farm near Montreal. *DCB* V, 500-501.

Lorimier, Jean-Baptiste, Chevalier de (c. 1786-1845) Indian agent, interpreter. He was born in

Quebec into a family with a distinguished military history. His father was Indian agent at Caughnawaga, and his mother was a Caughnawaga Iroquois. He served as an interpreter on the Niagara frontier in 1812 and was taken prisoner in 1813. After exchange in 1814, he became captain in the Embodied Indian Warriors, who saw service in the Great Lakes area. He was seconded in 1816 by Lord Selkirk* and was part of the force that captured Fort William in August of that year. He accompanied the NWC partners who were arrested by Selkirk back to Upper Canada, escaping their fate of drowning by a whisker. He was a witness in 1817 to the treaty between Selkirk and Peguis, and he escorted Roman Catholic missionaries J.-N. Provencher* and S.-J.-N. Dumoulin* to the colony in 1818. Provencher described him as a "gay, pleasant, polite, and honest man." Lorimier became involved in the legal battles between the HBC and NWC, but they did not affect his later career. He retired from the Indian Department in 1832. *DCB* VII, 516-17.

Lowe, John (1824-1913) Farm developer. Born in Warrington, England, he came to Montreal in 1841. By the late 1840s he was a journalist. In 1870 his printing and publishing firm went into bankruptcy, and he entered the Canadian civil service as temporary secretary at the Department of Agriculture, a post made permanent in 1873. Lowe used his departmental connections to accumulate land in Manitoba. By 1879 he held 16 square miles around Lowe Farm. Attempts to make the farm profitable were expensive, but failed. After 1895, when Lowe was retired against his will, he was still trying to make a go of the farm. He died in Ottawa. See his *The Lowe Farm Hydraulic-Colonization Syndicate* (1891). *DCB* XIV, 666-68.

Lower, Arthur Reginald Marsden (1889-1988) Historian. Born in Barrie, Ontario, he was educated at University College, University of Toronto, and then worked in the North until he enlisted in the Royal Navy during WWI. He received his PhD from Harvard in 1929 and began his teaching career at Wesley College in Winnipeg the same year, serving until 1949. He then took up an appointment at Queen's University, from which he retired in 1959. While in Winnipeg, Lower was an active opponent of Canadian isolation from affairs in Europe. He was president of the Canadian Historical Association in 1943. Although specializing in the history of

lumbering in early Canada, Lower was best known for his textbooks. *Colony to Nation* first appeared in 1946, followed by his pioneer social history, *Canadians in the Making*, in 1958. His autobiography, *My First Seventy-Five Years*, was published in 1967.

Lucow, Maurice (1918-1997) Journalist. Born in Winnipeg, he edited the *Western Jewish News* of Winnipeg before he was 20, and then was a *Free Press* reporter. He was a morse-code operator for the RCAF during WWII, then worked at the *Victoria Colonist*, for Maclean Hunter, and the *Financial Post*. A retail apparel expert, he spent a year as an executive for a women's wear firm. He then headed the public relations department of the United Jewish Appeal in Toronto before becoming editor of the *Canadian Jewish News* in 1980. He retired to Victoria in 1989 and died there.

Luining, Cecil Roy (1931-1998) Athlete, businessman. Born in Winnipeg, he graduated from Daniel McIntyre Collegiate Institute. From 1953 to 1963 he played football with the Winnipeg Blue Bombers, on five teams that went to the Grey Cup and won four Grey Cups. He was known as "the Selkirk Milkman" because he worked for the family dairy in Selkirk (later the Lakeland Dairies Limited). After retirement he served two terms as a Selkirk councillor and was president of the Gull Lake Ratepayers Association. He sold the dairy in 1988 and retired in 1989.

Lundy, Francis J. (1842-1912) Pioneer. Born in Canada, he taught school before coming to Winnipeg in 1872, where he was involved in erecting a gristmill. In 1876 he went to Weyburn, Saskatchewan, and then in 1880 moved to St. Laurent, Manitoba, where the nearby village of Lundyville was named after him. He was active in local affairs and the Conservative Party. He died in Winnipeg.

Lusted, Thomas (b. 1840) Baker. Born in England, he was described in 1872 as a carriage maker. In 1869 he was one of the most active members of the Canadian Party in Winnipeg, and was taken prisoner when those inside John Schultz's* house surrendered to Louis Riel in December. He was incarcerated in Upper Fort Garry until February 1870 and upon his release was forced to leave the country. When he returned to Manitoba later that year, he was one of the ex-prisoners who, with a few of the Ontario volunteers, actively sought revenge for past mistreatment by persecuting the Métis. He was Manitoba's first baker.

Luxton, William Fisher (1844-1907) Journalist. Born in Devon, England, he immigrated with his parents to Upper Canada in 1855. He began his newspaper career there in 1866 by establishing the *Strathroy Age*. He operated several other papers before moving to Winnipeg in 1871 to teach school. He served as a school trustee from 1879 to 1882 and as chair from 1885 to 1887. He began a Liberal newspaper, the *Manitoba Free Press*, in 1872, and it expanded with the city of Winnipeg, as did Luxton's career. He helped found the Winnipeg General Hospital in 1872, was president of the Agricultural Society in 1878, and was a founder of the Humane Society. He was MLA for Rockwood from 1874 to 1878 and MP for South Winnipeg from 1886 to 1888. His political goals were prohibition, a purely secular school system, the abolition of French as an official language, and the demise of the CPR. He defended himself successfully in 1890 from both civil and criminal libel charges brought against him by Joseph ("Fighting Joe") Martin,* the province's attorney general. His editorial opposition to the Greenway Liberals contributed to his loss of the newspaper when in 1893 Donald A. Smith* called in a loan Luxton had accepted while in earlier financial difficulties. Luxton started another paper, the *Daily Nor'Wester*, in 1893, but sold it in 1896 and became a reporter for the *St. Paul Globe*. After 1901 he was inspector of public buildings for the Manitoba government. He was noted for his veracity, his fearless editorial policies, and his assistance to young journalists. He died in Winnipeg. A school in Winnipeg has been named for him. See *The Luxton Expulsion! Why W.F. Luxton Has Been Expelled from the "Free Press" and Despoiled of the Fruits of His Life's Work* (1893). His extensive papers are in the PAM. *DCB* XIII, 605-6.

Lyall, Hugh Buxton (1877-1948) Businessman. Born in Sutton West, Ontario, he moved to Regina at age 13. In 1900 he came to Winnipeg, and soon began a machine and foundry business which eventually became Manitoba Bridge and Iron Works Ltd. He became a member of the Canadian Committee of the HBC. In 1915 he moved to Little Britain and became warden of St. Thomas Church, Lockport, a post he held for over 30 years. He died while chairing a vestry meeting of St. Thomas Church.

Lyde, Robert (1929-1992) Musician. Born in Raleigh, North Carolina, he grew up in Harlem. He won a teenage talent contest and played trombone during WWII for Leroy Anderson, subsequently spending three years as a sideman with Duke Ellington. He came to Canada in 1953 and worked as a CPR porter until 1963, when he returned to music. He helped found the Winnipeg Jazz Society. He died in Winnipeg.

Lynch, James Spencer (1841-1894) Physician. Born in London, Canada, he graduated in medicine from the University of Toronto and came to Red River in 1868. A fervent Canadian annexationist, he was a member of the party captured by Louis Riel at John Schultz's* house in December 1869 and was the last prisoner released in February, at which point he left the settlement. Lynch was in Ontario in April 1870 to be part of the various rallies protesting the "murder" of Thomas Scott,* and he testified that month before a Senate committee on affairs at Red River. In 1871 he lost a federal election in Marquette to Robert Cunningham,* and in 1872 he tied with Angus McKay* at 1,282 votes, the House dissolving before the tie could be resolved. He left politics and in 1872 became a staff member at the newly founded Winnipeg General Hospital. He testified before a parliamentary inquiry in 1874 that the Red River Rebellion of 1869-70 had been a plot by the Roman Catholic Church. In 1877 he was first president of the new College of Physicians and Surgeons of Manitoba. He served for many years as medical adviser to the HBC. His house was on the corner of Garry Street and St. Mary Avenue in Winnipeg.

Lynch, Walter (1835-1908) Cattleman. Born in Upper Canada, he came west with the Wolseley Expedition in 1870 and returned west with a party of 55 Canadian-Scots in 1871, ending up on the rivers of the Portage plains (White Mud River and Rat Creek). With Kenneth MacKenzie,* he brought the first registered Shorthorn cattle to Manitoba (via St. Paul) in 1873, and he became the province's first Shorthorn breeder. His bull "Scottish Canadian" was champion at the Winnipeg Industrial Fair in 1905. Lynch's herd provided foundation stock for western cattlemen. He was an early advocate of an agricultural college in Manitoba, and he served as first chair of the board of the Manitoba Agricultural College. He is a member of the Manitoba Agricultural Hall of Fame.

Lynn, Washington Frank (c. 1827-1906) Artist. Born in Chelsea, England, he studied at the Royal Academy of Arts and came to North America in 1861, serving as a reporter in the American Civil War. He returned to England to publicize British emigration to Canada, writing *Farming in Canada* and *Canada: Pamphlets for Working Men* in 1869. He came to Manitoba in 1872 and decided to remain. He began a series of letters to the *Toronto Globe*, as well as a series of popular paintings of the region. Late in 1872 he mounted a campaign against the corruption of the Dominion Lands Office in Manitoba, which produced reform but made him unpopular. He left Winnipeg for St. Paul in 1878, returned to England, and was back in Manitoba in 1885 as a shop proprietor. He was an unsuccessful aldermanic candidate in 1885, 1888, and 1889, and an active member of the Knights of Labor who wrote many letters to local newspapers. He died in Winnipeg. His paintings can be found in the Winnipeg Art Gallery and the PAM. See V.G. Berry, "Washington Frank Lynn: Artist and Journalist," *The Beaver* (1977-78): 24-31. *DCB* XIII, 606-7.

Lyon, George (b. 1880) Physician. Born in Ottawa, he was educated at McGill University, where he was a rugby player. He received a gold watch from the city of Ottawa for rescuing a drowning victim from the Rideau Canal. He graduated from McGill in 1906, and went on to postgraduate work in London, Dublin, and Edinburgh. He served with the 43rd Battalion in the first contingent in the Boer War, receiving a number of decorations. He served in WWI, including a stint as medical officer on the hospital ship *Mauretania* in the Dardanelles. After the war he came to Rivers, Manitoba, as medical health officer, also serving as Manitoba coroner.

Lyon, Robert Fern (b. 1856) Farmer. Born in Leeds County, Canada, he homesteaded in Manitoba in 1879, opening a store in Carberry, and running a 2,700-acre grain and stock farm, which was one of the largest farms in the province. He was also active in mining and milling operations. Lyon was elected a Conservative MLA from Norfolk in 1892, and re-elected in 1899, 1903, 1907, and 1910. He was defeated in the 1914 election.

Lyons, Manson Ainslie (b. 1879) Engineer. Born in Nova Scotia, he was educated at the Massachusetts Institute of Technology (1910). After teaching at the College of St. Francis Xavier and Lunenburg High School, he entered the engineering profession. He eventually came west, first to Calgary and then to Manitoba. In 1914 he was appointed chief engineer of the Good Roads Board of Manitoba, working on some of Manitoba's earliest paved highways.

Lysenko, Vera (1910-1975) Author. Born Vera Lesik in Winnipeg to Ukrainian Baptist parents, she was educated at the University of Manitoba, receiving her BA in 1929. She worked as a nurse and school-teacher in the West, then as a journalist on the *Windsor Star* until 1943, when she became a freelance journalist and writer. She wrote under the names Vera Lysenko and Luba Novak. She was the author of *Men in Sheepskin Coats* (1947). Her novels include *Yellow Boots* (1954) and *Westerly Wild* (1956). Lysenko's work tended to confound standard critical categories and has therefore been much neglected. There are papers, including manuscripts of unpublished works, at the NAC. See Beverly Rasporich, "Retelling Vera Lysenko: A Feminist and Ethnic Writer," *Canadian Ethnic Studies* 21, no. 2 (1989): 38-52.

Lyster, Lillie (fl. 1919-24) Municipal official. Born in Quebec, she was educated at St. Francis College (Richmond) and the Montreal Normal School. She taught school for many years before coming to Manitoba in 1919 to become a clerk in the office of the Rural Municipality of Whitewater. In 1924 she became secretary-treasurer of the municipality, one of the few women in the province to hold such a position before WWII.

Macallum, John (1806-1849) Cleric, educator. Born in Fortrose, Scotland, he received an MA from King's College, Aberdeen in 1832, and a year later came to Red River as a schoolteacher, working at £100 per annum at the academy established by David Jones. In 1836 he married one of his mixed-blood students, and he succeeded Jones as headmaster in 1837, purchasing the school for £350 in 1841. As head, he refused to permit mixed-blood or Native mothers not officially married, to visit their children at the school. He was ordained a priest in 1844 and became assistant chaplain to the HBC. An exponent of corporal punishment, he employed a rod more than three feet long. He was a member of the Council of Assiniboia from 1836, serving as its clerk in 1839. See T.F. Bredin, "The Red River Academy," *The Beaver* (winter 1974): 10-17. *DCB* VII, 526-27.

McArthur, Alexander (1842-1887) Merchant. Born in Nairn, Scotland, he came to British North America in 1862 and worked for the HBC. He went east to Toronto and returned to Red River in October 1869. He was a prisoner of Louis Riel at Upper Fort Garry in 1869-70. He subsequently operated the Northwest Navigation Company, and lumber operations. He was vice-president of the Manitoba Mortgage and Investment Company, but its failure in 1882 broke him financially. He helped found the Manitoba Historical Society, and wrote a number of papers on Red River history. He was also an active ornithologist. His letters are published in Valdene Mae and Edna Alexandra Medd, eds., *MacArthur Family Letters 1854-1934* (1992). *DCB* XI, 538-39.

MacArthur, Archibald A. (1845-1912) Farmer. Born in Middlesex County, Canada, he was educated at Komoka Seminary. He became a farmer specializing in stock breeding. He came to Winnipeg in 1882. From 1888 to 1891 he managed a farm at Gull Lake. He then returned to Winnipeg and founded MacArthur Grocery Company Limited. He was active in municipal politics, serving as alderman (1905-8) and several terms on the Board of Control. He was active in the Shoal Lake water supply business, as well as in locating a power plant in Lac du Bonnet. See Medd and Medd, eds., *MacArthur Family Letters*.

MacArthur, Duncan (1840-1907) Businessman. Born in Nairnshire, Scotland, he was educated at Free Church Academy in Nairn and entered the service of the HBC in 1864. He became senior clerk in the Montreal Department, succeeding his brother Alexander in 1868. In 1871 he resigned from the HBC to become manager of the Merchants' Bank of Canada in Winnipeg, then president of the Commercial Bank of Manitoba from 1885 to 1893, when the bank suspended payments and never resumed business. He was MLA from Assiniboia in 1888. During the 1870s and especially 1880s MacArthur was part of innumerable promotions and boards of directors for railways, insurance companies, and banks. He was also managing director of the Nelson Valley Railway and Transportation Company (1880), president of the Portage, Westbourne and North Western Railway (1882), and president of the Manitoba Central Railway (1883). In his prime he brought much investment to the province. In 1887 he withdrew a bid as Conservative candidate for Parliament, but ran provincially in a by-election in 1888 in Assiniboia. He ran against John Norquay* in Kildonan in the 1888 general election, but lost by two votes. He moved to Chicago in 1898 and died there. He was the author of *The Scottish Highlander: His Origin, Literature, Language, and General Characteristics* (1893). MacArthur also wrote a number of manuscript histories of the fur trade. There are papers at the PAM. His letters are published in Medd and Medd, eds., *MacArthur Family Letters* (1992). *DCB* XIII, 608-9.

MacArthur, John Alexander (b. c. 1860) Physician, community leader. Born in Lobo Township, Canada, he graduated from McGill University in 1886, having previously practised medicine in Iowa. He came to Winnipeg in 1884 and became a leading doctor, serving as surgeon for the Northern Pacific & Manitoba Railway from 1888 until its merger into the Canadian Northern. He was professor of diseases of children at the Manitoba Medical College. He was president of the Winnipeg branch of the Dominion Alliance, of the St. Andrew's Society, and of the Playgoers' Society. He contested Winnipeg Centre provincially in 1904 and 1907 as a Liberal.

MacArthur, John Duncan (1854-1927) Contractor. Born in Glengarry County, Canada, he farmed before coming to Winnipeg in 1879. He joined a railroad workgang and worked his way up to contractor for the CPR. He subsequently built the Manitoba line from Emerson in 1889. He boasted that he had built more miles of railroad than any other contractor in Canada. MacArthur also held extensive lumber and milling properties. He died immediately upon his return from health treatment at Battle Creek, Michigan.

MacArthur, Peter (1841-1936) Steamboat captain. Born in Scotland, he came to Red River in 1869 to work on the Snow road, which was being constructed by the federal government. He was listed in 1872 as a cabinetmaker. He was one of the group who were in John Schultz's* house when they surrendered to Louis Riel in December 1869. He escaped from Lower Fort Garry on 10 January 1870, but was soon recaptured. When released he travelled with A.W. Graham* and J. Latimer from Winnipeg to Minnesota on snowshoes in mid-March 1870. He later became a timberman and steamboat builder in Winnipeg. He built the first steamboat in Manitoba in 1872. His letters are published in Medd and Medd, eds., *MacArthur Family Letters* (1992). There are papers at the PAM.

McAskill, Roderick (b. 1874) Farmer, curler. Born in Stornoway, Scotland, he came with his family to Manitoba in 1887. He was educated at the Winnipeg Business College. After farming with his family, he became a machinery salesman and started his own farm implement business in 1908. He served as provincial auto licence inspector (1916-19), and was elected mayor of Gladstone in 1924. He was one of Manitoba's best-known curlers, winning a number of trophies, including the Empire in 1908 and the Dingwall in 1925.

MacAulay, John A. (1895-1978) Lawyer. Born in Morden, he received his BA and LLM from the University of Manitoba. He served overseas in WWI, then became a lawyer with Aikins MacAulay and Thorvaldson. A member of Westminister United Church, he taught one of the largest adult Bible classes in Canada in the 1930s and 1940s. He was president of the Manitoba and Canadian Red Cross during WWII. He was active with the Winnipeg Art Gallery and the National Gallery of Canada. He was president of the Canadian Bar Association in 1953-54 and was appointed to the Order of Canada in 1967.

McBain, Jean (d. 1986) Ballet dancer. She began her classical dance training in Vancouver, and had teaching degrees from the Royal Academy of Dance, London. She was the premier dancer with the Winnipeg Ballet in the 1930s and 1940s, until she moved to Montreal. McBain returned to Winnipeg in 1961 and was principal of the Royal Winnipeg Ballet School from 1962 to 1985.

McBean, Islay Ramona (Sinclair) (1905-1978) Actress, singer. Born in Winnipeg, she was for 58 years a singer in light opera across Canada. She died in Vancouver.

McBeth, Alexander (d. 1847) Farmer. Born in Sutherlandshire, he brought his family to Red River in 1815, originally settling on property now the site of St. John's Cathedral. According to family tradition he brought a pair of millstones to the settlement. In 1817, at the request of Lord Selkirk,* he exchanged his property for Lot 33, Old Kildonan, which is now McBeth Park.

MacBeth, George (1825-1870) Estate manager. Born in Red River, the eldest son of George MacBeth and Catherine Sutherland of Kildonan, Sutherlandshire, he accompanied his family east to Upper Canada in 1838. Shortly after, he began to work for Colonel Thomas Talbot, gradually becoming his business manager and later heir to half his estate, which was not a popular move with the family. With his inheritance he built a large house called Bleak House in London, Canada. He was involved in politics, the militia, and most of the business activity of the London region.

McBeth (McBeath), Robert (1805-1886) Farmer. He was the son of Alexander McBeth and was born in Sutherlandshire, coming to Red River in 1815. He was a jack of all trades in the settlement, farming on the family lot in Kildonan, running a store, and operating a freighting service to York Factory. He was appointed to the Council of Assiniboia in 1853, the first Selkirk settler so recognized. McBeth served as magistrate at 38 sessions of the General Quarterly Court of Assiniboia, including the investigation into the 1870 death of Elzéar Goulet.* He was not active in the Red River Rebellion, although he sheltered John Schultz* for a night upon his escape from Upper Fort Garry. *DCB*, XI, 539-40. There are papers at the PAM.

McBeth, Roderick George (1858-1934) Cleric, historian. Born in Kildonan, Manitoba, he was an early graduate of the University of Manitoba (BA 1882, MA 1885) and was called to the bar in 1886. He subsequently studied for the ministry at Manitoba College and Princeton Seminary, and was ordained in the Presbyterian Church in 1891. Most of his ministry was conducted in Vancouver. He wrote extensively about his ancestors in a series of autobiographical books on the early development of the Canadian West: *The Selkirk Settlers in Real Life* (1897), *The Making of the Canadian West* (1898), *The Romance of Western Canada* (1918), *Policing the Plains* (1922),

The Romance of the Canadian Pacific Railway (1924). He also wrote on church subjects, including *Our Task in Canada* (1912) and *The Burning Bush and Canada* (n.d.).

McBride, Albert Edward (b. 1886) Publisher. Born in Ontario and educated at the Toronto Normal School, he drifted into bookselling. In 1912 he opened in Winnipeg the first Canadian office of the Grolier Society, remaining at its head until he was transferred to Toronto in 1923. In 1949 he became president of the Grolier Society of Canada Limited, and he was instrumental in the creation of the *Encyclopedia Canadiana*

McBryde, Sydney Ronald ("Ron," 1941-1989) Politician. Born in British Columbia, he was raised in Oliver, and worked in the correctional system before coming to Manitoba in 1967 to work with the aboriginal community in The Pas. He was elected NDP MLA for The Pas in 1969, becoming minister without portfolio in the Schreyer government in 1971. From 1972 he served as minister of northern affairs, and was responsible for the Northern Affairs Act that granted self-government to northern communities. He retired from the legislature in 1981, subsequently serving for two years as deputy minister of northern affairs until 1983. He died in Calgary. There are extensive papers are in the PAM.

McCallister, Allen McCoag (1879-1949) Farmer. Born in Grey North County, Ontario, of Scots descent, he came to Manitoba in 1897, eventually operating a dairy in Prairie Grove. In 1913 he bought a half section six miles north of Portage la Prairie, which he organized as a demonstration farm. Beginning in 1924, he began growing peas as a seed crop, eventually organizing the McCallister Pea and Seed Cleaning Plant in Portage, which exported peas around the world. He also added other seed crops. He helped found the Portage Credit Union and was president of the local Manitoba Federation of Agriculture and the Manitoba Co-operative Livestock Association. He was councillor of his rural municipality (1932-40) and reeve (1940-49). He was a leading spirit in the building of a senior citizens' home in Portage la Prairie. He is a member of the Manitoba Agricultural Hall of Fame.

McCance, Gertrude Florence (1909-1989) Educator. Born in St. James, she graduated from the University of Manitoba and studied speech and voice in England. She taught at private schools before becoming head of the speech department of the Manitoba Normal School in 1943. A year later she became director of school broadcasts for Manitoba, and she was responsible for Manitoba's experiments with school television in 1958. She was the first woman named an honorary life member of the Canadian Education Association. She died in Winnipeg.

MacCharles, Malcolm Rutherford (1894-1991) Physician. Born in Cypress River, Manitoba, he moved to Manitou at an early age. He attended Manitoba College (1911-12), then Manitoba Medical College (1913-14) before serving with the medical corps in France. He was recalled to Canada in 1917 to complete his medical training. In 1926 he joined the University of Manitoba as a demonstrator in clinical surgery. In the 1930s he became a key figure in the establishment of the Manitoba Medical Service, which became the Manitoba Health Services Commission. Active in cancer research, he was president of the Canadian Cancer Institute in 1963-64. He died in Winnipeg.

McCliesh, Thomas (fl. 1698-1746) Fur trader. A carpenter by trade, he began with the HBC in 1698, served as a sloop captain, and became chief factor at Fort Albany in 1715. In 1722 he became governor-in-chief of the HBC operations on the Bay. With a year out in 1727 and again in 1734, he served as governor until 1737. He died in "low circumstances." *DCB* III, 414-15.

McClung, Nellie Letitia (Mooney) (1873-1951) Feminist, writer. Born in Ontario, she moved with her family to Manitoba in 1880. After attending normal school in Winnipeg she taught in rural Manitoba until her marriage in 1896 to Robert Wesley McClung, a druggist. Before her marriage she had been radicalized by her future mother-in-law, Annie McClung, into active work for temperance through the Woman's Christian Temperance Union, and for the universal franchise. As McClung later reported, her husband insisted that "I would not have to lay aside my ambitions if I married him." Her emergence to prominence began when she entered an American short-story competition in 1902 and was encouraged by an American publisher to expand the story into a novel, which became *Sowing Seeds in Danny* (1908). It sold 100,000 copies and brought its author a small fortune by contemporary standards. She and

her husband moved to Winnipeg with their four children in 1911, and she helped organize the Political Equality League in 1912. Frustrated with the difficulty in arousing male politicians to reform, she redoubled her political efforts, particularly as a platform speaker. After many early humiliations she became a good speaker. She satirized Premier Rodmond Roblin* — who had failed to respond to her calls for action — at the Mock Parliament of Women in 1914. McClung and her associates, supporting the Liberal Party, were unable to defeat Roblin's government in the 1914 election, but Roblin soon fell under the weight of the scandal associated with the construction of the new legislative building. Meanwhile, the McClungs had moved to Edmonton, where Nellie again led the fight for female suffrage, achieving success in 1916. She was an enthusiastic supporter of the war effort and the Red Cross, and in 1921 was elected to the Alberta Legislature, where she championed a host of radical measures ranging from mother's allowances, to dower rights for women, to sterilization of the mentally unfit. She was defeated in 1926 because of her temperance stance. Nellie subsequently helped lead the successful fight for Canadian women senators. The McClungs moved to Victoria in 1933. In her West Coast years, she was a CBC governor (1936-42), a delegate to the League of Nations (1938), and an advocate of divorce reform. She was throughout her life an active Methodist, prominent at the national and international level. Apart from her first novel, none of her fiction has withstood the test of time very well. McClung has done better with her autobiographical memoirs, *In Times Like These* (1915), *Clearing in the West* (1935) and *The Stream Runs Fast* (1945), all of which are highly regarded and have been reprinted. Like most early feminists, McClung was not as consistent in her liberated attitudes as she might have been. Her keen (almost bloodthirsty) support of WWI and her positive attitude toward eugenics unquestionably mark her as a figure of her time. For a biography, see Candace Savage, *Our Nell* (1979).

McColl, Ebenezer (1835-1902) Indian agent. Born in Aldborough Township, Upper Canada, into a Scottish family who were active Primitive Baptists, he studied in the United States and became a schoolteacher. In 1875 he worked briefly as field agent for the *Toronto Globe* before being named the Manitoba region's inspector of agencies and accounts for the Indian Affairs Branch of the Department of the

Interior. Soon after his arrival in Winnipeg, he helped investigate fraud charges in the Winnipeg office of the branch that resulted in the removal of lawyer J.-A.-N. Provencher* from his position as commissioner of Indian affairs. McColl travelled extensively to examine the reserves within his superintendency, and in 1890 was named superintendent of Indian Affairs for Manitoba and the North-West Territories. Many Native leaders regarded him as a friend. He died in Winnipeg. See Frances McColl, *Ebenezer McColl, 'Friend to the Indians,' Superintendent of Indian affairs for Manitoba and Northwest Territories: a biography, 1835-1902* (1989). *DCB* XIII, 617.

McConnell, George Newton (1894-1962) Farmer. Born in Hamiota, Manitoba, he graduated from the Manitoba Agricultural College in 1912. He began farming the "home" farm. Always active in farm organizations, he was vice-president of Manitoba Pool Elevators and in 1956 was appointed to the Board of Grain Commissioners of Canada, becoming its chair in 1961. He is a member of the Manitoba Agricultural Hall of Fame.

McCreary, William Forsythe (1855-1905) Lawyer. Born in Lanark County, Canada, he was educated in and studied law in Arnprior. He moved to Manitoba in 1881, becoming private secretary to John Schultz.* He later practised law in Winnipeg in partnership with George Elliott. He served as an alderman for Winnipeg in 1883, 1884, and 1886; and as mayor of Winnipeg in 1897. In the latter year he was appointed a commissioner of immigration, and he was active in encouraging immigration to the province. In 1900 he became Liberal MP for Selkirk. He died in Ottawa.

McCuaig, Duncan William (1855-1928) Grain grower. Born in Glengarry County, Canada, of Highland Scottish descent, he came to Manitoba in 1877, farming in the West Oakland district of the Portage plains. Active in the United Farmers of Manitoba movement, he became president of Manitoba Grain Growers' Association from 1904 to 1910. He was appointed president of the Manitoba Elevator Commission and was elected president of the Dominion Council of Agriculture. He also headed the Farmers' Trading Company of Portage la Prairie, and the Manitoba Farmer's Mutual Hail Insurance Company. He is a member of the Manitoba Agricultural Hall of Fame.

McCulloch, John K. ("Jack," 1868-1918) Sportsman. Born in Perth, Ontario, he moved to Winnipeg in 1874. He won the Canadian speed-skating championship at Montreal in 1893, the American championship at St. Paul in 1896, and the world speed-skating championship at Montreal in 1897. He turned professional in 1897, and gave exhibitions until at least 1907. He was also a successful competitive bicycle rider, and was Manitoba champion from 1890 to 1900. McCulloch also excelled at roller skating, track and field, canoeing, figure skating, and gymnastics. He designed and subsequently manufactured the McCulloch tube skate, as well as opening an early automobile repair shop specializing in racing machines. He was crippled in an automobile accident in 1908. He died in St. Paul, Minnesota. He is a member of Canada's Sports Hall of Fame and the Manitoba Sports Hall of Fame.

McDermid, Duncan Wendell (1858-1909) Educator. Born in Canada, he began working at the Ontario Institution for the Education and Instruction of the Deaf and Dumb in 1876, later serving as a teacher of articulation in a school that emphasized sign language. He moved to the Iowa Institution for the Education of the Deaf and Dumb at Council Bluffs in 1882, achieving considerable reputation as an educator. He came to Winnipeg in 1890 to become principal of the Deaf and Dumb Institute in Manitoba (later the Manitoba School for the Deaf), where he used both the oral and sign method and advocated the use of hypnosis to treat speech disorders. The school grew and prospered under his administration. He was extremely active in the community's elite organizations, and served as president of the Manitoba Club. He wrote a history of the early years of the Manitoba school for the deaf, which was published in E.A. Fay, ed., *Histories of American Schools for the Deaf, 1817-1893* (vol. 3, 1893). He died in Winnipeg. *DCB* XIII, 621-22.

McDermot, Andrew (1790-1881) Fur trader, merchant. Born in County Roscommon, Ireland, he was educated privately as a Roman Catholic. He was subsequently recruited by Lord Selkirk* for the HBC in 1812, and sailed from Sligo aboard the *Robert Taylor*. When there was a mutiny on ship, he supported the mutineers, and always claimed he learned to speak Gaelic on this voyage. He chafed at his slow advance in the HBC and retired to Red River in 1824, where he opened his own store and engaged in the fur trade under special licence. He speculated in land in what would become Winnipeg, and McDermot Avenue, located at the north edge of his property, is named after him. He was appointed to the Council of Assiniboia in 1839. In the 1840s he was a leading supporter of free trade in the fur trade. He resigned from the Council but returned in 1847, becoming *ex officio* president of the General Quarterly Court in 1849. He resigned his offices in 1851 because of lack of trust in Major William Caldwell* as governor of Assiniboia. He was a member of St. John's Cathedral after leaving the Catholic Church in 1866, and subsequently helped found Holy Trinity Church. He stayed out of the Red River Rebellion, and became an honoured senior citizen of Manitoba. He provided land for Winnipeg's first post office and for the Winnipeg General Hospital. He is buried in the cemetery of the Anglican St. John's Cathedral. *DCB* XI 545-46.

McDiarmid, James (b. 1855) Contractor. Born in Scotland, he immigrated to Canada in 1880 to join his brother in Stonewall, Manitoba. He moved to Winnipeg two years later and soon became a partner in a construction firm that eventually became J. McDiarmid Company, General Builders and Contractors, with branches in Calgary and Vancouver. His firm built many different kinds of structures, including the legislative building after the cancellation of the original contract that had led to the fall of the Roblin government. He designed many of the buildings himself, especially churches. As well as working as an architect, he was an amateur painter and a collector of art. He joined the art committee of the Winnipeg Industrial Bureau in 1906, and he proposed the construction of a civic art gallery, never built, in 1909.

McDiarmid, John Stewart (1882-1965) Merchant, politician. Born in Perthshire, Scotland, he came to Canada in 1887. His early years were spent on a farm at Portage la Prairie. He then went into the paint and glass business, then the lumber business, in Winnipeg with his brother Charles. In 1924 he was president of the Manitoba Curling Association. He was elected city alderman in 1925, and then was Liberal MP and MLA from 1926 to 1930. He was an MLA from 1932 to 1953. Retired from politics, he was appointed lieutenant-governor of Manitoba from 1953 to 1959. There are papers at the PAM.

Macdonald, Allan (1832-1901) Indian agent. Born in Fort Langley, British Columbia, the son of Archibald MacDonald* and his country-born mixed-blood wife Jane Klyne, he was baptized in Red River in 1834. He subsequently lived with his family at Fort Colvile, Washington, and was sent to Lower Canada for schooling. He inherited the family's farm at St. Andrews, Canada, in 1853. He was in British Columbia for the Cariboo gold rush, selling out in 1862 to return to St. Andrews. Active in the militia against the Fenians, he was appointed a captain in the Wolseley Expedition. In Manitoba he acquired land in Ste. Agathe, but became active in Indian affairs. In 1877 he became Indian agent in southeastern Saskatchewan and western Manitoba, based first at Swan River and then at Fort Qu'Appelle. He negotiated several Indian treaties and was part of the Qu'Appelle Syndicate, organized in 1881 among NWMP officers to acquire and deal in land. After the North-West Rebellion of 1885, he remained with a reorganized Indian Department as superintendent in the Qu'Appelle Valley. He supported Indian farming and was capable of opposing policy that he did not regard as appropriate for the Natives, becoming an Indian advocate in their continual struggles with settlers. Both his advocacy and his mixed-blood background hampered his promotion within the department. He was eventually transferred to Winnipeg to work as a clerk. He died in Winnipeg. *DCB* XIII, 622-24.

McDonald, Archibald (1790-1853) Fur trader. Born in Glencoe, Scotland, he became a protegé of the Lord Selkirk,* who sent him to study medicine in London before dispatching him to Red River with a party of Kildonan settlers under the command of Dr. Peter Laserre, who died during the voyage. McDonald took over command, wintered with the settlers at Fort Churchill, and led them first to York Factory and then to Red River in 1814. Appointed by Selkirk to the Council of Assiniboia, he became a lieutenant of Miles Macdonell.* In 1816 he published *Narrative Respecting the Destruction of the Earl of Selkirk's Settlement upon Red River, in the Year 1815* and a series of letters to the *Montreal Herald* answering a pamphlet by John Strachan highly critical of Selkirk. These letters became a pamphlet published that same year as *Reply to the Letter, Lately Addressed to the Right Honourable the Earl of Selkirk, by the Hon. and Rev. John Strachan, D.D.* McDonald accompanied Selkirk to Fort William in 1816, advocating the aggressive policy that Selkirk pursued at that point. In 1817 he brought a party of De Meuron soldiers west to Fort William, and in 1819 he was one of those indicted for conspiracy against the NWC. He joined the HBC in 1820, and a year later was posted to the Columbia District, where he remained throughout his career in the fur trade. He became chief trader in 1828, accompanied George Simpson* on his western inspection tour of that year, and was head at Fort Langley until 1833, when he established Fort Nisqually. He ran the agricultural Fort Colvile from 1835 to 1844, becoming chief factor in 1841. While in the West, he became an active correspondent of British scientific organizations and sent them many specimens. He also assisted several visiting botanists to collect specimens and information. Twice married according to the "custom of the country," he retired in 1844 and settled with his family on the Ottawa River in Lower Canada. See his *Peace River, a Canoe Voyage from Hudson's Bay to Pacific, by the Late Sir George Simpson (Governor, Hon. Hudson's Bay Company) in 1828*, edited by Malcolm McLeod (1872). For a biography, consult Jean M. Cole, *Exile in the Wilderness: The Biography of Chief Factor Archibald McDonald, 1790-1853* (1979). There are papers in the Selkirk Papers in the NAC. *DCB* VIII, 526-28.

Macdonald, Hugh John (1850-1929) Lawyer. Born in Kingston, Canada, he was the only surviving son of Sir John A. Macdonald and Isabella Clark. He was educated at University of Toronto (BA 1869), and took part as a private in the Wolseley Expedition, against his father's wishes. He was called to the bar in 1872, and returned to Winnipeg in 1882. He achieved the rank of captain in the North-West Rebellion of 1885. He was Conservative MP from Winnipeg from 1891 to 1893 and from 1896 to 1897, serving briefly as minister of the interior in the Tupper Cabinet of 1896. During this period he was closely connected with Lord and Lady Aberdeen. He was chosen to lead the Manitoba Conservatives in 1899 and became MLA for south Winnipeg and premier (also attorney general) in 1900. He served only briefly, then contested the federal seat of Brandon against Clifford Sifton.* When he lost, he retired to private life. He was created a Knight Baronet in 1912. From 1911 to 1929 he sat as police magistrate for the City of Winnipeg, coming down hard on aliens and the strikers of 1919. Like many sons of distinguished fathers, he was often elevated to positions beyond his capabilities. See H. Guest, "Reluctant Politician: a Biography of Sir John Hugh MacDonald" (MA thesis, University of Manitoba, 1973). There are papers at the PAM.

McDonald, John (le Borgne) (1770-1828) Fur trader. Born in Scotland, his family came to Glengarry in 1786. He joined the XY Company in 1798, and was soon stationed in Red River. He joined the NWC when the companies merged in 1804, remaining in the region, at Fort Dauphin (1808-10) and at Swan River (1810-13). In August 1816 he was arrested by Lord Selkirk* at Fort William and charged as an accessory to the murder of Robert Semple* and others. Brought by Selkirk's agents to Montreal, he was eventually tried in Upper Canada and acquitted. He became a chief factor in the HBC upon the merger, and was put in charge of the Upper Red River District. He retired to Upper Canada in 1827 because of ill health and died soon after. *DCB* VI, 435-36.

McDonald, John (of Garth) (1771-1866) Fur trader. Born in Perthshire, Scotland, he could not follow the family military tradition because of a withered right arm (he was later called "Le Bras Croche"). So he joined the NWC, and played an important role in the western fur-trade war with the HBC. In 1809 he was in charge of the Red River Department with John Wills,* went west to command Fort Astoria (arriving just after its sale to the NWC by the American Fur Company), and returned to Red River via a canoe brigade. He negotiated a peace between the settlers and the NWC in 1814, but his agreement was disavowed by the NWC annual meeting. He thereupon retired from the company and moved back east, ultimately purchasing a farm near Cornwall. His autobiography appears in L.-F.-R. Masson, ed., *Les Bourgeois de la Compagnie du Nord-Ouest*, II, 1-59 (1890). The original is at McGill University Libraries. *DCB* IX, 481-83.

Macdonell, Alexander (b. 1774) Colonial official. Born in Invernesshire, Scotland, he became a protegé of Lord Selkirk* in 1813. He was sent with Robert Semple* to bring settlers to Red River in 1815, and was appointed by Semple as second-in-command to Colin Robertson* and later to himself. He was known for his position as sheriff of the settlement in 1815-16. He assumed charge of the colony after Semple's death, and re-established it in 1817. For several years he seemed to be successful, although there were always rumours of veniality and partiality that Selkirk refused to believe. He became agent for Selkirk in 1820 and resumed his governorship of the settlement in June 1820. His later administration was replete with controversy and charges of favouritism, corruption, and immorality. He was dismissed by George Simpson* in 1822, having become known as the "grasshopper governor" because, said Alexander Ross* later, "he proved as great a destroyer within doors as the grasshoppers in the fields." He remained in the colony and attempted to undermine the authority of his successors while acquiring large amounts of land. He eventually returned to Upper Canada in 1828 and disappeared from view. *DCB* VI, 437-39.

Macdonell, Alexander (Greenfield) (1782-1835)

Fur trader. Born in Greenfield, Scotland, he emigrated with his family to Upper Canada in 1792, joining the NWC in 1803. Posted to Red River in 1809, he was there to welcome his cousin and brother-in-law Miles Macdonell.* In 1814 he was among the Nor'Westers criticized by the leadership for failing to resist Miles MacDonell's "pemmican proclamation" more vigorously, and he was apparently made a partner and placed (with Duncan Cameron) in charge of the Red River Department on the understanding that there would be more opposition to the settlement. For the next few years he and Cameron would lead a campaign against the colony, employing the local freemen, mixed-bloods, and Indians as the apparent actors. He helped promote a concept of Aboriginal rights among these people, and appears to have favoured intimidation short of the "shedding of blood." Cuthbert Grant's* men at Seven Oaks were under his orders, but the violence of that confrontation was probably inadvertent. He denied responsibility for the 1816 murder of Owen Keveny.* In 1819 *A Narrative of Transactions in the Red River Country* appeared under his name in London, in an attempt to exculpate him from the "calumnious libels" levelled against him by the Selkirk interests, who regarded him with such hostility that he was specifically excluded from employment with the HBC after the merger. He served as MLA from Glengarry from 1821 to 1824 in the Upper Canada Assembly and won the riding of Prescott as a Tory in 1835, dying of consumption while attending the assembly meeting. He served as sheriff of the Ottawa District from 1822 to his death. *DCB* VI, 445-46.

McDonell, Allan (c. 1776-1859)

Fur trader. Born in Glengarry, Scotland, he came to Upper Canada with his family. He joined Forsyth, Richardson and Company in 1799 and was sent west, serving as clerk in the NWC after the two companies merged. He was first posted to Fort Dauphin and later to Red River. He was arrested by Lord Selkirk* in 1816 at Fort William, sent east for trial, and later was indicted in Toronto. After the merger of the HBC and NWC in 1821, he was in charge of the Swan River district until posted to Timiskaming in 1826. There was mutual dissatisfaction between him and the HBC in his later years, and he retired in 1843. From 1839 to his retirement he served on the Council of Assiniboia. After 1843 he lived in Montreal. *DCB* VIII, 537-38.

MacDonell, John ("Le Prêtre," 1768-1850)

Fur trader. Born in Scotland, he was a brother of Miles Macdonell,* and came to America with his family in 1773, resettling in Canada. He held a militia commission in 1788 and entered NWC service in 1793, initially in the Qu'Appelle Valley. From 1806 to 1809 he was head of the Upper Red River Department. He helped create the corps of Canadian Voyageurs, in which he held the rank of captain. This unit captured Mackinac Island from the Americans in 1812, although he arrived too late to be involved in the victory, and was quickly captured by the enemy. In 1814 he considered settling in Red River, but instead he retired to Pointe Fortune, Upper Canada, where he kept a store and became a leading businessman and local political leader. Journals of his Red River service were published as "Mr. John MacDonell: Some Account of the Red River (about 1797)," in *Les Bourgeois de la Compagnie du Nord-Ouest*, ed. L. Masson, I, 265-95, and "The Diary of John MacDonell," *Five Fur Traders of the Northwest*, ed. C.M. Gates (1965), 61-119. *DCB* VII, 552-54.

Macdonell, Miles (1769-1828)

Colonial official, soldier. Born in Inverness, Scotland, he emigrated with his family, who were Roman Catholics, to the Mohawk Valley, New York, in 1773. The family resettled as Loyalists in Lower Canada in 1783. In 1782 Miles became an ensign in the King's Own Regiment of New York, serving until 1784. He began farming in Osnabruck Township, Upper Canada, and in 1794 was a lieutenant in the Royal Canadian Volunteer Regiment, rising to captain in 1796. He was stationed at Niagara-on-the-Lake from 1800 to 1802, and was often in financial difficulty. "Mere farming will hardly support my family in the manner I would wish," he commented in 1804, the year he first met Lord Selkirk,* who was touring Upper Canada. Thus he constantly sought military and civilian appointments, usually without much success. In 1811 Selkirk selected him as governor of Assiniboia, a role which he readily accepted, despite the difficulties of the endeavour and the association of most of his kinfolk with the NWC. Macdonell had trouble with the venture from the beginning. He treated the settlement's first recruits roughly when they became discontented before departure from Stornoway in 1811, and was never able to command their respect during the long winter the party had to spend on the Nelson River. After their arrival at Red River in late August 1812, the next few years went from bad to worse. Food for the new settlers was in short supply, and early in 1814 MacDonell issued the notorious "pemmican proclamation," which forbade the export of provisions from the jurisdiction over which he claimed authority, a claim contested by the NWC. No accountant, Macdonell had much difficulty with the double-entry bookkeeping insisted upon by Selkirk, and the local HBC people were not at all supportive. Harassed on all sides and clearly not in control of the situation, he experienced a nervous breakdown in August 1814. A year later he surrendered to the Nor'Westers and was taken east to stand trial on a number of charges, while most of his settlers went to Upper Canada in NWC canoes. Never tried, he returned west in 1816 and helped capture Fort William with Selkirk. He advised Selkirk to purchase the furs there from NWC partner Daniel McKenzie.* He subsequently led a party of De Meuron soldiers overland to recapture Fort Douglas in January 1817, serving again as governor of Red River in the spring and summer of 1817. He was soon back in Upper Canada, where he spent the remainder of his life attempting to hold Selkirk and his estate to the commitments made to him in 1811. He died at Pointe Fortune. Macdonell's papers are in the NAC; many of them, including a journal (1811-14), are in the Selkirk Papers, also in the NAC. A letterbook, "Selkirk settlement; letter book of Captain Miles Macdonell," was published in *PAC Report* (1886), clxxxvii-ccxxvi. There is no full biography. *DCB* VI, 440-44.

McDonell, Theresa (c. 1833-1917) Nun, nurse. Born in St. Andrews, Upper Canada, she was placed at the convent of the Sisters of Charity of Bytown and joined the order in 1851 as Sister Sainte-Thérèse. She was sent to Red River two years later. When the Grey Nuns ordered her to return east, the Métis, led by the elder Louis Riel,* surrounded the cart that was carrying her away and refused to let her go. She subsequently taught school in St. Vital, St. Norbert, and St. François Xavier, often combining the roles of superior and teacher. The temporary hospital she set up in 1871 became St. Boniface General Hospital. She died in St. Boniface. *DCB* XIV, 694-95.

McDougall, George Millward (1821-1876) Missionary. Born at Kingston, Upper Canada, to Highland Scots parents, he served in a militia unit in 1837 and later moved with his family to a farm near Barrie. He was converted to Methodism and attended Victoria College, Cobourg, 1849-50. He worked with the Indians and was ordained in 1854. In 1860 he took up a post at Rossville Mission, not far from Norway House, with responsibility for the huge Methodist district extending from Oxford House to the Rocky Mountains. He had much assistance from his family, especially his son John,* in this mission. In 1863 he established Victoria Mission on the North Saskatchewan River, 80 miles east of Edmonton House, which became his base until 1871, when he moved to Edmonton House itself. For a biography, see J.E. Nix, *Mission among the Buffalo: The Labours of the Reverends George M. and John C. McDougall in the Canadian Northwest, 1860-1876* (1960). *DCB* X, 471-72.

McDougall, John Chantler (1842-1917) Missionary. Born in Owen Sound, Canada, he attended Victoria College, 1857-60, and then joined his Methodist missionary father at Rossville Mission near Norway House in 1860. A fluent linguist, he was said to be more comfortable in Cree and Ojibway than English. He entered the ministry in 1866 and was ordained in the Methodist Church in 1874. He later was based in Edmonton. He often served as an unofficial agent of the government in its dealings with the Indians. He died in Calgary. He was the author of a biography of his father, *George Millward McDougall* (1895), and a multi-volume autobiography, published as *Saddle, Sled and Snowshoe* (1896), *Pathfinding on Plain and Prairie* (1898), *White Buffalo* (1908), *In the days of the Red River Rebellion* (1911), and *On Western Trails in the Early Seventies* (1911). See J.E. Nix, *Mission among the Buffalo* (1960). *DCB* XIV, 695-97.

McDougall, William (1822-1905) Erstwhile lieutenant-governor. Born near York, Upper Canada, he was educated at Victoria College, Cobourg. He practised as an attorney and was admitted to the Canadian bar in 1862. He was a leading Clear Grit and founder of the semi-weekly *North American,* which was absorbed by the *Globe* in 1857. McDougall became an associate of George Brown and entered politics in 1858. Rumours circulated in Red River later about his part in an "Indian rebellion" on Manitoulin Island in 1862, when he was Canadian superintendent of Indian affairs and commissioner of crown lands. According to the *Montreal Herald,* while commissioner he had allowed unscrupulous speculators to defraud people of their property. He served as provincial secretary in the government of the Great Coalition of 1864 and attended all the major Confederation conferences. He remained the leading Liberal in the Canadian coalition government of Sir John A. Macdonald, holding the public works portfolio from 1867 to 1869. McDougall had long advocated westward expansion, and in December 1867 he shepherded through Parliament a series of resolutions to incorporate Rupert's Land into the Dominion and extend Canadian sovereignty to the Pacific. He and Sir George-Etienne Cartier* went to London in 1868 to negotiate the transfer of Rupert's Land from the HBC to Canada. He was subsequently appointed the first lieutenant-governor of the newly acquired territory, and he was directly responsible for most of the clumsy Canadian actions that galvanized Métis hostility in the west. His arrival in the West with a sizeable entourage, including a government-in-waiting that contained no residents, touched off the 1869 Red River Rebellion. McDougall never got beyond Pembina, although he did briefly set foot on soil north of the 49th parallel. He made the supreme blunder when he issued a proclamation in early December that assumed the transfer to Canada had taken place as planned — it had not. He returned to Canada angry, embittered, and humiliated. He was very critical of the Manitoba Act in the House of Commons in 1870. His political career was not ended by Red River, but he never again held important office. He died in Ottawa. He was the author of *Eight Letters to the Hon. Joseph Howe on the Red River Rebellion* (1870), *Six Letters to the Hon. O. Mowat on the Amendment of the Provincial Constitution* (1875), and *An Open Letter to the Hon. H. Mercier on the Federalism of the Federal Constitution of 1867* (1887). His papers, including an unpublished autobiographical fragment (1837-69), are at the NAC. *DCB* XIII, 632-36.

MacDowell, Louise (1872-1965) Musician. Born in Ontario, she studied piano at the Toronto Conservatory of Music and then the Leipsic Conservatorium der Musick. She came to Winnipeg in 1903 and began teaching piano. She founded the Manitoba Music Teachers' Association in 1931. She left Winnipeg for Buffalo, New York, in the 1940s, then taught music at Kirkland Lake and Aurora, Ontario. Her memoirs, *Past and Present — a Canadian Musician's Reminiscences,* were published in 1957.

McEwen, Clifford Mackay ("Black Mike," 1897-1967) WWI flying ace. Born in Griswold, Manitoba, he served as a lieutenant in the Royal Air Force with 27 victories to his credit. After the war he achieved the rank of air vice-marshal in the RCAF. He died in Toronto.

McEwen, Jessie (Turnbull) (1845-1920) Feminist. Born in Montreal, she was an early advocate of higher education for women. In 1877 she helped form the Toronto Women's Literary Club, which in 1883 became the Canadian Women's Suffrage Association, with herself as president. She moved to Manitoba in 1884 when her husband began farming northeast of Brandon. The family built a large house called Tullichewen in 1893. McEwen became president of the Brandon branch of the National Council of Women of Canada in 1895, serving until 1916. She became a vice-president of the National Council in 1900. She helped organize the first branch of the Red Cross in Manitoba and helped found the Young Women's Christian Association in Brandon in 1907. She was an active Presbyterian and beginning in 1901 wrote for the *Canada Presbyterian* as well as the *Farmer's Advocate.* As a feminist, McEwen was not considered a radical militant so much as a "persuader." She died in Brandon.

MacFarlane, Roderick R. (1833-1920) Fur trader. Born in Stornoway, he was educated in that town's Free Church Academy and clerked at law before joining the HBC in 1852. A year later he was placed in charge of Fort Rae on Great Slave Lake, and worked at a number of posts in the far north before becoming chief trader in 1868. After a leave at home, he became head of Fort Chippewyan in the Athabasca in 1870, serving there for fourteen years and rising to become chief factor in 1875. He later served in New Caledonia and on the Lower Saskatchewan. MacFarlane spent many years in scientific investigation in the North and was a major contributor of specimens to the Smithsonian Institution in Washington, D.C. He was an intrepid northern traveller on foot, by dogsled, and on horseback. In 1908 he wrote, with Charles Mair, a volume entitled *Through the Mackenzie Basin*. He died in Winnipeg.

McFayden, Harris (d. 1941) Horticulturalist. Born in Caledon, Ontario, he received his BSA. from Ontario Agricultural College in the same class with John Bracken.* He became horticultural editor of the *Family Herald and Weekly Star*, then seed commissioner for Saskatchewan, then manager for the Garton Pedigree Seed Company in Winnipeg. In 1921 he started his own seed business, and by 1930 McFayden Seed Company was well established, with a field testing station at East Selkirk. Hallmarks of his trade were standard packaging, low prices, and a large catalogue business. He suffered a stroke in 1941.

McGillivray, John (1770-1855) Fur trader. Born in Highland Scotland, he was educated in Gaelic and English. He joined the NWC in 1794 and served in the Churchill River Department and later the Athabasca Department. In 1816 he was taken prisoner at Fort William by Lord Selkirk.* He retired in 1818 and moved to Glengarry County. He was a prominent Presbyterian and member of the Highland Society of Canada. *DCB* VIII, 546-47.

McGillivray, William (1764-1825) Fur trader. Born in Dunlichty, Scotland, he was brought by his uncle to Montreal to work for the NWC. In 1785, he was sent to Red River as a clerk, then moved further west before returning to the Rat River (now Manitoba) in 1789. After becoming a partner and being promoted to proprietor in 1790, he was put in charge of the English River department with headquarters at Île-à-la-Crosse; a year later he was given command of the Athabasca Department. McGillivray continued to advance gradually in the company, and became head of the NWC in 1804, arranging the amalgamation with the XY Company. He was prepared to fight the rejuvenated HBC and saw Lord Selkirk* and his settlement as the principal target. He was among those arrested at Fort William by Selkirk in 1816, although he was never tried. He negotiated the merger with the HBC in 1821. He was a member of the Beaver Club. For a biography, see Marjorie Wilkins Campbell, *Northwest to the Sea: A Biography of William McGillivray* (1975). *DCB* VI, 454-57.

McGregor, James Duncan (1860-1935) Cattle rancher, lieutenant-governor. Born in Amherstburg, Canada, he came to Manitoba in 1877, entering the livestock business in Portage la Prairie and Brandon, and later specializing in breeding Aberdeen Angus cattle. He became a mine inspector for the Yukon (1897-99), then formed Glencarnock Farms in Manitoba, and developed 200,000 acres near Medicine Hat. His Aberdeen Angus won the world grand championship in Chicago in 1913. He refused to become Manitoba minister of agriculture in 1915, but did agree in 1917 to serve as food controller for the four western provinces. He was lieutenant-governor of Manitoba from 1929 to 1934. He is a member of the Manitoba Agricultural Hall of Fame.

McGregor, Wilfrid Forrest (1902-1968) Farmer. Born in Acton, Ontario, he moved to Brandon in 1910, later farming on the family farm north of Brandon. He became secretary of Bloomsbury School District in 1932, serving in the post until 1966. He served for more than 10 years as a member of the board of Brandon College and was its chair when it became Brandon University. He received one of the university's first LLD degrees. He was active in many other farm organizations, including the Provincial Exhibition of Manitoba, which he served as president for three years. He is a member of the Manitoba Agricultural Hall of Fame.

Machray, John Alexander (1865-1933) Lawyer, embezzler. Born in Haddington, Scotland, he came to Winnipeg as a boy. A nephew and protegé of the Archbishop, he was a graduate of St. John's College School and the University of Manitoba (BA 1884, with First Class Honours and the Silver Medal). He then attended Sidney Sussex College at the University of Cambridge, receiving his LLB there in 1887. He became a partner in the law firm of Machray and Sharp and a KC. He also became bursar of the University of Manitoba, and in 1924 volunteered to become bursar of St. John's College without pay, adding the posts of chancellor of the diocese of Rupert's Land and chair of the University of Manitoba Board of Governors to his portfolio. In 1932, following an audit, it was revealed that all the endowment funds of the university, the college, and the diocese, as well as clients' trust funds, had been systematically embezzled by him over a period of several years. Machray had prevented audits for many years. What he had done with the money was never clear, although he may have lost it covering various bad investments, mainly in real estate. He was apparently not a successful investor. The collapse of the real estate market in the Depression broke him totally and he was unable to disguise the situation any longer. A royal commission inquiry later determined that he had been insolvent for 20 years. Dying of cancer, he was sentenced to seven years at Stony Mountain on lesser charges of theft, and died soon after in prison. The subsequent royal commission was unable to locate the money, although evidence given before it was front-page news for weeks. See Jim Blanchard, "The Machray Scandal," *Manitoba History* 33 (spring 1997): 27-37.

Machray, Robert (1831-1904) Cleric. Born in Aberdeen, Scotland, he was raised a Presbyterian but turned to the Anglican Church. He studied mathematics at King's College, Aberdeen, and Sidney Sussex College, Cambridge, and was ordained in 1856. He was appointed dean of Sidney Sussex College in 1859. He accepted the bishopric of Rupert's Land in 1865, the youngest bishop in the church at the time. He wrote to the colonial secretary in 1868, expressing concerns about squatters and recommending a small detachment of soldiers to facilitate the takeover of the HBC territory by Canada. In December 1869 he blamed the Canadian government for its lack of consultation, ignorance, and clumsy tactics. But he opposed the Métis resistance, and advocated the use of force to suppress it. When it was clear that the Métis had all the power, he counselled that Anglophone hotheads lay down their arms. At the same time that he facilitated the establishment of the provisional government, he wrote letters to Canada recommending military action. Machray feared the bloodshed of civil war and wanted outside military authority employed to suppress the Métis. He certainly distrusted Catholicism and looked hopefully to a Canadian future for Rupert's Land. He remained bishop until his death, adding the wardenship of St. John's College in 1874. As a schoolmaster at St. John's College School, he was famed for the quality of his breakfasts and of his corporal punishment. He was chosen first primate of Canada and archbishop of Rupert's Land in 1893, and served as chancellor of the University of Mantioba from 1877 to 1904. He was an ardent critic of the Greenway government's educational policy. He threatened to establish an Anglican system of parochial schools, but was outmaneuvered politically

and ended up being perceived as a supporter of the new educational system. Never married, he died in Winnipeg. For a biography see Robert Machray, *Life of Robert Machray* (1909). *DCB* XIII, 642-46. There are papers in the Rupert's Land Archives.

MacInnis, Grace (Woodsworth) (1905-1991) Politician. Born in Winnipeg, she was educated at Gibson's Landing, British Columbia, the University of British Columbia, the University of Manitoba, Ottawa Normal School, and the Sorbonne. She was a charter member of the CCF and NDP. She served as MLA for Vancouver-Burrard from 1941 to 1945, distinguishing herself in her campaign on behalf of Canadians of Japanese origin. She was later MP for Vancouver East (1965-72). MacInnis received the Order of Canada in 1974, and was granted a Governor General's Persons Award in 1979 for her work in aiding the status of women. She also won a 1982 Outstanding Service to Humanity Award from the Canadian Labor Congress, and was the only Canadian listed among the 50 most important women in the world by the French magazine *Marie Claire*. She won the medal for popular biography for her study of her father, *J.S. Woodsworth — A Man*.

McInnis, Stanley William (1865-1907) Dentist. Born in Saint John, New Brunswick, he was educated in Fredericton before his family moved to Manitoba. In 1880 he entered Manitoba College, graduating with a BA. He then apprenticed to a dentist and received a DDS from Philadelphia Dental College in 1888. He opened a practice in Brandon in 1890 as the province's first college-educated dentist. McInnis helped found the Canadian Dental Association in 1902 and served as its first registrar. He advocated successfully for a national standard of qualification for dentists. He supported the establishment of a sanatorium in Brandon, and in 1899 became an Independent-Conservative MLA from Brandon. He was re-elected in 1902 and 1907, and became provincial secretary in June 1907. He died suddenly in Brandon from blood poisoning resulting from appendicitis. McInnis was a fine baritone singer and a well-known cartoonist. *DCB* XIII, 649-50.

McIntyre, Daniel J. (1852-1946) Educator. Born in New Brunswick, he was educated at the Normal School, Fredericton, and at Dalhousie University. He taught in New Brunswick from 1872 to 1882, was admitted to the bar in the province in 1882, and came to Winnipeg that same year. He became principal of Carlton Street School. In 1885 he was named inspector of Protestant public schools and upon school reorganization in 1890 became superintendent of public schools. He was active on the advisory board of education and received an honorary LLD from the University of Manitoba in 1912. McIntyre worked with the Children's Aid Society (he was first president) and the Institute for the Blind. A Winnipeg high school is named after him. See William T. Wilson, *Daniel McIntyre and the Winnipeg Schools* (1981).

McIntyre, William Albert (1859-1938) Educator. Born in Canada, he was educated at Perth High School and the University of Manitoba. He became principal of the Boys' Central School of Winnipeg in 1880, and in addition was appointed mathematics master at the first Winnipeg Collegiate in 1882. He joined the Provincial Normal School in 1888 and become principal in 1892. He served on a commission to recognize the University of Manitoba, and was secretary of the Manitoba Educational Association. He was an editor of the "New Victorian" school readers in 1908.

McIvor, George Harold (1894-1991) Grain commissioner. Born in Portage la Prairie, he began work in a grain elevator at age 15, eventually joining the Winnipeg Grain Exchange. He became assistant chief commissioner of the Canadian Wheat Board in 1935 and its chief commissioner in 1937, serving until 1958. Associated for many years with C.D. Howe, McIvor's cautious approach to marketing and financing was increasingly seen as part of the farm policy of the Liberal government that was so unpopular with western grain farmers. Under attack by several members of the Diefenbaker government, he resigned in late 1957, although he agreed to stay on until after the 1958 election. He then became chair of the board of Robin Hood Flour, serving until 1969, when he retired to Calgary. He died in Scotland on holiday. See William E. Morriss, *Chosen Instrument: A History of the Canadian Wheat Board: The McIvor Years* (1987).

McKay, Angus (b. c. 1836) Indian agent, politician. A loyal mixed-blood in 1869-70, he was a defeated candidate to the 1870 Convention of Forty. He later served as MLA from Lake Manitoba (1870-76), and simultaneously as a Conservative MP from Marquette

(1871-72). Subsequently he was an Indian agent at Norway House. *DCB* XII, 640-41.

Mackay, Donald ("le malin," c. 1753-1833) Fur trader. Born in Clyne, Sutherlandshire, Scotland, he probably came to Canada with the British army. He joined the fur trade in 1779, but went to Montreal in 1781 to try to make money making potash. Failing at this, he returned to the fur trade on the Saskatchewan River, but was not employed by the NWC. He sailed to London in 1788 and joined in a new fur-trade partnership, but was pursued by creditors and headed back to Canada. In 1790 he was employed by the HBC as part of an expansion effort. The HBC admired his perseverence and knowledge of the country. In 1793 he was sent to Red River to explore the region, jousting continually with the NWC and establishing the HBC in the region. He visited Scotland in 1795 before returning to the Bay, where he was despatched to Brandon House at the beginning of 1796. About this time he began to exhibit symptoms of paranoia, which only worsened. He was sent home to England in 1800. Mackay's geographical knowledge was extensive, and was passed along through the HBC to the mapmakers, particularly to Arrowsmith. He later helped recruit for the HBC and was sent back to the Bay in 1805, where he had much trouble with William Auld. He made his final trip back to Scotland in 1807, eventually immigrating with his wife to Nova Scotia, where he died. The HBCA has his unpublished journals, while a manuscript diary is in the hands of descendants. See Harry W. Duckworth, "The Madness of Donald Mackay," *The Beaver* 68, no. 3 (June/July 1988): 25-42. *DCB* VI, 463-64.

MacKay, Douglas (1900-1938) Editor. Born in Woodstock, Ontario, he was educated at Woodstock Collegiate and Columbia University (1923). He served in public relations for several firms, becoming publicity director for the HBC's Canadian Committee. He edited the *The Beaver* from 1933 to 1938. He died in a plane crash in the United States. He wrote *The Honourable Company* (1936).

McKay, James (1825-1879) Trader, interpreter. Born at Edmonton House, he was educated at Red River and employed by the HBC. He was described by George Simpson* in 1859 as "Immensely broadchested and muscular . . . he weighed eighteen stone; yet in spite of his stoutness he was exceedingly hardy and active, and a wonderful horseman. His face — somewhat Assyrian in type — is very handsome: short, delicate, aquiline nose; piercing dark gray eyes; long dark-brown hair, beard, and moustaches; white, small, regular teeth; skin tanned to red bronze from exposure to weather." He favoured Red River dress — a capot (hooded frock-coat), flannel shirt, moccasins, trousers of homemade woollen material, and a sash. McKay lived at Deer Lodge. He was appointed to the Council of Assiniboia in 1868 and was a member of the Famine Relief Committee of 1868-69. He was a mixed-blood whose "father was Scotch, his mother French Half-Breed and though himself a Catholic he has two brothers Presbyterian." This made him the ideal first Speaker for the Manitoba Legislative Council. He later served as minister of agriculture from 1874 to 1878 before retiring due to ill health. A "quasi-king among halfbreeds," he had great authority with the Indians, and was instrumental in dealing with them throughout his life. See N. Jaye Goossen, "'A Wearer of Moccasins': The Honourable James McKay of Deer Lodge," *The Beaver* (autumn 1978): 44-53. *DCB* X, 473-75.

McKay, John (d. 1810) Fur trader. Probably born in Scotland, he had joined the fur trade by 1788, and the HBC by 1790. He became master at Brandon House in 1797 and remained there until his death. He was regarded as considerate, just and reliable, not always common attributes in the fur trade.

McKay, John Richards (c. 1792-1877) Fur trader. Born in Rupert's Land, he was educated in England before joining the HBC in 1808. He attempted to rebuild Qu'Appelle House in 1815 and was in command at Brandon House at the time of the merger. He retired to the Red River settlement in 1824. There he attempted to open a school to teach "writing, arithmetic, reading, English, French, dancing, fencing, and the Graces," but by 1830 he was back in the fur trade, rejoining the HBC in 1831 and serving at many posts. McKay was extremely popular with the Indians, who admired his abilities with horse, sword, and gun. He retired in 1859. *DCB* X, 475.

MacKay, Murdoch (1884-1962) Physician, politician. Born in Boularderie, Nova Scotia, he graduated from Manitoba Medical College in 1916. He served in the Canadian Army Medical Corps during WWI and was discharged as a Captain. He practised

medicine in Transcona for 40 years. He served as a Winnipeg MLA and as Manitoba Liberal leader from 1931 to 1936.

McKay, William (c. 1775-1849) Settler. Born in Caithness, Scotland, he came to Red River with the third Selkirk party, and was described as a shoemaker. Embarking at Stromness, he brought a pair of millstones and was accompanied by his wife and three children; a fourth child was born en route from York Factory to the settlement. In 1817 he was granted Lot 19 (now part of Kildonan Park) by Lord Selkirk.* He died at Red River.

McKeagney, James Charles (1815-1879) Lawyer, judge. Born in Ireland, his family came to Nova Scotia in 1822, and he was educated at McQueen's Academy in Halifax. He was called to the Nova Scotia bar in 1838. Initially a Reformer, he crossed the floor to support the Conservatives in 1857. Ten years later he was elected an anti-confederate MP from Cape Breton. Defeated in 1872, he was rewarded for running to split the Catholic vote with the appointment as puisne judge of the Manitoba Court of Queen's Bench. He was regarded as weak and fussy, described by one contemporary as a "right-minded and conscientious non-entity — or at best an old woman." Moreover, despite the requirement to be fluent in French, his lack of knowledge of the language was an embarrassment to the government, although it continued to support him. He refused to rule on the question of his court's jurisdiction in the Ambroise Lépine* trial and presided over the trial of André Nault.* He served several times as administrator of Manitoba and became acting lieutenant-governor of the North-West Territories for a time in 1876. He died in New Brunswick. *DCB* X, 475-76.

McKeand, Alfred (1849-1887) Soldier. Born in Glasgow, Scotland, he came to Hamilton with his family in 1854. He had joined the militia in 1869, and progressed to ensign by 1875. In 1879 he was sent by his family to Winnipeg to help open a branch of their wholesale grocery business. In 1881 he joined the Winnipeg Infantry Company, quickly rising to captain and command of the unit. He brought the company into the 90th Winnipeg Rifles in 1883, and led the 90th Battalion as its temporary commander in the North-West Rebellion of 1885 while William Kennedy* was in the Sudan. He was mentioned in dispatches. He became the battalion's regular commander upon Kennedy's death. *DCB* XI, 562.

McKechnie, John (1844-1918) Ironmaster. Born in Loch Lomond, Scotland, his parents came to Paris, Canada, in 1854. Apprenticed as a wheelwright, he came to Winnipeg in 1872 to work in a sawmill. A few years later he began the first foundry in the West, which gradually expanded into the Vulcan Iron Works, of which he was president. He was a member of the Winnipeg School Board from 1895 to 1911, was treasurer of the Grand Lodge of Manitoba, and a member of the Board of Managers of Knox Presbyterian Church. He was also a member of the St. Andrew's Society and the Carleton Club.

McKee, Samuel James (b. 1849) Educator. Born in Waterloo County, Canada, to Irish parents, he attended Stratford and Brantford grammar schools and graduated from the University of Toronto in 1872, winning the silver medal in metaphysics. Ill health brought him west in 1881, and he opened a private school in Rapid City, Manitoba, in 1881 which prospered until 1889. After a year in Ontario he returned to Brandon and opened another private academy, closing it to become a member of Brandon College's first faculty in 1899. He was professor of philosophy. On principle he did not belong to any secret societies or clubs. McKee was a Liberal in politics, but never ran for public office.

McKenney, Henry (1826-1886) Merchant. Born in Upper Canada, he came to Red River in 1859 and opened the first hotel (The Royal Hotel) in Manitoba. McKenney and Company also traded in furs and operated a general store at the intersection of the Portage la Prairie trail and the main road of Fort Garry (later famous as Portage and Main). He became sheriff of Assiniboia in 1862. McKenney had earlier been in partnership with his younger half-brother John Schultz,* but the two fell out in 1864 and engaged in a series of court battles that resulted in McKenney obtaining a judgment against Schultz and having him sent to jail. The two men were thereafter bitter enemies. McKenney erected a sawmill in 1861 on the east side of Lake Winnipeg, using a schooner (with too deep a draught) to haul the lumber to the settlement. During the Red River Rebellion of 1869-70 he advocated American annexation, but nevertheless was appointed sheriff by the provisional government in February 1870. When

Confederation with Canada appeared certain, he moved to Pembina, North Dakota, and soon became its sheriff. He returned to Winnipeg in 1874, but sold out in 1876 and moved to Oregon. He died in Washington Territory. *DCB* XI, 562-63.

McKenzie, Albert E. (1870-1964) Businessman, horticulturalist. Born in York, Ontario, he came with his family to Brandon and graduated from the Collegiate Institute there. He took over his father's seed and grain business, shifting the emphasis to the selling of seed, and building up in McKenzie Seeds the largest business of its kind in Western Canada, employing 100 people. He purchased the McFayden Seed Company in 1942. In 1945 he deeded 90 percent of the shares in his company to the province on condition that profits from the operation went to Brandon College. He was president of the Canadian Phoenix Fire Insurance Company and of the Brandon Board of Trade. A Christian Scientist, he was an active leader of the YMCA.

Mackenzie, Sir Alexander (1764-1820) Explorer, fur trader. Born in Stornoway, Scotland, he emigrated to New York with his father and siblings in 1774. His father joined a Loyalist regiment and sent Alexander to school in Montreal. In 1779 he became a clerk in the Montreal office of a fur-trading operation that would become the NWC, actually going into the field in 1784 and heading to the far West in 1785. He went to the Athabasca River in 1787 as second-in-command to Peter Pond,* succeeding him in 1788 as fur trader and explorer. His first journey of discovery in 1789 down the large river that flows from Great Slave Lake (now the Mackenzie River), which he hoped led to the Pacific Ocean, was predicated upon Pond's knowledge and theories. What Mackenzie discovered was that the river opened into the Arctic Ocean. Mackenzie was the ideal explorer, very strong and determined, and was anxious to try again. He learned a bit of surveying technique, and headed off in 1792 up the Peace River, then to the McGregor River and finally the Fraser, which he eventually followed to the Pacific in 1793. Although he remained in the fur trade until 1799, at this point he left for England and published his *Voyages from Montreal . . . to the Frozen and Pacific Oceans* in 1801 to wide acclaim. This work, written in collaboration with his cousin Roderick Mackenzie* and journalist William Combe, was extremely influential in a variety of quarters. It got Mackenzie his knighthood. It provided the NWC with a vision of a coast-to-coast trade, and its descriptions of Red River country first led Lord Selkirk to the region. Mackenzie and Selkirk joined forces in 1808 to buy HBC stock, although Mackenzie apparently did not understand the extent of the grant Selkirk wanted, for he opposed it in 1811. Soon after he retired to Scotland. He died near Dunkeld, probably of Bright's disease. There are papers in the PAM and in the HBCA. See W.K. Lamb, ed., *The Journals and Letters of Sir Alexander Mackenzie*, 4 vols. (1970). For biographies, see Roy Daniells, *Alexander Mackenzie and the North West* (1969) and J.K. Smith, *Alexander Mackenzie, Explorer: The Hero Who Failed* (1973). *DCB* V, 537-43.

McKenzie, Charles (1778-1855) Fur trader. Born in Scotland, he was employed by the NWC in 1802 for service around the Red and Assiniboine Rivers. Later he moved to Fort Dauphin and then to the upper Missouri River. After 1807 he moved to Upper Canada where he spent the remainder of his fur trading career until retirement in 1854. He spent his last year on his son's farm at Red River. His journals of his Missouri sojourn were published as "The Mississouri Indians: A Narrative of Four Trading Expeditions to the Mississouri, 1804-1805-1806," in Masson's *Les Bourgeois de la Compagnie du Nord-Ouest*, I, 315-93. *DCB* V, 556-57.

MacKenzie, Donald (1783-1851) Fur trader. Born in Scotland, he was one of five brothers who were partners in the NWC. He came to Canada in 1800 and entered the service of the Company. In 1810 he joined John Jacob Astor's Pacific Fur Company and journeyed overland in a difficult passage to Astoria in 1811, subsequently playing an important role in Astoria's purchase by the NWC in 1813. He may have sympathized with the Red River Settlement in 1814, but he became a NWC partner and returned to the Columbia in 1816. After the merger he led an expedition to the South Saskatchewan that so impressed George Simpson* that he was appointed to manage the HBC at Red River in 1823, becoming governor of Assiniboia in 1825. He steered the settlement successfully through the flood of 1826. He later broke with Simpson over his decision to "turn off" his native-born wife and marry a European. He retired to Lake Chatauqua, New York, in 1833. He died in Mayville, New York. For a biography, see C.W. Mackenzie, *Donald Mackenzie: "King of the Northwest"* (1937). *DCB* VIII, 557-58.

McKenzie, Frederick (d. 1888) Lawyer. Born in Toronto and educated at Upper Canada College, he came to Winnipeg and was admitted to the bar in 1872. He was the first treasurer of the Bar Society in 1877, as well as the first QC to be created in Manitoba. He later served as president of the Bar Society.

McKenzie, Kenneth (1822-1911) Cattle rancher. Born in Invernesshire, Scotland, he immigrated to Red River around 1867 and settled with his family on the banks of the Rat Creek near Portage la Prairie in 1869. He was an English delegate to the 1870 Convention of Forty from St. Mary's. In 1873, he and Walter Lynch* brought the first herd of registered Shorthorn cattle to Manitoba. He was Liberal MLA from Portage from 1874 to 1878, and in 1886 elected MLA from Lakeside. He was president of the Marquette St. Andrew's Society and the first postmaster at Burnside. He is a member of the Manitoba Agricultural Hall of Fame.

McKenzie, Nancy (c. 1790-1851) Fur-trade wife. The daughter of Roderick McKenzie* and an Indian woman, she was born in the Athabasca country. In 1813 she married NWC trader John George McTavish* according to the custom of the country. When the NWC and HBC merged, McTavish became chief trader responsible for York Factory, and his wife was the leading female at the post. In 1830, however, McTavish contracted a legal marriage in Scotland and left others to tell Nancy. George Simpson* used a dowry contributed by McTavish to arrange a marriage with Pierre Le Blanc,* celebrated on 7 February 1831. She moved west to the Columbia District with her husband in 1838. She died at Fort Victoria. *DCB* VIII, 561.

McKenzie, Roderick (c. 1772-1859) Fur trader. Born in Scotland, he worked with the NWC. After the merger with the HBC in 1821, he was made chief trader. In 1825 he headed Fort William. Promoted to chief factor in 1830, he came west and headed the English River District. In 1839 he was appointed to the Council of Assiniboia. He finally retired in 1852 for "the civilized world of Red River." He resided at Caberleigh Cottage, Red River. *DCB* VIII, 562-63.

Mackenzie, Sir William (1849-1923) Entrepreneur. Born in Kirkfield, Canada, of Scottish descent, he became involved in the railroad contracting business. He was responsible for the electrification of the tram system in Winnipeg in the 1890s. Beginning in 1896, he and Donald Mann* used the charter of the Lake Manitoba Railway and Canal Company as the first building block of the Canadian Northern railway system. He was knighted in 1911.

McLaughlin, John (fl. 1840s) Free trader, opponent of the HBC. He was a nephew of Andrew McDermot* and a British subject who had lived for some years in St. Louis. In 1845 he was reported to be carrying to Washington, D.C., a petition for assistance signed by 1,250 mixed-bloods and Canadian settlers of Red River asking for protection from the HBC monopoly. McLaughlin subsequently went to England, where he was sued for defamatory libel by the HBC for letters he had written to the British government about the situation in Red River. The case was dismissed. He testified at some length in 1857 before the parliamentary committee investigating the HBC monopoly.

McLean, Daniel (1854-1908) Politician. Born in Canada, he came to Manitoba to farm in the Pipestone area in 1882. He was reeve of the township from 1884 to 1886, when he became MLA. He was re-elected in 1888 and a year later became provincial secretary, then education minister. In 1892 he became sheriff of the Central Judicial District (Portage la Prairie) and in 1895 governor of the Central Judicial Jail, which became a reformatory in 1900.

McLean, James (1869-1945) Educator. Born in Mayfair, Ontario, he graduated from the University of Toronto in 1892, and received a PhD from Columbia in 1894. He became chair of the history and political science department at Colorado University, then president of the State University of Idaho in 1900. In 1912 he came to the University of Manitoba as president, retiring in 1934. He published *Essays in the Financial History of Canada*. He moved to Vancouver, then to Glencoe, Ontario. He died in London, Ontario.

McLean, John (b. 1815) Settler. Born in Perthshire, Scotland, he came to Wellington County, Upper Canada, in 1837. He and his family came to Red River aboard the steamer *International* on its maiden voyage in 1862, and settled on a farm at Portage la Prairie. He purchased land from a local Métis for

$375 in gold and subsequently added more from a neighbour, ultimately acquiring a lot seventeen and one-half chains wide on the slough. He sold this land in 1881 for $30,000. The McLeans had much trouble with their Aboriginal neighbours in the early years of settlement. McLean was one of the pioneer heroes of Robert B. Hill's* *Manitoba: History of its early settlement, development and resources* (1890).

McLean, John (1828-1886) Cleric. Born in Banffshire, Scotland, he was educated at King's College, Aberdeen, and ordained in the Church of England in 1858. He came to Canada as curate of St. Paul's Cathedral in London, serving to 1866 when he came to Red River as rector of St. John's Cathedral and archdeacon of Assiniboia, also serving as professor of divinity and warden of St. John's College. He was a college friend of Bishop Robert Machray* and his personal choice for these positions. During the Red River Rebellion McLean counselled moderation. He frequently served as a go-between in complex negotiations over Riel's prisoners, and helped convince Riel to spare the life of Charles Boulton.* In 1874 he was consecrated the first bishop of Saskatchewan, and he died in Prince Albert. *DCB* XI, 570-72.

McLean, John (1851-1928) Methodist missionary, writer. Born in Kilmarnock, Scotland, he came to Canada in 1873 and was educated at Victoria University (BA 1882, MA 1887) and Illinois Wesleyan University (PhD 1888). He served as a missionary to the Blood Indians in Alberta and held various charges in the West until he retired from the ministry in 1911. In 1895 he was president of the Manitoba and North West Conference of the Methodist Church. He founded the McLean Mission in Winnipeg, and from 1921 to 1928 was librarian of Wesley College. He wrote extensively on the Indians of the Northwest, publishing books such as *The Indians, Their Manners and Customs* (1889), *Canadian Savage Folk: The Native Tribes of Canada* (1896), *The Warden of the Plains and Other Stories* (1896). He also wrote many biographies of prominent Methodist pioneer churchmen in the West, and as "Robin Rustler" contributed children's fiction to many periodicals. He was an ardent opponent of the Winnipeg General Strike in 1919. His diary and extensive papers are in the Victoria University Archives, Toronto.

McLean, John (1882-1977) Lawyer. Born in Glasgow, Scotland, he graduated with a BA from

Manitoba College in 1904. He was Manitoba's first Rhodes Scholar that same year. After attending Oxford he applied to the Indian Educational Service, part of the civil service administering India, and served there eight years before joining the Canadian army. He was admitted to the Manitoba bar in 1920. He became president of the Winnipeg branch of the League for Social Reconstruction. He published actively in philosophy.

McLean, Stewart (1913-1996) Politician. Born in Dauphin, Manitoba, he was educated at Dauphin Collegiate and Dauphin Normal School. After one year of teaching he attended the University of Saskatchewan, then articled in Tisdale, Saskatchewan. He contracted tuberculosis before entering the RCAF. After WWII he practised law in Dauphin, served as mayor from 1955 to 1958, then became Conservative MLA from 1958 to 1969. He was the minister of education responsible for the major school consolidation of the province. Later he became a judge in Saskatchewan.

McLenaghan, James Osborne (1891-1950) Politician. Born in Balderson's Corner, Ontario, he was educated in Portage la Prairie and at the University of Manitoba. He read law with Arthur Meighen.* He was first elected Conservative MLA for Kildonan in 1927, and was re-elected in 1932, 1936, 1941, 1945, and for a new riding in 1949. He held many cabinet posts in the 1940s. He lived at Hawthorne Lodge, Little Britain. He sometimes farmed at Selkirk. There are some papers at the PAM.

MacLeod, Alan Arnett (1899-1918) War hero. Born in Stonewall, Manitoba, he joined the Royal Air Force upon his eighteenth birthday, and by November 1917 he was flying in France in a two-seated bomber. In March of 1918 he crashed his airplane in No Man's Land after it was hit six times with enemy fire. He dragged his airplane's observer from the burning wreckage at great personal risk, and the pair were saved by South African troops. He was awarded the Victoria Cross. He returned to Winnipeg in September, but died of influenza five days before the 11 November armistice.

McLeod, John (1788-1849) Fur trader. Born in Stornoway, Scotland, he joined the HBC in 1811 and helped Lord Selkirk* recruit in the Hebrides. He then sailed with Miles Macdonell* in 1811 as part of the settlement's advance party, arriving in Red River in 1812. McLeod spent the next few years founding posts in what is now southern Manitoba, and he was responsible for the HBC's Red River business in 1814-15. He was arrested in 1817 by the Nor'Westers for confiscating their property at Pembina with Robert Semple* in 1816, and was taken to Montreal for trial. The case was dismissed. In 1818 he returned to Red River with a brigade that included the earliest Roman Catholic missionaries to the settlement. He was made chief trader at the merger and sent west across the mountains. He returned to Norway House in 1826 and continued in HBC service until his death, although George Simpson* was highly critical of him. He died of cholera. Extracts from McLeod's journal of 1811-16 were published as "Diary, etc., of chief trader John MacLeod . . .," ed. H.G. Gunn, in North Dakota State Historical Society *Collections* 2 (1908): 115-34. His papers are in the NAC. There are also papers in the PAM. *DCB* VII, 570-71.

McLeod, John (1821-1920) Settler. Born in Red River, he carried the mail between HBC posts, and later worked at the first gristmill at Red River. A veritable giant, he was said to be six feet, 10 inches tall. He later trapped in the Whitemouth District.

MacLeod, Margaret Arnett (c. 1878-1966) Historian, writer. Born in Ontario, she lived in Brandon and Stonewall before moving to Winnipeg. Her husband, Dr. A.N. MacLeod, was a Stonewall dentist. Her son, Alan,* who died during WWI, was awarded the Victoria Cross. She began researching and writing history in the 1930s. Her first work, *The Frozen Priest of Pembina,* was published in 1935. She subsequently edited the letters of Letitia Hargrave* (1947) and co-authored a biography of Cuthbert Grant* with W. L. Morton.* She also researched the songs of Pierre Falcon.* She became a life member of the Manitoba Historical Society in 1964 and a member of the Order of the Buffalo. She died in a house fire at her home on Maryland Street. Her research papers are at the UML Archives, and her personal papers are at the PAM.

McLeod, Sarah (Ballenden) See Ballenden, Sarah.

McLuhan, Herbert Marshall (1911-1980) Educator, media guru. Born in Edmonton, he moved to Winnipeg in 1915. He attended Kelvin Technical High School before enrolling in the University of

Manitoba in 1928. He received a BA (Hons.) in 1933 and an MA in 1934. He then spent two years at Cambridge University (Trinity College) on an IODE fellowship. He was hired by the University of Wisconsin as a graduate asistant in 1936-37, at which time he converted to Roman Catholicism. In 1937 he moved to St. Louis to take up an appointment in English at Saint Louis University, a Jesuit institution. He taught the New Criticism and began doctoral work, receiving his doctorate from Cambridge in 1943 and producing the start of a long string of academic publications on literary subjects. While in St. Louis he struck up a friendship with the English polymath Wyndham Lewis, who was living in exile in North America. In 1944 he moved to Assumption College, Windsor, and in 1946 he joined St. Michael's College, University of Toronto. He remained at the University of Toronto until his death. His early writings in literary criticism, published in the academic journals, have been much neglected. An interest in popular culture — begun to facilitate communication with students, and fostered by Harold Adams Innis — led to *The Mechanical Bride: Folklore of Industrial Man* (1951). He wrote *Report on Project in Understanding the New Media* (1960) In 1962 he produced *The Gutenberg Galaxy: The Making of Typographic Man*. His most influential work appeared in 1964: *Understanding Media: The Extensions of Man*. Like all his work on the media, these were discursive tours of Western culture with some underlying theses. *Understanding Media* became unexpectedly popular, selling 100,000 copies in paperback soon after publication. McLuhan's major thesis, that electronic media had made books obsolescent, made him a guru for the electronic age, and he became the subject of increasing amounts of academic attention, much of it highly critical. In 1967 he went to Fordham University to take up an endowed chair in humanities for a year. While there he was operated on for removal of a brain tumour. His later books include *The Medium Is the Message* (1967), *War and Peace in the Global Village* (1968), *Counterblast* (1969), and *Culture Is Our Business* (1970). A number of his later works were done in collaboration, such as *From Cliché to Archetype* (with Wilfred Watson). He continued to expand upon his ideas in journalistic interviews. He enjoyed his fame, although he once said, "Temperamentally, I'm a stodgy conservative. If there are going to be McLuhanites, you can be sure that I'm not going to be one of them." He died following a stroke in 1979. A selection of his correspondence, edited by Matie

Molinaro, Corinne McLuhan, and William Toye, was published as *Letters of Marshall McLuhan* (1987). A biography written by W. Terrence Robinson was published in 1997. His papers are at the NAC.

McMicken, Alexander (1837-1916) Banker, politician. Born in Upper Canada, he was educated at the Toronto Academy. He entered the grain business in Windsor, and after Confederation became head of the western division of the government secret service. In 1871 he came to Winnipeg and became a banker, initially assisting his father at the Government Savings Bank and then opening his own bank (McMicken's Bank) in 1872. He was a member of early city councils in Winnipeg and was elected mayor in 1882; his term was marked by the failure of the city to recover from the economic bust after the boom of 1881-82. He lost heavily in land speculation, like many others. As banker he had raised funds for the City of Winnipeg through bond issues, and as mayor he became associated with overspending. Among his accomplishments were construction of the traffic bridge over the Assiniboine River at Osborne Street in 1882, the development of the first race track, and the establishment of the first cricket club. He was Provincial police magistrate from 1900 to 1913, and a founding member of Augustine Presbyterian Church. McMicken also established the IOOF in the province. He died in Winnipeg. *DCB* XIV, 727-29.

McMicken, Gilbert (1813-1891) Policeman, land agent. Born in Scotland, he came to Canada in 1832. He entered politics as MLA for Welland (1857-61). In 1870, he met the Red River delegates at the border between Ontario and New York while he was commissioner of police for the Dominion. He was very active in suppressing the Fenians. In 1871 he was appointed Dominion lands Agent for Manitoba, with instructions to settle the Métis land question. He served as acting inspector of the Manitoba penitentiary (1874-77). He was later elected MLA from Cartier (1879-83), serving as Assembly Speaker (1880-83). *DCB* XII, 675-80.

McMicken, Hamilton Grant (1852-1919) Railway executive. Born in Queenston, Canada, he came to Winnipeg in 1873, and opened a stagecoach service. In 1877 he entered the steamship business, and two years later began his years with various railroad companies, moving in 1892 to Toronto with the Great

Northern Railway, which employed him until his death in London.

MacMillan, Daniel Hunter (1846-1933) Soldier, politician, grain dealer. Born in Whitby, Canada, to a Scots father and an Irish mother, he served with the Canadian Volunteers on the Niagara Frontier in 1864, came west in 1870 as a captain under Garnet Wolseley,* and remained in Winnipeg. Entering the grain business, he founded the first steam-powered flour mill in the city. He remained active in military affairs, served as a major in the 1885 North-West Rebellion (winning a medal of honour), and in 1887 he became commanding officer of his regiment, the 95th Battalion Winnipeg Rifles. A Liberal, he served as MLA for Winnipeg (1880-83 and 1888-1900), and served as provincial treasurer (1889-1900). He was the first president of the Winnipeg Grain Exchange. He served for over 10 years as lieutenant-governor of Manitoba (1900-1911), and was created Knight Commander of the Order of St. Michael and St. George in 1902. There are papers at the PAM.

McMillan, James (1783-1858) Fur trader, farmer. Born in Scotland, he joined the NWC around 1803, spending most of his time on the Columbia River. He joined the HBC as chief trader and was promoted to chief factor in 1827, again serving on the West Coast. In 1830 he was brought to Red River to establish an HBC experimental farm, but the venture did not prosper and he hated the "Backbiting and Slander" of Red River society. After two years he was transferred near Montreal, and he retired in 1839 to Scotland. A number of his country-born children settled in Red River. *DCB* VIII, 583-84.

McMurachy, Malcolm S. Joseph (1878-1960) Agricultural researcher. Born in York County, Ontario, he came to Shoal Lake, Manitoba with his family in 1882. In 1935 he developed a rust-resistant wheat that would help lead to the development of the Selkirk seed variety. He supplied seed to the scientific community in that year. In 1954 he received an award from the Canadian government for his contribution. He is a member of the Manitoba Agricultural Hall of Fame.

McMurray, Edward James (1878-1968) Lawyer. Born in Thorndale, Ontario, he moved to Saskatchewan in 1878 and to Winnipeg in 1880. He graduated from Manitoba College in 1903, and

worked his way through law school by teaching at night. A criminal lawyer, he was defence counsel for the strike leaders of 1919, losing most of the cases. He was more successful with clients in murder trials, claiming that in 26 cases they had escaped the gallows. He was elected Liberal MP for Winnipeg North in 1921 and was named solicitor general in the MacKenzie King Cabinet in 1925. He became a QC in 1934.

McMurray, Mildred Beatrice (1900-1959) Lawyer. Born at Solsgirth, Manitoba, she taught school in northern Saskatchewan, entered the University of Manitoba in 1913, and graduated in 1917. She received her LLB in 1921 and was called to the bar in 1922. She was solicitor for the United Farmers of Manitoba and president of the Professional and Business Women's Club of Winnipeg and the Junior Service League of the CNIB. McMurray was the first and for years the only woman lawyer in the province.

McNaught, Kenneth (1918-1997) Educator, historian. Born in Toronto, he was educated at Upper Canada College and the University of Toronto and taught at United College in Winnipeg, resigning over the dismissal of a colleague, Harry Crowe,* in 1959. He then took up an appointment at the University of Toronto, where he taught until his retirement. He was a socialist called by many "the original Red Tory." McNaught was the author of a biography of J.S. Woodsworth, *A Prophet in Politics* (1959), *The Penguin History of Canada,* and (with David Bercuson) *The Winnipeg General.*

McNichol, Andrew Robert (1861-1931) Insurance executive. Born in Canada, he came to Manitoba with $12,000 to enter the real estate and insurance business. He became western Canadian manager of the Mutual Reserve Fund Life Association of New York, later promoted to General Manager of the North Western Department, which included six American states. He later became director of agencies of Mutural Reserve Life in New York, supervising 6,000 agents. He left the company over premium policies, eventually returning to Winnipeg to establish the firm of A.R. McNichol Limited with capital of $6 million. A bachelor, he lived at the Fort Garry Hotel and made substantial gifts to the Winnipeg General Hospital, the Children's Hospital, the Children's Home, the Margaret Scott Nursing Mission, and many other charities.

Macoun, John (1831-1920) Educator, botanist, publicist. Born in County Down, Ireland, he came to Canada in 1850. After farming he turned to the study of botany, and was appointed professor of natural history at Albert College in Belleville, Ontario, in 1868. In 1872 he accompanied the Sir Sandford Fleming* party west, and later joined several other expeditions. He joined the Geological Survey of Canada in 1879 and was appointed its botanist in 1881, and its assistant director and naturalist in 1887. A charter member of the Royal Society of Canada, he travelled and collected throughout his life. He moved to British Columbia in 1912. Macoun's work in the 1870s led him to believe that all the land of the southern prairies was cultivable, and he regarded it as his duty to publicize the potential of the Canadian West. His influential book *Manitoba and the Great North-West* (1882), popularized his theories but also helped to create an unrealistic public image of the West. He published other important books, such as *The Forests of Canada and their Distribution* (1895), but none were as significant as his Manitoba volume. His *Autobiography* (1922) was completed by his son. See also Doug Owram, *The Promise of Eden: The Canadian Expansionist Movement and the Idea of the West 1856-1900* (1980).

McPhail, James Roy (1889-1971) Farmer, farm agency executive. Born in Acton, Ontario, he came to Manitoba in 1901, and settled with his family on a farm near Brandon. He purchased his own land in 1910 and farmed until 1927, when he became president of the Manitoba Cooperative Livestock Producers Limited. In 1932 he became chair of the provisional board of the Canadian Livestock Cooperative (Western) Limited. In 1933-34 he was president of the United Farmers of Manitoba, and from 1937 he served as managing secretary of the Canadian Livestock Sales Agency. He was chair of the Milk Control Board from 1941 to 1961. He is a member of the Manitoba Agricultural Hall of Fame.

McPherson, Ewen Alexander (1879-1954) Lawyer, politician. Born in Missouri, he came to Portage la Prairie at an early age. Educated in Portage, he was a schoolmate of T.A. Crerar.* He was called to the bar in 1904, and first ran for public office in 1910. Over the next 15 years he contested seven elections, winning four. He was the leading local opponent of Arthur Meighen* for many years. He was elected to the Manitoba legislature in 1914, and in 1926 defeated Meighen to become Liberal MP for Portage la Prairie. In 1932 he became provincial treasurer in the Bracken* government, and was famous for not saying anything in the legislature. He was named chief justice of the Court of King's Bench in 1937, and was chief justice of Manitoba from 1944 to 1954. He was also chair of the Winnipeg Foundation. He died in Kenora.

McPherson, Stewart (1907-1996) Broadcaster. Born in Winnipeg, he was raised on Victor Street. He left a job as an undertaker's assistant in 1936 to travel to London, where he refereed hockey. During WWII he became the BBC's "voice from the air," covering the air war, and in 1942 won a listeners' poll as British Male Voice of the Year. After the war he worked for station WCCO in Minneapolis, then for Winnipeg Enterprises before joining CJAY (CKY-TV). He was a colour commentator for the early Winnipeg Jets hockey broadcasts.

McPhillips, Henry Thomas (1850-1913) Journalist. Born in York County, Canada, he learned the printing trade in Toronto. He came to Winnipeg in 1881 to publish a newspaper that would eventually (after his time) become the *North-West Review.* He moved to the Department of Inland Revenue in the North-West Territories, then to the United States as a journalist. In 1913 he ran a weekly newspaper in Assiniboia.

McRae, Duncan (1813-1898) Stonemason, architect. Born in the Hebrides, Scotland, he joined the HBC as a stonemason at Upper Fort Garry in 1837. In the 1840s he worked for the HBC and others along the Red River. Buildings he designed include St. Andrew's Rectory (1854), St. Peter's Church and Rectory (1853-54), Kildonan Presbyterian Church (1852-54), Little Britain Presbyterian Church (1874), and Twin Oaks (c. 1858). He was also probably largely responsible for the Church of St. Andrews-on-the-Red (1845-49). He also worked on St. John's Cathedral. All these buildings were executed in stone in early Gothic style.

McRae, John C. (1858-1921) Police chief. He first joined the Winnipeg Police in 1882, later becoming chief of police and serving for over 20 years in this position. He was a big man (over six feet tall) with a steely grey moustache. He advocated regulated prostitution and unwillingly conducted a series of raids on Winnipeg brothels in 1904. He continued to thwart the vice reformers through the early years of the century.

McRobie, William Orme (1838-1908) Fire chief. Born in Perthshire, Scotland he came to Montreal with his family in 1850. Soon after, he joined the Montreal fire brigade as a volunteer, and stayed on when the brigade became paid. He became captain of the salvage corps in 1872 and published his memoir, *Fighting the Flames,* in 1881. In 1882 he became Winnipeg's first fire chief, a post he held until his retirement in 1889, when he began manufacturing chemical fire extinguishers, based in part on his own inventions and designs.

McTavish, John George (d. 1847) Fur trader. Born in Argyllshire, Scotland, he joined the NWC in 1798, was stationed first at James Bay and later on the West Coast. He bought the Pacific Fur Company's assets for the NWC in 1813. He was captured at Grand Rapids (now in Manitoba) in 1817 and sent to England for trial on charges connected to the fur trade war, but soon returned and became a chief factor at the merger of the HBC and the NWC. George Simpson* had nothing but praise for his management skills, and after 1824 he presided at council in Simpson's absence. In 1830 he married in Scotland without making provision for his mixed-blood wife, an action that caused much criticism in the country, although Simpson (who had acted similarly) supported him fully. Nonetheless, he was becoming corpulent and intemperate, and was transferred to an undemanding post near Montreal in 1836, where he remained until his death. *DCB* VII, 577-78.

McTavish, John H. (1837-1888) Accountant. Born in Upper Canada, he was educated at the Jesuits' College and High School, Montreal. He married a daughter of John Rowand, an HBC chief factor, and joined the company in 1856. An accountant at Fort Garry in 1869-70, he was unrelated to Governor McTavish. He was a Roman Catholic and spoke French fluently. He was rumoured to be a sympathizer of the Métis. He was in charge of Upper Fort Garry after the departure of Governor McTavish* in 1870. He was elected Conservative MLA from Ste. Anne in the first Manitoba legislature. McTavish was made a member of the North-West Territories Council in 1874, but left to became land commissioner of the CPR instead. He became chief land

commissioner in 1881. McTavish was a close friend of Donald A. Smith* (Lord Strathcona).

McTavish, William (1815-1870) Fur trader, governor. Born in Edinburgh, Scotland, he came to the Bay in 1833 as an apprentice with the HBC under the patronage of his uncle, chief factor John George McTavish.* He worked at York Factory under James Hargrave,* soon to be his brother-in-law. In 1857 he moved to Red River to take charge of Upper Fort Garry, the most "troublesome and complicated charge" in the company. He was tall, sandy-haired, and he sported Palmerston whiskers with a heavy moustache. He soon married Mary Sarah McDermot, the mixed-blood Catholic daughter of Andrew McDermot* and sister of Annie McDermot Bannatyne.* Appointed governor of Assiniboia in 1858, he believed the governance of the fur trade and the settlement should be separated. Nevertheless, in 1869-70 he was governor of both Rupert's Land and Assiniboia. His lack of action in the Canadian crisis was partly due to his dislike of politics and his ill health, but also because of his sympathies with the old inhabitants. He believed the locals had a right to a proper arrangement with Canada, and he objected to Canadian imperialism. He criticized Canada for ignoring the inhabitants. From 16 November 1869 to February 1870 he was virtually (and sometimes actually) imprisoned in Fort Garry by Riel, mostly bedridden with advanced tuberculosis. What actions he took were through the agency of his private secretary, J.J. Hargrave* (his nephew) and A.G.B. Bannatyne,* his brother-in-law. He resigned on 15 January 1870. He and his family left for Scotland on 17 May, and he died upon disembarkation at Liverpool in July. McTavish had all sorts of power in 1869 that he refused to exercise. Why he did not act is a fascinating question. See F.E. Bartlett, "William Mactavish, the Last Governor of Assiniboia" (MA diss., University of Manitoba, 1964). *DCB* IX, 529-32.

McVicar, George Duncan (1846-1889) Merchant. Born in Chatham, Canada, he came to Winnipeg in 1869 and was imprisoned by Louis Riel in December 1869. He escaped and made his way overland with John Schultz* to Duluth, Minnesota. His health — like Schultz's — never recovered from this arduous winter journey. He returned to Manitoba in 1870, and with his brother opened the implement supply house of J. and G.D. McVicar. He then operated the West's first woollen mill, in St. Boniface, but lost the mill to fire. He became an appraiser in the Winnipeg Customs House, and later manager of a savings and loan company until his death.

McVicar, Victoria ("Vickie," c. 1842-1899) Heroine. Distantly related to George McVicar,* she was a cousin of Mrs. John Sutherland and of Mrs. Bernard Ross. Her father was Robert McVicar of the HBC. She visited Red River from Fort William over the winter of 1869-70. She was in Red River by 7 November 1869, when George McVicar wrote to Josephine Larwell, "I met here one evening a Miss McVicar from Fort William who claimed to be a cousin, and I have no objection to owning her for a relation for she is a jolly good girl. She is here for a visit and will remain all winter. I expect a bit of a flirtation; in fact she is the only girl I have met out here that would induce me to indulge in such a thing." She visited prisoners at the Upper Fort on 6 January 1870, and according to George McVicar, "when she heard that I had escaped, she came about twenty miles to see me; did anything in her power to aid me; gave letters to her mother and brothers at Ft. William; took charge of my things and now keeps me posted with regard to every movement in Red River." With A.G. Bannatyne* she helped plead in February 1870 for the release of the prisoners, and may have brought Mrs. Sutherland back from Kildonan to plead for the life of Captain Boulton.* There were rumours that she had some kind of flirtation with Louis Riel, but these have never been confirmed. She subsequently returned to Fort William (now Thunder Bay), where she was a successful real-estate speculator and assisted her sister in running the local post office. She was active in the Imperial Federation League and was an ardent spiritualist. She died in Fort William. *DCB* XII, 690-91.

McWilliams, Margaret (Stovell) (1875-1952) Feminist, historian. Born in Toronto, she graduated from the University of Toronto in 1898 and began her journalism career in Detroit. She came to Winnipeg in 1910 and was active in the women's movement for years. She was elected president of the University Women's Club in 1913. She was first president of the Canadian Federation of University Women in 1919, and president of the Women's Canadian Club in 1922. She was Winnipeg's second female city councillor, serving from 1933 to 1940. She wrote *Manitoba Milestones* (1928); with her husband Roland* and under the pseudonym Oliver Stowell, *If I Were King of Canada* (1931); and *This New Canada* (1948). She was frequently a Canadian representative at international conferences. McWilliams was instrumental in the resurrection of the Manitoba Historical Society in 1944, serving as president from 1944 to 1948. See the biography by Mary Kinnear, *Margaret McWilliams: An Interwar Feminist* (1991).

McWilliams, Roland Fairbairn (1874-1957) Lawyer, lieutenant-governor. Born in Peterborough, Ontario, he was educated locally and at the University of Toronto (BA 1896, LLB 1897). He was called to the bar in 1899, and practised law in Peterborough from 1899 to 1910, also serving as mayor in 1907. He moved to Winnipeg in 1910, joined the law firm of Sir James Aikins,* and lectured in constitutional law at the Manitoba Law School. A Liberal, he was appointed lieutenant-governor in 1940 and served until 1953. He and his wife Margaret,* after a visit in 1926, wrote *Russia in 1926* (1927), and he wrote *Does History Repeat Itself?* (1932). He was a champion football player and later a canoeist. A temperance man — alcohol was not served at Government House under his regime — he was also active in the YMCA. His papers are at the PAM.

Macenko, Paul (1897-1991) Musician. Born in Kyrykivka, Ukraine, he served in the Russian and Ukrainian armies during and after WWI. He was educated at the Prague Music Conservatory (doctorate in music) and came to Winnipeg in 1936 as choirmaster at the Ukrainian National Home. He co-founded the Ukrainian Cultural and Education Centre in Winnipeg and wrote extensively on Ukrainian music, especially church music. He died in St. Boniface.

Madill, Robert (1833-1921) Pioneer. Born in County Monaghan, Ireland, he came to Canada in 1852 and to Manitoba in 1877. He settled in Palestine (Gladstone), and in 1879 was one of the first settlers in the Murchison district around Riding Mountain.

Magar (or Mager), Victor (1849-1930) Businessman, politician. Born in Lorraine, then part of France, he came to Red River in 1859 with his family via Minnesota. In 1860 he enrolled in the Collège de Saint-Boniface, and then entered into business with his father, acquiring a sawmill and gristmill on the Red River on the present site of the St. Boniface Hospital. In 1870 he was present at the execution of Thomas Scott,* and he served in the Métis corps in the Fenian troubles of 1871. He later claimed that the band with Colonel Wolseley* had played "God Save the Queen" upon first raising the British flag at Upper Fort Garry in 1870. In 1872 he purchased land and began a business as a market gardener. He was elected councillor of St. Boniface in 1882, and began a 12-year term as reeve of St. Boniface in 1883. He was a prominent member of the Catholic parish of St. Boniface.

Magill, Robert (1873-1930) Educator, civil servant. He came to Canada in 1903, and was on the staff of Presbyterian College (Nova Scotia) as principal when Dalhousie University took it over in 1908. He served on royal commissions on coal fields in Cape Breton, and in 1915 became chair of the Board of Grain Commissioners of Canada and secretary of the Winnipeg Grain Exchange, which he served until his death. He represented Canada in grain-sale discussions with England in 1919-20. He died in Battle Creek, Michigan.

Magnusson, Johannes (1852-1917) Pioneer. Born in Iceland, he came to Canada in 1874 and settled in Gimli in 1875. He was a member of the provincial council that supervised the colony of New Iceland in 1875-76, and he homesteaded in the Arnes district, becoming reeve of Gimli municipality (1888-96 and 1900) and secretary (1901-8).

Mair, Charles (1838-1927) Poet. Born in Lanark County, Upper Canada, he attended Queen's University with John Schultz* but did not graduate. In the spring of 1868 in Ottawa he helped organize the secret movement "Canada First." About the same time he published *Dreamland and Other Poems*, an echo of John Keats. He received a patronage appointment from William McDougall* as secretary for the Canadian mission to London to negotiate the transfer of Rupert's Land, but was unable to go. He settled instead for an appointment as assistant on the Canadian road works near Red River, and was also named Red River correspondent of several Ontario newspapers, including the *Globe*. His comments about Red River mixed-blood ladies led to his being horsewhipped by Annie Bannatyne* in February 1869, and Louis Riel responded in print to his writing. He married a niece of John Schultz and was one of the most active of the pro-Canadian party in Red River in 1869. He was part of the group that surrendered to Louis Riel at John Schultz's house in December 1869, but he escaped a month later. He went first to Portage la Prairie, then south to St. Paul, travelling east with Donald A. Smith.* He appeared at a number of rallies in Ontario in 1870 to stir up hostility to Riel and the provisional government, and testified before the Senate subcommittee in April 1870. He received $1,910 compensation for lost property and $66 for imprisonment in 1873. He was a storekeeper in Portage la Prairie until 1883, and was an officer of the Governor General's Body Guards in 1885. Under pressure from his friends, he sought Canadian topics to write about, and in 1886 he published *Tecumseh*, a verse-drama well regarded at the time, subsequently being elected a fellow of the Royal Society in 1889. He later helped found Kelowna, British Columbia, and wrote *Through the Mackenzie Basin* (1908), based upon his work as secretary of the commission that negotiated with Indians there in 1899. He moved to Victoria in 1921. Once a highly regarded Canadian poet, his reputation has slipped into eclipse, at least partly because of the rawness of his Canadian nationalism. His papers are at Queen's University. For a biography, see Norman Shrive, *Charles Mair Literary Nationalist* (1965). Consult also Fred Cogswell, *Charles Mair and His Works* (1980).

Mair, Elizabeth Louise McKenney ("Eliza," 1849-1905) Postmistress. Born in Ontario, daughter of Augustus McKenney, she married Charles Mair* in Red River in 1869. Shortly after their honeymoon, the couple were imprisoned together in Upper Fort Garry by Louis Riel. After the Red River Rebellion, she accompanied Mair west to Portage la Prairie and then to Prince Albert (in present-day Saskatchewan). When the poet travelled in the 1890s, she remained in Prince Albert as postmistress to assure the family finances.

Major, William James (1881-1953) Lawyer, judge. Born in Yeovil, Somerset, England, he came to Canada in 1901 to farm. He read law in Winnipeg, was called to the bar in 1913, and ran for the provincial legislature in 1926. He became John Bracken's* attorney general in 1927, serving until 1941 when he took an appointment to the court of King's Bench. As attorney general he prepared Manitoba's briefs to the Rowell-Sirois Commission and supervised Manitoba's survey of enemy aliens in 1939 before the start of WWII. There are papers at the PAM.

Malaher, Gerald W. (1903-1984) Civil servant, conservationist. Born in England, he came to Canada in 1920. He attended St. John's College and the University of New Brunswick (BSc in Forestry, 1931). He served as a forester with Manitoba Natural Resources for many years. In 1942 he become Northern supervisor for the Department of Game and Fisheries, and in 1946 became director of Game and Fisheries, serving in that post to his retirement in 1967. He was a founding member of the Manitoba Museum of Man and Nature. An autobiography, *The North I Love,* was published in 1984. There are papers at the PAM.

Malcolm, George John Huntley (1865-1930) Politician. Born in Kussowie, India, son of a British army colonel, he was educated in England, attending the same school as Rudyard Kipling. He claimed to have been one of the characters in Kipling's *Stalky and Company*. He subsequently attended the Guelph Agricultural College and graduated in 1884. He came to Birtle in 1885 and was active in the Birtle Agricultural Society and the Manitoba Grain Growers' Association. He was elected to the Manitoba legislature as a Liberal in 1909, sitting until 1922. He entered the Norris Cabinet as minister of agriculture from 1920 to 1922. In 1922, it was rumoured that he was to become premier in a farmers' government. Instead, he did not contest the 1922 election and never again served in public life.

Malmros, Oscar (1826-1909) American consul. Born in Denmark, he settled in St. Paul, Minnesota, in 1853. Appointed American consul in Winnipeg on 1 July 1869, he arrived in the village on 13 August of that year. Publication in an official American

Senate document of his consular report of 11 September 1869 — which criticized both the HBC and the Roman Catholic clergy — led him to find his position in Fort Garry "untenable" by March of 1870. A small and very near-sighted man, he was on his way by dog train from Winnipeg to St. Cloud when he became separated from his dogs and driver. A.W. Graham's* party found him nearly exhausted in a snowbank. According to Graham, "we dug a bed in the snow, laid in it our robe and blankets, put him in, gave him a swallow of brandy and covered him up, and went on to Grand Forks. His man came back and found him by seeing a piece of the axe handle protruding through the snow, brought him to Grand Forks, where there was a log house and mail station." He spent the remainder of his life in the United States.

Maltman, William (1901-1971) Artist. Born in England, he moved to Canada in 1917. He came to Winnipeg that same year and worked for a commercial printer, than from 1918 to 1925 for Brigden's. He studied at the Winnipeg School of Art from 1921 to 1924. He spent much of his spare time sketching the scenery of Manitoba, often with Walter J. Phillips.* Maltman left Winnipeg in 1927, moving to Chicago and New York before settling in Toronto as an artist. He died in Victoria.

Mann, Donald (1853-1934) Entrepreneur. Born in Canada, he became a railway contractor in the West, often in association with William Mackenzie.* In 1896 the two men purchased the charter of the Lake Manitoba Railway and Canal Company, and used it as the basis for their Canadian Northern Railway.

Mann, Leslie Douglas (1923-1977) Musician. Born in Edmonton, he became principal clarinetist of the CBC Winnipeg Orchestra in 1958 and of the Winnipeg Symphony Orchestra in 1960. Largely self-taught, he became increasingly interested in composition, completing three symphonies before his early death.

Marest, Pierre-Gabriel (1662-1714) Missionary. Born in France and sent to Canada in 1694, he served as chaplain for the expedition led by Iberville* that year, keeping a journal for the entire period. He remained as chaplain at Fort Bourbon until 1696, when he was captured by the English. He subsequently was sent to the Illinois confederacy in 1698, which he evangelized until his death. *DCB* II, 454-55.

Mariaggi, Frank (c. 1847-1918) Restaurateur, hotelier. Born in Corsica, he came to Winnipeg with the Wolseley Expedition in 1870. He later opened a restaurant and was renowned as a chef. He also opened a hotel named after himself at the corner of Albert and McDermot streets, and acquired a fortune in real-estate speculation and hotels. He returned to Corsica in 1908 and died there.

Marion, Narcisse (b. 1805) Blacksmith. A Winnipeg blacksmith, he was regarded as a "loyal" Métis. After the Red River Rebellion he claimed for $130.50 for damages from the compensation commission. Commissioner Johnson recommended him for $100 as a special case of hardship, writing, "His service to the insurgents in the Fort was certainly rendered reluctantly, and under a species of duress, tho' not such as to entitle him strictly to compensation for imprisonment under the vote, as I understand it."

Marion, Roger (b. 1846) Politician. Born at York Factory, he was educated at the Collège de Saint-Boniface. He was employed by the Customs Service (1872-76), then served as Manitoba license commissioner (1879-85). He was a St. Boniface alderman (1883-86), then mayor of St. Boniface (1887-89). He was also Conservative MPP for Carillon (1886-88). In 1891 he was elected president of the Union Métisse Saint-Joseph.

Markle, Fletcher (1921-1991) TV producer. Born in Winnipeg, he was active on the CBC by the time he was 20. He served in the RCAF, worked for the BBC, and in the United States became the producer of *Studio One,* the famous CBS television drama series of the early 1950s. He returned to Canada in 1963 to produce television for the CBC, and became head of television in 1970, introducing the *Beachcombers* and *Jalna* series. One of his colleagues once commented that he had all the talents "except for the talent to make use of them." He died in California.

Marsh, Helen (1917-1995) Journalist, publisher. Born in Dauphin, Manitoba, she was educated locally. Her family had long published the *Dauphin Herald,* and she became its editor in 1949. She spent 18 years on the Dauphin town council and was Manitoba's first representative among Canada's United Nations delegation. She was the first female president of the Manitoba Association of Weekly Newspapers. She received an honorary doctorate from the University of Manitoba and served on its board of governors. Her memoir, *There's Lots of Bush — Between the Tea and the Green,* appeared in 1988.

Marshall, Henry John (1840-1911) Farmer. Born in Bombay, India, he came to Canada in 1850 with his family. A carpenter, he moved to Manitoba in 1871 to farm in the Springfield district. In 1882 he became superintendent of the Winnipeg city market, a post he held until his death.

Marten, Humphrey (c. 1729-c. 1792) HBC chief factor. First engaged by the Company in 1750, he was appointed second at York in 1759, acting head in 1761, and then became second at Fort Albany. He finally became chief at York Factory in 1775. He became quite ill but would not leave Rupert's Land until his resignation in 1786. *DCB* IV, 518-20.

Martigny et de La Trinité, Jean Baptiste, le Moyne de (1662-1709) Soldier. He spent most of the period from 1686 to 1709 as a French officer in Hudson Bay, first commanding an overland expedition to James Bay in 1686, which left Montreal on 30 March and arrived on 18 June. The detachment captured four HBC posts. Two years later he carried dispatches from James Bay to Quebec over the winter. He was part of Iberville's successful expedition of 1694 and served as commandant of Fort Bourbon in 1698. He was part of another invading party to James Bay in 1709. *DCB* II, 405-6.

Martin, Alfonse Fortunat (1849-1905) Surveyor, politician. Born in Rimouski, Canada, he was educated at Rimouski College, later studying surveying and civil engineering. He became a Dominion Land surveyor in 1871, and came to Manitoba in 1872 to settle in West Lynn, being employed over the years in various surveys. A Liberal, he became MLA for Ste. Agathe in 1874, and led the Opposition a year later. Defeated in the 1879 and 1883 elections, he was elected MLA from Morris in 1886. He supported "Manitoba First," the extension of the boundary to Hudson Bay, and the province's separate school system. He was the author of *Martin on Practical Surveys* (1883).

Martin, Archer Evans Springer (1865-1941) Lawyer, historian. Born in Canada, he was called to the Manitoba bar in 1887. He founded the *Western Law Times* and was western Canada's first legal historian.

He wrote also *Hudson's Bay Company Land Tenures* (1898). Martin was a constant advocate of legal reform of Manitoba's civil procedures.

Martin, Chester Bailey (1882-1958) Educator, historian. Born in Kings County, Nova Scotia, he was educated at the University of New Brunswick (BA, 1902) and Oxford (MA, 1907), winning the first Rhodes Scholarship awarded in North America in 1904. As professor of modern history at the University of Manitoba from 1909 to 1929, he founded the department of history. He was elected a fellow of the Royal Society of Canada in 1920. While in Manitoba he published *Lord Selkirk's Work in Canada* (1916), "*The Natural Resources Question": The Historical Basis of Provincial Claims* (1920), *The Colonial Policy of the Dominion* (1922), and *Empire and Commonwealth* (1929). He also served as president of the Canadian Historical Association (1928). Martin represented Manitoba at the commission of inquiry on the transfer of Manitoba's natural resources from federal to provincial responsibility. In 1929 he moved to the University of Toronto, where he chaired the history department until his retirement in 1952. Among his later works was *Foundations of Canadian Nationhood* (1956).

Martin, J.A. (fl. 1919) Veterans' leader. A returned soldier, he became involved in the Winnipeg General Strike. At a rally at Victoria Park on 12 June 1919 he warned strikers to "beware of camouflage and buncombe." His response to threats to evict workers behind with their rent was, "Well, they can't throw us all out." At a rally on 20 June, he referred to the proposed Saturday parade as "the only weapon we have left." He was part of the soldier-striker party that met with the mayor on the morning of 21 June but refused to call off the parade. He was charged by the government with seditious utterances but the grand jury refused to indict.

Martin, Joseph E. (1852-1923) Lawyer, politician. Born in Milton, Canada, he was educated at Toronto Normal School and the University of Toronto. He was called to the Manitoba bar in 1882, practising law in Portage la Prairie and Winnipeg. A Liberal, he was elected MLA from Portage 1883-92, serving as attorney general in the Greenway administration (1889-91) and introducing the notorious separate schools legislation. He became MP for Winnipeg (1893-96), and then moved to Vancouver, where he soon entered the provincial legislature and briefly became premier in 1900. He later became a British MP from East St. Pancras (1910-18). He thus sat in four different legislative bodies during his political career. See Henry Trachtenberg, "Ethnic Politics on the Urban Frontier: 'Fighting Joe' Martin and the Jews of Winnipeg, 1893-96," *Manitoba History* 35 (spring/summer 1998): 2-14.

Martin, William George (1886-1973) Cleric, politician. Born in Devonshire, England, he came to Canada in 1910. He attended Victoria College, University of Toronto, and received a DD from Wesley College. He served 19 years as the minister of Grace United Church in Winnipeg before becoming first minister of public welfare in Ontario from 1930 to 1934. In 1935 he was the historian on a Canadian Arctic expedition. In 1958 he was elected MLA from Winnipeg St. Matthews, subsequently becoming Speaker of the legislature.

Martin, William Steward (1924-1996) Lawyer, historian. Born in Winnipeg, he was educated at Kelvin High School and the University of Manitoba before doing graduate work at the University of Toronto, receiving a PhD in three disciplines. He practised labour law in Winnipeg for 40 years and was an active amateur historian, instrumental in the restoration of Dalnavert, the former home of Sir Hugh John Macdonald.* He was an honorary fellow and honorary degree recipient of St. John's College. He died in Rochester, Minnesota.

Mason, Bill (1929-1988) Filmmaker, artist. Born in Winnipeg, he was very tiny as a child and matured to only slightly over five feet. Despite his size he was an active athlete and quickly became a wilderness buff. He was educated at the University of Manitoba School of Art, then moved to Ontario where he became a filmmaker, first with Crawley Films, then with the National Film Board, specializing in wilderness themes. He published *Path of the Paddle* in 1980. A photographic collection of his paintings is in *Canoescapes* (1996). A Canada Post stamp was issued in his honour in 1998. See also the biography by James Raffin, *Fire in the Bones* (1996).

Mason, Sophia (Thomas) (1822-1861) Linguist. Born in Red River, she was the daughter of Chief Factor Thomas Thomas and an Indian mother. Upon her father's death in 1828, she inherited a small estate and was educated at the Red River Academy. She declined the opportunity to become a governess at the school in order to marry the Wesleyan missionary William Mason, who took over James Evans's mission to bring the printed word to the Indians. Fluent in Cree, she assisted her husband in his work and in preparing the translation of the Bible into Cree syllabics, which appeared in print in 1859 under her husband's name only. She died in London soon after the birth of her ninth child. *DCB* IX, 784.

Matas, Roy Joseph (1920-1986) Lawyer, judge. Born in Winnipeg, he was educated at St. John's High School and the University of Manitoba. He practised law until he was elevated to the Court of Queen's Bench in 1967. He was appointed to the Court of Appeal in 1973. He chaired subcommittees for the Manitoba Law Society from 1976 to 1979 on competence and legal education. Matas was a prominent member of the Winnipeg Jewish community.

Mather, William Allan (1885-1961) Railroad executive. Born in Oshawa, Ontario, he was educated at McGill University (BSc, 1908). He first joined the CPR in 1903, becoming engineer in 1908 and promoted to resident engineer at Winnipeg in 1910. In 1915 he became assistant general superintendent at Vancouver, subsequently becoming general superintendent in Moose Jaw (1918) and Calgary (1932). He was assistant to the vice-president in Montreal (1933) and then became general manager of western lines (1934), vice-president of western lines (1942) and of the prairie region (1947). He was president of the CPR from 1948 to 1955, and then chair of the board.

Mathers, Alvin T. (1889-1960) Psychiatrist, educator. Born in Neepawa, he graduated from the University of Manitoba Medical School in 1913 and was appointed an assistant professor of medicine there in 1914. During WWI he served in the Royal Canadian Army unit in Tuxedo. He was a pioneer psychiatrist, directing the Manitoba Psychopathic Hospital from 1919 to 1942. He served as provincial psychiatrist for 24 years. He served as president of the Royal College of Physicians and Surgeons in 1942-43, and was a founder of the Association of Canadian Medical Colleges. From 1931 to 1949 he was dean of the University of Manitoba Medical School, where he established an ethnic quota system of entry for which he was later heavily criticized.

Mathers, Thomas Graham (1859-1927) Lawyer, judge. Born in Lucknow, Canada, he served as solicitor for the Manitoba Government Railroad (1880-90), and was chief justice of the Manitoba Supreme Court from 1910. He was chair of the Krafchenko Commission in 1914. During WWI he was an ardent conscriptionist and was made honorary president of the Canadian Service League in 1916. He was also president of the Citizens' Recruiting League in 1916-17. He chaired the Industrial Commission of 1919 that bore his name and which found much unrest in Canada. It concluded that economic conditions rather than foreign aliens were responsible for this unrest, recommending as a way to a better future a package of reform measures that included minimum wage legislation, an eight-hour day, unemployment and health insurance, and free collective bargaining. As judge he granted bail to the eight leaders of the Winnipeg General Strike charged with seditious conspiracy, but he refused to allow bail to aliens arrested at the same time under the Immigration Act, on the grounds that his court had jurisdiction to grant habeas corpus only in criminal cases. See "Cases from Chief Justice Mathers' Legal Ethics," University of Manitoba Law School, 1983.

Matheson, Elizabeth (Beckett) (1866-1958) Physician, missionary. Born near Morris, Manitoba, she taught school before starting her medical course at Trinity College, Toronto. She spent two years in India in missionary service with the Presbyterian Church. Returning to Manitoba, she married John R. Matheson (d. 1916), a prominent Indian missionary. She graduated from the University of Manitoba in 1898, one of the first women students at the university and the second woman graduate from the medical school. She worked with her husband in India before returning to Winnipeg in 1918 to become assistant medical officer in the Winnipeg Public Schools. For a biography, see Ruth Matheson Buck, *The Doctor Rides Side-Saddle* (1974).

Matheson, Samuel Pritchard (1852-1942) Educator, cleric. Born in Kildonan to a distinguished local family, he was educated at St. John's College (BD, 1879), and served for many years at the college as professor of exegetical theology, bursar, and steward, and at the college school as headmaster. He was secretary of the provincial synod of Rupert's Land from 1883 to 1902, then was appointed coadjutor bishop of Rupert's Land in 1903 and archbishop of Rupert's Land in 1905. From 1909 to 1930 he was primate of all Canada. He also served as chancellor of the University of Manitoba and grand master of the Grand Masonic Lodge of Manitoba, as well as chair of the Provincial Advisory Board of Education. He founded Havergal Ladies' College in Winnipeg and was its first president. There are extensive papers at the PAM, some of which belong to the Diocese of Rupert's Land.

Matonabbee (c. 1737-1782) Interpreter, trader, "leading Indian." Born of Chipewyan (Dene) parents at Fort Prince of Wales, he was raised by Europeans at the fort. In the 1750s he was sent by the HBC to serve as a mediator between the Aboriginals and the fur traders. He and his wives accompanied Samuel Hearne on his journeys from 1769 to 1772. He was proclaimed a "leading Indian" by the HBC in 1772. He committed suicide after the destruction of Churchill Factory in 1782. *DCB* IV, 523-24.

Matthey, Jacques Frederick (1777-1850) Settler. Born in Switzerland, he was an officer of the de Meuron regiment which came to Canada in 1813 and was disbanded in Canada in 1816. He was engaged by Lord Selkirk* in 1816 to lead a band of soldiers from the de Meuron and Watteville Regiments to Red River. He was with Selkirk when Fort William was captured in 1816 and went with the Earl to Red River in 1817. He was required to leave by justice of the peace William Coltman,* but returned to the settlement in 1818 as military commander. Subsequently recruiting new settlers in Switzerland and accompanying them to the Red River, he became a centre of discontent before his departure for England in 1824.

Maw, Joseph (1854-1916) Motor racer, businessman. Born in Peel County, Canada, he came to Winnipeg in 1882 as agent for the Massey Manufacturing Company, later moving briefly to Calgary before becoming partner in the carriage firm Ross and Maw (founded 1892), which became Joseph Maw and Company in 1896. He won the Winnipeg Industrial Exposition five-mile motor race in 1905. He died in Los Angeles.

Maxwell, George (1823-1911) Contractor. Born in Northern Ireland, he emigrated to Canada in 1844 and to Manitoba in 1872. He joined an Orange procession in Fort Garry upon entering the town, and never looked back. He was a member of the first

Grand Orange Lodge and its grand secretary for 35 years. He was an early railroad contractor in Manitoba in the 1870s. Later, as a building contractor, he was responsible for many of Winnipeg's classic buildings, including the old Customs House and the Bannatyne Block.

Maxwell, J.S. (b. 1862) Business executive. Born in Wingham, Canada, he graduated from its Collegiate Institute in 1873. He joined the flour-milling industry, working his way up to founding manager of the Brandon branch of the Western Canada Flour Mills Company when it was organized in 1882. He was a vice-president of the Central Canada Insurance Company and a director of the Brandon General Hospital. He chaired the Brandon School Board and served as both grand master of the IOOF and a district high chief ranger of the Canadian Order of Foresters.

May, Wilfrid Reid ("Wop," 1896-1952) War hero, bush pilot. Born in Carberry, Manitoba, during WWI he was the pilot pursued by the "Red Baron" when the German ace was killed. May shot down 13 German aircraft during the war, eluding the "Red Baron" in the process, and was awarded the Distinguished Flying Cross in 1918. He became one of Canada's leading bush pilots in the post-war era, and received an Order of the British Empire in 1935. May helped set up the British Commonwealth Air Training Plan in 1939. He died near Provo, Utah, from injuries received in a rock-climbing accident.

May, William Sheppard (1907-1978) Swine breeder. Born in Dundee, Scotland, he immigrated to Canada in 1926 to farm in the Strathclair district. He specialized in purebred Yorkshire swine. He was also an elite seed grower. He served as president of the Manitoba Swine Breeders on several occasions, as well as on the board of directors of the Provincial Exhibition and Royal Manitoba Winter Fair. He was active in his community, with the United Church and the Strathclair Consumer Co-op, and the Strathclair Masonic Lodge. He is a member of the Manitoba Agricultural Hall of Fame.

Maybank, Ralph (1890-1965) Politician, judge. Born in London, Ontario, he was educated at the University of Manitoba (LLB, 1922). He entered politics as a Winnipeg alderman in 1930-31, serving as chair of the Unemployment Relief Administration.

He was Liberal MP from Winnipeg South Centre from 1935 to 1951, when he resigned to become a supreme court justice. His papers are at the PAM.

Maydanyk, Jacob (1891-1984) Cartoonist. Born in Syvdovi, Ukraine, he attended a textile-ornamenting academy in Krakow, and came to Canada in 1911. He attended Brandon College in 1912. He moved to Winnipeg and opened the Providence Church Goods Store, which he operated until 1979. A talented cartoonist, he created "Vykjo Shteef Tabachniuk" (Uncle Steve Tobacco), a satirical figure who appeared in the 1920s in the *Canadian Farmer* and other newspapers. He also did iconography and wrote both plays and poems. An exhibition of his work was held in Winnipeg in 1977. A book of his cartoons sold 10,000 copies in 1931 and was reprinted in 1974. See also the National Film Board's *Laughter in My Soul* (1983).

Mazzone, Carlo ("Charlie," 1905-1992) Night club owner. Born in Bovalino Marina in the Calabria region of Italy, he immigrated to Winnipeg in 1913. He worked for the CNR from 1917 as a sandblaster, spending his spare time playing his violin. He helped organize the Orchestra Stella d'Italia in the 1920s and left it in the early 1930s to form Curly's Music Weavers, which played at the Don Carlos Cabaret at Ellice and Donald. In WWII, he enlisted in the Canadian army. After the war he opened a cabaret, the Rancho Don Carlos, on Pembina Highway. Until he sold it in 1959, the Rancho was Winnipeg's most important nightspot, featuring some of the world's leading entertainers, including Bob Hope and Louis Armstrong. After some years in Edmonton he returned to Reggio di Calabria, Italy, where he established an automobile dealership. He died in Italy.

Meade, Roland (or Rollin) Pierce (b. 1838) Journalist. Born in Upper Canada, he was secretary pro tem of the Red River Famine Relief Committee in 1868-69 and editor of the *Nor'-Wester* in 1869. He was one of those captured at John Schultz's* house in December 1869. In 1872 the compensation commission listed him as a Winnipeg painter.

Medovy, Harry (1904-1995) Physician. Born in Russia, he moved with his family to Winnipeg at the age of 10 months. He was educated at St. John's High School and the University of Manitoba (BA, 1923) before entering the medical faculty, graduating with his MD in 1928. After postgraduate work at the University of Pennsylvania he returned to become a pediatrician in Winnipeg, acquiring a reputation for energy that was reflected in his nickname, "Hurricane Harry." Much of his work was done in the area of preventive pediatrics. He was head of the Department of Pediatrics and pediatrician-in-chief of the Children's Hospital from 1954 to 1970, and was president of the Canadian Paediatric Society in 1957. He received an honorary DSc from the University of Manitoba in 1975 and the Order of Canada in 1990. He wrote *A Vision Fulfilled*, an account of the history of the Winnipeg Children's Hospital (1979). There are papers at the PAM.

Meighen, Arthur (1874-1960) Lawyer, politician. Born in Perth County, Ontario, he graduated with honours in mathematics from the University of Toronto in 1896. He taught school before moving to Winnipeg to study law. He was called to the Manitoba bar in 1903 and practised until 1915 (with the firm of Meighen and Sexsmith) at Portage la Prairie. He was first elected as a Liberal-Conservative MP from Portage in 1908, winning re-election in 1911 and 1917. He became secretary of state in 1917 and minister of the interior in the Union government later that year. He was associated with many of the government's most controversial wartime measures, including repression of free speech, the Wartime Elections Act, the nationalization of the railroads, and the Military Service Act of 1917. Meighen also was responsible for the federal initiatives that put down the Winnipeg General Strike of 1919, thus incurring the enmity of organized labour. Despite these liabilities, he succeeded Sir Robert Borden as prime minister in 1921, but both he and his government went down to defeat shortly thereafter. Although his party won the largest number of seats in the 1925 election, he did not become prime minister until briefly in 1926, when his newly formed government was quickly defeated in the House. In the ensuing election the Conservatives were routed and Meighen resigned as leader. He was a member of the Hydro-Electric Power Commission of Ontario from 1931 to 1934, and entered the Senate in 1932 as government leader. In 1941 Meighen was again chosen leader of his party, but was defeated in the by-election in York South by a CCF opponent. His loss was a combination of his single-minded advocacy of conscription and his inability to think about national policy after the war was over. Disillusioned,

he retired from politics. He wrote *Overseas Addresses* (1921) and *Unrevised and Unrepentant Debating Speeches and Others* (1949). The standard biography, in three volumes, is by Roger Graham. His papers (on microfilm) are available at the PAM.

Mercury, John (1895-1990) Community leader. Born in Niata, Greece, he came to Canada in 1909 and moved to Winnipeg in 1941 to join his brothers in business. He helped found the Greek community centre in Winnipeg in 1943 and the first Hellenic Greek Orthodox Church in 1956. He died in Winnipeg.

Metcalfe, Thomas Llewellyn (1870-1922) Lawyer, judge. He articled in Manitoba and was called to the Manitoba bar in 1894. A leading Liberal, he was appointed to the Manitoba Court of King's Bench in 1909 and named by the federal government in May 1919 to be chair of the arbitration panel for the Winnnipeg Electric Railway. He subsequently became the judge in the trial of R.B. Russell* and the other strike leaders charged by the federal government with sedition. His charge to the jury was probably partly responsible for the subsequent convictions, since his definitions of sedition fit perfectly the actions of the men charged.

Metcalfe, William (1906-1990) Journalist. Born in Portage la Prairie, he was educated at the University of Wisconsin, where he captained the hockey team. He was a reporter for the *Winnipeg Free Press* (1931-40) and was head of the newsroom at CBC Radio in Winnipeg (1940-47). He became managing editor of the *Winnipeg Citizen* (1947-49), then managing editor of the *Winnipeg Free Press* (1952-59) and of the *Ottawa Journal* (1959-72). His autobiography was published as *The View from Thirty* (1984).

Mickle, Charles Julius (1848-1919) Lawyer, politician. Born in Canada, he was admitted to the Ontario bar in 1872. He migrated to Manitoba in 1882 to practise law in Birtle, serving as Liberal MLA for Birtle from 1888 to 1908. He was provincial secretary from 1896 to 1900 and led the Liberals after Greenway stepped down. He became a county court judge in 1909.

Middleton, Christopher (d. 1770) Explorer. Born in England, he served aboard privateers before joining the HBC in 1721 as second mate. He made 16 annual voyages to the Bay, many as captain, and his astronomical observations were published by the

Royal Society in 1726 (in 1737 he was chosen Fellow of the Royal Society). This publication drew the attention of Arthur Dobbs,* who chose him to lead the expedition he was organizing to search for the Northwest Passage. He helped lobby for the expedition at the Admiralty, and was appointed its commander in 1740-41, resigning from the HBC. His ships left England on 8 June 1741, so late that he was forced to winter at Churchill, where his crew suffered from scurvy. In 1742 he sailed further north than any previous explorer, but ended his expedition in Repulse Bay, having decided that there was no passage. He passed Chesterfield Inlet but did not enter it. Upon his return to England, Dobbs accused him of falsifying the record in order to preserve the trading monopoly of the HBC, and their controversy resulted in the publication of five books and pamphlets by Middleton and three by Dobbs. In most respects Middleton has been vindicated, although he did miss Chesterfield Inlet. He remained underemployed until 1748, when he was placed on the Admiralty's half-pay list. He stayed there until his death. Later historians have cast him as a victim of "a malicious campaign of denigration." See Glyndwr Williams, *The British Search for the Northwest Passage in the Eighteenth Century* (1962), and William Barr and Glyndwr Williams, eds., *The Voyage of Christopher Middleton 1741-1742* (1994). *DCB* III, 446-50.

Middleton, Katherine Major (Spinks) ("Kay," d. 1987) Journalist, writer. Born in Toronto, she was educated at Rupert's Land Ladies' College and the University of Manitoba in home economics. As food editor of the *Winnipeg Free Press* in the 1940s she wrote over 4,000 food columns. Middleton moved to Chicago in 1948 and hosted a daily television cooking show. She was the co-author of the best-selling *The Art of Cooking for the Diabetic,* which sold over half a million copies and won her many awards from health and diabetic organizations.

Miles, Henry John ("Harry," 1904-1990) Journalist. Born in Bristol, England, he came to Canada in 1911 and moved to Flin Flon in 1943, where he edited the *Flin Flon Daily Miner* for 30 years. He then edited the magazine *Northern Lights* from 1973 to 1983, when he retired to Winnipeg. In Flin Flon, Miles served as president of the Chamber of Commerce, on the board of directors of the Flin Flon General Hospital, and as a lobbyist for television broadcasting in the region. He died in Winnipeg.

Miles, Robert Seaborn (1795-1870) Fur trader. Born in Oxfordshire, he joined the HBC in 1818 as an accountant. He served at York Factory from 1821 to 1823 and from 1824 to 1834, and then as head of the Rupert's Land District until 1843. He became a chief trader in 1828 and a chief factor in 1844. He became sheriff of Rupert's Land in 1839. He retired to Brockville, Ontario.

Miller, C.C. (1900-1978) Lawyer, judge, politician. Born in Portage la Prairie and locally educated, he articled in the law firm of Meighen and Sexsmith. He was called to the bar in Portage la Prairie in 1920 and practised law there until he was appointed to the Court of Queen's Bench in 1959. He was MP for Portage la Prairie from 1946 to 1949. He went to the Court of Appeal in 1960 and was made chief justice of Manitoba in 1961, serving until 1967. He was a president of the Manitoba Conservative Association.

Miller, Edith Jane (1875-1936) Contralto. Born in Portage la Prairie, the daughter of W.W. Miller, she studied voice at the University of Toronto under Francesco D'Aurea. She taught at the Winnipeg Conservatory of Music, then went to Europe for further study, making her debut at Massey Hall as a contralto. She gave her first concert in London in 1905 and was chosen as a soloist in several early performances of Elgar's *Dream of Gerontius* and *The Kingdom*. She gave a recital at the Walker Theatre in Winnipeg before 3,500 people in 1909; it was the social event of the year. In 1911 she represented Canada at the Imperial Festival Canadian concert at the Crystal Palace. She was married to Max Charles Hamilton in 1913, the same week she appeared for the first time in grand opera, singing Gilda in *Rigoletto.* Miller subsequently disappeared from the spotlight. She died in England.

Miller, James Andrew (1839-1886) Lawyer, judge, civil servant. Born in Galt, Upper Canada, he graduated from Trinity College, Toronto, in 1859 and was called to the Upper Canada bar in 1863. He received an appointment to the Manitoba Court of Queen's Bench in 1880, serving until 1882. He resigned over patronage appointments to the court by the federal government. He was given an expensive silver tea service by the Law Society on his resignation. He subsequently ran unsuccessfully for the House of Commons as a Conservative in 1882, then was elected an MLA from Rat Portage in 1883, serving as provincial secretary and then attorney general until it was decided in 1884 that Rat Portage and area were part of Ontario, not Manitoba. He then became Manitoba registrar-general under the Torrens system until his death. *DCB* XI, 593-94.

Miller, Saul (1917-1993) Politician. Born in Winnipeg, he was educated at the Peretz School, St. John's High School, and the University of Manitoba. He launched his political career in West Kildonan in 1953 as a school trustee, becoming alderman in 1959 and mayor in 1967. He was first elected to the Legislative Assembly in 1966, serving until 1981. He held key portfolios, such as education, urban affairs, health, and finance, in the Schreyer government. He helped launch pharmacare and student aid, but often said that his greatest satisfaction was "being in the first NDP cabinet in Manitoba." He died in Winnipeg. Papers are at the PAM.

Miller, William Conrad (1896-1959) Politician. Born in Waterloo County, Ontario, he served in the Canadian Expeditionary Force from 1916 and was twice wounded. He was elected MLA from Morden-Rhineland in 1936, serving until 1955. First running as a Conservative, he became a Coalition Conservative in 1940 and a Liberal in 1950. He served as provincial secretary, Speaker of the Legislature, and minister of education. Many criticized him for his changes of party, but his constituents continued to support him through the changes.

Milliken, Lorene Frances (Ritz) (1907-1990) Author. Born in Humboldt, Saskatchewan, she grew up in Winnipeg, graduating from the University of Manitoba in 1928 and the normal school in 1929. She taught school for many years, and later was active in Winnipeg community affairs. She published seven books of poetry and short stories, beginning with *White Orchid* in 1952. Her papers are at the UML Archives. She died in Winnipeg.

Mitchell, James Bertram (1852-1945) Soldier, civil servant. Born in Ontario, he was educated at the Montreal Art School. He served in the militia in the Fenian raids of 1866 and 1870 before joining the NWMP in 1874 and serving until 1877. In 1893 he was appointed commissioner of School Buildings for the Public School Board in Winnipeg, and supervised the construction of many school buildings in the city. He was lieutenant-colonel of the 100th

Grenadiers from 1912 to 1920, taking them overseas in 1914. He retired from the School Board in 1928. He was a staunch imperialist. The J.B. Mitchell School in Winnipeg is named after him. There are papers at the PAM.

Moberly, Walter (1832-1915) Engineer, author. Born near Oxford, England, he came to Upper Canada in 1834 and studied engineering. He moved to British Columbia in 1858 and became the first professional engineer to explore there. In 1859 he laid out the new capital of British Columbia. (later New Westminster). In 1875 he was in charge of laying out Winnipeg's first sewer system. He also served as chief engineer of the Manitoba South Western Railway. He was the author of *The History of the Cariboo Wagon Road* (1908) and *The Early History of the Canadian Pacific Railway* (1909).

Mobius, R.M. (d. 1938) Educator. Supposedly born in Leipzig, Germany, and a sometime professor at a German university, Mobius appeared in Winnipeg around 1905 as principal of the Manitoba Institute of Mental Sciences, located on Main Street near William Avenue. He described himself as "Consulting Hygienist, Medical Electrician, Naturopath, and Phrenologist." The institute offered a lending library and served as an early centre for radical thought in Winnipeg. Mobius was a disciple of Henry George and a founder of the Single Tax League of Manitoba. He disappeared from Winnipeg around 1910. He died in Victoria, British Columbia.

Moffat, Leslie M. (1893-1952) Athlete, war hero. Born in Winnipeg, he played hockey as captain of the Victorias hockey team that won the Allan Cup in 1912. He also played halfback on the Winnipeg Rowing Club football team. During WWI he was a major with the 44th Battalion, winning the Military Cross at Vimy Ridge. He then joined the firm of Black and Armstrong, rising eventually to become vice-president.

Moffatt, James Irving (1919-1991) Manager. Raised in the Carroll district of Manitoba, he was a director of the Royal Manitoba Winter Fair for many years before serving as its president from 1957 to 1960. He was director of the Provincial Exhibition in 1970-71. From 1965 to 1985 he managed the Brandon assembly yard of the Manitoba Hog Commission, and he pioneered in barbecuing boneless smoked loins. He is a member of the Manitoba Agricultural Hall of Fame.

Moffatt, Louis Winfred (b. 1887) Educator, cleric, historian. Born in Ontario, he was educated at Toronto and Edinburgh Universities (PhD, 1921). He taught school in Ontario before entering the ministry in 1909. He joined the Canadian Expeditionary Force in 1914 and served as a chaplain and on hospital duty until the war ended. In 1922 he was appointed lecturer in history at Wesley College and was invited to become pastor of the Broadway Methodist Church. He wrote *England on the Eve of the Industrial Revolution*.

Mollot, Gabrielle (b. 1880) Musician. Born in Lyon, France, she studied piano there and in Paris before coming to Canada in 1897 to teach music. She later returned to Paris to study with Isidor Philippe and M. Mosskowski, then with Paul Brand. In 1919 and 1920 she studied with Percy Grainger. She taught piano at the Music and Arts Building in Winnipeg.

Molloy, John Patrick (1873-1948) Politician, senator. Born in Arthur, Ontario, he came with his parents by stagecoach to Winnipeg in 1876. He was educated at the Ontario Veterinary College and the McKillop Veterinary College in Chicago, and practised in Morris, Manitoba. He was an unsuccessful Liberal candidate on several occasions before he was elected MP for Provencher in 1908, being re-elected in 1911 and 1917. He was defeated in 1921. Molloy was appointed to the Senate in 1925, the first Irish-Catholic senator from Manitoba. He was a prominent member of the Knights of Columbus.

Moncrieff, John James (1865-1939) Journalist. Born in Scalloway, Shetland Islands, he moved with his family to St. Andrews in 1875. He was apprenticed to a printer at Rat Portage in 1883, and later helped found the *Winnipeg Daily News*. He bought the *Winnipeg Sun* and in 1890 became first news editor of the *Tribune*. He served as managing editor of the *Tribune* from 1903 to 1920, and then as associate editor from 1920 to 1936. He was elected Liberal MP for Lisgar in 1896 and 1900, later being elected in 1914 as a Union candidate for Springfield. He was soloist and choirmaster at Augustine Church from 1906 to 1925, and was first president of the Winnipeg Oratorio Society in 1907. There are papers at the PAM.

Monkman, Joseph (b. 1836) Farmer. Born in Red River, he was a Protestant mixed-blood who was given a commission by Colonel Dennis in 1869 to recruit Indian tribes to join in the war against the French Métis in Red River. He travelled south on snowshoes with John Schultz* in February 1870 and testified before the Special Senate Committee in May 1870. He met Colonel Wolseley* at Fort St. Frances with messages and intelligence, having obviously acted as a Canadian agent. On the 1872 compensation list he was described as a St. Peters farmer.

Montague, Walter Humphries (1858-1915) Politician, physician. Born in Middlesex County, Canada, he was educated at the School of Medicine (Toronto) and Victoria University, Cobourg (MD, 1882). After practising medicine at Dunnville, Ontario, he was elected as Conservative MP for Haldimand, serving from 1890 to 1900. He served briefly as secretary of state, then minister of agriculture under Mackenzie Bowell, but was accused by Bowell of conspiring against him. After another brief period of office with the Tupper government, he retired in 1896 and was defeated when he ran for office again in the election of 1900. In 1908, he moved to Winnipeg and later was MLA for Kildonan from 1913 to 1915. He served as minister of public works in the Roblin government, which involved him in the scandal over the construction of the Legislative Building.

Montgomery, Edward W. (c. 1874-1948) Physician, public health reformer. Born in Quebec, he came to Stonewall with his parents in 1877. He attended Manitoba College, taught school in Brandon, and entered Manitoba Medical College around 1890. He began medical practice in Winnipeg in 1892, and served as president of the Canadian Medical Association in 1922. He was active in the public health movement for many years, joining the Bracken government in 1927 to head a new department of health and welfare. He consolidated a number of disparate departments into a functioning unit before stepping down in 1932. In retirement he was an ardent gardener at his property on Henderson Highway.

Moor, William (d. 1765) Mariner. He advanced from ship's boy to first mate on HBC vessels under his cousin Christopher Middleton's* command, but later supported Arthur Dobbs* over Middleton in the great debate over the Northwest Passage. He commanded the private discovery expedition to the

Bay in 1746, but it returned to England with its goals unfulfilled and the crew in mutiny. *DCB* III, 471-72.

Moore, L.M. (b. 1848) Physician. Born in Nottawasage, Canada, he was educated at Duntroon before teaching school. He then entered Victoria College, Toronto, and completed his medical training at Trinity College in 1872, receiving that institution's first gold medal. He practised at Thornhill, Ontario, before coming to Brandon in 1882, where he accumulated substantial quantities of land inside and outside the city.

Moorhouse, Arthur Herbert Douglas (b. 1882) Author. Born in Bervie, Ontario, he was educated in London, Ontario, schools and the University of Western Ontario. He came to Manitoba in 1907 to become secretary to Premier Rodmond Roblin,* for whom he worked until 1910, when he became deputy minister of agriculture. In 1917 he went to work for the United Grain Growers. As "Hopkins Moorhouse" he was the author of *Deep Furrows* (1918), an account of farmer co-operatives in Western Canada, and several works of detective fiction, including *Every Man for Himself* (1920) and *The Gauntlet of Alceste* (1921). He worked as a journalist with many major Canadian newspapers during the 1920s.

Morice, Father Adrien Gabriel (1859-1938) Missionary, historian. Born in Brittany, France, he joined the Oblates in 1879 and came to British Columbia in 1880 to serve as a missionary to the Indians. He spent much time in the Chilcotin district, compiling maps and creating a syllabary for the Dene peoples. In later life he retired to St. Boniface and wrote a number of historical works, including *History of the Northern Interior of British Columbia* (1904); *Dictionnaire historique des Canadiens et des Métis français de l'Ouest* (1908); *History of the Catholic Church in Western Canada* (2 vols., 1910); and *A Critical History of the Red River Insurrection* (1935). For a biography, see T. O'Hagan, *Father Morice* (1928).

Morris, Alexander (1826-1889) Judge, lieutenant-governor. Born in Perth, Upper Canada, of self-conscious Scottish parents, he was educated in Scotland at Madras College, St. Andrews, and at the University of Glasgow. He became fluent in French, then studied law in Kingston under John A. Macdonald (and in company with Oliver Mowat). He attended Queen's College and then graduated from McGill. Morris was an early Canadian imperialist, publishing *Canada and its Resources* in 1855, and in his 1858 lecture "Nova Britannia: or, British North America, its extent and future" he predicted Confederation and transcontinental railroad expansion. He was an early advocate of the annexation of HBC territories (see *The Hudson's Bay and Pacific Territories*, 1859) and, as Conservative MLA and MP from Lanark from 1861 to 1872, was a leading Father of Confederation. He was appointed minister of inland revenue in 1869. When he retired from federal politics in 1872 due to ill health, he specifically requested to be sent to Manitoba as a judge, where "the work would be light" and he "could be of use." He served as the first chief justice of the Court of Queen's Bench of Manitoba, and acted as administrator of Manitoba and the North-West Territories when Adams Archibald* departed in October 1872. He once described his court as a "bear garden" where he had "a conflict of authorities & practices — the old Assiniboia ideas — the Ontario & the Quebec, *en lutte*." He regarded it as fortunate that the legislature had adopted English practice and English law. He "quietly enforced both" until appointed lieutenant-governor of the province and the North-West Territories in December 1872. As lieutenant-governor of Manitoba, he continued Archibald's insistence on responsible government and supported the foundation of the University of Manitoba. As lieutenant-governor of the Territories to 1876 he advocated the establishment of a police force and negotiated Treaties Three to Six with the Indians. His administration in Manitoba failed, however, to preserve Métis lands in that province, and he himself was an active investor and speculator. After he stepped down as lieutenant-governor, he attempted to enter Manitoba politics by running as MP from Selkirk, losing by 10 votes to Donald A. Smith.* He later ran unsuccessfully in 1878 in a by-election for the East Toronto seat in the Ontario legislature, although a year later he defeated Oliver Mowat in that same riding. In 1880 he published a book entitled *The Treaties of Canada with the Indians of Manitoba and the North-West Territories*. He was in ill health for many years before his death. He was president of the Montreal St. Andrew's Society, governor of McGill College, and trustee of Queen's College. Consult F.A. Milligan, "The lieutenant-governorship in Manitoba, 1870-1882" (MA diss., University of Manitoba, 1948). Morris's papers as Manitoba lieutenant-governor are in the PAM. *DCB* XI, 608-15.

Mortimer, John T. (d. 1908) Labour leader, reformer. Born in Scotland, he became president of Local 70 of the Journeyman Tailors' Union of America (JTUA) in 1897, and in 1899-1900 served as president of the Winnipeg Trades and Labor Council. He was closely associated with Arthur W. Puttee* and was Puttee's election agent when he was elected to the House of Commons in a by-election in 1900. From 1902 to 1906 he lived in Vancouver, running for office on several occasions. He returned to Winnipeg in 1906, eventually living with his wife's family just south of the Manitoba border. He was drowned when he fell through the ice near Emerson. Mortimer was an "impossiblist" who sought radical socialistic reform. *DCB* XIII, 718-19.

Morton, Ronald Edward Alfred (1901-1976) Soldier. Born in Toronto, he joined the army at the age of 19, graduating from the Royal Military College in 1923. He commanded the Fort Garry Horse in the Normandy invasion, and was frequently decorated for his service. After the war he took over Prairie command in 1949. In 1950 he was put in command of flood control in Manitoba during the flood emergency. He kept morale high and helped to keep casualties and injuries to a minimum. Under his command the authorities never lost control of the situation. He received an honorary degree from the University of Manitoba in 1951. He subsequently worked with the Canadian truce team in Laos before his retirement from the army in 1955. He died in Toronto.

Morton, Thomas Lewis (1846-1914) Farmer, politician. Born in Hull, England, he was educated at Edward VI College, Gloucester, and came to Manitoba in 1873 to farm at Gladstone. A Liberal, he became MLA for Westbourne from 1888 to 1905. He later moved to Winnipeg as a grain dealer with the firm of Morton and Pearson. His residence was on Mountain Avenue. He was the father of William Morton* (1884-1958).

Morton, William (1884-1958) Farmer, politician. Born in Gladstone, Manitoba, he was educated at St. John's College, where he was a champion athlete. He served 14 years on the Westbourne council, four as councillor and 10 as reeve, before his election as MLA in 1927. In 1939 he became minister of municipal affairs, then of telephones (1944), then public works (1950). He declined to succeed Premier Garson* in 1948. He was the father of William Lewis Morton.* There are papers at the PAM.

Morton, William Lewis (1908-1980) Educator, historian. Born at Gladstone, Manitoba, he was educated St. John's College and Oxford, where he was a Rhodes scholar. He returned to the University of Manitoba in 1942, where he was head of the history department from 1950 to 1964. In 1964 he went to Trent University to become master of Champlain College and Vanier professor of history. After retirement in 1975 he returned to the University of Manitoba, where he taught until his death. Morton began his historical work on the West with a collaboration with his sister, Margaret Morton Fahrni, *Third Crossing: A History of the Town and District of Gladstone in the Province of Manitoba* (1946). He then produced *The Progressive Party in Canada* (1950, rev. ed., 1967). Beginning in the mid-1950s, Morton entered into a decade of prodigious output which moved him from being a regional to a national historian. In 1956 he published two lengthy introductions to collections of documents: *The London Correspondence Inward from Eden Colvile 1849-1852* and *Alexander Begg's Red River Journal and Other Papers Relative to the Red River Resistance of 1869-70.* A year later he published his history of the province, *Manitoba: A History* (1957, rev. 1967). In 1957 he also produced *One University: A History of the University of Manitoba.* In 1960 he delivered a series of lectures at the University of Wisconsin that became *The Canadian Identity* (1961, rev. 1972), and in 1963 a survey of Canadian history, *The Kingdom of Canada,* appeared. He became co-editor of the Canadian Centenary Series, writing the volume on the confederation period, *The Critical Years: The Union of British North America, 1857-1973* (1964). He founded the Manitoba Record Society, editing its first volume, *Manitoba: The Birth of a Province,* in 1965. His collected essays are available in A.B. McKillop, ed., *Contexts of Canada's Past: Selected Essays of W.L. Morton* (1980). Morton was considered a "Red Tory." He died in Medicine Hat, Alberta. His papers are at Queen's University, but some are also at the PAM. See Charles Taylor, *Radical Tories: The Conservative Tradition in Canada* (1982): 49-76.

Mosienko, Bill (1921-1994) Hockey player. Born in Winnipeg's North End, he played 14 years and 711 games with the Chicago Black Hawks (1942-55), scoring 258 goals and 282 assists. He once scored three goals in 22 seconds in a game against the New York Rangers, still a record. He subsequently played for the Winnipeg Warriors. A five-time NHL all-star, he is a member of the Hockey Hall of Fame and the Manitoba Sports Hall of Fame. An ice arena in Winnipeg has been named for him.

Mowat, Edward (1786-1862) Fur trader. Born in the Orkney Islands, Scotland, he came to the Churchill region with the HBC in 1806, becoming head of Nelson House in 1819. After amalgamation he was in the Nelson River District. He settled in Red River in 1833 as a York boat freighter. He drowned in a boating accident.

Mulligan, James (1814-1891) Pensioner, constable. Born in Ireland, he served in the 17th Foot and lost an arm. He came to Red River in 1846 with the Chelsea pensioners and served as a constable in Winnipeg. He was one of those imprisoned by Louis Riel in December 1869. He was subsequently ill-treated by the Ontario volunteers of the Wolseley Expedition. Mulligan eventually became a prominent Winnipeg landholder, owner of the land now occupied by the Misericordia Hospital.

Mulvey, Stewart (1834-1908) Civil servant. Born in Ireland, he came to Canada in 1856 to teach at the behest of Egerton Ryerson. He came to Manitoba as an ensign with the Wolseley Expedition and remained, helping to found the first Orange lodge in the Northwest (number 1307) in September 1870. He became the first editor of *The Manitoba Liberal* in 1871, although he was a supporter of Sir John A. Macdonald. He and John Schultz* led a demonstration in 1872 that burned Louis Riel in effigy. He served for many years as a provincial school trustee, member of the Winnipeg School Board, and alderman (1883-88). In 1873 he became collector of Internal Revenue, serving until 1886. He became MLA for Morris in 1896 as an independent. He was a Mason and a leading Orangeman (grand master of the Orange Order in Manitoba and the North-West Territories, 1872-86). He died in British Columbia, having retired to North Vancouver in 1907. A street in Winnipeg is named after him. *DCB* XIII, 746-47.

Munck (Munk), Jens (1579-1628) Sailor, explorer. Born in present-day Norway, he became a captain in the Danish navy during the Swedish War, 1611-13.

In 1619, King Christian IV sent him in search of the Northwest Passage. He headed for Hudson Bay via Greenland, and was the first to produce a map which treated the entire bay as a single entity. Since he did not enter Hudson Bay until late August, he was forced to winter with his men and ships at Port Churchill in the estuary of the Churchill River (artifacts of his visit were later discovered). Scurvy attacked the party, and no one knew how to administer the drugs and herbs carried on board. Only Munck and two others survived, sailing home in the smaller of their two vessels. He had plans for a return, but never managed to accomplish one. See *The Expedition of Captain Jens Munk in Hudson's Bay in Search of a North-west Passage in 1619-20* (1624 and various translations and reprints). *DCB* I, 514-15.

Munro(e), Alexander (1824-1911) Fur trader. Born in Rosshire, Scotland, he came to Red River in 1857 in the service of the HBC, rising to senior chief factor. He retired in 1890.

Munroe, George (1797-1864) Weaver. Born in Sutherlandshire, Scotland, he worked as a weaver in Paisley. In 1830 he was brought to Red River to teach weaving, settling on Lot 55 in East Kildonan. He served as an elder of the Presbyterian Church.

Munroe, George Fraser (1849-1912) Lawyer. Born in Kildonan, he was educated at St. John's College and Manitoba College. He was admitted to the bar and practised law with the firm of Munroe, Mackenzie, and Macqueen. He was active in Kildonan local government, serving as secretary-treasurer of the East Kildonan School Board. He was also active in the Kildonan Presbyterian Church.

Murphy, Anne Ethel ("Nan," 1902-1990) Educator and community activist. Born in Arnaud, Manitoba, she graduated from Brandon Normal School and taught for some years before moving to Winnipeg. She became active in many community organizations and served on the boards of a number of philanthropic organizations. In 1956 she became the first female chair of the Winnipeg School Board and later became president of the Canadian School Trustees' Association. She received a Coronation Medal in 1953 and a Centennial Medal in 1967. The University of Winnipeg gave her an honorary doctorate in 1974. She died in Winnipeg.

Murphy, Emily Gowan (Ferguson) (1868-1933) Feminist, writer. Born in Cookstown, Ontario, she was educated at Bishop Strachan School in Toronto. Murphy had established herself as a writer and journalist before she accompanied her clergyman husband to Swan River, Manitoba, in 1903. The couple lived there until 1907, Emily collecting the material that would become *Janey Canuck in the West* (1910). She also served as literary editor of the *Winnipeg Tribune* from 1904 to 1912. Joining with like-minded women in the West and especially in Winnipeg, she was active in the suffrage and women's rights questions. She subsequently moved to Edmonton, where she became a Juvenile Court judge and leader of the move to recognize female senators. Under the pseudonym "Janey Canuck," Murphy wrote three books of essays and a travel account, while under her own name she exposed the drug trade in *The Black Candle* (1922). See Byrne Hope, *Emily Murphy, Crusader* (1945).

Murray, Alexander ("Sandy," 1839-1913) Politician. Born in Kildonan, he was educated at St. John's College. He became MLA for St. Charles in 1874 and was re-elected in 1878. In 1879 he was elected MLA for Assiniboia, and he was re-elected in 1883 as a Liberal-Conservative. He was Speaker of the House from 1883 to 1886 and was appointed minister of municipal affairs, serving 1887-88. He later worked in the municipal commissioner's office. He twice went to Ottawa as part of provincial delegations to negotiate better terms for Manitoba with the federal government.

Murray, Alexander Hunter (1818-1874) Fur trader. Born in Argyllshire, Scotland, he joined the American Fur Company in St. Louis, Missouri, in the 1840s, coming north to work for the HBC in 1846. He was sent to the Mackenzie River District and established Fort Yukon in 1847 inside Russian territory. His diary of this period has been published as *Journal of the Yukon, 1847-8,* ed. L.J. Burpee (1910). He became chief trader in 1856 and served at several posts in what is now Manitoba before retiring in 1867 to his house, Bellevue, near Lower Fort Garry. He wrote the satirical poem "Capture of Red River or Riel's Retreat." See M.M. Black, "Alexander Hunter Murray," *The Beaver* (June 1929): 211-13. *DCB* X, 540-41.

Murray, James Richard (1885-1963) Grain expert. Born in Limerick, Ireland, he attended Trinity College and came to Halifax in 1905, working his way to Winnipeg. He joined the Winnipeg Grain Growers' Company in 1909 as a clerk, and was appointed assistant general manager in 1916. After the merger with Alberta Elevator Company in 1917, he became manager of United Grain Growers' eastern division. He helped create the pool system. In 1930 he became general manager of the Alberta Pacific Grain Company. In 1937 he became chair of the Canadian Wheat Board, negotiated the sale of the 295-million-bushel surplus within eight months, and resigned because he said his job was done. He died in Victoria, British Columbia.

Musgrove, Alexander Johnston (1882-1952) Artist, educator. Born in Edinburgh, Scotland, he studied at the Glasgow School of Art from 1901 to 1910. In 1913 he immigrated to Winnipeg to become principal of the Winnipeg School of Art. He remained there until 1921, when he opened the Western Art Academy. Musgrove spent most of his adult life (except a year in Scotland in the early 1920s) in Winnipeg. He co-founded the Manitoba Society of Artists in 1925 and was a regular exhibitor at its shows. He specialized in watercolours. He also taught and wrote frequently on art for local newspapers. After 1932, he served for many years as curator for the Winnipeg Art Gallery. Musgrove was one of the handful of artists who kept art in Winnipeg alive during the dark days of the 1930s and 1940s. An exhibition of his work was held at the Winnipeg Art Gallery in 1986. See Nancy Dillow, *The Forgotten Innovator, Alexander J. Musgrove* (1985).

Mykytuck, Dymytri (1898-1983) Writer. Born in Selo Ratuwczyk, Ukraine, he fought with the Ukrainian army against the Russians during WWI. He came to Winnipeg in 1930 and became secretary of the Ukrainian Canadian Committee. He published 10 books about Ukrainska Halytsha Armia, the independent Ukrainian army. He died in Winnipeg.

Mynarski, Andrew Charles (1916-1944) War hero. Born in Winnipeg and educated at King Edward and Isaac Newton Schools, he was a Lancaster bomber pilot who was posthumously awarded the Victoria Cross for conspicuous bravery while in action. A park and a school in Winnipeg were named after him.

Nairn, Stephen (d. 1900) Businessman. Born in Glasgow, Scotland, he came to Canada in 1863 and joined his brother in the milling trade. He came to Winnipeg in 1884 to establish the Nairn Oatmeal Mills. He was active in Knox Presbyterian Church and was on boards for the Winnipeg parks and the Winnipeg General Hospital. He served as president of the Winnipeg Board of Trade and the Winnipeg Grain Exchange. Nairn Avenue in Winnipeg was named after him. *DCB* XII, 777-78.

Nanton, Augustus Meredith (1860-1925) Banker. Born in Toronto, he left school at age 13 and worked his way up in the banking business. He came to Winnipeg in 1883 as resident partner of Osler, Hammond and Nanton, investment bankers, and oversaw the financing of four railways in the 1890s. By 1900 he was on the boards of dozens of corporations and associations. His home in Winnipeg was called Kilmorie. He was president of the Manitoba Patriotic Fund during WWI, and was knighted in 1917 for his war work. During the Winnipeg General Strike of 1919 he personally patrolled his grounds at Kilmorie because of threats against him, and his barn at Rosser was burned down by an arsonist. He returned to Toronto in 1924 to become president of the Dominion Bank. See the biography by Roderick Macbeth (1931); Paul Nanton, "A.M. Nanton's Years in Winnipeg, 1883-1926," *Manitoba History,* no. 6 (fall 1983): 15-20.

Nanton, Edward A. (1901-1967) Banker. Born in Winnipeg, he was educated at Appleby College, Trinity College (Toronto), and Magdalen College (Oxford). He began to work for the Osler, Hammond and Nanton Company Limited in 1923, becoming director in 1933 and chair of the board in 1953. He went overseas with the RCAF in 1940 and served as a flying instructor until 1945. He moved to Calgary in 1957.

Nault, André (1829-1924) Insurgent. Although not a Métis, he commanded the Métis who captured Fort Garry in 1870, and also commanded the firing squad for Thomas Scott.* He escaped to the United States, returning to Manitoba in 1873. Arrested for the murder of Scott, he was released after a trial in 1874 resulted in a hung jury. There are scattered but extensive papers at the PAM.

Neale, Percy Reginald (1851-1906) NWMP officer. Born in England, he joined the NWMP in 1873 as a non-commissioned officer, serving first at Lower Fort Garry. He was rapidly promoted, and was superintendent by 1884. He was in active service during the North-West Rebellion of 1885, subsequently assuming command of the division at Fort Macleod. Neale was relieved of his post and sent on leave in 1888, then retired in 1890, ostensibly for health reasons. He was appointed to the customs service in 1892, and two years later he absconded to England with over $6,000 in funds. He was brought back for trial, convicted, and sentenced to seven years' imprisonment. Upon release he moved to Winnipeg, where he died.

Neil, George (b. 1870) Contractor, curler. Born in Ayrshire, Scotland, he came to Winnipeg in 1902 and established a contracting business. Neil was one of the major promoters of Scottishness in Winnipeg, belonging to the Clan Stuart Scottish Society and the St. Andrew's Society. Particularly active in curling, he was a member of the Thistle Curling Club and of the board of council of the Manitoba Curling Association. He was responsible for establishing the "Scottish Bonspiel" in 1907, in which, by 1913, 17 Scottish societies competed.

Neilson, William J. (1854-1903) Physician. Born in Perth, Lanark County, Canada, he received a medical education at McGill College. He moved to Winnipeg in 1881, where he lectured on anatomy at the Manitoba Medical School. In 1883 he became medical health officer for Winnipeg. He was chosen Conservative MLA for Winnipeg North in 1899.

Nelson, Earle a.k.a. Virgil Wilson (1898-1928) Serial rapist, murderer. Born in San Francisco, little is known of his early life. He was expelled from school in grade two, could not keep a job, and complained of pains in his head and of "spells." He spent some time in a mental institution. According to police, his career of violence began in San Francisco in 1926, when his first female victim was raped and strangled. He allegedly repeated the same modus operandi more than 20 times across the United States as far east as Philadelphia, becoming in the process notorious as the "Gorilla Strangler." His trail of violence ended in Winnipeg in 1927 with two killings in early June, one of a 14-year-old "flower girl" and the other of a 27-year-old housewife. Captured near Wakopa, Manitoba, on 15 June 1927, after Canada's largest manhunt, he escaped when his guard left the Killarney town hall lockup to find matches. He was subsequently recaptured and taken for trial to Winnipeg. Tried only for the death of the housewife, Nelson was hanged on 13 January 1928. He never confessed to any of the crimes, and the link to the American deaths was purely circumstantial.

Nelson, George (1783-1859) Fur trader. Born in Montreal, he became a clerk apprentice to Parker, Gerrard, and Ogilvy, a firm associated with the XY Company. He was first posted to what is now Wisconsin, and in 1804 became a clerk in the NWC, serving at various posts around Lake Winnipeg and the Dauphin River. He survived the explosion of a keg of gunpowder in 1807 with little ill effect. He later moved to Manitonamingan Lake north of Lake Superior, where competition with the HBC (for which he had little stomach) was severe. He retired briefly, but at the time of the amalgamation of the NWC and HBC was at Moose Lake, nursing a grievance against his treatment. He was made redundant in 1823, and he retired to Lower Canada, where he experienced continual family disaster. He was critical of his brother Wolfred for involvement in the Rebellion of 1837 in Lower Canada. Throughout his life Nelson wrote extensively of his experiences and observations. One journal was published as *A Winter in the St. Croix Valley: George Nelson's Reminiscences,* edited by Richard Bardon and G.L. Nute (1948), and another as *"The Orders of the Dreamed": George Nelson on Cree and Northern Ojibwa Religion and Myth, 1823,* edited by Jennifer Brown and Robert Brightman (1988). For a biographical sketch, see Sylvia Van Kirk, "George Nelson's 'Wretched' Career, 1802-1823," in *Rendezvous: Selected Papers of the Fourth North American Fur Trade Conference, 1981. DCB* VIII, 652-54.

Nesbitt, John Roger (1873-1948) Dairy executive. Born in Ontario, he came to Manitoba in 1896 and soon became associated with B. Scott's Creamery at Shoal Lake. He pioneered in packing butter in hermetically sealed containers, shipping them to the Yukon beginning in 1897. He was active in dairy associations and in local government. He is a member of the Manitoba Agricultural Hall of Fame.

Neufeld, Kornelius Herman (1892-1957) Musician. Born in Nikolajewa, Russia, he studied at the Moscow Conservatory and immigrated to Winkler in 1923. He organized church choirs in Winkler and elsewhere in Manitoba, seeking to make the Mennonites "a singing people." He founded the Winkler Music Festival in 1936. He acted as a music publisher, often of his own choral works.

Newton, Alison Houseon (Lockerbie) (1890-1967) Painter. Born in Edinburgh, Scotland, she was educated at Trinity Academy and the Art School of Edinburgh. She came to Winnipeg in 1923 and worked for Eaton's and Brigden's. An active painter, she was president of the Manitoba Society of Artists in 1943 and honorary president of the Canadian Federation of Artists in 1946. She moved to Toronto in 1955 and died there.

Newton, Chris H. (b. 1871) Police chief. Born near Sleaford, Lincolnshire, England, he was educated at Trent College Nottingham and Moravian College in Prussia. He came to Manitoba in 1891, working in commerce, then farming at Rounthwaite from 1893 to 1901. He joined the Winnipeg City Police Force in 1901, rising to patrol sergeant in 1904, sergeant in 1906, and inspector and chief of detectives in 1908. He served as deputy chief from 1911 to 1919 and became chief on 12 June 1919 in the midst of the Winnipeg General Strike, when the striking police force was replaced by temporary constables. He retired in 1934. He was the first president of the Manitoba Football Association in 1892 and an active cricketer. See Robert Hutchison, *A Century of Service* (1974).

Newton, Frederick Young (1870-1959) Farmer, municipal politician. Born in Cobourg, Ontario, he came to Manitoba as a child. He farmed in Carberry and then operated hardware businesses in Dauphin and Grandview. He was an ardent curler. He was reeve of Shellmouth and mayor of Roblin. Newton served as Conservative MLA from Russell from 1911 to 1932.

Newton, George Mode (b. 1877) Business executive, beekeeper. Born in Ontario, he came to Winnipeg in 1898 and became manager of Greenshields Limited. In 1919 he was appointed director and general manager of Greenshields for Western Canada. At his residence "Old England" in Fort Garry, he gardened extensively and was the owner of one of the largest apiaries in Western Canada. He was president of the Manitoba Beekeepers' Association.

Newton, Gertrude (1895-1972) Soprano. Born in England, she came to Winnipeg in 1910. She sang soprano solos at Fort Rouge United Church beginning in 1916 and at Knox United Church beginning in 1923. She spent some time in London, England, but returned to Winnipeg in 1933 to sing for many years with the Winnipeg Light Opera. From 1947 to 1954 she was soloist and choir leader at Harstone United Church. She then moved to California, returning to Canada (Victoria, British Columbia) in 1964.

Nicholson, Richard J. (1864-1890) Lacrosse player. Born in Montreal, he came to Winnipeg in 1885 and soon took the lead in local lacrosse as a member of the Winnipeg Lacrosse Club. He captained the Winnipeg Juniors in 1888. He died of typhoid fever.

Nisbet, James S. (1823-1874) Missionary. Born in Glasgow, Scotland, he came with his family to Canada in 1844. He graduated in theology from Knox College, Toronto, in 1849 and was ordained as a pastor in Oakville in 1850. In 1862 the Presbyterian Church of Canada chose him to assist John Black* in Kildonan and to study the possibility of an Indian mission in HBC territory. He finally managed to open an itinerant mission in Prince Albert in 1866 with the assistance of two mixed-bloods, George Flett and John McKay. The missionary party travelled overland by oxcart in the summer of 1866. Nisbet brought a schoolteacher to the mission in 1867. Teaching and church services were initially in both Cree and English, although English increasingly predominated. Nisbet was later criticized for this tendency, as well as for his emphasis on farming rather than evangelizing. His papers (1863-69) and his diary (1868-74) are in the PAM.

Noble, Robert M. (1901-1994) Journalist. Born in Halifax, he moved to Winnipeg after the Halifax Explosion. He joined the *Toronto Star* in the 1920s and returned to Winnipeg as a freelance journalist in the 1930s. He covered the building of the Alcan Highway. He joined the *Winnipeg Free Press* in 1950 on the cultural beat, writing about subjects ranging from the symphony to the Beatles' Minneapolis concert of 1964.

Nolin, Charles (1837-1907) Métis leader. Born in St. Boniface, he supported the Council of Assiniboia in 1869 along with other conservative Métis figures. In early 1870, however, he was elected a delegate from Ste. Anne des Chênes to the Convention of Forty, at which he opposed Louis Riel on several occasions, ultimately voting against the establishment of Red River as a separate province. He was subsequently elected to the Assembly that was to govern provisionally, but was soon arrested by Riel. Nolin attempted to gain the leadership of the Métis after Riel's exile. He was elected to the Manitoba legislature in 1874 and became minister of agriculture in 1875. He soon resigned to sit as an independent, in which capacity he was highly critical of the treatment of the Métis. He retreated to Saskatchewan in 1879, after losing out in a power struggle in the legislature and being reprimanded for election irregularities. He became a leader of the Métis in the South Saskatchewan River district, and was a supporter of Riel upon his return as leader. Arrested in 1885, he was freed in return for his testimony against Riel. He later received patronage support from the Tory government, but was never again politically successful. *DCB* XIII, 770-72.

Nolin, Jean-Baptiste (c. 1742-1826) Fur trader. For many years he controlled the fur trade in the region of the Sault as agent for the NWC. In 1816 Lord Selkirk* met him and urged that he and his family settle in Red River. In 1819, with the aid of many inducements from Selkirk, he did so, moving to Pembina. When the Pembina post and settlement were closed by John Halkett* in 1823, Nolin and his family moved to St. Boniface, where in his later years he lodged with Bishop Provencher.* His daughters opened the first girls' school in Western Canada in 1829 at St. Boniface. See Donald Chaput, "The 'Misses Nolin' of Red River," *The Beaver* (Winter 1975): 14-17. *DCB* VI, 546-48.

Nolin, Louis (fl. 1815-20) Interpreter. Probably born in Sault Ste. Marie, he was engaged for the HBC by Colin Robertson* in 1815, and he accompanied Robertson to Red River, acting as interpreter there. Robertson regarded Nolin as the only Canadian with "any talent for secret service," but did not trust him. Nolin made a deposition about Seven Oaks in 1816 and provided information about early flooding in the region. He accompanied the invasion party led by Proteus D'Orsonnens* to Fort Douglas in the winter of 1816-17. He was acquitted with Robertson in 1818 of charges of the destruction of Fort Gibraltar, and he returned to the settlement, where he operated as a private trader.

Noonan, Nancy (1920-1990) Musician. Born in Medicine Hat, Alberta, she was raised in Brandon. She studied piano at the Trinity School of Music in London and came to Winnipeg in the 1940s as a teacher, accompanist, and ensemble performer. She helped found the University of Manitoba Chamber Music Group. Noonan became a student again, attending Brandon University from 1979 to 1982. She died in St. Boniface.

Norquay, John (1841-1889) Politician, provincial premier. Born near St. Andrews of mixed-blood ancestry, he attended St. John's Collegiate School and became a schoolteacher before he began farming at High Bluff and fur trading on Lake Manitoba. Although not actively involved in the Red River Rebellion of 1869-70, at one point he served as a messenger from the Anglophone mixed-bloods to Louis Riel. High Bluff elected him as its MLA by acclamation late in 1870, and after he moved to St Andrews, he represented that constituency from 1874 until his death. He was a prominent Anglican, active in the diocese and in the St. John's Collegiate School. Like many leading mixed-bloods, he was a veritable giant of a man, over six feet tall and weighing over 300 pounds. He spoke a number of languages, including English, French, Cree, and Saulteaux. In the legislature he assumed the leadership of a major bloc of Anglophone mixed-bloods, becoming minister of public works and agriculture in 1871. In 1875 he was acknowledged as leader of one of the Anglophone factions in the province — the mixed-bloods — which had an equal number of legislative seats (eight) to the Francophones and also to the new settlers from Ontario. In 1878 he became premier, presiding over a province that was growing rapidly and shifting demographically towards Anglophone Protestants. Politics centred around railroads, with all Manitobans seeking a share of the CPR's hoped-for competitors. Ottawa disallowed Manitoba railroad charter legislation in 1882. The railroad controversy eventually brought Norquay down in 1887, when he was unable to find financing for the Red River Valley Railway, which was intended to link Winnipeg with the United States, and (with the assistance of Prime Minister Macdonald) ended up with a shortfall in the province's books. Norquay was known as one of the province's finest speakers, possessed of a "soft, clear, musical voice, notably resonant." He died unexpectedly in the summer heat of 1889. There is no full-length biography. His papers are at the PAM. *DCB* XI, 643-47.

Norris, Tobias Crawford (1861-1936) Provincial premier. Born in Brampton, Canada, of Irish descent, he migrated to Manitoba with his family and moved from farming into auctioneering, where he established a considerable reputation. In 1896 he was first elected as a Liberal MLA for Lansdowne, and in 1910 he became leader of the Liberal Party. Norris became premier of Manitoba in 1915 when Sir

Rodmond Roblin* resigned over a construction scandal involving the legislative building. During his term of office (1915-22), the government had to deal with wartime conditions and the return of peace, including the post-war challenges of the Winnipeg General Strike of 1919. The Norris ministry has been labelled "the centre of reform activity in Canada" for its progressive legislation. It introduced temperance legislation, female suffrage, compulsory education, workmen's compensation, and minimum-wage legislation, in addition to a public nursing system, rural farm credit, regulation of industrial conditions, and a mother's allowance for widowed dependent mothers. The province also increased road construction and public works, while balancing its books. Norris's great failure, perhaps, was his inability to intervene successfully in the labour unrest of 1919; the provincial government stood aside while the strikers in Winnipeg battled the city and the federal government. His government was defeated in 1922, but Norris remained in the legislature until 1925, when he unsuccessfully contested a federal seat. He then returned to the provincial legislature until taking up an appointment to the Board of Railway Commissioners. He died in office in Toronto. His premier's papers are in the PAM. There is no full-length biography.

Norris-Elye, Leonard (1884-1958) Lawyer, museum keeper. Born in England, he came to Winnipeg in 1912 and practised law until 1930, when he began teaching at Ravenscourt School. He remained at Ravenscourt until 1938, when he became director of the Manitoba Museum. He retired in 1952.

Northwood, George W. (1876-1959) Architect, war hero. Born in Ottawa, he was educated at McGill University. He came to Winnipeg in 1905 and established an architectural firm. He designed many Winnipeg buildings before 1914, when he went overseas with the 8th Battalion. Captured by the Germans in 1915, he returned to Winnipeg in 1918 as a major, having been awarded the Victoria Cross. He established the firm Northwood and Chivers, which designed the Civic Auditorium (now the Archives Building) and the Federal Building on Main Street. From 1931 to 1933 he was Dominion superintendent of unemployment and farm relief. He was elected a fellow of the Royal Architectural Institute of Canada in 1938. He was a president of the Manitoba Club.

Norton, Moses (c. 1735-1773) HBC chief factor. There is much uncertainty about his life, thanks to the hostility of Samuel Hearne,* who described him negatively in 1795. He contracted to serve with the HBC in 1753, becoming accountant and assistant at Fort Prince of Wales in 1756. In 1762 he was appointed chief factor at Churchill. He was much trusted by the London Committee, and he was particularly interested in northern expansion. He lived well at Fort Prince of Wales and was accused of being a "notorious smuggler." *DCB* IV, 583-85.

Norton, Richard (1701-1741) HBC governor, explorer. He first came to the Bay in 1714. He was a member of the advance party sent to establish a post at Churchill River in 1717, experiencing much privation and danger during the winter of 1717-18. He probably got as far north as latitude 60°. He commanded Fort Prince of Wales in 1723 and was moved as second-in-command to York in 1726. He returned to the Bay in 1731 as chief factor and commander of Fort Prince of Wales, and he spent much of his effort constructing a stone building on the site. He was reprimanded for disregarding orders in 1739, and he died shortly after his return to England in 1741. *DCB* III, 489-90.

Novak, Gregory (1888-1961) Physician. Born in Western Ukraine, he came to Saskatchewan with his parents in 1908. He later moved to Winnipeg, where he attended Manitoba College and the University of Manitoba before taking pre-medical training at the University of Alberta. In 1919 he graduated from McGill University, the first Ukrainian to do so. He came to Winnipeg in 1920 and was prominent as head of St. Joseph's Maternity Ward. He was active with the Red Cross.

Nursey, Walter R. (1847-1927) Journalist, librarian. He was justice of the peace for the Keewatin District from 1875 to 1877, then served as Manitoba's deputy minister of agriculture in 1878 and provincial auditor from 1879 to 1889. A reporter for the *Winnipeg Herald* and the *Winnipeg Times,* he co-authored *Ten Years in Winnipeg* (1879) with Alexander Begg.* He constantly tried to start new newspapers in Winnipeg. In 1908 he published a biography of Isaac Brock. He was appointed inspector of Ontario libraries in 1910.

O'Brien, Murrough Charles (1868-1955) Country doctor. Born in Delhi, India, he came to Canada in 1890, completing his MD at the Manitoba Medical College in 1897. He opened a country practice in Dominion City and spent a lifetime itinerating the Manitoba-Saskatchewan border region until his retirement in 1955. He delivered more than 9,000 babies. During WWI he served in Russia as a major with the British War Emergency Railroad. A biography by R. Tyre, *Saddlebag Surgeon*, appeared in 1954.

O'Bryan, Gregory (1858-1907) Educator. Born in Halifax, he studied at the Séminaire de Philosophie in Montreal. After studying with the Jesuits he entered teaching, and his career included two years at the Collège de Saint-Boniface in Manitoba (1885-87). In 1896 he became rector of Loyola College in Montreal. He died in Montreal. *DCB* XIII, 776.

O'Connor, William John ("Billy," 1837-1910) Hotelier, sportsman. Born in Dublin, Ireland, he ran away to Boston as a boy, eventually becoming part owner of the Boston Hotel. In ill health, he moved to St. Paul in 1876, where he was recruited by the owners of the Grand Central Hotel of Winnipeg as its first manager. He later opened the Merchants Hotel but experienced financial difficulties when the boom collapsed in 1882. Later he opened a succession of Winnipeg hotels, finally leasing and remodelling the old Bodega Hotel (renamed the O'Connor). In 1905 he opened the Corona Hotel. He was called "the dean of hotel men in Winnipeg." He was a member of the IOOF, the Elks, and the Catholic Order of Foresters, and was president of the local chapter of the Eagles (as well as president of the Hotel Men's Association of Winnipeg) at the time of his death. O'Connor was also president of the Fort Garry Turf Club and active in the Winnipeg Driving Club and the Buffalo Park Driving Club. In addition, he was a dog fancier.

O'Donnell, John Harrison (1838-1912) Physician. Born in Simcoe, Upper Canada, he received an MD from Victoria University College in 1862. After several years of medical practice, in 1869 he was invited by John Schultz* to come to Red River. He and his family arrived in early November 1869, just in time to become caught up in the Red River Rebellion. He and his wife were in Schultz's fortified house when its inhabitants were forced to surrender to Louis Riel's Métis in December, and they spent 10 weeks imprisoned in Upper Fort Garry. As a justice of the peace, he signed the arrest warrant for Louis Riel and Ambroise Lépine* in 1873, by which the latter was brought to trial for the murder of Thomas Scott. He framed the province's first medical act in the legislature. He served in the Manitoba Legislative Council and became its Speaker; he also opposed the council's abolition. He helped found the University of Manitoba and was president of the College of Physicians and Surgeons of Manitoba until 1877. See his autoobiography *Manitoba As I Saw It: From 1869 to Date* (1909). Some papers are at the PAM.

O'Donoghue, William Bernard (1843-1878) Insurgent. Born in Sligo, Ireland, he went to the United States as a boy. He was always an Irish patriot and hostile to Great Britain. In 1868 he volunteered for mission service in Red River, becoming a teacher of mathematics at the Saint Boniface College. In 1869 he became involved in the Red River Rebellion, and was chosen to represent St. Boniface at the first council of residents in November of that year. His relationship with Riel and the Métis was always a bit mysterious; it was apparently in his honour that the flag of the provisional government carried a shamrock. O'Donoghue did not always agree with Riel, but he helped Riel seize the HBC treasury in December 1869, and he became treasurer of the provisional government. He helped Ambroise Lépine* capture "the Portage boys" (a pro-Canadian force organized at Portage la Prairie which marched on the settlement) in February, and refused to intervene to save the life of Thomas Scott.* He accompanied Riel when the Métis leader fled in the face of the Wolseley Expedition. O'Donoghue subsequently broke with Riel, regarding the Métis as having sold out to the British. He petitioned the United States president U.S. Grant for intervention in Red River, and then turned to the Fenians for assistance in liberating the "Republic of Rupert's Land," of which he claimed to be president. The Fenian "invasion" of October 1871 was a disaster, thanks partly to opposition from Louis Riel, and O'Donoghue remained in Minnesota, where he sought employment as a teacher. He was exempted by name from the amnesty to Riel and Ambroise Lépine in 1875, although finally granted clemency in 1877. Despite rumours of his assassination on the streets of St. Paul, Minnesota, he died of tuberculosis in that city. *DCB* X, 556-57.

Ogilvie, William (d. 1912) Dominion astronomer. Born in Ottawa, he was educated locally. He came west as an engineer in 1875 and worked in the Dauphin region. He was made a fellow of the Royal Geographical Society in 1891. In 1896 he became Dominion astronomer. He became commissioner of police in the Yukon while working there in 1897 and then commissioner of the territory in 1898, resigning in 1901. Ogilvie was working on a book on the Yukon when he died in Winnipeg of septic poisoning.

Ogletree, Francis (1826-1916) Indian agent. Born in Cork, Ireland, he came to Canada with his family at a young age and was educated in Brockville, Upper Canada. He migrated to Manitoba in 1869 and farmed for years at Portage la Prairie, serving as police magistrate and Indian agent for the district. In 1871 he was appointed to the Legislative Council of Manitoba, in which he served until its abolition. He was briefly a member of the Manitoba Executive Council in 1874.

O'Grady, John Waller de Courcey (1854-1914) Banker, militia officer. Born in Canada, he was educated at Lennoxville before joining the Bank of Montreal in 1870. He left it in 1905 to organize the Northern Bank in Winnipeg. Always active in militia affairs, in 1911 he became commanding officer of the 90th Winnipeg Rifles. He died in Winnipeg.

O'Kelly, Christopher Patrick John (1895-1922) War hero. Born in Winnipeg, he attended local schools and was an undergraduate at St. John's College when he volunteered for the 144th Battalion. He was later transferred to the 52nd battalion of the Canadian Expeditionary Force, and was awarded the Victoria Cross at Passchendaele in October 1917. Subsequently he was promoted to captain. O'Kelly was among the first soldiers to return to Winnipeg, and was welcomed at a reception at Columbus Hall on 14 April 1918. Rejoining the Winnipeg Rifles in 1921 with the rank of major, he died in a boating accident at Lac Seul, Quebec, while prospecting for mining sites with a companion.

Olesków, Josef (1860-1903) Immigration publicist. Born in Galicia (Ukraine), he studied at the University of Lemberg and received his doctorate from the University of Erfurt in Germany. He became professor of agronomy at a teacher's college in Lemberg, and became an early advocate of the planned immigration of Ukrainian peasants to Canada, rejecting Brazil and Argentina as prospective destinations. In 1895 he established contact with the Canadian Department of the Interior and published *Pro vilni zemli* ("About Free Lands") in July 1895. Shortly after, he visited Canada to explore the possibilities of immigration, becoming enthusiastic about an area in Alberta. Upon his return to Ukraine he established an immigrant aid committee and published more pamphlets, including *O emigratsii* ("About emigration"). As a result, 30 families were sent to Alberta in 1896, and over the next few years Olesków encouraged thousands more to leave, many of them settling in Manitoba. Despite his vision, Olesków underestimated the capacity of peasants to become pioneers, and overstated assimilationism. See V.J. Kaye, *Early Ukrainian Settlements in Canada, 1895-1900: Dr. Josef Olesków's Role in the Settlement of the Canadian Northwest* (1964). *DCB* XIII, 784-6.

Oleson, Tryggvi Julius (1911-1963) Educator, historian. Born in Glenboro, Manitoba, he was educated at the University of Manitoba (where he received his BA and MA) and the University of Toronto. He became a member of the history department of the University of Manitoba, specializing in the history of Icelanders in North America. His volume in the Canadian Centenary Series, *Early Voyages and Northern Approaches, 1000-1632* (1963), offered a controversial interpretation of the Thule culture of the North.

Olive, George (1887-1963) Politician. Born in Leeds, England, he came to Canada in 1910 and settled in Transcona in 1914. He was employed with the CNR as a steamfitter from 1912 until 1952, when he retired. Olive served as Transcona mayor (1933, 1938-45) and as CCF MLA from Transcona-Kildonan (1945-53). He lived in New York after his retirement. He died in Winnipeg.

O'Lone, Robert ("Bob," d. 1872) Tavern-keeper. One of two brothers from the Hell's Kitchen district of New York City, he and Hugh O'Lone were proprietors of the Red Saloon. He served as a delegate from Winnipeg to the November 1869 council meeting between Métis and mixed-bloods, and his opinions were highly regarded by James Ross.* He was killed in a barroom brawl.

Olson, Shirley (c. 1955-1990) Lawyer, Native rights activist. Born on the Peguis Reserve, she was educated at various residential schools, the University of Manitoba (where she studied arts), and the University of British Columbia (where she studied law). She was called to the bar in 1986 and specialized in family law. Always concerned for Native rights, she became executive director of the Assembly of Manitoba Chiefs in 1989. She died suddenly during a demonstration in St. Boniface.

Omand, John (1823-1905) Missionary. Born in the Orkney Islands, he came to Red River in 1844 to engage in mission work in St. John's Parish. In 1858 he settled on land in St. James, and he resided there until his death. Omand's Creek bears his name.

O'Meara, James Dallas (1849-1901) Cleric, educator. Born on Manitoulin Island, he was educated at the University of Toronto and studied theology at Huron College. He came to Manitoba in 1873 and was ordained an Anglican priest. He later became a professor at St. John's College, first of exegeses, then of systematic theology and apologetics. In 1876 he became canon of the St. John's Cathedral Chapter and in 1882 deputy warden of St. John's College. In 1897 he was appointed dean of Rupert's Land.

Ooligbuck (d. 1852) Inuit interpreter. He first came to the HBC post at Churchill in 1824. He accompanied Captain Franklin* on his overland expedition that began in 1825. In 1827 he joined the service of the HBC. He later accompanied the 1839-40 overland expedition to the Mackenzie and Coppermine Rivers that was headed by Peter Dease* and Thomas Simpson,* then the John Rae* expedition of 1846. *DCB* VIII, 663-64.

Oozawekwuen See Yellow Quill.

Orchard, Harold (1878-1956) Horticulturalist. Born in Port Perry, Ontario, he moved with his family to Graysville, Manitoba, in 1887. In 1912 he established his own farm, the Glenorchie Farm Nursery, in the Miami district. On this facility he crossbred new apple varieties, including "White Lake." He was active on the show circuit and also in local government. He is a member of the Manitoba Agricultural Hall of Fame.

O'Reilly, John (1844-1914) Lawyer. Born in Canada, he was educated at Trinity College, Toronto. He joined his father's law firm in Manitoba in 1874, later becoming an associate of Daniel Carey.* From 1894 to 1910 he acted as Crown counsel in Selkirk, then was registrar for Portage la Prairie until his death. He died in Portage la Prairie and was buried outside St. John's Cathedral, Winnipeg.

Orlikow, David (1919-1998) Politician. Born in Winnipeg's North End, he was educated at the Workman's Circle School, St. John's High School, and the University of Manitoba, where he studied pharmacy. He was elected a school trustee in 1945, beginning an unbroken 43-year political run that graduated to Winnipeg City Council, then the Manitoba legislature, and finally Parliament. In the process he won 18 consecutive elections, including nine to the

House of Commons, where he sat as an NDP champion from 1962 until his defeat in 1988. He described himself as a "right-wing Social Democrat" and had little patience with the doctrinaire wing of the NDP.

Orlikow, Velma (Jessie) ("Val," 1917-1990) Plaintiff. Born in Winnipeg, she was one of nine Canadians who sued the United States Central Intelligence Agency in 1984 for subjecting them unknowingly to experimental mind-control techniques in Montreal between 1957 and 1962. The CIA settled out of court in 1988 but maintained that the settlement was not an admission of guilt. Orlikow died in Winnipeg.

Osborn, John Robert (1899-1941) War hero. Born in Norfolk, England, he served in the Royal Naval Volunteer Reserve in WWI, later moving to Saskatchewan and then Winnipeg, where he worked for the CPR. A member of the First Battalion, Winnipeg Grenadiers, he was called to active duty in 1939 as company sergeant-major. He won a Victoria Cross in Hong Kong when he saved members of his company by yelling "Duck, lads" and throwing himself on top of a grenade.

Osborne, Helen Betty (1952-1971) Murder victim. Born in Norway House to Cree parents, she was locally educated before being sent to Margaret Barbour Collegiate in The Pas in 1969. On 12 November 1971 she was abducted by four males in a car. She was subsequently sexually assaulted, beaten, and stabbed many times with a screwdriver. Although the identity of her killers was known to many people in The Pas, no arrests were made until 1986. The trial of two accused men took place in 1987 — two others were granted immunity in return for their testimony — with the media national following it closely. Only one, Dwayne Johnston, was convicted. This case, along with the shooting of J.J. Harper,* prompted the Manitoba government in 1988 to begin an inquiry into the treatment of Aboriginal people under the province's criminal justice system. See Lisa Priest, *Conspiracy of Silence* (1989).

Ostenso, Martha (1900-1963) Author. Born in Norway, she came with her parents to North America at an early age, living in various American towns before settling in Brandon, Manitoba. She was educated at Brandon Collegiate, Kelvin Technical High School in Winnipeg, and the University of Manitoba. She taught school in the Interlake region before

becoming a *Winnipeg Free Press* reporter. She became romantically involved with novelist/teacher Douglas Durkin,* and he helped her with her writing. The two lived together for many years and married in 1945. In 1925 she published *Wild Geese*, a novel that in manuscript won a $13,500 prize for best first novel in competition with 1,700 others. Like many Prairie novels, it features a patriarchal father (whose tyranny is compared to the land he farms) and intergenerational conflict. Ostenso subsequently lived in the United States, publishing a number of other novels and other writings as well as spending much time in Hollywood writing film scripts. See David Arnason, "The Development of Prairie Realism" (PhD diss., University of New Brunswick, 1980).

Ostrander, Alice (1893-1970) Educator. Born in Colchester, England, she became blind at an early age. She attended the Royal School for the Blind, Surrey, and came to Canada with her parents in 1912. During WWI she used a knitting machine to knit 14,000 pairs of socks and leggings for the troops, winning a special commendation from the Prince of Wales for this effort. In 1918 she was appointed by the CNIB as the first home teacher for the blind in Western Canada, and she continued in this work until her marriage in 1927. She returned to teaching in 1949 after the death of her husband.

Owen, David Dale (1807-1860) Surveyor. Born in Scotland, the son of reformer Robert Dale Owen, he went to the United States in 1828, graduating from the Ohio Medical College in 1836 and taking up a career as a geological surveyor. In 1848 he surveyed in Wisconsin, Iowa, and Minnesota, making his way as far north as Lake Winnipeg and continuing along the Winnipeg River system to Lake of the Woods and Lake Superior. He described the countryside along the Red River and listed fossils in the rock at Lower Fort Garry. See his *Report of a Geological Survey of Wisconsin, Iowa, and Minnesota* (1852).

Oxton, Stephen C. (d. 1927) Stonemason, civil servant. Born in Liverpool, England, he came to Canada in 1914. A stonemason, he was involved in the construction of the Manitoba legislative building. He was appointed deputy minister of public works in 1916, serving until 1922, when he became chair of the Manitoba Fair Wages Board.

Padwick, Percy Graham ("Paddy," 1888-1938) Music educator. Born in England, he came to Winnipeg in 1914. He taught at Lord Roberts Junior High School in 1920 and founded the Winnipeg Youth Orchestra in 1923. He then taught music at Kelvin Technical High School from 1926 to 1938. He founded the Western Canada Junior Symphony Orchestra to perform concerts over CKY to a national audience. He died in Winnipeg.

Pahtahsega, a.k.a. Peter Jacobs (c. 1807-1890) Missionary. Born in Upper Canada, he converted to Methodism at a young age and began preaching to Indians in 1836. He subsequently accompanied James Evans* westward, helping to found the Rossville Mission near Norway House before establishing his own base at Fort Alexander. In 1842 he left there to journey to England for ordination. He later was established at Fort Frances on Rainy Lake, leaving in 1850. He journeyed west again in 1852 before returning to Ontario to hold intermittent postings. His later years were troubled by excessive drinking. He wrote *Journal of the Reverend Peter Jacobs, Indian Wesleyan Missionary, from Rice Lake to the Hudson's Bay Territory, and Returning: Commencing May 1852; With a Brief Account of His Life, and a Short History of the Wesleyan Mission to That Country* (1853). *DCB* XI, 660-61.

Painchaud, Robert (1941-1978) Educator, historian. Born in St. Boniface, he was educated at the Collège de Saint-Boniface, United College, the University of Manitoba, and the University of Winnipeg before receiving his PhD from the University of Toronto. A member of the history department at the University of Winnipeg, he was killed in a plane crash in Newfoundland while travelling as a member of the National Sites and Monuments Board.

Palliser, John (1817-1887) Explorer. Born in Dublin, Ireland, to a distinguished Anglo-Irish family, he was educated abroad before intermittent attendance at Trinity College, Dublin. He was fluent in three foreign languages (French, German, and Italian). He had an appointment as a captain in the Waterford Artillery Militia, but was seldom on active service. In 1847 he travelled to North America to hunt big game, visiting New Orleans and Panama before returning to Ireland in 1849. This tour produced his *Solitary Rambles and Adventures of a Hunter in the Prairies* (1853). In 1856 he offered the Royal Geographical Society a proposal for a journey of exploration through what is now Western Canada. The society upgraded the journey to a scientific expedition and obtained the support of the British government and the HBC. Palliser left for New York on 16 May 1857. He and his associates (Dr. James Hector,* Eugene Bourgeau,* Lieutenant Thomas Wright Blakiston, John William Sullivan) travelled to Red River by canoe through British territory, and then spent several years criss-crossing the West. The result was a series of reports appearing in 1859, 1860, and 1863, and a large map finally published in 1865. These added considerably to what was known about the southern prairies and Rocky Mountains. Particularly notable was Palliser's insistence on a fertile belt suited for agriculture on the edge of the semi-arid land of what became known as Palliser's Triangle. The expedition expressed concern about the future of the Native peoples. Palliser inherited the Irish estates of his family in 1862, and he made several later voyages to remote places. He died unmarried. See *The Papers of the Palliser Expedition, 1857-6* (1968) and Irene Spry, *The Palliser Expedition: An Account of John Palliser's British North American Exploring Expedition 1857-1860* (1963). *DCB* XI, 661-64.

Pambrun, Pierre-Chrysologue (1792-1841) Soldier, fur trader. Born in Lower Canada, he enlisted in the Voltigeurs Canadiens and was promoted from the ranks to second lieutenant for his service with distinction at the battle of Chateauguay. Left at loose ends when his unit was disbanded, he joined the HBC, departing for Red River with Colin Robertson.* While accompanying a fur brigade from the West in 1816, he was captured and taken prisoner by Métis led by Cuthbert Grant* as part of the fur-trade war. He was forced to accompany the Métis from Fort Qu'Appelle to Fort Douglas to Fort William, where Lord Selkirk* freed him. He testified for the HBC against the NWC in the court trials in Canada, and was in turn charged by the NWC. After the merger of the two companies he headed further west, ending up in the HBC's service in the Columbia District. He became a chief trader in 1839, his career progress hampered by his being a French Canadian and by his lack of formal education. He died at Fort Walla Walla after falling off a horse. See *Narratives of John Pritchard, Pierre Chrysologue Pambrun, and Frederick Damien Heurter, Respecting the Aggressions of the North-West Company, against the Earl of Selkirk's Settlement upon Red River* (1819); K.L. Holmes, "P.C. Pambrun" in *The Mountain Men and the Fur Trade of the Far West,* vol. 3, ed. L.R. Hafen (1968), 239-47. *DCB* VII, 671-72.

Pangman, Peter (1744-1819) Fur trader. Born in New Jersey, he was active in the fur trade out of Michilimackinac by 1767. In 1773 he came to York Factory to seek a shipping route to England but was sent packing by the HBC. He subsequently moved to the Saskatchewan River, where he spent most of his fur-trading career before retiring from the NWC in 1793. He died on his seigneury in Mascouche, Lower Canada. *DCB* V, 656-57.

Parfitt, Gilbert C. (1887-1966) Architect. Born in England, he studied architecture there. He remained in Winnipeg in 1912 after a visit, and worked with various local architectural firms. After service in the Canadian Expeditionary Force during WWI, he became a leading Winnipeg architect, noted for his medieval churches, stately monuments (the Winnipeg Cenotaph), and university buildings (the Tier and Buller Buildings at the University of Manitoba). He became president of the Manitoba Architects' Association in 1927. He was an amateur painter, and he studied at the Winnipeg School of Art in 1927-28, serving on the Art Committee thereafter. He later became provincial architect, retiring in 1957. He then became head of Manitoba's office of Planning and Development until 1961. He was a fellow of the Royal Architectural Institute of Canada.

Parisien, Norbert (1814-1870) Victim. Born in the West, little is known of Parisien before his capture as a "spy" by the Portage expedition of 1870 on its way to Kildonan. Held overnight at the Kildonan Church, Parisien escaped, seized a gun, and fatally wounded Hugh John Sutherland, who came upon him inadvertently on horseback. Parisien attempted to get away across the ice, but was soon captured and was treated very roughly by the crowd of men who had gone after him. He died a few weeks later, apparently of head wounds suffered in the scuffle on the ice. Ironically, the date of his death was 4 March 1870, the same day as the execution of Thomas Scott.* Parisien was sometimes included (with Thomas Scott and Hugh John Sutherland) as one of the few casualties of the Red River Rebellion. Métis supporters often attempted to place his death on one side of a balance sheet that put Thomas Scott on the other side. *DCB* IX, 617-18.

Parker, Matthew A. (1871-1953) Educator. Born in Glasgow, Scotland, he was educated at Glasgow University, receiving his BSc in 1902. He came to Canada in 1904 to become the first professor of chemistry at the University of Manitoba and founder of the chemistry department there. He helped found the Scientific Club of Winnipeg and the Canadian Institute of Chemistry. He received an honorary doctorate from the University of Manitoba in 1921. He retired in 1937 and died in Winnipeg. His papers are at the UML Archives.

Parker, William James (1896-1971) Business executive. Born in Sanford, Manitoba, he graduated with a BSc from the University of Manitoba. After many years as director of elevator associations, he became president of the Manitoba Pool Elevators in 1940, also serving as president of Canadian Seed Sales Limited and Pool Packers Limited. He was a member of the Order of the British Empire, and he held the Medal of Service of the Order of Canada. He is a member of the Manitoba Agricultural Hall of Fame. See W.L. Hamilton, *Service at Cost: A History of Manitoba Pool Elevators 1925-1975* (1975).

Pasichny, Michael (1924-1997) Cantor. Born in Winnipeg, he was educated at St. Nicholas Ukrainian Catholic School and the Basilian Fathers' monastery near Edmonton. After returning to Winnipeg in 1949, he worked as a bookkeeper. His real work, however, was as principal cantor to St. Nicholas Ukrainian Catholic Church, where in the 1970s he helped introduce English versions of Ukrainian liturgical songs to enable non-Ukrainian speakers to participate in the services. He died in a road accident in Wawa, Ontario.

Patmore, Henry Lewis (1861-1946) Nursery owner. Born in Essex, England, he first moved to London, Ontario. In 1888 he bought a nursery in Brandon and became a leading exponent of shelterbelts and tree planting. He served on the Exhibition Board and was the first president of the Brandon Pool. He is a member of the Manitoba Agricultural Hall of Fame.

Patrick, William (1852-1911) Educator, cleric. Born in Glasgow, Scotland, he graduated from Glasgow University. After teaching there for three years he served as a Free Kirk minister, first in Kirkintilloch, then in Dundee. He received an honorary DD from Glasgow University in 1893. He was appointed principal of Manitoba College in 1900, and he served until 1910. He was active in the temperance movement and was the author of *James, the Lord's Brother* (1906).

Patterson, James Colebrook (b. 1838) Lawyer, lieutenant-governor. Born in Ireland, he was educated at Dublin. He came to Canada in 1857 and studied law in Windsor, Canada. He became reeve of Windsor and MP for Essex County. He served as lieutenant-governor of Manitoba from 1895 to 1900. His papers from his lieutenant-governorship are at the PAM.

Paulley, Andrew Russell ("Russ," 1909-1984) Politician. Born in the Weston district of Winnipeg, he moved to Elmwood at an early age. Upon his marriage in 1938 he moved with his bride to Transcona, where he spent the remainder of his life. He worked in the CNR shops before entering politics, first as mayor of Transcona and then in 1953 as CCF (later NDP) member of the Manitoba legislature. He served as Transcona's MLA in the legislature from 1953 to 1978. He was leader of the Manitoba CCF from 1959 to 1969, and later served as minister of labour in the Schreyer government from 1969 to 1977. For ten years he was rector's warden of St. George's Anglican Church in Transcona and he was a past master of the Grand Lodge of Manitoba AFAM. His papers (1957-77) are at the PAM.

Paupenakis, Edward (1840-1911) Cleric. He was born at Norway House. His father was a Swampy Cree hunter who joined James Evans's* Methodist mission in the early 1840s and became a church leader. Edward worked for the HBC before joining Rev. John Semmens* at Norway House as an interpreter in 1874. He accompanied Semmens to Berens River in 1876, stayed at Nelson House as a missionary until 1880, and returned to preach at Norway House until 1888. He was the first northern Manitoba Cree to be ordained, on 23 June 1889. He served at several postings until his death in Warrens Landing. *DCB* XIV, 826-27.

Pearce, William (1848-1930) Civil engineer. He was in charge of land surveys in Manitoba and the North-West Territories from 1873 to 1881, later serving as superintendent of mines in Manitoba and the West. He was a member of the royal commission to inquire into freight rates in the West.

Pearl, Bert (1913-1986) Entertainer. Born in Winnipeg, he attended Aberdeen School and St. John's High School before taking the pre-medical course at the University of Manitoba on an Isbister scholarship. He moved to Toronto during the Depression to earn money to continue medical training, and found work with the CBC. He formed the Happy Gang, a radio musical troupe, in 1937. He was the "Gang's" star and emcee for over 20 years in Canada and the United States. In 1959 he went to Hollywood to write for Jimmy Durante. He later served as musical director for Gisele MacKenzie. Pearl was also well known as a pianist, appearing in nightclubs and with the Winnipeg Symphony Orchestra. He was a member of the Order of the Buffalo. He died in Hollywood.

Pearson, William (1865-1940) Developer. Born in Bowden, Cheshire, England, he came to Canada in 1883 and settled in St. François Xavier, Manitoba, where he established the first creamery in Western Canada in 1886. He later moved to Winnipeg and organized the National Land Company, which developed the Wildwood subdivision. He helped found the Winnipeg Real Estate Exchange and the Fort Rouge Bowling Club, as well as the Social Welfare Commission. He died in Winnipeg.

Pedley, Hugh (1852-1923) Cleric. The pastor of Winnipeg's Central Congregational Church, he was a keen curler and was chaplain of the Manitoba Curling Association at the end of the nineteenth century. He introduced the curlers' service at the Manitoba Bonspiel in 1895. His papers are in the United Church Archives, Toronto.

Peebles, Adam John Laing (1812-1902) Soldier. Born in Kent, England, of Scottish ancestry, he was educated at Royal Military College Sandhurst, and he served in the British army as an engineer. He came to Canada in 1849, eventually becoming active in the militia. In 1870 he was appointed deputy commissary officer (with the rank of captain) on Colonel Garnet Wolseley's* staff, and he remained in Winnipeg after the militia was disbanded in 1871. He soon became supply officer of Military District No. 10. In 1880 he became the first full-time police magistrate in Winnipeg, hearing hundreds of cases every year. He was occasionally criticized for his lack of legal training but was generally respected. He was on the first Board of Commissioners of Police, founded in 1884 to oversee the Winnipeg force. He died in Winnipeg. *DCB* XIII, 824.

Peel, William (1839-1932) Fruit grower. He came to Winnipeg with the Wolseley Expedition in 1870 and remained. He won a Gold Medal for Canadian fruit products at the Paris Exhibition in 1900 and repeated the feat at the Glasgow Exhibition in 1901.

Peguis (c. 1774-1864) Chief. Born near what is now Sault Ste. Marie, Ontario, he led a band of his people to the Red River around the turn of the century. The Selkirk settlers found a good friend in Peguis, who used his relationship with the settlement to cement his claims to the land his people had earlier occupied. Peguis assisted the settlers in retreating from Red River after the battle of Seven Oaks in 1816, and he helped Selkirk's de Meuron soldiers in recapturing Fort Douglas in January 1817. Later in 1817 Lord Selkirk* made a treaty with him, and after 1855 he received an annual pension from the HBC. In 1832, Missionary William Cockran* persuaded Peguis and a few of his people to settle in a community just north of present-day Selkirk, which by 1836 was known as St. Peter's. He was baptized into the Anglican Church in 1840, giving up three of his four wives to do so. He took the name William King, and his children used the last name Prince. In 1860 he protested to the Aborigines' Protection Society that he had been deprived of land he had never formally surrendered; the case was not resolved until after his death. Colin Inkster* recalled him as "short in stature, with a strong, well-knit frame, and the voice of an orator." His nose had been bitten off in a fracas around 1802, and he was often known as "Chief Cut-Nose." See A E. Thompson, *Chief Peguis and his Descendants* (1971). *DCB* IX, 626-27.

Pelly, Robert Parker (1790-1825) Governor. Born in England, he served in the East India Company army as a captain before becoming governor of Assiniboia from 1823 to 1825. He was not a great success. It was Pelly who took a series of watercolours by Peter Rindisbacher* to England and had oil copies made which replaced the original figure of Andrew Bulger* with himself.

Pennefather, John Pyne (1833-1913) Physician. Born in India, he attended Trinity College, Dublin, and eventually received a medical degree there. After practising medicine in London, England, he settled in Manitoba near Holland in 1880. He served as medical officer of the Winnipeg Light Infantry in 1885, and later practised medicine in Winnipeg. From 1903 to 1906 he ran a sanitorium in Holland. He wrote *Thirteen Years on the Prairies* (1892).

Penner, Jacob (1880-1968) Municipal politician. Born in Ukraine, he came to Manitoba in 1904 and taught school in Gretna. He subsequently moved to Winnipeg where he worked as a florist and an accountant. He helped found the Socialist Party of Canada in 1905 and the Social Democratic Party a few years later. He joined the Communist Party in

1921 and was its national chair in 1958. In 1934 he was elected to the Winnipeg City Council as a North End Communist, serving almost continuously until 1961. He insisted that his chief concern was to protect "those on the lower rung of the social ladder," and was particularly noted for his advocacy of low-rental housing.

Penrose, James (1845-1918) Civil servant, photographer. Born in England, he came to Manitoba in 1871. After a brief encounter with farming, he opened the third photography shop in Fort Garry, later turning to livestock importing. In 1893 he became chief inspector of the provincial liquor licence department, a post he held for many years.

Pentland, Harry Clare (1914-1978) Educator, historian. Born in Justice, Manitoba, he attended the Brandon Normal School, Brandon College (BA and University Gold Medal 1940), and the University of Oregon (MA 1941). He served in the Canadian army from 1942 to 1945, then attended the University of Toronto (studying for his PhD in economics, completed in 1961). He joined the University of Manitoba Department of Economics in 1949. He was president of the Manitoba Historical Society and the Manitoba Record Society. His major work, which was originally his doctoral thesis, was published posthumously as *Labour and Capital in Canada 1650-1860* (1981).

Pentreath, Edwyn Sandys Wetmote (1846-c. 1913) Cleric, temperance leader. Born in New Brunswick, he was educated in England, and he returned to Canada in 1865. He graduated from the General Theological Seminary in New York in 1872, and in 1874 became pastor of St. George's Church, Moncton. In 1882 he came to Christ Church, Winnipeg. He was chaplain of the 91st Battalion in 1885, received a doctorate from St. John's College in 1889, and became an honorary canon of St. John's Cathedral in 1891. He was noted for his work with the temperance movement, and he served as president of the Dominion Alliance. In 1897 he came out of retirement to become archdeacon of Columbia (in British Columbia). He died in California.

Perdue, William Edgerton (1850-1933) Lawyer, judge. Born in Brampton, Canada, he was educated at the University of Toronto, and he articled in the Winnipeg law offices of Macdonald, Macdonald, and Marsh. He was appointed judge of the Court of Queen's Bench in 1903, judge of the Court of Appeal in 1906, and chief justice of Manitoba in 1918. He retired in 1929.

Peregrine, David (1955-1989) Ballet dancer. Born David Evans in Llay, Wales, he moved to Ottawa as a child. He trained at the Nesta Tournaine School in Ottawa, the Banff School of Fine Arts, and the Royal Winnipeg Ballet school. He made his debut at the Royal Winnipeg Ballet in 1975 and became noted as a partner for Evelyn Hart. He died while flying his own airplane when it crashed in Alaska.

Peterson, Rudolph Frederick (1900-1975) Agricultural researcher. Born in Winnipeg, he graduated from the University of Manitoba in 1930 and did graduate work at the University of Minnesota. Appointed a wheat breeder in 1935, he served from 1948 to 1965 as head of cereal breeding at the research station in Winnipeg. He was associated in the 1950s with the development of the spring wheat variety "Selkirk," which resisted wheat rust. He served as a wheat breeder in Kenya after his retirement in 1965. He was the author of *Wheat — Botany, Cultivation and Utilization* (1965). He is a member of the Manitoba Agricultural Hall of Fame.

Pfimister, Alexander ("Sandy," c. 1886-1963) Entertainer. Born in Edinburgh, he attended Heriot-Watt College and came to Winnipeg in 1907. He worked the vaudeville circuit in Canada and the United States as a "Scotch Comedian" for some years. During WWI he served as a sergeant major in the 43rd Cameron Highlanders, singing with the Dumbells and with the 43rd Pipe and Drum Band. He was invalided home to Deer Lodge Hospital in 1918. After the war he became an entertainer on the charity circuit. He was also a vocalist on Winnipeg's first radio show, broadcast on 17 April 1922. He appeared with Ernie Holden (d. 1943) as "Alec and Sandy," doing Scottish comic dialogues. He retired from the stage in 1962. He died in Winnipeg.

Pfimister, Marshall Cameron ("Marsh," 1914-1971) Entertainer, producer. Born and educated in Winnipeg, he became a producer while performing at the Cave, a popular Winnipeg supper club. He subsequently ran Jack's Place, a nightclub on Pembina Highway, and was the original host of the Hollow Mug. He made many appearances on radio and television, and played on Rainbow Stage. At the time of his death — in an automobile accident in Selkirk involving a collision with a moving house — he was a public relations officer.

Phillips, Walter Joseph (1884-1962) Artist, educator. Born in England, the son of a Primitive Methodist minister, he moved with his family from manse to manse. At age 14 he was enrolled in Bourne College (near Birmingham) and at Birmingham's Municipal School of Art. In 1901 he became an assistant instructor at Yarmouth College, then emigrated to the Transvaal for five years. By the time of his return he was committed to being an artist. With his wife and baby he immigrated to Winnipeg in 1912, choosing the city "for no particular reason." He soon found a job at St. John's Technical High School, and he began sketching and exhibiting with LeMoine FitzGerald* and Cyril Barraud.* When the latter joined the Canadian Expeditionary Force in 1917, Phillips acquired his press, plates, paper, and tools, enabling him to fulfill a lifelong ambition to make prints. He and his family spent a year in England in 1924-25 to enable him to improve his technique, particularly with woodcut blocks, and he acquired a reputation as the nation's finest woodcut artist. Economic conditions in Winnipeg in the 1930s were as hard on Phillips as on any other artist, and he was anxious to leave. Election to full membership in the Royal Canadian Academy did not alleviate his fear that he was "getting older and getting nowhere" in a "more moth-eaten" city. Life seemed little more than a constant scramble for survival. In 1940 he began a 20-year run of teaching in the summers at the Banff School of Art, and a year later he accepted a position teaching at Calgary's Institute of Technology and Art. Finances improved and he built a house at Banff, to which he moved in 1948. He and his wife later moved to Victoria, where he died. Phillips was a fine watercolourist in the English tradition, and his woodcuts fetch astounding prices. Although there are signs of critical change, he still has not made his way into the first rank of Canadian artists, however; not least because his exquisite miniature landscapes did not shout their emotions. See Michael J. Gribbon, *Walter J. Phillips* (1978); Roger Boulet, *The Tranquility and the Turbulence: The Life and Work of Walter J. Phillips* (1981); Maria Tippett and Douglas Cole, eds., *Phillips in Print: The Selected Writings of Walter J. Phillips on Canadian Art and Nature* (1982).

Phillips, Wilford (1858-1918) Engineer. Born in Canada, he studied engineering in Toronto and held several engineering positions before being appointed manager of the Winnipeg Electric Railway Company in 1900 and serving until 1917. He died in Rochester, Minnesota.

Picard Destroismaisons, Thomas-Ferruce (1796-1866) Cleric. Born in Lower Canada, he was educated at the Séminaire de Quebec and the Collège de Nicolet, and was ordained in 1819. He was selected in 1820 to be a missionary in Red River, but was not very successful. Despite goodwill, he proved incapable of learning Native languages and returned east in 1827, where he had a long if ineffectual career in the priesthood.

Pickersgill, Frank (1915-1944) War hero. Born in Ashern, Manitoba, he was educated at United College. He then went to Paris to study French, and in 1940 volunteered for a mission behind enemy lines with British intelligence. Captured, he died in the Buchenwald Concentration Camp.

Pickersgill, John Whitney ("Jack," 1905-1997) Federal Cabinet minister, historian. Born in Wyecombe, Ontario, on 23 June 1905, he moved when young to a Manitoba homestead. He graduated from the University of Manitoba with a BA in 1927, moving on to Oxford to study history. In 1929 he accepted a lectureship at Wesley College in Winnipeg, and he taught history there until 1937, when he wrote the civil service examination and finished first that year. He was appointed to the Prime Minister's Office and remained there until 1949, rising to become clerk of the Privy Council in the St. Laurent government. Pickersgill was one of the most ardent supporters of Newfoundland's entry into Confederation in 1949. With Joey Smallwood's assistance, he ran for Parliament for the riding of Bonavista-Twillingate in 1949, serving in Parliament until 1967. He held several Cabinet portfolios (secretary of state, minister of citizenship and immigration, transport minister) before arranging his own appointment as chair of the transport commission, which he as minister had created. He retired from that post in 1975. Pickersgill was an active writer on politics and political biography, as well as a memoirist. His first work was *Canadian Responsible Government from British Hansard and Other Sources* (1927). He also wrote *The Mackenzie King Record* (1960), *The*

Liberal Party (1962), *My Years with Louis St. Laurent: A Political Memoir* (1975), *Louis St. Laurent* (1981), and *The Road Back* (1986). He was the author of an autobiography, *Seeing Canada Whole: A Memoir* (1994).

Pinkham, William Cyprian (1844-1928) Born in England, he attended St. Augustine College, Canterbury, graduating in 1868. That same year he became incumbent of St. James Church, Winnipeg, serving until 1882. From 1871 to 1883 he was superintendent of education for Manitoba's Protestant Schools, and in 1887 he was consecrated as Bishop of Saskatchewan and Calgary. There are papers in the Rupert's Land Archives. See Keith Wilson, *William Cyprian Pinkham* (1986).

Pitblado, Charles Bruce (1836-1913) Cleric. Born in Scotland, he came to Canada in 1851. After his father's death, he carried on the family contracting business until beginning his studies for the ministry at Presbyterian College, Halifax. He held several pastoral positions in the Maritimes before touring the West in 1880 and becoming pastor of St. Andrew's Presbyterian Church (Winnipeg) in 1881. He was chaplain of the 90th Rifles in 1885. He served at a church in San Francisco from 1888 until 1893, when he returned to Winnipeg as pastor of Westminster United Church. He eventually retired to California and died there.

Pitblado, Isaac (1867-1964) Lawyer. Born in Glenelg, Nova Scotia, he was educated at Dalhousie University and the University of Manitoba, where he earned his BA in 1886 and MA in 1893. He received an honorary LLD from Dalhousie in 1919. Pitblado came to Winnipeg in 1882 and was called to the Manitoba bar in 1890. A prominent lawyer, he was president of the Manitoba Law Society from 1917 to 1920. He also served as registrar of the University of Manitoba from 1893 to 1900. Regarded as an expert on the intricacies of railroad freight rates and grain marketing, he served on a number of royal commissions. He was a member of the Committee of 1,000 in the Winnipeg General Strike of 1919. An avid golfer and curler, he was president of the Manitoba Curling Association in 1910-11. His papers are at the UML Archives.

Plainval, Louis de See Frasse de Plainval, Louis.

Polson, Alexander (1777-1857) Wheelwright. Born in Kildonan, Scotland, he came to Red River in 1815 with Lord Selkirk's* third party of settlers. A carpenter, he was also a farmer and the owner of one of the early windmills in the country. He constructed spinning wheels for the settlement. He was an elder of the Kildonan Presbyterian Church, and is buried in Kildonan Cemetery.

Polson, Alexander (1840-1905) Civil servant. Born in Kildonan and educated at St. John's College, he taught school and farmed in Kildonan. Eventually he was able to sell his farm property when the city expanded. He represented Ward Six on the board of aldermen in 1887 and 1888, was the first trustee in the North End, and from 1893 was city licence inspector and relief officer.

Pond, Peter (1739/40-1807) Fur trader. Always adventurous, Pond was from a Connecticut family whose members were, by his own account, "all waryers Ither by Sea or Land." After military service in the Seven Years War, he entered the fur trade around Detroit in 1765 and began to move west from Michilimackinac in 1773. By 1775 he had joined Alexander Henry* at the mouth of the Winnipeg River and wintered at Dauphin Lake. From there he moved into the Athabasca watershed, which he helped open to fur trading. Accused of murdering a trading rival over the winter of 1786-87, Pond left the West in 1788 and never returned. He spent most of his later years in Connecticut. Not a Loyalist, he was always suspect in Canada for his American background. See H.R. Wagner. *Peter Pond, Fur Trader and Explorer* (1955). *DCB* V, 681-86.

Pooh, Winnie the See Winnipeg Bear.

Poole, Alfred (1910-1988) Stock breeder. Born in Kemnay, Manitoba, he was an important animal breeder (of Belgian horses, Hereford cattle, and Yorkshire swine) and winner of many championship awards. He and his wife Edith (née Gauld) are both members of the Manitoba Agricultural Hall of Fame.

Popovich, Matthew (1890-1943) Journalist. Little is known of his early life. He was a member of the Ukrainian Social Democratic Party in Winnipeg and editor of the journal *Toiling People* in the 1910s. He was converted to Bolshevism in 1917, and he participated in the Winnipeg General Strike in 1919. He was assistant editor of the *Ukrainian Labour News* in 1919 and editor of the *Voice of Labour* from 1922 to 1924. As leader of the Ukrainian Socialists of Canada, he was arrested in 1931 and jailed for five years. See Peter Krawchuk, *Matvii Popovych* (1986).

Porteous, Mark (1952-1996) Dance administrator. Born in Montreal, he studied arts administration at Ryerson Polytechnic and worked for various theatre groups before joining the Royal Winnipeg Ballet as tour manager in 1978. He was noted for his efficiency and his patience. He became co-general manager of the RWB in 1992, but retired to Vancouver a year later. He died of AIDS in Vancouver

Potts, John (d. 1764) HBC surgeon. He came to the Bay in 1738, serving first at York Factory and then at Moose Factory. He later was a factor on the East Main coast, where he found few furs and proved a failure. In 1761 he returned to Fort Prince of Wales as surgeon. *DCB* III, 533-34.

Pratt, Charles (c. 1816-1888) Missionary. An Aboriginal baptized at Red River by John West* in 1823, he worked for the HBC before studying with William Cockran* in the late 1840s. In the early 1850s he went to the Qu'Appelle River district as an Anglican lay preacher to the Cree-Assiniboine, and he remained there, often discontented because he had little status with the Church Missionary Society. He died on the Gordon Indian Reserve in what is now Saskatchewan. *DCB* XI, 710-11.

Pratt, Walter ("Babe," 1916-1988) Hockey player. Born in Stony Mountain, Manitoba, he started his NHL career with the New York Rangers in 1935 and played for 12 years as a defenceman with Toronto and Boston as well as New York. He played on two Stanley Cup teams, and he was elected to the Hockey Hall of Fame in 1966. In later years he lived in British Columbia and worked for the Vancouver Canucks from 1970 until his death, which occurred while he was watching a hockey game between Vancouver and Calgary.

Prefontaine, Edmund (1897-1971) Politician. He graduated from the University of Manitoba in 1918. A Liberal, he was elected MLA for the Carillon riding in 1935, serving until his death. He replaced his father, Albert, who had been minister of agriculture under John Bracken* and had served as an MLA for 30 years. Edmund was minister of municipal affairs from 1951 to 1958 and provincial secretary from

1956 to 1958. He was the major critic in the House of the Roblin government's plans to build the Winnipeg Floodway. He died in Quebec City.

Prendergast, James Emile Pierre (1858-1945) Judge, writer. Born in Quebec City, he was educated at the Commercial Academy and Laval University, graduating with a BA in 1878 and LLB in 1881. He was admitted to the Quebec bar in 1881 and came to Manitoba in 1882. From 1884 to 1890 he was a member of the Catholic section of the Board of Education. He was an MLA from 1885 to 1897, and he served as provincial secretary in the Greenway government in 1888, resigning over the schools question. He subsequently led the opposition to new school laws in the House and was elected mayor of St. Boniface in 1893 and 1896. He was appointed county court judge in 1897 and judge of the Supreme Court of the North-West Territories in 1903. He was a member of the Saskatchewan Supreme Court (1905-10), a member of the Manitoba Court of King's Bench (1910-22), and a judge of the Manitoba Court of Appeal (1922-29). In 1929 he became chief justice of Manitoba. Prendergast was also a poet and an author. See Roy St. George Stubbs, *Lawyers and Laymen of Western Canada* (1939).

Prendergast, Joseph Albert (1862-1918) Librarian. Born in Quebec City, he came to Manitoba in 1882, serving as assistant librarian of the province until 1889. In 1904 he became French clerk at the Dominion Lands Office. He was active in the Catholic Foresters and the Société Saint-Jean-Baptiste.

Primeau, Louis (fl. 1749-1800) Fur trader. Originally a Canadian trader, he lived with the Aboriginals for several years before joining the HBC in 1765. He advocated the expansion of inland posts, and he rejoined the Canadians in 1773, working for the Frobisher interests. He helped the Nor'Westers compete against the HBC at York and Churchill. *DCB* IV, 647.

Prince, Henry (b. 1819) Native leader. He was a son of Peguis,* chief of the Saulteaux Indians, who had taken the European name William King. In his own tongue Prince was known as Pa-bat-or-kok-or-sis. He complained in 1869-70 that the Métis were not sympathetic to the Native people, and he was a firm supporter of the Canadian annexation of Red River. He met the arriving Wolseley Expedition in his canoe at the mouth of the Red River.

Prince, Rufus (1920-1989) Native leader. Born on the Long Plain Indian Reserve in Manitoba, he was educated at the Portage la Prairie Indian Residential School before serving with the Canadian army in Italy during WWII. Upon his return he was elected chief of the Long Plain Indian Band. Prince later became vice-president of the Manitoba Indian Brotherhood, and he helped found the Dakota Ojibway Tribal Council and the Dakota Ojibway Police Force (the first Aboriginal law enforcement agency in Canada) in 1977. He died at Portage la Prairie.

Prince, Tommy (1915-1977) War hero. A Saulteaux Indian born in Manitoba (the grandson of Chief Peguis*), he was Canada's most decorated Aboriginal soldier in WWII, awarded 10 medals, most with the Canadian-American detachment known as the "Devil's Brigade." After the war he toured the province agitating for Indian treaty rights. He then served with Princess Patricia's Canadian Light Infantry during the Korean War and was crippled by machine-gun fire in battle. He later lived in poverty in Winnipeg.

Pritchard, Hugh (1830-1912) Postmaster. Born in Kildonan, he moved to Middlechurch in 1870, where he became one of the backbones of the community. He ran a grinding mill, was postmaster, and was sometimes reeve, councillor, and school trustee. He was churchwarden of Middlechurch Anglican Church for over 40 years.

Pritchard, John (1777-1856) Fur trader. Born in Shropshire, England, he came to Canada in 1800, and in 1802 joined Forsyth, Richardson and Company, part of the XY Company. He served near Lake Winnipeg until 1805, when he went to the Souris River (and became lost on the prairies, where he wandered for 40 days). He refused to resist the use of force by Miles Macdonell* in 1814 and was forced to leave the NWC service branded as a coward. In Montreal, he warned Colin Robertson* of the dangers to Red River, and with Robertson's approval he returned to Red River during the winter of 1814-15 overland on snowshoes. He attempted to farm but soon found himself one of the leaders of the loyal colonists who retreated to Jack River House in the summer of 1815. He was taken prisoner at the Battle of Seven Oaks and removed to Fort William, where he was liberated by Lord Selkirk.* He subsequently testified in the fur-trade trials in Montreal and York.

In 1819 he travelled to London to present a petition to Parliament on behalf of the settlers, which led to James Montgomery's parliamentary speech that was printed as *Substance of the Speech of Sir James Montgomery, Bart., in the House of Commons, on the 24th of June 1819, On Bringing Forward His Motion Relative to the Petition of Mr. John Pritchard, of the Red River Settlement* (1819). This speech led Parliament to ask for the Colonial Office papers on the settlement and the fur-trade war, which were subsequently printed. Pritchard was one of those who pleaded for a schoolmaster, and he convinced the HBC to organize the Buffalo Wool Company with himself as general manager. George Simpson* saw him as "a wild visionary speculative creature," and indeed the Buffalo Wool Company soon failed. Pritchard later taught school at Middlechurch and was part of the tallow company disaster of the 1830s. He was a councillor of Assiniboia until 1848. He was a co-author of *Narratives of John Pritchard, Pierre Chrysologue Pambrun, and Frederick Damien Heurter, Respecting the Aggressions of the North-West Company, against the Earl of Selkirk's Settlement upon Red River* (1810), and his letters were collected and edited by George Bryce* as *Glimpses of the Past in the Red River Settlement from Letters of Mr. John Pritchard, 1805-1836* (1892). *DCB* VIII, 713-15.

Pritchard, William John (1888-1975) Labour leader. Born in England, he was educated at Swinton and attended night classes at the Royal Institute of Technology and the Manchester School of Technology. He immigrated to Vancouver in 1911 and quickly became a socialist leader. He edited the *Western Clarion* from 1914 to 1917 and led the British Columbia contingent to the Calgary Western Labour Conference in March 1919 which founded the One Big Union. He arrived in Winnipeg on 10 June 1919 with James Farmer,* and was soon involved in the Winnipeg General Strike. A warrant was issued for his arrest, and he was captured in Calgary and put on trial for sedition with other leaders singled out by the federal government. He defended himself and was sentenced to one year in prison. His *Address to the Jury* was published in 1920. He then returned to Vancouver, where he was elected to the Burnaby council in 1928 and chosen reeve in 1930. He also became president of the Union of British Columbia Municipalities. After the death of a daughter in 1938 he moved to Los Angeles, where he became active in the Socialist Party of America. See Harry and

Mildred Gutkin, *Profiles in Dissent: The Shaping of Radical Thought in the Canadian West* (1997), 93-134.

Provencher, Joseph-Alfred-Norbert (1843-1887) Lawyer. Born in Canada, he was educated at the Séminaire de Nicolet and was eventually called to the Montreal bar in 1864. He worked as editor of *La Minerve* while running unsuccessfully for Parliament in 1867. In 1869 he was appointed secretary to William McDougall,* becoming a member of the notorious carpetbagging administration that McDougall brought west with him late that year. He was appointed because his uncle, Bishop J.-N. Provencher,* had been well liked by the Red River Métis. He was described as a "tall, bulky fellow, with an odd-looking head, hands of a Hercules, sloppy garb, heavy gait, and enormous bushy mop of hair." He was briefly captured by Riel but released. He returned to Manitoba in October 1871 as immigration commissioner, spent 1872 in Paris, and came back to Manitoba as commissioner of Indian Affairs. In this post he helped conclude Treaty Three with the Lake of the Woods Ojibwa. After 1876 he practised law, helped found the University of Manitoba, and in 1879 was badly defeated in St. Boniface in provincial elections. By 1880 he was back in Montreal working as a journalist, and he died in that city. *DCB* XI, 716-17.

Provencher, Joseph-Norbert (1787-1853) Cleric. Born in Nicolet, Quebec, he attended the Collège de Saint-Raphael in Montreal, the Séminaire de Nicolet, and the Grand Séminaire de Quebec. He was ordained in 1811, and proved a zealous evangelical worker. In 1818 he was posted by Bishop Plessis to Red River, financed by a subscription campaign throughout Lower Canada. Accompanied by Sévère Dumoulin* and William Edge, he reached the Forks on 19 May 1818. Provencher was a big man, standing six feet four inches tall, and dressed in his clerical garb he created a great stir among the inhabitants. Large numbers were baptized, and many assisted in building a house that would serve as chapel and residence. He was appointed an auxiliary bishop and suffragan for the new territory in 1820, finally agreeing to serve as titular bishop of Juliopolis in 1821. He was consecrated in 1822. As bishop, Provencher took the lead in providing education for the local inhabitants, in supporting agriculture, and in converting both Europeans and Native peoples. He got on well with the Anglican missionaries and, after some initial problems, with the HBC directors as well. He travelled to Europe in 1835 to raise funds for his work in the West, and the Pope extended his jurisdiction to the Pacific Coast. He became a member of the Council of Assiniboia in 1837. He toured Lower Canada in 1843 to recruit more priests and raise more money. In later years he fought for a coadjutor bishop (finally getting A.-A. Taché* in 1851). Most of his papers are in the Archives of the Archdiocese of Quebec, but some copies are in the PAM. His early correspondence, edited by Grace Nute, was published in English as *Documents Relating to Northwest Missions, 1815-1827* (1942). For a biography, see Donatien Frémont, *Mgr Provencher et son temps* (1935). *DCB* VIII, 718-24.

Prowse, S.W. (1859-1931) Surgeon. Born in Charlottetown, Prince Edward Island, he was educated at Mount Allison University (1889) and the University of Edinburgh (MD 1896). He became a member of the Royal College of Surgeons in Edinburgh in 1898 and returned to Canada, settling in Winnipeg. He was elected president of the Winnipeg Medico-Chirurgical Society in 1910. In 1916 he took a mobile field hospital to France, and while there in 1917 he was elected dean of the Manitoba Medical College. He served in that position until his death.

Pruden, John Peter (1778-1868) Fur trader. Born in England, he entered HBC employment in 1791 and served for many years in the Saskatchewan District. After the amalgamation of the HBC and NWC he took a leave in England. He headed Norway House and Carlton House before retiring in 1837 to Red River, where he farmed Lot 67 in St. Andrew's Parish. In retirement he married Ann Armstrong, who was governess of the Red River Academy. He was appointed councillor of Assiniboia in 1843 and chair of the Board of Public Works in 1847. He died in Red River. *DCB* IX, 648-49.

Prud'homme, Louis Arthur (1853-1941) Lawyer, judge. A law partner of Joseph Royal,* he was appointed as judge in the Eastern Judicial District in 1885 to deal with Francophone areas. While not a strong lawyer, he made a humane and equitable judge. He retired in 1925. He contributed many historical articles on the Métis and the Catholic Church in the West to periodicals and the Royal Society of Canada.

Puttee, Arthur W. (1868-1957) Politician, labour leader. Born in Folkstone, Kent, England, he was apprenticed as a printer. He came to Brandon in 1888, but worked for some years in the United States, chiefly in Seattle and St. Paul, before settling in Winnipeg in 1891. He was active in the International Typographical Union and was Canada's first labour MP (Independent Labour), winning a hotly contested by-election in January 1900 against Edward Martin. One campaign jingle went, "The Martin is a summer bird/Uncertain of his flight/But year round Puttee sticks and hears/The stalwart's 'Voice for Right.'" There were charges that he was Clifford Sifton's* candidate, particularly in the November 1900 election, which Puttee again won. It was true he had much Liberal support. In 1904, he found labour sentiment had moved leftward and the Liberals no longer trusted him. He was easily defeated, even losing his deposit. From 1897 he was a moderate labour leader, editor of the radical newspaper the *Voice*, in which he had a financial interest until its collapse in July 1918. He was one of the strongest voices in favour of the organization of a Canadian Labour Party based on the British Labour Party model. He and R.A. Rigg* were nominated early in 1918 to meet with Prime Minister Borden on the conduct of the war, but neither man attended. Puttee was a member of First Unitarian Church of Winnipeg. He lived on College Avenue. There are scattered but extensive papers at PAM.

Queen, John (1882-1946) Politician. Born in Lanarkshire, Scotland, in a family of Plymouth Brethren, he was educated in Dunfermline. He came to Winnipeg in 1906 and, although a cooper by trade, was employed by North-West Laundry as a driver of a horse-drawn delivery wagon. He was a member of the Social Democratic Party, co-founder of the Winnipeg Socialist Sunday School, as well as business agent and advertising manager for the *Western Labor News*. He was Winnipeg alderman for Ward Five from 1916 to 1919. Queen was active in opposing the Lord's Day Act in Winnipeg. He served as chair of a meeting at the Walker Theatre of 22 December 1918 which passed several radical resolutions. He was arrested on 17 June 1919 by the Mounties on charges of sedition connected with the Winnipeg General Strike, defended himself, and was sentenced in 1920 to one year in prison. He was a MLA from 1920 to 1932 and served for many years as leader of the Independent Labor Party. He served as mayor of Winnipeg seven times (1935, 1936; and from 1938 to 1942) , and was elected in part as a moderate alternative to Communist Party candidates. See Harold and Mildred Gutkin, *Profiles in Dissent: The Shaping of Radical Thought in the Canadian West*(1997), 343-381.

Queen, Katherine (Ross) (d. 1933) Feminist and socialist. She opposed conscription in 1917, and after WWI she organized the Labor Women of Greater Winnipeg, which lobbied for birth control clinics and equal opportunities for women. In 1931 she represented the Winnipeg West-End Independent Labor Party at a Calgary conference that called for "the socialization of economic life in the country." She died of pneumonia, and her coffin was, at her own insistence, draped in a red flag.

Radisson, Pierre-Esprit (c. 1640-1710) Explorer, fur trader. Born in France, he came to New France at an early age. In 1651 he was captured by Mohawk Indians and adopted into an Indian family. He escaped once, was tortured, and was saved from death by his adopted family, only to escape again. He became an interpreter and guide for the Jesuits before joining his brother-in-law, Médard Chouart des Groseilliers,* in the fur trade. The two returned from Hudson Bay to New France laden with furs in 1660, only to have their cargo confiscated and themselves thrown into prison for trading without official permission. Not surprisingly, they turned to the English for support, first in New England and then in London. In 1668 they headed for the Bay in English ships, returning with such an impressive load of beaver skins that Charles II chartered the HBC in 1670. The two men continued to work for the HBC until 1675, when they were persuaded to return to the French. Radisson spent several years in Africa in a disastrous naval campaign against the Dutch colonies, and in 1681 managed to become connected with an unofficial French fur-trading/military expedition to the Bay, which in 1682 virtually eliminated the

English from the region. But he and his brother-in-law fell afoul of European dynastic politics, and Radisson returned to the employ of the HBC in 1684. He made his last voyage to Hudson Bay in the years 1685-87, returning to retire in a London suburb. Radisson was clearly a survivor. His changes of national allegiance demonstrate how tenuous such matters were in the seventeenth century. His autobiographical account of his travels was published in 1885 as *Voyages of Peter Esprit Radisson, Being an Account of His Travels and Experiences among the North American Indians, from 1652 to 1684, Transcribed from Original Manuscripts in the Bodleian Library and the British Museum*, ed. G.D. Skull. See also Grace Nute, *Caesars of the Wilderness* (1943). *DCB* II, 535-40.

Rae, John (1813-1893) Surgeon, explorer. Born near Stromness, Scotland, he studied medicine at the University of Edinburgh and was appointed surgeon on an HBC ship in 1833. He served as resident surgeon at Moose Factory from 1835 to 1844. From 1846 to 1854 he was active in Arctic exploration, and he received the Founder's Medal of the Royal Geographical Society in 1862. He was regarded as the principal Arctic explorer of his day. He made two expeditions to search for Sir John Franklin.* The second one, in 1853, ascertained what had happened to Sir John. Rae was something of a polymath, and his writings on economics were admired by John Stuart Mill. In 1864 he worked for the HBC in surveying a route for a continental telegraph from Fort Garry to Victoria. He was elected a fellow of the Royal Society in 1880. He wrote A Narrative of an Expedition to the Shores of the Arctic Sea in 1846 and 1847 (1850) and Report of the Proceedings of the Arctic Searching Expedition (1852). He spent his last years in London. See E.E. Rich, ed., John Rae's Correspondence with the HBC on Arctic Exploration 1844-55 (1953); Robert L. Richards, Dr. John Rae (1985). *DCB* XII, 876-79.

Ransom, Edgar J. (1874-1956) Artist. First treasurer of the Manitoba Society of Artists in 1903. He was the head of Ransom Engraving Company, which printed most of Winnipeg's promotional material before 1922. Ransom Engraving Company papers are at the PAM.

Ransom, Fawcett Wright (1852-1957) Farm leader. Born in Bedford, England, he immigrated to Manitoba in 1897. He was actively involved in the cooperative movement, serving as the first secretary of the Manitoba Pool Elevators from 1925 to 1949. He also lectured on soil conservation, in person and on the radio. He is a member of the Manitoba Agricultural Hall of Fame.

Ransom, Sidney Edwin (1909-1990) Farm leader. Born in Morton, Manitoba, he served as provincial president of the Manitoba Federation of Agriculture in 1958. He won many awards for soil conservation. He is a member of the Manitoba Agricultural Hall of Fame.

Rastel De Rocheblave, Pierre de (1773-1840) Fur trader. He was born in Kaskaskia (now Illinois). His father had fought with the French colonial troops in the Seven Years War and emerged as British commandant at Kaskaskia in 1778, when he was taken prisoner by the Americans. Pierre was a founder of the New North West Company (or XY Company) in 1798, and he survived the merger with the HBC in 1804 to head the Red River Department until 1807, when he was posted to the Athabasca region. He became a captain in the Corps of Canadian Voyageurs organized by the NWC in 1812, receiving a militia commission for the "Indian and conquered countries" in 1814. He was at Fort William when it was seized by Lord Selkirk* in 1816, and he helped William McGillivray* recapture it in 1817. A year later he helped transport the first Catholic priests to Western Canada. Upon the merger of the NWC and HBC, he drew up the NWC inventory. He later became active as a seigneur and went into politics in Lower Canada. His papers were destroyed in a fire in 1860. *DCB* VII, 735-39.

Reader, Joseph (d. 1928) Missionary. Born in England, he came to Manitoba in 1874, serving as an Anglican missionary at The Pas from 1878 to 1881. He then became an Indian agent and converted to the Church of the Plymouth Brethren. He began printing in Cree syllabics in 1890, and published a number of books over the following years, thus spreading syllabic literacy among Aboriginal peoples.

Rebchuk, Slaw (1907-1996) Municipal politician. Born in Winnipeg, he graduated from St. John's High School in 1924. He was first elected to Winnipeg City Council in 1950, and served until 1978. He was known as the "mayor of the North End." An independent, he was deputy mayor from 1966 to 1969.

He served on 68 committees during his years on council, and Slaw Rebchuk Bridge (Salter Street Bridge) was named for him in 1984. He was granted the knighthood of the Order of St. Gregory the Great by the Vatican in 1991. He was famed for his "Rebchukisms," such as "You've buttered your bread — now lie in it" or "A verbal agreement is not worth the paper it's written on."

Redekopp, Elsa (Sawatsky) (1922-1992) Musician, author. Born in Russia, she came with her family to Canada in 1923, settling in Gnadenthal, Manitoba. An active musician, she played the viola in the Winnipeg Symphony Orchestra and founded the Holiday String Quartet. She also wrote several children's books, including *Wish and Wonder: A Manitoba Village Childhood* (1982) and *Dream and Wonder: A Child's View of Canadian Village Life* (1986).

Reimer, Klaas R. (1837-1906) Businessman. Born in Rosenort, Molotschna, Russia, he came to Steinbach, Manitoba in 1874 with the Kleine Gemeinde Mennonites. In 1877 he opened a store in his log house, and by 1880 was investing in a flour mill and a lumberyard. By 1885, he and his family controlled two blocks of downtown Steinbach, running three general stores, four cheese factories, a sawmill, and most of a flour mill. By the end of the century, the Reimer family paid almost half of Steinbach's taxes. Reimer later opened a large greenhouse operation and an irrigation system.

Reimer, Peter (1902-1988) Cleric. Born in Steinbach, Manitoba, he taught school for many years before becoming pastor of the Evangelical Mennonite Church of Steinbach in 1944. His early ministry was distinguished by his work with Mennonite conscientious objectors in prison camps in Western Canada. He later helped found the Manitoba Mennonite Historical Society and the Mennonite Museum, and he wrote extensively on Mennonite history. He died in Honolulu.

Renouf, George P. (1879-1961) Farmer, politician. Born in Jersey, the Channel Islands, he came to Bowsman, Manitoba, in 1899 and farmed in the Swan River Valley until 1955. He entered politics in 1907, when he was elected to the Bowsman school board. As a politician he never lost an election. He served as reeve and school board secretary for Minitonas from 1921 to 1932, before entering the Manitoba

legislature. He was also president of the Minitonas Red Cross from 1922. He was first elected as Conservative MLA for Swan River in 1932, and sat in the Legislative Assembly until 1958. He left the Progressive Conservatives in 1949 to serve as leader of an Independent coalition group. In the House he was known as a man who looked after his constituents. He retired to Victoria in 1959.

Rice, Samuel Dwight (1815-1884) Cleric. Born in Houlton, Maine, he was converted to Methodism in 1834 and became a preacher, first in New Brunswick and later in Canada. From 1880 to 1882 he held a pastorate in Winnipeg, where he served on the board of education in 1880-81. *DCB* XI, 729-30.

Richards, Cecil Clarence (1907-1982) Sculptor, educator. Born in Cornwall, England, he came to Canada in 1925 and attended the Ontario College of Art. Richards served in the Canadian army during WWII and then taught at the Cranbrook Academy of Art in Bloomfield Hills, Michigan, before coming to the University of Manitoba to open the Department of Sculpture in 1951. He served as head of the department until his retirement in 1966. His large sculpture *Night and Day* is at the entrance steps of the School of Architecture at the University of Manitoba, and he also did "the doors" of St. George's Anglican Church, Crescentwood. He died in Lakefield, Ontario. See Vaughan L. Baird, *The Sculptor: Cecil Clarence Richards, R.C.A.* (1980).

Richards, Robert Whitla (1909-1989) Athlete. Born in Winnipeg, he won many Canadian and international rowing titles, including the gold pairs medal at the 1930 British Empire Games. He worked for many years as a stockbroker, retiring in 1974 as a partner of Richardsons Securities Canada. Richards was chair of the board of the Winnipeg Symphony Orchestra and commodore of the Lake of the Woods Yacht Club. He was elected to the Manitoba Sports Hall of Fame in 1988. He died in Winnipeg.

Richardson, Gertrude (Twilley) (1875-1946) Feminist, reformer. Born in Leicester, England, she trained as a costumer and became active with anti-war socialists during the Boer War. After a prolonged nervous breakdown following the breakup of her marriage, she became active in the suffrage movement, writing many poems on feminist subjects. She immigrated with her mother to Swan River, Manitoba, in 1911 to join her siblings. In 1912 she married Robert Richardson, and she soon became active in the Manitoba feminist movement. She opposed WWI from the beginning and became an anti-conscriptionist in 1915. This stance cost her an outlet for her writing in the magazine *Women's Century*, sponsored by the National Council of Women in Canada. In 1917 she began a friendship with Helen Armstrong* and continued her involvement with the Christian Peace Crusade. After the war she became ill again, and in 1921 was admitted to the Hospital for Mental Diseases at Brandon, where she remained until 1925. After several years on the farm in Swan River, she returned to Brandon in 1930, remaining there until her death. See Barbara Roberts, *A Reconstructed World: A Feminist Biography of Gertrude Richardson* (1996).

Richardson, James Armstrong (1885-1939) Grain executive, aviation executive. Born in Kingston, Ontario, and educated at Queen's University, he supervised the operations of the Richardson family in Toronto from 1907 to 1912 and came to Winnipeg as vice-president in charge of western branches in 1912. In 1918 he worked for the Allied Wheat Commission, and in 1919 became president and general manager of James Richardson and Sons, Limited. In 1926 he helped found Western Canada Airways, a pioneer enterprise in northern flying, and merged it with other operations into Canadian Airways Ltd. (of which he was president) in 1929.

Richardson, John (1787-1865) Surgeon, explorer, field naturalist. Born in Dumfries, Scotland, he studied at the Royal College of Surgeons in Edinburgh, served with the Royal Marines in the War of 1812, and obtained an MD in 1826. He also studied natural history and was appointed to the Franklin expedition in 1819. On that expedition, which travelled from York Factory to Melville Sound, he collected and identified many specimens of plants, birds, and animals. He was also on the second expedition of 1825-27. He later became recognized as a major field naturalist and received many honours. He led a search for Sir John Franklin* in 1848 in company with Dr. John Rae.* His journal of the first Franklin expedition, edited by C. Stuart Houston, was published in 1984 as *Arctic Ordeal: The Journal of John Richardson, Surgeon-Naturalist with Franklin.* See Houston's "John Richardson: First Naturalist in the Northwest," *The Beaver* (November 1984): 10-15. *DCB* IX, 658-61.

Richardson, Muriel (1891-1973) Business executive, volunteer leader. Born in Belleville, Ontario, she came to Winnipeg at the time of her marriage in 1919. She was active in war work and volunteer work in the community. She served on the board of trustees of Queen's University from 1939 to 1966 and on the board of regents of United College in Winnipeg from 1940 to 1951. She was honorary chair of many local and national charities. From 1939 to 1966 she was president of James Richardson and Sons Limited. She was awarded honorary degrees by Queen's University in 1951 and the University of Manitoba in 1953.

Richardson, Robert Lorne (1860-1921) Journalist, politician. Born near Perth, Canada, he was educated in Lanark County before moving to Toronto, where he soon joined the *Globe*. He came west in 1882 to help found the *Manitoba Sun*, which in 1889 became the *Tribune*. He was elected to Parliament as a Liberal for Lisgar in 1896 on a revenue tariff platform, but he was thereafter unsuccessful at the polls until 1917, when he was elected to Parliament as a Conscriptionist. He published two novels, *Colin of the Ninth Concession* (1903) and *The Camerons of Bruce* (1906).

Riddell, James (1880-1926) Farm leader, politician. Born in Jedborough, Scotland, he came to Carman, Manitoba, in 1880, where he farmed for many years. He was president of the Dufferin Agricultural Society. He was elected to the Manitoba legislature as a Liberal representing Lorne in 1896, and he served until 1903, when he was defeated by Rodmond Roblin* after a redistribution of seats. He subsequently ran unsuccessfully for Parliament from Macdonald. In later years he was president of the Caledonia Box and Manufacturing Company of Winnipeg.

Riddell, John Henry (1863-1952) Educator, cleric. Born in Bolton, Canada, he was educated locally and at the model school in Brampton. After teaching briefly, he returned to Collingwood High School for matriculation and then attended Victoria University, Cobourg, graduating with a BA in 1889. After several years of circuit preaching in Manitoba, he accepted a dual appointment as lecturer in Latin and Greek at Wesley College in Winnipeg and as assistant minister at Grace Church. He founded Alberta College in 1903 and returned to Wesley College in

1917 as principal. He remained for 21 years, fending off several challenges to his authority. Never a great scholar, he regarded one of his greatest academic feats as defending a downtown campus for undergraduates in arts at the University of Manitoba. Riddell received an honorary doctorate from the University of Alberta in 1913. An unpublished autobiography and papers are in the United Church Archives, Toronto. A building at the University of Winnipeg is named for him. See Gerald Friesen, "Principal J.H. Riddell: The Sane and Safe Leader of Wesley College," in *Prairie Spirit*, ed. Dennis L. Butcher et al. (1985), 251-64.

Riddell, Robert Gerald ("Gerry," 1908-1951) Diplomat, historian. Born in Edmonton, he came to Manitoba in 1917 with his father, John Riddell,* who became principal of Wesley College. He received a BA from the University of Manitoba in 1930 and went on to an MA at the University of Toronto and a BLitt at Oxford (1934). His specialty was imperial history, which he taught at the University of Toronto from 1934 until 1942, when he joined the External Affairs Department in Ottawa. He became head of the United Nations division in 1946, special assistant to the minister for external affairs in 1949, and Canada's permanent UN delegate in June 1950. He died soon thereafter.

Riel, Louis (1844-1885) Métis leader, politician. Born in Red River, he was the eldest of 11 children in a close family of Métis elite. He was educated in St. Boniface and then sent to the Pétit Seminaire de Montreal. He withdrew from college after his father's death, perhaps because of romantic problems, and became a law clerk. He returned to Red River around 1868, and soon became embroiled in the prospective Canadian annexation of the settlement, gradually coming to lead Métis hostility to the transfer. At the beginning he sheltered behind the titular leadership of John Bruce,* listening carefully to the advice of Father Joseph-Noel Ritchot,* but gradually he asserted his own voice. His direction of the Red River Rebellion 1869-70 as president of the provisional government was for the most part brilliant, marred only by the execution of the Orangeman Thomas Scott,* which enabled the Canadian government to turn him into an outlaw. In 1871 he helped raise a Métis force to support the new province against the Fenians. He was subsequently elected to Parliament from Provencher on several occasions,

but was expelled. In 1875 he was granted an amnesty for deeds committed in 1869-70, providing he remained in exile for five years. Unhappy and frustrated in the United States, he spent some time in mental asylums in Quebec from 1876 to 1878 before going to Montana, where he married and became an American citizen. In June 1884 he was asked by a group of settlers in the Saskatchewan Valley to lead them in protest against the Canadian government. The protest turned to violence in 1885, and the Métis and Indians led by Riel were quickly and brutally suppressed after military defeat at the battle of Batoche. He was tried for treason, rejecting a plea of insanity advanced by his lawyers, and was hanged at Regina on 16 November 1885. Five volumes of his papers, which demonstrate his prose style and his competence as a poet, have been edited by George F.G. Stanley and others. The best biographies are by Stanley, Thomas Flanagan, and Maggie Siggins. *DCB* XI, 736-52.

Riel, Louis (Sr.) (1817-1864) Métis leader. Born at Île-à-la-Crosse in what is now Saskatchewan, he went east to Lower Canada with his family in 1822 and was educated there as a wool carder. At age 21 he joined the HBC at Rainy River, where he served from 1838 to 1840. He later returned to Lower Canada for a brief spell with the Oblates, but he left the order for want of a sense of vocation. When he came west to Red River, he married Julie, the daughter of Jean-Baptiste Lagimodière* and Marie-Anne Gaboury.* He supported the free traders within the Métis, and also insisted that the Council of Assiniboia have Métis representation and that the courts of Red River employ French. He was less successful in business; a textile mill that he opened with equipment purchased in the East failed in the late 1850s. *DCB* IX, 663.

Rigg, Richard Arthur ("Dickie," 1872-1964) Labour leader, socialist. Born in Todmorton, Lancashire, England, he worked in a cotton mill while in grade school and was employed full-time from the age of 12. He began his theological studies in 1891 and had abandoned the Methodist ministry on coming to Canada in 1903. By 1909 he was the Winnipeg representative of the Bookbinders' Union. He was the first nominee of the Labour Representation Committee to win a seat on the Winnipeg City Council when elected in 1913. A year later he was sent to represent the Trades and Labor Council at the American Federation of Labor convention in Philadelphia. He was elected to the provincial legislature in 1915 from Winnipeg North. He agreed to co-operate with the government's national registration program in 1916 when he was assured that registration was not a prelude to conscription, but he subsequently withdrew his support. He joined the army in 1917 and insisted on being sent overseas. In 1917 he resigned his provincial seat to contest the federal election in Winnipeg North as the nominee of the Manitoba section of the Canadian Labor Party. He was described by the *Manitoba Free Press* in 1918 as "the outstanding figure in the labour and radical world of Winnipeg," but was not active in the Winnipeg General Strike. Rigg subsequently opposed the One Big Union. From 1930 to 1937 he was director of the Employment Service of Canada. His papers are at the PAM.

Riley, Conrad (1875-1960) Oarsman. His eight-oar crew won the Steward's Cup at the Henley Regatta of 1910, and many other championships. He later became a Winnipeg businessman. See his *Rowing Memories* (1934).

Riley, Robert Thomas (1851-1944) Insurance executive. Born in Beverley, Yorkshire, England, to Quaker parents, he was educated at Argyle College and St. Thomas Charterhouse School. He won an appointment as a clerk in the Horse Guards in an open civil-service competition, and after service there for several years, he came to North America (Hamilton) in 1879. He first arrived in Manitoba in 1881. He founded a number of financial and insurance companies in Winnipeg, including the Northern Trusts Company, the Northern Mortgage Company, and the Canadian Fire Insurance Company. He was also chief manager of the Westbourne Cattle Company for many years. In addition, Riley was one of the founders of the Great-West Life Assurance Company. He was a great believer in the future of Western Canada.

Riley, W. Culver (1907-1970) Insurance executive, sportsman. Born in Winnipeg, he was educated in local schools and at McGill University. He was an active sportsman who gained international recognition as a sculler. He served with the Royal Canadian Ordnance Corps in WWII, emerging as a lieutenant-colonel. From 1925 he was connected with the Canadian Fire Insurance Company, serving as branch

manager until his appointment as chair in 1963. He was president of the Winnipeg Blue Bombers in the early 1950s, and a founder of the Winnipeg Enterprises Corporation, which in 1953 opened the Polo Park stadium-arena sports complex. He was a commissioner on the Flood Cost-Benefit Study from 1956 to 1958, and in 1963 he organized the Pan Am Games for Winnipeg. Riley is a member of the Manitoba Sports Hall of Fame.

Rindisbacher, Peter (1806-1834) Artist. Born in Switzerland, he came with his family, German-speaking Lutherans, to Red River in 1821. He became a clerk for the HBC but supplemented the family income with his watercolour painting, mainly of life around the settlement. Word of his talent spread, and he received commissions from as far away as London, often filling them by making traced copies of his own works and finishing them in watercolour. Robert Pelly* had oil copies made in England of some of his works, and colour lithographs of these were sold without remuneration to the artist. Most of Rindisbacher's subjects were the Native peoples of the settlement, rather than his own people. The Rindisbachers and other Swiss fled the colony after the flood of 1826, re-establishing themselves in the United States. Rindisbacher went to St. Louis, where he became a successful artist and a volunteer in the St. Louis Grays. He died of cholera in 1834. A collection of his work, given to St. John's College, was later sold to the Provincial Library and Archives. His work is also held by the Glenbow Institute and the PAM. See A.M. Josephy, *The Artist Was a Young Man: The Life Story of Peter Rindisbacher* (1970), which includes a thorough bibliography. *DCB* VI, 648-50.

Ritchot, Noel-Joseph (1825-1905) Cleric. Born in Lower Canada, he was educated at the Collège de l'Assomption and was ordained to the priesthood in 1855. In 1862 he volunteered for mission service in Manitoba and was posted to the Métis parish of St. Norbert. In 1869 he was actively involved with his parishioners — some said he was Louis Riel's chief adviser — in the opposition to the transfer of the West from the HBC to Canada, although his role lessened after the establishment of the provisional government in December 1869. He was selected in February 1870 as a delegate of the provisional government (with John Black* and Alfred H. Scott)* to negotiate an agreement with Canada based upon a "List of Rights" drafted by the Convention of Forty and revised by the executive of the provisional government. He began travelling to Ottawa in late March 1870, arriving in Ontario at about the same time as the news of the death of Thomas Scott.* He was briefly arrested on charges of complicity in Scott's "murder," but was soon released. Although the Canadian government refused to accept the delegates as officially representing the provisional government, since it did not wish to recognize that government, Sir John A. Macdonald and Sir George-Étienne Cartier* did open discussions with Ritchot and his companions. Ritchot took the lead in the negotiations, which led to the passage of the Manitoba Act. Ottawa granted provincial status, bilingualism and biculturalism, and a large amount of land (1,400,000 acres) in compensation for the Métis loss of Aboriginal rights, and privately agreed to a general amnesty for all resisters. The amnesty question would prove a thorny one, since pressure from Ontario made a public announcement of an amnesty impossible. Land claims proved equally difficult to settle. In the end, of Ritchot's major concerns in 1870, only provincial status really stood the test of time. Ritchot felt increasingly betrayed by the government. He tried desperately to keep his parishioners in Manitoba and eventually accumulated much Métis land in the parish to provide for incoming Francophones. He died in St. Norbert. A rural municipality in Manitoba has been named for him. Ritchot's journal of his negotiations with Ottawa (translated into English) has been published by W.L. Morton in *Manitoba: The Birth of a Province* (1965), 131-60. See also Philippe Mailhot, "Ritchot's Resistance: Abbé Noel Joseph Ritchot and the Creation and Transformation of Manitoba" (PhD diss., University of Manitoba, 1986). There are papers at the PAM. *DCB* XIII, 876-78.

Robbins, John Everett (1909-1995) Publisher, educator. Born in Hampton, Ontario, he taught school in Saskatchewan from 1922 to 1925, then attended the University of Manchester, where he received an MA. He worked for the Dominion Bureau of Statistics from 1930 to 1952, serving as director of its Education Division from 1936. In 1943 he helped found the Canadian Youth Commission. He was editor-in-chief of the *Encyclopedia Canadiana* from 1952 to 1960, and then served as president of Brandon University from 1960 until 1969, when he was appointed first Canadian ambassador to the Vatican, a post he held until 1973. From the late 1930s, he was involved in the founding of at least a dozen Canadian cultural organizations. Robbins was an officer of the Canadian Social Science Research Council (1940-61), the Humanities Research Council (1943-61), and the Canada Foundation (1950-61). In 1929 he published *A Study of the Revenue System of the Dominion of Canada*. For a biography, see John A.B. McLeish, *A Canadian for All Seasons: The John E. Robbins Story* (1978).

Roberton, Thomas Beattie (1879-1936) Journalist. Born in Glasgow, Scotland, of Scotch-Ulster descent, he moved to Canada in 1910. He farmed in Alberta, set type in Calgary and Victoria, and ended up in Winnipeg working as a printer for the labour newspaper the *Voice*. He joined the *Free Press* in 1918 and remained there until his death. Roberton had no experience as a reporter, and was a critic/commentator from the outset of his journalistic career. He wrote on a variety of topics under the *nom de plume* "T.B.R." His subject matter ranged from Robbie Burns to a defence of political agitators, to jazz, to Canadian literature. A collection of his essays, edited by J.B. McGeachy, appeared in 1936 as *TBR: Newspaper Pieces*.

Roberts, John Hamilton (1892-1962) Soldier. Born in Pipestone, Manitoba, he was educated at Epsom College in England, Upper Canada College, and the Royal Military College. He served in the Royal Canadian Horse Artillery in WWI and remained in the peacetime army until he went overseas with the First Canadian Division Artillery in 1940. As a major-general he commanded the Canadian force in the Dieppe raid in 1942, winning the Distinguished Service Order and the Military Cross, as well as the French Croix de Guerre. He always defended the Dieppe raid, although many thought he had been made a scapegoat for its failure. He retired in 1945 and served as chief administrative officer of the northwest European district of the Imperial War Graves Commission from 1945 to 1950. He died in Jersey in the Channel Islands.

Robertson, Colin (c. 1779-1842) Fur trader. Born in Perth, Scotland, he entered NWC service around 1803. He left the NWC in 1809, borrowed money from the HBC's William Auld,* and sailed for London with an introduction to the HBC's London Committee. He advocated an active push into the Athabasca territory with Canadian voyageurs. This proposal was rejected at the time, and Robertson went into trade in Liverpool. He submitted a revised plan in 1814, which was accepted with himself in charge. His motto was "When among wolves, howl." He understood the need for the flamboyant gesture and often made it. In Red River, he seized Fort Gibraltar from the NWC and returned it only under conditions. He subsequently disagreed with Robert Semple* over strategy for defending the settlement, and went back to England at the end of 1816. He returned to Montreal to stand trial for the Fort Gibraltar business, and was acquitted. He then organized his Athabasca venture, eventually collecting 27 canoes and 190 men. The strategy was successful and brought the NWC to the bargaining table with the HBC. He was made a chief factor in the reorganized HBC in 1821, but George Simpson* did not like him. Simpson and Robertson contested over the latter's effort to introduce his mixed-blood wife into Red River society. Simpson forced Robertson to plan retirement. Before he could retire, however, he had a stroke, and therefore did not leave the Company officially until 1840. He died in Quebec, shortly after election to the Canadian Legislative Assembly. A letter-book (1817-22) was published in 1939 by the Hudson's Bay Record Society, edited by E.E. Rich as *Colin Robertson's Correspondence Book, September 1817 to September 1822. DCB* VII, 748-50.

Robertson, Hugh John (1868-1952) Cleric, artist. Born in Woodstock, Ontario, he went to British Columbia in 1892 as a Presbyterian student missionary. In 1907 he founded a Presbyterian church on Home Street in Winnipeg, and he served there until 1919, when he moved to John Black United Church in Kildonan. In 1934 he went to a church in Emerson, where he remained until his retirement in 1943. In retirement he took up oil painting, and had a number of exhibitions.

Robertson, James (1839-1902) Cleric. Born in Scotland, he came to Canada in 1855. He studied at the University of Toronto, Princeton Theological Seminary, and Union Theological Seminary. In 1874 he became the first pastor of Knox Presbyterian Church in Winnipeg, and he served until 1881. He was active in Manitoba College and helped found the University of Manitoba. In 1881 he became superintendent of missions in the Northwest for the Presbyterian Church, devoting his energies to building churches and staffing them with ministers. He died in Toronto but was buried in Kildonan. There is a biography by

C.W. Gordon (Ralph Connor), *The Life of James Robertson*, published in 1908. See also Catherine Macdonald, "James Robertson and Presbyterian Church Extension in Manitoba and the North West, 1866-1902," in *Prairie Spirit: Perspectives on the Heritage of the United Church of Canada in the West*, ed. D.L. Butcher et al. (1985), 85-99. *DCB* XIII, 880-81.

Robertson, John Palmerston (1841-1919) Journalist, curling enthusiast. Born in Perthshire, Scotland, he came to Canada during his childhood. He attended the Toronto Normal School and was principal of the Central School in Ottawa for nearly a decade before turning first to law, then to journalism. In 1879 he came to Winnipeg to become night editor of the *Winnipeg Times*, and he joined the *Manitoba Free Press* in 1881. He was appointed legislative librarian in 1884. In 1887 he published *The Political Manual of Manitoba and the Northwest Territories*. He was deputy royal chief of the Order of Scottish Clans. He helped found the Manitoba Curling Club, was general manager of the Mammoth Winnipeg Annual Bonspiel for a quarter century (1888-1919), and represented the Assiniboine curlers on the Canadian team that travelled in Britain in 1909. He also compiled annual yearbooks of curling in Manitoba. He died in Los Angeles. There are papers at the PAM.

Robinson, Henry Martin (1845-1907) Journalist. An American, he was editor of the *New Nation* from January 1870 until he was fired by Louis Riel in March of that year for showing too much sympathy to American annexationism. He later wrote *The Great Fur Land, or Sketches of Life in the Hudson's Bay Territory* (1879), which perpetuated many of the stereotypes about the fur trade and the Métis.

Robinson, Jeremiah (1846-1930) Merchant, farmer. Born in Canada, he came to Manitoba in 1878 and moved to Winnipeg in 1882, after a fire had destroyed his store in Emerson. He soon opened a large dry-goods store at the foot of Notre Dame Avenue, which expanded substantially over the years. In later years he purchased a farm in Warren and raised horses.

Robinson, Mary Augusta (Ruttan) (1912-1993) Athlete and sportswoman. Born in the St. James area of Winnipeg, she was locally educated. As Mary Ruttan she was one of Manitoba's top athletes of the 1930s and early 1940s. She was Manitoba champion in fencing in 1933 and 1936, and she won countless national ski titles. She also was an active horsewoman on her horse Teddy. She helped found the Puffin Ski Club and pioneered the women's/mothers' exercise course at the YWCA. For 30 years she ran a dance school in Winnipeg, from which she retired in 1966. She moved to Victoria in 1972. She is a member of the Manitoba Sports Hall of Fame.

Robison, Herbert Edward (1869-1933) Lawyer. Born in Consecon, Ontario, he taught school at Alexander, Manitoba, before studying law in Brandon and Winnipeg. He moved to Carman in 1899 in partnership with F. Brown. He served as mayor of Carman in 1912-13, and was created a KC in 1913. He was an active curler, a Mason, a Methodist, and a prominent Conservative politician who was never elected to office.

Roblin, Rodmond Palen (1853-1937) Premier. Born in Canada of Loyalist ancestry, he was educated locally before attending Albert College, Belleville. He worked as a cheese buyer and in 1877 moved to Winnipeg. He then moved to Carman as a merchant before returning to Winnipeg. He was elected to the legislature as an Independent in 1888, and in 1892 he ran unsuccessfully as a Conservative for the Morden seat. In 1896 he was elected as Conservative member for Woodlands, and he was soon chosen leader of the party. Roblin became premier in October 1900, serving until his resignation in 1915 in the midst of a corruption scandal over the construction of the Manitoba legislative building. He promoted the grain trade and railway construction, and introduced the first government-owned telephone system in North America. Manitoba extended its boundary and doubled its territory in 1912 under his premiership. He was made knight commander of the Order of St. Michael and St. George in 1912. He died in Hot Springs, Arkansas. See Hugh Robert Ross, *Thirty-Five Years in the Limelight: Sir Rodmond P. Roblin and His Times* (1936). There are papers at the PAM.

Robson, Hugh Ames (1871-1945) Lawyer, politician. Born in Barrow, England, he came to Canada in 1882. He was an eyewitness at the trial of Louis Riel in Regina in 1885, and he practised law in the North-West Territories before joining the law firm of James Aikins* in Winnipeg. He was appointed to

the King's Bench in 1909, but resigned to take up the chair of the public utilities commission for the province (1911-14), introducing public hydroelectric power. He was chosen Liberal leader in 1927 and elected to the provincial legislature. He was appointed to the Court of Appeal in 1930, serving until 1943.

Robson, Joseph (fl. 1733-63) Surveyor. Engaged in 1733 as a stonemason to build Fort Prince of Wales, he also worked as a surveyor and kept a journal of his experiences, which he published as *An Account of Six Years Residence in Hudson's Bay* (1752). This was the first book on the Bay written by someone who had lived there, and its criticism of the HBC was very influential. It was he who wrote, "The Company have for eighty years slept at the edge of a frozen sea." He later published *The British Mars* (1763), a manual about fortifications. *DCB* III, 561-62.

Robson, Leslie Victor (1893-1977) Cattle breeder. Born at Deleau, Manitoba, he graduated from the Manitoba Agricultural College in 1915. He was active in the cooperative movement. He specialized in purebred polled Herefords and in 1947-48 served as president of the Canadian Hereford Association. He is a member of the Manitoba Agricultural Hall of Fame.

Robson, William (1865-1941) Farmer, farm leader. Born in Yorkshire, England, he came to Canada with his parents in 1867. He moved to Manitoba in 1889 on his honeymoon, settling in Deleau. As a farmer, he one year threshed 36,000 bushels of wheat. He was an early exponent of mixed farming, however. Active in the Grain Growers' movement and in the cooperative movement (he was president of Manitoba Co-Op Dairies from 1947 to 1962), he was elected an independent member of the provincial legislature in 1920. He turned down offers of the premiership and suggested John Bracken* instead. He was superintendent of the Sunday school at Bethel Methodist Church in Deleau for 43 years.

Roddick, George (1831-1910) Cleric. Born at sea en route from Scotland to Nova Scotia, Roddick grew up in West River, Nova Scotia. He attended Durham Hall theological school and entered a 20-year pastorate at West River Presbyterian Church. In 1879 he led a party of immigrants west to Manitoba, where he met much suspicion from the Presbyterian

Church, which was more accustomed to Ontario newcomers. Nevertheless, he was put in charge (without pay) of the Presbyterian Church's Grand Valley and Big Plains district, which included the present-day city of Brandon. James Robertson* described him in 1881 as "a disgruntled missionary, unequal to the task of shepherding the flock," but recommended paying him a stipend. Roddick retired in 1883 and joined the Methodists. In the early 1890s he spearheaded a movement to build a Union church at Brandon Hills.

Rogers, Edith (McTavish) (1877-1947) Feminist, social reformer. Born in Norway House, Manitoba, the daughter of D.C. McTavish, chief factor of the HBC, she was the first woman to be elected to the Manitoba legislature (1920), representing Winnipeg. She was an active advocate of the Child Welfare Act. A Liberal, she was re-elected in 1922 and 1927. During WWI she had been very involved in volunteer work, and was particularly active in social-welfare work. She served as the only woman on the Winnipeg General Hospital Board, and was secretary of the Central Council of the Battalion Auxiliaries. She moved to Ontario in 1942. There are papers at the PAM.

Rogers, Robert ("Bob," 1864-1936) Politician. Born in Canada, he came to Clearwater, Manitoba, in 1881 and to Winnipeg in 1896. He ran for the Conservatives in the Manitou riding in the provincial election in 1899, and became minister of public works in the Roblin government. He was a firm believer in public ownership of essential utilities, and thousands of acres of farmland were put into drainage districts under his supervision. He was also responsible for a major public building program.

Rosner, Mina (1915-1997) Writer. Born into a Jewish family in Buchach, Poland, she spent the years of German occupation in hiding. After WWII she and her husband (who had served in the Russian army) immigrated to Canada and settled in Winnipeg's North End, where they ran a grocery store. In her later years she wrote an autobiographical account of her wartime experiences in the Holocaust entitled *I Am a Witness*, and she often lectured on the subject.

Ross, Alexander (1783-1856) Fur trader, historian. Born in Morayshire, Scotland, he came to Lower Canada in 1804 and worked as a schoolmaster there

and in Glengarry, Upper Canada. In 1810 he signed on as a clerk with the Pacific Fur Company and sailed aboard the *Tonquin* for the Pacific Northwest, arriving in March 1811 to help establish Fort Astoria. He went to the NWC when it took over the Pacific Fur Company in 1813, working mainly in the interior until his forced retirement to Red River in 1825. In the settlement he farmed and traded. Although George Simpson* did not like him, he gradually acquired positions of responsibility. He became sheriff of Assiniboia in 1835 and a councillor of Assiniboia a year later. As sheriff and head of the Volunteer Corps of 60 men used as a police force, he refused to enforce the fur-trade monopoly of the HBC. His demeanour was pedantic, and in later years he was known in the settlement as "the Professor." In 1850 he and a number of other judges and magistrates refused to continue their work while Governor William Caldwell* remained in office. He fought for years to create a Presbyterian church in the settlement. In his later years he wrote three autobiographical books, *Adventures on the Columbia* (1849), *The Fur Hunters of the Far West* (1855), and *The Red River Settlement* (1856). This made him the pre-Confederation Northwest's most prolific author, and its finest as well. He may also have written the novel *Selma: A Tale of the Sixth Crusade* (1839). There are some papers in the PAM, but there is no full-scale biography, his own writings serving in its place. *DCB* VIII, 765-68.

Ross, Anne Glass (1912-1998) Social reformer. Born in Winnipeg's North End, she attended United College and the University of Manitoba. She studied nursing at Winnipeg General Hospital and psychiatric nursing in New York City. She was first employed by Mount Carmel Clinic in Winnipeg in 1948 as its only full-time staff member, and she built up the clinic through her personal efforts. She was known as "Anne of the Milk Subsidies." In 1995 she established AGR Health Services for seniors. She was the author of several books, including *Teenage Mothers Teenage Fathers* (1982) and a history of the Mount Carmel Clinic entitled *Clinic with a Heart* (1998).

Ross, Arthur Wellington (1846-1901) Politician. Born in Canada to Scottish parents, he entered teaching and in 1871 rose to inspector of public schools for Glengarry County. Soon afterward he received his BA from the University of Toronto, and he moved to Winnipeg in 1877. He was admitted to the bar in

1878. Ross was one of the leading real estate promoters and speculators in the infamous Winnipeg Boom of the early 1880s, holding most of the Fort Rouge area. He was active in acquiring Métis scrip, perhaps because of inside information he had received. But in 1882 the collapse of the boom ruined him, and he spent years in court over his complex finances. He was elected Liberal MLA from Springfield in 1878 and re-elected in 1879. He was an opponent in the legislature of the CPR monopoly, and he was elected Liberal MP from Lisgar (the riding that included the town of Selkirk) in 1882. In Ottawa he became an eloquent defender of the CPR, and he became active in Vancouver real estate speculation associated with the railroad's arrival in that city. He was vice-president of the Manitoba and Northwest Railway. By 1887 he was a Conservative, and he remained in the House of Commons with tacit CPR support until 1896. According to one of his colleagues in Ottawa, Joseph Royal,* "Ross was elected for Ross." Ross suffered a stroke in British Columbia in 1901 and died in Toronto while seeking medical treatment. See his *Speeches on the Canadian Pacific Railway and the Canadian Northwest* (1884). *DCB* XIII, 898-900.

Ross, Bernard Rogan (1827-1874) Fur trader. Born in Ireland, he immigrated to Canada in 1843 and later obtained a post with the HBC through the intervention of a relation. He began as an apprentice clerk at Norway House. He subsequently served at many posts, including York Factory, Fort Simpson, Fort Norman, and Fort Resolution. He became a chief trader in 1856. Ross was well read, boasting in 1859 of a library of over 500 volumes, and extremely active in various cultural activities, including music and natural history. During his 24 years of service to the HBC he collected many natural history specimens which in later years he sent to the Smithsonian Institution. He also sent collections to the Royal Scottish Museum in Edinburgh and the British Museum in London. He was a correspondent of several American learned societies, and he wrote a number of scientific papers. In late 1869 Ross was in Red River, advising against the formation of a provisional government. Instead, he and his coterie recommended the continuation of HBC government with a popularly elected executive council to deal with Canada. His library is housed in the HBC Archives. See Debra Lindsay, ed., *The Beginnings of Subarctic Ornithology: Northern Correspondence with the Smithsonian Institution,* *1856-68* (1991). *DCB* X, 629. There are papers at the PAM.

Ross, Charlotte (Whitehead) (1842-1916) Physician. Born in Darlington, England, she came to Montreal with her parents in 1847. She completed the medical course at the Women's Medical College in Philadelphia in 1875. When her husband, David Ross, came west to build the railroad, the family settled in Whitemouth, in territory disputed between Manitoba and Ontario. Special legislation was introduced to enable her to practise in Manitoba, but it was never approved. She continued to practise for many years although she was never formally licensed by the Manitoba College of Physicians and Surgeons. She moved to Winnipeg in 1916 and died there. The Charlotte W. Ross Gold Medal in obstetrics was first awarded by the Manitoba Medical College in 1917. See Barbara Angel and Michael Angel, *Charlotte Whitehead Ross* (1982); Fred Edge, *The Iron Rose: The Extraordinary Life of Charlotte Ross*, M.D. (1992). *DCB* XIV, 1054-55.

Ross, Donald (1797-1852) Fur trader. Probably born in Scotland, he joined the HBC in 1816 and spent his years serving at Cumberland House, York Factory, and Norway House. He became a chief trader in 1829, and he retired to the Red River Settlement. He died in Red River. An extensive correspondence is on microfilm at the PAM.

Ross, Hugh (1856-1894) Building contractor. Born in Pictou County, Nova Scotia, he moved to Winnipeg in 1880, where he joined his brothers Duncan and Neil as a building contractor. He became valuator for the Permanent Mortgage and Trusts Company. He was Sunday school superintendent of St. Andrew's Church. Ross resided at 146 Mayfair Avenue.

Ross, Hugh MacKay (1912-1992) Fur trader, memoirist. Born in Rothes, Scotland, he was educated there and at Elgin, Scotland. He joined the HBC in 1930 and spent 42 years with the Company, mainly working in the North as a fur trader. He wrote two memoirs of his experiences, *The Apprentice's Tale* (1986) and *The Manager's Tale* (1989).

Ross, James (1835-1871) Journalist. Born in Red River, the son of Alexander* and Sarah Ross,* he was educated at St. John's College and the University of Toronto. He married Margaret Smith (b. 1835 in Scotland) in 1858. He returned to Red River that same year. In 1859 he became postmaster of Assiniboia and helped start the *Nor'-Wester*, which became identified with the Canadian Party in the settlement. Ross became sheriff and governor of the jail in 1862, but all his appointments were revoked on 25 November 1862 because of his opposition to a government effort to bring imperial troops to Red River and his criticism of the HBC. In 1863 he was chief defence counsel in the abortion trial of G.O. Corbett.* He left Red River in 1864 to study law in Toronto, and turned to journalism to support himself and his family while obtaining his qualifications, working for the *Toronto Globe*, the *Hamilton Spectator*, and then the *Globe* again between 1865 and 1869. He returned to Red River on the eve of the Red River Rebellion, quickly becoming the spokesman and leader of the English mixed-bloods in the November council meeting with the Métis, to which he was a delegate from Kildonan. His advocacy of cooperation with the Métis at this council, although falling far short of an advocacy of rebellion, separated him from the Canadian Party in the settlement. Ross served as a delegate from St. John's to the Convention of Forty, and was chosen as the convention's interpreter and a member of the influential Bill of Rights committee. He opposed provincial status for Red River but supported the general aims of the resistance, and was appointed chief justice in Riel's provisional government. He worked unsuccessfully to defeat John Schultz* in the election campaigns of 1870 and 1871, but continued to drink heavily, and died on 20 September 1871. Ross was the only Anglophone mixed-blood in the colony who had the stature and the ability to oppose Louis Riel on equal terms, and his equivocal support for the resistance was a crucial factor in its success. Ross was tall and slender, with black hair and a widow's peak. His face was aristocratic and he was extremely handsome. In later years he sported a full black beard and moustache, and he had bushy eyebrows and piercing eyes. See Leonard Remis, "James Ross: 1834-1871: The Life and Times of an English-speaking Halfbreed in the Old Red River Settlement," (MA thesis, University of Manitoba, 1987). There are substantial if scattered papers at the PAM. *DCB* X, 629-31.

Ross, John Hugo (1875-1912) Realtor. Born in Toronto, he came to Winnipeg with his family at an early age, later moving with them to Vancouver. Educated at Upper Canada College, he became a junior stock broker in Toronto before opening the Hugo Ross Realty Company in Winnipeg in 1894. He was secretary-treasurer of the Winnipeg Stock Exchange and president of the Winnipeg Real Estate Exchange. He was an active clubman and yachtsman. Ross died in the Titanic disaster. There is a plaque dedicated to his name in Winnipeg City Hall.

Ross, Sarah ("Sally," c. 1798-1884) Community leader. The daughter of an Okanagan Indian chief, she married the fur trader Alexander Ross* "by the custom of the country" in 1812 and in the Anglican Church at Red River in 1828. She and her children accompanied her husband to Red River in 1826, and she lived there until her death. Although she seldom appeared in public, she was a well-known figure in the community, serving as a link between the Aboriginals and Europeans in the settlement. *DCB* XI, 775-76.

Roy, Gabrielle (1909-1983) Author. Born in St. Boniface, she attended the Winnipeg Normal School, taught school in rural Manitoba, and travelled to Europe, where she began to write. Her first novel, *Bonheur d'Occasion* (translated as *The Tin Flute*), appeared in 1945 and won the Governor General's Award. She was thoroughly bilingual and had a deceptively simple writing style. She wrote about ordinary people and strong women. Her work tended to celebrate the brief moments of joy in otherwise difficult lives. She wrote a number of collections of short stories set in Manitoba: *La Petite Poule d'Eau* (1950; translated as *Where Nests the Water Hen*); *Rue Deschambault* (1955; translated as *Street of Riches*); *La Route d'Altamont* (1966; translated as *The Road Past Altamont*); *Un jardin au bout du monde* (1975; translated as *Garden in the Wind*); and *Ces enfants de ma vie* (1977; translated as *Children of My Heart*). Several books were set in the Arctic and in Quebec. Roy also wrote two children's books. She won three Governor General's Awards and the Prix Duvernay. See Marc Gagné, *Visages de Gabrielle Roy* (1973).

Royal, Joseph (1837-1902) Lawyer, politician. Born in Lower Canada to poor parents, he was educated by the Sulpicians and the Jesuits. He articled in law with George-Étienne Cartier's* firm in 1857 and became an active journalist, in 1858 founding *L'Ordre*, devoted "to the church, to our faith, to the homeland, to our nationality." In 1867 he helped create *Le Nouveau Monde*, and he was editing the paper in 1869 when the Red River Rebellion began. He printed much material favourable to the Métis, and soon came to the attention of Bishop Taché,* who was on the lookout for Francophone professionals for the new province. He founded *Le Métis* in St. Boniface in 1871 and opened a law practice with Joseph Dubuc.* Royal was soon one of the leaders of the Francophones in Manitoba, with his finger in almost every possible pie. He was elected MLA for St. François Xavier West in 1870, was chosen first Speaker of the House in 1871, and soon became provincial secretary. He later also served as minister of public works and attorney general. He was a member of the team defending Ambroise Lépine* in the notorious murder trials of 1873-74. He was a consistent supporter of the Métis and their cause (including an amnesty for Louis Riel and Lépine), anxious to incorporate them in a Francophone bloc in the provincial legislature. He was eventually forced out of the government by John Norquay* in 1879, and he soon shifted to the federal scene, where he became Conservative MP for Provencher, retaining the seat in 1882 and 1887. In 1888 he was named lieutenant-governor for the North-West Territories, but he was uncomfortable with the loss of French rights during his term of office, which ended in 1893. He hoped to become a senator but was never nominated. In his last years he worked as a journalist in Montreal, and he died in that city. Although he was arguably the most important Francophone politician of his generation in Manitoba, there is no proper full-length biography. *DCB* XIII, 910-13.

Ruddell, John Henry (1859-1906) Realtor. Born in Halton County, Canada, he came to Manitoba to establish a harness business in Nelson in the early 1880s. He later moved to Morden and opened a real-estate firm, Ruddell, Pickel, and Hobbs. He was mayor of Morden and successfully ran for the Conservatives as Morden MLA in 1899 and 1903.

Ruh, Philip (1883-1962) Cleric, architect. Born in Lixheim on the Franco-German border, he studied with the Oblates in Holland and joined the order there. He was sent to Ukraine to learn the language and then to Canada as a missionary to the Ukrainians in 1911. He designed and built a huge church at Mountain Road in the Riding Mountains in 1924, then another at Portage la Prairie 1926-30, and another at Cook's Creek, which was begun in 1930 and not completed until 1952. As well, he designed over 50 other churches across the prairies. Ruh was famous for not only designing his churches, but for contracting the construction and raising the funds himself. See his *Misioner i budivnychyi* (Missionary and Architect, 1960).

Russell, John Alonso (1907-1966) Architect, educator. Born in Hindsdale, New Hampshire, he was educated at the Massachusetts Institute of Technology, and he had a diploma from the Fontainebleu School of Fine Arts. He came to Winnipeg in 1928 to teach architecture, and at the time of his death was dean of the Faculty of Architecture at the University of Manitoba. Russell was a fellow of the Royal Architectural Institute of Canada.

Russell, John Hamilton Gordon (1862-1946) Architect. Born in Toronto to parents who were natives of Scotland, he was educated at the Model School of Toronto before apprenticing as an architect. He worked as an architect in the United States until 1893, when he came to Winnipeg, where he opened an office in 1895. He designed the McArthur Building, the Trust and Loan Building, and the Great West Permanent Loan Building, as well as the Westminster and Knox Churches. He served as president of the Royal Architectural Institute of Canada in 1912-13. He was also a vice-president of the Manitoba Provident Mortgage Company. He was a director of the Rotary Club.

Russell, Norman Campbell Hill (d. 1978) Architect. Born in Winnipeg, he was a graduate of the University of Manitoba School of Architecture. He practised architecture in Winnipeg for many years and was responsible for the architecture survey of Manitoba for the Manitoba Historical Society. He served on the National Board of Church Architecture of the United Church. He died in Summerland, British Columbia.

Russell, Robert Boyd ("R.B.," 1888-1964) Labour leader, socialist. Born in Glasgow (Springburn), Scotland, he came to Canada in 1911. A member of the Socialist Party of Canada, he was not active in labour's opposition to WWI or to conscription. He attended the Calgary Convention in early 1919, and was chosen one of the five Manitoba delegates to "carry on the propaganda" for the One Big Union. Leader of the International Association of Machinists Local 122, and secretary (a paid position) of district number 2 in 1919, he was a main leader of the Winnipeg General Strike and a member of the Central Strike Committee. He was arrested on 17 June 1919, and two months later became secretary-treasurer of the Winnipeg Labor Council formed by the One Big Union. Russell was the only member of the 15-person Central Strike Committee charged with seditious libel. His trial began on 25 November 1919 and the verdict of guilty was delivered on 23 December 1919. The court was not sympathetic to Russell's insistence that he was only acting as a paid agent of the strikers, and sentenced him to two years in prison. His appeal to the Manitoba Court of Appeal was unanimously dismissed, the court finding that his actions amounted to a seditious conspiracy. He tried to appeal to the Judicial Committee of the Privy Council, but failed because the matter was held to be a criminal rather than civil one. He subsequently successfully defended the OBU against a Communist Party takeover, but was unable to win elected office. He held on through the Depression as secretary of the OBU in Winnipeg. A new junior vocational school in Winnipeg was named after him in 1966. See Harry and Mildred Gutkin, *Profiles in Dissent: The Shaping of Radical Thought in the Canadian West* (1997), 135-180; Kenneth Osborne, *R.B. Russell and the Labour Movement* (1978).

Russenholt, Edgar Stanford (1890-1991) War hero, historian. Born in Uxbridge, Ontario, he came to Hartney, Manitoba, in 1898, then moved to the Swan River Valley. He served in the 44th Battalion of the Canadian Expeditionary Force in WWI, being wounded at Vimy Ridge and earning a battlefield commission. He later wrote the unit's war history. He served with the Winnipeg Grenadiers (Reserve) in WWII. He was an active historian and environmentalist, as well as CWBT-TV's first weatherman. His opening "Ah, yes, the heart of the continent" was a Manitoba catchphrase and became the title of his published history of Assiniboia. As well as *Heart of the Continent* (1968), his books included *Six Thousand Canadian Men* (1932), *The Power of a City*, and *Grains of History* (1960). His papers are at the PAM.

Rutherford, Gwladys Mary ("Banky," 1878-1961) Actor. Little is known of her early background. "Banky," as she was always called, was the first lady of the Winnipeg theatre for many years, and well known to audiences in Winnipeg and across Canada through her appearances on the CBC.

Rutherford, Thomas (1835-1912) Entrepreneur. Born in Glenmorris, Upper Canada, he came to Winnipeg in 1872 and established a lumber mill. He and his partner Alexander Brown also opened a sawmill at Fisher River, Manitoba. They later founded Brown and Rutherford Lumber. He built the first Knox Church.

Rutherford, W. George (1878-1963) Musician. Born in Haldimand County, Ontario, he came to Hamiota, Manitoba, with his parents in 1882. He started playing the violin at an early age. He attended the Toronto Conservatory of Music and studied in Prague before settling in Winnipeg as a violin teacher in 1909. He was active in Manitoba musical affairs, and for years was a member of the syllabus selection committee of the Winnipeg Music Festival.

Ruttan, Arthur Charles (1878-1918) Soldier. Born in Kingston, he was educated at Queen's University. He moved to Winnipeg in 1899 as western manager for James Richardson. Active in the 90th Winnipeg Rifles, in 1916 he helped raise the 144th Battalion with rank of major. He returned to Winnipeg on furlough in 1918 and died suddenly.

Ruttan, Henry Noland (1848-1925) Soldier. Born in Cobourg, Canada, he was educated locally. He worked as a railway engineer from 1866 until 1877, when he came to Winnipeg and established an engineering practice. In 1885 he became Winnipeg city engineer, a post he held until his death. He served under General Middleton in the North-West Rebellion in 1885, and later became commanding officer of the 90th Battalion (1895-1900). He was president of the Canadian Society of Civil Engineers in 1910. His papers are at the PAM.

Ruttan, Mary See Robinson, Mary Augusta (Ruttan).

Ryan, Matthew (1810-1888) Magistrate. Born in St. John's, Newfoundland, he became a journalist in St. John's and Montreal before being called to the Lower Canada bar. He served as private secretary to Sir Francis Hincks. In 1875 he was made a commissioner to investigate "half-breed" claims in Manitoba, and he was subsequently appointed a stipendiary magistrate for the North-West Territories. He lost his office in 1881. He died in St. Boniface.

Sabourin, Joseph Adonias (1880-1960) Cleric. He joined the Eastern Rite of the Catholic Church in 1908 to administer to Ukrainian immigrants, whom he served until 1917, where he became director of the seminary at St. Boniface. He became chancellor of the archbishopric of St. Boniface in 1922, and parish priest at St. Pierre-Jolys in 1926. He published extensively on education and religion.

St. Amant, Beatrice (1888-1957) Health care pioneer. Born in Morice, Quebec, she came to St. Jean Baptiste in 1914 as a schoolteacher. In 1939 she established Youville Hospital in a Transcona farmhouse as a facility for mentally challenged children, running it until 1956 when she moved her patients to the St. Amant ward in the St. Boniface seniors' home run by the Sisters of Charity. She supervised the ward until her death.

St. Godard, Emile (1906-1948) Dogsled racer. Born in The Pas, he won his first race at the age of 16. Over the next six years he worked to within one win of the World Championship Trophy. He finished second in several dogsled derbies at The Pas. He was regarded as one of the finest dog drivers of his generation. He died in The Pas.

St. John, Frederick Edward Molyneux (1838-1904) Journalist, office-holder. Born in Newcastle, England, he was educated at Rossall College, Lancashire. He entered the Royal Marines as second lieutenant in 1855, and subsequently left the service after a promotion to first lieutenant. He came to Canada in 1868, joining the staff of the *Toronto Globe*, and served as special correspondent on the Wolseley Expedition. He stayed in Manitoba after the troops went home, becoming first clerk of the legislature, first secretary of the Protestant Board of Education, and later first sheriff and Indian Commissioner of the North-West Territories. In 1884 he became Canada's first emigration agent in England, and London secretary to the CPR. He served as editor of the *Winnipeg Standard,* and then the *Manitoba Free Press,* resigning in 1895 when the newspaper changed its editorial policy. He wrote *A Sea of Mountains* (1877) and was also a playwright.

St. John, Jack (1906-1965) Politican. He was educated at the University of Manitoba, and played on its 1928 Allan Cup hockey team. He later played professionally for St. Louis and Buffalo. A pharmacist, he was a Ward Two alderman from 1944 to 1953, then served as MLA for Winnipeg Centre from 1953 to 1958. While alderman he was an advocate of metropolitian government. As MLA, he led the attacks against the coloured margarine ban and the CBC's Winnipeg monopoly.

Saint Pierre, Télesphore (1869-1912) Journalist, author. Born in Lavaltrie, Quebec, he moved with his family to Michigan in 1878. He began his journalism career in 1885 as editor of *Le Progrès* in

219

Windsor. He later served on a succession of newspapers in Michigan in the early 1890s, Montreal papers in the later 1890s, and then Winnipeg newspapers after the turn of the century, including the *Manitoba Free Press*. After years of exhaustive research in the Detroit Public Library, he wrote the authoritative *Histoire des Canadiens du Michigan* (1895). He was president of the parliamentary press gallery in Ottawa in 1894 and 1895. He died in St. Boniface. *DCB* XIV, 903-05.

Salaberry, Colonel Charles de (1820-1882) Explorer. Born in Quebec, the son of the victor of the battle of Chateauguay (1813), he grew up in a family of private means and public service. In 1857 he accompanied the Hind Expedition to Red River, and in 1869 he was appointed a Canadian government emissary to Red River. He arrived in Pembina on Christmas Eve and in Red River in early January, 1870. Because he was not empowered to negotiate on behalf of Canada with Red River, the provisional government ignored him. His most important contribution to Red River was his training of a boys' band in St. Boniface. He later served as superintendent of woods and forests in Quebec. *DCB* XI, 441-42.

Salverson, Laura (Goodman) (1898-1970) Author. Born in Winnipeg, she grew up in a family which spoke only Icelandic. She spent her early working years as an itinerant nurse, dance hostess, factory worker, and maid, before marrying in 1913 and settling in Winnipeg. A few years later she joined her husband on a homestead north of Prince Albert, Saskatchewan, later moving to Regina. She turned to writing with the encouragement of Austin Bothwell, and published *The Viking Heart* in 1923. She subsequently produced eight more novels, including *Dark Weaver* (which won the Governor General's Award for fiction in 1937) and *Immortal Rock* (which won the Ryerson Press Fiction Award for 1954). She served for many years as president of the Winnipeg branch of the Canadian Authors' Association. She also published poetry and a highly acclaimed autobiography, *The Confessions of an Immigrant's Daughter* (which won the Governor General's Award for nonfiction in 1940).

Samborski, Daniel James ("Sam," 1922-1989) Scientist. Born in Hampton, Saskatchewan, he studied at the University of Saskatchewan and McGill University. He worked at the Agriculture Canada Research Station in Winnipeg from 1956 to 1987, developing several strains of rust-resistant wheat. He received the gold medal of the Professional Institute of the Public Service of Canada for his contributions to Canadian agricultural science. He died in Winnipeg.

Samuel, Herbert J. (b. 1882) Rabbi. Born in Glasgow, Scotland, he was educated at Jews College, London, and University College, London. After serving as rabbi in Swansea, Wales, from 1906 to 1914, he came to Winnipeg to become rabbi of the Congregation Shaarey Zedek. He moved to Montreal in 1925.

Sanders, Nellie (McNichol) ("Nic," 1906-1990) Lawyer, judge. Born in Westover, Ontario, she graduated from the University of Manitoba in arts in 1928 and in law in 1932. She was called to the bar, and also became a social worker with the Manitoba Department of Welfare. She was secretary of the Manitoba Welfare Supervision Board from 1936 to 1942. In 1957 she was the first woman in Manitoba to be named to the bench, serving various courts before her retirement in 1977. She often awarded custody rights to fathers in family cases. Sanders was made QC in 1971. She died in Winnipeg.

Sanderson, George William (1846-1936) Memoirist. Born in Athabasca Landing to a mixed-blood family, he grew up in Portage la Prairie. In 1870 he was part of the Portage party captured by Louis Riel and imprisoned in Upper Fort Garry. According to his autobiography, Thomas Scott* was a real nuisance to both his captors and his fellow prisoners. The autobiography, published as "The 'Memories' of George William Sanderson," ed. Irene Spry, *Canadian Ethnic Studies* 17 (1985): 115-34, provides one of our best accounts of frontier mixed-blood life in the years after 1870.

Sanderson, James Francis (1848-1902) Interpreter, author. Born at Athabasca Landing, he moved with his mixed-blood mother (who had remarried) to Portage la Prairie. Unlike many Anglophone mixed-bloods, his family was associated with the plains buffalo hunters. He and his brother George joined the militia group that marched in early 1870 to liberate the prisoners held by Riel at Upper Fort Garry. He was captured and imprisoned with others, including

Thomas Scott.* In 1872 he married Maria McKay of Red River, and the couple moved to the Cypress Hills with her family. Sanderson became an interpreter for the NWMP in 1875, an association that continued for many years. He later became a successful cattle rancher and author of *Indian Tales of the Canadian Prairies* (1965). He died in Medicine Hat, Alberta. *DCB* XIII, 921-22.

Sanderson, John S. (1841-1930) Farmer. Born in East Lothian, Scotland, he came to Manitoba in 1872 and was the first homesteader to file a claim in the Canadian West. "After I had built my log shack, had broken a few acres of land, and harvested my first crop of wheat, things were easier for me," he later recalled. He is a member of the Manitoba Agricultural Hall of Fame.

Saunders, Michael Graham (1920-1975) Medical researcher, doctor. Born in London, England, he received a BSc degree from Victoria University, Manchester, and worked at an EEG laboratory in Manchester before entering medical school. He immigrated to Winnipeg in 1949, and systematically developed the EEG laboratory at the Winnipeg General Hospital, introducing computer technology into clinical medicine. He was awarded a doctorate in medicine by Manchester in 1963.

Saunderson, Hugh Hamilton (1904-1984) Scientist, educator. Born in Winnipeg, he attended local schools and the University of Manitoba, obtaining a BA in 1924 with the gold medal. He obtained a BSc in 1929 and an MSc in chemistry in 1930 from the University of Manitoba, then studied at McGill University, where he was awarded a PhD in chemistry in 1932. He then taught at the University of Manitoba, becoming professor of chemistry and dean of arts and sciences in 1945. From 1947 to 1951 he was director of the Division of Information Services for the National Research Council, then went to the Department of Defence Production until 1954, and finally returned to the University of Manitoba as sixth president in 1954, the first graduate of the university to hold its highest office. He retired in 1970, after having shepherded the university through a major growth period. His autobiography was published in 1981 as *The Saunderson Years*. He held many important national and provincial offices, including the presidency of the National Conference of Canadian Universities and Colleges from 1959 to 1960,

and presidency of the Winnipeg Symphony Orchestra. Saunderson had honorary degrees from the University of Alberta, the University of Saskatchewan, the University of Winnipeg, the University of Manitoba, and McGill University. His papers are at the University of Manitoba.

Savage, Alfred (1889-1970) Animal pathologist. Born in Montreal, he was educated at McGill University (BSA 1911), Cornell University (DVM 1914), and Edinburgh Royal Dick (MRCVS 1928). He joined the Manitoba Agricultural College in 1921. From 1930 to 1945 he was professor of animal pathology and bacteriology, and dean of agriculture from 1933 to 1937, during which time he insisted on keeping the faculty open despite the hard times of the Depression. He was provincial animal pathologist from 1938 to 1957. He served as president of the Canadian Veterinary Medical Association in 1952. He is a member of the Manitoba Agricultural Hall of Fame.

Sawchuk, Terrence Gordon ("Terry," 1929-1970) Hockey goalie. Born in Winnipeg, he played junior hockey in the city and in Galt, Ontario, before turning professional in 1946 with Omaha. He joined the Detroit Red Wings as goalie in 1951, winning the Calder Cup as rookie of the year. In his first five years in the NHL, Sawchuk won the Vezina Trophy (for fewest goals allowed per game) three times, producing 56 shutouts. His style was based on superb reflexes and many acrobatics. Like many goalies, however, Sawchuk had trouble living with the psychological stresses of the game. Especially after expansion of the league, he shifted from team to team, although he won one of his five Vezina trophies with the Toronto Maple Leafs in 1965 and the Stanley Cup with the same team in 1967. He holds many NHL records, including a record 103 shutouts that is more secure than almost any other career record in sports. Sawchuk had a lifetime goals-against average of 2.52 per game. He died in Long Beach, New York from injuries suffered accidentally in a scuffle with a teammate. A Winnipeg hockey arena is named after him. He is a member of the Canadian Sports Hall of Fame, the Hockey Hall of Fame, and the Manitoba Sports Hall of Fame.

Sayer, Pierre-Guillaume (c. 1795-c. 1849) Trader. Born in the Fond du Lac District southwest of Lake Superior, he came to Red River in 1824 and settled at Grantown. He farmed, traded, and hunted buffalo. In 1849 he was tried in the General Quarterly Court of Assiniboia for illegal trading in furs. The jury found Sayer guilty but recommended mercy because Sayer genuinely believed that Métis could trade freely. Sayer was freed, and the Métis responded to this action by declaring that "Le commerce est libre!" *DCB.* VII, 776-77.

Scallion, James William (1847-1926) Farmer, farm leader. Born in County Wexford, Ireland, he came to Canada at the age of eight. He grew up in Hamilton, then attended the University of Toronto before teaching school in Thorold, Ontario, for 11 years. In 1882 he and his brother Thomas came to Stonewall, Manitoba, later moving to Virden, where they farmed 960 acres. Scallion was the founder and first president of the United Farmers of Manitoba (when it was the Grain Growers' Association in 1903) and a founder of the Progressive Party of Manitoba. He led the battle against excessive freight rates in 1910.

Scarth, William Bain (1837-1902) Merchant, politician. Born in Aberdeen, Scotland, he came to Canada in 1855 and became a successful shipowner and timber merchant. He invested heavily in Manitoba land and prospered mightily during the boom of the early 1880s. He also fell on hard financial times when the boom collapsed. He did his best to make peace between the federal Conservatives of Sir John A. Macdonald and the provincial Conservatives under John Norquay* in the 1880s. In the 1886 provincial election he ran as an Independent but lost by 39 votes. He was then pressed into service as a federal candidate, and won by eight votes early in 1887. The Canada Northwest Land Company, of which he was managing director, was never happy with his career as a politician, but Sir John A. regarded him highly. His prominence in the party ended with Macdonald's death, although he was eventually rewarded for loyal party service with an appointment as federal deputy minister of agriculture in 1895. A Liberal investigation of his earlier land dealings criticized him but did not find much real corruption. Scarth was incapacitated from 1898 to his death in Ottawa. *DCB* XIII, 929-31.

Schmidt, Louis (1844-1935) Métis leader. A mixed-blood of German descent, he was educated at the Collège de Saint-Boniface and then sent (with Louis Riel and Daniel MacDougall) to Quebec for further education. Schmidt attended the Collège de Saint-Hyacinthe and returned to Red River in 1861. He was a French delegate to the Convention of Forty from St. Boniface. He served as a member of the committee of six which prepared the bill of rights debated by the convention. He served as French secretary to the convention and as secretary in the provisional government. He was elected to the first Manitoba Assembly. He later held an appointment in the land office at Prince Albert (now Saskatchewan), and he kept his distance from Louis Riel during the Rebellion of 1885. A typescript of his memoirs is at the PAM.

Schofield, Frank Howard (1859-1929) Educator, historian. Born in Black River, Nova Scotia, he was educated locally, at the Horton Academy, and at Acadian University (BA 1882). He taught at Horton Academy, then at the Winnipeg Collegiate Institute, where he became principal in 1899. He retired in 1919 and moved to Victoria, where he died. In 1913 he published in three volumes *The Story of Manitoba*, perhaps the most thorough provincial history produced to that date.

Schultz, Agnes Campbell (Farquharson) (1840-1929) Born in British Guiana, she came to Manitoba with her father James Farquharson* in 1864, and married John Schultz* in the Catholic Church in 1867. She helped her husband escape from jail in 1868 and was imprisoned with him by Louis Riel in 1870. She later served as hostess at Government House from 1888 to 1895. She died at her home in Armstrong Point, Winnipeg.

Schultz, Ivan (1891-1974) Lawyer, politician. Born in Belmont, Manitoba, he was educated at Baldur schools, Wesley College, and the University of Manitoba. Called to the bar in 1920, he practised law in Baldur and was first elected a Liberal MLA in 1930. From 1936 to 1944 he served as minister of education, adding the post of minister of libraries and archives in 1942. As minister, he introduced a program of rural scholarships. From 1944 to 1953 he was minister of health and public welfare, and was responsible for establishing rural hospitals in the province. He was attorney general from 1953 until 1955, when he became a justice of the Manitoba Court of Appeal. During his last six months on the bench he was acting chief justice. He retired in 1966.

Schultz, John Christian (1840-1896) Doctor, merchant, politician. Born in Amherstburg, Canada, he claimed to have attended Oberlin College, as well as Victoria University, Cobourg, and to have graduated from Queen's University, Kingston. Oberlin has no record of his attendance. He attended one term at Victoria, and two terms at Queen's, but received no degree. Thus there is no evidence of his having received a medical degree or having been licensed by Victoria University, as he later claimed. Soon after his arrival in Red River in 1861 he advertised in the *Nor'wester* as "Physician and Surgeon." He spoke some French, helped his half-brother, Henry McKenney,* manage the Royal Hotel, and was elected secretary of the Institute of Rupert's Land (claiming to be a Fellow of the Botanical Society of Canada). He became proprietor of the *Nor'wester* newspaper and was the leader of the pro-Canadian party in Red River. He was one of the founders of the Masonic Lodge in Winnipeg. In 1867 he was found unacceptable as a councillor of Assiniboia. On 7 January 1868 he was jailed for resisting a sheriff. Eleven days later, with the help of a party led by his wife, he escaped from jail. He was renowed for his prodigious strength. A.C. Garrioch* once saw him singlehandedly move an oxcart weighing 900 pounds. In 1870 he marched over 450 miles of prairie on snowshoes. A.W. Graham* described him in December 1869 as a "genial, powerfully built man, over six feet, red, sandy complexion." In December 1869 he and a party defending his house were captured by the Métis and imprisoned at Upper Fort Garry. Schultz escaped, attempted to organize an opposition to Louis Riel, and eventually left the settlement via an overland route through Minnesota for eastern Canada, where he helped organize Ontario agitation against the Métis for the murder of Thomas Scott.* He returned to Manitoba in September 1870, and was elected as a Conservative to represent Lisgar in the House of Commons from 1871 to 1882, when he was called to the Canadian Senate. He served as lieutenant-governor of Manitoba from 1885 to 1895. He was still dining on stories of his captivity more than 20 years after the event. There is no full-length biography, but there are extensive papers at the PAM. *DCB* XII, 949-54.

Scoble, Thomas Clarkson (1840-1900) Soldier, engineer. Born in Devonshire, he studied civil engineering at the University of Toronto 1857-1860. He joined the militia in 1861 and advanced rapidly, becoming a Lieutenant-Colonel in 1871 and Brigadier-Major (district quarter-master in Winnipeg) in 1885. He worked as an engineer for the Ontario government, and subsequently worked for the Ontario government in various capacities, including deputy inspector of asylums and prisons. He came to Winnipeg in 1881 and devoted most of his civilian energy to promoting a Hudson Bay Railroad. He was managing editor of the Great West Publishing Company 1898-9. He wrote many articles and one book, *Canadian Volunteers' Hand-Book for Field Service*, published in 1868.

Scorer, Mary (1911-1988) Bookseller, publisher. Born in Newcastle, England, she came to Canada aged three. Educated in Winnipeg, she worked as a secretary for Purity Flour for many years. During WWII she went to Britain as an ambulance driver, then worked for an English publisher after the war. She returned to Canada in 1950, worked at Eaton's book department from 1950 to 1959, and then opened her own bookstore in 1959. She established Peguis Publishers in 1967, which was Manitoba's first full-time publishing company. At Peguis, Scorer published many books on Manitoba history. The bookstore initially financed the publishing, but she gradually moved full-time into the publishing business and sold the bookstore to other parties. She was named YWCA Woman of the Year in 1982 and was inducted into the Order of the Buffalo Hunt in 1984. An annual prize for the best book by a Manitoba publisher is named in her honour.

Scott, Alfred H. (c. 1840-1872) Insurgent, diplomat. He had no known history before 1869, when he began work as a barkeeper in the saloon of Bob O'Lone,* later working as a clerk in the store of Henry McKenney.* Both employers were American. He was elected a delegate from Winnipeg to the 1870 Convention of Forty with the aid of the American vote. He was later a delegate from the provisional government to Ottawa, and was arrested as a party to the murder of Thomas Scott.* He appears to have supported Father Ritchot* in the negotiations, but left before they were completed. He returned to Red River via the United States, and converted to Roman Catholicism in 1871-2 during a long illness. He died as the first patient of the Saint Boniface Hospital. *DCB* X, 645-46.

Scott, Margaret (Boucher) (1856-1931) Reformer. Born in Coburg, Canada, she grew up in

Campbellford and married there. Her husband died in 1881 and in 1886 she moved to Winnipeg, where she worked in a law office and was noted as the most expert stenographer in the city. She soon began assisting Reverend C.C. Owen of Holy Trinity Church with his relief work, and before long had organized a facility for assisting wayward girls, which was gradually partially financed by the city. In 1904 the facility became the Margaret Scott Nursing Mission. Scott initiated a local woodyard to provide work for unemployed men; it was taken over by the city. In 1911 the mission began a child's hygiene department. In 1929, the mission's report indicated that nearly 3,000 cases had come under its care. The papers for the Scott Mission are at the PAM.

Scott, Thomas (1841-1915) Politician. Born in Lanark County, Upper Canada, he apprenticed to a newspaper publisher and became publisher himself of the *Perth Expositor*. Always active in the militia, he came west as an officer with the Wolseley Expedition of 1870, and remained in the army until he retired in 1874. He was defeated in a bid for the provincial legislature in 1874, but won in 1878. He ran successfully for MP against Donald A. Smith* in 1880. At the same time, he served as a Winnipeg alderman from 1874, as school trustee from 1875 to 1877, and as mayor of Winnipeg from 1876 to 1878. He subsequently became collector of customs for Winnipeg in the early 1880s, and fell from public view.

Scott, Thomas (c. 1842-1870) Adventurer. Born in Ireland and an Orangeman, he was one of the workmen who threatened John Snow* with physical violence at Oak Point in October 1869. Scott was fined £4 at the 19 November 1869 General Quarterly Court. According to Alexander Begg* he said on leaving court "it was a pity they had not ducked Snow while they were at it as they had not got their money's worth." He was one of a delegation of three sent by those in John Schultz's* house to negotiate with Riel on 7 December 1869; he was held by Riel as a prisoner. He escaped along with others on 9 January 1870, by digging for nights at the windows of Upper Fort Garry with pocket knives until he had removed the iron bars from one of the windows. He went to Portage la Prairie, where he helped encourage the attempt of February 1870 to free the remaining prisoners. He was captured 17 February 1870 and was tried by a Métis tribunal on 3 March 1870 for insubordination and rebellion against the provisional government. He was condemned to death and executed on 4 March, 1870, becoming the martyr of the resistance. The people of Ontario, especially Orangemen, were very angry about his death. See J.M. Bumsted, "Thomas Scott and the Daughter of Time" *Prairie Forum* 23, no. 2 (fall 1998): 145-170. *DCB* IX, 707-9.

Scott, William (1834-1926) Contractor. Born in County Tyrone, Ireland, he came to Canada with his family and moved to Winnipeg in 1881. A contractor, he undertook the laying of the first block pavement in Winnipeg on Main Street, and also the city's first granolithic sidewalk. He operated the Crystal Ice Company for many years. He owned extensive property in the Riverview area of Winnipeg. He died in Santa Monica, California.

Scott, William Duncan (1861-1925) Civil servant. Manitoba immigration agent from 1887 to 1899, he was Canadian commissioner at various international exhibitions from 1899 to 1903, and superintendent of the Federal Immigration Branch from 1903 to 1925. From 1911 Scott was also chief controller of Chinese immigration.

Selkirk, Earl of See Douglas, Thomas

Semmens, John (1850-1921) Missionary. Born in Perran Downs, Cornwall, England, he came to Canada with his family in 1860. He graduated from the preparatory department of Victoria College, Toronto, before entering the Methodist ministry. In 1872 he relieved Egerton Ryerson Young* at Norway House, where he became an authority on the Cree language. In 1880 he became pastor of Zion Methodist Church in Winnipeg, then Emerson Methodist Church, before heading north again in the 1880s. In 1890 he became pastor of Wesley Church, and then McDougall Methodist Church, both in Winnipeg. In 1895 he organized the Industrial School at Brandon for the education of Indian children, leaving in 1900. Ill health led him to retire from the ministry and to accept an appointment with the federal department of Indian Affairs. He published *Mission Life in the Northwest* and *The Field and the Work: Sketches of Missionary Life in the Far North* (1884). He also published several books in the Cree language.

Semmens, John Nelson (1879-1960) Architect. Born in Toronto, he graduated from Wesley College,

Winnipeg, and took a degree in architecture from the University of Pennsylvania. He returned to Winnipeg around 1910 and designed many of the city's leading buildings, including the RCMP barracks, the St. Boniface Sanatorium, Grace Maternity Hospital, and Daniel McIntyre School. He was active in the Winnipeg Grenadiers from 1910 and went overseas as a major, becoming commanding officer of the 78th Battalion in 1917. He ultimately received the Distinguished Service Order. He organized the second battalion of the Grenadiers during WWII, becoming commandant at Camp Shilo during the war. He retired to Victoria, British Columbia in 1957.

Semple, Robert (1777-1816) Colonial official. Born in Boston to Loyalist parents, he travelled widely at the time of the Napoleonic Wars as a merchant (and probably as a British spy), producing a number of travel books and a novel, *Charles Ellis, or the friends* (1807). In 1815 Lord Selkirk* named him governor of Assiniboia, and he arrived at York Factory in August 1815 with settlers from Sutherlandshire, Scotland. At Red River, he soon ran into conflict with Colin Robertson,* who persisted in calling him "Mr. Simple." Robertson found him both too conciliatory and too contemptuous of the Métis. He was killed leading a party of armed settlers (about 20 of whom were also killed) by a group of Métis under Cuthbert Grant* at the area known as Seven Oaks on 19 June 1816. Lord Selkirk and the HBC always referred to this skirmish as a "massacre," although evidence of who was the aggressor and what actually happened at Seven Oaks is not at all conclusive. Although a number of the Grant party were tried in Upper Canada for murder on Selkirk-initiated indictments, not surprisingly, none were ever convicted. *DCB* V, 749-751.

Sénécal, Joseph-Azarie (1841-1917) Architect, contractor. Born at St. Marc, Canada, he was a factory owner in Montreal before coming to Baie St. Paul, Manitoba in 1877 to farm. He was reeve of St. François Xavier from 1881 to 1884. In 1891 he moved to St. Boniface and became an architect, where he designed the St. Boniface Cathedral, the St. Boniface CNR station, and various other buildings. Sénécal also designed buildings in Saskatchewan and Alberta, being best known in the Prairie West for his Catholic churches. He was mayor of St. Boniface in 1901 and was a school trustee for many years. He died in St. Boniface. *DCB* XIV, 921-23.

Sergeant, Henry (fl. 1683-89) HBC governor. Little is known of Sergeant apart from his service to the HBC. In 1685 he sailed for the Bay with the first clergyman sent to the region and three women including his wife, a companion, and a maidservant — the first European women to winter in James Bay. The HBC had planned to replace him in 1685, but the order to do so was lost at sea. He lost Albany Factory to the French in 1686, was taken prisoner, and was subsequently ordered home "with the whole parcell of women appertaining to him." The HBC sued him for damages caused by his "neglect or cowardice" but dropped the case in 1689. *DCB* I, 605-6.

Seton, Ernest Thompson (1860-1946) Naturalist, writer. Born in County Durham, England, he moved to Canada with his family at age five, settling on a farm near Lindsay, Ontario, and then moving to Toronto, where he was educated at Toronto Collegiate and the Ontario College of Art. He then studied at the Royal Academy of Painting and Sculpture in London as a scholarship student, all the while pursuing his interest in natural history. Upon his return from England in 1882, in ill health, he joined his brother on a homestead in Manitoba just east of Carberry. He always regarded the next five years as his "golden days," as he walked around the Carberry countryside taking notes and making sketches. At Carberry he also began to write. In 1891 he published *The Birds of Manitoba*, which in 1892 led to his appointment as Provincial Naturalist by the Manitoba government. In the early 1890s he made several trips to Paris to study art, discovering upon his return to Manitoba that settlement had disrupted much of the natural habitat. *Wild Animals I Have Known* (1898) was the publication that made Seton famous. It was the first successful attempt to present animals realistically in story form. In 1902 he organized the Woodcraft Indians, a boys' organization, and wrote a manual, *The Birch Bark Roll of the Woodcraft Indians*. This organization later merged with the Boy Scouts, as Seton was one of the founders of the Boy Scouts of America in 1910 and helped to write its first manual. He was expelled from the organization in 1915, after constantly criticising its militarism, officially because he was not an American citizen. He continued to publish books about woodcraft, however, throughout his life. In 1908 he published *The Life Histories of Northern Animals: An Account of the Mammals of Manitoba* (2 vols.) in the midst of a continued outpouring of animal stories. In his later life he was often accused of anthropomorphism in his animal stories, but no one disputed his naturalist work, such *as Lives of Game Animals* (4 vols., 1925-27). In 1930 he moved to Santa Fe, New Mexico, and in 1931 he became an American citizen. Here he admired the Indians, producing *Gospel of the Redman* (1936). His autobiography was *Trail of an Artist-Naturalist* (1940). For a biography, see John Henry Wadland, *Ernest Thompson Seton: Man in Nature and the Progressive Era, 1880-1915* (1979). There are papers at the NAC.

Settee, James (c. 1809-1902) Missionary. Born near Split Lake (in present day Manitoba) to mixed-blood parents, he went to school at Red River and was baptized as an Indian in 1827. He became a protégé of the Reverend William Cockran* and eventually an Anglican missionary, serving as a catechist and schoolteacher. He was a firm believer in agricultural settlement. A Swampy Cree, he had little in common with the Plains Cree of the southern Prairies, but he persevered at The Pas and later at the Lac La Ronge-Stanley Mission, which he founded. In 1853 he enrolled in St. John's College School, and in 1854 he went to Swan River, where he was ordained in 1856 to the Anglican priesthood. Settee later attempted to establish a mission in the Qu'Appelle Valley, but met hostility from the local Indians. He spent many years in what is now Saskatchewan before retiring to Manitoba. He resented his treatment by the Anglican Church, but rejoiced in the gains made by the Native Church. He died in Winnipeg. *DCB* XIII, 937-39.

Shantz, Jacob Yost (1822-1909) Immigration promoter. Born in Ebytown (Berlin), Upper Canada, he farmed and ran various businesses, including a button factory. In 1872 the Canadian government asked him to accompany a Russian Mennonite to Manitoba to investigate a possible settlement there. He described the visit in *The Narrative of a Journey to Manitoba* (1873), which became an important immigration tract. He served at the behest of the Canadian government as Canadian director of Mennonite immigration, raising considerable money through gifts and loans. He was recompensed with land in the Mennonite reserves near Schanzenfeld and Schanzenberg. He later began a Mennonite colony in Didsbury, Alberta. In later years he joined the reform Mennonites and ended up in the Christian Science Church. He died in Berlin, Ontario. See S.J. Steiner, *Vicarious*

Pioneer: The Life of Jacob Y. Shantz (1988). *DCB* XIII, 939-41.

Sharpe, Thomas (1866-1929) Contractor, municipal politician. Born in County Sligo, Ireland, he was locally educated. He immigrated to Canada in 1885 and to Winnipeg in 1892, where he introduced the cement sidewalk to the city. A Conservative, he was elected mayor of Winnipeg in 1903, serving for two more terms as a staunch supporter of municipal ownership. At one time he was grand master of the Orange Lodge of Manitoba.

Shepperd, William (1841-1916) Civil servant. Born in Goderich County, Canada, he came to Portage la Prairie in 1882, where he established a successful hotel business and farmed. He was captain of the Portage la Prairie regiment in the North-West Rebellion in 1885, subsequently retiring at that rank. In 1907 he was appointed governor of the Central Judicial District Jail.

Sherman, Louis Ralph (1886-1953) Archbishop. Born in Fredericton, New Brunswick, he was locally educated and graduated from the University of New Brunswick in 1907 with honours in classics. He received an MA from the University of New Brunswick, then studied divinity at Bishop's College. In 1909 he was chosen Rhodes Scholar for New Brunswick, and attended Christ Church College, Oxford. He was ordained deacon in 1912 and priest in 1913, both in London, England. He returned to New Brunswick as curate of Trinity Church, St. Johns, in 1914, becoming rector at Holy Trinity, Toronto in 1917. He was appointed rector of the Cathedral of the Holy Trinity in Quebec in 1925, and then bishop of Calgary in 1926. In 1943 he was elected sixth archbishop of the ecclesiastical province of Rupert's Land. He was an ardent supporter of a self-supporting Canadian Church. He died in Brandon.

Shewman, Harold P. (1900-1969) Politician. Born in Winnipeg, he moved with his parents to Morris, Manitoba, in 1915. He was for many years in partnership with his father in a road construction business. He later worked as an auctioneer and insurance agent. He served on the school board from 1925 to 1938. Shewman was mayor of Morris from 1948 to 1954, and was elected to the Manitoba legislature in 1949, re-elected as an Independent in 1953 and as a Progressive Conservative in 1958. He was active as a flood fighter in the 1950 flood and supervised the evacuation of the town of Morris. In the legislature he was an advocate of flood protection and crop insurance for farmers.

Shillinglaw, Walter H. (1864-1957) Engineer and architect. Born in Staffa, Perth County, Canada, he was educated in Missouri before moving with his parents to Brandon in 1882. He attended the School of Science in Toronto. His father had been a builder, erecting the house at 302 Russell Street in which Shillinglaw lived all his life. He designed many houses while working as city engineer in Brandon from 1906 to 1910, after which he joined David Marshall in the architectural firm of Shillinglaw and Marshall, which was responsible for the design of the exhibition buildings for the 1913 Dominion Fair at Brandon. After military service in WWI, he designed a number of buildings in Brandon, including First Presbyterian Church (1928) and the Federal Building (1930). He was a member of the Royal Architectural Institute of Canada and the Curling Club of Brandon.

Shipley, Herbert Rowland (1903-1977) Farm leader. Born in Epworth, England, he came to Birtle, Manitoba, with his parents. He joined his father in business, helping to run an auctioneering and meat-marketing operation in Russell. In 1942 he became an inspector for the Trust and Loan Company of Canada, which later joined the Canada Permanent Trust Company. He was an authority on land values and an advocate of better farming practices. He is a member of the Manitoba Agricultural Hall of Fame.

Shipley, Nancy Evelyn (Sommerville) ("Nan," 1902-1990) Writer. Born in Glasgow, Scotland, she came to Canada at an early age. After her marriage to George Shipley she moved to Winnipeg in the 1920s. She published her first book, *Frances and the Crees*, in 1957. In the years thereafter she published 10 more books, some of them children's stories, some historical studies, and a biography (*The James Evans Story*, 1966). Much of her writing focussed on Indian and Métis women. In 1959 she organized Manitoba's first Indian handicrafts sales centre, and she was elected Woman of the Year in Manitoba by the Women's Sales and Advertising Council in 1965. She died in Winnipeg. Some of her papers are at the University of Mississippi, and others are at the PAM.

Siemens, Jacob John (1896-1963) Farm leader. Born near Altona, Manitoba, he was educted at the Mennonite Educational Institute and at the Manitoba Normal School. He was an active member of the co-operative movement, and helped found over 30 co-operatives in the region. An advocate of agricultural education, he organized the Rhineland Agricultural Institute for youth training in 1937 and helped found the Western Co-operative College at Saskatoon. During WWII he advocated the growth of sunflowers and marketed the idea of extracting oil from them, eventually organizing Co-op Vegetable Oils Ltd. in Altona. He is a member of the Manitoba Agricultural Hall of Fame. See R.R. Myer, *The Spirit of the Post Road* (1955) and E.K. Francis, *In Search of Utopia* (1955).

Sifton, Sir Clifford (1861-1929) Publisher, politician. Born in London, Canada, he was educated at Victoria University, Cobourg (1880), and was called to the Manitoba bar in 1882. He practised law in Brandon and was MLA for North Brandon from 1888 to 1896, serving as attorney general and minister of education from 1891 to 1896. He was responsible for dealing with the federal government over the Manitoba School Question, and was a constant opponent of the principle of separate schools. He was subsequently Liberal MP for Brandon from 1896 to 1911, and served as minister of the interior and superintendent general of Indian affairs from 1896 to 1905. He is associated with an aggressive immigration policy that brought many settlers, including those from eastern Europe, to the Prairie region. Although he broke with the Liberals over reciprocity in 1911, as owner of the *Manitoba Free Press*, he continued to have an influential voice in Canadian affairs, and was awarded a knighthood. His papers are in the NAC. For a favourable biography, see J.W. Dafoe, *Clifford Sifton in Relation to His Times* (1931). A more balanced effort is David Hall's *Clifford Sifton* (1981, 1985) (2 vols.).

Sifton, John Wright (1833-1912) Publisher, politician. Born in Middlesex County, Upper Canada, of Irish origins, he came to Selkirk, Manitoba, in 1875 and became a successful contractor, mainly involved with railway and telegraph construction. He spent several years in California in the 1880s. He served as Liberal MLA from St. Clements from 1878 to 1879, becoming Speaker in the latter year. From 1881 to 1883 he sat as Brandon MP, and later held a variety of government appointments. He became vice-president of the Manitoba Free Press Company in 1902 and subsequently its president. Sifton was an active temperance advocate, serving four years as president of the Manitoba branch of the Dominion Alliance.

Sifton, Victor (1897-1961) Publisher. Born in Ottawa, he left the University of Toronto to serve in WWI, demobilized with the rank of major and the Distinguished Service Order. He worked as a broker during the 1920s, and then took over the *Regina Leader-Post* when the Sifton empire gained control of it. In 1935 he moved to Winnipeg as general manager of the *Free Press*. During part of WWII he served as an executive assistant to the defence minister; he was named a Commander of the Order of the British Empire. He served as president of the Canadian Press from 1948 to 1950 and as chancellor of the University of Manitoba from 1952 to 1959. He was the author of *Rights and Citizenship: The Threat to Our Freedom* (1954). He died in Winnipeg.

Sigfusson, Svein Olafur (1912-1992) Athlete, businessman. Born in Lundar, Manitoba, he was an outstanding athlete, winning a bronze medal in the discus at the 1950 British Empire Games. He was also a Canadian champion hammer thrower. He won nine Manitoba championships and nine Canadian championships in the years he competed in the Amateur Athletics Union. For many years he ran a transportation company in northern Manitoba which operated on a road system of 3,500 miles; most of this road system had been developed by Sigfusson. The company employed over 400 people, nearly half of whom were of Native origin. He received the Manitoba Centennial Medal in 1970, the Order of Canada in 1974, and was elected to the Manitoba Sports Hall of Fame in 1982. In 1992 he published *Sigfusson's Roads*, describing his northern transportation network. He is a member of the Manitoba Sports Hall of Fame.

Sigurdson, Snjolaug (d. 1971) Pianist. Born in Arborg, Manitoba, she studied piano in Winnipeg with Eva Clare before heading to New York in 1946 on an Icelandic Canadian Club scholarship. She made her New York debut in 1950, and performed often in major venues. She returned to Winnipeg in 1958, and served as organist and choir director of First Lutheran Church. She also taught piano and served as a music adjudicator. She died in Winnipeg.

Sigurdsson, Stefan (1864-1917) Businessman. Born in Iceland, he came to Big Island (Hecla Island) with his parents in 1876. He took an early lead in commercial ventures on Lake Winnipeg, organizing fish packing and, with his brother Johannes, establishing the firm Sigurdsson Brothers at Hnausa in 1890. The brothers launched the lake steamer *Lady of the Lake* in 1896. Stefan captained the vessel himself for a time. He served as reeve of Gimli in 1893-4, and the Rural Municipality of Bifrost in 1909.

Silvy, Antoine (1638-1711) Missionary. Born in France, he came to Quebec as a Jesuit neophyte in 1673, taking his vows as a professed in 1675. He served as a missionary to the aboriginals out of a base at Michilimackinac, and was chaplain to the expedition led by Sieur Bermen de la Martinière to Hudson Bay in 1684, during which he kept a journal. He later accompanied the Chevalier de Troyes overland to Hudson Bay, and evangelized among the First Nations of the Bay until 1693, when he became a teacher at the Jesuit College. He is usually regarded as the founder of the northern mission of the Catholic Church. *DCB* II, 607-09.

Simkin, Frank ("Feivel," "Pops," 1885-1983) Publisher. Born in Magilio, Russia, he came to Winnipeg in 1905. In 1911 he established the *Israelite Press,* for many years the only Jewish newspaper in Western Canada. He was also active in the Jewish community, a leader of the Arbeiter Ring School and later the I.L. Peretz School. He became president of Universal Printers when it was founded in 1949, remaining head of the company until its sale and his retirement in 1960. He died in Winnipeg.

Simon, Frank Worthington (1863-1933) Architect. Born in England, he was educated in Wolverhampton and Birmingham before attending the École des Beaux Arts in Paris. He commenced practice as an architect in Edinburgh in 1888. In 1912 he won a competition against 64 other architects for the design of the Manitoba legislative buildings, and he moved to Winnipeg to supervise the construction, leaving shortly after their completion in 1920 for Mentone, France, where he died. Simon also designed the Edinburgh International Exhibition Building, the Liverpool Cotton Exchange, and buildings at Liverpool University. He was the author of *Etchings of Old Edinburgh.*

Simonite, Charles Edward (1879-1973) Municipal politician. Born in Paris, Ontario, his family moved to Rapid City, Manitoba in 1880. He moved to Winnipeg in 1895, and was active in the real-estate business. He was first elected to city council in 1930, serving until 1955 with only one two-year break. He was chair of the welfare committee in the 1930s, and subsequently chair of the finance committee for 17 years, including in 1950, the year of the flood. He was also deputy mayor for many years. He helped found Winnipeg Enterprises. There are personal papers at the PAM.

Simpson, Allan John (1939-1998) Advocate for the handicapped. Born in Ottawa, he was educated in Starbuck, Manitoba. He contracted polio at age 14 while living in Winnipeg and graduated University of Manitoba (B Com) in a wheelchair in 1962. He managed the first Pan Am Wheelchair Games in 1967, and organized the Manitoba and Canadian Wheelchair Sport Associations. Simpson spent 30 years working on behalf of Canadians with disabilities, and was one of Canada's most successful lobbyists. After some years with Monarch Life Assurance Company, in 1984 he became managing director of the Independent Living Resource Centre. He became a member of the Order of the Buffalo Hunt in 1995 and was awarded the Order of Canada in 1998.

Simpson, Frances Ramsay (1812-1853) Fur-trade wife. Born in London into a merchant family, Frances married her cousin George Simpson* when she was eighteen and he was on furlough in England. The couple left soon after the ceremony for North America. Frances was one of the first European women to travel west by canoe from Lachine to York Factory, and in Red River she created a new social standard before her withdrawal back to London because of ill health in 1833. She had continual trouble with pregnancy, but returned to North America (to Lachine) in 1845. She found her husband's autocratic behaviour and his constant absence to be major problems, particularly given her continual physical suffering. Her correspondence is in the HBCA. *DCB* VIII, 811-12.

Simpson, Sir George (c. 1787-1860) HBC Governor. An illegitimate son of a London merchant, he served as a clerk in the sugar brokerage firm of Andrew Wedderburn-Colvile* before his appointment as HBC governor-in-chief locum tenens in 1820. In North America, he ran the tough Athabaska Department until the union of the HBC and NWC in 1821, when he became governor of the Northern Department of Rupert's Land, with headquarters at Red River. After 1826 he was governor-in-chief of the HBC and its territories in North America. For the first part of his tenure he ran his vast empire from Red River, although after 1826 he also established a headquarters in Lachine, Lower Canada. Simpson married his cousin Frances Simpson* in 1830 and brought her to Red River, where the couple lived until 1833. His marriage, which involved disposing of a Native wife and family, brought about a new fashion in the HBC for European wives. It also eventually led Simpson to make his permanent headquarters at Lachine, where his wife could be more comfortable. In the course of his work, Simpson became one of the great business travellers of the nineteenth century. Except for three years in London, no year passed without a major journey somewhere. He travelled North America by canoe, often accompanied by a piper, and insisted his health improved the moment he stepped into a canoe. Despite failing eyesight, he travelled to Hawaii in 1841 and continued around the world via Alaska and Siberia. He was a great autocrat and brooked no opposition to his decisions. Simpson's heyday was before the railroad, but he recognized that the railroad would change the HBC and the nature of the West. Most of his papers are in the HBCA in Winnipeg. Several selections of his letters have been printed, including Joseph Shafer, ed., *Letters of Sir George Simpson 1841-1843* (1908). His account of his around-the-world tour was published as *Narrative of a Journey round the World, during the Years 1841 and 1842* (1847) (2 vols.); his journal of the trip appeared, edited by Frederick Merk as *Fur Trade and Empire* (1931). For a biography, see J.S. Galbraith, *The Little Emperor: Governor Simpson of the Hudson's Bay Company* (1976). *DCB* VIII, 812-19.

Simpson, Isobel Graham (Finlayson) (1811-1890) Memoirist. Born in London, she was "amiable & accomplished," and was successfully wooed by Duncan Finlayson* in 1838. She joined her husband in Rupert's Land in 1840, keeping a journal of the journey. She moved to Lachine in 1844. She died in London, England. For her diary, see *The Beaver* (September 1951): 32-35; (December 1951): 32-37. *DCB* XI, 824.

Simpson, Robert Mills (b. 1865) Physician. Born in Canada, he was educated at Manitoba College and the Manitoba Medical College. He subsequently studied medicine in England and was the first graduate from Manitoba College to become qualified in England. He served for many years as chief surgeon to the Hudson's Bay Company and taught medicine at the University of Manitoba. He joined the Canadian Expeditionary Force in 1915 as a lieutenant, and served in the medical corps until the end of WWI.

Simpson, Thomas (1808-1840) Explorer. Born in Dingwall, Scotland, he was educated at King's College, Aberdeen University. A cousin of George Simpson,* he came to Norway House in 1829 as George's secretary. In 1836 he was appointed by the HBC as co-leader of an arctic expedition. Over the winter of 1836-37 he snowshoed from Fort Garry to Fort Chipewyan on Lake Athabasca, a distance of 1,277 miles, in 46 marching days. In 1837 the expedition explored the arctic coastline west of the Mackenzie River, then in 1838 journeyed down the Coppermine River. In December 1839 Simpson set out for Red River from the Boothia Peninsula, making it back over the 1,800 miles in 61 days. He had demonstrated that he was very fit, but over the years of the expedition also that he was extremely conceited. He hastened back to England to gain approval for further discoveries, not knowing that the authorization was already on its way. Unwilling to wait for the ships at Hudson Bay, he decided to travel overland by horse through the United States. According to companions with him, he became increasingly anxious and even deranged during the journey, which ended with two colleagues shot dead and Simpson with his head blown off. It seemed to contemporaries a clear case of murder and suicide. His *Narrative of the Discoveries on the North Coast of America . . . during the years 1836-9* was published by his brother in 1843. See also Alexander Simpson, *The Life and Travels of Thomas Simpson* (1845).

Simpson, William John (1869-1928) Jeweller. A manager for Robinson and Company in Winnipeg in 1904, he also operated a wholesale jewellery business. In WWI he became purchasing agent for Canadian headquarters in England, then director of contracts with rank of lieutenant-colonel. He was awarded the Order of the British Empire. After the war he was responsible for the sale of all the Canadian goods left in English warehouses and military depots, as well as for disposition of 27 hospitals. All were sold at a profit. He later became secretary-treasurer of the Canada Colonization Association.

Sinclair, James (1811-1856) Trader. Born in Rupert's Land, the son of an Orcadian HBC officer and an Indian or mixed-blood wife, he was educated in Scotland. Returning to Rupert's Land in 1826, he worked briefly for the HBC before entering into private trade, eventually in partnership with Andrew McDermot.* In 1841 he led a party of 23 Red River families to the Columbia River. He later fought with the HBC over trading rights and went to London to submit a petition to the British government. He was briefly in California in 1848 and then acted as counsel for Pierre-Guillaume Sayer* in 1849. He then decided to migrate to the Oregon Territory and proposed leading another party of emigrants there. He spent some time in Oregon and California before joining the HBC as head of Fort Walla Walla. He was killed in an Indian attack at Walla Walla. See D.G. Lent, *West of the Mountains James Sinclair and the Hudson's Bay Company* (1963). *DCB* VIII, 819-20.

Sinclair, Thomas (b. 1880) Architect. Born in Edinburgh, Scotland, he was educated there and at the University of Edinburgh. He served an apprenticeship in Scotland as an architect before coming to Brandon. In that city he designed the Alexandra School, the King George School, the McKenzie Building, and the Arena, the largest indoor arena in Canada in its day.

Sinclair, William (1794-1868) Fur trader. Born in Rupert's Land, son of an Orkney fur trader and an Indian or mixed-blood wife, he joined the HBC in 1808, demonstrating considerable initiative and a spirit of adventure in his early years. He began a lengthy service in the Winnipeg River/Rainy River Districts in 1824, but his advancement was limited by his inability to speak French. He finally became chief trader in 1844 and chief factor in 1850. He organized troop transportation between York Factory and Red River on a number of occasions and served from 1851 to 1863 as a member of the Council of the Northern Department. Sinclair was one of the few successful country-born mixed-bloods in the HBC. Although he owned property in Red River, he retired to Brockville, Canada, in 1863.

Sinkevich, Joanne (1942-1990) Dancer. Born in Grimsby, Ontario, she came to Winnipeg at the age of eight with her parents. She began dancing with the Ukrainian National Youth Federation, and in 1962 founded the Rusalka Dance Ensemble, which she led for most of its first decade. She later moved to Thunder Bay to teach dance. She died in Winnipeg after a long illness.

Sinnott, Alfred Arthur (1877-1954) Cleric. Born in Crapaud, Prince Edward Island, he studied at Prince of Wales College, St. Dunstan's College, Laval University, the Grand Seminary at Montreal, and the Appolinaire in Rome. He taught at St. Dunstan's until appointed private secretary to several apostolic delegates to Canada in Ottawa. He was appointed first Roman Catholic Archbishop of Winnipeg in 1915 and was consecrated on 21 September 1916, serving until his retirement in 1952.

Sirett, Ruby (1882-1972) Nurse. Born in Wiarton, Ontario, she came to Manitoba in 1905. She trained for nursing at the Brandon General Hospital, winning the silver medal upon graduation in 1908. She was one of the first public-health nurses appointed in the province, nursing for many years in the Roblin District. She died in Winnipeg.

Sirett, William Flowers (1879-1971) Veterinarian. Born in the Muskoka district of Ontario, he moved with his parents to Mentmore, Manitoba in 1881. He received a diploma in agriculture from the University of Wisconsin, subsequently attending the veterinary college in Ontario, which granted him a DVM. Sirett began his veterinary practice in 1911 at Minnedosa, extending it far into the surrounding territory by Model T and horse. He retired 50 years later. He was active in local government, serving 20 years on town council and four years as mayor. He was a member of the Board of Stewards of the United Church.

Sisler, William James (1868-1954) Educator. Born in Ontario, he graduated from the University of Chicago. From 1905 to 1921 he was principal of Strathcona School in Winnipeg, then he became principal of Isaac Newton High School, from which he retired in 1938. Sisler developed the "direct method" of teaching English to immigrant students, which was widely copied in Manitoba and elsewhere. He opened at Strathcona the city's first night school and encouraged sports for his students. In 1919-20 he was president of the North Winnipeg Canadian Club. He was the author of a school textbook entitled *Peaceful Invasion* (1944) and *Pioneers of Rockwood and Woodlands* (1949). A Winnipeg school is named for him. His papers are at the PAM.

Siveright, John (1779-1856) Fur trader. Born in Scotland, he joined Forsyth, Richardson, and Company in 1799 and remained in the employ of the North West Company after the mergers of 1804. He was stationed in Manitoba at the time of the confrontation between the settlers at Red River and the NWC in 1815 and 1816, and he was one of those tried (and acquitted) in York in 1818 as accessory to the murder of Robert Semple.* From 1816 to 1823 he served at the Sault, and then on the upper Ottawa, where he was unable to stem the advance of the lumbering interests. From 1843 to 1847 he served at Timiskaming, and he retired as chief factor in 1849. He died in Edinburgh. *DCB* VIII, 820-22.

Skaptason, Johanna Gudrun (1878-1960) Volunteer. Born near Gimli, her family later moved to Arnes, where she taught after completing normal school training. After marriage she lived in Selkirk, and later in Winnipeg. She organized the Jon Sigurdson Chapter of the IODE, and was an active member of the Western Canada Alliance of Unitarian Women. She died in Winnipeg.

Skinner, Frank Leith (1882-1967) Horticulturalist. Born in Scotland, in 1985 he immigrated with his family to the Dropmore district of Manitoba. Located at latitude 51°, elevation 550 metres, it was an ideal area for testing northern farming. After losing a lung to pneumonia, he turned to gardening, soon acquiring a substantial expertise in horticulture and plant breeding through self-study. Encouraged by several experts, he began to commercialize his hobby of plant propagation in the mid-1920s. His major accomplishments were in hybridization; he introduced 248 species of plants to the Prairies, 144 of which were improved varieties. He was particularly successful with trees, producing a number of rapid-growing and disease-resistant hybrids of poplars, elms, and ornamental fruit trees, as well as early-blooming lilacs and lilies. Throughout his career he managed to balance scientific research with the demands of the small nursery that provided his income. He received an honorary Doctor of Laws degree from the University of Manitoba in 1947. He published his autobiography, *Horticultural Horizons: Plant Breeding and Introduction at Dropmore, Manitoba,* in 1967. Skinner's papers are in the PAM. The Skinner Memorial Library at the University of Manitoba is named in his honour.

Skinner, Morden H. L. ("Ducky," 1914-1991) Althlete. Born in Selkirk, he played hockey for the Selkirk Fishermen, Flin Flon Bombers, and later professionally for the Indianapolis Caps. He managed and coached the Hamilton Cubs in the Ontario Hockey Association. He was a co-founder of the famous Skinner's Restaurant at Lockport and hosted at the restaurant for many years. He died in Selkirk.

Slotin, Louis (1910-1946) Scientist. Born in Winnipeg's North End, he attended St. John's Technical High School and the University of Manitoba, winning the gold medal in chemistry and physics and completing an MSc in 1933. He received his PhD in biochemistry from London University in 1936. He was also an amateur boxer. He became a research associate at the University of Chicago, working on an atom-smashing cyclotron. He began work in the Metallurgical Laboratory of the Manhatten Project in Chicago in 1942, and moved to Los Alamos in December 1944. Slotin became an expert at hand-assembling the core of atomic bombs, and it was an accident during the process of assembly that led to his death. In order to save his colleagues, he terminated a connection in a bomb core, and as a result exposed himself to a fatal dose of radiation. Slotin's tale is told in the 1955 novel *The Accident* by Dexter Masters. See also Martin Zeilig, "Dr. Louis Slotin and 'The Invisible Killer,'" *The Beaver,* 75, no. 4 (August-September 1995): 20-26.

Smart, James Allan (1858-1942) Mayor, civil servant. Born in Ontario of Scottish descent, he opened a hardware business in Brandon, and served two terms as mayor in 1885 and 1886. He become provincial minister of public works in 1888, and federal deputy minister of the interior under Clifford Sifton* from 1896 until 1903, when he resigned because of ill health.

Smith, Albert Edward (1872-1947) Cleric, agitator. Born in Guelph, Ontario, he was a Methodist minister and became president of the Manitoba Methodist Conference before leaving the church to organize a Labour Church in Brandon. Speaking during the Winnipeg General Strike of 1919, he argued the strike was as religious a movement as a church revival. He was elected to the Manitoba legislature in 1920, and later became president of the Ontario section of the Canadian Labor party. As a member of the Communist Party, he was arrested in 1934 on charges of sedition under section 98 of the Criminal Code and was acquitted. His papers are in the United Church Archives, Toronto.

Smith, Charles Rhodes (1896-1993) Civil servant. Born in Portage la Prairie, he was educated at the University of Manitoba, winning gold medals in history and economics. After service in WWI, he became a Rhodes Scholar at Queen's College, Oxford. Called to the bar in 1923, he was a cabinet member in the Garson government, serving as minister of labour (1946-8) and later minister of education and attorney general. He was appointed chair of the Restrictive Trade Practices Commission in 1952 and chair of the Canadian Labour Relations Board in 1953. For many years he was president of the Canadian Legion. He also chaired the commission of inquiry into The Pas Forestry and Industrial Complex, which reported in 1974.

Smith, Sir Donald Alexander, 1st Baron Strathcona and Mount Royal (1820-1914) Businessman. Born in Scotland, he joined the HBC in 1838, serving mainly in Labrador 1848-68, where he was promoted to chief trader (1852) and chief factor (1862). In 1869 he was appointed a special commissioner to Red River to deal with the recalcitrant Métis. Arriving in late December, he spent most of his stay in Red River under house arrest, but did manage to meet with the people of Red River in public assembly on 19-20 January 1870, where he encouraged the rebels to call the Convention of Forty to present their demands to Ottawa. Although the mission was officially successful, the Canadian government privately felt he had failed, since his real assignment had been to bribe the rebels into complete submission. Smith then became chief commissioner for the HBC, serving until 1874 when he became land commissioner for the company. One of his first acts as chief commissioner was to negotiate with the North American partners of the HBC, agreeing that they would not share in the payment for the territory. In 1883 he became a director and in 1889 governor of the HBC; by this time he was its largest stockholder. During his years as commissioner, Smith spent much time in Manitoba. He served as MLA from Winnipeg from 1870 to 1874, and as MP from Selkirk from 1871; his break with Sir John A. Macdonald in 1873 helped lead to the fall of the government. He was frequently criticized for election corruption. He later served as Montreal West MP from 1887 to 1896, retiring when he was appointed Canadian high commissioner in London, a post he held until his death. Smith used his HBC position to make shrewd investments in other endeavours, including railways, and his involvement in the CPR gave him the right to drive the last spike in 1885. He became a pillar of the Bank of Montreal and had his hand in all sorts of business activities. Raised to the peerage in 1897, in 1898 he raised, equipped, and maintained a unit of mounted rifles (Lord Strathcona's Horse) for service in the South African War. In later years he received innumerable honours from government and the private sector. He died in London. There is no completely satisfactory biography, but see Beckles Willson, *The Life of Lord Strathcona and Mount Royal* (1915), and Donna McDonald, *Lord Strathcona: a Biography* (1996). *DCB* XIV, 939-47.

Smith, Gordon Charles (1886-1977) Gallery owner. Born in O'Neill, Nebraska, he moved with his parents to Winnipeg at an early age. He spent his business life in the art business, beginning with A.J. Cranston, then Eaton's, then the Bay, and finally as proprietor of the Little Gallery from 1939 to 1954, when he retired.

Smith, Henry Hall (1847-1928) Civil Servant. A lawyer in Peterborough, Ontario, he was a personal friend of Sir John A. Macdonald. After serving as an organizer for the Ontario Conservative Party, he was rewarded in 1884 with the post of Dominion Lands Commissioner for Manitoba and the North-West Territories. He moved to Winnipeg to take up this job and remained in the city for the remainder of his life.

Smith, Hugh Pollit (1912-1998) Bush pilot. Born in Liverpool, England, he came to Winnipeg in 1920. In 1927, he joined Arrow Airways Ltd. of The Pas as a pilot-engineer, later barnstormed through western Manitoba. Smith joined the Manitoba Government Air Service in 1940, serving as chief superintendent at Lac du Bonnet in 1948 and Director from

1962 to 1975, when he retired. He was president of the Lac du Bonnet Water Co. Ltd. from 1954 to 1971 and was active in many other community organizations.

Smith, J. Lawrence (1889-1967) Municipal politician, flood-damage assessor. Born in Dundee, Scotland, he came to Canada at the age of 22, and settled in the Sidney district of Manitoba, where he farmed until 1928. He subsequently farmed in the MacDonald District and northeast of Portage la Prairie. He served as Portage mayor from 1949 to 1961. He served as president of the Union of Municipalities in 1959-60, and as its secretary from 1960 to 1967. Smith was appointed a flood damage assessor for the province in 1950, and served on the Red River Valley Board, 1966-67. In 1956, he received the Golden Boy Award for his public service.

Smith, John Obed (1864-1937) Civil Servant. Born in Birmingham, England, and educated at Liverpool College, he immigrated to Winnipeg in 1882 and then farmed at Turtle Mountain. He later articled in the law office of Munson and Allan, then under the former attorney general Joseph Martin,* in Winnipeg, and was called to the Manitoba bar in 1891. He served the Manitoba government until 1899, when he became commissioner of immigration in Western Canada. In 1908 he was transferred to London to supervise European immigration to Canada, serving at this post until his retirement in 1924. He remained in England after his superannuation.

Smith, Norman Stanley (1882-1946) Newspaper publisher. Born in Drayton, Ontario, he came to Portage la Prairie with his parents at an early age. He was educated locally, and then became a newspaper apprentice, working for a number of newspapers before joining the staff of the *Daily Graphic* in Portage la Prairie, which he purchased in 1922. Smith was active with the Red Cross, the hospital board, and the horticulural society. He died in Portage la Prairie.

Smith, Sidney Earle (1897-1959) Educator. Born in Port Hood, Cape Breton Island, he was educated at King's College (BA, MA) and Dalhousie University (LLB). After service in the Canadian Expeditionary Force during WWI, he was called to the bar in 1921 and appointed to the faculty at Dalhousie. He taught at Osgoode Hall 1925-9, then became dean of law at Dalhousie from 1929 to 1934, when he was appointed president of the University of Manitoba. In 1941 he was mentioned as a possible leader of the Conservative Party, but John Bracken* got the position instead. Smith helped restore the University of Manitoba after the disastrous Machray defalcation. His great triumph was the creation of a new interdisciplinary humanities curriculum (called the "Western Civilization" curriculum) in the middle of WWII. For financial reasons, it was never introduced. Smith left Manitoba to become principal of University College (Toronto) in 1944, and became president of the University of Toronto a year later. He saw the University of Toronto through the crucial post-war years and was elected Fellow of the Royal Society of Canada in 1950. In 1957 he left Toronto to become John Diefenbaker's minister for external affairs, and MP for Hastings-Frontenac. He died in Ottawa. See E. A. Corbett, *Sidney Earle Smith* (1961).

Smith, William Osborne (1833-1887) Soldier. Born in Wales, he was educated for the army, which he joined in 1855. He served in the Crimea and retired after coming to Canada with his regiment. During the American Civil War he organized the Victoria Rifles in Montreal and was appointed assistant adjutant general of Canada in 1865. In 1871 he commanded the second expedition to Fort Garry, and remained in Manitoba for a year. He resigned from his post in 1881 and moved to Winnipeg, where he several times ran for the House of Commons. During the North-West Rebellion he raised and commanded the 91st Battalion, the "Winnipeg Light Infantry." He died on a visit to Wales. *DCB* XI, 838-39.

Smithurst, John (1807-1867) Cleric. Born in Derbyshire, England, he was educated at Islington College and ordained in 1839, on the eve of his departure for Red River. He took up a position as missionary and HBC chaplain at Netley Creek, where he attempted to learn Cree. Smithurst produced some translations, but James Evans's* linguistic work was preferred by his church. His ordination became a subject of controversy in 1842 when Adam Thom* insisted that the bishop of Quebec did not have the authority in Rupert's Land to ordain Smithurst as a priest. Smithurst became the man in the middle, criticized by both the HBC and the Church Missionary Society. In attempting

to gain support from his Native parishioners in 1846, Smithurst ruffled more feathers. In 1849 he became a councillor of Assiniboia. He left Red River in 1851 for Elora, Canada, where he spent the remainder of his life. His memorial sermon for the Duke of Wellington was published in Elora in 1852. See F.A. Peake, "John Smithurst and the Ordination Controversy: Reflections on Red River Society in the 1840s," in B. Ferguson, ed., *The Anglican Church and the World of Western Canada 1820-1970* (1991), 72-82. His letters and journals are in the Rupert's Land Archives. *DCB* IX, 732-33. His papers are at the PAM.

Snodie, Adam (b. c. 1783) Fur trader. Born in the Orkney Islands, he joined the HBC in 1801 and served at Churchill Factory until 1807. From 1808 to 1811 he was master at Nelson House, and then was in the Nelson River and Severn Districts until he took charge at Churchill from 1815 to 1819. He then became district master at York Factory, and served there as trader after the merger. He resigned in 1822 and retired to Stromness. George Simpson* described him as an "excellent trader and tolerable Clerk, but deficient in Education."

Snow, John Allan (1824-1888) Surveyor. Born in Hull Township, Lower Canada, he was educated at St. Lawrence Academy in Potsdam, New York, and trained as a surveyor. Chosen in 1868 to head the road-building team constructing the road from Lake of the Woods to Upper Fort Garry that would become the Dawson Road, he was assaulted by some of his workmen, who were subsequently convicted in the Red River Court. He was himself convicted of selling liquor to the Indians. His critics said he supplied liquor in return for being allowed to purchase Indian land, especially at Oak Point. He was virtually the only Canadian official left at liberty in the Red River Settlement in December 1869, and he supplied food to the prisoners at Upper Fort Garry. He later worked as an engineer and surveyor in Quebec and in Western Canada. He died in Ottawa. *DCB* XI, 841-43.

Snow, Matthew (1858-1930) Farmer, grain dealer. Born in Edinburgh, Scotland, he came to Canada in 1880 and homesteaded at Wolseley, in present day Saskatchewan, in 1882. He farmed there until 1905, when he moved to Winnipeg and entered the grain business. He served as secretary of the North-West Grain Dealers' Association 1922-23, and in the latter year was appointed Canadian Grain Commissioner. He was a pioneer fox farmer and a keen curler (at the Granite Curling Club).

Sokolowiski, Mike (d. 1919) Victim. Little is known about him apart from his death, on 21 June, in the midst of a melee in front of Winnipeg City Hall during a demonstration connected with the Winnipeg General Strike. He was shot through the heart. According to one newspaper account he was of Austrian birth and lived with a wife and three children at 552 Henry Avenue. That same account had him shot while in the act of throwing a stone at the Mounted Police. *DCB* XIV, 951-52.

Solomon, John Roman (1910-1985) Jurist. Born in Zoria, Manitoba, he graduated from the University of Manitoba in 1934 with a bachelor of law degree. He was admitted to the bar in 1935. In 1941 he was elected an MLA from Emerson, serving until 1957. From 1953 to 1957 he was Deputy Speaker. In 1957 he was appointed to the County Court, and from 1971 to his retirement in 1983 he served on the Court of Queen's Bench. He was active in many community agencies, especially within the Ukrainian-Canadian Community. He helped develop St. Andrew's College and the Holy Trinity Ukrainian Orthodox Cathedral. He died in Winnipeg.

Somerset, John Beaufort (1843-1901) Educator. Born in Ireland, he immigrated to Canada in 1861. He soon received a teaching certificate and advanced rapidly up the administrative hierarchy. He was appointed inspector of schools for Lincoln County in 1871, and became inspector of Protestant schools for Winnipeg in 1882. A year later he became superintendent for Protestant schools in the province, serving until 1889. During his tenure, the schools were considerably expanded in number and modernized, with a central system of inspection and regulation. His model was the non-denominational public school in Ontario. He served on the board of Wesley College, and became business manager of the *Winnipeg Free Press* from 1891 until retirement in 1900. He died in Peachland, British Columbia. *DCB* XIII, 978.

Spall, Robert (1890-1918) War hero. Born in Suffolk County, England, he immigrated to Canada with his parents in 1892. Working in a Winnipeg office in 1914, he enlisted in the 90th Winnipeg Rifles and later transferred to the Princess Patricia's Light Infantry, holding the rank of sergeant. He won the Victoria Cross at Parvillers by sacrificing his life to save his platoon.

Sparling, John Kerr (1872-1941) Lawyer. Born in Montreal, he came to Winnipeg in 1888. He was a leading attorney and a partner in Hull, Sparling, and Sparling. Active in municipal affairs, he was a Winnipeg alderman from 1917 to 1922, and chair of the Police Commission. He later chaired the board of governors of United College. Sparling was a pioneer Boy Scout leader in Manitoba.

Sparling, Joseph Walter (1843-1912) Cleric, educator. Born in Blanshard Township, Canada, he was educated at St. Mary's High School and attended Victoria University, Cobourg, from which he received a BA and MA. He received divinity degrees from the Garrett Biblical Institute (Northwestern University) in Illinois. He was ordained in 1871 and served many Methodist churches before coming to Winnipeg in 1888 to become principal of Wesley College. He was awarded a DD by Northwestern University in 1889. Under his administration, Wesley College grew from a handful of students to 400. At his death in office the college was free of debt and had an endowment of $250,000. He had recruited a number of important teachers, including Salem Bland.* Sparling was a prominent member of the board of education of the Methodist Church in Canada, and was the chair of the social-work committee of Winnipeg Methodism. *DCB* XIV, 952-53.

Speakman, R. E. (b. 1857) Engineer. Born in Cheshire, England, he graduated from Shrewsbury Grammar School and in 1876 apprenticed to an engineer. He came to Brandon in 1892, and began his engineering career in Canada with involvement in the city's sewage and waterworks system. He moved to Toronto in 1895 and established a large engineering consultancy business. In 1903 he became city engineer at St. Catharines, then city engineer at Calgary where he designed the sewage system, erected the waterworks, installed the municipal electric light plant, and designed the Calgary Street Railway System. He was lured to Brandon in 1909 and was offered inducements to remain.

Speechly, Henry Martindale (1866-1951) Physician. Born in England, he served as medical officer at Mostyn Hall School before immigrating to Canada in 1901 to practise medicine in Pilot Mound, Manitoba. He left for England in 1916 to serve as a medical officer in WWI, and subsequently became provincial coroner. He was a distinguished horticulturalist, the first president of the Manitoba Horticultural and Forestry Association in 1911; and he helped found the Natural History Society of Manitoba in 1920.

Speechly, Mary (Barrett) (1873-1968) Social reformer. Born in London, England, she received a BA from University College, Liverpool in 1892 and subsequently studied at Cambridge. She married Henry Speechly* in 1895 and joined him in Manitoba in 1902, where he had established a general medical practice in Pilot Mound. Having studied photography, she worked as a professional photographer. She became president of the Pilot Mound Home Economics Society in 1912 and was active in the home economics societies of the time, a major advocate of home economics and domestic science. She was also a member of the Agricultural Women's Association and the Women's Institute. She moved to Winnipeg in 1916, became a prominent proponent of the birth control movement and became the first president of the Winnipeg Birth Control Society in 1934. She also helped found the Family Planning Association of Manitoba. Speechly had been appointed to the council of the Manitoba Agricultural College in 1924 and to the board of governors of the University of Manitoba in 1933, serving to her retirement in 1946. A student residence at the University of Manitoba is named for her. See Angela Davis, "Mary Speechly: A Life of Service," *The Beaver* 74, no. 5 (October/November 1994): 35-39.

Speers, R. James ("R.J." or "Jim," 1892-1955) Sportsman. Born in Ontario, he moved to Battleford, Saskatchewan in 1908, and become a grain and livestock dealer. He gradually acquired race horses, and came to Winnipeg in 1920. He took over racing at River Park in St. Boniface in 1922, introducing parimutuel betting in 1923. He built the first of four racetracks associated with him at Whittier Park in 1924, then opened Polo Park in 1925. He entered the thoroughbred-breeding business in St. Boniface in 1925, and raced horses throughout the remainder of his life.

Spence, Thomas (1832-1900) Author, local character. Born in Scotland, he came to Canada in 1852 and to Red River in 1867, marrying Charlotte Cook. He worked initially as a general handyman. In 1867, he became president of the "Republic of Manitobah," in the area of what is now Portage la Prairie. According to his parliamentary testimony in 1874, he "had organized a Provisional Government in 1867 over a part of the territory which was occupied by about four hundred people," and "had communicated this organization to the Imperial Government, and upon hearing from the Imperial authorities that our proceedings were illegal, the organization was broken up. This matter had nothing whatever to do with the outbreak or disturbances in 1869 or 1870. This organization was made simply as a matter of protection for ourselves, as we were outside the Government of the Council of Assiniboia, as Governor McTavish* informed me himself." He was arrested briefly by Louis Riel on 25 January 1870, and was an English delegate to the Convention of Forty from St. Peter's. Initially residing in St. Boniface, by 1872 he had moved to Point Douglas. He was later described by J.H. O'Donnell* as having "quite a few of the characteristics of Wilkins Micawber; he was always living in great expectations, and when they were not materializing he became depressed, and would tell dramatically how shamefully his services had been overlooked by the federal government." He was a Roman Catholic and friendly with Bishop Taché. He later served as clerk of the Legislative Assembly of Manitoba and as an immigration pamphleteer, producing such items as *Manitoba and North-West of the Dominion* (1876) and *The Prairie Lands of Canada* (1879). *DCB* XII, 982-84.

Spencer, John (1790-c. 1863) Colonial official. Born in England, he was educated at Christ's Hospital and joined the HBC as a writer in 1806. In 1814, upon the recommendation of William Auld,* he became a councillor and the sheriff of Assiniboia. He was responsible for enforcing the pemmican proclamation, and was subsequently arrested by the North West Company. From 1819-23 he served as an accountant at York Factory, and after several years service further west he was made a chief trader in the Columbia District. He retired in 1828, rejoined the Company in 1834, and finally retired in Red River in 1857. He subsequently moved to Goderich, Canada, where he probably died.

Spivak, David (1873-1961) Social reformer. He came to Canada in 1906 and settled on a farm at

Bird's Hill, Manitoba. He was active in every Winnipeg Jewish welfare organization, particularly the Jewish Orphanage and the Jewish Old Folks Home (later the Sharon Home). In the 1930s he was a member of the Refugee Settlers' Committee of the Canadian Jewish Congress and travelled extensively to assist in bringing refugees to Canada. He died in Vancouver.

Spry, Graham (1900-1983) Civil servant. Born in St. Thomas, Ontario, he served in the ranks in WWI and graduated from the University of Manitoba with a BA in 1922. The gold medallist at the University of Manitoba, he was appointed a Rhodes Scholar and attended University College, Oxford. He worked on the staff of the *Free Press* even before his graduation. In the early 1930s he was a leading advocate of public broadcasting in Canada and has been called the "Father of the CBC." He served in a variety of international administrative capacities before becoming personal assistant (1942-45) to British statesman and politician Sir Stafford Cripps. He later became a member of the Board of Broadcast Governors (1958-67) and the Canadian Radio and Television Commission (1968-1972). See Rose Potvin, ed., *Passion and Conviction: The Letters of Graham Spry* (1992).

Stack, Frank (1906-1987) Speed Skater. Born in Winnipeg, he won the western indoor speed-skating championship in Chicago in 1929. He set many records in the 1930s, including one for five miles which stood for years. He won bronze at the 1935 Olympics, then sat out the 1936 games. He finished fifth at the Olympics in Switzerland in 1948. He coached the 1960 Canadian Olympic speed-skating team. He was awarded the Order of the Buffalo Hunt in 1973, became a member of the Canadian Sports Hall of Fame in 1974, and a member of the Manitoba Sports Hall of Fame 1981. A street in Winnipeg is named after him.

Stansfield, Margaret Mary (Speechly) (1896-1990) Consumer activist. Born in Neston, England, she came to Manitoba at an early age with her parents, and graduated in home economics from the Manitoba Agricultural College. She worked as an editor for the *Grain Growers' Guide* in the 1920s, and later became a pioneer in the consumer rights movement, being honoured by the Consumers' Association of Canada in 1976 for her work. She was awarded an honorary doctorate in 1977 from the University

of Manitoba and was given the YWCA Woman of the Year Award in 1979. She died in Winnipeg.

Stead, Hay Strafford (1871-1924) Journalist, cartoonist. Born in England, he came to Gilbert Plains, Manitoba, with his family in 1889. From 1892 to 1905 he worked for the HBC in Winnipeg. He ultimately worked for all the Winnipeg newspapers of his day. He was a cartoonist for the *Manitoba Free Press* and also for the *Saturday Post*. First president of the Manitoba Society of Artists in 1903, he left Winnipeg in 1922 to join Maclean Publications. Stead also painted, although little of his work appears to have survived. See Virginia G. Berry, *Vistas of Promise* (1987).

Stead, Robert James Campbell (1880-1959) Author. Born in Middleville, Ontario, he moved with his family to Cartwright, Manitoba, in 1882. After attending Winnipeg Business College he edited a weekly newspaper in Cartwright for some years, then the *Crystal City Courier* from 1908-9. He moved to Calgary in 1912 and by 1913 was director of publicity for the colonization branch of the CPR. In 1919 he became publicity director for the federal Department of Immigration and Colonization, and from 1936 to 1946 he was director of publicity for the Department of Mines and Resources. He was president of the Canadian Authors' Association in 1923. Stead began his literary career by writing a number of volumes of patriotic verse, such as *Kitchener and Other Poems* (1917). He was best known for his prairie novels, particularly *The Bail Jumper* (1914), *The Homesteaders* (1916), *The Cow Puncher* (1918), *Dennison Grant* (1920) *Neighbours* (1923), *Smoking Flax* (1925), and *Grain* (1926). Although most of his work was neglected by critics for many years as being popular writing of only regional interest, he has in recent years been recognized as one of the founders of prairie realism and an important Canadian novelist. There are papers at the NAC.

Steen, Robert Ashley (1933-1979) Lawyer, politician. Born in Winnipeg, he graduated with a BA from the University of Manitoba and received a law degree from the University of Manitoba Law School. He was involved in politics from an early age, participating in mock Parliaments. In 1966 he was elected Progressive Conservative MLA for St. Matthews, but was defeated in 1969. He then moved into municipal politics, and won by acclamation as councillor for Westerminster Ward. He sat first as an Independent. He ran for mayor in 1977 and was supported by Stephen Juba* and Ed Schreyer. In that election, he defeated Bill Norrie by 1,819 votes. After only two years in office, he died of cancer. The 1977 mayoralty campaign is the focus of a NFB documentary, *The New Mayor.*

Stefanson, Eric (1913-1977) Farmer. Born in Winnipeg, he operated a dairy farm from 1935 to 1948 at Oak Point, later opening a store and insurance agency at Gimli. He was active in Gimli government and served 10 years in the federal Parliament. In 1970 he was made general manager of the Interlake Development Corporation, and worked to promote the region until his death. He is a member of the Manitoba Agricultural Hall of Fame.

Stefansson, Vilhjalmur (1879-1962) Explorer. Born in Arnes, Manitoba, he was educated at State University of North Dakota, State University of Iowa (BA 1903) Harvard Divinity School (1903-4), Harvard Graduate School (1905-6), and received an LLD, University of Michigan (1921). He undertook his first archaeological expedition to Iceland under the auspices of the Peabody Museum of Harvard in 1905. From 1906-7 he accompanied the Leffingwell-Mikkelsen ethnological expedition to the Inuit of the Mackenzie Delta. From 1903 to 1912 he made a series of ethnological surveys of the arctic coast, ending with a year's residence among the Inuit. From 1913 to 1918 he headed a Canadian Arctic Expedition, making a 600-mile overland journey with sleds and dogs in 1914. He discovered new islands and learned much about the Inuit. After 1919 he wrote and lectured about the Arctic from a base in the United States. His library went to Dartmouth College in 1951. Stefansson wrote extensively. His major works include: *My Life with the Eskimo* (1913), *The Friendly Arctic* (1921), *The Northward Course of the Empire* (1922), *Hunters of the Great North* (1922), and *Ultima Thule* (1940). He died in the United States. His autobiography appeared posthumously in 1964. Microfilm of his Arctic diaries 1906-1918 are at the University of Manitoba. See Alexander D. Gregor, *Vihljalmur Stefansson and the Arctic* (1978); Richard Diabaldo, *Stefansson and the Canadian Arctic* (1979); William Hunt, *Stef: A Biography* (1986).

Steinhauer, Henry Bird (1818-1884) Missionary, linguist. Born near Lake Simcoe in the Chippewa tribe, he adopted the name of the German family that raised him. In 1840 Steinhauer went with the Rev. James Evans* to Norway House and was instrumental in helping Evans develop the Cree syllabic alphabet. He did much of the translation of the Bible into Cree. Posted to Lac la Biche (in present-day Alberta) in 1855, he was ordained a minister of the Methodist Church in 1858 and spent the last years of his life at Whitefish Lake, now in the Northwest Territories. See Gayle Simonson, "The Prayer Man," *The Beaver* 68, no. 5 (October/November 1988): 28-33; John Maclean, *Henry B. Steinhauer, his work among the Cree Indians of the western plains of Canada* (n.d.). His papers are in the Alberta Archives. *DCB* XI, 848-50.

Steinkopf, Maitland Bernard (1912-1970) Lawyer, politician. Born in Winnipeg, he graduated in law from the University of Manitoba in 1936. As a student he had organized the athletic board of control and was vice-president of the students' union. He succeeded his father Max* as honorary consul for Czechoslovakia in 1937. During WWII he served in the Canadian army. In 1962 he was elected MLA for River Heights, serving as provincial secretary and minister of public utilities from 1963 to 1966. He was chair of the Manitoba Centennial Corporation from 1963 until his death. He also served as chair of a special committee of the Manitoba Legislative Assembly on consumer credit in 1966.

Steinkopf, Max (1881-1935) Lawyer. Born in Prague, he came to Canada at an early age. He was called to the bar in 1905, becoming the first Jewish lawyer on the Prairies. Active in community life, he was president of the Winnipeg Talmud Torah and the Winnipeg Zionist Council.

Stephens, Donald McGregor (1903-1968) Engineer. Born in Reston, Manitoba, he was educated locally and graduated from the University of Manitoba in 1931 with a degree in civil engineering. He joined the Manitoba Department of Mines and Natural Resources in 1933, serving as deputy minister from 1938 to 1951. In the 1950 flood he organized an emergency flood-forecasting unit, and subsequently served on the Greater Winnipeg Dyking Board. In 1951 he became chair and general manager of the newly created Manitoba Hydroelectric Board, continuing as general manager after 1961 when he stepped down as chair. He was a member of the International Joint Commission, and from 1958 a member of the board of Atomic Energy of Canada, Ltd. He was active in his profession, serving as president of the Engineering Institute of Canada. He was also active in the United Way. He held an honorary doctorate from Clarkson College of Technology and an honorary Doctor of Laws from the University of Manitoba (1966).

Stephenson, Sir William (1896-1989) War hero, espionage administrator. Born in Winnipeg as William Samuel Clouston Stanger, he attended Argyle School and subsequently delivered telegrams in the city. During WWI, he joined the Royal Flying Corps and shot down 26 enemy aircraft, receiving both the Military Cross and the Distinguished Flying Cross. During WWII he headed the New York-based organization called British Security Coordination, work he later described in the books *A Man Called Intrepid* (1976) and *Intrepid's Last Case* (1983) and for which he received a knighthood. In 1979 he received an honorary degree from the University of Winnipeg. For a biography, see H.M. Hyde, *The Quiet Canadian* (1962). See also Thomas Tory, *Wild Bill and Intrepid: Donovan, Stephenson, and the origins of the CIA* (1996); and Bill Macdonald, *The True "Intrepid": Sir William Stephenson and the Unknown Agents*(1998).

Stevens, Frances Elizabeth Eleanor (1876-1955) Missionary. As a bride she travelled to Oxford House by scow and canoe with her missionary husband. She set hymns to music that her husband had translated into Cree. She lived in many parts of Manitoba. Her life was described by Nan Shipley in *Frances and the Crees*. She died in Sault Ste. Marie.

Stevenson, Alexander P. ("Sandy," 1854-1922) Horticulturalist. Born in Perthshire, Scotland, he came to Winnipeg in 1874, soon moving to a farm near Morden where he developed the Pine Grove Nursery and apple orchard. He was soon known as the "Apple King of Manitoba," and was active in breeding from apple stock imported from the United States. He also introduced cherries and bred plums. Stevenson demonstrated that horticulture could work on the Canadian prairies. The Stevenson Memorial Gold Medal of the Manitoba Horticultural Association was named for him in 1932.

Stevenson, Frederick J. (1896 -1928) Pilot. An officer in the air force in WWI, he won the DFC and the Croix de Guerre. During the Russian civil war after the 1917 revolution, he trained White Russian pilots in the Crimea to fight the Bolsheviks. At home he became Canada's leading commercial pilot. In 1927 he flew 30 tonnes of cargo from The Pas to Sherritt-Gordon Mines, proving that heavy and bulky material could be flown into remote areas. He died in a plane crash in The Pas. Stevenson Field, now the Winnipeg International Airport, was named after him.

Stewart, Andrew (1851-1925) Cleric, educator. Born in Albion, Canada, he graduated from Victoria University, Toronto, in 1879 and came to Manitoba shortly afterwards. For 10 years he did organizational work for the Methodist Church in southern Manitoba and served as a public school inspector for Turtle Mountain and Souris River. He was an advocate of a uniform public-school system for the province. In 1889 he became pastor of Fort Rouge Methodist Church in Winnipeg, and in 1890 he took on the chair of systematic theology, Hebrew, and Old Testament exegesis at Wesley College. He acted as principal of Wesley College from 1912 to 1915. A recognized expert on church law and policy, he was an advocate of church union. He died in Winnipeg.

Stewart, Arthur (1854-1913) Businessman. Born in Belfast, Ireland, he came with his family to Ottawa in 1867, and worked in a variety of businesses before joining the NWMP in 1872. Coming to Winnipeg, he was paymaster sergeant before becoming government commissary in 1875. In March of 1887 he founded the Permanent Mortgage and Trust Company (which subsequently merged into the Manitoba Trust Company and then the National Trust Company). He retired as manager in 1913. He founded the Arts Publication Company, Ltd., of Winnipeg, "publishers of high-class music."

Stewart, David Alexander (1874-1937) Physician. Born in Kent County, Ontario, he moved to Manitoba with his family in 1891 and entered normal school in 1892. He later enrolled in the Manitoba College Faculty of Arts and prepared for ordination as a Presbyterian clergyman. He worked his way through Manitoba Medical College (which he entered in 1902) as a reporter for the *Manitoba Free Press*. Graduating in 1906, he became a senior intern at the Winnipeg General Hospital and began to specialize in epidemiology. In 1908 he became executive director of the Tuberculosis Society, and contracted the disease himself in 1909. Later that year he became building administrator, then medical superintendent of the province's new sanitorium at Ninette, located 160 miles southwest of Winnipeg on Pelican Lake. The sanitorium grew from 65 beds to 300 beds under his leadership, and tuberculosis mortality rates were greatly cut in the province. Stewart was also an active researcher in western Canadian history, especially the fur trade. He was president of the Manitoba Medical Association in 1926 and served from 1929 to 1934 as president of the Manitoba Historical Society. His papers are at PAM.

Stewart, James (b. 1827) Drapier. Born in the Orkney Islands, he joined the service of the HBC and later moved to Winnipeg, where he became a resident of St. James and worked in John Schultz's* store dispensing pharmacological supplies. He headed the party which freed Reverend G.O. Corbett* in 1863. He was himself imprisoned and in turn freed by a group led by William Hallett* and John Bourke.* He was one of those who surrendered in Schultz's house in December 1869 amd was imprisoned in Upper Fort Garry for 66 days. He later was described as a Winnipeg drapier.

Stewart, James Green (1825-1881) Fur trader, explorer. Born in Quebec City, he joined the HBC in 1844 and became active in arctic travel and exploration, travelling 1,100 miles to Fort Simpson from Frances Lake for supplies in 1850. His later exploration activities were less successful, although he was involved in an overland expedition searching for the Franklin Expedition in 1855. He served at Oxford House from 1865 to 1867 and Norway House from 1867 to 1871, becoming chief trader in 1869 but not surviving into the new deed poll of 1871. He died near Edmonton. There are papers at the PAM. See also E. J. Holmgren, "The diary of J.G. Stewart, 1855, describing his overland journey in search of the Franklin expedition," *The Beaver* (spring 1980): 12-17. *DCB* XI, 854-55.

Stinson, Lloyd C. (1904-1976) Cleric, political leader. Born in Treherne, Manitoba, he was ordained as a United Church minister at an early age. He served as provincial secretary of the Manitoba CCF from 1943 to 1944, simultaneously acting as alderman for Winnipeg Ward Two. From 1945 to 1959, he was the MLA for Osborne, and he led the Manitoba CCF

from 1953 to 1959. His political memoir was published in 1975 as *Political Warrior*. He died in Vancouver. His papers are at the PAM.

Stinson, Robert George (1879-1961) Publisher. Born in Flesherton County, Ontario, he taught school before coming to Manitoba to work with the *Winnipeg Telegram*. In 1929 he became publisher of *Waghorn's Guide and Pocket Directory to Manitoba and the North West*, retiring in 1956 to publish "Stinson Maps." He died in Winnipeg.

Stokes, George Ford (c. 1913-1977) Restaurateur. Born in Winnipeg, he was for many years a prominent musician. He also operated the first drive-in restaurant in Winnipeg, called "The Riverside Club," in St. Vital..

Story, Myfanwy (Evans) (1921-1970) Contralto. Born in Winnipeg of Welsh parents, she won the Rose Bowl at the Manitoba Music Festival Competition at an early age. She then sang in a NFB film about the Festival (*Listen to the Prairies*), and soon was performing on the CBC. She travelled to London to study in 1950, returning to be married. She moved to Washington, D.C., in 1956 and became a soloist at Westmoreland Congregational Church and other Washington area churches. She died in Washington. There is a recording of her singing, entitled "With Tender Affection: Myfanwy Evans Story. In Memorium."

Stoughton, Arthur A. (1867-1955) Architect. Born in New York City, he studied at Columbia College, as well as the École des Beaux Arts in Paris. In 1913 he became head of the Department of Architecture at the University of Manitoba, and organized its curriculum on American and Canadian models. He was also a strong advocate of city planning and the "city beautiful" movement. He served on the art committee of the Winnipeg Industrial Bureau from 1914 to 1933. He continued to design buildings and monuments, few of which were ever built. His cenotaph design (with Marguerite Taylor) did not win in Winnipeg, but was put up in Prince Albert, Sasktachewan. He won the 1929 design competition for the Richardson Building. He designed many of the buildings erected in the 1920s at the University of Manitoba, particularly the Arts and Sciences buildings, before he returned to the United States. Stoughton was a member of the Manitoba

Association of Architects, the Royal Architecture Institute of Canada, and the Winnipeg Sketch Club. He died in Mount Vernon, New York.

Stovel, A. Burton (1921-1977) Architect. Born in Winnipeg, he served as a pilot in the RAF during WWII, flying Mosquitoes and Wellingtons; he was awarded the DFC. He graduated from the University of Manitoba as gold medallist in architecture in 1947, and worked as an architect for Frank Lount and Son before forming his own firm in 1968. He was active in local St. James affairs.

Stovel, Augustus B. (1865-1921) Printer. Born in Mount Forest, Canada, he learned printing in Chicago. He came to Winnipeg in the 1880s and in 1889 founded the Stovel Printing Company, which became a major Winnipeg printer. He died in Hot Springs, Virginia.

Strachan, Alfred John (1915-1978) Horticulturalist. Born in Pope, Manitoba, he was educated at Carman before attending the University of Manitoba, from which he graduated in 1938 with a BSc in Agriculture. He subsequently joined the Dominion Department of Agriculture at Brandon, Melita, and Minnedosa. He formed the Strachan Feed Company in 1943. He became a specialist in breeding gladioli, and developed six new varieties. He is a member of the Manitoba Agricultural Hall of Fame.

Strange, Henry George Latimer (1882-1964) Engineer, researcher, writer. Born in London, England, he studied engineering, served in the Boer War, and worked as a gas-processing engineer around the world. During WWI he worked in a special section of the Royal Engineers developing flame projectors. In 1918 he was badly wounded by shrapnel. He moved to North America in 1919, and worked for some years in agricultural research before joining the Searle Grain Company of Winnipeg in 1930 to head its research department. He developed a new crop-testing system which was adopted around the world. Throughout his career he wrote on agriculture and other areas of interest, often in collaboration with his wife Kathleen. Strange was the author of *A Short History of Prairie Agriculture* (1951). He retired in 1954, first to England, then to British Columbia. He died in Vancouver. A partial biography is provided in *With the West in Her Eyes* (1937) and a partial autobiography by *Never a Dull Moment* (written with Kathleen Strange, 1941).

Strange, Kathleen (Redman) (1896-1968) Writer. Born in London, England, she came to North America with her husband, Henry Strange,* after WWI, travelling around the West until settling in Winnipeg in 1930. She told the story of these years in her book *With the West in Her Eyes: The Story of a Modern Pioneer* (1937). In Winnipeg she served as president of the Canadian Authors' Association for many years, and later became national bursar. She also continued her writing, producing with her husband *Never a Dull Moment* (1941), another memoir of family adventures. Moving to England in 1954, she became involved with the movie industry in Europe, producing several screenplays. She retired to Vancouver in 1964, where she died.

Stronach, Esther Frances (d. 1980) Music teacher. Born in Winnipeg, she attended Riverbend School for Girls before studying music in Toronto and London. She was a long-time music teacher in Winnipeg, a member of the Manitoba Music Teachers' Association and the Professional and Business Women's Club. She was a member of St. Andrew's United Church, River Heights. She died in Winnipeg.

Stuart, William (c. 1678-1719) Fur trader. He first went to Hudson Bay in 1691, rejoining the service in 1714 with James Knight,* whom he accompanied on a treaty-making expedition to the Cree in 1715 because he spoke Aboriginal languages. Stuart's part of the expedition, which crossed the Barrens to Great Slave Lake, was one of enormous hardship, from which he never recovered. He became "lunatick" in 1719 and had to be tied to his bed, dying soon after. He was the first European to cross the Barrens. *DCB* II, 615-16.

Stubbs, Lewis St. George (1885-1958) Lawyer, judge, gadfly. Born in the West Indies, he was educated at Denniston College in England. He came to Manitoba in 1902 and was called to the Manitoba bar in 1906. He practised at Birtle and Winnipeg. Stubbs assisted F.J. Dixon* in preparing his defence against charges of sedition in 1919. He was later dismissed from the bench in 1933, officially for "judicial misbehaviour," but probably more for advocating unpopular views, particularly the view that justice be dispensed by an independent judiciary to both rich and poor without distinction. In 1936 he was elected an MLA and became a political gadfly. See the biography by his grandson of the same name, entitled *A Majority of One* (1983).

Stubbs, Roy St. George (1907-1995) Lawyer, judge, author. Born in Winnipeg, he worked for the *Winnipeg Tribune* before attending the University of Manitoba (law degree, 1936). He served in the RCAF from 1941 to 1945. After years of family practice, in 1970 he was appointed senior judge of the juvenile and family court, serving until his retirement in 1982. He published a number of books, including *Lawyers and Laymen* (1939), *Men in Khaki* (1941), *Prairie Portraits* (1954) and *Four Recorders of Rupertsland* (1967). He was also an ardent advocate of the work of the Icelandic poet Guttormur J. Guttormson, who became the subject of his last book, *In Search of a Poet* (1975).

Stutsman, Enos (1826-1874) Lawyer. Born in Indiana with no legs, he used crutches throughout his life. Despite the handicap he went to the Dakota Territory in 1858 and served as a member of the territorial legislature. He was hired in 1868 as an attorney to defend Alex McLean from a charge of manslaughter. In 1869 he was promoting the American annexation of Red River from Pembina, and he was often consulted by Louis Riel and the Métis leadership. He arrived in Winnipeg 22 November 1869 and met with the Métis about a Bill of Rights, the first four clauses of which echoed his own earlier submission of a Dakota bill to a St. Paul newspaper. With the growing disfavour shown by Riel to the Americans, Stutsman disappeared from the Red River scene. See the biography by Dale Gibson, *Attorney for the Frontier* (1983). *DCB* X, 669.

Summers, Danny (1924-1999) Athlete. Born in Winnipeg, he was educated locally. After military service in WWII, he played the 1945 season with the Winnipeg Blue Bombers. He then enjoyed a lengthy career in hockey, playing as a defenceman for the Calder Cup champion Providence Reds in 1949; for the President's Cup and Edinburgh Trophy champion Winnipeg Maroons of 1956; for the International Hockey League's Turner Cup champions the St. Paul Saints in 1960-61; and for the Allan Cup champion Winnipeg Warriors in 1964. He subsequently spent many years as a hockey scout with the Detroit Red Wings, New York Rangers, and San Diego Sharks, drafting stars like Marcel Dionne and Brian Leetch. He is a member of the Manitoba Hockey Hall of Fame and the Manitoba Sports Hall of Fame.

Sutherland, Hugh McKay (1843-1926) Businessman. Born in New London, Prince Edward Island, he was descended from Scottish Highlanders from Sutherlandshire. His parents moved to Oxford County, Canada, when he was nine. Sutherland had little formal education, but was a successful railroad contractor before coming to Manitoba in 1874. He served as dominion superintendent of public works for the Prairie district from 1874 to 1878, then entered into the lumbering business at Kenora and Winnipeg. He became Liberal MP for Selkirk in 1882, and soon was busy organizing and then constructing (in 1884) the Winnipeg and Hudson Bay Railway Company. He was defeated for a Winnipeg seat in the Commons in 1887 by William Scarth* (Conservative) in a bitter campaign. He then entered the mining business in British Columbia, then became the Canadian Northern's chief executive agent in 1901. He again promoted a railway to Hudson Bay in 1908 and was always remembered as being the strongest advocate that the railway ever had. He died in London and was buried in Winnipeg.

Sutherland, James (c.1751-1797) Fur trader. Born probably in the Orkney Islands, he joined the HBC as a tailor in 1770. He was ordered to London in 1775 and re-signed with the HBC in 1777. He was extremely versatile and became a successful inland trader, establishing posts on the Winnipeg River. He headed Osnaburgh House in 1794 and took over Brandon House in 1796, dying there shortly after his arrival. See Shirlee Smith, "James Sutherland: Inland Trader 1751-1797," *The Beaver* (winter 1975): 18-23. *DCB* IV, 727-28.

Sutherland, James (b. 1768) Settler. Born in Sutherlandshire, Scotland, he came to Red River with the third Selkirk party in 1815. A weaver by trade, he was also authorized by the Church of Scotland to perform baptisms and marriages. He exercised this authority often in Red River and became known as "The Parson." He was granted Lot one by Lord Selkirk in 1817. He left the settlement in 1819 to visit his family in Upper Canada, and apparently never returned.

Sutherland, James (c. 1777-1844) Fur trader. Born in Ronaldshay, Orkney Islands, he joined the HBC in 1797. He was master of Cumberland House from 1808 to 1813 and was imprisoned by the NWC in 1816. He was in charge of Swan River from 1819 to 1821, when he became chief factor. He retired in 1827 to the Red River Settlement. He served as a councillor of Rupert's Land from 1815, a councillor of the governors of the HBC from 1822, and a councillor of Assiniboia from 1839. He died in Red River.

Sutherland, John (1821-1899) Farmer, senator. Born at Point Douglas, he moved to Lot 86, East Kildonan, after the flood of 1852 to establish a farm and a general store. He was a member of the Council of Assiniboia from 1866 to 1870, and a member of the Convention of Forty. He recognized Riel's provisional government only after visiting with Governor William McTavish* who Sutherland claimed had advised the delegation to do so. His son was killed in February 1870 by Norbert Parisien. Sutherland was the first sheriff of Manitoba, and was appointed to the Senate on 18 December 1871. He helped found Manitoba College. There are papers at the PAM.

Swan a.k.a. Captain Swan (fl. 1715-1719) Cree leader. He served as a middleman between Aboriginals and fur traders at Hudson Bay from 1715 to 1719, having been sent in 1715 by Governor James Knight* to trade with the inhabitants of the Lake Athabasca region. *DCB* II, 617.

Sweatman, Travers (1879-1941) Lawyer. Born in Pembroke, Ontario, he came to Winnipeg as a small boy. He was educated in Winnipeg public schools and worked his way through St. John's College. In 1900 he was an honours graduate in classics from the University of Manitoba. He articled with Isaac Pitblado* and was called to the bar in 1906, forming his own firm in 1913. He defended Thomas Kelly* in the litigation over the construction of the Manitoba legislative buildings, and was a Crown lawyer in the Winnipeg General Strike trials. He was a member of the Committee of 1,000 in 1919, and president of the Board of Trade from 1921 to 1925. He was a founding member of the Winnipeg Winter Club. There are papers at the PAM.

Swystun, Wasyl (1893-1964) Lawyer. Born in Sorotske, Western Ukraine, he attended colleges in L'vov and Rumania. He immigrated to Canada in 1913 and attended the University of Saskatchewan, graduating with a BA with honours in economics and philsophy. He taught in Saskatchewan before becoming a high-school principal in Ethelbert, Manitoba. In 1925 he came to Winnipeg to found the Ukrainian Institute of Peter Mohyla, of which he was principal until 1931. From 1928 to 1932 he attended the University of Manitoba law school, and he practised law for the remainder of his life. After 1946 he became an expert in Soviet law. He wrote *Ukraine: the sorest spot of Europe* (1931). Swystun was active in the Ukrainian Greek Orthodox Church and in various Ukrainian national organizations. He founded the Ukrainian Self-Reliance League and was pro-Communist in his later years.

Taché, Alexandre-Antonin (1823-1894) Cleric. Born in Rivière-du-Loup, he was educated at the Collège de Saint-Hyacinthe and the Theological Seminary of Montreal. He entered the Oblate Order in 1844 and was sent to Red River a year later, becoming bishop of St. Boniface in 1853. He became archbishop and metropolitan in 1871. Taché was in Rome for a Vatican Council during the Red River Rebellion of 1869-70, and many observers thought his absence from Red River had encouraged the Métis to rebelliousness. Upon returning to Red River in March 1870 after meeting with the Canadian government, he stated that the government had promised a general amnesty to those involved in the uprising and that Canada had in principle accepted the bill of rights passed by the Convention of 1870. Taché spent the next few years attempting to get the Canadian government to honour his promise of a general amnesty, without much visible success. At the same time, he recruited a large number of Francophone professionals to attempt to give some substance to the guarantees of bilingualism and biculturalism in the Manitoba Act. In the end, he fought a losing battle on this front and lived to see legislation creating unilingual schools and the Manitoba School Question. He wrote a number of books, including *Vingt Années de missions dans le Nord-Ouest de l'Amérique* (1866) and *Esquisse sur le Nord-Ouest de l'Amérique* (1869). For a biography, see Dom Benoit, *Vie de Mgr Taché*, 2 vols. (1904). *DCB* XII, 1,002-12.

Tait, Robert (1830-1912) Businessman. Born in Red River, he apprenticed as a blacksmith at Lower Fort Garry in 1843, moved to St. Paul in 1845, and returned to Red River in 1850 with a reaping machine. A year later he brought a threshing machine. He farmed in St. James, opened a store, and in 1869 built the first steam grist mill in St. James. He later operated a steam ferry on the Red River between Winnipeg and St. Boniface. His funeral was a huge one.

Tait, William Auld (1826-1900) Politician. Born in Kildonan, he attended St. John's School. He moved to Headingley in 1860, and in 1869 he attended the Council of Twenty-Four, which met in November. He became a councillor of the North-West Territories in 1874 and ran without success as Headingley MLA that same year.

Talbot, Alphonse Laurent Phillip Adjutor (1872-1961) Politician. Born near Quebec City, he came to Manitoba around 1900, becoming an insurance and real estate agent. He was first elected to the legislature in 1915 as a Liberal, but left the party in 1916 over the school question in Quebec. His motion of censure forced the Norris government to call an election, which it lost, in 1922. Under the successor Bracken government, Talbot was chosen Speaker of the House, serving until 1936, when he could not win renomination in his riding. He became clerk of the Executive Council in 1937 and remained there until his retirement in 1948.

Talbot, Stuart Richard ("Stu," 1895-1965) Amateur radio operator. Educated in Fairburn and Boissevain, Manitoba, he served overseas in WWII with the RCAF as a squadron leader and radar instructor. He was a founder of the Amateur Radio League of Manitoba. His call letters were VE4SR. In the 1948 and 1950 floods he was active in private radio communications, and this earned him a Public Service Award.

Tallin, George Percy Raymond ("Pete," 1894-1970) Educator. Born in Petrolia, Ontario, he came to Winnipeg at an early age and graduated from Wesley College in arts in 1916. As an undergraduate, he was noted for having studied Greek at the university level with no previous exposure to the language. He rose from private to captain in the army during WWI. He was a Rhodes Scholar at Queen's College, Oxford, and was called to the bar at the Inner Temple in 1921. After returning to Manitoba, he practised law until he was appointed dean of the Manitoba Law School in 1945, serving until 1964. During WWII he commanded the University of Manitoba Contingent, COTC Tallin was known for his prodigious talents, having acquired, among other accomplishments, an ability to speed-type and to take shorthand.

Tanner, John ("The American," c. 1780-1846) Indian captive, interpreter. Born on the Kentucky River, he was kidnapped by Indians in 1789 and ended up in Red River. His memoirs of his captivity were some of the most interesting published in the nineteenth century and were translated into several languages. He lost command of English and wrote that he could not speak it "so as to be at all understood." He was able to observe the Saulteaux society during a time of great transition, and his account is extremely ambivalent about his attitudes toward his situation. Tanner was present at Red River when the first Selkirk settlers arrived, and he assisted them without at first joining them. By 1816 he was guiding Lord Selkirk's hired soldiers from Fort William to Fort Douglas. Selkirk* himself was fascinated with Tanner's story, and he assisted Tanner in trying to establish contact with his family. Tanner met with his brother in 1817 but eventually returned to the Northwest. In 1830 Edwin James, an army surgeon, recorded the former captive's recollections at Sault Ste. Marie and published them. Like most children taken captive by Indians in their early years, Tanner assimilated to Native ways. He never managed to be comfortable with his own people again. See Edwin James, ed., *A Narrative of the Captivity and Adventures of John Tanner (U.S. Interpreter at the Sault de Ste. Marie) during Thirty Years Residence among the Indians in the Interior of North America* (1830); John T. Fierst, "Strange Eloquence: Another Look at *The Captivity and Adventures of John Tanner*," in *Reading Beyond Words: Contexts in Native History*, ed. Jennifer Brown and Elizabeth Vibert (1996), 220-41. *DCB* VII, 844-45.

Tarasiuk, Hryhorij (1895-1982) Ukrainian activist. Born in Perevodiv, Sokal, Ukraine, he was recruited into the Austrian army, subsequently joining the Ukrainian army (Halychyna Division, Fifth Sokal Brigade), where he fought from 1918 to 1922 for Ukrainian independence. He came to Canada in 1929, serving in the Queen's Own Cameron Highlanders in WWII. Employed for many years by Ontario Hydro in Kapuskasing, he came to Winnipeg upon his retirement in 1966, becoming very active in the Ukrainian-Canadian community in the city. He was a founding member of the Carpathia Credit Union and recipient of an award from the Ukrainian Canadian Committee for his contributions to Ukrainian culture.

Taraska, Peter (1907-1984) Accountant, commission chair, judge. Born in Winnipeg, he was a local businessman who worked as an accountant from 1945 to 1957. In the 1950s he was an unsuccessful Liberal candidate at both the provincial and federal levels. In 1962 he served as financial chair of the Metropolitan Corporation of Greater Winnipeg. He was appointed a citizenship court judge in 1968. In 1971 he chaired the Electoral Boundaries Commission, which recommended the ward boundary system for a proposed regional government for Greater Winnipeg. In this task he sought to preserve the historical and cultural background of the city. He later chaired another commission which reviewed the City of Winnipeg Act, recommending in 1976 a parliamentary system for Unicity. He was a knight commander of the Order of Saint Gregory the Great. He received the Order of Canada in 1982.

Tarr, Edgar Jordan (1881-1950) Insurance executive, international affairs expert. Born in Ottawa, he was educated at Ottawa Collegiate and McMaster University. In 1902 he came to Manitoba on a harvest excursion and remained in Winnipeg. He was called to the bar in 1905 and eventually became president of Monarch Life Insurance Company. An original member of the Canadian Institute of International Affairs (he served as president) and international chair of the Institute of Pacific Relations, he often represented Canada at international conferences in the post-WWII years. In 1939 in a Winnipeg speech he advocated a national unemployment insurance scheme and repatriation of the Constitution. He died in Winnipeg.

Tattannoeuck ("Augustus," d. 1834) Interpreter. An Inuk born 200 miles north of Fort Churchill, he was employed at the fort beginning in 1812. In 1820 he was engaged as an interpreter for Sir John Franklin,* and he accompanied Franklin down the Coppermine River. He was converted to Christianity by John West in 1823, and he served again as interpreter to Franklin's second expedition in 1825. He perished while trying to join George Back's* expedition of 1834. He was much beloved by those of the various Franklin parties. A butterfly and a lake in the Northwest Territories were named for him. *DCB* VI, 753-55.

Taylor, Fawcett Gowler (1878-1940) Lawyer, judge. Born in Meadow Lea, Manitoba, he was educated at Winnipeg Collegiate. He studied law with W.J. Cooper in Portage la Prairie and was called to the bar in 1900. During WWI he served as a major with the First Canadian Mounted Rifles, and he was awarded the Distinguished Service Order in 1917. Taylor was elected to the Manitoba legislature in 1920 and became leader of the Manitoba Conservative Party in 1922. He declined to join a coalition government in 1931. In 1933 he was appointed to the Court of King's Bench.

Taylor, George S. (1839-1919) Explorer. Born in York Factory, he was a sailor for the HBC before accompanying the Palliser Expedition across the West in 1857. He later settled near Lower Fort Garry and in 1879 moved west to Prince Albert to homestead. He died in Edgerton, Alberta.

Taylor, James Wickes (1819-1893) Diplomat. Born in Starkey, New York, he was educated at Hamilton College before studying law. He was admitted to the Ohio bar in 1843. He subsequently became a newspaper owner (the *Cincinnati Morning Sentinel*) and politician, serving as state librarian from 1852 to 1856. He then moved to St. Paul, which served as the base for his work with the United States Treasury Department from 1859 to 1869 on reciprocal trade and transportation links with British North America. Taylor served as an intelligence agent for the State Department in Red River in 1869-70 and was in Ottawa at the time of the negotiations leading to the Manitoba Act. In 1870 he became American consul at Winnipeg, serving until his death. Taylor was a leading booster of the West and especially of Canadian-American relations. See Theodore Blegen, "James Wickes Taylor: A Biographical Sketch," *Minnnesota Historical Bulletin* 1 (1915-16): 155-212. Taylor's letters to Washington were edited by Hartwell Bowsfield as *The Correspondence of James Wickes Taylor, 1859-1870* (1968). *DCB* XII, 1,029-31.

Taylor, John (1812-1884) Missionary, immigrant promoter. Born in Barbados, he was educated in Halifax and at Oxford University. He became a missionary for the British-American Bible Society in 1865 and became interested in Icelandic settlement in 1874. He helped Icelanders get a federal grant for a journey to the West to find a location for settlement, and he brought a party to Gimli, where he remained until moving to Argyle, Manitoba. He later lived in Carberry. He died in Milwaukee.

Taylor, John (1834-1925) Educator, politician. Born in Middlechurch, he attended St. Paul's School there and was chosen by Bishop David Anderson* to be trained to teach in the Indian settlements. He was the first schoolteacher in Headingley, serving in 1853-54 at an annual salary of $150. He was a supporter of G.O. Corbett,* and as a magistrate he became involved in the Corbett scandal of 1862-63. In 1870 he was elected to the January Convention of Forty, and later he joined the armed party from Portage la Prairie that was imprisoned by Louis Riel. He had carried the flag in this company, and later commented, "It was so cold in Fort Garry that we never had our greatcoats off during all that time." Elected MLA for Assiniboia in 1871, he served as minister of agriculture in 1878-79.

Taylor, John (1838-1908) Sloop captain. Born in the Orkney Islands, he joined the HBC as a sailor in 1866 at Moose Factory. He skippered the schooners *Otter* and *Mink* out of Moose Factory for 37 years, eventually retiring to Winnipeg.

Taylor, Marguerite (Judd) (1883-1963) Sculptor. Born in Paris, she studied with French sculptor

Antoine Bourdelle and came to Winnipeg in 1906. She later moved to London, England, to be near her husband. Among her Winnipeg commissions were the bust of Victoria Cross-winner Alan McLeod,* the soldier memorial on the legislative grounds, and the Chief Peguis monument in Kildonan Park. She kept a small studio on Langside Street for many years. See Vaughan L. Baird, *The Sculptress Marguerite Taylor* (1966).

Taylor, Thomas Wardlaw (1833-1917) Lawyer, judge. Born in Auchtermuchty, Scotland, he was educated at Edinburgh University, graduating in 1852. He came to Canada with his parents in 1852 and graduated from the University of Toronto, receiving his MA in 1856. He was called to the bar in Canada in 1858. He came to Manitoba in 1872 to be master in Chancery, serving until 1883, when he became puisne judge of the Court of Queen's Bench. The latter appointment was part of a complex political controversy of the day. In 1887 he was appointed chief justice, a post he held until 1899. He administered the government of Manitoba from 1890 to 1893 and served as Exchequer Court judge in Ottawa from 1900 to 1908. He was the judge in the Riel treason case in 1885 and one of the judges who supported the government's law to abolish separate schools in 1892. Taylor wrote a number of books on legal matters, such as *Grand Orders of the Court of Chancery* (1865) and *Commentaries on Equity Jurisprudence, Founded on Story* (1875). He was regarded as an expert on Canadian church law. Among his works written in Manitoba were *The Public Statutes Relating to the Presbyterian Church in Canada* (1879). In 1895 he published *The Individual and the State: An Essay on Justice*. He was created a knight bachelor at the diamond jubilee of Queen Victoria in 1897. He died in Hamilton. *DCB* XIV, 990-93.

Taylor, Thomas William (1852-1924) Businessman. Born in Portsmouth, England, he came to Winnipeg in 1877 as a bookbinder. By 1901 he was president of T.W. Taylor, Limited, a printing business that was highly mechanized and that specialized in business forms. He introduced the first paper-rolling machine in Western Canada. He served as Ward Four alderman from 1889 to 1892 and was elected mayor by acclamation in 1893. In 1900 he was elected at a by-election as MLA from Winnipeg Centre First, and he served for many years. He was chair of the Winnipeg Public Parks Board in 1904-5.

He was a leading Mason. Taylor Avenue in Winnipeg was named after him.

Taylor, William Agutter (1846-1914) Law librarian. He became librarian of the Manitoba Law Society (as well as sub-secretary and Society solicitor) in 1883, helped edit the *Manitoba Law Journal* in 1884, and assisted with the Manitoba Law Reports from 1886 to 1894.

Taylor, William Henry (1820-1873) Cleric. Born in Bristol, England, he spent some years in Newfoundland before arriving in Rupert's Land as the first missionary of the Society for the Propagation of the Gospel. He was ordained by Bishop David Anderson* in St. Andrew's Church on 22 December 1850. He opened a Sunday school in 1851 and did all the painting inside and outside the church, which was consecrated in 1855 as "St. James." He also established a lending library of 200 volumes and was elected to the council of the Institute of Rupert's Land in 1862. Taylor retired in ill health to England in 1867. *DCB* X, 673-74.

Tees, Francis William (c. 1895-1976) Journalist. Born in Oak Lake, Manitoba, he was brought up in Prince Albert, Saskatchewan, and he moved to Winnipeg to work for the *Winnipeg Telegram*. He subsequently spent 40 years with the Stovel Publishing Company and Sanford Evans Publishing Limited as editor and advertising manager of the *Prairie Grocer and Provisioner* and advertising manager of the *Western Canada Coal Review*.

Tees, James (1854-1906) Broker, musician, sportsman. Born in Montreal, he apprenticed to a metal engraver. In 1881 he came to Winnipeg to manage the Canadian Lead Works, later becoming a manufacturing broker. For many years he was choirmaster of Grace Church, and he was also associated with the Winnipeg Operatic Society, the Winnipeg Oratorio Society, and the Male Voice Choir of Winnipeg. He was active in sports as well as music. An avid curler at the Assiniboine Curling Club, he was a cyclist and lacrosse enthusiast as well.

Teeter, George G. (d. 1949) Architect. Born in Ste. Anne's, Ontario, he was educated at the University of Toronto, where he received a degree in architecture. He became a junior partner of a North Bay firm of architects, and came to Winnipeg in 1908.

He worked as an independent architect in the city for many years. He was a president of the Manitoba Association of Architects. His buildings include King Edward Memorial Hospital and Trinity Baptist Church.

Telford, D. McLeod (1845-1921) Community leader. A prominent businessman and customs appraiser, he was the leading spirit of the Scottish community in Winnipeg for many years, and served as sometime president of the St. Andrew's Society, the Highland Society, and the Caithness Society. He resigned as customs appraiser in 1921.

Tennant, Edith Irene (1898-1989) Municipal politician. Born and educated in Winnipeg, she taught in the Winnipeg public schools for many years until 1934. She later served for six years on the school board and for 10 years on Winnipeg City Council as alderwoman. She was deputy mayor in 1964-65.

Tessier, Joseph (1891-1948) Beekeeper. Born in Quebec, he came to Manitoba as a young man, living at Elm Creek and Starbuck before settling in St. Pierre in 1923. He was a prominent fur farmer and beekeeper and one of the founders of the Manitoba Co-operative Honey Producers' Association. He also served as a local school trustee and councillor for the Municipality of De Salaberry.

Thanadelthur ("The Slave Woman," d. 1717): Interpreter. A Chipewyan (Dene), she was captured by Crees and enslaved before escaping to York Fort, which she reached late in 1714. She subsequently accompanied William Stuart* and a party of Crees on a peace mission to the Chipewyans. While most of the mission gave up the task, Thanadelthur pursued her people and talked them into negotiating peace. Governor James Knight* described her as being of "great Courage." *DCB* II, 627-28.

Thibault, Jean Baptiste (1810-1874) Cleric. Born in Saint-Joseph-de-Lévis, Lower Canada, he was educated at the Quebec Seminary. In 1853 he was posted to the Northwest, and he spent many years as a missionary, first in St. Boniface and later among the Native peoples. He was in Quebec in 1869 when he was asked to return to Red River as a special envoy of the Canadian government, along with Charles de Salaberry* and Donald A. Smith.* Thibault was intended to provide credibility for the government's

sincerity. He arrived in Red River on Christmas Day 1869 and was immediately placed out of the way in the bishop's palace by the provisional government when it discovered he had no power to negotiate an agreement on behalf of Canada. He played little role in the unfolding events of 1870, although he may have assisted Riel to assert his authority over wavering supporters on several occasions. *DCB* X, 676-78.

Thom, Adam (1802-1890) Polemicist, judge. Born in Brechin, Scotland, he graduated from King's College Aberdeen in 1819. He first tried to find a career in London, then came to Canada in 1832 to make his way in journalism. He published several important pamphlets and, from 1836 to 1838, he was editor of the *Montreal Herald*. Thom's mind was that interesting combination of radical sentiments and acceptance of the prevailing climate of opinion, a sure-fire formula for reactionary positions. In 1836 he attacked the French-Canadian party in the legislature in a pamphlet called *Anti-Gallic Letters*. He began to read law, and he was called to the bar of Lower Canada in 1837. At first a critic of the Durham mission, Thom became a secretary to Lord Durham and an adviser on the famous Durham Report. At least one obituary claimed that Thom was responsible for most of Durham's document. While in London Thom met George Simpson,* who offered him the job as Recorder of Rupert's Land. He arrived in Red River to take it up in the spring of 1839. His eyesight was bad, his French virtually non-existent, his knowledge of the law dubious and his attitude toward ethnic minorities not good. Moreover, Thom saw himself as an advocate for the HBC. In his court he ran roughshod over the constitution of the settlement, hanging an Indian in 1845 despite the Act of Parliament requiring all capital cases to be tried in Canada. In 1843 he heard a lawsuit against him brought by Anne Rothney, one of his own servants, and refused to order the jury's verdict against him. His most notorious cases were the Sayer trial and *Foss* v. *Pelly*. In the first he lost the confidence of the Francophone community, in the second the confidence of the Anglophone. On the positive side, he did prepare in 1851 an extensive report on the state of the law in Red River. He remained in Red River for four years after his replacement as judge, and then in 1854 retired to Edinburgh. He died in London. A prolific author and controversialist, he wrote *Letter to the Right Hon. E.G. Stanley, secretary of state for* *the colonies, by an Emigrant*(1834);*Remarks on the Convention and on thePetition of the Constitutionalists, by Anti-Bureaucrat*(1835);*Review of the Report made in 1828 by the Canada Committee of the House of Commons*(1835); *Anti-Gallic Letters, Addressed to His Excellency, the Earl of Gosford, by Camillus*(1836);*The Claims to the Oregon Territory Considered*(1848), and *Chronology of Prophecy* (1848). See Roy St. George Stubbs, *Four Recorders of Rupert's Land* (1967); and Dale Gibson, "A Scandal at Red River," *The Beaver* 70, no. 5 (October/November 1990): 30-38. *DCB* XI, 874-77.

Thomas, Alfred Vernon (1875-1950) Journalist. Born in Manchester, England, he attended Manchester Grammar School and served in Europe as a representative of a lace manufacturer. He regularly contributed to the *Guardian* while living abroad. Thomas embarked for Canada in 1905 as part of a round-the-world tour. He remained in the country, reaching Winnipeg around 1914. After three years with the *Manitoba Free Press* he lost his job because of his anti-conscription attitudes. He went to New York, returning to Winnipeg in 1923 to begin a career with the *Tribune* that ended only with his retirement in 1944. Municipal editor of the *Tribune,* he held strong views in favour of municipal ownership of utilities.

Thomas, Catherine Elizabeth (1921-1982) Physician. Born in Assiniboia, Saskatchewan, she received her BA from the University of Saskatchewan in 1942 and her MD from the Manitoba Medical College in 1945. In 1948 she joined the Red Cross, and she was the first physician involved in beginning the Blood Transfusion Service in Manitoba. She joined the Manitoba Medical College as a faculty member in 1959 and was later associated with the departments of pathology and anatomy until her retirement in 1978.

Thomas, Lillian (Beynon) (1874-1961) Journalist, feminist, author. Born in King, Ontario, she came to Manitoba in 1889 with her family and graduated from Wesley College in Winnipeg in 1905. She taught in Morden and then, in 1906, joined the *Free Press,* where she served as assistant editor of the *Weekly Free Press* and wrote as "Lillian Laurie." Her first successful short story won a prize from *Maclean's* magazine and was published by the *American Magazine.* She was an active feminist and advocate of women's suffrage, and was especially involved in the Political Equality League. She worked in New York from 1918 to 1923 but returned to Canada with her husband,

A.V. Thomas,* to write. She authored several successful plays, including *Among the Maples, Jim Barber's Spite Fence* (winner of the Dominion Drama Award for Manitoba) and *As the Twig Is Bent.* Her first novel, *New Secret,* was published in 1946. See Manitoba Department of Cultural Affairs and Historic Resources, *Lillian Beynon Thomas* (1983).

Thomas, Maria (c. 1846-1867) Domestic servant. Born in Mapleton to a mixed-blood family, she was employed as a maid at age 13 by the cleric G.O. Corbett,* who resided in Headingley. According to her later testimony, she was initially drugged and raped by Corbett, subsequently falling into a regular sexual relationship with him, usually in the barn. When she became pregnant, Corbett (who practised medicine in the Red River Settlement) unsuccessfully attempted five times to procure an abortion. The affair became the talk of the settlement. Thomas was the star witness in the case of *The Queen v. Corbett,* heard early in 1862, which charged the cleric with the abortions but not the rape. She stuck by her story, and Corbett was convicted. A complete trial transcript was published in the *Nor'-Wester.* She died in Mapleton.

Thomas, Sophia See Mason, Sophia (Thomas).

Thomas, Thomas (c. 1766-1828) Fur trader. Born in Wales, he joined the HBC as a surgeon in 1789 and became master of Severn House from 1796 until 1810, when he became superintendent of the Southern Department. In 1814 he became governor of the Northern Department and in 1815 a councillor of Assiniboia. He refused to succeed Robert Semple* in 1817 as temporary governor-in-chief of Red River. He retired to Red River in 1819 and was again appointed to the Council of Assiniboia in 1822. Both Colin Robertson* and George Simpson* regarded him as timid and weak. He died in Red River. *DCB* VI, 767-68.

Thomas, Wilfred William Henry (1875-1953) Cleric. Born in Tenby, South Wales, he attended St. Paul's Missionary College in England and St. Augustine's College in Canterbury. He came to Hamilton in 1898 and was ordained although under the canonical age. He came to St. Luke's Anglican Church in Winnipeg as rector in 1899, then was appointed to Selkirk in 1901. He became archdeacon in 1915, and was elected first Anglican bishop of

Brandon in 1924. He was an early supporter of the Bishop's Messengers, founded by Rita Fowler in 1926. He was awarded an honorary degree by St. John's College. He retired in 1949 and died in Brandon.

Thompson, David (1770-1857) Explorer and fur trader. He was educated at Grey Coat Hospital in London, and he joined the HBC in 1784. He spent his first year at Fort Churchill, then moved inland for several years. In 1790 he was posted to York Factory, and in 1792 was sent west to the Athabasca country. He joined the NWC in 1797 and spent the next 15 years exploring and mapping in Western Canada, mainly west of the Rocky Mountains. He retired in 1814 and bought a farm in Williamston, Upper Canada. Later he was employed by the boundary commission working on the border with the United States, and in the 1830s he worked on the surveys in the Eastern Townships for the British American Land Company. In his last years he wrote about his travels, and his account was published as *David Thompson's Narrative*, ed. J.B. Tyrrell (1916). See J.K. Smith, *David Thompson: Fur Trader, Explorer, Geographer* (1971). *DCB* VIII, 878-84.

Thompson, Florence Daly Lucas (1865-1915) Illustrator, librarian. Born in Hitchin, England, she was privately educated. She married William Henry Thompson of Winnipeg in 1892. She joined her husband in Winnipeg and soon began exhibiting watercolour paintings at the Winnipeg Industrial Exhibition. She became involved in scientific research and illustration in collaboration with professors at the university. In 1908 she became librarian at the University of Manitoba, a post she held until her death from appendicitis. Employing a small budget, she built the library up substantially. Thompson was active in a number of women's organizations and was elected the first honorary member of the University Women's Club. She died in Winnipeg. *DCB* XIV, 668-69.

Thompson, Frederick George (1886-1972) Lawyer, municipal politician. Born in Winnipeg, he attended Manitoba College and graduated from the Manitoba Law School. He served in the 78th Battalion, Winnipeg Grenadiers in WWI. He was a school board member from 1929 to 1935 and a city councillor from 1936 to 1943.

Thompson, Gisli M. (1863-1908) Journalist, publisher. Born in Iceland, he homesteaded near Gimli.

He brought a printing press to Gimli in 1891 and began publishing three periodicals, *Dagsbrun* (Dawn), *Svava*, and *Bergmalid* (The Echo). He was reeve of the Gimli municipality in 1896.

Thompson, John W. (1858-1914) Politician. Born in Ravenswood, Canada, he came to Manitoba in 1878 and eventually homesteaded in Minnedosa. He was a lieutenant in the 91st Battalion in the North-West Rebellion of 1885, and he became a homestead inspector for the federal government in 1897. He was elected as a Liberal to represent Minnedosa in the provincial legislature in 1910.

Thompson, Samuel Jacob (1845-1909) Veterinarian. Born in Caledonia, Canada, he was trained at the Ontario Veterinary College, and he practised as a veterinarian at Brantford. He moved to Manitoba in 1881 and settled in Carberry. He represented Norfolk in the 1886 provincial Assembly and was re-elected in 1888. He later became provincial veterinarian. He moved to St. James to farm in 1899 and served as reeve of Assiniboia for several years.

Thompson, Ernest Seton See Seton, Ernest Thompson.

Thomson, William Davidson (1886-1961) Musician. Born in Scotland, he came to Manitoba in 1903 and to Winnipeg in 1906 to study voice. He was already well known as a natural baritone, and he continued to have that reputation despite considerable formal training. He became associated with Knox United Church, the United Scottish Society and the St. Andrew's Society male choirs. In 1931 he directed the *Winnipeg Tribune*'s "Nights of Community Song" in the city's parks to a cumulative audience of over 100,000 people. He later was a music reviewer for the *Winnipeg Free Press*.

Thorlakson, Paul Henric Thorbjorn (1895-1989) Physician. Born in Park River, North Dakota, he enrolled in the Manitoba Medical College in 1914, volunteering for military service in 1916. He graduated from Manitoba Medical College in 1917, then undertook postgraduate studies in surgery in London. He helped form the Maclean-Thorlakson Clinic (later renamed the Winnipeg Clinic in 1938), and in the 1940s was organizer of the corporation that promoted the Manitoba Medical Centre. He served as president of many medical organizations, was active in Icelandic affairs, and served three terms as chancellor of the University of Winnipeg, from 1969 to 1978. In 1951 he was named to the Order of the Falcon by the Icelandic government, and in 1971 became a Companion of the Order of Canada. He died in Winnipeg.

Thorlaksson, Paul (1841-1882) Cleric. Born in Húsavík, Iceland, he attended the Grammar School in Reykjavík and then accompanied his relatives to the United States in 1872. He studied theology at Concordia Seminary in St. Louis from 1872 to 1875 and joined the Norwegian Synod of the Lutheran Church, where he was ordained on 8 July 1875. He immigrated to New Iceland (in Manitoba) with a number of settlers in 1877 and organized three congregations in the district, serving them on foot during the long winter months. A doctrinal conservative, he became involved in considerable theological controversy in his new home. In March 1878 the three congregations organized into the "Icelandic Lutheran Congregations in Iceland" in opposition to the "Association of Icelandic Lutheran Churches in America" led by Rev. Jón Bjarnason.* In 1880 Thorlaksson moved to Pembina. Long ill with tuberculosis, he died in 1882 near Pembina in Mountain, North Dakota. See George J. Houser, *Pioneer Icelandic Pastor: The Life of the Reverend Paul Thorlaksson* (1990).

Thornton, Robert Stirton (1863-1936) Physician, politician. Born in Edinburgh, Scotland, he attended George Heriot School and the University of Edinburgh, which awarded him an MD in 1884. He came to Canada shortly after graduation and became the first physician in the Deloraine area of Manitoba. In 1908 he was elected MLA from Deloraine, and in 1915 he became minister of education in the government of Tobias Norris.* He served as president of the Medical Council of Canada in 1914, and shortly thereafter received an honorary degree from Queen's University. Thornton was active in the Masons, serving as grand master for Manitoba from 1900 to 1902. He died in British Columbia.

Thorpe, Jack (1881-1965) Lumberman. A bachelor, he lived his entire adult life in Winnipeg hotels. He began with the Queen's Hotel, moved to the Royal Alexandra Hotel when it opened in 1906, and then to the Fort Garry Hotel in 1913. He continued to live at the Fort Garry for another 52 years (until his death), staying longer than any other resident of the hotel. Thorpe was a well-known Winnipeg character.

Thorson, Charles (1890-1967) Film animator. Born in Winnipeg, he moved to Hollywood in 1934 as a Disney Studios character designer. He has been credited with the creation of Snow White, based on a Winnipeg waitress he had met in the 1920s. He also worked at Warner Brothers, and is credited there with the creation of Bugs Bunny. In the 1940s he returned to Winnipeg, where he created and drew the cartoon character Punkinhead, featured for many years in children's booklets produced by Eaton's. See Gene Walz, *Cartoon Charlie* (1998).

Thorsteinsdóttir, Torfhildur (Holm) (1845-1918) Author. Born in Skagastrond, Iceland, she studied in Reykjavík. In 1876 she accompanied Rannveig Jónasson to New Iceland (in Manitoba), remaining there on and off for nine years. She moved to Winnipeg in 1885 to teach, and she returned to Iceland in 1889. In Manitoba she recorded many stories of Icelandic immigrants, which were published posthumously in 1962 as *Folktales and Stories*. While in the province she also wrote a popular historical novel, *Brynjólfur Sveinsson biskup*, published in 1882, and completed several volumes of short stories. In 1891 she was awarded a controversial pension by the Icelandic government for her literary success. *DCB* XIV, 1,000-1,001.

Tinline, Milton John (1880-1968) Educator. Born in York County, Ontario, he came with his parents to the Elkhorn district of Manitoba and helped clear the family homestead. He was the first student to register at the Manitoba Agricultural College, graduating in 1911, when he was made assistant superintendent at the Brandon Experimental Farm. After some years there and in Saskatchewan, he became superintendent of the Brandon Experimental facility in 1924, serving until his retirement in 1946. He then became superintendent at the International Peace Gardens, directing the landscaping work there for many years. He is a member of the Manitoba Agricultural Hall of Fame.

Tipping, Frederick G. (1885-1973) Labour leader. Born in England, he came to Manitoba in 1905 as a Baptist preacher. He drifted from preaching into carpentry and then into industrial education as a schoolteacher (later associate principal) at Lord

Roberts School. Tipping was a moderate socialist and a member of the Social Democratic Party. He was elected president of the Winnipeg Trades and Labor Council later in 1917, and deposed a year later because as a member of the Mather Industrial Commission he had signed a report more critical of labour than of management. He objected especially to the Metal Trades Union going on strike while its dispute was before the commission, which intended to settle it. The vote calling for his suspension passed the council on 5 September 1918 by a vote of 49 to 10, and his resignation was accepted two weeks later. The movement to depose him was led by R.B. Russell,* and was indicative of a growing split between moderates and radicals on the Trades and Labor Council. He later helped to found the Manitoba CCF. He received the Manitoba Centennial Medal in 1970, and a senior citizens' block on Osborne Street was named after him in 1974. A frequent source for later interviews with historians about the Winnipeg General Strike, he was regarded by many of his contemporaries as discredited and outside the mainstream of events in that period.

Tisdale, Walter F. (1887-1960) Physician, wildlife conservationist. Born near Greenway, Manitoba, he was educated at Baldur and the University of Manitoba Medical School (1917). During WWI he went overseas to France with a British Field Hospital Unit, and he worked with the Red Cross in the Canadian North after the war. Tisdale opened his own medical practice in Winnipeg in 1925. He was very involved with the conservation of wildlife, becoming president of Ducks Unlimited, president of the Manitoba Game and Fish Association, and chair of the Manitoba Museum Board. He died in Winnipeg. There are papers at the PAM.

Tod, John (1794-1882) Fur trader. Born in Dumbartonshire, Scotland, he came to the HBC with the first party of Selkirk settlers in 1811. He was stationed at several posts in what is now Manitoba before being sent to New Caledonia in 1823. He was back in York Factory in 1834 when he met the governess Eliza Waugh, who was returning to England from Red River. They were married in England. The couple spent 1835-36 in Red River but soon moved to the Pacific coast again. Tod died in Oak Bay, British Columbia. *DCB* XI, 881-83.

Todd, William (c. 1784-1851) Physician. Born in Ireland, he joined the HBC in 1816 and spent a season in the Athabasca country in the midst of the competition with the NWC, in which he distinguished himself for his competence. He subsequently served in Red River (1821-22), at York Factory (1822-27), and at Fort Vancouver (1827-29). He then became a clerk at Brandon House. He was not regarded as a good trader, but he acquired a considerable reputation as a physician and surgeon. He held a number of modern views. He refused to bleed George Simpson* during his wife's troublesome pregnancy. Although Todd ended a spell of illness at York Factory called the "York Factory complaint," he himself became sick in the process and was weakened for the remainder of his life. At Fort Pelly in 1837, he began a program of cowpox inoculation among the Indians to prevent smallpox, the first use of the vaccine in the West. In the spring of 1851 he retired to Red River, where he died soon after. *DCB* VIII, 888-90.

Tolton, James Harvey (1898-1987) Farmer. Born in Bruce County, Ontario, he moved with his family to Woodnorth, Manitoba. He attended the Manitoba Agricultural College, where he was the gold medallist. He began breeding Shorthorn cattle and Yorkshire pigs in the 1920s, as well as growing registered seed grain. He was the youngest farmer to receive the Master Farmer's Award, which he won in 1934. He was active in his community and in livestock organizations. He was a long-time member of the Brandon University board of governors, and he received an honorary doctorate from that institution in 1976. After his retirement to Brandon he was active as an exhibitor at agricultural exhibitions. He is a member of the Manitoba Agricultural Hall of Fame.

Tomison, William (c. 1739-1829) Fur trader. Born in South Ronaldsay, Orkney Islands, he joined the HBC in 1760, spending seven years at York Factory. In 1767 he was sent inland to winter with the Aboriginals, and he remained there until 1790, when he became chief at York Factory. There he tenaciously defended the internal trade on the Saskatchewan River. He was called home by the HBC committee in 1796, and he returned a year later as inland chief. He retired in 1803 but was called back into service to head an unsuccessful expedition to the Athabasca country, finally returning home in 1810. *DCB* VI, 775-77.

Topolnicky, William (1893-1978) Credit union leader. Born in Serafenci in Western Ukraine, he attended the University of Prague, graduating in 1924. He came to Canada in 1927, and in 1930 he organized the Kalyna Ukrainian Co-operative Limited in Winnipeg. In 1940 he organized the Carpathia Credit Union Limited, which employed him from 1940 to 1974, and he assisted in the organization of many other credit unions in Manitoba. He was active in the Ukrainian War Veterans' Association and the Ukrainian Cultural and Educational Centre. He was awarded the Taras Shevchenko Medal in 1974. He died in Winnipeg.

Town, Tommy (1893-1957) Runner. Born in London, he came to Brandon in 1910. A long-distance runner, he won eight Canadian championships between 1919 and 1924, and ran in the Olympic Games of 1920 and 1924. He died in White Rock, British Columbia. He is a member of the Manitoba Sports Hall of Fame.

Traill, Walter J.S. (1847-1932) Fur trader, memoirist. Born in Canada, the youngest son of Catherine Parr Traill, he came west to Rupert's Land in 1866 as a clerk with the HBC. He was briefly imprisoned by Louis Riel in 1870 before being sent out of Red River. A memoir of his adventures in the West from 1866 to 1870 was compiled by Mae Atwood from his letters and journals and published as *In Rupert's Land: Memoirs of Walter Traill* (1970). Traill was appointed as postmaster of Fort Ellice in 1870 although he was only an apprentice clerk. By 1874 he was in charge of five HBC posts in the United States, including one at Grand Forks. From 1874 to 1876 he liquidated the HBC's holdings in North Dakota, and then, exhausted by the effort, he took a leave of absence and travelled in the southern United States for a year. He resigned from the HBC in 1877 and took charge of a St. Paul elevator company. He married Mary Gilbert in 1881. The couple lived in Pembina, then St. Paul, and from 1890 to 1910 in Kalispell, Montana, where Traill ran a ranch. He then moved to Grand Forks, British Columbia, where he built a fruit farm but was not successful. He subsequently headed south to the American Okanogan Valley, returning to British Columbia in 1927. For a biography, see Mae Atwood, *Dawn Across Canada: Oxcart to Railway in Ten Years* (1986).

Trémaudan, Auguste Henri de (1879-1929) Journalist, historian. Born in Saint-Chrysostome, Quebec, he was educated in France, returning to Canada in 1893. He founded *The Herald* at The Pas in 1911, and then ran several other Francophone newspapers. During the 1920s he published extensively on Louis Riel and the Red River Rebellion, based chiefly on access he was given to unpublished Riel papers. He was employed by the Union Nationale Métisse Saint-Joseph to write the *Histoire de la Nation Métisse,* which was completed in 1929 and published in 1936. He died in Los Angeles, where he had retired for his health in 1924.

Trifunov, Jim (1903-1993) Wrestler and wrestling administrator. Born in Regina, he won ten Canadian wrestling championships between 1923 and 1932 and wrestled in the 1924, 1928, and 1932 Olympics, winning a bronze medal in 1928. He was transferred to Winnipeg by the Sifton Publishing Company in the 1930s. In 1967 he organized the Pan Am wrestling championships, and he subsequently lobbied for a permanent home for the Manitoba Sports Hall of Fame, of which he is a member. He received the Order of Canada in 1981.

Trueman, Walter Harley (1870-1951) Lawyer. Born in New Brunswick, he practised law there before coming to Winnipeg in 1908. He drafted the Initiative and Referendum Act in 1915, major legislation based on American populist precedents. He defended William Ivens* and John Queen* against charges of sedition springing from the Winnipeg General Strike in 1919, insisting in his jury address, "you cannot indict ideas." He was retained to take R.B. Russell's* appeal to the Privy Council, but could not get the appeal heard because it was a criminal matter. He was appointed to the Court of Appeal in 1923. He had a hair-trigger temper and was regarded as erratic. In 1928 he conducted a federal enquiry into the Maulson affair, involving the dismissal of a judge. He retired finally in 1947 with his deteriorating mental state quite evident.

Tuckwell, Alfred J. (1854-1911) Educator, musician. Born in England, he was educated at Leeds Grammar School and Queen's College, Oxford (BA). He moved to Winnipeg in 1887 to establish the Winnipeg Preparatory School, which he headed until he retired in 1909. Tuckwell was one of the early choirmasters of Winnipeg, serving as musical director of several Anglican churches, including Holy Trinity, All Saints', and Christ Church. He was an active golfer and a member of the Winnipeg Cricket Team.

Tupper, James Stewart (1851-1915) Lawyer. Born in Amherst, Nova Scotia, he was the eldest son of Sir Charles Tupper. He was educated at McGill University and called to the Ontario bar in 1875. In 1882 he moved to Winnipeg to go into partnership with Hugh John Macdonald* in a firm that later became Macdonald, Tupper, Phippen, and Tupper. He built and resided in a large mansion in Armstrong's Point.

Tupper, R. La Touche (1845-1904) Office-holder. Born in Omemee, Canada, he came to Manitoba in 1874 as a surveyor after service in the Union army in the American Civil War. He subsequently explored for oil in the Riding Mountain district. He served with the 91st Battalion in the North-West Rebellion in 1885. Tupper held a number of municipal, provincial, and federal offices during his career, including superintendent of government telegraphs in the North-West Territories, Winnipeg licence inspector, Manitoba chief of police, and superintendent of the fish hatchery in Selkirk.

Turnbull, Jessie See McEwen, Jessie (Turnbull).

Turner, James (1826-1889) Wholesale merchant, senator. Born in Glasgow, Scotland, he was educated at Glasgow High School. He came to Canada in 1848 and established a wholesale grocery business in Hamilton a few years later. He added a branch of his business at Fort Garry in 1867 and was a major booster of the Northwest. In 1869 he toured the region with Joseph Howe.* He constructed the first brick store in Winnipeg in 1875, and he was appointed a senator in 1884.

Turner, Ronald David (1915-1965) Aviation pioneer. Born in Carman, he was educated at Winnipeg schools and the University of Manitoba (BA 1935).

He was a champion swimmer at university, setting a record for a swim at Lake of the Woods. He received his law degree in 1939 and joined the RCAF as a pilot officer, being discharged in 1946 as a wing commander. He was elected MLA for RCAF veterans in 1945, and later served as MLA for Winnipeg South. In 1951 he became provincial treasurer, later adding the portfolio of industry and commerce, then that of provincial railway commissioner. His budget presentations were highly prized for their detail. He resigned all his appointments in 1956 to become president of TransAir Limited.

Turnor, Philip (c. 1751-c. 1800) Fur trader, surveyor. Originally a Middlesex farmer, he joined the HBC in 1778 and served at York Factory as a surveyor. He was ordered to map the route to Cumberland House, and in 1780 he surveyed the route from Albany House to Henley House and Gloucester House. He was in charge of Brunswick House in 1782, and he established a new post at Abitibi in 1784. The HBC paid him 20 guineas for his maps in 1788. He taught surveying to Peter Fidler* and David Thompson* in 1789-90 at Cumberland House. After his retirement he taught navigation. *DCB* IV, 741-42.

Tuttle, Charles Richard (b. 1848) Journalist, author. Born in Nova Scotia, he taught school there and engaged in newspaper work in Boston before coming to Winnipeg in 1879 to found the *Winnipeg Daily Times*. He was editor only until 1880. He served as census commissioner for Manitoba in 1881, and later was a member of an exploring party to Hudson Bay. He moved to Chicago around 1885, and there he wrote extensively on American local history. While in Manitoba he assisted Donald Gunn* in preparing for publication *A History of Manitoba from the Earliest Times* (1880). He also wrote *Tuttle's Popular History of the Dominion of Canada* (1877), *Royalty in Canada* (1878), and *Our North Land* (1885).

Umfreville, Edward (c. 1755-c. 1789) Fur trader, writer. First engaged by the HBC in 1771, he worked as an accountant at Severn House, then at York Factory. He was imprisoned by the French in 1782, and after his return to London he wrote newspaper letters highly critical of the HBC. He later worked for the NWC on the North Saskatchewan River. In 1790 he published *The Present State of Hudson's Bay,* a knowledgeable account based largely on the work of HBC officers. *DCB* IV, 742-43.

Usher, Janet Wilkie (1902-1979) Administrator. Born in Graysville, Manitoba, she was educated at the University of Manitoba. In 1926 she became secretary to the dean of Agriculture at the university, a position she held to her retirement in 1967. A reference section in the Agriculture reading room is named after her. She died in Vancouver.

Ustvolsky, Stefan (fl. 1902-8) Clergyman. Little is known about his early life. He came to the United States in 1903, claiming to have been consecrated by a dissident Russian orthodox patriarch, and moved to Winnipeg in 1903, where he soon established the All-Russian Patriarchal Orthodox Church, independent of both Catholic and Orthodox control. Within a few years he left for Russia, and upon his return without legitimacy or funds his church disintegrated. He returned to Russia for good in 1908. *DCB* XII, 1044-45.

Valade, Marie Louise (1809-1861) Grey Nun. Born in Sainte-Anne-des-Plaines, Lower Canada, she was one-quarter Indian. In 1843 she was proclaimed superior-foundress of the convent that her order intended to set up in Red River, and she led three of her colleagues west via canoe in 1844, arriving at the Forks on 21 June. She was re-elected superior in 1848, and she travelled east to Montreal for a general chapter meeting of her order in 1849, returning in 1850 with reinforcements for the convent. She headed east again in 1850, accompanying Louis Riel, Daniel McDougall, and Louis Schmidt* to schools in Lower Canada and again returning with fresh recruits after a difficult journey. Under Mother Valade's supervision, by 1857 the Grey Nuns had added a boarding school and an orphanage to the mission schools they had created in 1844, and they undertook nursing services for the community as well. Mother Valade died of cancer at Red River in 1861, only a few months after the destruction of the second St. Boniface Cathedral. See Estelle Mitchell, *The Grey Nuns of Montreal and the Red River Settlement 1844-1984* (1984).

Van Bellegham, Joseph B. (1902-1967) Politician. Born in St. Vital, he attended Provencher School and St. Boniface College. He was joint owner of the Tourist Hotel until his retirement in 1960. He served as MLA for St. Boniface from 1953 to 1957 and as mayor of the City of St. Boniface from 1954 to 1960. He was a St. Boniface alderman for 18 years between 1932 and 1965. For many years he was the Belgian consul for Manitoba. Van Bellegham was a fourth-degree Knight of Columbus. He died in St. Boniface.

Van Slooten, Harriet (1910-1965) YWCA official. Born in Holland, she was a leader in the Dutch underground during WWII. In 1952 she immigrated to Canada and became an executive director of the YWCA, first in Brantford and latterly in Winnipeg, where she died.

Van Slyck, Winnifred (1910-1992) Community worker. Born in Winnipeg, she moved to Dugald, Manitoba, in 1929, and there she became involved in all aspects of community life. She was an active painter and was co-author and illustrator of a history of the Springfield district, published in 1977. Van Slyck was the moving force behind the establishment of the Dugald Costume Museum, which opened in 1983 with herself as president emeritus and curator. She was awarded the Margaret McWilliams Medal in 1972 and the gold seal from the Red River Valley Historical Society in 1978. She became a member of the Order of Canada in 1985.

Vanstone, Charles Morley (1870-1953) Physician, insurance executive. Born in Kincardine, Ontario, he moved to Manitoba with his family in 1878. He attended Winnipeg Collegiate and the University of Manitoba, where he finished his medical studies. In 1894 he moved to Wawanesa to open a medical practice and pharmacy. He worked as a country doctor in Wawanesa until 1912, when he moved to North Battleford, Saskatchewan, to raise thoroughbred horses. In 1922, he was invited to return to Wawanesa to head the troubled Wawanesa Mutual Insurance Company, which had been founded in the town in 1896 during Vanstone's tenure as local doctor. Despite having no insurance experience, he led the company to recovery and to new sources of insurance business, especially in automobile insurance.

He retired in 1943, moved to Burnaby, Britsh Columbia, and eventually returned to Winnipeg, where he died. See Dr. Robert Harvey, *Pioneers of Manitoba* (1970), and Wawanesa Mutual Insurance Company, *Old Pathways, New Horizons: A History of the Wawanesa Mutual Insurance Company 1896-1996* (1996).

Veitch, Henry George (1881-1960) Printer. Born in Scotland, he came to Winnipeg in 1910 and established the Wallingford Press. He was president until his retirement in 1954. He died in Trail, British Columbia.

Verey, George (c. 1830s-1881) Physician. Educated in London, England, he studied medicine at St. Bartholomew's Hospital before beginning a peripatetic life in Australia, the Far East, and Montana. In 1871 he moved to Fort Edmonton as an HBC clerk, and in 1877 he opened a medical partnership in Winnipeg with James Stewart. He soon returned to Edmonton and died there of a drug overdose. *DCB* XI, 900-901.

Vincent, Arthur James (1913-1998) Aviator, businessman. Born in Toronto, he learned to fly while working for Inco. During WWII he was a flying instructor for the RCAF, becoming chief instructor of the Air Commonwealth Training Program. He moved to Winnipeg after the war and became a grain dealer, serving as president of Smith, Vincent and Company Limited from 1958. He headed the Murphy Foundation, which contributed to many Winnipeg cultural institutions. Vincent was active in the summer life of Winnipeg Beach.

Vincent, Thomas (c. 1776-1832) Fur trader. He joined the HBC in 1790 and became head of Brandon House in 1806. In 1814 he became governor of the Southern Department. He was made a chief factor when the HBC and NWC merged in 1821. *DCB* VI, 794-95.

Wachna, Theodosy (1874-1960) Immigrant agent. Born in the Carpathian Mountains of Ukraine, he emigrated to Pennsylvania in 1894 and to Canada in 1897. He became a local agent for immigration officials, helping many of his countrymen to homestead in the Stuartburn area of Manitoba. He and his wife opened several general stores in the region, which served as post offices and social centres. He helped organize the Municipality of Stuartburn. He is a member of the Manitoba Agricultural Hall of Fame. See Mary Paximadis, *Look Who's Coming: The Wachna Story* (1976).

Wade, Frederick Coate (1860-1924) Journalist, politician. Born in Bowmanville, Canada, he was educated at the University of Toronto and worked for the *Toronto Globe* before coming west in 1886. He was called to the Manitoba bar that year and was elected first president of the Young Liberal Club of Winnipeg. Wade wrote editorials for the *Manitoba Free Press* from 1886 to 1888, and later was an active essayist on the Manitoba School Question. His style was described as "slashing" and ad hominem. He wrote a large number of controversial pamphlets on issues of the day, especially the Manitoba School Question. He left Manitoba for the Yukon in 1896 and finally settled in British Columbia. He was appointed agent general for British Columbia in the United Kingdom in 1918. He died in London.

Wade, Henry Gerald (1875-1953) Community pioneer. Born in Port Hope, Ontario, he was educated at Ridley College, where he was an active rugby player. He came to Winnipeg in 1910 to manage the municipal department of the Willson Stationery Company, where he remained until his retirement in 1947. He was a charter member of the Winnipeg Rugby Club. In 1914 he was president of the Canadian Literary Society. Wade lectured widely on literary matters, gave an annual reading of "A Christmas Carol," and was honorary life president of the Dickens Fellowship. In 1921 he published *When Dickens Came to Canada*. His papers are at the PAM.

Wagner, William (1820-1901) Immigration promoter, politician. Born in Prussia, he was educated as an engineer and architect there before becoming active in the revolutions of 1848, which resulted in his immigration to the United States. He came to Canada in 1850 and worked as a land surveyor. In 1860 he was appointed immigration commissioner, and he spent several years in Germany promoting immigration to Canada. He came to Manitoba in 1870 as a government land surveyor and wrote about his experiences in articles that were published in 1872 as *Einwanderung nach Manitoba*. This work, along with others written by Wagner, served as a German immigration pamphlet for many years. Wagner settled at Ossowa near Poplar Point and was an active promoter of dairy farming in Manitoba, becoming president of the Manitoba Dairy Association. A Conservative, he served as the representative for Woodlands in the provincial legislature from 1883 to 1886 and held a federal appointment as swamp lands commissioner from 1886 to 1896. He was later appointed an assistant sergeant-at-arms in the legislature. He died in Winnipeg. In addition to the work previously mentioned, he was the author of *Anleitung für Diejenigen, welche sich in Canada . . .*(1861),*Canada, ein Land für deutsche Auswanderung*(1861), and *Das Petroleum, aus Canada bezogen, in seinem Werthe für Deutschland* (1863). His survey field books are at the PAM. *DCB* XIII, 1,062-63.

Walker, Corliss Powers ("C.P.," 1853-1942) Impresario. Born in the United States, he moved to Winnipeg in 1897 as a theatrical impresario. He began with the Bijou Theatre as part of his Red River Valley Theatre Circuit, which was connected with a New York syndicate and possessed several touring theatres in North Dakota. Walker's venues made it possible for him to bring touring companies to Winnipeg and the adjacent United States for major runs. He developed the Walker Theatre (1906) in conjunction with Montreal architect Howard Colton Stone. For some time it was managed by William Blake Lawrence. See Reg Skene, "C.P. Walker and the Business of Theatre: Merchandizing Entertainment in a Continental Context," in *The Political Economy of Manitoba*, ed. James Silver and Jeremy Hull (1990), 128-50; Ruth Walker Harvey, *Curtain Time* (1949).

Walker, David Mair (1835-1920) Lawyer, judge. Born in Woodhouse, Norfolk, Upper Canada, he was admitted to the bar in 1861 and was subsequently gazetted a captain in the 39th Regiment, seeing active service in 1864-65. He came to Winnipeg in 1875 to become city solicitor, serving until 1878, when he was elected MLA. He then served as attorney general from 1878 to 1882, when he was appointed to the county court. He retired from the court in 1914. From 1911 he was also a police magistrate for the City of Winnipeg. He helped to found the Manitoba Jockey Club and the Manitoba Club. His papers are at the PAM.

Walker, Harriet (Anderson) ("Hattie," 1865-1943) Theatrical producer. Born in New York City, she won an elocution contest at the age of 13 and was soon on the stage. Her first part on Broadway was in *The Lost Children* in 1879. In her first years she played boys. She later appeared in light opera. In 1897 she accompanied her husband, C.P. Walker,* to Winnipeg.

She never appeared on the stage professionally in Manitoba, but she produced musical comedy, light opera, and drama in the city for many years. She was a charter member of the Canadian Women's Press Club, and for many years she wrote a theatre column under the pen name "Rosa Sub." She founded the American Women's Club of Winnipeg in 1917. See Ruth Walker Harvey's autobiographical memoir, *Curtain Time* (1949). There is also a manuscript biography by Victoria Morris at the Manitoba Legislative Library.

Walker, John Bruce (b. 1861) Immigration agent. Born in Troon, Ayrshire, Scotland, he was educated at Ayr Academy. He was a member of the Scottish football team that defeated England in 1882, the year he came to Canada as editor of the *Brantford Expositor*. In 1903 he entered the federal service, working for several years as government agent in Glasgow. There he publicized Canada in all ways possible, distributing handbills at football matches and employing the cinemas in the larger towns. He himself lectured with stereopticon slides. He disguised himself as an immigrant on one occasion to expose a steamship agent who was luring people with false promises. Canadian immigration from Scotland increased substantially while he was in Glasgow. He was subsequently sent to London, and he was recalled to Winnipeg in 1908 to become commissioner of immigration. He was a Presbyterian and a member of the Greenock Burns Club.

Wallace, Lila Bell (Acheson) (1890-1984) Publisher. Born in Virden, Manitoba, the daughter of a Presbyterian minister, she was educated at the University of Oregon (graduated 1917) and then worked as a social worker in the United States. She married book salesman DeWitt Wallace in 1921, and the two founded the *Reader's Digest* in 1922. She owned 48 per cent of the stock and was active in the editing for many years. She was a director of the New York Central Railroad from 1954 to 1959, the first woman to serve as a railway director in the United States. Her estate at her death was valued at half a billion dollars.

Wallace, Robert Charles (1881-1955) Educator. Born in the Orkney Islands, he was educated at Edinburgh University and the University of Goettingen. In 1910 he was appointed a lecturer in geology at the University of Manitoba. Wallace was elected a fellow of the Royal Society of Canada in

1921 and became a Companion of the Order of St. Michael and St. George in 1944. He published extensively on the geology of Manitoba, his works including *The Geological Formations of Manitoba* (1925). He became president of the University of Alberta in 1928 and principal of Queen's University in 1936, and retired in 1951. In later years he became interested in humanistic questions, and he was the author of *A Liberal Education in the Modern World* (1932) and *Religion, Science, and the Modern World* (1952).

Wallace, William ("Willie," 1859-1943) Pioneer. Born in Scotland, Wallace immigrated to Manitoba in 1881 with his father and younger brother. The family acquired a homestead in the Shellmouth region in 1882. Wallace became an organist, choir director, and music teacher in the Presbyterian Church of Shellmouth in 1886, continuing until 1930. In 1887 he became secretary-treasurer of the Municipality of Shellmouth, while still continuing to work the family farm. Unmarried, he was joined by his sister and her husband in 1904. After being injured in 1909 he moved to Shellmouth and became postmaster, a position he held until 1936. He donated his extensive manuscript correspondence to Brandon College (now Brandon University) in 1943. A selection of these letters, covering 1881-86 and edited by Kenneth S. Coates and William R. Morrison, was published in 1991 as *My Dear Maggie . . . Letters from a Western Manitoba Pioneer.*

Wallbridge, Lewis (1816-1887) Politician, judge. Born in Belleville, Upper Canada, he studied at Upper Canada College and articled at law in the office of Robert Baldwin. He was called to the bar in 1839. He won the riding of Hastings South as a moderate Reformer in 1857, especially advocating representation by population. He became Speaker of the Canadian House in 1863, presiding over the historic debates on Confederation in 1865 before retiring from politics in 1867. He re-entered the political arena 10 years later as a Conservative but was defeated in Hastings West. In 1882 he was named chief justice of Manitoba, ostensibly because he was familiar with many Manitoba lawyers and understood land law, but probably more because he was a crony of Sir John A. Macdonald. His appointment provoked the resignation of Mr. Justice Miller.* His early involvement in the trial of Louis Riel before improperly sitting on the Appeal Court panel has recently provided a legal argument for parliamentary reversal of the 1885 sentence of treason against Riel. He acted as a mediator between John Norquay* and Sir John A. Macdonald until his death. Wallbridge had a nasty temper and on one occasion threw a statute book across the courtroom. He died in Winnipeg. There are family papers in the NAC. See Ronald J. Olesky, "Louis Riel and the Crown Letters," *Canadian Lawyer* (February 1998): 12-15. *DCB* XI, 908-9.

Walsh, Aquila (1823-1885) Civil servant. Born in Upper Canada, he was educated in London District Grammar School and became a civil engineer. He was first elected MLA in 1861. In 1867 he was elected to the Commons. He aspired to the speakership, the first of a number of appointments he hoped to receive for his loyalty to the Conservative Party. Finally, in 1882, he was appointed commissioner of Crown lands for Manitoba and the North-West Territories. He then started to complain about his salary and continued to do so until his death in Winnipeg. *DCB* XI, 909-10.

Walsh, Irene (1888-1954) Liberal leader, sportswoman. Born in Arnprior, Ontario, she came to Winnipeg in 1918. She was prominent in Liberal circles in Manitoba, serving as president of the Liberal Women's Association of Greater Winnipeg in 1937 and of the South Winnipeg Women's Liberal Club in 1946. She also served as president of the Manitoba Ladies' Curlers Association, the Riverview Ladies' Lawn Bowling Association, and the Fort Rouge Curling Club. She organized the Catholic Women's League in Manitoba for many years.

Walsh, James Morrow (1843-1905) Police officer. Born in Prescott, Canada, he was active in the militia during the Fenian troubles and was appointed an ensign in the first Ontario Battalion of the Wolseley Expedition, resigning in April 1870 to get married. He was appointed in 1873 as sub-inspector of the NWMP, and helped recruit the first contingent. He was soon promoted to inspector (1874) and superintendent (1875). He was sent to the Cypress Hills to command B division in 1875, where he became involved with Sitting Bull and the Sioux Indians. American journalists referred to him as "Sitting Bull's boss." The Canadian government regarded him as too sympathetic to the Sioux and he was removed from active service in 1881 and pushed into retirement in 1883. He subsequently managed the Dominion Coal, Coke and Transportation Company, which opened the coal mines of the Souris district of Manitoba. Walsh got his revenge on the NWMP in 1897, when he was appointed Commissioner of the Yukon District, and also became superintendent of the NWMP and commissioner of police for the North-West Territories. A year later he was criticised for his failure to put the administration of mining claims on a judicious footing, and retired to Brockville, Ontario, where he died. See "James Walsh: Frontiersman," in *Canada: An Historical Magazine* 2, no.1 (1974-75), 28-42. A fictional account is in Iris Allan, *White Sioux: Major Walsh of the Mounted Police* (1969). See also Sharon Pollock, *Walsh* (1973). His papers are at the PAM. *DCB* XIII, 1071-72.

Walsh, William James (1917-1971) Sportsman. Born in Haileybury, Ontario, he moved with his parents to Winnipeg in 1917 and attended Lord Roberts and Kelvin Schools. After graduation he entered the Comptroller General's Office of the Province of Manitoba and worked there all his life. Walsh served with the Royal Winnipeg Rifles in WWII, winning the Oak Leaf and the Croix de Guerre. He skipped Canadian-championship curling teams in 1952 and 1956 and was an active member of the Fort Rouge Curling Club.

Walton, Charles H.A. (1906-1981) Physician. Born in Winnipeg, he grew up in Mather, Manitoba, and Victoria, British Columbia. He was educated at the University of Manitoba, where he was the president of the students' union in 1930-31. In 1932, he published a study of the racial incidence of tuberculosis in Manitoba. Appointed demonstrator in medicine at the University of Manitoba in 1935, he worked with Dr. Margaret J. Dudley on atmospheric studies of pollen, spores and dust. Walton also built up a medical practice in East Kildonan and served as municipal health officer. During WWII he served in the Royal Canadian Army Medical Corps, stationed in England at No. Five Canadian General Hospital. Upon demobilization he joined the Winnipeg Clinic and was its chair from 1961 to 1971. In 1952 he was appointed to the Medical Council of Canada, serving until 1977. His memoirs, mainly about medical service during the war, were published in 1980 as *A Medical Odyssey: Vignettes of People and Events at Home and Abroad.*

Wapinesiw (fl. 1755-72) Cree "leading Indian." First noted by Anthony Henday in 1755, he commanded

20 canoes and was lured to York Factory, which he visited regularly for 15 years. The number of his canoes grew from 20 to 30. After 1770 he worked for the Canadian fur traders from Montreal. *DCB* IV, 761.

Warkentin, John (1850-1948) Cleric. Born in Niederchortiza, Russia, he immigrated to Manitoba in 1879 with his parents and settled in Haskett. He taught in the village school of Hoffnungsfeld from 1881 to 1887 and began farming on the outskirts of Winkler in 1888. In 1891 he was baptized and became an avid churchgoer. He became leader of the Mennonite Brethren congregation of Winkler in 1906, remaining in that capacity until his retirement in 1931. He died in Winkler.

Waterhouse, John Fereday Preston (1877-1970) Musician. Born in Bilston, England, he came to Winnipeg in 1914 from Minneapolis, where he had been a violinist in the Minneapolis Symphony. He was concertmaster of the Winnipeg Orchestral Club from 1923 to 1927 and conductor of the Winnipeg String Orchestra from 1934 to 1936. In both his teaching and his performing, he introduced many English works previously unfamiliar to his audience. He taught violin for over fifty years from his house on Furby Street. He was made a fellow of the Associated Board of the Royal Academy of Music and received an honorary doctorate from the University of Manitoba in 1965. A file of his reviews is at the PAM.

Watson, Gordon Pendrigh (1915-1998) Born in Winnipeg, he attended Lord Roberts and Kelvin Schools. After studying music under F.D. Bull and Gwendda Owen-Davies* of Winnipeg, he received a scholarship at the Royal Academy of Music. During WWI, he was employed as a pianist by the London County Council and the BBC, as well as touring to entertain soldiers. He was a prominent accompanist in England until returning to Canada in 1952, and he accompanied Gracie Fields on her Canadian tour in 1953. He taught music at Portage la Prairie schools from 1952 to 1975, and composed a good deal of music, some of which is still used as test pieces by music festivals. His entry for a centennial song won first prize in Manitoba. He twice served as organist and choir leader at St. Mary's Anglican Church, Portage la Prairie, the last time from 1975 to 1995.

Watson, Robert (1853-1913) Politician. Born in Elora, Canada, to Scottish parents, he became a mill-wright and moved to Manitoba in 1876. He was elected to the Commons as a Liberal in 1882 and 1887, and was the only Liberal from west of the Lakehead in those parliaments. He was re-elected in 1891 but resigned to become minister of public works in the Greenway government. He was elected to the legislature in 1892 and 1896 but was defeated in 1900, the year he was called to the Senate. His correspondence (1893-1900) is at the PAM.

Watson, Robert (1882-1948) Editor, author. Born in Scotland, he came to Canada in 1908. He was employed by the HBC from 1917 to 1932, serving as editor of *The Beaver*, among other duties. He published a number of children's books, such as *A Boy of the Great North West* (1930).

Watson, Rosetta Ernestine Carr (1845-1907) Photographer. Born in Drummond Township, Canada, she trained as a photographer with William Notman. She moved to Winnipeg in 1883 and a year later purchased a local photographic business, which she named the American Art Gallery. The work of this studio was technologically advanced and of high quality. Watson was especially admired for her portraiture, and she won many prizes. In 1893 her competitors boycotted the Winnipeg Industrial Exhibition because she had been given exclusive rights to photograph it. She entered all the photography classes and won all the prizes. She died in Ottawa. *DCB* XIII, 1,077.

Watt, Mary Jane ("Jennie," 1867-1933) Women's leader. Born in Woodstock, Ontario, she came west to Birtle, Manitoba, with her husband in 1892. She was secretary of the Birtle Women's Institute when it was organized in 1910, later serving as president until she became provincial president of Women's Institutes. Subsequently she was elected the national president, in which capacity she promoted a women's exhibit at the CNE in Toronto. She was awarded an honorary diploma in home economics by the Manitoba Agricultural College in 1926. She is a member of the Manitoba Agricultural Hall of Fame.

Waugh, Harriet Lily (d. 1931) Volunteer worker. Born in Winnipeg, she was educated at St. Mary's Academy and the girls' department of St. John's College. She was the first president of the first women's curling club in Manitoba. In 1915, when her husband, Richard Deans Waugh* was mayor of Winnipeg, she helped organize the Returned Soldiers' Association, and she served as president of its women's auxiliary for five years.

Waugh, Richard (c. 1830-1908) Journalist. Born in Melrose, Scotland, he worked as a builder and mason, designing and constructing farmhouses and churches across Scotland. He came to Manitoba in 1881 and continued as a builder. He gradually moved into agricultural journalism and developed a connection with the *Nor'West Farmer,* becoming a member of the paper's editorial staff by 1886 and serving as co-editor or editor until 1904. He was an advocate of mixed farming, including the dairy industry. For many years he was active as "A Scot Abroad," writing a column under that name for the *Scotsman* of Edinburgh and encouraging Scots in Winnipeg to maintain their ties to the motherland. He was so well regarded that, at the time of his death in Winnipeg, the *Nor'West Farmer* organized a subscription for a portrait to be hung at the Manitoba Agricultural College. *DCB* XIII, 1,078-79.

Waugh, Richard Deans (1868-1938) Municipal politician. Born in Melrose, Scotland, he came to Manitoba in 1881 with his parents. After spending six years in the law office of Glass and Glass, he turned to real estate, becoming a founder of the Winnipeg Real Estate Exchange and the Winnipeg Industrial Bureau. He served as chair of the Winnipeg Public Parks Board from 1904 to 1908, when he was elected to the Board of Control. In 1911 he was elected mayor, and he served, with a one-term break, until 1916. While mayor he championed the cause of public playgrounds. In 1920 he was appointed by the British government to the Saarland Commission, which administered the Saar area while its coal assets were taken over by the French. He resigned because he felt the arrangement, which was part of the Treaty of Versailles, was unfair. He was an ardent curler who served as president of the Granite Curling Club and the Manitoba Curling Association, and he was also honorary president of the Winnipeg Cricket Association and the Winnipeg Swimming Club. A gardening enthusiast, he created the Children's Garden Competition in the city's elementary schools. His papers are at the PAM.

Webb, Ralph Humphreys (1887-1945) Municipal politician, military officer. Born on a British liner sailing between England and India, he was educated at Westminster. He came to Canada in 1902 and to Winnipeg in 1906. He operated his own lumber business until he went overseas in August 1914 as a lieutenant. He had a distinguished military career in WWI, winning the Military Cross, the Distinguished Service Order, and the Croix de Guerre. By December 1917 he was a lieutenant-colonel commanding the 47th Battalion. Upon his return to Winnipeg in the 1920s he managed the Marlborough Hotel. He was noted for attempting to attract conventions to Winnipeg and for publicizing the city as a tourist destination. He was a seven-time mayor of Winnipeg, from 1925 to 1928 and 1930 to 1934. He was elected MLA in 1932 and re-elected in 1936. In 1939 he was appointed to organize the Canadian army's catering and messing services, and he spent WWII in the quartermaster-general's department at Ottawa. He died in Ottawa.

Weir, Frederick James (1912-1976) Horticulturalist. Born in Lakehurst, Ontario, he was educated at Lindsay Collegiate Institute and the Ontario Agricultural College. He served with the RCAF from 1941 to 1946, participating in WWII as a bomber navigator in Egypt, Malta, and Libya and later as a squadron bombing leader on Sunderland flying boats. In 1949 he became the Manitoba provincial horticulturalist. He wrote hundreds of articles on horticulture and was an active judge at horticultural events. He was a deacon of Oxford United Church and an amateur musician. He died in Kenora, Ontario.

Weir, Walter (1929-1985) Politician. Born in High Bluff, Manitoba, he was educated there and in Portage la Prairie. In 1953 he moved to Minnedosa, where he owned a funeral home until 1963. He was active in municipal affairs in Minnedosa and was elected MLA for Minnedosa in 1959. He became minister of municipal affairs in 1961 and minister of public works in 1962. When Duff Roblin stepped down from the premiership in 1967, Weir was elected as his successor by the Progressive Conservative Party at a convention in November. He was an outspoken fiscal conservative. He and his government were defeated at the polls in the 1969 election. Soon after, he left politics and moved to Ontario, but he returned to Minnedosa in 1976. Two years later he was appointed vice-chair of the Manitoba Public Utilities Board and later to the Manitoba Assessment Review Committee. He died in Minnedosa.

Wells, David (c. 1897-1918) Conscientious objector. Born in England, he was a student at a Pentecostal school in Winnipeg in 1918 when he was sentenced to two years' imprisonment for refusing to be conscripted. He was pronounced mad within a few days of his arrival at Stony Mountain Penitentiary, and died soon thereafter, many maintaining he had been brutally treated in prison. *DCB* XIV, 1,046-47.

Wells, John Hampson ("Cactus Jack," 1911-1999) Sports broadcaster. Born in Moose Jaw, Saskatchewan, and educated locally, he began broadcasting hockey in Saskatoon in 1935. In 1941 he moved to Winnipeg to CJRC radio, becoming known for his curling and football announcing. For many years he was the play-by-play announcer for the Winnipeg Blue Bombers, and he was Winnipeg CBC's first sportscaster in 1954. In a 58-year broadcasting career in Winnipeg, he worked for CJRC, CJOB, CJAY (CKY), and CBC. Wells was notorious for his loud sports coats and his mispronunciation of names. A member of the Canadian Football and Broadcasting Halls of Fame, he died in Winnipeg.

West, J. Pender (b. 1868) Architect. Born in Suffolk, England, he was educated in Bungay before apprenticing as an architect. He spent 10 years practising his profession in the Cape Colony before coming in 1909 to Winnipeg, where he joined the architectural staff of the city power department. He designed Hydro Sub-Station No. 1 at 54 King Street (1910-11). He was also active in the city planning movement before WWI. In 1912 he entered private practice with D.W.F. Nichols, designing the Skjaldbreid Apartments at 745 Wolseley (1912).

West, John (1778-1845) Cleric. Born in Surrey, England, he was educated at St. Edmund Hall, Oxford, and assumed curacies in Essex until he volunteered for missionary service with the Church Missionary Society. He was appointed chaplain to the HBC in 1819 and left for Red River in May 1820, fully committed to evangelization of the Indians rather than service to the settlers. He saw the education of children as the most promising technique, and quickly established a school in a log cabin in Kildonan which taught Christianity and practical subjects. Unlike the earlier education scheme recommended by Lord Selkirk,* however, he did not emphasize the need to remain in touch with Native skills. West upset the settlers by opposing marriage "according to the custom of the country," and forcing some Company officers to formalize their relationships with Indian and Métis women. He refused to baptize an illegitimate child. He travelled widely across Rupert's Land, but the fur traders became fearful that his evangelization would ultimately harm the fur trade. He went home in 1823, supposedly temporarily, but he never returned. He published his journal in 1824. West spent the remainder of his life as rector of Chettle, Dorsetshire, England, becoming a domestic chaplain to Baron Duncannon in 1831. See his *The Substance of a Journal during a Residence at the Red River Colony, British North America; and Frequent Excursions among the North-West American Indians, in the years 1820, 1821, 1822, 1823* (1824). W. B. Heeney's *John West and His Red River Mission* (1920) is a standard study, but see also I.H.S. Stratton, "The Work and Ideas of John West, 1778-1845" (MA diss., University of Durham, 1977) and Vera Fast, "The Protestant Missionary and Fur Trade Society: Initial Contact in the Hudson's Bay Territory, 1820-1850" (PhD diss., University of Manitoba, 1984). There are papers at the PAM. *DCB* VII, 900-903.

West, Phyllis Ellen (1905-1991) Actor. Born in Yorkshire, England, she immigrated to Canada in 1952 to work with Sanford Evans Publishers. In 1960 she auditioned for a part in *Gaslight* at the Manitoba Theatre Centre and began an acting career that kept her busy for the remainder of her life. She subsequently appeared with Actors Showcase, Fantasy Theatre for Children, and Rainbow Stage. West did television appearances with Burton Cummings and a film entitled *Gentle Sinners*, and was well known for her television commercials as the "Birt's Saddlery lady." She was known as "the Grand Duchess." Her last performance was in 1990. She died in Winnipeg.

Westbrook, Henry Shaver (1842-1913) Municipal politician. Born in Oakland, Canada, he came to Winnipeg in the mid-1870s to open an implement dealership in partnership with Frank Fairchild. In 1885 he won a highly contested mayoralty campaign, but he returned to private business after his term in office. He retired to Selkirk, Manitoba.

Westwood, William James (1888-1962) Politician. Born near Rapid City, Manitoba, he attended Brandon College. He was a bank manager at Roblin when he was first elected MLA for the Roblin constituency in 1917. In 1920 he became secretary-treasurer of the Municipality of Shell River, serving until 1946, when he moved to Russell to operate a hardware store. Westwood represented Roblin again as a Liberal Progressive MLA from 1932 to 1936.

Wheeler, Charles Henry (1838-1917) Architect, musician, and critic. Born in Lutterworth, England, he immigrated to Winnipeg with his wife and six children in 1882. He first came to public notice as a bass soloist at Holy Trinity Anglican Church and subsequently designed a new church building for Holy Trinity. By 1889 his architectural firm, which included two of his sons, was a major one in the city. His last building was designed in 1906. Wheeler described himself as an "ardent Gothicist." He remained active in music and drama, becoming choirmaster at Knox Presbyterian Church in 1885 and a columnist for the *Sun* in 1887. A weekly column in the *Winnipeg Tribune* began in 1890 and continued until he died of injuries suffered from falling on an icy sidewalk. Wheeler worked hard for many years to improve the city's cultural scene. *DCB* XIV, 1,049-1,050.

Whellams, Creasey J. (1842-1918) Immigration promoter. Born in St. Ives, England, he was privately educated in Cambridge before entering business in Liverpool. He first came to Canada in 1872 as an agent for agricultural immigrants. Four years later he visited Manitoba and was so taken with its agricultural possibilities that he obtained a number of townships on the Little Saskatchewan River and established Rapid City. From 1892 to 1910 he was in St. Paul, but he came back to Winnipeg in 1910, becoming secretary of the Million for Manitoba League and later the Western Canada Development Bureau. Throughout his life Whellams was a regular author of literature promoting settlement in Manitoba.

Whimster, Peter (c. 1852-1919) Municipal official. Born in St. Mary's, Canada, he came to Red River in 1860. He served as secretary-treasurer of Portage la Prairie for many years and also served with the Land Titles Office in that city. He volunteered for service in South Africa in 1898 and entered business when he returned from the Boer War. In 1916 he became clerk of the provincial Executive Council.

White, Stella Rebecca (1892-1991) Nurse. Born in Akureyi, Iceland, she immigrated to Canada in

1910. She graduated from the St. Boniface Hospital School of Nursing in 1914 and then trained further in obstetrics at the Soane Hospital for Women in New York City. She engaged in private nursing in Winnipeg while her husband served overseas in WWI. During the flu epidemic of 1918-19 she performed heroic service, nursing whole families through the illness. In 1920 she moved with her husband to Snowflake, Manitoba, where she continued her nursing career while raising seven children.

White, William James (1850-1940) Journalist. Born in Stouffville, Upper Canada, he apprenticed at his father's newspaper. In 1881 he was persuaded by Thomas Greenway* to start a newspaper in Brandon, where he founded the *Brandon Sun*. He later was lured to Ottawa by Clifford Sifton,* and he worked for the federal department of immigration. After 1896 he helped create the great advertising campaigns that attracted thousands of immigrants to the Prairies. He retired to a farm in Lockwood, Saskatchewan, where he died.

Whitehead, Anne Marie Collier (1914-1991) Historian. Born in Arizona, Manitoba, she moved with her family to Sidney, where she was raised and educated. After her marriage in 1934 she moved to Austin, where she and her husband ran a service station and a small restaurant. In 1958 they opened a new location on the Trans-Canada Highway. They retired to Portage la Prairie in 1965. In retirement Whitehead became a historian and writer. Her *History of Portage la Prairie* was published in 1970, and *My Roadside Restaurant* appeared in 1988. She also helped write the lyrics for both the Manitoba centennial song and the Portage la Prairie centennial song. She died in Portage la Prairie.

Whitehead, Charles (1836-1919) Contractor. Born in England, he moved with his family to Canada in 1850 and came to Manitoba in 1877 to work with his father on railway grading. He and his father Joseph* brought the *Countess of Dufferin,* the West's first locomotive, to Winnipeg by barge in 1877. He later went into the lumber business and then contracted for the construction of the CPR and the drainage of the Boyne Marsh south of Carman. He headed the board of the Brandon General Hospital from 1904 to 1918. He died in Brandon.

Whitehead, Ernest Christie (1895-1961) Newspaper publisher. Born and educated in Brandon, he succeeded his father as publisher of the *Brandon Sun* in 1941. He was a director of The Canadian Press from 1945 to 1947, and served as president of the Canadian Daily Newspaper Publishers' Association in 1951-52. He died in Brandon.

Whitehead, Gladys, née Marion Mannin (b. 1903) Musician. Born in Portsmouth, England, she came to Manitoba with her family at a young age. She studied piano, violin, and voice in both England and Canada. A soprano, she appeared frequently as a soloist on CKY in Winnipeg and on the CBC. She sang solos at St. Andrew's River Heights Church from 1933 to 1948 and St. Stephen's Broadway United Church from 1951 to 1957. After 1949 she commuted from Kenora to Winnipeg, teaching privately and, from 1952 to 1957, at the Mennonite Bible College. She became principal of the Royal Hamilton College of Music from 1968 to 1975 and later taught voice at McMaster University. Whitehead was a frequent music festival adjudicator in Canada and abroad.

Whitehead, Joseph (1815-1894) Railway builder. Born in Darlington, England, he served for several years as a fireman and engineer on early railroads before becoming a railroad builder. He helped build the Caledonian Railway in Scotland. He subsequently immigrated to Canada, where he built the entire Buffalo and Goderich Railway. In 1867 he was elected to the first Canadian Parliament as a Liberal, and in the 1870s he began contracting on the railroads that were being built in Western Canada. He began building the Pembina Branch Railroad in 1877, bringing the first steam engine in Western Canada into Manitoba by barge. Whitehead was an active contractor on the CPR before his retirement to Clinton, Ontario, where he died.

Whitelock, William (1881-1974) Farm leader. Born in Glasgow, Scotland, he came to Manitoba in 1903, settling in the Roskeen district, where he farmed for almost 60 years. He was famous for his cereal grain crops, growing what was recognized as Western Canada's best Marquis wheat in 1922. He received orders for seed from around the world thereafter. He was president of the Manitoba branch of the Canadian Seed Growers Association from 1940 to 1945. He was also active in local government and the 4-H movement. He is a member of the Manitoba Agricultural Hall of Fame.

Whitla, Robert J. (1846-1905) Merchant, sportsman. Born in Ulster County, Ireland, he was educated there before immigrating to New York in 1867. He later moved to Canada, where he opened a series of retail stores, including one at Arnprior, Ontario. He came to Winnipeg in 1878 and opened a retail and wholesale dry-goods firm on Main Street, later concentrating on the wholesale trade. In 1885 he served as a captain of E Company of the 90th Regiment. He was a prominent member of the Board of Trade and a leading Methodist at Broadway Methodist Church. He was also president of the Fort Garry Gun Club and the Winnipeg Gun Club, and he headed the Winnipeg Kennel Club. He helped found Wesley College and the Young Men's Christian Association. His business papers are at the PAM.

Whyte, William (1843-1914) Railway executive. Born in Dunfermline, Scotland, he came to Canada in 1863 to work for the Grand Trunk Railway. In 1884 he joined the CPR and in 1886 became general superintendent of its western division. A year later he was manager of western lines. He became assistant to the president in 1899 and advanced to vice-president by 1910. Whyte was responsible for expanding the branch line system of the CPR in order to improve grain movement. He was knighted in 1911. Fort Whyte in Winnipeg was named after him. He died in California. *DCB* XIV, 1,062-63.

Wiebe, Cornelius W. (1893-1999) Country doctor. Born in Altona, Manitoba, he was educated at Wesley College, the University of Manitoba and the Manitoba Medical College (graduating in 1924). He began to practise medicine in Winkler in 1925. During the course of his medical career, which ended in 1978, he delivered more than 6,000 babies, often after journeys by sleigh to farm homes. He served as Liberal MLA from 1932 to 1936, founded Bethel Hospital in Winkler in 1935, and established a school for mentally challenged children in Winkler. Wiebe served on the Winkler school board from 1929 to 1953 and was a life member of the Liberal Party. He was awarded the Order of Canada in 1999. See Mavis Reimer, *Cornelius W. Wiebe: A Beloved Physician* (1983).

Wild, Eric (1910-1989) Musician. Born in Sault Ste. Marie, he studied music at the University of Michigan and, from 1933 to 1936, arranged for the Canadian Radio Broadcasting Corporation. He worked for the BBC from 1936 to 1939, then returned to Toronto, where he was musical director of *Meet the Navy* from 1942 to 1945. In 1947 he was appointed conductor of the CBC Winnipeg Orchestra, and he served until 1974. While in Winnipeg he was musical director of the Royal Winnipeg Ballet from 1955 to 1962 and of CBC TV's *Hymn Sing* from 1965 to 1977. He composed a number of short works, including "The Red River Jig." Wild was notorious for beginning musical works on an upbeat. He died in Florida.

Wilder, H.E. (1881-1948) Zionist leader. Born in Romania, he was educated in Bucharest and came to Canada in 1903. He was managing editor of the *Israelite Press* for nearly 20 years. He served as first secretary of the Jewish Orphanage and Children's Aid of Western Canada, and in 1934 became its superintendent. He also helped found the Winnipeg Hebrew Free School. He was Winnipeg president of the Zionist Organization of Canada and at his death was an honorary Canadian vice-president of the Zionist Organization.

Wilder, Joseph (1896-1993) Pharmacist, memoirist. Born in Romania, he came to Canada in 1904 and delivered and sold newspapers in his youth. He was a member of the first graduating class from the Manitoba School of Pharmacy in 1916. He served as a medical sergeant in WWI, then set up as a pharmacist in Winnipeg. He helped found Mount Carmel Clinic and the Jewish Orphanage, and was active in the Canadian Legion. He published two books chronicling his life, *Read All About It: Reminiscences of an Immigrant Newsboy* (1978) and *Lotions, Potions and Liniments Pure* (1982).

Williams, Eston Kenneth (1889-1970) Lawyer. Born in Parkhill, Ontario, he was called to the bar in 1911 and then came to Winnipeg. He was a prominent member of the Committee of 1,000 in 1919. He was active in drafting the Canadian Bar Association's canon of legal ethics in 1920, and he taught at the Manitoba Law School for most of his professional years. In 1921 he published *Canadian Law of Landlord and Tenant,* which became a landmark Canadian legal textbook. A non-driver, he drafted a Highway Traffic Act, which was the first comprehensive motor vehicle statute in Canada, in 1930. He also chaired a committee that in 1939 produced new rules for the Court of King's Bench. He served as chief counsel for the Royal Commission on Espionage that was appointed in 1946 to investigate the charges by Igor Gouzenko, and he recommended procedures highly criticized by civil libertarians. Soon after, he was appointed chief justice of the Court of King's Bench over considerable local opposition because he was not a Liberal. As a judge, Williams was a stickler for form and tradition, introducing coloured gowns and sashes for judges in 1949. Between 1947 and 1951 he tried five men charged with murder, and sentenced all of them to be hanged. He became chair of the board of trustees of the Manitoba Law School in 1947. Williams retired unexpectedly, in ill health, in 1962. His extensive papers are at the PAM.

Williams, William (d. 1837) Fur trader. His early history is unknown, but he was apparently a sailor, possibly in the East India Company's service. He was appointed governor-in-chief of Rupert's Land in 1818, probably because of his courage and aggression. He arrived at York Factory in August of that year to continue the HBC's struggle with the NWC, which ended only with the merger of the two companies in 1821. In 1819 he took the offensive against the Nor'Westers, arresting a number of the opposition at Grand Rapids. He was given the Southern Department of the HBC while George Simpson* got the Northern Department. The two men did not get on, and Williams was insufficiently familiar with the fur trade to hold his own. Simpson got the ear of the London Committee in 1825 and Williams was recalled in 1826. He died in Brixton. *DCB* VII, 912-14.

Willis, Errick French (1896-1967) Politician. Born in Boissevain, Manitoba, he was educated there. He received his BA from the University of Toronto and his MA from the University of Alberta, and graduated in law from the University of Manitoba in 1922. He first ran for Parliament in 1926. He was elected to Ottawa in 1930. After he was defeated in the federal election of 1935 by three votes (following a recount), he became leader of the Conservative Party of Manitoba in 1936 and the leader of the Opposition. He entered the provincial legislature in 1936 as MLA for Deloraine. When a coalition government was formed in Manitoba in 1939 he became deputy premier, serving until 1952. He surrendered the Conservative leadership to Duff Roblin in 1954 and became deputy premier and minister of agriculture

in the Roblin government. He was appointed the first native-born lieutenant-governor of Manitoba in 1960. Willis operated a livestock farm for many years and was an ardent curler and golfer. He skipped the Manitoba rink that won a gold medal at the 1932 winter Olympics. His extensive papers are at the PAM.

Wills, John (d. 1814) Fur trader. A partner in the XY Company in 1798, he became a wintering partner of the NWC in 1804, building Fort Gibraltar at the Forks and serving as head of the Red River District until 1806, when he went to Rat Portage. Elected to the Beaver Club in Montreal in 1807, he returned to the Red River in 1809. He stepped down in ill health in 1814.

Wilson, Norman R. (1879-1944) Educator. Born in Cobourg, Ontario, he graduated from the University of Toronto in 1899. After a year teaching mathematics at the Royal Military College he came to Wesley College in Winnipeg in 1900 as professor of mathematics. He joined the University of Manitoba in 1914. In 1916 he went overseas with the 196th University Battalion, later switching to the Royal Garrison Artillery. After demobilization he obtained his doctorate from the University of Chicago. With L.A.H. Warren, he wrote *Higher Algebra,* which for years was a popular university text. He became head of the University of Manitoba mathematics department in 1927, serving until his death in Winnipeg.

Wilton, John W. (1879-1942) Politician. Born in High Bluff, Manitoba, he was a Liberal lawyer who supported T.J. Norris* in the legislature. In 1916 Wilton introduced the Workmen's Compensation Bill, which provided for private coverage by insurance companies rather than state funding. He then enlisted as a private in the Canadian army, returning as a captain. His unpublished autobiography is at the PAM.

Winkler, Valentine (1864-1920) Merchant, politician. Born in Grey County, Canada, he moved to Manitoba in 1879 and opened his own grain and lumber business in Morden in 1883. In 1892 the village of Winkler, where he had a flourishing grain elevator and lumber operation, was named after him. Fluent in German, he was elected MLA in 1892, and he served until his death. He spent five years as minister of agriculture and immigration (1915-20), introducing many legislative initiatives vital to farmers. A legislative scheme to provide cows on credit to settlers in the Interlake region was always known as the "Winkler Cow Scheme." He died in Morden, probably of complications from diabetes. He is a member of the Manitoba Agricultural Hall of Fame. His extensive papers are at the PAM. *DCB* XIV, 1,072-73.

Winning, James (fl. 1906-41) Labour leader. Born in Scotland, he came to Winnipeg in 1906 as a bricklayer. He was an alderman and the president of the Trades and Labor Council at the time of the Winnipeg General Strike. He served as a member of the Manitoba Minimum Wage Board from 1918 to 1941. In 1919 Winning testified before the Robson Commission that was inquiring into the Winnipeg General Strike, and his assertions that the strike was not revolutionary in intent formed one of the bases for the commission's conclusions.

Winnipeg Bear ("Winnie," 1914-1934) Mascot. Born in White River, Ontario, he was bought by Lieutenant Harry Colebourn of the Fort Garry Horse as the regimental mascot on the regiment's train ride to the East (and Europe) in 1914. Known as "Winnie," he was soon deposited in the London Zoo, where he was seen in the early 1920s by author A.A. Milne and his son Christopher, serving as the inspiration for "Winnie the Pooh."

Winter, Kurt (1946-1997) Musician. Born in Winnipeg, he attended Daniel McIntyre High School. He started playing the guitar at age 12. He played with many local bands, and was lead guitarist for the Guess Who during their most successful period. In 1974 he left the band. He lived in the Winnipeg neighbourhood of Fort Garry during his last years. He died in Winnipeg.

Wiseman, Adele (1928-1992) Author. Born in Winnipeg to parents who were Jewish immigrants from Ukraine, she was educated at the University of Manitoba, where she received her BA in 1949, and was employed as a social worker. Her first novel was *The Sacrifice*, published in 1956 and the recipient of the Governor General's Award for fiction. It recounted the travails of a Jewish patriarch in Winnipeg against a setting of immigration and the garment trade. *Crackpot* (1974) also dealt with Jewish themes and was set in Winnipeg's North End during the Depression. The protagonist was a prostitute and the style was satirical. Never a prolific writer, Wiseman published much of her work privately or in journals. She was a close friend of Margaret Laurence, and their correspondence, edited by John Lennox and Ruth Panofsky, was published as *Selected Letters of Margaret Laurence and Adele Wiseman* (1997).

Wolseley, Garnet Joseph, First Viscount (1833-1913) Army officer. Born near Dublin, Ireland, to an Anglo-Irish military family, he entered the British army in 1852. He served in Burma, the Crimea, India, and China before being posted to Canada from 1861 to 1870 as assistant quartermaster-general and deputy quartermaster-general. He wrote a field manual on supply, and in 1870 led the joint Anglo-Canadian expedition to Red River. It secured Manitoba to Canada without firing a gun or losing a life. Subsequently he was active in the Ashanti War of 1873, and in 1882 he commanded the British force that was sent to Egypt. In 1884-85 he led the unsuccessful expedition to Khartoum, employing Canadian voyageurs on the Nile. Wolseley was the classic British soldier of the "small war" period of 1870-1914, more skilled at supplying an army far from its headquarters than at fighting battles. He continued advancing in rank until he became commander-in-chief of the British army from 1895 to 1900. His autobiography, *The Story of a Soldier's Life*, was published in 1903. The standard biography is Sir F. Maurice and Sir G. Arthur, *The Life of Lord Wolseley* (1924). See also Sir G. Arthur, ed., *The Letters of Lord and Lady Wolseley* (1922). Wolseley's extensive papers are housed at Hove, near Brighton. There are papers at the PAM.

Wood, Edmund Burke (1820-1882) Lawyer, judge. Born in Upper Canada to Irish-American parents, he graduated from Oberlin College in 1848 and was called to the bar in 1854. He lost an arm in a shooting accident on the farm. He was industrious, highly talented, and very abrasive as a lawyer. Throughout his career he mixed railroad promotion, politics, and the law. He was elected as a Reform MLA from West Brant in 1863, and he served for four years as treasurer of Ontario in the government of John Sandfield Macdonald. He was also elected to the House of Commons in 1867. He resigned his office in 1871 in a huff and became known as a difficult colleague. In the House of Commons he was familiar as "Big Thunder," his booming voice frequently attacking the Tories. He accepted the appointment as chief justice of Manitoba in March 1874 and presided at the Ambroise Lépine* trial that same year. That performance demonstrated his style, which was assertive and unquestioning in its support for English law and British values. But he also tended to shoot from the hip, and he became embroiled with John Schultz* to the detriment of any reputation for impartiality he might once have enjoyed. In later years paralyzed by strokes and heavy drinking, he died on the bench one step ahead of his removal. See R. St. George Stubbs, "Hon. Edmund Burke Wood," *HSSM Papers*, 3rd ser., no. 13 (1958): 27-47. His papers are at the PAM. *DCB* XI, 934-35.

Wood, Howard ("Pappy," 1888-1978) Curler and athlete. Born in Winnipeg, he played lacrosse, soccer, and hockey in his youth. He was a member of the "Winnipeg Scottish" team that became the senior soccer champions of Canada in 1915, and he won three Canadian curling championships. He competed in 71 Manitoba bonspiels and won 23 trophies. He is a member of the Canadian Sports Hall of Fame and the Manitoba Sports Hall of Fame.

Wood, Janet (Jaffray) (1863-1944) Women's leader. Janet Jaffray was born in Bannockburn, Scotland. She spent her childhood in Ontario and moved with her family to Kildonan, Manitoba. After her marriage she moved to Elkhorn and then Oakville. She helped organize the first local of the women's section of the Manitoba Grain Growers' Association in 1915 and became first president of the provincial organization in 1918, when it became the United Farm Women of Manitoba. She served in that capacity until 1922. She received an honorary diploma from the University of Manitoba in 1931. She is a member of the Manitoba Agricultural Hall of Fame.

Woodhouse, Arthur Sutherland Pigott (1895-1964) Educator. Born in Port Hope, Ontario, he was educated at the University of Toronto, from which he graduated in 1919, and at Harvard, where he received his MA in 1923. He became an assistant professor of English at the University of Manitoba from 1923 to 1929. He then returned to the University of Toronto (University College), where he served as editor of the *University of Toronto Quarterly* from 1933 to 1945. He wrote extensively, his best-known work being *Puritanism and Liberty* (1938), a study of Christian political idealism in seventeenth-century England.

Woodsworth, James Shaver (1874-1942) Social reformer, politician. Born near Islington, Ontario, his father superintended Methodist missions in Western Canada. He was educated at Wesley College of the University of Manitoba (BA, 1896), the University of Toronto, and Oxford University. He became active in social reform and threatened to leave the Methodist Church in 1907, being persuaded to remain by being put in charge of All People's Mission in the North End of Winnipeg. There Woodsworth worked chiefly with new immigrants, his efforts and ideas discussed in his books *Strangers within Our Gates* (1909) and *My Neighbour* (1911). While sympathetic to the plight of new Canadians, he feared their ability to assimilate into Canadian society and the ways in which extensive immigration from eastern Europe would change Canada. A pacifist and opponent of national-service registration during WWI, he served at a mission on the Sechelt Peninsula in British Columbia before finally leaving the church in 1918. He worked briefly on the Vancouver docks before embarking on a lecture tour in 1919 that brought him to Winnipeg in the midst of the Winnipeg General Strike. After becoming editor of the strikers' newspaper, he was arrested on charges of seditious libel and later released. Although his involvement in the Winnipeg General Strike was minimal, his strike work and his subsequent arrest made Woodsworth's reputation among supporters of labour, and he was elected to Parliament from Winnipeg North Centre in 1921 as an Independent Labour candidate, serving the riding until his death. He and his fellow labourite A.A. Heaps* actually held the balance of power in the 1926 House of Commons, and they forced the King government to pass old-age pension legislation. Woodsworth was involved in the creation of the Co-operative Commonwealth Federation and became House Leader of the seven CCF members elected to Ottawa in 1935. He was an ardent socialist and social reformer of the moral perfectionist variety. Because of his pacifism, he was forced to step down as leader of the CCF when war again broke out in 1939. Although he was re-elected to Parliament in 1940, he was already quite ill and died soon after. There are two biographies: Grace MacInnes (his daughter), *J.S. Woodsworth: A Man to Remember* (1953) and Kenneth McNaught, *A Prophet in Politics* (1959). See also Allen Mills, *Fool for Christ: The Political Thought of J.S. Woodsworth* (1991). The Woodsworth Papers are in the NAC, although there are some papers at PAM.

Work, John (c. 1792-1861) Fur trader. Born in County Donegal, Ireland, he came to York Factory in 1814 as a servant of the HBC. In 1823 he was transferred to the Columbia District, and he spent the remainder of his life on the Pacific coast. His journals (1823-35), held in the Provincial Archives of British Columbia, are a valuable source of information on the coastal fur trade.

Wright, Archibald (1842-1912) Saddler and merchant. Born near Glasgow, Scotland, he came to Canada with his parents in 1852 and learned the saddlery trade in the American South. He came to Fort Garry as a saddler in 1869, later founding the Winnipeg Saddlery Company. Wright subsequently imported British woollens and linens. He owned large amounts of land along the Assiniboine River, which the City of Winnipeg bought for Assiniboine Park, and was the first resident of the Tuxedo neighbourhood of Winnipeg.

Wrigley, George Weston (1847-1907) Radical journalist. Born in Wrigley Corners, Canada, he was raised near Galt and became a teacher, then a school principal. He entered journalism and in 1886 founded the *Canada Labour Courier*, which was associated with the Knights of Labor. In 1892, convinced that farmers and workers had a common goal, he created the *Canada Farmers' Sun*. He founded one more paper, *Citizen and Country*, which was taken over by his son. Wrigley moved to Vancouver Island in 1902 to become a labour organizer and a socialist journalist. A series of strokes in 1904 led him to retire to Winnipeg, where a son had a business. He died there a few years later. *DCB* XIII, 1,111-15.

Wynne, Thelma Alma (1904-1992) Volunteer worker. Born in Toronto, she moved to Winnipeg with her parents at a young age. An active layperson in the Anglican Church, Wynne was awarded the Order of Rupert's Land in 1988. Her major accomplishment was the foundation of the layette program of St. Matthew's Anglican Church, which helped new mothers in need throughout the province. The program was eventually extended throughout the Rupert's Land diocese and has been renamed the Thelma Wynne Project in honour of its founder.

Yakimischak, Dmytro (b. 1888) Born in Ukraine, he came to Manitoba in 1898 and was educated at the University of Manitoba (BA, LLB). He was director of the Ukrainian Publishing Company, and was elected to the Manitoba legislature in 1920 as an Independent and re-elected in 1922. He was one of the first Ukrainian-Canadians to serve as an MLA.

Yakimischak, William (1906-1988) Pharmacist. Born in Pleasant Home, Manitoba, he became a school teacher in 1926 and later worked in Detroit making automobiles. He returned to teaching while building up a drug store in Vita, apprenticing as a pharmacist in his own store. He graduated from the University of Manitoba in pharmacy in 1941. He also provided veterinary services for the surrounding community, and manufactured his own analgesic ointment which he sold internationally. Yakimischak was active in community affairs and politics, especially in Ducks Unlimited.

Yellow Quill ("Ozawekwun," 1821-1910) Native leader. Little is known of his eary life. He was reputed one of the best hunters in Red River. Not a hereditary chief, around 1860 he was "clothed" by the HBC as chief of the mixed Ottawa and Ojibway band that claimed the land around Portage la Prairie. He did not take an active role in the negotiations for Treaty No. 1 at Lower Fort Garry in August 1871, and subsequently was more willing to agree to government proposals than were his councillors. He selected the present Swan Lake Indian Reserve No. 7 for his band in 1876, but he was unable to convince many of his people to follow him. Instead, the band remained at Hamilton's Crossing and was rejoined by Yellow Quill. In 1890 he opposed provincial attempts to enforce game laws against the aboriginal people of Manitoba. After his death, the federal government in 1913 agreed to establish a reserve at Hamilton's Crossing, known as Indian Gardens Reserve No. 8. Yellow Quill was highly respected by government agents, and his leadership eventually came to be accepted by his people.

Yeomans, Amelia (Le Sueur) (1842-1913) Physician, suffragist. Born in Canada into a civil-service family, she married Dr. Augustus Yeomans, who died in 1878. After his death she decided to join her daughter Lillian in medical studies at Michigan State University, and she graduated in 1883. Lillian Yeomans took up medical practice in Winnipeg in 1882 and was joined by her mother a year later, although Amelia was not licensed until 1885. Amelia became an active practitioner of "social medicine" in the city's tenement districts, speaking out for better working conditions, housing reform, and the eradication of venereal disease through an ending of prostitution. She helped found the Winnipeg Humane Society in 1894. She quickly came to see alcohol as the symbol of the deterioration of society, becoming a leader of the Woman's Christian Temperance Union and its president in 1896-97. Reform would not be possible without the enfranchisement of women, she believed. She thus acted the part of premier in the mock parliament organized by the WCTU in 1893 and helped demonstrate in favour of the suffrage in 1894, subsequently leading in the founding of the Equal Franchise Association, which was committed to empowering women. Yeomans joined her daughters in Calgary in 1906 in semi-retirement. See Carlotta Hacker, *The Indomitable Lady Doctors* (1974); Manitoba Historic Resources Branch, *Dr. Amelia Yeomans* (1985). *DCB* XIV, 649-50.

Young, Alexander Lovelace (1860-1928) School inspector. Born in St. Rose, Canada, he was bilingual. He was wounded at Batoche and in 1893 was appointed school inspector for the eastern part of Manitoba. He was charged with dealing with the Franco-Manitobans who were offended by the Greenway legislation of 1890, and especially with reconciling them to the Laurier-Greenway Compromise after 1897. Young retired in 1925. He died in Winnipeg.

Young, David (1847-1913) Pioneer mental health worker. Born in Sarnia, Canada, he graduated from Queen's University in medicine in 1871. He came west that same year to set up a medical practice at St. Andrew's Rapids (Lockport), and he provided medical service for the Manitoba Penitentiary at Lower Fort Garry from 1871 to 1877. In 1877 he became Indian agent and medical officer for the Clandeboye Indian agency, and later he served as first superintendent of the hospital for the mentally ill at Selkirk, retiring in 1912. He died in Winnipeg. Many of his daily journals are at the PAM.

Young, David (1848-1887) Merchant, sportsman. Born near Glasgow, Scotland, he came to Canada as an orphan in 1858. He ran away from his uncle and travelled around North America in a number of occupations, including a stint as a quartermaster sergeant in the Union army. He came to Manitoba in 1870 as a volunteer with the Third Company of Ontario Rifles, and remained. By 1880 he had acquired a fortune in the dry-goods business, was active in Winnipeg social and sports circles, and was a supporter of the city's railroad interests, especially the Manitoba Southwest Railway. Young

was first president of the Granite Curling Club and was an active promoter of lacrosse, baseball, and cricket. He was active in the Dufferin Park Association that built Winnipeg's first stadium. He was associated with many cultural organizations such as the Winnipeg Dramatic and Literary Society. He was also active in politics, though never elected to office. Ill health led him to Florida in 1881, and he left Manitoba permanently in 1885. He died in Saratoga Springs, New York. *DCB* XI, 941-42.

Young, Egerton Ryerson (1840-1909) Missionary, author. He was born in Crosby Township, Upper Canada. His family admired his namesake but was not related to him. Young was educated at the Toronto Model School, and he taught briefly. After several years of missionary work, he was ordained in 1867 and soon became a missionary in Rupert's Land, taking charge of the Rossville mission at Norway House in 1868. He and his wife remained in Manitoba until their children began to need schooling, when they returned to Ontario. Young later wrote a number of books based on his missionary experience, mostly for juveniles. They included *By Canoe and Dog-Train among the Cree and Salteaux Indians* (1890) and *Stories from Indian Wigwams and Northern Camp-fires* (1893). The latter provoked criticism from Rev. John Chantler McDougall* in the *Christian Guardian* over the liberties Young had taken with his material and the extent of stereotyping he employed. Young also wrote *The Apostle of Truth: Rev. James Evans* (1900). He died in Bradford, Ontario. A bit of his correspondence has appeared as "Letters of Egerton Ryerson Young," ed. Harcourt Brown, *Manitoba Pageant* 17, no. 1 (1971): 2-11. *DCB* XIII, 1,121-22.

Young, Finlay McNaughton (1852-1916) Politician. Born in St. Chrystostome County, Canada, he came to Manitoba in 1879 to farm near Turtle Mountain. He later entered the grain business at Killarney. He was elected to the Manitoba legislature in 1883, then moved to Killarney for the 1888 election. He represented Killarney until 1899, when he was defeated. He was Speaker of the legislature from 1896 to 1899 and was appointed to the Senate in 1900. He was a Liberal.

Young, George (1821-1910) Cleric. Born in Prince Edward County, Upper Canada, he attended local school and was ordained to the Wesleyan Methodist Church in Canada in 1846. In 1868 he joined George McDougall* as a western missionary, eventually establishing a mission church in Winnipeg in 1871. During the Red River Rebellion of 1869-70 he supported the Canadian Party, ministering to the spiritual needs of Thomas Scott* and serving as one of Scott's principal hagiographers. In October 1871 he became chaplain to the volunteer defence force raised against the Fenians. He founded Grace Church (1871) and the Wesleyan Institute (1873) in Winnipeg. He returned to Toronto in 1876 but came back to Emerson, Manitoba, in 1879, finally retiring in 1883 to Toronto, where he died. His autobiography was published as *Manitoba Memories* (1897). *DCB* XIII, 1,122-23.

Young, John (1913-1991) Native leader. Born in The Pas, Manitoba, he was active in politics on The Pas Reserve for over 50 years. He served as chief of The Pas band for many years and was a senator of the Manitoba Indian Brotherhood. He founded the McGillivray Care Home on the reserve.

Young, Norman Andrew Thomson (1901-1942) Educator. Born in Montreal, he was brought up by his aunt and uncle, who moved to Winnipeg in 1907. He graduated from the University of Manitoba in 1923 with a gold medal in history and a Rhodes Scholarship to Balliol College, Oxford. He went to Africa in 1925 with the education branch of the British Colonial Service, serving at Achimota College in British West Africa until 1929, when he returned to Winnipeg. In 1930 he became first headmaster of Ravenscourt School, and it was his vision that shaped the school in its first decade. An officer in the Queen's Own Cameron Highlanders from 1937, he was mobilized in 1939 and went overseas as a captain with the Sixth Infantry Brigade, Second Canadian Division, in November 1940. On 19 August 1942 he was killed leading "B" Company of the Camerons in the Dieppe raid. He is buried at Hauteville-sur-mer, France.

Young, Richard (1843-1905) Cleric. Born in England, he was educated at Louth Grammar School and Clare College, Cambridge, receiving a BA in 1868. After a promising career as an evangelist, he accepted a Canadian Missionary Society appointment in St. Andrew's in 1875. He was a missionary

to the Saulteaux, and he served on the diocesan finance committee from 1877 to 1885. He helped divide the huge Diocese of Athabasca in the 1880s and was appointed bishop of the new Diocese of Athabasca. In 1884 he became the first Anglican bishop to be consecrated in Western Canada (at St. John's Cathedral, Winnipeg). He moved his residence to Athabasca Landing, Alberta. He retired in 1903 and died in England. *DCB* XIII, 1,123-25.

Young, Robert Evans (1861-1911) Surveyor. Born in Georgetown, Canada, he trained as a surveyor and re-surveyed Winnipeg under the Torrens system in the 1870s, also surveying the old trails of Manitoba. He served with the 90th Rifles in 1885. He was Manitoba lands surveyor before his appointment in 1902 as federal superintendent of railway lands. In 1909 he published *Canada's Fertile Northland*. He became chief geographer of Canada in 1910 and died in Ottawa soon after.

Zaplitny, Frederick Samuel (1913-1964) Politician. Born in Oak Brae, Manitoba, he was educated at Fork River and Ethelbert. He operated an insurance and real estate brokerage in Dauphin, and he was president of the Dauphin Chamber of Commerce at the time of his death. He was first elected to the House of Commons for the CCF in 1945 and was re-elected in 1953 and 1957.

Zengel, Ralph Louis ("Ray," 1894-1977) War hero. Born in Faribault, Minnesota, he moved with his widowed mother to Saskatchewan at an early age. He was working on a farm at Virden when he enlisted in the 45th Battalion. In 1917 he won a Victoria Cross for bravery at Warvillers. After the war he moved to Alberta and later British Columbia. During WWII he served as a regimental sergeant major.

Zuken, Joseph (1912-1986) Municipal politician. Born in Ukraine, he came to Canada with his family in 1914 and grew up in Winnipeg's North End, attending St. John's High School. He graduated as a lawyer in 1936 from the University of Manitoba, but was unable to gain employment because of his Communist affiliations. He taught Yiddish for six years and eventually opened his own law office. He was very active in the Progressive Arts Club and New Theatre in the 1930s. A long-time Communist, Zuken served on the Winnipeg School

Board from 1942 to 1962, and was a Winnipeg city councillor from 1962 to his retirement in 1983. He also ran unsuccessfully for mayor in 1979. Called both a "gadfly" and the conscience of city council, Zuken was noted for his concern for the underdog, and never voted for a city budget because he claimed they did not help the poor and unemployed. He was a supporter of low rental housing and a champion of Seven Oaks Hospital. See the biography by Doug Smith (1990). There are extensive papers at the PAM.

Zvankin, Peter (1879-1975) Composer. Born in Kherson, Russia, he came to Winnipeg in 1906. He became a textile broker and began composing music at the age of 55. His music was performed frequently by the Winnipeg Symphony Orchestra and the Winnipeg CBC Orchestra. His papers are at the UML Archives. There are also papers at the PAM.

Zwicker, Linda (1945-1993) Writer. Born in Swan River, Manitoba, she was educated there and in Russell before her family moved to Alberta. She was an award-winning playwright and radio dramatist who also wrote novels for young people.